General Liability Insurance Coverage

General Liability Insurance Coverage

Key Issues in Every State

Fifth Edition

Volume II

Randy Maniloff
Jeffrey Stempel
Margo Meta

ISBN: XXXXXXXXXX
ISBN 13: XXXXXXXXXXXXX

Note to Readers
This publication is designed to provide accurate and authoritative information in regard to the subject matter covered. It is based upon sources believed to be accurate and reliable and is intended to be current as of the time it was written. It is sold with the understanding that the publisher and authors are not engaged in rendering legal, accounting, or other professional services. If legal advice or other expert assistance is required, the services of a competent professional person should be sought. Also, to confirm that the information has not been affected or changed by later developments, traditional legal research techniques should be used, including checking primary sources where appropriate.

About the Authors

Randy J. Maniloff is an attorney at White and Williams, LLP in Philadelphia. He concentrates his practice in the representation of insurers in coverage disputes over primary and excess obligations under a host of policies, including commercial general liability and various professional liability policies. Mr. Maniloff is an adjunct professor, teaching insurance law, at Temple University Beasley School of Law. Mr. Maniloff publishes *Coverage Opinions* [CoverageOpinions.info], an electronic newsletter that addresses recent insurance coverage developments, looks at the lighter side of the law and features interviews with the nation's most unique, accomplished and celebrated lawyers. For the past twenty years, Mr. Maniloff has published a year-end article that addresses the ten most significant insurance coverage decisions of that year. Mr. Maniloff has published dozens of articles addressing a variety of insurance coverage subjects, is a frequent lecturer at industry seminars and has been quoted on insurance coverage topics by such media as *The Wall Street Journal*, *The New York Times*, *USA Today*, *Dow Jones Newswires and Associated Press*. He has also published numerous editorials in *The Wall Street Journal* addressing various legal issues. Mr. Maniloff received his B.S., with distinction, in 1988 from Pennsylvania State University and his J.D. in 1991 from Temple University School of Law in Philadelphia.

    Jeffrey W. Stempel, the Doris S. & Theodore B. Lee Professor of Law, teaches legal ethics, civil procedure, insurance, and contracts at the William S. Boyd School of Law, University of Nevada Las Vegas. He is the author or co-author of many law journal articles and six previous books, including *Fundamentals of Litigation Practice* (2014), *Fundamentals of Pretrial Litigation* (11th ed. 2020), *Principles of Insurance Law* (5th ed. 2020), *Stempel and Knutsen on Insurance Coverage* (4th ed. 2016), and *Foundations of the Law* (1994). A member of the bar in both Minnesota and Nevada, he served on the State Bar of Nevada Committee on Ethics and Professional Responsibility and the Bar's Ethics 2000 Committee. Prior to joining the UNLV law faculty in 1999, he taught at Florida State University College of Law and Brooklyn Law School and has been a practicing attorney and judicial clerk. He is a graduate of the University of Minnesota and the Yale Law School.

Margo E. Meta is an attorney at White and Williams, LLP. She focuses her practice on advising major property and casualty insurance companies on complex insurance coverage issues under general and professional liability, homeowner's liability, commercial property and excess policies. Ms. Meta has handled a wide variety of coverage and litigation matters, including construction defect (with related risk transfer issues), premises and product liability, business interruption, educator's legal liability, sexual misconduct, rescission and bad faith. Prior to joining White and Williams, Ms. Meta served as Associate General Counsel for Universal Property and Casualty Insurance Company. Ms. Meta received her B.A., with the highest distinction, from the University of Pittsburgh and her J.D. from Rutgers Law School.

Table of Contents (Volume I)

CHAPTER 1   Commercial General Liability Insurance—An Overview
CHAPTER 2   Choice of Law for Coverage Disputes
CHAPTER 3   Late Notice Defense Under "Occurrence" Policies:
             Is Prejudice to the Insurer Required?
CHAPTER 4   Coverage for Pre-Tender Defense Costs
CHAPTER 5   Duty to Defend Standard:
             "Four Corners" or Extrinsic Evidence?
CHAPTER 6   Insured's Right to Independent Counsel
CHAPTER 7   Insurer's Right to Reimbursement of Defense Costs
CHAPTER 8   Prevailing Insured's Right to Recover Attorney's
             Fees in Coverage Litigation
CHAPTER 9   Number of Occurrences
CHAPTER 10   Coverage for Innocent Co-Insureds: "Any" Insured vs.
             "The" Insured and the Severability of Interests Clause
CHAPTER 11   Is Emotional Injury "Bodily Injury"?

Table of Contents (Volume II)

CHAPTER 12   Is Faulty Workmanship an "Occurrence"?   1
CHAPTER 13   Permissible Scope of Indemnification in
              Construction Contracts   82
CHAPTER 14   Qualified Pollution Exclusion   143
CHAPTER 15   "Absolute" Pollution Exclusion   182
CHAPTER 16   Trigger-of-Coverage for Latent Injury and
              Damage Claims   243
CHAPTER 17   Trigger-of-Coverage for Construction Defects and
              Non-Latent Injury and Damage Claims   277
CHAPTER 18   Allocation of Latent Injury and Damage Claims   323
CHAPTER 19   Insurability of Punitive Damages   373
CHAPTER 20   First- and Third-Party Bad Faith Standards   409
CHAPTER 21   The ALI Restatement of the Law of
              Liability Insurance   514

CHAPTER
12

Is Faulty Workmanship an "Occurrence"?

When it comes to claims for latent injuries and damages, such as asbestos and hazardous waste, some would say that they were never contemplated under the historic policies that were later—sometimes decades later—called upon to respond. That being so, it is not surprising that questions such as trigger of coverage and allocation have been viewed by courts as particularly vexing, with the result being a lack of unanimity in their handling as different schools of thought developed in response to the issues.

But claims for coverage for construction defects, and the damage they cause, present a different situation. It is unquestionably contemplated that such claims will be made under commercial general liability policies—especially when the insured is in the construction business. For this reason, it is surprising that so much disparity has developing around the country in the case law over the treatment of such claims, especially those involving relatively similar facts and oftentimes identical policy language.

Many construction defect claims follow a typical pattern. A general contractor is hired to build a residential or commercial building. The general contractor employs various subcontractors to assist with the completion of the project, such as to pour the foundation, frame the building, or install the plumbing, windows, HVAC, etc. The house or building is completed. After taking possession, the owner discovers defects in the construction—such as defectively installed windows that are now leaking or an improperly poured foundation that is causing the building to shift. The owner and general contractor are unable to resolve the problem in a manner that is satisfactory to both parties. Left with no choice, the owner files suit against the general contractor. The general contractor then files a third-party complaint against the allegedly at-fault subcontractors. And all defendants turn to their commercial general liability policies seeking coverage for a defense and any liability that may be assessed against them.

As a general rule, courts have concluded that defects in the insured's work product are not covered—unless a certain exception applies, as discussed below.

As another general rule, with a few exceptions, defective workmanship that *causes* "property damage" to something *other than* the insured's work product, is covered. While these general rules accurately describe the outcome of most construction defect claims, there is a fracture among courts in the rationales used to get there. And the choice of rationale employed can have a dramatic effect on the extent of coverage owed.

While insurers' handling of claims for coverage for construction defects may vary widely, they generally all begin with the same initial questions: Are any of the damages being sought from the insured (1) for "property damage"; and (2) if so, was such "property damage" caused by an "occurrence"?

The source of such questions is the insuring agreement of the commercial general liability coverage form, which often provides that the insurer "will pay those sums that the insured becomes legally obligated to pay as damages because of … 'property damage' to which this insurance applies" (*See, e.g.,* Ins. Servs. Office, Inc., Commercial General Liability Coverage Form, No. CG 00010413, § I1a (2012)), provided that the "'property damage' is caused by an 'occurrence.'" ISO Form, CG 00010413 at § I1b1. "Occurrence" is typically defined as "an accident, including continuous or repeated exposure to substantially the same general harmful conditions." ISO Form, CG 00010413 at § V13. It is also a requirement that any "property damage" occur during the policy period. ISO Form, CG 00010413 at § I1b2. This "timing" issue is addressed separately. *See* Chapters 16 and 17.

The principal schools of thought that have emerged, in response to the question whether coverage for construction defects is available under a commercial general liability policy, are as follows.

Some courts have held that defective workmanship, standing alone, which results in damage solely to the insured's completed work product, is not an accident, and, hence, not an "occurrence." *Essex Ins. Co. v. Holder*, 261 S.W.3d 456, 459–60 (Ark. 2007). The Arkansas high court's rationale, which is not an uncommon one, was that its "case law has consistently defined an 'accident' as an event that takes place without one's foresight or expectation—an event that proceeds from an unknown cause, or is an unusual effect of a known cause, and therefore not expected. Faulty workmanship is not an accident; instead, it is a foreseeable occurrence, and performance bonds exist in the marketplace to insure the contractor against claims for the cost of repair or replacement of faulty work." *Id.* at 460 (citation omitted).

Other courts have likewise held that defective workmanship, which results in damage solely to the insured's completed work product, is not covered—but for a different reason. These courts initially conclude that defects in the insured's work product *do* constitute an "occurrence." *See Bituminous Cas. Corp. v. Kenway Contracting, Inc.*, 240 S.W.3d 633, 639–40 (Ky. 2007) (holding that a claim against a contractor, who was supposed to demolish a carport, but instead also demolished half of the attached residential structure, qualified as an "occurrence" because such outcome was not the plan, design, or intent of the insured). However, such courts then usually conclude that, despite the existence of an "occurrence," damage that is solely to the insured's completed work product is nonetheless excluded from coverage on account of the policy's so-called "your work" exclusion, which applies to "'property damage' to 'your [named insured's] work' arising out of it or any part of it and included in the 'products-completed operations hazard.'" ISO FORM, CG 00010413 at § I2l.

Given the extraordinary number of decisions addressing coverage for construction defects – many from state high courts, but many have also not addressed the issue – and their incredibly factual nature, it is difficult to provide a scorecard of which side is winning. Consider that, even after states decide the fundamental question, whether faulty workmanship is an "occurrence," litigation of coverage for construction defects often marches on. A testament to the issue not being so cut and dry.

Whether it is because defective workmanship is not an "occurrence" or the operation of the "your work" exclusion, damage to the insured's completed work product is not covered. While these outcomes are the same, which rationale a court employs to reach it can make a world of difference. The reason being that the "your work" exclusion also contains what is commonly referred to as the "subcontractor exception," which provides: "This exclusion does not apply if the damaged work or the work out of which the damage arises was performed on your [named insured's] behalf by a subcontractor." *Id.*

The "subcontractor exception" restores coverage for "property damage" to the insured's own work, that would otherwise be excluded by the "your work" exclusion, if the cause of the damage to the insured's work was the operations of the insured's subcontractor. *See Am. Family Mut. Ins. Co. v. Am. Girl, Inc.*, 673 N.W.2d 65, 83–84 (Wis. 2004) ("There is coverage under the insuring agreement's initial coverage grant. Coverage would be excluded by the business risk exclusionary language, except that the subcontractor exception to the business risk exclusion applies, which operates to restore the otherwise excluded coverage.").

In *Travelers Indem. Co. of Am. v. Moore & Assocs., Inc.*, 216 S.W.3d 302, 309 (Tenn. 2007), the Supreme Court of Tennessee illustrated the significant impact that the "subcontractor exception" can have on the extent of coverage available for a construction defect claim. The insured was the building contractor for the construction of a hotel. *Id.* at 304. The insured hired a subcontractor to provide and install the windows. *Id.* The owner of the hotel alleged that the windows were negligently designed and installed, resulting in damage to other components of the interior and exterior of the building. *Id.*

The *Moore* court concluded that the entire hotel qualified as the insured's work for purposes of the "your work" exclusion. *Id.* at 310. Therefore, *all* of the damages to the hotel were *initially* excluded by the "your work" exclusion. *Id.* However, because the policy at issue contained a "subcontractor exception" to the "your work" exclusion, the court's analysis did not end there: "It is alleged that the installation of the windows was performed by subcontractors hired by [the insured]. Therefore, damages resulting from the subcontractors' faulty installation of the windows are not excluded from coverage, even if those damages affected [the insured's] work." *Moore*, 216 S.W.3d at 301. On account of the "subcontractor exception," coverage was restored for the otherwise excluded damage to the hotel caused by the subcontractor's negligent design and installation of the windows. *Id.*

So while coverage is not owed for damage to an insured's defective workmanship, the "subcontractor exception" to the "your work" exclusion demonstrates, in stark terms, why it matters whether a court reaches that conclusion based on the absence of an "occurrence" or the operation of the "your work" exclusion. Many courts hold that, if damage to an insured's defective workmanship is not covered, because it does not qualify as an "occurrence," then the insured has not satisfied the requirements of the insuring agreement. As a result, coverage is excluded and the court's analysis ends there, without any need to address the potential applicability of policy exclusions. In other words, by resting its decision on the insured's failure to satisfy the insuring agreement, it is unnecessary for the court to reach the "your work" exclusion. Translation—policyholders are denied the opportunity to invoke the "subcontractor exception" to such exclusion to restore coverage for damage to their own work that was caused by the operations of a subcontractor. *See Amerisure, Inc. v. Wurster Constr. Co.*, 818 N.E.2d 998, 1005 (Ind. Ct. App. 2004) ("Because Wurster's claim fails the definitional requirements of the terms 'property damage' and 'occurrence' in order for coverage to apply, we do not reach the applicability of the various policy exclusions [including the 'your work' exclusion]."); *see also Nabholz Constr. Corp. v. St. Paul Fire & Marine Ins., Co.*, 354 F. Supp. 2d 917, 923 (E.D. Ark. 2005) ("The Court need not reach CONARK's argument that coverage exists based on the Policy's completed work exclusion, or more accurately, based upon an exception to this exclusion. Because the Court's finding is based upon its conclusion that coverage is lacking under the basic insuring clause, it is unnecessary to consider this exclusion. An exception to an exclusion cannot create or extend coverage where none exists under the terms the policy's basic insuring agreement.").

Some courts use this interplay, between the "occurrence" requirement and "subcontractor exception" to the "your work" exclusion, to conclude that faulty workmanship must be an "occurrence." As they see it, the "subcontractor exception" has no purpose if it cannot be reached. *See Sheehan Construction Co., Inc. v. Continental Cas. Co.*, 935 N.E.2d 160 (Ind. 2010).

The availability of coverage, for damage to an insured's completed work product, depends upon certain legal and factual issues: Does defective workmanship qualify as an "occurrence" and did the insured use subcontractors that caused damage to the insured's work? Given these variables, courts vary in their answers.

Despite the debate whether faulty workmanship qualifies as an "occurrence," most courts are uniform in their conclusion that, if faulty workmanship *caused* property damage, to something *other than* the insured's work product, such injury or damage was caused by an "occurrence" and coverage exists. *Auto-Owners Ins. Co. v. Home Pride Cos.*, 684 N.W.2d 571, 577–78 (Neb. 2004) ("[A]lthough faulty workmanship, *standing alone*, is not an occurrence under a CGL policy, an accident caused by faulty workmanship is a covered occurrence. Stated otherwise, although a standard CGL policy does not provide coverage for faulty workmanship that damages only the resulting work product, if faulty workmanship causes bodily injury or property damage to something other than the insured's work product, an unintended and unexpected event has occurred, and coverage exists.") (citations omitted and emphasis on original).

While it is almost universally held that coverage exists for such consequential damages caused by an insured's faulty workmanship, a few courts have deviated from this path. For example, Pennsylvania courts have rejected this principle adopted by the vast majority of courts. In *Kvaerner Metals Division of Kvaerner U.S., Inc. v. Commercial Union Insurance Co.*, 908 A.2d 888, 899 (Pa. 2006), the Supreme Court of Pennsylvania held that damage to the insured faulty workmanship did not constitute an "occurrence." Then in *Millers Capital Insurance Co. v. Gambone Brothers Development Co.*, 941 A.2d 706, 713 (Pa. Super. Ct. 2007), the Superior Court of Pennsylvania addressed coverage for damage caused by the insured's faulty workmanship. Despite confronted with a paradigm example of property damage caused by a contractor's faulty workmanship—water intrusion damage caused by defective residential windows and stucco—the Pennsylvania appellate court concluded that no coverage was owed for such consequential damages. *Id.* Addressing *Kvaerner Metals, Gambone Brothers* held that "natural and foreseeable acts, such as rainfall, which tend to exacerbate the damage, effect, or consequences caused *ab initio* by faulty workmanship also cannot be considered sufficiently fortuitous to constitute an 'occurrence' or 'accident' for the purposes of an occurrence based CGL policy." *Id. See also Cincinnati Specialty Underwriters Ins. Co. v. Green Prop. Sols. LLC,* No. 19-00010, 2019 U.S. Dist. LEXIS 220161 (D. Utah Dec. 23, 2019) (finding moisture buildup and water damage which was the "natural and probable result of the lack of ventilation caused directly by Green Property's allegedly defective work" did not constitute "property damage" caused by an "occurrence").

There are massive numbers of state laws and regulations that govern insurance. But when it comes to coverage issues under commercial general liability policies, state legislatures have generally been content to stay on the sidelines and let courts be the ones to get their hands dirty. But over the past few years some state legislatures have no longer been able to hold their tongues in the face of what they see as dissatisfaction with courts ruling that damage to an insured's defective workmanship does not qualify as having been caused by an "occurrence."

Legislative involvement in construction defect coverage kicked off in May 2010, when the Colorado General Assembly enacted "An Act Concerning Commercial Liability Insurance Policies Issued to Construction Professionals." *See* C.R.S.A. § 13-20-808. The Colorado Act addresses several issues relevant to coverage for construction defects, most notably declaring that: "In interpreting a liability insurance policy issued to a construction professional, a court shall presume that the work of a construction professional that results in property damage, *including damage to the work itself* or other work, is an *accident* unless the property damage is intended and expected by the insured." (emphasis added).

The Colorado legislature's decision was a direct response to the Colorado Court of Appeals' decision in *Gen. Sec. Indem. Co. of Ariz. v. Mountain States Mut. Cas. Co.,* 205 P.3d 529 (Colo. Ct. App. 2009), which held that a claim for damages arising from defective workmanship, standing alone, does not qualify as an "occurrence," regardless of the underlying legal theory pled (tort, contract, or breach of warranty). The Colorado Act specifically described the Court of Appeals' decision in *General Security* as not properly considering a construction professional's reasonable expectation that an insurer would defend the construction professional against a construction defect claim.

In 2011, three states followed Colorado's lead and adopted legislation directly in response to court decisions in their states that they believed did not provide adequate coverage to contractors for construction defects. Interestingly, while these three states, and Colorado, all set out with the same motivations, each one adopted a different approach to achieve its objective.

In June 2011, Hawaii adopted legislation that takes direct aim at *Group Builders, Inc. v. Admiral Ins. Co.*, 231 P.3d 67 (Haw. Ct. App. 2010). In *Group Builders*, the Hawaii court held that "under Hawaii law, construction defect claims do not constitute an 'occurrence' under a CGL policy. Accordingly, breach of contact claims based on allegations of shoddy performance are not covered under CGL policies. Additionally, tort-based claims, derivative of these breach of contract claims, are also not covered under CGL policies." *Id.* at 73–74. Following several pages of findings, that paint the *Group Builders* decision in very problematic terms for the state's economy, the Hawaii legislature announced that, in a policy issued to a construction professional, for liability arising from construction-related work, the meaning of the term "occurrence" "shall be construed in accordance with the law as it existed at the time that the insurance policy was issued." *See* HAW. REV. STAT. § 431:1(a). Thus, only policies that were issued after the May 19, 2010 decision in *Group Builders* will be subject to its holding that construction defect claims— contract and tort—do not constitute an "occurrence" under a CGL policy.

In March 2011, Arkansas adopted legislation that a CGL policy shall contain a definition of "occurrence" that includes "[p]roperty damage or bodily injury resulting from faulty workmanship." *See* ARK. CODE § 23-79-155(a)(2). The statute places no restriction on exclusions in the policy. The Arkansas statute's findings and purpose make clear that it was passed in response to legislative dissatisfaction with court decisions, no doubt including its Supreme Court's in *Essex*.

In May 2011, South Carolina adopted legislation that a CGL policy shall contain or be deemed to contain a definition of "occurrence" that includes "[p]roperty damage or bodily injury resulting from faulty workmanship, exclusive of the faulty workmanship itself." *See* S.C. CODE § 38–61-70. The statute places no restriction on exclusions in the policy. The South Carolina law was passed in response to legislative dissatisfaction with its Supreme Court's decision in *Crossmann Communities v. Harleysville Mutual Insurance Co.*, No. 26909, 2011 S.C. LEXIS 2 (S.C. Jan. 7, 2011). Then, in August 2011, the Supreme Court of South Carolina, after granting re-hearing, withdrew its January decision in *Crossmann* and replaced it with one that essentially follows § 38–61-70 (*See* South Carolina, *infra*).

In essence, all four states that have passed laws to address the "occurrence" issue come at it in a different manner. In Colorado, damage to the insured's work itself is an occurrence. In South Carolina, damage to the insured's work itself is not an occurrence. The Arkansas statute does not specifically speak in terms of damage to the insured's work itself. In Hawaii, it depends when the policy was issued.

The most significant aspect of this legislative avenue for finding coverage for construction defects is this. Once the "occurrence" issue has been decided in a particular state, via the judicial route, it is difficult to change the outcome, especially if the issue has been decided by the state's highest court. And even if it remains an open issue with the highest court, the right case still needs to come along, not to mention that the judicial system is not known for its speediness. But the legislative route—especially for insureds who did not find success in the judicial branch and have exhausted their viable options—would offer insureds the proverbial second bite at the apple, and a speedier one at that. Further, while lobbying judges has significant restrictions—being limited to skillful advocacy, in public and under very precise conditions—lobbying legislators is a whole different kettle of fish. And construction trade associations are no strangers to legislative hallways.

In summary, and putting aside a few exceptions, the general rules concerning coverage for construction defects are as follows. No coverage is owed for damage solely to the insured's completed work product—either because it is not an "occurrence" or the applicability of the "your work" exclusion. However, if damage to the insured's completed work product qualifies as an "occurrence," then coverage is owed for such damage if its cause was the operations of an insured's subcontractor. And notwithstanding the varying rules and rationales concerning coverage for damage to the insured's work product, "property damage" to something other than the insured's work product is an "occurrence," and covered.

50-State Survey: Is Faulty Workmanship an "Occurrence"?

Alabama: The Supreme Court of Alabama held that "faulty workmanship itself is not an occurrence but that faulty workmanship may lead to an occurrence if it subjects personal property or other parts of the structure to 'continuous or repeated exposure' to some other 'general harmful condition' … and, as a result of that exposure, personal property or other parts of the structure are damaged." *Town & Country Property, L.L.C. v. Amerisure Ins. Co.*, 111 So. 3d 699 (Ala. 2011). *See also Shane Traylor Cabinetmaker, L.L.C. v. American Resources Ins. Co., Inc.*, 126 So. 3d 163 (Ala.

2013) (explaining that the court's decision in *Town & Country* was a reconciliation of the Alabama Supreme Court's decisions in *Moss v. Champion Insurance Co.*, 442 So. 2d 26 (Ala. 1983), which found an "occurrence" when a contractor's poor workmanship resulted, not merely in a poorly constructed roof, but damage to the plaintiff's attic, interior ceilings and furnishings and *United States Fidelity & Guaranty Co. v. Warwick Development Co.*, 446 So. 2d 1021 (Ala. 1984), which found no coverage for the cost of repairing or replacing the portions of a new house that had been defectively constructed by the insured); *Pa. Nat'l Mut. Cas. Ins. Co. v. St. Catherine of Siena Parish*, 790 F.3d 1173 (11th Cir. 2015) ("When a contractor performs faulty work (that is, fails to use reasonable skill), there is no accident or occurrence, but, when the contractor's faulty work creates a condition that in turn damages property, under Alabama law, that damage results from an accident. Thus, the question of whether poor workmanship can lead to an occurrence . . . depends on the nature of the damage that results from the faulty workmanship. For example, when a contractor hired to repair a roof performs the work poorly so that the roof must be replaced, there is no accident covered by the Policy. In contrast, when a contractor is hired to repair a roof and his work causes a leak that damages the building's ceilings, walls, or floors, there is an accident, and the cost of repairing the ceilings, walls, or floors is covered."); *FCCI Ins. Co. v. Capstone Process Sys.*, LLC, 49 F. Supp. 3d 995 (N.D. Ala. 2014) ("In this case, the only harmful condition was the failure of the rubber installed by Capstone, which necessitated that the Vessel be taken offline and thus resulted in a loss of use. While the policy does define 'property damage' to include the loss of use of property that is not physically damaged, that property damage must still be caused by an 'occurrence' under the policy. In this case, the faulty workmanship did not lead to any additional harmful condition; rather, the rubber failure was the only condition that lead to the Vessel being taken offline. The faulty workmanship of Capstone, by itself, is not an occurrence, and therefore the accident is not covered under the policy."). In *Owners Ins. Co. v. Jim Carr Homebuilder, LLC*, 157 So. 3d 148 (Ala. 2014), the Alabama Supreme Court explained its decision in *Town & Country*, but thought it "prudent to restate that principle in more precise terms -- faulty workmanship itself is not 'property damage' 'caused by' or 'arising out of' an 'occurrence.'" *Id.* at 155. The *Jim Carr* court added: "[T]o read into the term 'occurrence' the limitations urged by Owners would mean that, in a case like this one, where the insured contractor is engaged in constructing an entirely new building, or in a case where the insured contractor is completely renovating a building, coverage for accidents resulting from some generally harmful condition would be illusory. There would be no portion of the project that, if damaged as a result of exposure to such a condition arising out of faulty workmanship of the insured, would be covered under the policy." *Id. See also Nationwide Mut. Fire Ins. Co. v. David Grp., Inc.*, 294 So. 3d 732 (Ala. 2019) (noting that, "although there is no coverage for replacing poor work, there may be coverage for repairing resulting damage caused by the poor work").

Alaska: The Supreme Court of Alaska held that the failure of an improperly constructed curtain drain (device designed to prevent groundwater from penetrating a septic system's leach field), that caused a septic system to stop functioning, constituted an "occurrence." *Fejes v. Alaska Ins. Co.*, 984 P.2d 519, 523 (Alaska 1999). "The mere fact that a complaint against a contractor is based on a theory of misrepresentation or deceit does not mean that the facts underlying the claim did not arise from an accident." *Id.; see also Clear, LLC v. Am. & Foreign Ins. Co.*, No. 07-00110, 2008 U.S. Dist. LEXIS 23355 (D. Alaska Mar. 24, 2008) ("This court has no trouble extending the reach of *Fejes* to say that defective work by the general contractor which damages other property falls within the CGL coverage, because the same analysis by which the Alaska court concluded that the subcontractor's work was an accident supports the conclusion that the general contractor's own defective work damaging other property was an accident.").

Arizona: The Court of Appeals of Arizona held that the use of defective soil at a residential development, which resulted in expansion, leading to cracking of drywall and tile grout in completed homes, qualified as an "occurrence" for purposes of the resulting damage. *Lennar Corp. v. Auto-Owners Ins. Co.*, 151 P.3d 538, 545 (Ariz. Ct. App. 2007). "The Pinnacle Hill plaintiffs … do not claim faulty work alone; they also claim that property damage resulted from the faulty work. This is sufficient to allege an occurrence under the policies at issue." *Id.* (noting that, pursuant to *U.S. Fid. & Guar. Corp. v. Advance Roofing & Supply Co.*, 788 P.2d 1227 (Ariz. App. Ct. 1989), faulty workmanship, standing alone, cannot constitute an occurrence); *see also U.S. Home Corp. v. Maryland Cas. Co.*, No. 06–15092, 2007 U.S. App. LEXIS 29886 (9th Cir. Dec. 20, 2007) ("Appellant's complaint fails to allege any property damage other than the defective stucco and damage resulting from repair of that stucco. Under Arizona law, the faulty stucco, standing alone, does not constitute an 'occurrence' as defined in the insurance policy.") (citing *Advance Roofing* and *Lennar*); *Desert Mountain Props. Ltd. P'ship v. Liberty Mut. Fire Ins. Co.*, 236 P.3d 421, 431 (Ariz. App. Ct. 2010) ("We decline to hold that as a matter of law, a CGL policy does not cover liability arising out of contract. While there is some appeal to the notion that a breach of contract is not the sort of accidental risk to which liability insurance is designed to apply, we are reluctant to read such a limitation into a CGL policy when the parties have not chosen to write it for themselves.") ("Instead, we hold that the proper inquiry is whether an 'occurrence' has caused 'property damage,' not whether the ultimate remedy for that claim lies in contract or in tort.") (citation and internal quotes omitted); *Am. Family Mut. Ins. Co. v. Spectre West Builders Corp.*, No. CV09-968, 2011 U.S. Dist. LEXIS 11328 (D. Ariz. Feb. 4, 2011) ("[P]hysical damage caused by faulty workmanship can constitute an occurrence under a commercial liability policy.") (addressing *Lennar, Advance Roofing*, and *Desert Mountain*); *Quanta Indem. Co. v. Amberwood Development Inc.*, No. 11–01807, 2014 U.S. Dist. LEXIS 40211 (D. Ariz. Mar. 26, 2014) ("Arizona law is clear that property damage that is 'a natural consequence of faulty construction' constitutes an 'occurrence.'") (quoting *Lennar*); *Groth v. Owners Ins. Co.*, No. 12-1846, 2014 U.S. Dist. LEXIS 71884 (D. Ariz. May 27, 2014) ("Faulty soil compaction in this case constitutes a 'general harmful condition'; therefore, the improper soil compaction is an 'accident,' which in turn means the subcontractor work was an 'occurrence.' It is undisputed that exposure to the improperly prepared soils resulted in settling of the foundation, thereby causing distress to the home. At some point, the strain damaged the concrete slab. Thus, physical injury 'resulted from exposure to faulty construction.'") (citing *Lennar*); *Double AA Builders, Ltd. v. Preferred Contractors Ins. Co., LLC*, 386 P.3d 1277 (Ariz. Ct. App. 2016) (because of the "your work" exclusion, court did not need to reach the "question whether the Named Insured's faulty work constitutes an 'occurrence' unless an exception to the exclusion applies"); *Adams Craig Acquisitions, LLC v. Atain Specialty Ins. Co.*, No. 18-00817, 2019 U.S. Dist. LEXIS 150227 (D. Ariz. Sept. 4, 2019) (citing *Desert Mountain* in support of a finding that "the cost of repairing defective work, including the 'get to' costs required to make repairs to defective work" do not allege an "occurrence," while "the costs of repairing resulting damage, including the 'get to' costs" does allege an "occurrence"); *Sunwestern Contrs. Inc. v. Cincinnati Indem. Co.*, 390 F. Supp. 3d 1009 (D. Ariz. 2019) (finding that inadequate installation of flanges, which caused serious damage to a water main collector system's pipeline and surrounding areas, constituted an "occurrence" because the damage caused by the flanges was not limited to the flanges themselves); *United Specialty Ins. Co. v. Dorn Homes, Inc.*, No. 18-08092, 2020 U.S. Dist. LEXIS 138431 (D. Ariz. Aug. 4, 2020) (relying upon *Advance Roofing* and *Lennar* in rejecting the argument that faulty workmanship by a subcontractor, standing alone, could constitute an "occurrence").

Arkansas: The Supreme Court of Arkansas held that claims against a builder, for damages resulting from delays, defective construction, and employment of incompetent subcontractors, in the construction of a residence, did not qualify as an "occurrence." *Essex Ins. Co. v. Holder*, 261 S.W.3d 456, 460 (Ark. 2007). The court chose to side with what it viewed as the majority rule—that defective workmanship, standing alone, which results in damages only to the work product itself, is not an "accidental occurrence." *Id.* at 459–60. The court was persuaded that faulty workmanship is a foreseeable occurrence and performance bonds exist to insure a contractor against claims for the cost of repair or replacement of faulty work. *Id.* at 460. While one of the policies at issue defined "occurrence" to specifically exclude defective construction, the court's decision was based on the definition of "occurrence" without regard to the express exception. *Id.* at 457; *see also Cincinnati Ins. Cos. v. Collier Landholdings*, 614 F. Supp. 2d 960, 966 (W.D. Ark. 2009) ("[B]ecause the defective construction alleged by Collier is not an 'occurrence' under the CGL policy issued by Cincinnati, Benchmark is not entitled to recover the repair and remediation cost *arising from* its defective workmanship under the policy.") (emphasis added); *id.* at 967 ("The focus of the Arkansas approach is on the act or event that caused the underlying damage and not on the foreseeability of the resulting damage."); *Lexicon, Inc. v. ACE American Ins. Co.*, 634 F.3d 423 (8th Cir. 2011) (addressing *Holder* and concluding that "Absent some applicable exclusion in the policies or other defense, the Insurers are obligated to reimburse Lexicon for all property damage other than to the silo itself, including the lost DRI and damage to the nearby equipment. Under Arkansas law, it was foreseeable that faulty subcontractor work would damage the silo, but not foreseeable that faulty subcontractor work would cause millions of dollars in collateral damage."). However, in March 2011, Arkansas adopted legislation that a CGL policy shall contain a definition of "occurrence" that includes "[p]roperty damage or bodily injury resulting from faulty workmanship." *See* ARK. CODE § 23-79-155(a)(2). The statute places no restriction on exclusions in the policy. The Arkansas statute's findings and purpose make clear that it was passed in response to legislative dissatisfaction with court decisions, no doubt including its Supreme Court's holding in *Essex. See also J-McDaniel Const. Co., Inc. v. Mid-Continent Cas. Co.*, 761 F.3d 916 (8th Cir. 2014) (holding that "an insurance policy is governed by statutes in effect at the time of its issuance" and declining to apply § 23-79-155 retroactively); *S.E. Arnold & Co. v. Cincinnati Ins. Co.*, 507 S.W.3d 553 (Ark. Ct. App. 2016) ("No one disputes that faulty workmanship is an 'occurrence.' *See* Ark. Code Ann. § 23-79-

155 (Supp. 2015). The parties appear to agree that the insuring language in Arnold's CGL policy was triggered. Although the Griffiths complained about the installation of the flooring, which could be considered faulty workmanship, the only resulting damage alleged in the complaint was to the flooring itself, which was a product admittedly sold by Arnold. We hold that there was no uncertainty as to the effect of the damage-to-your-product exclusion—it excluded coverage for property damage to Arnold's product arising out of it or any part of it.").

In *Columbia Ins. Grp., Inc. v. Cenark Project Mgmt. Services*, 491 S.W.3d 135 (Ark. 2016) the Supreme Court of Arkansas – in a case where § 23-79-155 was not applicable -- addressed the following questions certified by the Eastern District of Arkansas: "(1) Whether faulty workmanship resulting in property damage to the work or work product of a third party (as opposed to the work or work product of the insured) constitutes an 'occurrence?' and (2) If such faulty workmanship constitutes an 'occurrence,' and an action is brought in contract for property damage to the work or work product of a third person, does any exclusion in the policy bar coverage for this property damage?" *Id.* at 136. The court held: "We reaffirm this court's previous position that a CGL policy does not extend basic coverage for a claim of breach of contract. Because there is no coverage, we consider the certified questions to be moot." *Id.* In explaining its decision, the court stated: "[T]he Home Owners' claim is that AII breached the contract by not adhering to the plans, specifications, and drawings prepared by the engineering firm. As damages, the Home Owners are seeking the economic losses flowing from AII's alleged breach. Although the underlying litigation touches upon damage to property, this does not alter the nature of the lawsuit, which is strictly a claim for breach of contract." *Id.* at 140-41.

California: The Supreme Court of California held that defects in aluminum doors sold to a building contractor were unexpected, undesigned, and unforeseen and constituted an "accident." *Geddes & Smith, Inc. v. St. Paul-Mercury Indem. Co.*, 334 P.2d 881, 884 (Cal. 1959). "Accident, as a source and cause of damage to property, within the terms of an accident policy, is an unexpected, unforeseen, or undesigned happening or consequence from either a known or an unknown cause." *Id.* (citation and internal quotes omitted). "They [door failures] were not the result of normal deterioration, but occurred long before any properly constructed door might be expected to wear out or collapse." *Id.* In general, unlike most states, California courts have not approached coverage for construction defects by focusing on whether faulty workmanship constitutes an "occurrence." Rather, coverage has turned on more overarching principles. *See Maryland Casualty Co. v. Reeder*, 221 Cal. App.3d 961, 971 (Cal. Ct. App. 1990) ("Generally liability policies, such as the ones in dispute here, are not designed to provide contractors and developers with coverage against claims their work is inferior or defective. The risk of replacing and repairing defective materials or poor workmanship has generally been considered a commercial risk which is not passed on to the liability insurer. Rather liability coverage comes into play when the insured's defective materials or work cause injury to property other than the insured's own work or products."). *Reeder* went on to hold that, under the policy language that is now the "sub-contractor exception" to the "your work" exclusion, the insured would have coverage for damage to his work arising out of a subcontractor's work, and the insured would have coverage for damage to a subcontractor's work arising out of the subcontractor's work. *Id.* at 971–72; *see also Clarendon America Ins. Co. v. General Sec. Indem. Co. of Arizona*, 193 Cal. App.4th 1311 (Cal. Ct. App. 2011) (quoting above passage from *Reeder*); *Ameron Intern. Corp. v. American Home Assur. Co.*, No. CV 11–1601, 2011 U.S. Dist. LEXIS 61486 (C.D. Cal. June 6, 2011) ("The policies provide coverage for liability arising from 'bodily injury or property damage,' including loss of use of property, caused by an 'occurrence' that takes place in the 'coverage territory.' Under California law, Brown's allegation that the concrete supplied by plaintiff was substandard constitutes an 'occurrence' under the policies. As discussed *supra*, under California law, the unintentional supplying of defective products constitutes an 'occurrence' within the meaning of commercial general liability policies."); *Regional Steel Corporation v. Liberty Surplus Insurance Corporation*, 226 Cal. App. 4th 1377 (2014) (noting that the basic purpose of liability policies, as explained in *Reeder*, is that they "are not designed to provide contractors and developers with coverage against claims their work is inferior or defective. The risk of replacing and repairing defective materials or poor workmanship has generally been considered a commercial risk which is not passed on to the liability insurer. Rather liability coverage comes into play when the insured's defective materials or work cause injury to property other than the insured's own work or products."); *Am. Home Assur. Co. v. SMG Stone Co.*, 119 F. Supp. 3d 1053 (N.D. Cal. 2015) ("But those California cases that have found coverage under general liability policies for property damage resulting from construction defects involved physical injuries to *other* parts of the construction project.") (emphasis in original); *S. Patterson Constr., Inc. v. Peerless Ins. Co.*, No. 16-01165, 2017 U.S. Dist. LEXIS 166693 (C.D. Cal. Apr. 27, 2017) ("Defendants argue that, because the Anderson complaint alleges that Patterson intentionally utilized defective materials, there was no 'occurrence.' However, the Anderson complaint alleges *both* that Patterson intentionally utilized defective materials and that Patterson did so negligently and carelessly. Therefore, the Anderson complaint does allege an 'occurrence.'") (emphasis in original); *Navigators Specialty Ins. Co. v. Moorefield Construction, Inc.*, 6 Cal. App. 5th 1258 (2016) ("We emphasize that we need not and do not decide whether all construction defects are 'occurrences' under a standard CGL policy. We only decide whether, based on the record before us, Moorefield's conduct for which liability was sought to be imposed constituted an accident under California law. We conclude Moorefield's conduct was not an accident because it was a deliberate decision made with knowledge that the moisture vapor emission rate from the concrete slab exceeded specifications. This was not a case in which a contractor engaged in conduct only later discovered or revealed to constitute a construction defect. Navigators proved that Moorefield knew about and intended to perform defective work with the hope or mistaken belief the defect would not cause property damage. Although there was no evidence that Moorefield intended to cause property damage, under California law, [t]he insured's subjective intent is irrelevant."). However, despite some decisions addressing coverage for construction defects based on general principles, the California Court of Appeal stated in *Global Modular, Inc. v. Kadena Pacific, Inc.*, 15 Cal. App. 5th 127 (2017) that "any preconceived notion that a CGL policy is only for tort liability [for damage to third party property] must yield to the policy's actual language." *Id.* at 143 (citing *Lamar Homes* (*see* Texas) and calling it a decision that rejected an invitation "to ignore policy language in favor of a general principle against insuring against 'business risks.'"); *Mesa Underwriters Specialty Ins. Co. v. Universal Constr. Grp.*, No. 18-08802, 2019 U.S. Dist. LEXIS 222632 (C.D. Cal. Aug. 21, 2019) (noting that allegations of negligently building and installing certain aspects of a construction project in an unintended manner, which compromised the property's structural integrity and functionality, toed the line between "intentional acts with unintended consequences and unintentional acts," but ultimately concluding that the "occurrence" requirement was met).

Colorado: The Colorado Court of Appeals held that a claim for damages arising from defective workmanship, standing alone, does not qualify as an "occurrence," regardless of the underlying legal theory pled (tort, contract, or breach of warranty). *Gen. Sec. Indem. Co. of Ariz. v. Mountain States Mut. Cas. Co.*, 205 P.3d 529, 534 (Colo. Ct. App. 2009). However, the court also adopted a "corollary" to such rule—an "accident" and "occurrence" are present "when consequential property damage has been inflicted upon a third party as a result of the insured's activity." *Id.* at 535;

see also United Fire & Cas. Co. v. Boulder Plaza Residential, LLC, No. 06-CV-00037, 2010 U.S. Dist. LEXIS 14257 (D. Colo. Feb. 1, 2010) (addressing *General Sec.* in detail and rejecting the insured's effort to separate out "loss of use" of the work product, from the work product itself, as it would cause the consequential damage exception to swallow the rule). However, on May 21, 2010, the Colorado General Assembly enacted An Act Concerning Commercial Liability Insurance Policies Issued to Construction Professionals, H.B. 10–1394. *See* C.R.S.A. § 13-20-808. The Act specifically described the Court of Appeals's decision in *General Security* as not properly considering a construction professional's reasonable expectation that an insurer would defend the construction professional against a construction defect claim. *Id.* at § (1)(b)(III). The Act addresses several issues relevant to coverage for construction defects, most notably declaring that: "In interpreting a liability insurance policy issued to a construction professional, a court shall presume that the work of a construction professional that results in property damage, including damage to the work itself or other work, is an accident unless the property damage is intended and expected by the insured." *Id.* at § 3. However, nothing in the Act "[r]equires coverage for damage to an insured's own work unless otherwise provided in the insurance policy; or [c]reates insurance coverage that is not included in the insurance policy." *Id.* at § 3(a), (b). *See Crossen v. Am Family Mut. Ins. Co.*, No. 09-cv-02859, 2010 U.S. Dist. LEXIS 68108 (D. Colo. July 7, 2010) (concluding that, because the policy could cover the injury alleged, notwithstanding *General Security*, it was not necessary to address the impact of C.R.S.A. § 13-20-808); *United Fire & Cas. Co. v. Boulder Plaza Residential, LLC*, 633 F.3d 951, 959–60 (10th Cir. 2011) (applying Colorado law) (addressing the motivation behind the passage of C.R.S.A. § 13-20-808 but concluding that it was not necessary to consider the statute to reach a decision); *Continental Western Ins. Co. v. Shay Const., Inc.*, 805 F. Supp. 2d 1125 (D. Colo. 2011) (addressing C.R.S.A. § 13-20-808 and concluding it was not applicable because policy not in force on effective date) (noting that, in any event, even under *General Security*, the claim might allege an occurrence); *Greystone Constr., Inc. v. Nat'l Fire & Marine Ins. Co.*, 661 F.3d 1272 (10th Cir. 2011) (applying Colorado law) (holding that statute did not apply retroactively, even though it states that it applies to "all insurance policies currently in existence" (or issued after the act's effective date), as this means that the Act applies to policies whose policy period have not yet expired; fact that coverage can still be obtained, under an expired policy, does not qualify as "currently in existence") (characterizing *General Security* as "persuasive," noting that it agreed with "most of it" but also pointed out that it was non-binding) (holding that "the CGL policies at issue may cover damage to nondefective property arising from poor workmanship. In our view, the policyholders' complaints adequately allege an 'accident' that fits within the policies' definition of a covered 'occurrence.' Accordingly, we hold that injuries flowing from improper or faulty workmanship constitute an occurrence so long as the resulting damage is to nondefective property, and is caused without expectation or foresight."). The real difference between *Greystone Construction* and *General Security* is in a case that involves the application of the "sub-contractor" exception to the "your work" exclusion. *See also Colorado Pool Systems, Inc. v. Scottsdale Ins. Co.*, 317 P.3d 1262 (Colo. Ct. App. 2012), *cert granted* 2013 Colo. LEXIS 619, *appeal dismissed* 2014 Colo. LEXIS 77 (holding that § 13-20-808 was not applicable) (applying *Greystone* test and concluding that policy did not cover damage incurred in demolishing and replacing a pool itself; but "rip and tear damage to nondefective third-party work (including damage to a deck, sidewalk, retaining wall, and electrical conduits) is covered. Under the *Greystone* test, this damage is the result of an 'accident'"); *TCD, Inc. v. American Family Mut. Ins. Co.*, 296 P.3d 255 (Colo. Ct. App. 2012) (under *General Security*, "claim for damages arising from poor workmanship, standing alone, does not allege an accident that constitutes a covered occurrence, regardless of the underlying legal theory pled," but noting that *Greystone* provides a corollary that "an 'accident' and 'occurrence' are present when consequential property damage has been inflicted *upon a third party* as a result of the insured's activity") (emphasis in original) ("A plain reading of 'currently in existence' supports the conclusion that section 13-20-808 applies only to policies for which the policy period had not yet expired on May 21, 2010."); *Wardcraft Homes, Inc. v. Emplrs Mut. Cas. Co.*, 70 F. Supp. 3d 1198 (D. Colo. 2014) (addressing whether there was the property damage, to nondefective property, to satisfy *Greystone*); *Cool Sunshine Heating & Air Conditioning, Inc. v. Am. Family Mut. Ins. Co.*, No. 14-1637, 2014 U.S. Dist. LEXIS 174818 (D. Colo. Dec. 17, 2014) ("Faulty workmanship can constitute an occurrence that triggers coverage under a [commercial general liability] policy if (1) the property damage was not caused by purposeful neglect or knowingly poor workmanship, and (2) the damage was to non-defective portions of the contractor's or subcontractor's work or to third-party property. The Court presumes that Cool Sunshine did not purposefully or knowingly install an inferior compressor at the Residence, thereby fulfilling the first prong. However, as set forth below, there is no allegation of 'property damage' to any 'non-defective portion' of Cool Sunshine's work. Thus, the Court finds that neither the CDARA Letter nor the Underlying Complaint contain allegations that could reasonably come within the coverage of the Policy."); *Peerless Indem. Ins. Co. v. Colclasure*, No. 16-424, 2017 U.S. Dist. LEXIS 22193 (D. Colo. Feb. 16, 2017) ("[I]t fairly appears that Defendant Colclasure and/or his subcontractor did not intend and expect the damage to Defendant Weed's property, thus applying the presumption required by § 13-20-808 to the Policy, the Court finds that Defendant Colclasure's work resulting in property damage was an 'accident' and, therefore, is a covered 'occurrence.'"); *Owners Ins. Co. v. Tipton*, No. 15-02638, 2017 U.S. Dist. LEXIS 231555 (D. Colo. Mar. 29, 2017) ("Arguably, the case law on whether improper or faulty construction workmanship is an 'occurrence,' as that term is used in the Owners Policy, has produced varying conclusions. That leaves some doubt about the meaning of this key term in the context of the underlying suit and, thus, some doubt about the precise limits of the coverage provided by the Policy...Here, there is reasonable doubt about whether the alleged improper or faulty workmanship by Tipton constitutes an 'occurrence' which triggers the duty to defend. That doubt must be resolved in favor of insurance coverage for Tipton.").

Connecticut: The Supreme Court of Connecticut held that "unintended construction defects may form the basis of an 'occurrence' or 'accident' under commercial general liability policies. Furthermore, damage to an insured's nondefective work is 'property damage' within the commercial general liability policy's initial grant of coverage. Claims limited to damages for the replacement of defective components or poor workmanship, however, without more, do not constitute 'property damage' under the policy." *Capstone Bldg. Corp. v. American Motorists Ins. Co.*, 67 A.3d 961, 985 (Conn. 2013). *See also Travelers Cas. and Sur. Co. of America v. Netherlands Ins. Co.*, 95 A.3d 1031 (Conn. 2014) ("[W]e conclude that defective workmanship can give rise to an 'occurrence' under the insuring agreement. This is, however, only the first step in determining whether the damage at issue in the present case is covered under the policy. The terms of the insuring agreement require both an 'occurrence' and 'property damage' for coverage.") (quoting *Capstone*); *New London County Mut. Ins. Co. v. Sielski*, 123 A.3d 925 (Conn. Ct. App. 2015) (describing *Capstone* as "rejecting a per se rule for or against including all damages related to defective construction in the initial grant of coverage and requiring, instead, that any damages claimed be considered individually") ("'Although we reject [the insurance company's] argument that the insuring agreement never covers damage to the insured's project, whether an insured party makes a viable claim for property damage is a highly fact-dependent determination in each case. The allegations detailed in the District Court's memorandum of law may be divided into four categories: (1) damage to nondefective property stemming from defective construction; (2) carbon monoxide; (3) defective work, standing alone, including building and fire safety code violations; and (4) repairs to damaged work.' *Capstone Building Corp. v. American Motorists Ins. Co.*, supra, 308 Conn. 777-78. The court then proceeded to examine each of these categories, holding that the first ground, if properly alleged, would set forth a claim for property damage within the terms of the policy, and that the remaining three would not provide a basis for such an allegation.") (*appeal granted* 125 A.3d 533 (Conn. 2015)) (addressing whether a claim of negligent misrepresentation was covered under a homeowner's policy)).

Looking at pre-*Capstone* cases, a Connecticut trial court held that the loss of use of property, caused by the need to relocate tenants and lost rental revenue, on account of the insured's installation of unsuitable telephone cable in residential units, did not qualify as an "occurrence." *Times Fiber Commc'ns, Inc. v. Travelers Indem. Co. of Ill.*, No. CVX05CV030196619S, 2005 Conn. Super. LEXIS 335 (Conn. Super. Ct. Feb. 2, 2005). "[T]he 'accident' is 'the event' causing the injury, not the cause of that event. In this case the alleged 'accident' would have to be the removal of the cable because this was and will be the event causing the injury to the [multi-dwelling units]. The alleged loss of use of property is therefore based entirely on harm which resulted from repair activities necessary to replace the nonconforming cable. The accident was therefore not the installation of the non-conforming cable as claimed by plaintiff." (quotation omitted). A Connecticut District Court held that claims against a swimming pool builder, for defective construction of pools (cracking in the concrete walls and floors), did not qualify as an "occurrence." *Scottsdale Ins. Co. v. R.I. Pools, Inc.*, 742 F. Supp. 2d 239 (D. Conn. 2010). "[A]lthough an accident can be a consequence of faulty workmanship, faulty workmanship alone is not an accident." *Id.* at 246, *vacated by* 710 F.3d 488 (2d Cir. 2013) (noting that "the district court erred in ruling that defects in the insured's work are not within the scope of an 'occurrence'" because it "never considered the crucial question whether the defects come within the subcontractor exception to the express exclusion for the insured's own work"); *See also Barbar v. Berthiaume*, No. CV054009532S, 2009 Conn. Super. LEXIS 2477 (Conn. Super. Ct. Aug. 25, 2009) (noting that the insured contractor raised house in order to construct new piers and the house toppled causing damage) ("[I]t is clear that the toppling of the house was an accident or an occurrence and clearly covered by the policy. No evidence was presented to the court that the toppling of the house was as a result of faulty work by [the insured].") ; *Peterbilt of Conn., Inc. v. First Financial Ins. Co.*, No. 3:10cv1575, 2011 U.S. Dist. LEXIS 106740

(D. Conn. Sept. 20, 2011) ("Faulty workmanship does not constitute an accident or occurrence.") (citing *R.I. Pools* and *Times Fiber*).

Delaware: A Delaware District Court held that a claim against a homebuilder for construction deficiencies, including missing flashing, fiberglass installation, and improper installation of a wrap system, did not qualify as an "occurrence." *Brosnahan Builders, Inc. v. Harleysville Mut. Ins. Co.*, 137 F. Supp. 2d 517, 526 (D. Del. 2001). "[T]he Pinkerts claim that plaintiffs were directed to install specific water proofing materials and failed to do so, and that the materials used were installed improperly .... The situation that led to the damage to the Pinkerts' home was clearly within the control of plaintiffs, as general contractor of the construction project, and not a fortuitous circumstance happening 'without human agency.'" *Id.* (*aff'd* 2003 U.S. App. LEXIS 1204 (3rd Cir. Jan. 21, 2003)); *see also AE-Newark Associates, L.P. v. CNA Ins. Cos.*, No. Civ. A 00C-05-186JEB, 2001 Del. Super. LEXIS 370 (Del. Super. Ct. Oct. 2, 2001) (holding that damage to apartment buildings and tenants' personal property, caused by faulty installation of a roof system, was "clearly" "property damage" that was caused by an "occurrence"); *Goodville Mut. Cas. Co. v. Baldo*, No. 09–338, 2011 U.S. Dist. LEXIS 59526 (D. Del. June 3, 2011) (addressing coverage for claims by a builder against an insured–condominium property manager) ("The [builder's] third party complaint alleges that, as a result of defendant's [property manager's] efforts to 'repair purported leaks to roofs, windows, siding and other areas' of the Condominium, it is 'responsible for or exacerbated the issues' for which damages are sought. Therefore, as in *Brosnahan Builders*, the property damage was not caused by an occurrence because the situation that caused the damage was not an accident, but was within the control of the insured."); *David A. Bramble, Inc. v. Old Republic Gen. Ins. Corp.*, No. S16C-06-025, 2017 Del. Super. LEXIS 34 (Del. Super. Ct. Jan. 20, 2017) (citing *Baldo* and *Brosnahan Builders*) ("I agree that for this case defective workmanship does not constitute an 'occurrence' because Georgetown is only seeking breach of contract damages arising out of Bramble's allegedly defective workmanship in the construction of the spray irrigation system. That is the type of risk that many courts have concluded is not covered by a commercial general liability policy. However, if Bramble's defective workmanship had caused injury to a person or damage to property other than the spray irrigation system, then this well might qualify as an 'occurrence.' That is simply not the case here though.").

District of Columbia: No instructive authority. *See* Maryland. "When District of Columbia law is silent, it has been the practice of the federal courts in this Circuit to turn to the law of Maryland for historical and geographical reasons." *Gray v. American Exp. Co.*, 743 F.2d 10, 17 (D.C. Cir. 1984).

Florida: The Supreme Court of Florida held that faulty workmanship that is neither intended nor expected from the standpoint of the insured can constitute an "accident" and, thus, an "occurrence." *U.S. Fire Ins. Co. v. J.S.U.B., Inc.*, 979 So. 2d 871, 888 (Fla. 2007). "[W]e reject a definition of 'occurrence' that renders damage to the insured's own work as a result of a subcontractor's faulty workmanship expected, but renders damage to property of a third party caused by the same faulty workmanship unexpected." *Id.* at 885. The court next examined whether there was "property damage," holding that "faulty workmanship or defective work that has damaged the otherwise nondefective completed project has caused 'physical injury to tangible property' within the plain meaning of the definition in the policy. If there is no damage beyond the faulty workmanship or defective work, then there may be no resulting 'property damage.'" *Id.* at 889. In *Auto-Owners Insurance Co. v. Pozzi Window Co.*, 984 So. 2d 1241 (Fla. 2008), the Supreme Court of Florida held that a subcontractor's defective installation of defective windows was not itself "physical injury to tangible property," and, therefore, was not "property damage," thereby precluding coverage for the costs of repair or replacement of the defective windows. *Id.* at 1249. "Conversely, if the claim is for the repair or replacement of windows that were not initially defective but were damaged by the defective installation, then there is physical injury to tangible property. In other words, because the windows were purchased separately by the Homeowner, were not themselves defective, and were damaged as a result of the faulty installation, then there is physical injury to tangible property, i.e., windows damaged by defective installation." *Id.*; *see also Arnett v. Mid-Continent Cas. Co.*, No. 08-2373-T-27, 2010 U.S. Dist. LEXIS 71666 (M.D. Fla. July 16, 2010) ("It is settled that defective construction does not constitute 'property damage' within the meaning of GAIC's policy. However, faulty workmanship or defective work that has damaged the otherwise nondefective completed project has caused physical injury to tangible property within the plain meaning of the definition in the policy. Coverage therefore extends to costs to repair damages caused by construction defects, but not to repair or replace the defective work itself.") (citing *J.S.U.B.* and *Pozzi Window*); *Palm Beach Grading, Inc. v. Nautilus Ins. Co.*, No. 10–12821, 2011 U.S. App. LEXIS 14576 (11th Cir. July 14, 2011) ("The problem with PBG's claim is that the defective pipe did not cause damage independent of the repair and replacement of the pipe. For example, the pipes never burst, caused sinkholes, or caused back-ups. Rather, PBG's claim is solely for the costs of repairing and removing the defective pipe, which is not a claim for 'property damage.'") (citing *J.S.U.B.* and *Pozzi Window*); *Amerisure Mut. Ins. Co. v. Auchter Co.*, 673 F.3d 1294 (11th Cir. 2012) (addressing *J.S.U.B.* and *Pozzi Windows* at length) ("Although the loss of roof tiles may be said to have 'damaged' the structural integrity of the roof, thereby rendering it defective, 'there is no damage beyond the faulty workmanship' because the defective roof has not damaged some 'otherwise nondefective' component of the project."); *Nationwide Mut. Fire Ins. Co. v. Advanced Cooling and Heating, Inc.*, 126 So. 3d 385 (Fla. Ct. App. 2013) ("Property damage as contemplated by the plain meaning of the insurance policy refers to damage to property other than the property being repaired. A complaint seeking recovery for costs of repair and removal of defective work does not involve a property damage claim."); *J.B.D. Construction, Inc. v. Mid-Continent Cas. Co.*, 571 Fed. Appx. 918 (11th Cir. 2014) ("The Florida Supreme Court has been clear that the cost of removing or repairing defective work does not qualify as a claim for 'property damage.' However, a claim for the costs of repairing damage to other property caused by defective work does qualify as a claim for 'property damage.'") (discussing *J.S.U.B.* and *Pozzi Windows*); *Core Constr. Servs. Southeast v. Crum & Forster Specialty Ins. Co.*, 658 Fed. Appx. 534 (11th Cir. 2016) ("Crum & Forster owed no duty to provide a defense to Core Construction because the complaint against it did not allege a claim for 'property damage.' Empire failed to allege that the defective installation of roofing caused 'physical injury to tangible property' such that there was 'damage to the completed project caused by the subcontractor's defective [roofing] work,'. . . or that the defective work 'caused the roof to fail in such a way as to allow the elements to damage other components of the project,' Empire, like the owner of the inn in *Amerisure*, 'never alleged that any part of the [buildings or development] other than the roof was damaged by the defective roof.'"); *Addison Ins. Co. v. 4000 Island Blvd. Condo Ass'n*, 721 Fed. Appx. 847 (11th Cir. 2017) ("The Florida Supreme Court has shed additional light on the 'property damage' and 'occurrence' terms in commercial general liability insurance policies. The term 'property damage' does not include an insured's faulty workmanship, but it does include physical injury to otherwise nondefective property that results from that faulty workmanship. Damage to otherwise nondefective property that is caused by faulty workmanship constitutes an 'occurrence,' so long as the faulty workmanship was unintentional.") (citing *J.S.U.B.*); *S. Owners Ins. Co. v. Gallo Bldg. Servs.*, No. 15-01440, 2018 U.S. Dist. LEXIS 212961 (M.D. Fla. Dec. 18, 2018) (citing *J.S.U.B.* and *Auchter* in support of the conclusion that the insurer had a duty to defend a complaint alleging "damage to other building components," "damage to other property," "water intrusion" and "relocation of residents"); *Glass-On Solutions, Inc. v. Blackboard U.S. Holdings, Inc.*, No. 19-14027, 2020 U.S. Dist. LEXIS 73711 (S.D. Fla. Apr. 24, 2020) (relying on *J.S.U.B.* for the proposition that "defective workmanship can constitute an 'occurrence' under Section I.A.1 of the 1986 standard form CGL policy").

Georgia: The Supreme Court of Georgia addressed a general contractor's claim against a plumbing subcontractor for faulty workmanship and held that "an occurrence can arise where faulty workmanship causes unforeseen or unexpected damage to other property." *Am. Empire Surplus Lines Ins. Co. v. Hathaway Dev. Co.*, 707 S.E.2d 369, 372 (Ga. 2011). "In this case, Whisnant was a subcontractor for Hathaway on three projects. On one project, Whisnant installed four-inch pipe on an underslab, although the contract specified six-inch pipe. On another project, Whisnant improperly installed a dishwasher supply line. On the third project, Whisnant improperly installed a pipe which separated under hydrostatic pressure. Each of these missteps damaged neighboring property being built by Hathaway. The Court of Appeals correctly determined that these acts constituted an 'occurrence' under the CGL policy. *SawHorse v. S. Guar. Ins. Co.*, etc., *supra*. Accordingly, we answer the question posed at the outset of this opinion in the negative and hold that an occurrence can arise where faulty workmanship causes unforeseen or unexpected damage to other property." *Id.* at 371–72. Then, in *Taylor Morrison Services, Inc. v. HDI-Gerling America Ins. Co.*, 746 S.E.2d 587 (Ga. 2013), the Supreme Court of Georgia held that, for an "occurrence" to exist under a standard CGL policy, it is not required that there be "damage to 'other property,' that is, property other than the insured's completed work itself." *Id.* at 588. "[W]e find a number of recent decisions in our sister states that construe 'occurrence' without reference to the identity of the person whose property or work is damaged thereby." *Id.* at 593. The *HDI-Gerling* Court also overruled *Forster v. State Farm Fire & Cas. Co.*, 704 S.E.2d 204 (2010) "which relied on the dicta in *Custom Planning [& Development, Inc. v. American Nat. Fire Ins. Co.]*, 606 S.E.2d 39 (Ga. Ct. App. 2004) to affirm the grant of summary judgment to an insurer with regard to any construction defects constituting a breach of warranty, without any further consideration of whether an 'occurrence' was involved." *See also Builders Ins. v. Tenenbaum*, 757 S.E.2d 669 (Ga. Ct. App. 2014) (citing *HDI-Gerling* and not disturbing trial court's decision that damage to nondefective work, caused by other defective work, constituted an occurrence: "damages to framing, support beams, sheathing, sheetrock, and interior walls caused by improperly installed windows, improperly installed roofing materials, and improper flashing"); *Auto-Owners Ins. Co. v. Unit Owners Ass'n of Riverview Overlook Condo.*, No. 13-3012, 2014 U.S. Dist. LEXIS 152452 (N.D. Ga. Oct. 28, 2014) ("An occurrence does not require damage to property other than that of the insured. Faulty workmanship alone may therefore constitute an occurrence. . . . The Underlying Complaint here alleges that defects in the PDQ Defendants' work have caused damage to the common areas of the property. Overlook has alleged both faulty workmanship, which is enough to constitute an occurrence, and damage to nondefective property, which is enough for property damage. It is at least arguable, therefore, that the underlying claims fall within the main policy coverage."). In *Evanston Ins. Co. v. DCM Constr., Inc.*, 441 F. Supp. 3d 1336 (N.D. Ga. 2020), the United States District Court for the Northern District of Georgia analyzed the "occurrence" requirement in the context of an amended definition of "occurrence." The policy revised the definition of "occurrence" to include "'[b]odily injury' or 'property damage' resulting from faulty workmanship, exclusive of the faulty workmanship itself." *Id.* at 1343. The District Court noted that, pursuant to the "plain language of the contract" and well-settled Georgia law, a lawsuit seeking "damages to repair DCM's work and economic losses" did not allege an "occurrence." *Id.*

Hawaii: The Court of Appeals of Hawaii held that "under Hawaii law, construction defect claims do not constitute an 'occurrence' under a CGL policy. Accordingly, breach of contact claims based on allegations of shoddy performance are not covered under CGL policies. Additionally, tort-based claims, derivative of these breach of contract claims, are also not covered under CGL policies." *Group Builders, Inc. v. Admiral Ins. Co.*, 231 P.3d 67, 73–74 (Haw. Ct. App. 2010). While the *Group Builders* court did not address the issue in these terms, it appears that the decision precluded coverage for not only defects in a contractor's own work, but also any consequential damages caused by the contractor's faulty workmanship. Consider that the claim at issue involved the availability of coverage for an insured that installed, among other things, an EIFS system on a hotel, which then experienced mold growth in guest rooms, followed by the closure of 20 floors of rooms.

In June 2011, Hawaii adopted legislation that takes direct aim at *Group Builders*. Following several pages of findings that paint the *Group Builders* decision in very problematic terms for the state's economy, the Hawaii legislature announced that, in a policy issued to a construction professional, for liability arising from construction-related work, the meaning of the term "occurrence" "shall be construed in accordance with the law as it existed at the time that the insurance policy was issued." *See* HAW. REV. STAT. 431:1(a). Thus, only policies that were issued after the May 19, 2010 decision in *Group Builders* will be subject to its holding that construction defect claims—contract and tort—do not constitute an "occurrence" under a CGL policy. Therefore, Hawaii law, prior to *Group Builders*, will still be relevant for some time.

Looking at Hawaii law, prior to *Group Builders*, the Supreme Court of Hawaii held that "[w]ater damage to an exposed building is the foreseeable result of a contractor's abandonment of a roofing contract, such that this class of damages did not arise from an 'occurrence' as defined by the CGL policy." *Keneke Roofing, Inc. v. Island Ins. Co., Ltd.*, No. 24726, 2004 Haw. LEXIS 663 (Hawaii Oct. 5, 2004); *see also Burlington Ins. Co. v. Oceanic Design & Constr., Inc.*, 383 F.3d 940, 948 (9th Cir. 2004) (applying Hawaii law) ("General liability policies … are not designed to provide contractors and developers with coverage against claims their work is inferior or defective. The risk of replacing and repairing defective materials or poor workmanship has generally been considered a commercial risk which is not passed on to the liability insurer. Rather liability coverage comes into play when the insured's defective materials or work cause injury to property other than the insured's own work or products.") (citation omitted); *State Farm Fire and Cas. Co. v. Vogelgesang*, No. 10–00172, 2011 U.S. Dist. LEXIS 72618 (D. Haw. July 6, 2011) (examining HAW. REV. STAT. 431:1 and concluding that it did not alter decision of no coverage because no coverage was owed based on the state of Hawaii law prior to 2006, the year that the first potentially applicable policy was issued); *State Farm Fire & Cas. Co. v. Kaaihue*, No. 13–00185, 2013 U.S. Dist. LEXIS 175395 (D. Haw. Dec. 13, 2013) ("*Burlington, Group Builders*, and [*Illinois Nat. Ins. Co. v. Nordic PCL Const., Inc.*, 870 F.Supp.2d 1015 (D. Haw. 2012)] involved CGL insurance policies. Here, Kaaihue seeks insurance coverage under his homeowner's and personal umbrella insurance policies for claims arising out of a contract to help construct a house. This case therefore presents an even stronger case than *Burlington, Group Builders*, and *Nordic* for a determination that the state-court complaint does not allege anything that can be considered an 'occurrence' for purposes of the policies.") ("Even if section 431: 1–217(a) applies [and the court concluded that it didn't], the law in effect at the time the insurance policy issued was that of *Burlington* and *Group Builders*."); *Am. Auto. Ins. Co. v. Haw. Nut & Bolt, Inc.*, No. 15-00245, 2017 U.S. Dist. LEXIS 149571 (D. Haw. Sept. 14, 2017) ("Subsequent to the passage of Act 83 [Section 431:1], courts in this district have continued to find that policies issued before *Group Builders* and after *Burlington* continue to fall within the Ninth Circuit's *Burlington* analysis."); *State Farm Fire & Cas. Co. v. GP West, Inc.*, 190 F. Supp. 3d 1003 (D. Haw. 2016) ("While it is true that the legislature strongly denounced *Group Builders* in House Bill No. 924 (which ultimately resulted in Act 83), it is also true that no court has criticized or overturned *Group Builders* — or *Burlington*, the case upon which *Group Builders* so heavily relied — in the six years since the decision was rendered and the five years since the enactment of Act 83. Additionally, the District of Hawaii has already recognized that nothing in Act 83 purports to nullify any of the decisions preceding *Group Builders*, and that *Group Builders* is consistent with prior case law. To the extent that *Group Builders*, as a result of Act 83, no longer represents appropriate case law for policies issued prior to that decision, the case still serves as helpful insight into how Hawaii courts will construe and apply the multiple cases, including *Burlington*, upon which *Group Builders* relies. Those cases remain good law and stipulate the rule that CGL policies do not provide coverage for contract or contract-based tort claims.") (construing *Group Builders* to mean that "faulty construction work giving rise to 'other property' damage does not constitute an 'occurrence' under a CGL policy.").

In *Gemini Ins. Co. v. ConstRX Ltd.*, 360 F. Supp. 3d 1055 (D. Haw. 2018), the Hawaii District Court examined the "occurrence" requirement under a policy which modified the definition of "occurrence." The policy provided that "[f]aulty workmanship does not constitute an 'occurrence.' But when faulty workmanship performed by you or on your behalf causes 'bodily injury' or causes 'property damage' to property other than 'your work,' then such 'bodily injury' or 'property damage' will be considered caused by an 'occurrence.'" *Id.* at 1061. The District Court found that "the plain language of the Revised Occurrence Endorsement, when appropriately 'construed in accord with the reasonable expectations of a layperson,' indicates that coverage exists even for contract-based 'faulty workmanship' claims so long as the damage is to property other than [the insured's] work." *Id.* at 1066. The District Court noted that other Hawaii cases, including *Group Builders*, which held that "contract and contract-based tort claims are not within the scope of typical CGL policies do not bar coverage under the circumstances alleged here." *Id. See also Nautilus Ins. Co. v. RMB Enters.*, 497 F. Supp. 3d 936 (D. Haw. 2020) (concluding that allegations of faulty workmanship did not allege an "occurrence" within the meaning of the policies because the property damage was limited to the insured's own work) (applying the revised definition of "occurrence").

Idaho: No instructive authority. *See W. Heritage Ins. Co. v. Green*, 54 P.3d 948 (Idaho 2002) (addressing various business risk exclusions and acknowledging that the parties conceded that the nonapplication or insufficient application of fertilizer and weed control chemicals to farm ground, resulting in damage to potato crops, constituted an "occurrence" within the meaning of the policy); *see also Am. States Ins.*

Co. v. Edgerton, No. CV 07-239, 2008 U.S. Dist. LEXIS 79866 (D. Idaho Sept. 3, 2008) (addressing the "your work" exclusion but not whether faulty workmanship is an "occurrence") ("The policy is clear that there is no coverage for property damage to work or operations performed by Pioneer or on its behalf and materials, parts or equipment furnished in connection with such work or operations. The parties agree on this point. They do dispute what the exact amount of damages to Pioneer's work would be."); *Employers Mut. Cas. Co. v. Donnelly*, 300 P.3d 31 (Idaho 2103) (containing some discussion in the context of a construction defection claim that could be relevant to the "occurrence" issue); *Bingham Mech., Inc. v. CNA Ins. Co.*, No. 10-00342, 2014 U.S. Dist. LEXIS 46028 (D. Idaho Mar. 31, 2014) (addressing whether damage caused by a contractor's work qualified as "property damage," but not addressing the "occurrence" issue) ("[T]he damages could include Mountain View Hospital's inability to use rooms and/or equipment due to the defects or during the time when the piping alleged to be defective was being replaced. This type of 'loss of use' could amount to property damage as defined in the policies. The damages also could include the cost of replacing ceiling tiles and drywall, and repainting, as part of accessing the already-installed piping to replace it with that specified in the project plans.").

Illinois: The Appellate Court of Illinois stated that "Illinois courts have held in numerous cases that construction defects that damage something other than the project itself will constitute an 'occurrence' under a CGL policy." *CMK Dev. Corp. v. W. Bend Mut. Ins. Co.*, 917 N.E.2d 1155, 1164 (Ill. App. Ct. 2009) (citations and quotations omitted). The court examined several alleged construction defects and concluded that none qualified as damage to something other than the home itself. *Id.* at 1166–67; *see also Stoneridge Dev. Co., Inc. v. Essex Ins. Co.*, 888 N.E.2d 633, 656–57 (Ill. App. Ct. 2008) (holding that the "subcontractor exception" to the "your work" exclusion did not provide coverage for damage to a home, even though it was a subcontractor's defective soil compaction that caused the damage, because such damage was not "property damage" caused by an "occurrence" and an exception to an exclusion cannot create coverage); *Fireman's Fund Ins. Co. v. Amstek Metal, LLC*, No. 07 C 647, 2008 U.S. Dist. LEXIS 75879 (N.D. Ill. Aug. 27, 2008) ("[A]lthough *Viking* establishes that, generally, a CGL policy does not cover a general contractor's claim for breach of contract in construction cases, 358 Ill.App.2d at 42, 831 N.E.2d at 6, other courts suggest that there are exceptions to this general rule. Most recently, the *Stoneridge* court made clear that a construction defect that damages something other than the project itself can constitute an 'occurrence'"); *Nautilus*

Ins. Co. v. 1735 W. Diversey, LLC, No. 10 C 425, 2011 U.S. Dist. LEXIS 82246 (N.D. Ill. July 21, 2011) (noting that Illinois courts have consistently concluded that damage to a construction project resulting from construction defects is not an "accident" (citing numerous cases), but that a construction defect that damages something other than the project itself is an "occurrence"); *Nautilus Ins. Co. v. Board of Directors of Regal Lofts Condominium Ass'n*, 764 F.3d 726 (7th Cir. 2014) (addressing several prior Illinois decisions) ("Nautilus points out, and the Board does not seriously dispute, that the allegations in the original and first amended complaint in the underlying action involved only damage to the building itself, nothing more. Damage of this nature is clearly not an 'occurrence' under Illinois law."); *Donven Homes, Inc. v. Amerisure Ins. Co.*, No. 1–10–2790, 2012 Ill. App. Unpub. LEXIS 791 (Ill. App. Ct. Mar. 30, 2012) (addressing several prior Illinois decisions) ("Since the underlying complaints in this case did not allege damage to or loss of use of any property other than the houses themselves, the underlying complaints did not allege property damage caused by an occurrence."); *Acuity v. Lenny Szarek, Inc.*, 128 F. Supp. 3d 1053 (N.D. Ill. 2015) ("[W]here faulty workmanship results in cracks in the load-bearing elements of a home, there is no occurrence causing covered property damage, but where faulty workmanship results in leaks that cause water damage to the homeowner's furniture, clothing and antiques, there *is* an occurrence causing covered property damage.") (emphasis in original); *West. Bend Mut. Ins. Co. v. Pulte Home Corp.*, No. 1-14-0355, 2015 Ill. App. Unpub. LEXIS 1039 (Ill. Ct. App. May 15, 2015) (parsing the language of a complaint to determine if its alleges resultant damage from faulty work); *Westfield Ins. Co. v. West Van Buren, LLC*, 59 N.E.3d 877 (Ill. Ct. App. 2016) ("[W]e must reject the Developer's argument that the underlying complaint triggered a duty to defend because the complaint alleged actual physical harm to personal property. While construction defects that damage something other than the project itself *can* constitute an occurrence and property damage, they do not in this case. We agree with the trial court that these allegations were meant to simply bolster the contention that water infiltration generally occurred and caused damages."); *Westfield Ins. Co. v. Nat'l Decorating Serv.*, 863 F.3d 690 (7th Cir. 2017) ("When the policy defines the term ['occurrence'] to include the 'continuous or repeated exposure to substantially the same harmful conditions,' as it does here, the condominium association's allegation that the painting subcontractor acted negligently is sufficient under Illinois law to constitute an 'occurrence.'") (complaint included allegations that the painting subcontractor caused damage outside the scope of its own work); *Certain Underwriters at Lloyd's London v. Metro.*

Builders, Inc., 158 N.E.3d 1084 (Ill. App. Ct. 2019) (stating general rule that "[i]f the underlying complaint against the insured contractor merely alleges construction defects that require repair and replacement (or that cause a diminution in value) of the contractor's work product, no 'accident,' and thus no 'occurrence' under the CGL policy, has been alleged. But if the damage extends to other people or things that were not part of the contractor's work product, we have held that this damage is alleged to have resulted from an 'accident,' and thus an 'occurrence' has been alleged to trigger coverage under the CGL policy") (allegations of damage to owner's personal property were sufficient to allege an "occurrence"); *Owners Ins. Co. v. Precision Painting & Decorating Corp.*, No. 19-0926, 2019 Ill. App. Unpub. LEXIS 2425 (Ill. App. Ct. Dec. 31, 2019) (allegations that a contractor hired to paint the exterior of a property caused lead dust to infiltrate the interior of the property and surrounding land constituted an "occurrence") (collecting cases); *Lexington Ins. Co. v. Chi Flameproof & Wood Specialties Corp.*, 950 F.3d 976 (7th Cir. 2020) (finding that the cost to rip and tear out inadequate materials that were deliberately supplied is the "natural and ordinary consequence" of supplying such materials) (noting that faulty workmanship may constitute an "occurrence" "if it results in damages that exceed the scope of the insured's work product" or if the insured "'was unaware of the defective nature' of its component until after it was incorporated into a finished product"); *West Bend Mut. Ins. Co. v. Trapani Constr. Co.*, No. 19-1772, 2020 Ill. App. Unpub. LEXIS 1783 (Ill. App. Ct. Oct. 19, 2020) (insurer had a duty to defend because "the requested relief for the damages to the unit owners' tangible personal property was beyond the cost to repair or replace the faulty workmanship that caused water to infiltrate into the Condominium causing damage").

In *Acuity Ins. Co. v. 950 West Huron Condo. Ass'n*, 138 N.E.3d 189 (Ill. App. Ct. 2019), the Appellate Court of Illinois considered whether an insurer had a duty to defend a lawsuit "where a subcontractor's allegedly poor workmanship caused damage to the overall project and individual condo units within the building—damage that went beyond the scope of its own work." The court noted that "[f]rom the eyes of the subcontractor, the 'project' is limited to the scope of its own work, and the precise nature of any damage that might occur to something outside of that scope is as unknown or unforeseeable as damage to something entirely outside of the construction project. The portions of the construction project that are completely outside the scope of the subcontractors' responsibility seem to us very similarly situated (from the subcontractors' point of view) to the 'carpeting, drywall, antique furniture, clothing, personal mementoes and pictures,' of unit owners, as to which we long ago recognized allegations of damage would trigger a duty to defend." *Id.* at 198. The court concluded that "when an underlying complaint alleges that a subcontractor's negligence caused something to occur to a part of the construction project outside of the subcontractor's scope of work, this alleges an occurrence under this CGL policy language, notwithstanding that it would not be an occurrence from a general contractor or developer's perspective." *Id.* at 199.

Indiana: The Indiana Supreme Court held that claims against a general contractor, for defective construction of a home—lack of adequate flashing and quality caulking around the windows, lack of a weather resistant barrier behind the brick veneer, improperly installed roof shingles, among other things—constituted an "occurrence." *Sheehan Construction Co., Inc. v. Continental Cas. Co.*, 935 N.E.2d 160 (Ind. 2010). The court held that it was aligning itself "with those jurisdictions adopting the view that improper or faulty workmanship does constitute an accident so long as the resulting damage is an event that occurs without expectation or foresight." *Id.* at 169. "[I]f the faulty workmanship is 'unexpected' and 'without intention or design' and thus not foreseeable from the viewpoint of the insured, then it is an accident within the meaning of a CGL policy." *Id.* at 170. Among other reasons, the Indiana high court was persuaded that, if property damage to an insured's own work cannot be an "occurrence," then there would be no reason for the policy to contain a "your work" exclusion. *Id.* at 171 (discussing Clifford J. Shapiro, "The Good, the Bad, and the Ugly: New State Supreme Court Decisions Address Whether an Inadvertent Construction Defect is an 'Occurrence' Under CGL Policies," 25 *Constr. Law.*, Summer 2005, at 9, 12). The court distinguished *Indiana Ins. Co. v. DeZutti*, 408 N.E.2d 1275 (Ind. 1980) on the basis that it relied on exclusions to determine that no coverage existed and it was not the intent to suggest that faulty workmanship, that damages the contractor's own work, can never constitute a covered "occurrence." *Id.* at 166–67. The Indiana Supreme Court granted rehearing in *Sheehan* and modified its opinion concerning late notice. *Sheehan Constr. Co., Inc. v. Cont'l Cas. Co.*, 938 N.E.2d 685 (Ind. 2010) (*See* Chapter 3). *See also Gen. Cas. Ins. v. Compton Const. Co., Inc.*, No.10-134, 2011 U.S. Dist. LEXIS 27269 (N.D. Ind. Mar. 16, 2011) (following *Sheehan*); *American Ins. Co. v. Crown Packaging Int'l.*, No. 2:05CV68, 2011 U.S. Dist. LEXIS 94552 (N.D. Ill. Aug. 24, 2011) (discussing *Sheehan* and concluding that arguments went both ways on whether insured's manufacturing problems were unexpected so as to constitute an "occurrence"); *Indiana Ins. Co. v. Kopetsky*, 11 N.E.3d 508 (Ind. Ct. App. 2014) (discussing *Sheehan* and explaining that an occurrence need not have been caused by the insured) (*transfer granted and then vacated*, 2015 Ind. LEXIS 276 (Ind. 2015)).

Iowa: The Supreme Court of Iowa held that claims against an insured who built basements and other portions of homes below the floodplain, in violation of a city ordinance, necessitating that the level of the homes be raised, did not qualify as an "occurrence." *Pursell Const., Inc. v. Hawkeye-Security Ins. Co.*, 596 N.W.2d 67, 71 (Iowa 1999). "If the policy is construed as protecting a contractor against mere faulty or defective workmanship, the insurer becomes a guarantor of the insured's performance of the contract, and the policy takes on the attributes of a performance bond." *Id.; see also W.C. Stewart Constr., Inc. v. Cincinnati Ins. Co.*, No. 08–0824, 2009 Iowa App. LEXIS 273 (Iowa Ct. App. Apr. 8, 2009) (holding that no coverage was owed for defective grading performed by insured, causing building movement and cracks in walls, because the damages sought were to the very property upon which the insured performed work and rejecting insured's argument that coverage was owed because its faulty workmanship required reconstruction of walls that it had not built); *Cont'l W. Ins. Co. v. Jerry's Homes, Inc.*, 713 N.W.2d 247 (Iowa Ct. App. 2006) (table) ("Defective work itself, regardless of who performs the work, is not an occurrence that is covered under a CGL policy. Defective work is not covered under a CGL policy if the only damage is the work product itself. *Pursell Constr., Inc.*, 596 N.W.2d at 70–71 … . Our supreme court has stated it agrees with the majority rule that defective workmanship, standing alone, that is, resulting in damages only to the work product itself, is not an occurrence. To rule otherwise would make a CGL policy more like a performance bond, and the insurer more like the guarantor of the insured's work.") (citations and internal quotations omitted); *Liberty Mut. Ins. Co. v. Pella Corp.*, 650 F.3d 1161, 1176 (8th Cir. 2011) ("[T]he *Pappas* complaint alleged that Pella knew that its windows had a defect that allowed water to leak through the window frame. Similarly, all of the claims in the *Saltzman* complaint derived from the allegation that Pella knew 'that its windows contained an inherent defect that permitted [water] leakage.' In both cases, the property damage—whether to the windows themselves or the structure of the building near the windows—was caused by a defect that Pella was alleged to have known about. Under Iowa law, such defective workmanship, as alleged in the *Pappas* and *Saltzman* Suits, cannot be considered an occurrence, i.e., 'an undesigned, sudden, and unexpected event.'") (following *Pursell* and *W.C. Stewart*).

More recently, the Iowa Supreme Court held in *National Surety Corp. v. Westlake Invs., LLC*, 880 N.W.2d 724 (Iowa 2016) that "the insuring agreement in the modern standard-form CGL policy provid[es] coverage for property damage arising out of defective work performed by an insured's subcontractor unless the resulting property damage is specifically precluded from coverage by an exclusion or endorsement. In addition, we conclude the defective work performed by the insureds' subcontractors falls within the definition of 'occurrence' in the insuring agreement appearing in the Arch policy." *Id.* at 740. "Most importantly, our holding in *Pursell* was limited by its plain language to situations in which the insured performed defective work and sought coverage for the cost of repairing the defective work product. By implication, *Pursell* anticipated that a CGL policy might provide coverage for at least some claims arising from defective construction, just not claims seeking coverage for repairing or replacing the insured's own defective work product." *Id.* at 738. "Reading the Arch policy as a whole, we conclude it plainly contemplates coverage for some property damage caused by defective work performed by an insured's subcontractor. In short, interpreting the term 'accident' or the term 'occurrence' so narrowly as to preclude coverage for all property damage arising from negligent work performed by an insured's subcontractor would be unreasonable in light of the exceptions and exclusions the Arch policy contains." *Id.* at 739. *See also Hudson Hardware Plumbing & Heating, Inc. v. AMCO Ins. Co.*, 888 N.W.2d 682 (Iowa Ct. App. 2016) (analyzing difference between *Pursell* and *Westlake*); *Pella Corp. v. Liberty Mut. Ins. Co.*, 221 F. Supp. 3d 1107 (S.D. Iowa 2016) (analyzing Iowa law and holding that "claims of defective workmanship manifesting in water intrusion that damages property other than the work itself include the allegations of an accident -- namely, unexpected and unintended water intrusion-- and thus can support the finding of an 'occurrence.' This may be the case even where the claims are based in negligence and the property damage is alleged to have been foreseeable."); *Artistic Iron Works, Inc. v. Selective Ins. Co. of Am.*, No. 15-00315, 2017 U.S. Dist. LEXIS 174902 (S.D. Iowa 2017) (reviewing Iowa case law regarding the interpretation of the words "accident" and "occurrence" in the context of commercial general liability policies and concluding that "an insured's defective workmanship can constitute an accident under Iowa law" to the extent the defective workmanship causes damage to other property) (holding that a claim against a metal railing installer, who used the wrong grout to stabilize posts in a retaining wall, alleged an "occurrence" because "the damage in this case extends beyond the insured's work product and is not for faulty workmanship standing alone").

Kansas: The Supreme Court of Kansas held that moisture leakage over time, caused by defective windows installed by the insured's subcontractor, which led to structural damage within a constructed home, qualified as an "occurrence." *Lee Builders, Inc. v. Farm Bureau Mut. Ins. Co.*, 137 P.3d 486, 495 (Kan. 2006). "The damage in the present case is an occurrence—an even more expansive coverage term than 'accident'—because faulty materials and workmanship provided by Lee's subcontractors caused continuous exposure of the Steinberger home to moisture. The moisture in turn caused damage that was both unforeseen and unintended." *Id.*; *see also Wilson v. Farmers Ins. Exch.*, 233 P.3d 767, *8 (Kan. Ct. App. 2010) (table) (holding that damage caused by the continuous and repeated exposure of a home to moisture and foreign intrusion is an "occurrence") ("Just like the insurance policy in *Lee Builders*, the insurance policy in this case specifically defined an 'occurrence' as 'an accident, including continuous or repeated exposure to substantially the same general harmful conditions.' And, just like the homeowner in *Lee Builders*, the Wilsons allege faulty materials and workmanship by subcontractors caused the home to be continuously exposed to moisture and that the moisture in turn caused damage that was both unforeseen and unintended.").

Kentucky: The Supreme Court of Kentucky held that a claim against a contractor, who was supposed to demolish a carport, but instead also demolished half of the attached residential structure, qualified as an "occurrence." *Bituminous Cas. Corp. v. Kenway Contracting, Inc.*, 240 S.W.3d 633, 640 (Ky. 2007). "The damage to the Turners' property was unexpected and unintended by the insured. It was not the plan, design, or intent of the insured. Therefore, the fortuity requirement in the definition of accident is satisfied." *Id.* at 639; *see also Cemex, Inc. v. LMS Contracting, Inc.*, No. 3:06-CV-124, 2008 U.S. Dist. LEXIS 85209 (W.D. Ky. Oct. 21, 2008) ("LMS did not intend or expect for explosives to be left on the job site, and as such the damage caused by leaving the explosives resulted from an accident.") (following *Kenway Contracting*). However, in *Cincinnati Ins. Co. v. Motorists Mut. Ins. Co.*, 306 S.W.3d 69 (Ky. 2010) the Supreme Court of Kentucky held, as a matter of first impression, that a claim against a builder, for defective construction of a home, did not qualify as an "occurrence". *Id.* at 76. Since the builder had control over the construction of the home, it could not be said that the allegedly substandard construction was a fortuitous, truly accidental event. *Id.* The court rejected any notion that its decision in *Bituminous Cas. Corp.* compelled a different result: "[T]he quick destruction of a residence is manifestly a completely different undertaking than the protracted improper construction of a residence. The home construction in the case at hand occurred over a period of weeks; the mistaken destruction of a carport in *Bituminous Cas. Corp.* occurred in a short flurry of activity on only one day. Because of this inescapable, material factual difference, *Bituminous Cas. Corp.* is not controlling on the narrow issue presented in this case: whether a claim of faulty construction may qualify as an 'occurrence' under a standard CGL policy."

Id. at 77; *see also Acuity v. Krumpelman Builders, Inc.*, No. 09–9-DLB, 2010 U.S. Dist. LEXIS 34777 (E.D. Ky. Apr. 8, 2010) (following *Cincinnati*) ("A claim for faulty workmanship, standing alone, is not an 'occurrence' under a CGL policy."); *Global Gear & Machine Co., Inc. v. Capitol Indemnity Corp.*, No. 5:07-CV-00184, 2010 U.S. Dist. LEXIS 86745 (W.D. Ky. Aug. 23, 2010) (observing that the court in *Cincinnati* did not address whether property damage to something other than the insured's faulty workmanship is an "occurrence" and concluding that it is) (coverage precluded on other grounds); *Liberty Mut. Fire Ins. Co. v. Kay & Kay Contracting, LLC*, 545 Fed. Appx. 488 (6th Cir. 2013) (holding that, even if the Supreme Court of Kentucky adopted a rule that coverage could be owed if an allegedly improperly constructed home damaged another's property, the facts at issue did not warrant coverage) ("[T]he fact that Kay and Kay was hired for the express purpose of preparing a pad site for the pending construction of a building thereon, coupled with the alleged fact that Kay and Kay's faulty workmanship produced a defective pad site that resulted in settling as well as cracking in the building's walls, indicates to us that what happened here was not a 'fortuity,' as the Supreme Court of Kentucky has defined and explained that term.").

The Kentucky Supreme Court accepted review of *Acuity v. Martin/Elias Props., LLC*, No. 2013-CA-001428, 2016 Ky. App. Unpub. LEXIS 237 (Ky. Ct. App. Mar. 25, 2016), *review granted* 2016 Ky. LEXIS 592 (Ky. Dec. 8, 2016), where the Kentucky appeals court held: "The Supreme Court's holding in *Cincinnati Ins. Co.* governs the issue before us. Martin/EliasProperties misinterprets the holding of that case. Gosney had control of and contracted to construct a new foundation under the entire home. Gosney's stabilization of the home, excavation of the basement floor, underpinning and construction of a new concrete foundation were all within the scope of work and, therefore, were his work product. Likewise, Gosney's decision to undertake the project without consulting an engineer was part of Gosney's work. Martin/Elias Properties alleged it suffered collateral injury to its property by Gosney's improper excavation of the basement floor and removal of material from beneath the structure's foundation. Martin/Elias Properties did not allege there had been an accident. It likewise did not allege Gosney intentionally performed shoddy work or inflicted damage upon the structure. It merely alleged Gosney's substandard workmanship had caused damage throughout the structure. . . . Since the allegedly substandard workmanship undertaken in this case cannot be considered unintended or fortuitous as a matter of law, there are no material facts in dispute. Based on the current state of the law, we conclude there was no 'occurrence' which would trigger coverage under the CGL policy for the claims asserted against Gosney by Martin/Elias Properties." *Id.* at *11-13.

The Supreme Court affirmed, finding that a "contractor's faulty workmanship on the basement and foundation of an existing structure, resulting in extensive damage to the entire building, was not an accident triggering coverage as an occurrence under the contractor's CGL policy." *Martin/Elias Props., LLC v. Acuity*, 544 S.W.3d 639, 640 (Ky. 2018). "We make clear today that the legal analysis used to determine whether something constitutes an accident for issues of CGL coverage is the doctrine of fortuity, which encompasses both intent and control." *Id.* at 642-43. The court noted that the principles of control and intent are compelling because "[o]ne would not purposefully perform substandard work for the purpose of damaging property. So the emphasis should not be whether the damage done is the type of damage that would be expected by the contractor, but rather whether the damage resulted from the actions purposefully taken by the contractor or those working under the contractor's control." *Id.* at 644. Because the contractor's work was entirely under his control and executed as intended, the court concluded that "we cannot say that the resulting damage throughout the property was an accident." *Id.* at 644-45.

Louisiana: The Court of Appeal of Louisiana held that a claim against a pile driving contractor, for damage to a newly constructed home, qualified as an "occurrence." *Rando v. Top Notch Props., L.L.C.*, 879 So. 2d 821, 833 (La. Ct. App. 2004). Following a comprehensive survey of Louisiana law, the court held that "the clear weight of authority in more recent cases considers defects in construction that result in damage subsequent to completion to be accidents and occurrences when they manifest themselves. However, a clear signal from the Supreme Court on this issue would surely do much to eliminate expensive future litigation." *Id.; see also Joe Banks Drywall & Acoustics, Inc. v. Transcon. Ins. Co.*, 753 So. 2d 980, 983 (La. Ct. App. 2000) (holding that a claim against a sheet vinyl flooring subcontractor, for staining of a floor that it installed, qualified as an "occurrence" because there was no allegation that the damage at issue was intentional); *Supreme Servs. & Specialty Co. v. Sonny Greer, Inc.*, 958 So. 2d 634, 643 (La. 2007) (holding that a CGL policy containing a "work product" exclusion did not insure any obligation of the policyholder to repair or replace his own defective product) (not addressing whether the damage was caused by an "occurrence"); *Travelers Cas. and Sur. Co. of America v. University Facilities, Inc.*, No. 10–1682, 2012 U.S. Dist. LEXIS 49970 (E.D. La. Apr. 10, 2012) ("The failure to use workmanlike practices by prematurely installing wall board and using nails instead of screws constitutes an occurrence under Louisiana law.") (citing *Rando*); *Gootee Constr., Inc. v. Travelers Prop. Cas. Co. of Am.*, No. 15-3185, 2016 U.S. Dist. LEXIS 50911 (E.D. La. Apr. 15, 2016) ("Although Satterfield's petition is inartfully drafted, the Court can reasonably infer from the allegations that Gootee performed subcontracting work on the St. Mary's immovable property, in connection with the reconstruction of St. Mary's high school. The allegation that St. Mary's has incurred damages or will incur damages 'as a result [of]' Gootee's allegedly defective or incomplete construction work sufficiently implies that St. Mary's seeks to recover for damage to tangible property, potentially including, but not limited to, the defective work itself.") (insurer did not challenge insured's ability to prove an "occurrence"); *JEI Sols., Inc. v. Burlington Ins. Co.*, No. 19-156, 2019 U.S. Dist. LEXIS 95068 (E.D. La. June 6, 2019) (Although "defects in construction, alone, do not trigger coverage under a CGL policy," allegations of damage to other property, including water damage to walls, "[p]laces where outsides can be seen from inside" and "[s]tud integrity weakened by excessive cutouts" constituted an "occurrence"); *Specialty Ins. Co. v. Siegen 7 Devs., LLC*, No. 18-850, 2019 U.S. Dist. LEXIS 152525 (M.D. La. Sept. 6, 2019) ("The failures to achieve the proper finish slab elevation, to provide position storm water drainage, and to prepare a drainage plan for the house and lot constitute 'occurrences' under Louisiana law.").

Maine: The Supreme Judicial Court of Maine held that a claim against a contractor, for failure to frame two houses in accordance with the plans and specifications, did not qualify as an "occurrence." *Peerless Ins. Co. v. Brennon*, 564 A.2d 383, 386 (Me. 1989). "An 'occurrence of harm risk' is a risk that a person or property other than the product itself will be damaged through the fault of the contractor. A 'business risk' is a risk that the contractor will not do his job competently, and thus will be obligated to replace or repair his faulty work. The distinction between the two risks is critical to understanding a CGL policy. A CGL policy covers an occurrence of harm risk but specifically excludes a business risk." *Id.* (citation omitted); *see also Baywood Corp. v. Maine Bonding & Cas. Co.*, 628 A.2d 1029, 1031 (Me. 1993) ("[G]eneral comprehensive liability policy affords coverage when faulty work causes an accident resulting in physical damage to others, but not for contractor's product or complete work, which is a business expense.") (citing *Brennon*, 564 A.2d at 386); *Boothbay Harbor Shipyard, LLC v. N. Am. Specialty Ins. Co.*, No. 12-005, 2012 U.S. Dist. LEXIS 123525 (D. Me. Aug. 30, 2012) ("Although the complaint is fairly specific with respect to the ways in which the Shipyard's workmanship was faulty, it does not exclude claims for damages caused by leaking of the vessel after it was put back into service. Indeed, the complaint's reference to damages including 'repair and restoration of the vessel' is broad enough to reasonably encompass any number and kind of damages, including replacing materials or repairing finishes not touched by the Shipyard but ruined by the leaking. Accordingly, at least a portion of the *Coastwise* complaint's allegations may fall within the Policy's broad general grant of coverage." (citing *Brennon* and noting that the parties disputed whether any allegations in the complaint "could possibly relate to a Policy-covered 'occurrence of harm risk' or whether, instead, the allegations relate exclusively to 'business risks'"); *Lyman Morse Boatbuilding, Inc. v. Northern Assur. Co. of Am.*, 772 F.3d 960 (1st Cir. 2014) ("Irwin's complaint alleged damages to the yacht; the policy excludes damages to 'your product'; 'you' is defined as, inter alia, LMB; the yacht is LMB's product; thus, the policy unambiguously excludes the allegations of the complaint. Accordingly, on these facts, we find that Northern Assurance had no duty to defend Cabot Lyman in the arbitration proceeding. To hold otherwise would undercut the well-recognized purpose of CGL insurance policies, as articulated by the Maine Law Court. CGL policies are designed to cover 'occurrence of harm risks' but not 'business risks.'") (citing *Brennon*).

Maryland: The Court of Special Appeals of Maryland held that an insured contractor's liability for the negligent installation of a façade on a building was not unexpected or unforeseen and, therefore, did not result from an accident. *Lerner Corp. v. Assurance Co. of Am.*, 707 A.2d 906, 911 (Md. Ct. Spec. App. 1998); *see also French v. Assurance Co. of Am.*, 448 F.3d 693, 706 (4th Cir. 2006) (holding that the CGL policy does not provide coverage to a general contractor for the cost to correct defective workmanship performed by a subcontractor, but coverage is owed for the cost to remedy unexpected and unintended property damage to the contractor's otherwise nondefective work-product caused by the subcontractor's defective workmanship); *Travelers Indem. Co. of Am. v. Tower-Dawson, LLC*, 299 Fed. App'x 277, 282 (4th Cir. 2008) (following *French*) ("[I]t is evident that the cost of installing the new retaining wall and the cost of repairing the damage to the federally-protected wetlands brought about by the installation of the new retaining wall are not covered losses under the Policies."); *Clipper Mill Federal, LLC v. Cincinnati Ins. Co.*, No. JFM-10-1647, 2010 U.S. Dist. LEXIS 112172 (D. Md. Oct. 20, 2010) ("In order to determine whether property damage is the result of an 'occurrence' where there is potential contractual liability, the focus of the inquiry is on the nature of the damages: If the damages suffered relate to the satisfaction of the contractual bargain, it follows that they are not unforeseen. Specifically, the courts uniformly hold that when property damage arising out of the insured's defective workmanship is confined to the insured's own work product, the damage is not caused by an 'occurrence.' Where other property incurs damage, however, this constitutes an 'occurrence,' which may be compensable under the CGL Policy. Accordingly, the critical inquiry in determining whether alleged damages were 'expected' by the insured is whether the damages relate to the satisfaction of the insured's contractual obligations to construct its product or whether the damages relate to something other than the insured's product.") (citations and internal quotes omitted); *Pa. Nat. Mut. Cas. Ins. Co. v. Alliance Roofing & Sheet Metal, Inc.*, No. WDQ–12–1427, 2013 U.S. Dist. LEXIS 38567 (D. Md. Mar. 14, 2013) ("*Lerner* . . . emphasized that coverage may exist when the alleged defect causes unrelated and unexpected personal injury or property damage to something other than the defective object itself."); *State Auto. Mut. Ins. Co. v. Old Republic Ins. Co.*, 115 F. Supp. 3d 615 (D. Md. 2015) ("In *French*, as here, the insured contracted with a sub-contractor to perform a subset of the insured's work. The subcontractor's defective work then allegedly damaged other parts of the insured's project. The non-defective parts affected by the sub-contractor's negligence were thus a component of the larger project for which the insured was responsible. In this case, Hydro-Logic's failure to treat the water may have resulted in damage to other parts of the HVAC system. Although Fidelity contracted to provide a HVAC system, its sub-contractor's defective work caused the damage to non-defective HVAC components. As in *French*, this damage is an 'occurrence' that triggers Old Republic's duty to defend."); *Depositors Ins. Co. v. W. Concrete, Inc.*, No. 16-1018, 2017 U.S. Dist. LEXIS 123923 (D. Md. Aug. 4, 2017) ("[W]hen property damage arising out of the insured's defective workmanship is confined to the insured's own work product, the damage is not caused by an 'occurrence' within the meaning of the CGL policy. . . . The corollary of this rule is that there is an 'occurrence' under a CGL policy when a subcontractor's defective workmanship causes 'property damage' to another contractor's otherwise non-defective work-product.") (citing *Lerner* and *French*).

Massachusetts: The Appeals Court of Massachusetts held that an insured's subcontractor's negligent installation of a concrete slab, in the course of construction of a school building, did not qualify as an "occurrence." *Mello Constr., Inc. v. Acadia Ins. Co.*, No. 06-P-100, 2007 Mass. App. LEXIS 1063 (Mass. App. Ct. Oct. 5, 2007); *see also Friel Luxury Home Constr., Inc. v. ProBuilders Specialty Ins. Co. RRG*, No. 09-cv-11036, 2009 U.S. Dist. LEXIS 121775 (D. Mass. Dec. 22, 2009) (holding that a claim against an insured contractor, for faulty construction and renovation work on a home, did not qualify as "property damage," nor caused by an "occurrence"); *Am. Home Assurance Co. v. AGM Marine Contractors, Inc.*, 467 F.3d 810, 813 (1st Cir. 2006) ("Whether Massachusetts would follow the 'occurrence' cases is not certain. In *Caplette [Commerce Ins. Co. v. Betty Caplette Builders, Inc.*, 647 N.E.2d 1211 (Mass. 1995)] the Supreme Judicial Court bypassed the issue in a case involving damage to the insured's product, going instead directly to the exclusions. This might suggest that the SJC thought that the occurrence and property damage requirements were satisfied, but the parties did not dispute the issue. In all events, one of the exclusions in this case bars coverage even if we assume *arguendo* that there was an occurrence and property damage within the meaning of the policy."); *Mello Const., Inc. v. Acadia Ins. Co.*, 874 N.E.2d 1142, *3 (Mass. App. Ct. 2007) (table) ("The risk intended to be insured is the possibility that the goods, products or work of the insured, once relinquished or completed, will cause bodily injury or damage to property other than to the product or completed work itself, and for which the insured may be found liable. … The coverage is for tort liability for physical damages to others and not for contractual liability of the insured for economic loss because the product or completed work is not that for which the damaged person bargained.") (quoting Henderson, "Insurance Protection for Products Liability and Completed Operations-What Every Lawyer Should Know," 50 Neb. L. Rev. 415, 441 (1971)); *Nat'l Union Fire Ins. Co. of Pittsburgh, PA v. Modern Cont'l Constr. Co., Inc.*, No. 082015BLS1, 2009 Mass. Super. LEXIS 413 (Mass. Super. Ct. Dec. 11, 2009) (table) ("The Court rejects National Union's argument that the ceiling collapse was not an occurrence. The policies define 'occurrence' as an 'accident.' The term 'accident' is to be broadly construed in a policy insuring against damage by accident. In its common signification the word means an unexpected happening without intention or design. While a crack in the ceiling or a leak might be expected to result from Modern's faulty workmanship, it is unlikely that Modern intended for or expected a portion of the concrete ceiling to completely collapse.") (citations and internal quotations omitted) (also noting that the complaints alleged damage beyond the insured's work); *E.H. Spencer & Co., LLC v. Essex Ins. Co.*, 944 N.E.2d 1094, *1 (Mass. App. Ct. 2011) (table) (addressing business risk exclusions) ("The purpose of such exclusions is to prevent the insured from using its product liability coverage as a form of property insurance to cover the cost of repairing or replacing its own defective products or work. Where an insured is a builder of homes, as is the case here, the *entire* house is considered the product of the builder. Thus, the exclusions serve to deny coverage when the insured builder or its subcontractor has caused any damage to the home itself. Conversely, coverage will not be excluded when a builder or its subcontractor, while constructing a home, causes damages to *other* persons or property.") (emphasis in original and citations and internal quotes omitted); *General Cas. Co. of Wisconsin v. Five Star Bldg. Corp.*, No. 11–30254, 2013 U.S. Dist. LEXIS 134122 (D. Mass. Sept. 19, 2013) ("Although the Supreme Judicial Court has not decisively circumscribed the bounds of what constitutes an occurrence under Massachusetts law, other courts applying Massachusetts law have endorsed the distinction that Five Star posits. For example, the Massachusetts Appeals Court, in deciding *Davenport [v.* USF&G, 778 N.E.2d 1038 (Mass. Ct. App. 2002)] noted that although [f]aulty workmanship, alone, is not an 'occurrence,' insurance coverage would extend to faulty workmanship which causes an accident.") ("Five Star does not seek coverage for faulty workmanship itself, but rather coverage of the damage resulting from the rainstorm even if such allegedly faulty workmanship contributed to the leaking. The rain damage to the roofing system, therefore, is an 'occurrence' under the Policy."); *All Am. Ins. Co. v. Lampasona Concrete Corporation*, 120 N.E.3d 1258 (Mass. Ct. App. 2019) ("The claim here is not simply that Lampasona's work was substandard and needs to be replaced, but that this work caused damage to particular parts of the hospital property outside of its own work.") (finding that "[t]he puncturing of the vapor barrier and the migration of water through the concrete slab causing damage to the layer above it fit readily within the definition of an occurrence"); *Fontaine Bros. v. Acadia Ins. Co.*, No. 18-11636, 2019 U.S. Dist. LEXIS 148056 (D. Mass. Aug. 29, 2019) (finding that a complaint alleged an "occurrence" when it did not "foreclose the possibility that the corrosion resulting from Plaintiff's alleged faulty workmanship and maintenance might be shown to be an unforeseen or unintended consequence of reckless or negligent conduct") (rejecting argument that "as a matter of Massachusetts law, faulty workmanship cannot constitute an occurrence").

Michigan: The Court of Appeals of Michigan held that an insured–mobilehome seller's provision of defective instructions to contractors hired by the home's purchaser, for the construction of a basement foundation and erection of the home on such foundation, qualified as an "occurrence." *Radenbaugh v. Farm Bureau Gen. Ins. Co. of Mich.*, 610 N.W.2d 272, 280 (Mich. Ct. App. 2000). "[I]t is clear that the underlying complaint alleged damages broader than mere diminution in value of the insured's product caused by alleged defective workmanship, breach of contract, or breach of warranty." *Id.* at 276; *see also Ahrens Constr., Inc. v. Amerisure Ins. Co.*, No. 288272 (Mich. Ct. App. Feb. 10, 2010) ("[T]here is little dispute that damages arising solely from faulty workmanship are not considered as resulting from an 'occurrence.'"); *Groom v. Home-Owners Ins. Co.*, No. 272840, 2007 Mich. App. LEXIS 1068 (Mich. Ct. App. Apr. 19, 2007) ("[W]here the 'damage arising out of the insured's defective workmanship is confined to the insured's own work product, the insured is the injured party, and the damage cannot be viewed as accidental within the meaning of the standard liability policy.'") (quoting *Radenbaugh*, 610 N.W.2d at 280) (citation omitted); *Houseman Construction Co. v. Cincinnati Ins. Co.*, No. 08-719, 2010 U.S. Dist. LEXIS 39961 (W.D. Mich. Apr. 23, 2010) (holding that a sinking floor, which was the result of defective workmanship, was not an "occurrence"); *Christman Co. v. Renaissance Precast Indus., L.L.C.*, No. 296316, 2011 Mich. App. LEXIS 1104 (Mich. Ct. App. June 21, 2011) (holding that damage to the components of a parking structure itself, with no damages beyond this work product, was not an occurrence or an accident); *Kent Cos., Inc. v. Wausau Ins. Cos.*, No. 295237, 2011 Mich. App. LEXIS 810 (Mich. Ct. App. May 3, 2011) ("The undisputed facts show that plaintiff is attempting to recover the expenses it incurred for replacing its own product due to its own defective work. As explained in *Hawkeye–Security Ins. Co. v. Vector Constr. Co.*, 185 Mich. App. 369, 377–378, 460 N.W.2d 329 (1990), plaintiff's defective workmanship does not involve an 'occurrence' as defined in defendant's policy."); *Oak Creek Apartments, LLC v. Garcia*, No. 308256, 2013 Mich. App. LEXIS 550 (Mich. Ct. App. Mar. 21, 2013) ("[T]he trial court correctly applied *Radenbaugh* to the undisputed facts of this case when it concluded that the loss was an 'occurrence' or 'accident' within the meaning of the general liability policy. The damage to the building resulting from Manuel Roofing's failure to adequately or properly secure the open roof area, which allegedly led to rainwater intrusion, was not confined to the insured's work product. It is undisputed that the scope of Manuel Roofing's work was limited to the roof of the building, yet the building sustained damage beyond the roof, including extensive water and mold damage to its interior and its contents."); *Michigan Ins. Co. v. Channel Road Const., Inc.*, No. 315837, 2014 Mich. App. LEXIS 1981 (Mich. Ct. App. Oct. 21, 2014) ("When an insured's defective workmanship results in damage to the property of others, an 'accident' occurred according to a standard liability policy; but, when an insured's defective workmanship results in damage confined to the insured's own work product, the insured is the injured party and the damage was not an 'accident.'") (*leave to appeal denied*, 866 N.W.2d 427 (Mich. 2015)); *Steel Supply & Eng'g Co. v. Ill. Nat'l Ins. Co.*, 620 Fed. Appx. 442 (6th Cir. 2015) (citing *Radenbaugh* and *Hawkeye–Security* and calling Michigan's treatment of the "occurrence" issue "intuitive" -- "the purpose of such insurance contracts is to protect the insured against the sort of *accidents* that give rise to liability. It is not to insure against malpractice"); *Employers Mutual Casualty Co. v. Mid-Michigan Solar*, No. 325082, 2016 Mich. App. LEXIS 791 (Mich. Ct. App. Apr. 19, 2016) (discussing *Radenbaugh* and *Hawkeye–Security* and, following a detailed analysis of the property damage at issue, that it was confined to the work product of the insured, and, therefore, did not result from an "occurrence"); *Skanska United States Bldg. v. M.A.P. Mech. Contrs.*, 952 N.W.2d 402 (Mich. 2020) ("[G]iven the plain meaning of the word 'accident,' we conclude that faulty subcontractor work that was unintended by the insured may constitute an 'accident' (and thus an 'occurrence') under a CGL policy.") (limiting the Court of Appeals' decision in *Hawkeye* "to cases involving pre-1986 comprehensive general liability insurance policies").

Minnesota: The Supreme Court of Minnesota addressed the potential for coverage for construction defects without regard to whether the claim qualified as "property damage" caused by an "occurrence." *Thommes v. Milwaukee Ins. Co.*, 641 N.W.2d 877 (Minn. 2002). Instead, the court's analysis was based on the general principle that business risks arising from contractual liability for defective materials and workmanship are not covered, while risks arising from tort liability to third parties are covered. *Id.* at 881 (addressing *Bor-Son Bldg. Corp. v. Employers Commercial Union Ins. Co. of Am.*, 323 N.W.2d 58 (Minn. 1982) and *Knutson Constr. Co. v. St. Paul Fire & Marine Ins. Co.*, 396 N.W.2d 229 (Minn. 1986)). However, the analysis did not end with the business risk principles: "If parties to an insurance contract demonstrate their intent, using clear and unambiguous language, to exclude the risk of damage to the real property of third parties, then there is no need to look to business risk principles to ascertain whether the policy was intended to cover such risks." *Id.* at 882. Other Minnesota cases have addressed coverage in the context of an "occurrence" analysis. *See Aten v. Scottsdale Ins. Co.*, 511 F.3d 818 (8th Cir. 2008) ("Just as the partial floor collapse and cracking of floors and walls caused by defective structural supports in *O'Shaughnessy [v. Smuckler Corp.*, 543 N.W.2d 99 (Minn. Ct. App. 1996)] constituted a covered occurrence, so would Aten's water damage to other property resulting from an improperly poured and graded basement floor which caused water to flow away from a floor drain."); *Remodeling Dimensions, Inc. v. Integrity Mut. Ins. Co.*, 819 N.W.2d 602 (Minn. 2012) ("Both negligent construction claims allege moisture damage resulting from 'continuous or repeated exposure' to water intrusion into the house. Pursuant to the insurance policy, both of the homeowners' negligent-construction claims, if proven, satisfy the meaning of 'occurrence' under the policy."). Recently, a Minnesota federal court addressed coverage in term of "business risk" concepts: "The business-risk doctrine excludes coverage for property damage caused by the insured's faulty workmanship where the damages claimed are the cost of correcting the work itself. The business-risk doctrine is a complement to the basic purpose of CGL policies — to cover tort liability for physical damages to others and not for contractual liability of the insured for economic loss because the product or completed work is not that for which the damaged person bargained." *Interlachen Props. v. State Auto Ins. Co.*, No. 14-4380, 2017 U.S. Dist. LEXIS 123499 (D. Minn. Aug. 4, 2017) (citing Minnesota's early decisions in *Bor-Son* and *Knutson*) (referring to the "damage to your work" exclusion as "a contractual adoption of the business-risk doctrine"). *But see Owners Ins. Co. v. Equal Access Homes, Inc.*, No. A12–186, 2013 Minn. App. Unpub. LEXIS 467 (Minn. Ct. App. May 28, 2013) ("[W]e reiterate that the general contractor is responsible by contract for performing in a good and workmanlike manner, satisfying not only its contract but also the building regulations and codes. . . . When, as here, the damages are not due to an accident, we decline to equate a breach of contract (or 'shoddy workmanship' as the district court called it) with an 'occurrence.' The CGL policy at issue does not cover poor workmanship and/or errors and omissions that occurred; instead the remedy was on the contract, which, in this case, required arbitration. Expansion of the interpretation of 'occurrence' would convert a CGL policy into a 'guaranty' of contractor performance, which is exactly what the insurance industry has tried to avoid. Further, EAH knew it was purchasing an insurance policy, not a performance bond, as does every contractor."); *King's Cove Marina, LLC v. Lambert Commer. Constr. LLC*, 937 N.W.2d 458 (Minn. Ct. App. 2019), *rev'd, in part, on other grounds* 958 N.W.2d 310 (Minn. 2021) (concluding that claims against a contractor who "did not make 'willful and knowing violations of contract specifications' or of expected standards of workmanship" alleged an "occurrence").

Mississippi: The Supreme Court of Mississippi held that a claim against a contractor, for damages caused by a subcontractor's failure to install rebar in the foundation of a building, qualified as an "occurrence." *Architex Ass'n, Inc. v. Scottsdale Ins. Co.*, 27 So. 3d 1148, 1162 (Miss. 2010). "While the alleged 'property damage' may have been 'set in motion' by Architex's intentional hiring of the subcontractors, the 'chain of events' may not have 'followed a course consciously devised and controlled by [Architex], without the unexpected intervention of any third person or extrinsic force.'" *Id.* at 1159 (citation omitted) (alteration in original). The opinion does not address the "occurrence" issue outside the subcontractor context. *See also Nat'l*

Builders and Contractors Ins. Co. v. Slocum Const., L.L.C., No. 10–60601, 2011 U.S. App. LEXIS 12260 (5th Cir. June 15, 2011) ("Slocum [insured] intended to build a house on the land that Anderson staked out. It may not have intended to build one on property that did not belong to Anderson, but that is the unintended result of its intentional actions. Therefore, its actions were not an accident under the terms of its policy."); *Lafayette Ins. Co. v. Peerboom*, 813 F. Supp. 2d 823 (S.D. Miss. 2011) (holding that, because the complaint left open the possibility that the "property damage" at issue was proximately caused by an accident (an inadvertent act), and, thus, the result of an "occurrence," summary judgment could not be granted for the insurer); *National Builders and Contractors Ins. Co. v. Slocum*, No. 2:10cv253KS, 2011 U.S. Dist. LEXIS 81694 (S.D. Miss. July 26, 2011) (finding no "occurrence") ("It is clear that at no point in Peterson's state Complaint does she allege that Slocum inadvertently failed to perform any of the actions complained of related to her breach claims. Instead, Peterson's Complaint makes clear that she alleges specific failures of Slocum in carrying out its duties in constructing the home pursuant to the contract in a workman like manner resulting in faulty construction and the specifically alleged defects set forth in the Complaint."); *W.R. Berkley Corp. v. Rea's Country Lane Const., Inc.*, 140 So. 3d 437 (Miss. Ct. App. 2013) ("Broom alleged that the various defendants acted *intentionally*—by digging pits, removing topsoil, dumping clay, disobeying her requests, and failing to plant grass and lay gravel—and that it was these intentional acts or refusals to act that damaged her real property. Nowhere in her complaint does she allege there was an inadvertent act or accident that damaged her property. And without an accident, there was no 'occurrence,' and without an occurrence, there was no duty to defend.") (emphasis in original); *Accident Ins. Co. v. Byrd*, No. 11–367, 2013 U.S. Dist. LEXIS 141523 (S.D. Miss. Sept. 30, 2013) ("The Mississippi Supreme Court has held that an act is not an 'accident,' and thus not an 'occurrence' if: (1) the act is committed consciously and deliberately without the unexpected intervention of any third force; and (2) the likely (and actual) effect of the act was well within the actor's foresight and anticipation.") ("The Byrds allege that a BBH employee, Chad Thompkin, submitted an inaccurate report and failed or refused to locate and repair the source of the leak, even after learning the actual source. When viewed through the chain of events leading to the Byrds' injuries, Thompkin intentionally set in motion the injuries by providing an inaccurate report of the leak, even if he did not intend to harm the Byrds. There was no unexpected intervention of a third force and Thompkin could have or should have reasonably foreseen that a client would rely on his assessment and report. These facts meet the two-step test employed by Mississippi law. Thus, Thompkin's actions, as alleged, were intentional and are not considered an 'accident' or 'occurrence.'") (*adopted at* 2013 U.S. Dist. LEXIS 141523 (S.D. Miss. Sept. 30, 2013)); *Emplrs Mut. Cas. Co. v. West*, No. 16-4, 2017 U.S. Dist. LEXIS 113951 (N.D. Miss. July 21, 2017) ("[Insured] testified that the method he used to fasten the deck, using nails secured into oriented strand board, would not be an appropriate method of fastening a deck used for live loads. Furthermore, he testified that he knew people would use the decks. Therefore, given [insured's] contemporaneous knowledge of his failure, it cannot be said that his actions constitute an accident. While the notion of a 'failure' or 'omission' intuitively may seem less intentional than an overtly affirmative act, logic does not bear this out.").

Missouri: The Missouri Court of Appeals held that a claim against a contractor, for the cost to remove and replace a home's subfloor and framing, on account of defective concrete supplied by the insured's subcontractor and used for a foundation, qualified as an "occurrence." *Columbia Mut. Ins. Co. v. Epstein*, 239 S.W.3d 667, 673 (Mo. Ct. App. 2007). "Epstein sold and delivered to the Doerrs concrete for a basement foundation, that through no fault of Epstein, the concrete was defective, that the defective nature of the concrete damaged the sub-floor and framing of the home in that it all had to be torn down and replaced, and that neither the defect in the concrete nor the damage to the home was foreseeable to Epstein." *Id.* at 672–73. The court distinguished *American States Insurance Co. v. Mathis*, 974 S.W.2d 647 (Mo. Ct. App. 2007), which held that failure to construct ducts according to contract specifications did not qualify as an "occurrence" because it was within the insured's control and management and it did not cause damage to other property. *Id.* at 672; *see also D.R. Sherry Const., Ltd. v. Am. Family Mut. Ins. Co.*, 316 S.W.3d 899, 905 (Mo. 2010) ("The determinative inquiry into whether there was an 'occurrence' or 'accident' is whether the insured foresaw or expected the injury or damages. *Columbia Mut. Ins. Co. v. Epstein*, 239 S.W.3d 667, 672 (Mo. App. 2007). While an 'accident' does not include expected or foreseeable damage, it is also true that an 'accident' is not necessarily a sudden event; it may be the result of a process."); *Employers Mut. Cas. Co. v. Luke Draily Const. Co., Inc.*, No. 10–00361, 2011 U.S. Dist. LEXIS 69929 (W.D. Mo. June 29, 2011) (noting that claims denominated as negligence were truly contract claims by another name) ("The parties agree that Draily expressed concerns about the 'quality of work' from Roof Toppers during the project, describing it as a 'major concern.' For Draily to argue now that problems on the roof were unforeseeable is not supported by the record, because problems were in fact *foreseen*. Whatever happened in the interim to assuage Draily's concerns does not change the fact that it actually foresaw roof problems during construction. In the event that the faulty workmanship claim can survive the initial occurrence threshold, *Sherry* states that the 'determinative inquiry … is whether the insured foresaw or expected the injury or damages.") (emphasis in original) ("*Sherry* does not state any abrogation or negative view of *Mathis*."); *Assurance Co. of Am. v. Secura Ins. Co.*, 384 S.W.3d 224 (Mo. Ct. App. 2012) ("*Mathis* was purely a breach-of-contract case. *Hawkeye* [*Hawkeye-Sec. Ins. Co. v. Davis*, 6 S.W.3d 419 (Mo. Ct. App. 1999)] was a breach-of-contract and breach-of-warranty case. Here, in contrast, MVG is not charged with breach of its contractual obligations. Rather, it is only alleged that MVG was negligent.") ("Allowing negligent conduct to be encompassed by a liability policy providing coverage for an 'occurrence' defined as an 'accident' comports with a reasonable person's expectation of liability coverage."); *Village at Deer Creek Homeowners Ass'n, Inc. v. Mid-Continent Cas. Co.*, 432 S.W.3d 231 (Mo. Ct. App. 2014) ("Mid–Continent concedes that water damage caused by the defective exterior cladding systems is covered 'property damage' under its CGL policies. It persists, however, in its claim that any damages awarded to replace the exterior cladding system are not 'property damage.' Our discussion, above, dispels Mid–Continent's argument. Once defective construction causes damage, the cost to repair the damage is covered 'property damage.' That cost to repair damage may include the cost to replace the defective construction if it too has been damaged or must be removed to access other damaged areas. Substantial evidence supports the conclusion that components of the defectively installed exterior cladding system were damaged by water intrusion, and that removal of some or all of the exterior cladding system will be necessary to repair water intrusion damage caused 'behind the walls' of the townhomes. As a result, the trial court did not error in determining that the judgment in the Underlying Lawsuit awarded the Association a recovery for 'property damages' as that term is defined in Mid–Continent's policies."); *Davies v. Barton Mut. Ins. Co.*, 549 S.W.3d 472 (Mo. Ct. App. 2017) (discussing and reconciling several Missouri cases and concluding that "no evidence described in the judgment supports a conclusion that Builder was negligent or did not foresee the water problem so as to support a ruling that the water problem suffered by Homeowners was an occurrence and an accident covered by the policy."); *View Home Owners Ass'n v. Burlington Ins. Co.*, 552 S.W.3d 726 (Mo. Ct. App. 2018) ("Because the ability to resolve these construction deficiencies was within The View's control and management, its failure to address them cannot be described as an 'undesigned or unexpected event,' and thus there was no 'accident.' Because there was no 'accident,' there was no 'occurrence' within the meaning of the policy, no 'property damage' to which the policy applied, and hence no duty on the part of TBIC to defend The View."); *Westfield Ins. Co. v. Miller Architects & Builders*, 949 F.3d 403 (8th Cir. 2020) (allegations of water coming through a defectively installed roof, which caused damage to the "finishes and electrical work in the building's interior" alleged "property damage" caused by an "occurrence"); *Am. Family Mut. Ins. Co. v. Mid-American Grain Distribs., LLC*, 958 F.3d 748 (8th Cir. 2020) ("Just like the damages resulting from the insured's work in *Mathis*, *Davis*, and *View Home Owner's Association*, Lehenbauer's damages are the 'normal, expected consequence' of Mid-American's work. They are thus foreseeable as a matter of law, so Mid-American's work is not an 'accident,' and thus not an 'occurrence,' under the CGL.") (internal citations omitted).

Montana: The Supreme Court of Montana held that an insured's subcontractor's defective manufacturing of disposable sanitary bags, for use in another party's portable toilets, qualified as an "event," defined in the policy as an "accident." *Revelation Indus., Inc. v. St. Paul Fire & Marine Ins. Co.*, 206 P.3d 919, 929 (Mont. 2009). The court rested its decision, in part, on the following example contained in the policy of the operation of the "your work" exclusion and "subcontractor exception," which the court deemed to be indistinguishable from the situation before it: "You construct a building as a general contractor. Some of the work is done by you while the rest is done for you by subcontractors. The building is accepted by the owner. If it's damaged by a fire caused by electrical wiring installed by a subcontractor, we won't apply the exclusion. However, if the wiring was installed by you, we'll apply the exclusion to property damage to your completed work done by you." *Id.*; *see also King v. State Farm Fire & Cas. Co.*, No. CR 09–96-M-DWM, 2010 U.S. Dist. LEXIS 49029 (D. Mont. May 18, 2010) (holding that claims against the seller of a log home kit, for misrepresentations about the quality of the logs and refusal to correct deficiencies, did not allege an "occurrence") (*affirmed* 500 Fed. Appx. 699 (9th Cir. 2012)); *Haskins Const., Inc. v. Mid-Continent Cas. Co.*, No. CV–10–163, 2011 U.S. Dist. LEXIS 127231 (D. Mont. Nov. 3, 2011) ("[S]ince the Montana Supreme Court has held that, from the insured's standpoint, the term 'accident' means 'any unexpected happening that occurs without intention or design on the part of the insured,' *Blair v. Mid–Continent Casualty Co.*, 167 P.3d 888, 891 (Mont. 2007), 'occurrence' encompasses the faulty workmanship alleged in the … Amended Complaint."); *Thomas v. Nautilus Ins. Co.*, No. 11–40, 2011 U.S. Dist. LEXIS 108915

(D. Mont. Aug. 24, 2011) ("That faulty workmanship is an 'occurrence' that may ultimately, under certain circumstances, be covered, is evidenced by the fact that the Policy contains a subcontractor exception to the 'your work' exclusion, which otherwise precludes coverage for property damage to the insured's completed or abandoned work.") (*adopted at* 2011 U.S. Dist. LEXIS 109018 (D. Mont. Sept. 19, 2011)); *Northland Cas. Co. v. Mulroy*, No. 13-232, 2015 U.S. Dist. LEXIS 94631 (D. Mont. July 21, 2015) (citing a treatise for the following proposition: "A claim for faulty workmanship, in and of itself, is not an occurrence under a commercial general liability policy because a failure of workmanship does not involve the fortuity required to constitute an accident. Instead, what does constitute an occurrence is an accident caused by or resulting from faulty workmanship, including damage to any property other than the work product and damage to the work product other than the defective workmanship. In other words, although a commercial general liability policy does not provide coverage for faulty workmanship that damages only the resulting work product, the policy does provide coverage if the faulty workmanship causes bodily injury or property damage to something other than the insured's work product."); *Phoenix Ins. Co. v. Ed Boland Constr., Inc.*, 229 F. Supp. 3d 1183 (D. Mont. 2017) ("Montana federal courts, applying Montana law, have concluded that defective workmanship is not considered an 'occurrence' under the insuring language of a CGL policy.") (citing *King* and *Mulroy*); *W. Heritage Ins. Co. v. Slopeside Condo. Ass'n*, 371 F. Supp. 3d 828 (D. Mont. 2019) ("The Court finds that Slopeside's damages arose from the unanticipated and unexpected consequences of Folkman's conduct. Folkman's installation of the T-panel systems constitutes an 'occurrence,' and the underlying dispute between Slopeside and Folkman falls within the policy's insuring agreement."); *Atl. Cas. Ins. Co. v. Quinn*, No. 18-76, 2019 U.S. Dist. LEXIS 103566 (D. Mont. June 20, 2019) (rejecting argument that "faulty workmanship is not a covered occurrence because it is not a fortuitous event" because "[a]s this Court recognized in *Western Heritage*, faulty workmanship can be an occurrence under *Fisher Builders* if the consequences were not objectively intended or expected by the insured, notwithstanding the work was intentional").

Nebraska: The Supreme Court of Nebraska held that damage to roof structures and buildings, caused by an insured's subcontractor's negligent installation of shingles, qualified as an "occurrence." *Auto-Owners Ins. Co. v. Home Pride Cos.*, 684 N.W.2d 571, 579 (Neb. 2004). "[A]lthough a standard CGL policy does not provide coverage for faulty workmanship that damages only the resulting work product, if faulty workmanship causes bodily injury or property damage to something other than the insured's work product, an unintended and unexpected event has occurred, and coverage exists." *Id.* at 578. The court described the damage to the roof structures and buildings as "an unintended and unexpected consequence of the contractors' faulty workmanship" which went beyond damages to the contractors' own work product, and, therefore, qualified as an occurrence. *Id.* at 579. *See also Alsobrook v. Jim Earp Chrysler-Plymouth, Ltd.*, 740 N.W.2d 785 (Neb. 2007) (restating holding of *Auto-Owners*); *Cizek Homes, Inc. v. Columbia Nat. Ins. Co.*, 853 N.W.2d 28 (Neb. Ct. App. 2014) (noting that the evidence revealed "that the damage was only to the home itself and that no other property was damaged") ("[T]he allegations of the complaint support a conclusion that the damage to the home was caused by faulty workmanship or a similar impropriety in Cizek's performance. According to *Auto–Owners Ins. Co. v. Home Pride Cos.*, this does not constitute an 'occurrence' under the terms of the policy."); *Drake-Williams Steel, Inc. v. Cont'l Cas. Co.*, 883 N.W.2d 60 (Neb. 2016) ("There is a fundamental distinction between the noncovered business risk of having to correct faulty products or work and the covered risk of liability when faulty products or work cause damage to other property that cannot be corrected through the correction of the faulty products or work. A CGL policy is intended to cover an insured's tort liability for physical injury or property damages, not economic losses due to business risks.") ("The facts in the case at bar are distinguishable [from *Auto-Owners*]. Here, the insured's defective work product did not damage other property. And the inadequacies of the product could be remedied through modification of the integrated pile caps, so as to conform to the required specifications."); *Grinnell Mut. Reinsurance Co. v. Fisher*, No. 16-1047, 2018 Neb. App. LEXIS 47 (Neb. Ct. App. Mar. 13, 2018) ("Smith's allegations of property damage represent unintended and unexpected consequences of Fisher's alleged faulty workmanship and go beyond damages related to Fisher's own work product; accordingly, such claims of property damage sufficiently allege an occurrence within the meaning of the CGL insurance policy.").

Nevada: A Nevada District Court held that claims against an insured framing contractor, for water damage to homes allegedly caused by its defective work, qualified as an "occurrence." *Gary G. Day Constr. Co. v. Clarendon Am. Ins. Co.*, 459 F. Supp. 2d 1039, 1047 (D. Nev. 2006). The court noted that the Supreme Court of Nevada, interpreting similar "occurrence" language, defined "accident" as "a happening that is not expected, foreseen, or intended." *Id.* (quoting *Beckwith v. State Farm Fire & Cas. Co.*, 83 P.3d 275, 277 (Nev. 2004)). "The Court finds that water intrusion is a 'happening that is not expected, foreseen, or intended' and thus falls within the definition of 'occurrence.' Certainly, neither the Plaintiff nor the homeowners intended to have water intrude into the 20 homes. Nor can it be said that either the Plaintiff or the homeowners expected or foresaw the water intrusion." *Id. See also Big-D Const. Corp. v. Take it for Granite Too*, 917 F. Supp. 2d 1096 (D. Nev. 2013) (predicting that the Nevada Supreme Court "would hold that faulty workmanship itself does not fall under the common meaning of an accident, and therefore is not an occurrence" but "that an unexpected happening caused by faulty workmanship could be an occurrence") ("Nevada therefore likely would follow the courts which recognize that although faulty workmanship itself is not an accident, the unexpected consequences of that faulty workmanship is an accident."); *Evanston Ins. Co. v. Western Community Ins. Co.*, No. 13–01268, 2014 U.S. Dist. LEXIS 136129 (D. Nev. Sept. 26, 2014) (agreeing with the analysis in *Big-D*); *Gemini Ins. Co. v. N. Am. Capacity Ins. Co.*, No. 14-00121, 2015 U.S. Dist. LEXIS 14836 (D. Nev. Feb. 6, 2015) ("Although faulty workmanship itself cannot constitute an occurrence under Nevada law, an unexpected happening caused by faulty workmanship could be an occurrence. Accordingly, Olsen's alleged faulty workmanship could constitute an occurrence under Nevada law, and thereby create a possibility of coverage under the Policy even if the faulty workmanship occurred when Olsen conducted its repairs.") (citing *Big-D*) (vacated pursuant to a settlement between the parties, 2015 U.S. Dist. LEXIS 80239 (D. Nev. June 18, 2015)); *Ariz Civ. Constructors v. Colony Ins. Co.*, 481 F. Supp. 3d 1141 (D. Nev. 2020) ("While [the Nevada Supreme Court] has yet to clarify whether faulty workmanship itself constitutes an accident, other judges in this district have reasoned that faulty workmanship, on its own and without other, independent damage, is hardly an unexpected occurrence during and after construction. This reasoning accords with decisions from courts nationwide interpreting other states' laws and similar liability insurance policies, including the Ninth Circuit. I agree with those courts' reasoning and adopt their interpretation.").

New Hampshire: The Supreme Court of New Hampshire held that a claim against a landscaper, for faulty workmanship in constructing a leach field and performing landscaping, did not qualify as an "occurrence." *McAllister v. Peerless Ins. Co.*, 474 A.2d 1033, 1036–37 (N.H. 1984) (Souter, J.). "The fortuity implied by reference to accident or exposure is not what is commonly meant by a failure of workmanship." *Id.* at 1036; *see also Webster v. Acadia Ins. Co.*, 934 A.2d 567, 573 (N.H. 2007) (distinguishing *McAllister* and holding that the "occurrence" requirement was satisfied because the claim alleged damage to property other than the work of the contractor-insured); *see also Concord Gen. Mut. Ins. Co. v. Green & Co. Building &*

Develop. Corp., 8 A.3d 24, 28 (N.H. 2010) (acknowledging that defective work, standing alone, does not constitute an "occurrence," but, rather, an "occurrence" is damage to property other than the work product and damage to the work product other than the defective workmanship) (holding that the entry of carbon monoxide into homes, caused by defective chimneys, was not an "occurrence" because the carbon monoxide caused no physical, tangible alteration of the property, homeowners continued to occupy their homes and no homeowners suffered bodily injury) ("The only effect caused by the faulty chimneys was their loss of use. The loss of use of the insured's work product, standing alone, is not sufficient to constitute an 'occurrence' under the policy."); *Brown v. Concord Group Ins. Co.*, 44 A.3d 586 (N.H. 2012) (citing *Green & Co.* for the proposition that "to constitute an 'occurrence,' the damage at issue must have been to property other than Spencer's work product") ("[T]he factual dispute as to whether the damage was caused by the 2007 repair work or the 2003 original construction of the house is material to whether the damage was caused by an 'occurrence.' If the 2007 work caused damage to the 2003 work, then the damage was caused by an 'occurrence' because the 2007 work is not the same work product as the 2003 work. Conversely, if the damage at issue was actually caused by the 2003 work, then it was not caused by an 'occurrence' because the damage was not to a separate work product."); *Fletch's Sandblasting & Painting, Inc. v. Colony Ins. Co.*, No. 15-490, 2017 U.S. Dist. LEXIS 86488 (D.N.H. June 6, 2017) ("Thick Tech's claim is a noncovered claim for defective workmanship because the costs it seeks to recover were incurred to repair Fletch's defective work rather than to compensate Thick Tech for damage to other property that resulted from the defective work.") (citing *McAllister* and *Concord Gen.*); *Patriot Ins. Co. v. Holmes Carpet Ctr.*, No. 17-73, 2017 U.S. Dist. LEXIS 175643 (D.N.H. Oct. 24, 2017) ("[T]he policy at issue provides coverage only for personal injury or property damage caused by an occurrence, and an insured's defective work does not satisfy this requirement because it lacks the requisite fortuity. This principle applies regardless of whether the claim is for damage to the property that the insured worked on directly or other property that requires repair or replacement in order to correct the defective work. In both instances, the sole cause of the property damage is the insured's defective work, which cannot qualify as an occurrence. In the present case, any property that will be damaged when the defective tile is replaced will be solely the result of the Carpet Center's defective workmanship rather than some intervening fortuitous event or exposure. Therefore, the Carpet Center is not entitled to a defense because the underlying action does not seek to recover for property damage caused by an occurrence."); *Wallace v. Nautilus Ins. Co.*, No. 18-747, 2019 U.S. Dist. LEXIS 122219 (D.N.H. July 23, 2019) ("Plaintiffs do not dispute that New Hampshire law holds that defective workmanship alone is not an occurrence under the Policy's language. They argue, however, that the occurrence for purposes of the Policy in this case is not the defective workmanship itself, but rather the leaking caused by the defective roofs, which resulted in property damage. The court agrees.").

New Jersey: The New Jersey Supreme Court, in *Cypress Point Condominium Assoc. v. Andria Towers*, 143 A.3d 273 (N.J. 2016), after stating that it "had never addressed questions of coverage for consequential damages caused by faulty workmanship under the 1986 ISO standard form CGL policy," concluded: "[U]nder our interpretation of the term 'occurrence' in the policies, consequential harm caused by negligent work is an 'accident.' Therefore, because the result of the subcontractors' faulty workmanship here—consequential water damage to the completed and nondefective portions of Cypress Point—was an 'accident,' it is an 'occurrence' under the policies and is therefore covered so long as the other parameters set by the policies are met. *See Weedo, supra*, 81 N.J. at 249, 405 A.2d 788 (noting that CGL policies do 'not cover an accident of faulty workmanship but rather faulty workmanship that causes an accident')." *Id.* at 289. The court looked at cases nationally and observed that they "represent a strong recent trend in the case law [of most federal circuit and state courts] interpet[ing] the term 'occurrence' to encompass unanticipated damage to nondefective property resulting from poor workmanship." *Id.* at 285. The court went on to address the impact of the "subcontractor exception" to the "your work" exclusion: "This exception to the 'your work' exclusion was not contained in the 1976 ISO CGL form, but unquestionably applies in this case. Accordingly, the third and final step of our inquiry compels the conclusion that, because the water damage to the completed portions of Cypress Point is alleged to have arisen out of faulty workmanship performed by subcontractors, it is a covered loss. *Id.* at 289. In *Travelers Prop. Cas. Co. of Am. v. USA Container Co.*, 686 Fed. Appx. 105 (3rd Cir. 2017), the court rejected the insurer's argument -- that the CGL Policy does not provide coverage to replace or repair defective work – on the basis of *Cypress Point:* "[I]n *Cypress Point*, the New Jersey Supreme Court rejected this very argument: '[R]elying on *Weedo*, the insurers assert that damage to an insured's work caused by a subcontractor's faulty workmanship is foreseeable to the insured developer because damage to any portion of the completed project is the normal, predictable risk of doing business. . . . We disagree.' The court also cited favorably to *U.S. Fire Insurance Co. v. J.S.U.B., Inc.*, 979 So.2d 871 (Fla. 2007), where the Florida

Supreme Court rejected an insurer's argument that faulty workmanship can never be an accident because it results in reasonably foreseeable damages; and confirm[ed] that the 1986 revisions to the standard CGL policy ... specifically cover[ed] damage caused by faulty workmanship to other parts of work in progress; and damage to, or caused by, a subcontractor's work after the insured's operations are completed." *Id.* at 108-09. *See also 313 Jefferson Trust, LLC v. Mercer Ins. Cos.*, No. 2907-15, 2018 N.J. Super. Unpub. LEXIS 35 (N.J. Super. Ct. App. Div. Jan. 8, 2018) (finding no "occurrence" because "although there may have been unintended or unexpected expenses because of the contractor's poor workmanship, there was no finding by the trial court that there was harm to any completed, nondefective portions of a building") ("We do not read *Cypress Point* so broadly as to define occurrence without some damage to nondefective property.").

New Mexico: The New Mexico Court of Appeals, noting that "that some jurisdictions have recently disapproved of the view that faulty workmanship cannot constitute an accident," held that "because the definition of 'occurrence' in this case does not expressly state that faulty workmanship can never constitute an accident and does not limit the term's effect to a particular class of tangible property, we conclude that the alleged property damage in this case was caused by an alleged 'occurrence' as the policy defines that term." *Pulte Homes of N.M., Inc. v. Ind. Lumbermens Ins. Co.*, 367 P.3d 869 (N.M. Ct. App. 2015). "We conclude that (1) claims of defective or defectively installed windows and doors in Pulte's two defense tenders to ILM constituted claims for 'property damage' caused by an 'occurrence' under the policy at issue; (2) the 'your work' policy exclusion precluded coverage for this occurrence with regard to Pulte's May 2009 defense tender because no facts were alleged tending to show that the defective or defectively installed windows and doors caused damage to property other than the windows and doors themselves." *Id.* at 871. *See also Mid-Continent Cas. Co. v. Circle S Feed Store, LLC*, 754 F.3d 1175 (10th Cir. 2014) (adopting "the majority approach" that "the insured's act is not accidental only if the insured intended both the act *and* to cause some kind of injury or damage.") ("Intent to cause the injury or damage can be actual or it can be inferred from the nature of the act when the consequences are substantially certain to result from the act."); *King v. Travelers Ins. Co.*, 505 P.2d 1226 (N.M. 1973) (addressing whether water damage had been caused by "accidental discharge, leakage or overflow," as required by a first-party property policy) (court cited with approval the holding of the Supreme Court of Minnesota in *Hauenstein v. Saint Paul-Mercury Indemnity Co.*, 65 N.W.2d 122 (Minn. 1954): "There is no doubt that the property damage to the building caused by the application of the defective plaster was 'caused by accident' within the meaning of the insurance contract, since the damage was a completely unexpected and unintended result. Accident, as a source and cause of damage to property, within the terms of an accident policy, is an unexpected, unforeseen, or undesigned happening or consequence from either a known or an unknown cause.").

New York: The Supreme Court of New York, Appellate Division, held that a claim against a construction manager for failing to adequately and properly supervise the installation of (1) a building's wood flooring, leading to its buckling and cracking, and (2) a curtain wall and windows that caused widespread water infiltration, did not qualify as an "occurrence." *George A. Fuller Co. v. U.S. Fid. & Guar. Co.*, 613 N.Y.S.2d 152, 155 (N.Y. App. Div. 1994). The policy "does not insure against faulty workmanship in the work product itself but rather faulty workmanship in the work product which creates a legal liability by causing bodily injury or property damage to something other than the work product. The policy was never intended to provide contractual indemnification for economic loss to a contracting party because the work product contracted for is defectively produced." *Id.*; *see also Transp. Ins. Co. v. AARK Constr. Group, Ltd.*, 526 F. Supp. 2d 350, 357 (E.D.N.Y. 2007) (following *Fuller* and holding that the costs of repair of a garage, and loss of use of the building incident to the closure of the garage, did not qualify as an "occurrence" because the alleged negligence only affected the property owner's economic interest in the insured contractor's completed work product); *Saks v. Nicosia Contracting Corp.*, 625 N.Y.S.2d 758, 760 (N.Y. App. Div. 1995) (distinguishing *Fuller* and finding an "occurrence" because the claim against the contractor was not that the house it built was defective, but, rather, was for damage to real property on which the house encroached); *Continental Ins. Co. v. Huff Enterprises, Inc.*, No. 07-CV-3821, 2010 U.S. Dist. LEXIS 71272 (E.D.N.Y. June 21, 2010) ("[I]f the damage to be remedied is faulty work or the product itself, rather than an injury to a person or other property because of the faulty work product, the alleged act is not an 'occurrence' under standard insurance contracts."); *Exeter Bldg. Corp. v. Scottsdale Ins. Co.*, 913 N.Y.S.2d 733, 735–36 (N.Y. App. Div. 2010) ("[B]ecause the complaint seeks relief for conduct that falls solely and exclusively under the work product exclusions of the CGL policies, and the damages sought therein do not arise from an occurrence resulting in damage to property distinct from the work product of Exeter or its hired subcontractors, Scottsdale is not obligated to provide Exeter with a defense or to indemnify it in the underlying action."); *QBE Ins. Corp. v. Adjo Contracting Corp.*, 121 A.D.3d 1064 (2014) ("New York courts have generally acknowledged that, while a commercial general liability policy does not insure for damage to the work product itself, it insures faulty workmanship in the work product which creates a legal liability by causing bodily injury or property damage to something other than the work product.") (citing *Fuller*); *Savik, Murray & Aurora Const. Mgmt. Co., LLC v. ITT Hartford Ins. Group*, 927 N.Y.S.2d 634 (N.Y. App. Div. 2011) (same) (citing *Fuller*); *I.J. White Corp. v. Columbia Cas. Co.*, 964 N.Y.S.2d 21 (N.Y. App. Div. 2013) ("Courts have held that commercial general liability policies do not insure against faulty workmanship in the work product itself. However, such policies do insure against property damage caused by faulty workmanship to something other than the work product.") (citing *Fuller* and concluding that coverage owed because plaintiff did "not seek coverage simply for allegedly faulty workmanship that caused the defect in the freezer. Rather, it seeks defense and indemnity for property damage that Hill Country, a third party, alleged that it suffered because of a defect in the freezer."); *Ohio Cas. Ins. Co. v. Lewis & Clinch, Inc.*, No. 12–872, 2014 U.S. Dist. LEXIS 159720 (N.D.N.Y. Nov. 13, 2014) (citing *Fuller* and concluding that coverage owed for 'property damage' resulting from an 'occurrence.'"); *Rosewood Home Builders, LLC v. National Fire & Marine Ins. Co.*, 11–1421, 2013 U.S. Dist. LEXIS 45374 (N.D.N.Y. Mar. 29, 2013) ("The Second Circuit Court of Appeals has stated that an 'occurrence' does not include claims for mere faulty workmanship but 'rather for consequential property damage inflicted upon a third party as a result of the insured's activity.' Therefore, 'this circuit has held that a CGL policy [does] not provide coverage for a claim against an insured for the repair of faulty workmanship that damaged only the resulting work product.'") (quoting *J.G.Z. Res. Inc. v. King*, 987 F.2d 98, 102 (2d Cir. 1993)); *Maxum Indem. Co. v. A One Testing Labs., Inc.*, 150 F. Supp. 3d 278 (S.D.N.Y. 2015) ("There can be no doubt that the allegations 610 West includes in the UAC bring this matter within the 'no occurrence, no coverage' rule for commercial general liability policies under New York law. The damages 610 West seeks to recover represent the cost of repairing the allegedly defective work in order to bring it into compliance with the underlying contracts, industry standards, and legal requirements. New York law is clear that the recitation of a cause of action labeled 'negligence' in the underlying complaint does not suffice to create coverage for faulty work product under a commercial general liability insurance policy."); *Am. Home Assur. Co. v. Allan Window Techs., Ltd.*, No. 15-5138, 2016 U.S. Dist. LEXIS 101118, (S.D.N.Y. Apr. 2, 2016) ("Here, it is entirely possible that some or all of the claims alleged in the Underlying Complaint are for tort damage caused to third-party property, distinct from Allan's work product.

Because American Home cannot reasonably claim that the allegations of the complaint allow for *no interpretation* that the unit owners' claims relate to third-party property damage, and thus fall within the coverage afforded by the policy, the Court cannot conclude that American Home does not have a duty to defend Allan in the Underlying Action.") (emphasis in original); *Black & Veatch Corp. v. Aspen Ins. (UK) Ltd.*, 882 F.3d 952 (10th Cir. 2018) (applying New York law) (noting that "New York state court decisions have not resolved whether subcontractor damages can be deemed an 'occurrence' under a CGL policy containing a subcontractor exception" to the your work exclusion) (predicting that the New York Court of Appeals would hold that a subcontractor's faulty workmanship causing damage to a contractor's own work would constitute an "occurrence" because the damages were "accidental and harmed a third party's property" and to find otherwise would render a subcontractor exception to the your work exclusion and an endorsement excluding "property damage to the 'particular part of real property' that [the contractor] or its subcontractors were working on when the damage occurred" during ongoing operations "mere surplusage, in violation of New York law"); *East 111 Assoc. LLC v. RLI Ins. Co.*, No. 653890/2018, 2019 N.Y. Misc. LEXIS 5331 (N.Y. Sup. Ct. Oct. 4, 2019) ("As the Underlying Complaint carries the possibility that Walsh's allegedly faulty workmanship damaged other parts of the building—which was not, as a whole, Walsh's work—an 'occurrence' giving rise to 'property damage' may exist under the Selective Policy issued to Walsh."); *Interstate Fire & Cas. v. Aspen Ins. UK Ltd.*, No. 153512/2017, 2019 N.Y. Misc. LEXIS 5800 (N.Y. Sup. Ct. Oct. 25, 2019) ("GCL policies such as Aspen UK's cover consequential property damage caused by a contractor's faulty workmanship as 'property damage' caused by an 'occurrence', even if the cost of repairing the defective work itself is not covered."); *Greater N.Y. Mut. Ins. Co. v. Harleysville Worcester Ins. Co.*, No. 151179/2016, 2020 N.Y. Misc. LEXIS 799 (N.Y. Sup. Ct. Feb. 21, 2020) (allegations of damage to other property, due to faulty construction, including mold growth and a water damaged balcony door saddle, constituted an "occurrence").

North Carolina: The Supreme Court of North Carolina held that a claim against a roofer, for water damage resulting from its failure to cover a partially removed roof, qualified as an "accident." *Iowa Mut. Ins. Co. v. Fred M. Simmons, Inc.*, 128 S.E.2d 19, 25 (N.C. 1962). "[W]e do not subscribe to the view that the term 'accident,' used in the liability policy here, considered in its usual, ordinary, and popular sense necessarily excludes human fault called negligence, because negligence would most probably be the predicate of any likely liability against appellant." *Id.* More recent decisions addressing North Carolina law have focused on the "property damage" requirement of the insuring agreement—and not the "occurrence" requirement—and have held that damage solely to an insured's work does not qualify as "property damage." *See Production Systems, Inc. v. Amerisure Ins. Co.,* 605 S.E.2d 663, 666 (N.C. Ct. App. 2004) ("The term 'property damage' in an insurance policy has been interpreted to mean damage to property that was previously undamaged, and not the expense of repairing property or completing a project that was not done correctly or according to contract in the first instance."); *see also Breezewood of Wilmington Condominiums Homeowners' Assn. Inc. v. Amerisure Mut. Ins. Co.,* 335 Fed. Appx. 268, 271 (4th Cir. 2009) ("North Carolina state courts and federal courts sitting in diversity have consistently held that 'property damage' in the context of commercial general liability policies means 'damage to property that was previously undamaged' and does not include 'the expense of repairing property or completing a project that was not done correctly or according to contract in the first instance' by the insured.") (citing cases); *Builders Mut. Ins. Co. v. Mitchell,* 709 S.E.2d 528, 531–32 (N.C. Ct. App. 2011) ("It is true that a claim for faulty workmanship, in and of itself, is not an occurrence under a commercial general liability policy. ... Faulty workmanship is not included in the standard definition of 'property damage' because a failure of workmanship does not involve the fortuity required to constitute an accident. ... Thus, for any damages regarding the cost of repairing the faulty workmanship itself, the Maryland Casualty policy would not apply, because the damages for such repair costs would not constitute 'property damage' as defined by the policy. However, we agree with BMI that McKinney's claims were not limited to costs associated only with repairs to the faulty workmanship itself.") (citations and internal quotes omitted); *National Union Fire Ins. Co. of Pittsburgh, PA v. Intercoastal Diving, Inc.,* No. 10–115, 2012 U.S. Dist. LEXIS 76291 (E.D.N.C. June 1, 2012) ("[S]tate and federal courts applying North Carolina law have held that damage caused by the insured's defective work to property other than the insured's work product may constitute 'property damage.'"); *Erie Ins. Exchange v. Builders Mut. Ins. Co.,* 742 S.E.2d 803 (N.C. Ct. App. 2013) (discussing *Mitchell*) ("[A]lthough the Hardison Action complaint alleges that the bank collapse was a result of TPD Builder's negligent construction and faulty workmanship, there is no indication in the record that the destructive bank collapse was 'expected or intended' by TPD Builder. Rather, the collapse of the altered slope and retaining wall was an accident resulting from the alleged faulty workmanship of TPD Builder according to the allegations in the Hardison Action complaint.").

North Dakota: The Supreme Court of North Dakota held that water damage to the interior of a building, caused by the insured's failure to protect it against rain during a roof replacement project, qualified as an "occurrence." *ACUITY v. Burd & Smith Constr., Inc.*, 721 N.W.2d 33, 39 (N.D. 2006). "We agree with the rationale of those courts holding that faulty workmanship causing damage to property other than the work product is an accidental occurrence for purposes of a CGL policy. That rationale is consistent with the coverage risks for a CGL policy and the plain and ordinary language of the policy. We conclude property damage caused by faulty workmanship is a covered occurrence to the extent the faulty workmanship causes bodily injury or property damage to property other than the insured's work product." *Id.* However, in *K & L Homes, Inc. v. American Family Mut. Ins. Co.*, 829 N.W.2d 724 (N.D. 2013), the North Dakota high court, following a comprehensive national survey of the "occurrence" issue, overruled *Burd & Smith* and held: "We conclude faulty workmanship may constitute an 'occurrence' if the faulty work was 'unexpected' and not intended by the insured, and the property damage was not anticipated or intentional, so that neither the cause nor the harm was anticipated, intended, or expected. This is consistent with our definition of 'accident' for purposes of a CGL policy." *Id.* at 736. "There is nothing in the definition of 'occurrence' that supports that faulty workmanship that damages the property of a third party is a covered 'occurrence,' but faulty workmanship that damages the work or property of the insured contractor is not an 'occurrence.'" *Id. See also SW Design Build, Inc. v. Auto-Owners Ins.*, No. 16-82, 2017 U.S. Dist. LEXIS 215504 (D.N.D. Sept. 29, 2017) ("The North Dakota Supreme Court has held that faulty workmanship may constitute an 'occurrence' so long as 'the faulty work was unexpected and not intended by the insured, and the property damage was not anticipated or intentional'…This is true whether the property damage is to a third party's property or to the work or property of the insured. The three claims against SW Design in the underlying complaint—negligence, breach of implied warranties of good and workmanlike design and construction, and breach of contract—arise out of alleged faulty workmanship…neither the property damage nor its cause was anticipated or intended. Accordingly, the claims fall within the initial grant of coverage.") (citing *K & L Homes*); *Selective Way Ins. Co. v. Glosson Group*, No. 17-230, 2020 U.S. Dist. LEXIS 115278 (D.N.D. Mar. 25, 2020), *rev'd on other grounds* 994 F.3d 952 (8th Cir. 2021) (finding that the parties failed "to apply the fundamental legal principle that several courts, including the North Dakota Supreme Court, have recognized — that is, 'defective workmanship, standing alone, which results in damages only to the work product itself [(i.e., the concrete parking lot)] is not an accidental occurrence under a CGL policy.'") (citing, in support, *Burd & Smith*, despite the fact that it was overruled in *K&L Homes*).

Ohio: The Supreme Court of Ohio held that "claims for faulty workmanship, such as the one in the present case, are not fortuitous in the context of a CGL policy like the one here. In keeping with the spirit of fortuity that is fundamental to insurance coverage, we hold that the CGL policy does not provide coverage to Custom for its alleged defective construction of and workmanship on the steel grain bin. Our holding is consistent with the majority of Ohio courts that have denied coverage for this type of claim. The majority view is that claims of defective construction or workmanship are not claims for 'property damage' caused by an 'occurrence' under a CGL policy." *Westfield Ins. Co. v. Custom Agri Sys., Inc.*, 979 N.E.2d 269 (Ohio 2012).

Relying upon *Custom Agri*, the Supreme Court of Ohio has additionally held that "[p]roperty damage caused by a subcontractor's faulty work is not an 'occurrence' under a CGL policy because it cannot be deemed fortuitous." *Ohio N. Univ. v. Charles Constr. Servs.*, 120 N.E.3d 762 (Ohio 2018). The court acknowledged that its reasoning "contrasts with recent decisions of other courts" but that "the language requiring that 'property damage' be caused by an 'occurrence' remains a constant in the policies. And under our precedent, faulty workmanship is not an occurrence as defined in CGL polices like the one before us. Regardless of any trend in the law, we must look to the plain and ordinary meaning of the language used in the CGL policy before us." *Id.* at 771 (noting that the Ohio General Assembly has the power to legislate the definition of "occurrence" to include "property damage" resulting from faulty workmanship). *See also Cincinnati Ins. Cos. v. Motorists Mut. Ins. Co.*, 18 N.E.3d 875 (Ohio Ct. App. 2014) ("In the instant matter, Nationwide's complaint sought damages caused by the fire, not damages caused directly by G & S' allegedly defective work. In other words, the complaint did not exclusively seek to recover damages stemming from G & S's work in installing the lighting. Rather, it sought damages from the consequential risks that stemmed from the work of G & S. Accordingly, we cannot say that Motorists' duty to defend is negated by *Westfield*."); *Reggie Constr. v. Westfield Ins. Co.*, No. 2013–L–095, 2014 Ohio App. LEXIS 3703 (Ohio Ct. App. Sept. 2, 2014) ("[C]ourts generally conclude that the policies are intended to insure the risks of an insured causing damage to other persons and their property but that the policies are not intended to insure the risks of an insured causing damage to the insured's own work. In other words, the policies do not insure an insured's work itself; rather, the policies generally insure consequential risks that stem from the insured's work.") (quoting *Westfield*, quoting *Heile v. Herrmann*, 736 N.E.2d 566 (Ohio Ct. App. 1999)); *Weitz Co., LLC v. Acuity*, No. 12-855, 2016 U.S. Dist. LEXIS 150433 (S.D. Ohio Oct. 31, 2016) ("[T]he Panel found that Weitz failed to perform in a workmanlike manner. The Panel also found that Weitz breached its contract with Twin Lakes, and that Weitz's breach of contract caused the moisture intrusion and the resulting moisture damage to all of the units. These claims cannot be considered a fortuitous accident, since neither the claims for faulty workmanship nor breach of contract are claims for 'property damage' caused by an 'occurrence.'"). Pre-*Westfield* cases were mixed on the "occurrence" issue. *See Beaverdam Contracting v. Erie Ins. Co.*, No. 1–08–17, 2008 Ohio App. LEXIS 4136 (Ohio Ct. App. Sept. 29, 2008) ("We note that many courts in Ohio have reached different conclusions as to whether claims of negligence and/or failure to perform in a workmanlike manner constitute an accident for purposes of establishing an 'occurrence' under CGL insurance contracts.").

Oklahoma: An Oklahoma District Court held that a claim for damages resulting from the insured's delivery of defective concrete to a bridge construction project qualified as an "occurrence." *Employers Mut. Cas. Co. v. Grayson*, No. CIV-07–917, 2008 U.S. Dist. LEXIS 43255 (W.D. Okla. May 30, 2008). "[I]t is undisputed that Ready Mix [the insured] did not knowingly deliver concrete containing fly ash. Nor is there any suggestion that a reasonable supplier in its position would have known the concrete contained fly ash or was otherwise non-conforming. Thus, the damage to the bridge deck and to its structural components during the required removal of the defective concrete was the unintended consequence of Ready Mix innocently supplying a non-conforming product."; *Am. Modern Select Ins. Co. v. Crum*, No. 07-CV-315, 2008 U.S. Dist. LEXIS 93748 (N.D. Okla. Nov. 17, 2008) ("In this case, the Allens contracted with Crum to remodel their existing home. The Allens complain of improper and deficient workmanship. The Allens do not allege any event or series of events that could be construed as an accident. The alleged deficiencies and substandard construction did not constitute an accident or an occurrence under the plain-meaning rule, even if the resulting work was unexpected, unforeseen, or unintended by the insured. The purpose of a CGLP policy is to protect the insured from liability for damages to property other than his own work or property that is caused by the insured's defective work product.") (citation omitted); *North Star Mut. Ins. Co. v. Rose*, 27 F. Supp. 3d 1250 (E.D. Okla. 2014) ("Faulty workmanship can constitute an occurrence that triggers coverage under a CGL policy if (1) the property damage was not caused by purposeful neglect or knowingly poor workmanship, and (2) the damage was to non-defective portions of the contractor's or subcontractor's work or to third-party property.") (quoting an unpublished Colorado District Court opinion, which is evidence of the paucity of Oklahoma authority). *See National American Ins. Co. v. Gerlicher Co., LLC*, 260 P.3d 1279 (Ok. Ct. Civ. App. 2011) ("We do not determine in this Opinion whether the moisture intrusion due to alleged defective workmanship that led to interior and structural damage constitutes an 'occurrence' as defined in the CGL policies."); *Essex Ins. Co. v. Sheppard & Sons Constr., Inc.*, No. 12-1022, 2015 U.S. Dist. LEXIS 89096 (W.D. Okla. July 9, 2015) (noting that "no Oklahoma case directly addresses whether an insured's negligent construction or faulty workmanship constitutes an accident for purposes of determining whether occurrence coverage exists under a commercial general liability insurance policy") ("Under controlling Oklahoma law faulty workmanship may constitute an accident (and, therefore, an occurrence) under the Policy. . . . [I]t is undisputed that Essex makes no assertions that Sheppard or C&D Dozer intentionally provided allegedly defective work. Because it is alleged that the property damage to the dental facility resulted from negligent conduct, such conduct may constitute an accident, and therefore an occurrence, under the Policy."); *MTI, Inc. v. Emplrs Ins. Co.*, No. 15-716, 2017 U.S. Dist. LEXIS 136869 (W.D. Okla. Aug. 25, 2017), *rev'd on other grounds* 913 F.3d 1245 (10th Cir. 2019) (noting that no Oklahoma state cases define the term "occurrence"); *Country Mut. Ins. Co. v. AAA Constr. LLC*, No. 17-486, 2019 U.S. Dist. LEXIS 115935 (W.D. Okla. July 12, 2019) ("Here, CMIC points to no evidence that AAA Construction purposefully built the garage on top of the gas line or intentionally or deliberately intended to construct the garage in violation of the utility easement…Because at trial 'the jury could [find AAA Construction] guilty merely of negligence or other nonintentional conduct' by failing to ascertain the location of the easement, the possibility of coverage exists and gives rise to a duty to defend."); *Evanston Ins. Co. v. A&S Roofing, LLC*, No. 17-870, 2019 U.S. Dist. LEXIS 142828 (W.D. Okla. Aug. 22, 2019) ("[T]he Court finds, under the prevailing view, that faulty workmanship does give rise to an occurrence where, as here, the work at issue is not that performed by the insured but by a subcontractor of the insured, the property damage was not caused by purposeful neglect or knowingly poor workmanship and the damage includes damage to the non-defective work product of the contractor and damage to third-party property.").

Oregon: The Supreme Court of Oregon held that a claim against a general contractor on a residential construction project, for the removal and replacement of a subcontractor's interior painting work that had failed to cure properly, did not qualify as an "occurrence." *Oak Crest Constr. Co. v. Austin Mut. Ins. Co.*, 998 P.2d 1254, 1258 (Or. 2000). "Had the facts demonstrated that the claimed problem with the cabinets and woodwork was the result of that kind of breach [of the duty to act with due care—as opposed to breach of contract], or that plaintiff might be liable to the owners in tort for other damage, that might have qualified as an 'accident' within the meaning of the commercial liability policy." *Id.*; *see also MW Builders, Inc. v. Safeco Ins. Co. of Am.*, 267 Fed. App'x 552, 554 (9th Cir. 2008) (applying Oregon law) (holding that damage to a hotel as a result of faulty installation of EIFS, as opposed to any damages associated with the actual replacement of the EIFS, qualified as an "occurrence"); *Ohio Cas. Ins. Co. v. Ferrell Developments, LLC*, No. 10–162, 2011 U.S. Dist. LEXIS 135819 (D. Or. July 27, 2011) ("To the extent Ferrell's damages are based on its breach of contract claim, they were not the result of an 'accident' and, therefore, not caused by an 'occurrence' under the Policy. However, the courts also recognize that damage caused by the negligent performance of a contract can in certain instances be recoverable in tort.") (relying on, among other decisions, *Oak Crest*). *But see Willmar Dev., LLC v. Illinois Nat. Ins. Co.*, 726 F. Supp. 2d 1280, 1286 (D. Or. 2010) ("*Oak Crest* is also distinguishable from the case at bar. First, in *Oak Crest*, the damage involved repair work required to complete the project. By contrast, here, the alleged damages arose after the project was complete and did not result from repairs required to complete the project. Second, in *Oak Crest*, the complaint only alleged a breach of contract. Conversely, here, the complaints include allegations of negligence. The cases on which AIG rely do little to persuade this court that the alleged damages in the complaints are not 'occurrences' as defined under the Policy. Moreover, this court is reluctant to find that the alleged damages in the complaints sound only in contract, especially when considering that Oregon courts have previously held that damages caused by the negligent performance of a contract can, in certain circumstances, be recoverable in tort.") (citations omitted) (*affirmed* 464 Fed. Appx. 594 (9th Cir. 2011)); *Houston Specialty Ins. Co. v. Rodriguez Corp.*, No. 18-01886, 2019 U.S. Dist. LEXIS 225601 (D. Or. Oct. 25, 2019) (finding a complaint alleging damage to "something other than the insured's work" sufficiently alleged an "occurrence").

Pennsylvania: The Supreme Court of Pennsylvania held that claims against the insured, for defective design and construction of a coke oven battery, did not qualify as an "occurrence." *Kvaerner Metals Div. of Kvaerner U.S., Inc. v. Commercial Union Ins. Co.*, 908 A.2d 888, 899 (Pa. 2006). "We hold that the definition of 'accident' required to establish an 'occurrence' under the policies cannot be satisfied by claims based upon faulty workmanship. Such claims simply do not present the degree of fortuity contemplated by the ordinary definition of 'accident' or its common judicial construction in this context." *Id.; see also Millers Capital Ins. Co. v. Gambone Bros. Dev. Co., Inc.*, 941 A.2d 706, 713 (Pa. Super. Ct. 2007) (addressing *Kvaerner*) ("[N]atural and foreseeable acts, such as rainfall, which tend to exacerbate the damage, effect, or consequences caused *ab initio* by faulty workmanship [of windows, roofs and stucco exteriors] also cannot be considered sufficiently fortuitous to constitute an 'occurrence' or 'accident' for the purposes of an occurrence based CGL policy."); *Specialty Surfaces International, Inc. v. Continental Cas. Co.*, 609 F.3d 223 (3rd Cir. 2010) (holding that, based on *Kvaerner* and *Gambone*, no coverage was owed to an insured for its faulty workmanship, nor for any damage to other property that was a reasonably foreseeable result of such faulty workmanship, on the basis that neither constituted an "occurrence"); *Nationwide Mut. Ins. Co. v. CPB International, Inc.*, 562 F.3d 591 (3rd Cir. 2009) (holding that no coverage was owed for the consequential damages caused by combining the insured's defective chondroitin, with glucosamine, to form nutritional tablets, because it was foreseeable that the product that the insured sold would be used for the purpose for which it was sold); *Erie Ins. Exchange v. Abbott Furnace Co.*, 972 A.2d 1232 (Pa. Super. Ct. 2009) (holding that no coverage was owed for damage to property caused by the insured's defective furnace); *Bomgardner Concrete v. State Farm Fire & Cas.*, No. 10-1287, 2010 U.S. Dist. LEXIS 96379 (E.D. Pa. Sept. 14, 2010) (holding that no coverage was owed to a cement installer, for a defective floor, notwithstanding that the spalling and delamination of the concrete was caused by the concrete itself (excess water and failing to properly cure)—that had been supplied by a party other than the insured); *Zurich American Ins. Co. v. R.M. Shoemaker Co.*, 519 Fed. Appx. 90 (3d Cir. 2013) ("*Kvaerner* and *Gambone* control the outcome of this dispute. Faulty workmanship—whether caused by the contractor's negligence alone or by the contractor's negligent supervision, which then permitted the willful misconduct of its subcontractors—does not amount to an 'accident' or 'occurrence.'") (citing *CPB, Specialty Surfaces* and *Bomgardner*). *But see Indalex Inc. v. National Union Fire Ins. Co. of Pittsburgh, PA*, 83 A.3d 418 (Pa. Super. 2013) ("[W]e are constrained to conclude that neither *Kvaerner, Gambone*, nor *Abbott*, bar coverage. As acknowledged by the trial court in this case, the *Kvaerner* holding was limited to situations 'where the underlying claims were for breach of contract and breach of warranty, and the only damages were to the [insured's] work product.' *Gambone* was a suit against a property developer and builder of homes, not a typical product manufacturer, with the 'product' being the home itself. In the instant case, we have an off-the-shelf product that failed and allegedly caused property damage and personal injury. Also, the court in *Gambone* framed the issue as faulty workmanship in the application of the stucco and other items. Here, there are issues framed in terms of a bad product, which can be construed as an 'active malfunction,' and not merely bad workmanship."); *Nat'l Fire Ins. Co. of Hartford v. Robinson Fans Holdings, Inc.*, No. 10–1054, 2011 U.S. Dist. LEXIS 77367 (W.D. Pa. July 18, 2011) (denying reconsideration of April 7, 2011 decision holding that, in context of the duty to defend, because the failure of the insured's work or product was caused by the insured's faulty design, and such design predated the contract, *i.e.*, was not an obligation undertaken specifically on account of the contractual relationship, then the insured did not breach its contract, but, rather, breached a duty imposed by social policy, and, as such, any damage was caused by a occurrence); *Hagel v. Falcone*, No. 614 EDA 2014, 2014 Pa. Super. Unpub. LEXIS 464 (Pa. Super. Ct. Dec. 23, 2014) (declining to distinguish *Kvaerner* and *Gambone*) ("[T]he most critical element in *Indalex* was that the appellant's claims were product-liability/tort claims that were based on damages to persons or property, other than the insured's product. Such claims are absent here, where workmanship is at issue, rather than an active malfunction or product liability, as such. Hence, *Indalex* cannot carry the day for Appellants."); *Northridge Vill., LP v. Travelers Indem. Co.*, No. 15-1947, 2017 U.S. Dist. LEXIS 140541 (E.D. Pa. Aug. 31, 2017) (citing over a dozen Pennsylvania cases that have relied on *Kvaener* and/or *Gambone* to hold that faulty workmanship does not constitute an "occurrence") ("[E]ven if these vague references to consequential damage can be construed to allege damage to property other than Plaintiffs' work, the *Kvaerner* Court's holding has been extended to other property where the damage is a foreseeable result of the insured's faulty workmanship.") (also noting that "*Indalex* did not announce a new majority rule, but instead carved out a discrete scenario where a claim based in products liability could constitute an 'occurrence'" and that the claims at issue did not "amount to an 'active malfunction' in any product, nor do they state a product liability claim"); *MMG Ins. Co. v. Floor Assocs.*, No. 15-4814, 2017 U.S. Dist. LEXIS 124883 (E.D. Pa. Aug. 8, 2017) ("Because this case is about shoddy workmanship, Floor Associate's reliance on *Indalex, Inc. v. National Union Fire Insurance Co.*, is misplaced."); *Quality Stone Veneer,*

Inc. v. Selective Ins. Co. of Am., 229 F. Supp. 3d 351 (E.D. Pa. 2017) ("[F]aulty workmanship by a contractor which results in damage to additional property of the other party to the underlying contract is not an 'occurrence'....It does not matter that the insured was a developer or a subcontractor. All that matters for the analysis is whether the insured performed the work that is alleged to have been faulty."); *Northridge Vill., LP v. Travelers Indem. Co.*, No. 15-1947, 2017 U.S. Dist. LEXIS 140541 (E.D. Pa. Aug. 31, 2017) ("Courts in this Circuit have consistently applied *Kvaerner* and held that claims based upon faulty workmanship do not amount to an 'occurrence,' and thus do not trigger an insurer's duty to defend...The same conclusion has been reached in this Circuit in cases where the faulty workmanship results in foreseeable damage to property other than the insured's work product."); *Pa. Mfrs. Indem. Co. v. Pottstown Indus. Complex, LP*, 215 A.3d 1010 (Pa. Super. Ct. 2019) ("Because the Underlying Action alleges damage to other property, not property that Insured contracted to provide, and that the damage was caused by an accident, a flood, it includes claims for property damage caused by an 'occurrence.'") (finding that *Kvaerner*, *Gambone*, and *Abbott Furnace* "do not hold that the fact that liability is based on failure to properly perform contractual duties precludes the existence of an 'occurrence' where the claim is for damage to property not supplied by the insured and unrelated to what the insured contracted to provide"); *Sapa Extrusions, Inc. v. Liberty Mut. Ins. Co.*, 939 F.3d 243 (3d Cir. 2019) (rejecting insured's contention that third-party property damage constitutes an "occurrence" on the basis that "any distinction between damage to the work product alone versus damage to other property is irrelevant so long as both foreseeably flow from faulty workmanship"); *Nautilus Ins. Co. v. 200 Christian St. Partners LLC*, 819 Fed. Appx. 87 (3d Cir. 2020) (complaint alleging "the use of faulty materials, and the active malfunction of products, such as the windows and moisture barriers" alleged an "occurrence"); *Burlington Ins. Co. v. Shelter Structures, Inc.*, 484 F. Supp. 3d 237 (E.D. Pa. 2020) (noting that the court in *Pottstown* "merely held that faulty workmanship does not preclude the finding of an occurrence when third-party property is damaged" and that "[a]n underlying complaint must still allege that the damage was caused by 'an unexpected and undesirable event' that 'falls within the definition of the term 'occurrence' under the [policy]' for there to be a duty to defend"); *Berkley Specialty Ins. Co. v. Masterforce Constr. Corp.*, No. 19-01162, 2021 U.S. Dist. LEXIS 14006 (M.D. Pa. Jan. 26, 2021) (noting that "there remains an open question whether, under Pennsylvania law, an 'accident' occurs when the underlying claims are based upon faulty workmanship when the faulty workmanship results in damage to third-party property—i.e., property that belongs to someone other than the insured") (predicting that, despite Superior Court decisions to the contrary, "the Supreme Court of Pennsylvania would determine that damage to third-party property caused by faulty workmanship does not qualify as an accident sufficient to trigger insurance coverage").

Rhode Island: A Rhode Island trial court held that claims against an insured, for damages allegedly caused by its negligent preparation of specifications used by others on a sewer project, qualified as an "occurrence." *Aetna Cas. & Sur. Co. v. Consulting Envtl. Eng'rs, Inc.*, No. P.C. 88–2075, 1989 R.I. Super. LEXIS 136 (R.I. Super. Ct. June 20, 1989). "The installation of the manholes and pipes at the wrong level in one location and their settlement to the wrong level at another may well have been the foreseeable consequence of some negligence of the defendant [insured] … . But, one cannot say that the defendant expected the damaging consequences of its conduct unless one can say that the defendant knew that its conduct would result in the harmful consequence and pursued it anyway, taking what has been called a 'calculated risk.'" *See also Boisse v. Miller*, No. WC 2003-0281, 2013 R.I. Super. LEXIS 155 (R.I Super. Ct. Aug. 8, 2013) ("Mr. Miller's incorrectly performed work cannot be considered an 'occurrence' under the Assurance policies. The United States District Court for the District of Massachusetts has stated that most commercial general liability policies 'exclude the insured's faulty workmanship from coverage . . . [because] faulty workmanship fails to constitute an accidental occurrence in a commercial general liability policy.' (citation omitted) As such, poor workmanship is a business risk to be borne by the insured; construing a policy as providing coverage for faulty workmanship, therefore, would improperly transform the insurer into a guarantor of the insured's work.") (citing all non-Rhode Island decisions).

South Carolina: South Carolina has taken a winding road in its treatment of the "occurrence" issue. The Supreme Court of South Carolina held that the deterioration of roads, caused by a contractor's faulty workmanship, did not qualify as an "occurrence." *L-J, Inc. v. Bituminous Fire & Marine Ins. Co.*, 621 S.E.2d 33, 36 (S.C. 2005). The court concluded that the roadway contractor's faulty workmanship, which caused damaged to only the roadway system, was not something that is typically caused by an accident, and, therefore, did not constitute an "occurrence." *Id. See also Auto Owners Ins. Co. v. Newman*, 684 S.E.2d 541 (S.C. 2009) (holding that, unlike the damage in *L-J*, which was merely for the insured's faulty workmanship itself, there was "property damage" beyond that of the defective work product (stucco), such as damage to the walls and exterior sheathing; while the defective application of the stucco did not, on its own, constitute an occurrence, the continuous moisture intrusion resulting from the subcontractor's negligence was an occurrence).

In January 2011, in *Crossmann Communities v. Harleysville Mut. Ins. Co.*, No. 26909, 2011 S.C. LEXIS 2 (S.C. Jan. 7, 2011), the Supreme Court of South Carolina revisited its decision in *Newman* and overruled it. The *Crossmann* Court held that "where the damage to the insured's property [project] is no more than the natural and probable consequences of faulty workmanship such that the two cannot be distinguished, this does not constitute an occurrence." In other words, unlike *Newman*, which held that the consequential damages of an insured's faulty workmanship qualifies as an "occurrence," *Crossmann* held that the consequential damage of an insured's faulty workmanship does not automatically qualify as an "occurrence." In particular, property damage that is the natural and probable consequences of faulty workmanship does not constitute an "occurrence."

In May 2011, South Carolina enacted § 38–61-70 of the South Carolina Code, which goes to the heart of *Crossmann*, and provides, in part, that commercial general liability insurance policies shall contain or be deemed to contain a definition of "occurrence" that includes "property damage or bodily injury *resulting from* faulty workmanship, exclusive of the faulty workmanship itself." (emphasis added). The statute does not alter *L-7*, that damage that is merely to an insured's faulty workmanship itself does not qualify as having been caused by an "occurrence."

In August 2011, the Supreme Court of South Carolina, after granting re-hearing, withdrew its January decision in *Crossmann* and replaced it with one that essentially follows § 38–61-70. *See Crossmann Communities v. Harleysville Mut. Ins. Co.*, 717 S.E.2d 589 (S.C. 2011). The *Crossmann* II court held: "Returning to *Newman* and viewing those facts through the lens of both 'property damage' and 'occurrence,' we clarify that the costs to replace the negligently constructed stucco did not constitute 'property damage' under the terms of the policy. The stucco was not 'injured.' However, the damage to the remainder of the project caused by water penetration due to the negligently installed stucco did constitute 'property damage.' Based on those allegations of property damage and construing the ambiguous occurrence definition in favor of the insured, the insuring language of the policy in *Newman* was triggered by the property damage caused by repeated water intrusion." Under *Crossmann* II, while no coverage is owed to an insured for defective construction, coverage is owed for the consequential damages of defective construction. *Newman* is no longer overruled.

South Carolina courts, post-*Crossmann* and the statute, have continued to address the "occurrence" issue. *See Harleysville Mut. Ins. Co. v. State*, 736 S.E.2d 651

(S.C. 2012) (holding that South Carolina's "occurrence" statute is constitutional, except retroactivity provision; statute only applies prospectively to contracts executed on or after its effective date of May 17, 2011); *Builders Mut. Ins. Co. v. Lacey Const. Co., Inc.*, No. 11–400, 2012 U.S. Dist. LEXIS 41588 (D.S.C. March 27, 2012) ("[T]he court concludes that Section 38–61–70 does not modify the rule set down in *Crossmann* which clarified the reasoning but did not change the result in *Newman* and *L–J*. It follows that Builders Mutual is not obligated to indemnify the Lacey Defendants for any damages which a jury in the State Action may award for repair or reconstruction of defectively constructed components at Waverly Place. By contrast, Builders Mutual may be obligated to indemnify the Lacey Defendants to the extent there is a finding that some defectively constructed component at Waverly Place caused injury to some other component. For reasons explained below, when applied to the evidence presented to this court, this conclusion establishes that, at most, Builders Mutual may be obligated to indemnify the Lacey Defendants for replacing and packing eroded soil above the North Retaining Wall."); *Auto-Owners Ins. Co. v. Rhodes*, 748 S.E.2d 781 (S.C. 2013) (reviewing South Carolina's history of the issue and concluding that *Crossmann's* expansive view of an "occurrence" is not limited to progressive property damage cases); *Harleysville Group Ins. v. Heritage Cmtys., Inc.*, 803 S.E.2d 288 (S.C. 2017) (reviewing South Carolina's history of the issue); *UFP E. Div., Inc. v. Selective Ins. Co.*, No. 15-2801, 2017 U.S. Dist. LEXIS 17082 (D.S.C. Feb. 6, 2017) ("Under South Carolina law, insurance coverage for property damage does not cover defective construction, though it may cover consequential damages to otherwise non-defective components resulting from negligent or defective construction.") (citing *Crossmann II*).

South Dakota: The Supreme Court of South Dakota, addressing a policy that contained a Broad Form Property Damage Endorsement (BFPDE) (now the "your work" exclusion with "subcontractor exception") held that a subcontractor's faulty workmanship, that resulted in damage to the insured's work, was covered, provided that such damage was caused by an "occurrence." *Corner Constr. Co. v. U.S. Fid. & Guar. Co.*, 638 N.W.2d 887, 894 (S.D. 2002). "As required by the insuring clause, there was an accident or unintended event, resulting in property damage that was neither expected nor intended by the insured, at least in respect to the following: Cub [subcontractor], which was hired to do the insulation work, left voids in the insulation between the studs and failed to securely attach the vapor barrier. The vapor barrier fell, causing temperature fluctuations and other ventilation problems. As a result, Corner's [insured] own work was damaged by the faulty work of its subcontractor .... Such damage is covered by the insuring clause in connection with the BFPDE." *Id.* at 894–95. *See also Swenson v. Auto Owners Ins. Co.*, 831 N.W.2d 402 (S.D. 2013) ("[W]e acknowledge that the issues regarding the existence of 'property damage' caused by an 'occurrence' are threshold issues. However, even if the record contained sufficient allegations of 'property damage' caused by an 'occurrence,' DJ Construction was not entitled to defense or indemnity from Owners if the Policy exclusions applied. Consequently, because we conclude that the circuit court correctly determined the Policy exclusions were applicable, we need not address the parties' disputes regarding whether Swenson and Stewart's claimed damages to their home constitute 'property damage,' and if so, whether the 'property damage' was caused by an 'occurrence.'"); *Owners Ins. Co. v. Tibke Construction*, 901 N.W.2d 80 (S.D. 2017) ("[I]f inadvertent faulty workmanship causes unexpected injuries to people or property, it may constitute an accident and thus an occurrence. Currently, the majority of state supreme courts who have decided the issue of whether inadvertent faulty workmanship is an accidental 'occurrence' potentially covered under the CGL policy have decided that it can be an 'occurrence.'") ("Owners' argument that the alleged faulty work was intentional and thus not an accident is unavailing. The failure to test the soil was not an intentional or deliberate action but an unplanned omission, which caused an unexpected result.").

Tennessee: The Supreme Court of Tennessee held that various types of damage to a hotel construction project, caused by the insured's subcontractor's negligent installation of windows, qualified as an "occurrence." *Travelers Indem. Co. of Am. v. Moore & Assocs., Inc.*, 216 S.W.3d 302, 309 (Tenn. 2007). The court concluded that, because it must be assumed that the windows would be installed properly, the insured could not have foreseen the water penetration, and, therefore, the damage qualified as an accident and an "occurrence." *Id.* The court also addressed the "subcontractor exception" to the "your work" exclusion: "It is alleged that the installation of the windows was performed by subcontractors hired by [the insured]. Therefore, damages resulting from the subcontractors' faulty installation of the windows are not excluded from coverage, even if those damages affected [the insured's] work." *Id.* at 310; *see also Cincinnati Ins. Co. v. Grand Pointe, LLC*, Nos. 105-CV-161, 105-CV-157, 2007 U.S. Dist. LEXIS 39784 (E.D. Tenn. May 30, 2007) (addressing *Moore & Associates* and holding that damage solely to a condominium building that the insureds were contracted to design and build did not qualify as "property damage") (declining to address the "subcontractor exception" to the "your work" exclusion because "it is futile to consider the exclusions to the policy since there is no initial coverage under the insuring agreement"); *Forrest Const., Inc. v. Cincinnati Ins. Co.*, 728 F. Supp. 2d 955, 964 (M.D. Tenn. 2010) ("[I]n light of *Moore*, the counter complaint alleged 'property damage.' The alleged cracking in the foundation is analogous to the water penetration in *Moore*—it is physical damage to the property that occurred *after* the relevant component had been incorrectly installed. Whatever the precise construction defect was here, that defect resulted in further, tangible damage to the house. This was not a case where the 'sole damages' were for 'replacement of a defective component or correction of faulty installation.'") (emphasis in original) (quoting *Moore* at 309–10). *See also Forrest Const., Inc. v. Cincinnati Ins. Co.*, 703 F.3d 359 (6th Cir. 2013) (*Travelers* did not effect a sea change in the law, but clarified that 'property damage' occurs when one component (here, the faulty foundation) of a finished product (the house) damages another component. This is not a case where the 'sole damages' alleged were the 'replacement of a defective component or correction of faulty installation.'"); *Columbia Nat'l Ins. Co. v. JR Livingston Construction, LLC*, No. 14-01781, 2016 U.S. Dist. LEXIS 41499 (M.D. Tenn. Mar. 28, 2016) (noting that, while some allegations alleged faulty workmanship or materials in the construction repair of a home, homeowners also alleged "physical injury to tangible property beyond merely a recitation of alleged faulty workmanship or materials") ("Applying *Travelers Indemnity*, the Court concludes that the above allegations present claims for property damage because of an occurrence under the Policy. In addition, the Lynches' request for damages is not limited to replacement costs of a defective component or correction of faulty installation.").

Texas: The Supreme Court of Texas held that a claim against a general contractor, for damage to a home's sheetrock and veneer, caused by the contractor's negligence in designing and constructing the home's foundation, qualified as an "occurrence." *Lamar Homes, Inc. v. Mid-Continent Cas. Co.*, 242 S.W.3d 1, 9 (Tex. 2007). The court concluded that there is no logical basis within the definition of "occurrence" for distinguishing between damage to the insured's work and damage to a third party's property. *Id.* "Both types of property damage are caused by the same thing—negligent or defective work." *Id.* (quoting *Erie Ins. Exch. v. Colony Dev. Corp.*, 736 N.E.2d 950, 952 n.1 (Ohio Ct. App. 2000)); *see also Century Sur. Co. v. Hardscape Constr. Specialties Inc.*, 578 F.3d 262, 266 (5th Cir. 2009) (discussing *Lamar Homes*) (allegations of unintended construction defects may constitute an "accident" or "occurrence" under commercial general liability policies); *Pine Oak Builders, Inc. v. Great Am. Lloyds Ins. Co.*, 279 S.W.3d 650, 652 (Tex. 2009) ("Great American urges us to hold that Pine Oak's faulty-workmanship claims do not allege 'property damage' caused by an 'occurrence' under the terms of the policies. This argument is foreclosed by *Lamar Homes v.* Mid-Continent Cas., where we held that a claim of faulty workmanship against a homebuilder was a claim for property damage caused by an occurrence under a CGL policy."); *Sigma Marble & Granite-Houston, Inc. v. Amerisure Mut. Ins. Co.*, No. H-09-3942, 2010 U.S. Dist. LEXIS 137096 (S.D. Tex. Dec. 28, 2010) ("The [*Lamar Homes*] Court noted that the policy did not define 'accident' but concluded that the ordinary meaning encompassed a deliberate act, performed negligently, such that the result was not intended and would have been different given correct performance. 'Thus, a claim does not involve an accident or occurrence when either direct allegations purport that the insured intended the injury ... or circumstances confirm that the resulting damage was the natural and expected result of the insured's actions, that is, was highly probable whether the insured was negligent or not.'") (quoting *Lamar Homes* at 9); *Ewing Const. Co., Inc. v. Amerisure Ins. Co.*, 420 S.W.3d 30 (Tex. 2014) ("In *Lamar Homes* we focused on whether the underlying allegations for defective construction or faulty workmanship fell within the broad coverage granted by the CGL policy's insuring agreement— not whether any of the policy's exclusions applied to exclude coverage. . . . We explained that more often . . . faulty workmanship will be excluded from coverage by specific exclusions because that is the CGL's structure. We mentioned some of the business risk exclusions in the policy having specific application to the construction industry, but did not determine their applicability. Because the policy contains exclusions that may apply to exclude coverage in a case for breach of contract due to faulty workmanship, our answer to the first certified question is not inconsistent with the view that CGL policies are not performance bonds."); *Crownover v. Mid-Continent Cas. Co.*, 772 F.3d 197 (5th Cir. 2014) ("Here, the defective installation of the HVAC system caused the system to be deficient and eventually required the stressed mechanical units to be replaced. There can be no doubt that the HVAC units were themselves 'tangible property,' and therefore the loss of their use amounted to property damage. The HVAC units fall within the plain meaning of 'tangible property.' . . . Therefore, Arrow's defective work was an 'occurrence' that caused the HVAC system and the foundation to require repairs, which amounted to 'property damage.'"); *Atlantic Casualty Ins. Co. v. PrimeLending*, No. 15-1475, 2017 U.S. Dist. LEXIS 34425 (N.D. Tex. Mar. 10, 2017) ("Considering the nature of the claims and the facts alleged in the third amended petition, it is reasonable to infer that PrimeLending was only alleging that the construction work that First Choice performed in renovating and improving White's residence was of poor quality and was not completed in a timely manner, not that First Choice accidentally (or through continuous or repeated exposure to substantially the same general harmful conditions) caused damage to White's property. In fact, it is difficult to draw the reasonable inference that PrimeLending was alleging that First Choice damaged White's property through poor and untimely construction work caused by an 'accident.'"); *Greystone Multi-Family Builders, Inc. v. Gemini Ins. Co.*, No. 17-921, 2018 U.S. Dist. LEXIS 55610 (S.D. Tex. Mar. 30, 2018) (counterclaim which stated that "the framing subcontractor allegedly failed to construct frames with the required amount of studs, often using only one when the plans called for two or three; Greystone installed power conduits under the building's garage and these were later lost or destroyed when concrete was poured over them; the masonry subcontractor installed the trash-chute walls without leaving access to install the trash chutes, which required retrofitting of the doors; Greystone builders 'forgot to install' pipe; and the emergency exit door was literally installed backwards" alleged an "occurrence," despite other "inflammatory language" which "may lead one at first glance to conclude that the alleged damages were the 'natural and expected result' of Greystone's actions"); *Siplast, Inc. v. Emplrs. Mut. Cas. Co.*, 489 F. Supp. 3d 603 (N.D. Tex. 2020) ("The origin of the property damage the underlying plaintiffs allege is defects with the workmanship and materials that comprised the roof membrane and system. As in *Lamar Homes*, there is nothing in the underlying pleading that alleges Siplast intended or expected its roofing system to fail. It is immaterial that the legal theory the Archdiocese asserts against Siplast is for breach of its Siplast Guarantee. The underlying complaint alleges property damage caused by an accident or occurrence.").

Utah: A Utah District Court held that a claim against a contractor, for inadequate preparation of a soil pad at a construction site, did not qualify as an "occurrence." *H.E. Davis & Sons, Inc. v. N. Pac. Ins. Co.*, 248 F. Supp. 2d 1079, 1084 (D. Utah 2002). The failure to adequately compact the soil led to its natural consequences— removal and replacement of the soil pad and the concrete footings. *Id.* "So long as the consequences of plaintiff's work were natural, expected, or intended, they cannot be considered an 'accident.'" *Id.* In *Great American Insurance Co. v. Woodside Homes Corp.*, 448 F. Supp. 2d 1275 (D. Utah 2006), the court distinguished *H.E. Davis* and held that a subcontractor's faulty work is an "occurrence" from the standpoint of the insured. *Id.* at 1283. "Given the Utah Supreme Court's focus on the acts of the insured when determining whether there has been an occurrence, it follows that the negligent acts of Woodside's subcontractors can be considered an occurrence from Woodside's 'point of view.'" *Id.* at 1281. "[T]he conclusion that defective subcontractor work can be considered an occurrence harmonizes other provisions contained in the policy that might otherwise be in tension." *Id.* at 1282 (analyzing the "occurrence" issue in conjunction with the "subcontractor exception" to the "your work" exclusion); *see also Cincinnati Ins. Co. v. Linford Bros. Glass Co.*, No. 2:08-CV-387, 2010 U.S. Dist. LEXIS 11226 (D. Utah Feb. 9, 2010) ("Because the reasonably foreseeable consequences of negligently manufacturing windows and doors include damage to the property in which the defective products are installed, there can be no 'occurrence' here under Utah law."); *Utah Property & Cas. Ins. Guar. Ass'n v. Travelers Indem. Co. of Illinois*, No. 12-00224, 2013 U.S. Dist. LEXIS 120299 (D. Utah Aug. 23, 2013) (distinguishing *Woodside* to conclude that coverage was not owed) ("[T]he subcontractor whose faulty work caused the case in *Woodside* was a third party, not a named insured or additional insured on the insurance policy at issue. In contrast, here the subcontractor, Valley, is the named insured on the Policy not a third party. Second, the named insured on the insurance policy at issue in *Woodside* was the general contractor, whereas in this case the general contractor . . . was only an additional insured on the Policy. Due to these important distinctions, *Woodside* does not control the outcome of this case."); *Cincinnati Ins. Co. v. AMSCO Windows*, 593 Fed. Appx. 802 (10th Cir. 2014) (discounting the analysis in *H.E. Davis*, *Woodside* and *Linford* "to the extent they elide the concepts of foreseeability and intent or expectation," noting that, "[u]nder Utah law, only the latter are relevant") ("Whether damaged property underlying a claim is the direct product of negligent conduct or, instead, is one or more steps removed from the alleged product of negligent conduct may determine whether an insured expected that damage to result. . . . The Utah Supreme Court has spoken clearly that negligence *can* give rise to an occurrence, and federal case law does not require us to find otherwise.") (emphasis in original); *Auto-Owners Ins. Co. v. Fleming*, 701 Fed. Appx. 738 (10th Cir. 2017) ("Applying Utah law, this court has previously determined that the natural results of an insured's negligent and unworkmanlike construction do not constitute an occurrence triggering coverage under a CGL policy. . . . Two exceptions to this general rule might exist where defective workmanship causes damage to property other than the work product itself or where damage is caused by the negligent acts of the insured's subcontractors.") ("The Flemings allege only faulty construction causing damage to the insureds' own work. There are no allegations in the pleadings, nor factual findings in the final judgments against the insured, that the defective workmanship caused damage to property other than the work product itself. The

Flemings' vague assertions, without citations to record evidence, that LC Builders and Timbersmith caused 'latent defects' or 'dangerous,' 'unsafe,' and 'hazardous' conditions in the home are insufficient to demonstrate coverage."); *Cincinnati Specialty Underwriters Ins. Co. v. Green Prop. Sols. LLC*, No. 19-00010, 2019 U.S. Dist. LEXIS 220161 (D. Utah Dec. 23, 2019) (finding moisture buildup and water damage which was the "natural and probable result of the lack of ventilation caused directly by Green Property's allegedly defective work" did not constitute "property damage" caused by an "occurrence").

Vermont: A Vermont District Court held, without analysis, that claims against a construction company, for negligent construction or design of the dormers and heating system of a hotel, qualified as an "occurrence," because an accident is "an unexpected happening without intention or design." *Transcon. Ins. Co. v. Engelberth Constr., Inc.*, No. 1:06-CV-213, 2007 U.S. Dist. LEXIS 83187 (D. Vt. Nov. 8, 2007) (quoting *Commercial Union Ins. Co. v. City of Montpelier*, 353 A.2d 344, 346 (Vt. 1976)); *see also Fine Paints of Europe, Inc. v. Acadia Ins. Co.*, No. 08-81, 2009 U.S. Dist. LEXIS 24188 (D. Vt. Mar. 24, 2009) ("A CGL policy may cover an intentional act that results in unintended injury. . . . The relevant inquiry is not whether Fine Paints breached a contract or warranty, but whether Fine Paints by its actions expected or intended the harm to the Cottage.") (finding that there being no dispute that the insured paint retailer did not intend the injury caused by its faulty paint (cracking, chipping, peeling, loss of adhesion, and separation from the primer), the paint failure constituted an "occurrence" under Vermont law); *Down Under Masonry, Inc. v. Peerless Ins. Co.*, 950 A.2d 1213, 1216 (Vt. 2008) ("Neither 'physical injury' nor 'loss of use' occurred in this case. The undisputed facts show that Down Under's subcontractor installed shingles that were inferior in quality and different in color from those specified in the original contract with the Cranes. Nothing in the record, however, suggests that any physical defect existed in the shingle material used or in the manner in which the shingles were installed, or that the Cranes were unable to use their new garage as a result of the inferior shingles. ... To find that the aesthetic impact on property value caused by the installation of inferior shingles equates to 'property damage' would extend coverage beyond the contemplation of the parties as it is expressed by the plain language of the CGL policy.").

Virginia: The Fourth Circuit Court of Appeals, applying Virginia law, held that clams against a general contractor, for damages to homes caused by mold contained in trusses supplied by a subcontractor, qualified as an "occurrence." *Stanley Martin Cos. v. Ohio Cas. Group*, 313 Fed. App'x 609, 614 (4th Cir. 2009). "Stanley Martin's obligation to repair or replace the defective trusses was not unexpected or unforeseen under the terms of its building contracts for the townhouses and does not trigger a duty to indemnify. However, any mold damage that spread beyond the defective trusses and the gypsum fire walls to nondefective components of the townhouses was an unintended accident, or an occurrence that triggered coverage under the Ohio Casualty policy." *Id.* The court distanced itself from its seemingly opposite decision in *Travelers Indemnity Co. of America v. Miller Building Corp.*, 142 Fed. App'x 147 (4th Cir. 2005) (applying Virginia Law), on the basis that the holding in *Miller Building* rested on "case law that addressed damage that a general contractor's defective work caused to its own finished product, not damage that a subcontractor's defective work caused to the general contractor's nondefective work." *Id.* at 613; *see also Dragas Mgmt. Corp. v. Hanover Ins. Co.*, 798 F. Supp. 2d 766 (E.D. Va. 2011) ("This court sees no reason why the decisions in *Stanley Martin* and *French* [*see* Maryland] should not control the results in this case. Therefore, under the Fourth Circuit's precedent, this court holds that the replacement of the defective drywall is not an occurrence under the policy; however, any repair or replacement of non-defective components of the homes at The Hampshires and Cromwell Park or personal property of the homeowners constituted an occurrence under the Citizens policies at issue."); *Breezewood of Wilmington Condos. Homeowners' Ass'n, Inc. v. Amerisure Mut. Ins. Co.*, 335 Fed. Appx. 268, 274 (4th Cir. 2009) ("Breezewood CHOA's allegations in the Underlying Complaint squarely allege faulty workmanship by the insured and damages associated with repairing the deficient construction. Under North Carolina law, such allegations do not constitute property damage. *Prod. Sys. Inc. v. Amerisure Ins. Co.*, 167 N.C. App. 601, 607, 605 S.E.2d 663, 667 (2004) (holding 'property damage' does not include 'repair of defects in, or caused by, the faulty workmanship in the initial construction'). Breezewood CHOA also charges that Quality Built did not construct the Condominium Development according to contract in the first instance. Costs associated with bringing the project into compliance with Breezewood CHOA's contractual expectations is not 'property damage' covered by a CGL policy.") (citations omitted); *Nautilus Ins. Co. v. Strongwell Corp.*, 968 F. Supp. 2d 807 (W.D. Va. 2013) ("Although the Supreme Court of Virginia has not been presented with this issue, federal courts applying Virginia law have considered whether damage caused by a subcontractor's defective work constitutes an 'occurrence' under a commercial general liability policy. These courts have drawn a distinction between a claim for the cost of repairing the subcontractor's own defective work and a claim for repairing damage to non-defective property resulting from the subcontractor's faulty workmanship.") (concluding that the possibility of an "occurrence" existed because "the damages sought in the underlying action are not limited to the costs of repairing or replacing [the insured's] purportedly defective work product."); *Erie Ins. Exch. v. Salvi*, 86 Va. Cir. 132 (Va. Cir. Ct. 2013) (comparing *Stanley Martin* and *RML Corp. v. Assurance Co. of Am.*, No. CH02-127 (Va. Cir. Ct. Dec. 31, 2002) and holding that structural defects caused to otherwise nondefective components of a home, by the subcontractor's defective workmanship, were not an "occurrence"); *Builders Mut. Ins. Co. v. J.L. Albrittan, Inc.*, No. 19-1315, 2020 U.S. Dist. LEXIS 81211 (E.D. Va. May 7, 2020) ("Although the Virginia Supreme Court has not appeared to consider this question, the decision in *Hotel Roanoke* has been cited favorably by courts within the Fourth Circuit with regard to its conclusion that an insured's defective performance of a contract is not an occurrence under a commercial general liability policy."); *W. World Ins. Co. v. Air Tech, Inc.*, No. 17-518, 2019 U.S. Dist. LEXIS 53683 (W.D. Va. Mar. 29, 2019) (holding that when "damages sought in the underlying action are limited to the costs of replacing the insured's purportedly defective work product, the allegations do not give rise to coverage").

Washington: The Court of Appeals of Washington held that a claim against a construction company, for damage to a building, caused by dry rot which resulted from dirt having been piled against the box sills of the building by backfilling during construction, qualified as an "occurrence." *Gruol Constr. Co., Inc. v. Ins. Co. of N. Am.*, 524 P.2d 427, 429 (Wash. Ct. App. 1974). "We recognize that dry rot is the expected result when moisture is introduced to dirt which is too close to wood but the fact that the condition (defective backfilling) was not detected during construction supports the finding that the dry rot which resulted from the unknown condition was unexpected. It cannot be disputed that it was undesigned." *Id.* at 430; *see also Mid-Continent Cas. Co. v. Titan Constr. Corp.*, 281 Fed. App'x 766, 768 (9th Cir. 2008) (applying Washington law) ("Absent any allegation that the substandard construction in this case resulted from an intentional breach of contract by Titan, we conclude that the negligent construction of the Williamsburg project that resulted in breach of contract and breach of warranty claims constituted an 'occurrence.'"); *Indian Harbor Ins. Co. v. Transform LLC*, No. C09-1120, 2010 U.S. Dist. LEXIS 94080 (W.D. Wash. Sept. 8, 2010) ("Pure workmanship defects are not considered accidents or 'occurrences,' since CGL policies are not meant to be performance bonds or product liability insurance. On the other hand, damages arising from workmanship defects can give rise to an 'occurrence.' The Court looks to the 'kind of losses' resulting from defective construction to determine if the property damage constitutes an 'occurrence.'") (citations omitted) ("Whether there is an 'occurrence' depends on whether the mismanufacture was unintentional rather than intentional, not on whether the action is for negligence or breach of contract."); *Big Const., Inc. v. Gemini Ins. Co.*, No. C12–5015, 2012 U.S. Dist. LEXIS 71350 (W.D. Wash May 22, 2012) ("A general liability policy is not intended to encompass the risk of an insured's failure to adequately perform work. Rather, the policies are most often intended to cover unforeseeable accidents. Pure workmanship defects are not considered accidents or occurrences, since commercial general liability policies are not meant to be performance bonds or product liability insurance. Commercial general liability policies are designed generally to provide coverage for a number of risks, including employee injuries while on the work site and physical damage to property other than the work of the insured. When an insurer issues a general liability policy, it is not issuing a performance bond, product liability insurance, or malpractice insurance. Liability insurance policies therefore do not cover an insured's business risk of performing faulty work. There is no coverage for repairing or replacing an insured's defective work. For faulty workmanship to give rise to property damage there must be property damage separate from the defective product itself.") (numerous citations and internal quotes omitted).

West Virginia: The Supreme Court of Appeals of West Virginia, following a national survey of the "occurrence" issue, held that defective workmanship causing bodily injury or property damage is an 'occurrence' under a policy of commercial general liability insurance." *Cherrington v. Erie Ins. Property and Cas. Co.*, 745 S.E.2d 508, 521 (W. Va. 2013). "Application of our prior holdings to find that the defective work of subcontractors does not constitute an 'occurrence' and thus is not covered by the subject CGL policy would, indeed, create an absurd result when the policy expressly provides coverage for damages occasioned by subcontractors acting on behalf of the insured. Therefore, we conclude that the more sound approach to interpreting the subject policy is to find that defective work performed by a subcontractor on behalf of an insured does give rise to an 'occurrence' under a policy of CGL insurance to maintain consistency with the policy's stated intention to provide coverage for the work of subcontractors." *Id.* at 520-21. The *Cherrington* court overruled *Webster County Solid Waste Auth. v. Brackenrich & Assocs., Inc.*, 617 S.E.2d 851 (W. Va. 2005), among other opinions, which held that claims for poor workmanship, standing alone, did not constitute an "occurrence." *See also Westfield Ins. Co. v. Carpenter Reclamation, Inc.*, No. 13–12818, 2014 U.S. Dist. LEXIS 130752 (S.D.W.Va. Sept. 18, 2014) (distinguishing *Cherrington*) ("[T]here [*Cherrington*] the defective workmanship during the construction of a residential home led to the following property damage: water damage, cracked walls, sagging beams, and an uneven concrete foundation. Here, by contrast, Carpenter was retained to excavate and prep the site before the actual construction of the LES, and its alleged non-conforming or 'defective workmanship' did not otherwise damage the tangible property of the school or finished project. There was no resulting property damage akin to the water leakage, sagging beams, cracks in the drywall or uneven concrete floor that was found in *Cherrington*.") (also distinguishing *Cherrington* because "the presence of any overblasting was an expected, quasi-intentional and/or foreseen event, and cannot now be considered an accident or occurrence under the terms of the CGL Policy and applicable West Virginia case law") (*affirmed* 614 Fed. Appx. 622 (4th Cir. 2015)); *State ex rel. Nationwide Mut. Ins. Co. v. Wilson*, 778 S.E.2d 677 (W. Va. 2015) ("According to the Nelsons' complaint, Mr. Hlad negligently built their house, and thereby 'adversely impacted the structural integrity of [their] home, [and caused] cracks in the foundation of [their] home and water leaks and structural and other property damages[.]' The Nelsons also assert that as a result of Mr. Hlad's defective work, they had to replace 'various doors, windows, walls, lights;' 'vinyl siding and flashing;' 'kitchen cabinets, tiles, and appliances;' etc. These damages were caused by an 'occurrence.'") (also concluding that "to the extent that the amended complaint alleged that Mr. Hlad's actions were intentional misconduct or purely breach of contract, his actions are not "occurrences").

Wisconsin: The Supreme Court of Wisconsin held that damage to a warehouse constructed by an insured–general contractor, caused by a soil engineering subcontractor's faulty site-preparation advice, qualified as an "occurrence." *Am. Family Mut. Ins. Co. v. Am. Girl, Inc.*, 673 N.W.2d 65, 76 (Wis. 2004). "The damage to the 94DC occurred as a result of the continuous, substantial, and harmful settlement of the soil underneath the building. Lawson's inadequate site-preparation advice was a cause of this exposure to harm. Neither the cause nor the harm was intended, anticipated, or expected." *Id.* The court also addressed the "subcontractor exception" to the "your work" exclusion and rejected the insurer's argument that it creates coverage where none existed: "There is coverage under the insuring agreement's initial coverage grant. Coverage would be excluded by the business risk exclusionary language, except that the subcontractor exception to the business risk exclusion applies, which operates to restore the otherwise excluded coverage." *Id.* at 83–84; *see also Toldt Woods Condominiums Owner's Ass'n, Inc. v. Madeline Square, LLC*, No. 2007AP1763, 2008 Wisc. App. LEXIS 638 (Wis. Ct. App. Aug. 13, 2008) (examining several Wisconsin decisions and concluding that faulty workmanship is not an "occurrence," but, rather, faulty workmanship that causes damage to other property is an "occurrence"); *Mantz Automation, Inc. v. Navigators Ins. Co.,* No. 2009AP1681, 2010 Wisc. App. LEXIS 358 (Wis. Ct. App. May 12, 2010) (holding that faulty workmanship in itself does not constitute an "occurrence" and there was no evidence of subsequent property damage); *Acuity v. Society Ins.,* 810 N.W.2d 812 (Wis. Ct. App. 2012) ("The lessons of *American Girl, Glendenning's [Limestone & Ready-Mix Co., Inc. v. Reimer,* 721 N.W.2d 704 (Wis. Ct. App. 2006)], and *Kalchthaler [v. Keller Const. Co.,* 591 N.W.2d 169 (Wis. Ct. App. 1999)] are that while faulty workmanship is not an 'occurrence,' faulty workmanship may cause an 'occurrence.' That is, faulty workmanship may cause an unintended event, such as soil settling in *American Girl,* the leaking windows in *Kalchthaler,* or, in this case, the soil erosion, and that event—the 'occurrence'—may result in harm to other property."); *Henshue Const., Inc. v. Terra Engineering & Const. Corp.,* 833 N.W.2d 873 (Wis. Ct. App. 2013) ("Based on its review of engineering drawings, Henshue mistakenly believed that the storm sewer pipe that crossed its excavation was connected only to two small inlets in a driveway. For this reason, Henshue did not install a temporary diversion pipe. The storm sewer pipe, however, was connected to the storm sewer for a large parking lot. The result of Henshue's failure to divert the storm water was that significant amounts of water entered the excavation when heavy rains fell in the area. The flooding was not an event that Henshue anticipated. As Henshue points out: 'Henshue did not divert the storm pipe precisely because it did not expect any water to travel through the pipe and into the excavation.' Henshue did not anticipate that its work would result in flooding that would cause damage, and thus the flooding event was an accident and an occurrence requiring coverage under the policy."); *Yeager v. Polyurethane Foam Insulation, LLC,* 808 N.W.2d 741 (Wis. Ct. App. 2011) ("Yeager contends that, because PFI's conduct led to unexpected or accidental property damage, PFI's conduct must have constituted an occurrence under the CGL policy. However, an unexpected or accidental bad result does not qualify as an 'occurrence' for purposes of insurance coverage; instead, it is the act which causes the bad result that must qualify as an 'occurrence' or 'accident' under the policy.") (faulty workmanship, and not an "occurrence," took place where the insured came into a house to spray insulation and sprayed more than he should, did not protect the areas where he was spraying, allowed his hoses to leak, did not properly fill the voids in the wall, or sprayed the material on too thin); *Dahl v. Peninsula Builders, LLC,* 855 N.W.2d 904 (Wis. Ct. App. 2014) ("[A]pplying the rule of *Glendenning's* here, there is no alleged event that could constitute an occurrence.")

(describing *Glendenning's:* "We therefore conclude that faulty workmanship in itself is not an 'occurrence'—that is, 'an accident'—within the meaning of the CGL policy. An 'accident' may be caused by faulty workmanship, but every failure to adequately perform a job, even if that failure may be characterized as negligence, is not an 'accident,' and thus not an 'occurrence' under the policy.") ("The buildings that gave way in *American Girl* and *Acuity* were better supported than Peninsula's argument."); *Smith v. Anderson*, 893 N.W.2d 790 (Wis. 2017) (dissenting opinion from the court dismissing the petition for review as improvidently granted) ("The 'occurrence' that R&B Construction is alleged to have caused in the instant case is the continuous and repeated exposure to water leaking into the basement and matter flowing into and clogging the drain tiles. Like the faulty workmanship in [*American Girl* and *Acuity v. Society Ins.*, 810 N.W.2d 812 (Wis. Ct. App. 2012)], R&B Construction's allegedly faulty workmanship in the instant case led to our conclusion that R&B Construction's alleged negligence led to leaking basement walls and clogging of the drain tiles. Either of these conditions continually caused unexpected water damage to Smith's house. Water damage, when it is a condition that unexpectedly results from faulty workmanship, is an 'occurrence' under the policy. Therefore, we conclude that the complaints allege facts that Smith's residence experienced property damage caused by an occurrence.").

Wyoming: A Wyoming District Court held that claims against a contractor for water damage to a resort, caused by improper installation and waterproofing of siding, did not qualify as an "occurrence." *Great Divide Ins. Co. v. Bitterroot Timberframes of Wyoming, LLC*, No. 06-CV-020, 2006 U.S. Dist. LEXIS 94826 (D. Wyo. Oct. 20, 2006). "[T]he allegations demonstrate losses resulting from breach of contract, as water damage is the natural and foreseeable result of improper installation and waterproofing of exterior siding, and therefore can not constitute an 'accident' for purposes of determining coverage." "Defendant's inadequate preparation and installation of the siding on the resort was not an 'accident' since defendant intended to perform in compliance with the contract, but allegedly failed to do so. Defendant could foresee the natural consequences of any negligence or poor workmanship, thus, any resulting damage is not considered an 'accident' triggering an 'occurrence' under the Policy."; *Employers Mut. Cas. Co. v. Bartile Roofs, Inc.*, 618 F.3d 1153, 1174–75 (10th Cir. 2010) ("[E]ven though the underlying complaints plead claims under several labels, the claims all arise out of Bartile's allegedly negligent roofing work and its alleged breach of its contractual duties to perform roofing work, indemnify the general contractor, and obtain insurance for the general contractor. Under Wyoming and Utah law, 'the natural results of [an insured's] negligent and unworkmanlike construction do not constitute an occurrence triggering coverage under a [CGL] policy.'") (quoting *Great Divide* and characterizing its holding as "an event is not an 'accident' under Wyoming law if defendant breached the underlying construction contract and the damages are 'the natural and foreseeable result' of an insured's negligent construction work") (*Bartile I*); *Employers Mut. Cas. Co. v. Bartile Roofs, Inc.*, 478 Fed. Appx. 493 (10th Cir. 2012) ("In *Bartile I* we repeatedly insisted that both Utah and Wyoming would agree that the natural results of an insured's unworkmanlike or negligent construction do not constitute an occurrence (i.e. accident) triggering coverage under a CGL policy. Again, Bartile makes no argument that the consequential water damage at issue here was *not* a natural result of Bartile's own unworkmanlike or negligent construction. This being the case, under the very law we repeatedly emphasized in *Bartile I*, Bartile has not established an 'accident' subject to policy coverage.") (emphasis in original) (characterizing *Bartile I* as adopting a "natural results" standard).

CHAPTER
13

Permissible Scope of Indemnification in Construction Contracts

Indemnification agreements are not "coverage" issues in the purest sense of the word. Yet the extent of an insurer's coverage obligation for a claim is sometimes tied—and inextricably so—to its insured's agreement to indemnify another party for loss.

An indemnification agreement is a "contract between two parties whereby the one undertakes and agrees to indemnify the other against loss or damage arising from some contemplated act on the part of the indemnitor, or from some responsibility assumed by the indemnitee, or from the claim or demand of a third person, that it, to make good to him such pecuniary damage as he may suffer." BLACK'S LAW DICTIONARY 393 (5th ed. 1979). *See also Walsh Const. Co. v. Mutual of Enumclaw*, 104 P.3d 1146, 1148 (Or. 2005) (defining "indemnify" to mean: "[t]o restore the victim of a loss, in whole or in part, by payment, repair, or replacement. To save harmless; to secure against loss or damage; to give security for the reimbursement of a person in case of an anticipated loss falling upon him. To make good; to compensate; to make reimbursement to one of a loss already incurred by him") (quoting BLACK'S LAW DICTIONARY 393 (5th ed. 1979)) (alteration in original).

Indemnification agreements, however, become insurance issues because commercial general liability policies typically provide coverage for an insured's obligation to "assume the tort liability of another party to pay for bodily injury or property damage to a third person or organization," i.e., an indemnification agreement. *See, e.g.,* INS. SERVS. OFFICE, INC., COMMERCIAL GENERAL LIABILITY COVERAGE FORM, No. CG 00010413, §§ I2b, V9f (2012). In other words, notwithstanding that indemnification agreements are formed between two parties—neither of which is an insurance company—in certain circumstances the party that is taking on the indemnification obligation likely has insurance to satisfy such obligation.

A common indemnification scenario that gives rise to potential insurance coverage obligations is one that involves bodily injury that occurs in the course of construction. For example, take a worker that sustains bodily injuries on a construction project. He will very likely bring an action against the project's general contractor, alleging, among other things, that the general contractor breached an obligation to maintain a safe working environment. The general contractor likely retained subcontractors for some or all of the work being performed, including entering into written agreements with such subcontractors governing their work. If so, such agreements likely contain a provision that obligates the subcontractor to indemnify the general contractor for the general contractor's liability for bodily injuries sustained by third parties (here, the injured worker). Therefore, despite the general contractor's duty to maintain the premises in a safe condition, the general contractor will likely seek to be indemnified by its subcontractors for the general contractor's liability for breaching this obligation.

If the factual scenario contemplated under the indemnity agreement to trigger the indemnitor's obligation has been satisfied, and provided the indemnity agreement is enforceable, discussed below, the subcontractor will be required to indemnify the general contractor for the general contractor's liability (likely including defense) for the bodily injuries sustained by the third-party injured worker. In this situation, the subcontractor's contractual indemnification obligation is likely covered under its general liability policy as an "assum[ption] of the tort liability of another party [the general contractor] to pay for bodily injury or property damage to a third person or organization [the injured worker]." *Id.*

Therefore, not surprisingly, an insurer that stands to be required to provide coverage to its insured, for its insured's contractual indemnification obligation, is likely to have a lot of interest in whether its insured will in fact be liable for such obligation. It is for this reason that, despite indemnification agreements existing outside of the insurance relationship, those handling claims that arise out of such agreements often pay close attention to their scope and enforceability.

While indemnification agreements have long been a part of commercial transactions, so too have been concerns by courts and legislatures over their permissibility. *See Weckerly v. German Lutheran Congregation*, 3 Rawle 172 (Pa. 1831) (addressing public policy concerns in the context of the enforceability of an indemnification agreement). Virtually all states recognize the potential for problems caused by the use of indemnification agreements. Courts and legislatures have particular concern with indemnification contracts in which an indemnitee is seeking to be indemnified for its *own* negligence. Such agreements have been referred to as "hazardous" and "unusual and extraordinary." *Perry v. Payne*, 66 A. 553, 557 (Pa.

1907). It is for this reason that there can be no presumption that the indemnitor intended to assume the responsibility for the negligence of the indemnitee "unless the contract puts it beyond doubt by express stipulation." *Id.* But despite being in accord that, as a general matter, indemnification agreements that purport to indemnify a party for its own negligence are potentially problematic, and must be examined with a cautious eye, states differ in their response to the concern.

On one hand, the requirement that an indemnification agreement, that purports to indemnify the indemnitee for its own negligence, must be expressed in unequivocal terms, has survived to this day and become the clear majority rule. *See Bridston v. Dover Corp.*, 352 N.W.2d 194, 196 (N.D. 1984) ("It is almost universally held that an indemnity agreement will not be interpreted to indemnify a party against the consequences of his own negligence unless that construction is very clearly intended."); *see also Tateosian v. Statet*, 945 A.2d 833, 841 (Vt. 2007) ("[W]e adopt the general rule that an indemnity clause covers the sole negligence of the indemnitee only where it clearly expresses that intent."). *But see Brown Ins. Agency v. Star Ins. Co.*, 237 P.3d 92, 96–97 (Nev. 2010) (discussing, but declining to adopt the "modern minority view," which provides that, because indemnity contracts are "so common in the modern business world that courts should leave the parties with their bargain for 'any and all liability'") (citations omitted).

On the other hand, despite the fact that almost all courts are willing to allow a party to be indemnified for its own negligence, provided that the contractual language is expressed in unequivocal terms, many of the legislatures in those same states have adopted a different rule in the context of construction contracts. Here many states have enacted legislation that prohibit a party to a construction contract from being indemnified for its own negligence—no matter how unequivocal the terms of the agreement. *See* DEL. CODE ANN. tit. 6, § 2704 (stating that indemnification of a party to a construction contract for any aspect of its own negligence is void and unenforceable as against public policy "even where such covenant, promise, agreement or understanding is *crystal clear and unambiguous* in obligating the promisor or indemnitor to indemnify or hold harmless the promisee or indemnitee from liability resulting from such promisee's or indemnitee's own negligence") (emphasis added). The court in *Wilhelm Constr., Inc. v. Secura Ins.*, No. 49A02-1604-CT-811, 2017 Ind. App. Unpub. LEXIS 642 (Ind. Ct. App. May 24, 2017) counted up the score and concluded that "the vast majority of states have adopted some form of a general anti-indemnity statute relating to construction contracts." *Id.* at 26, n.7 (citing 40 statutes).

In general, there are two overarching reasons why construction contracts are often singled out for special treatment when it comes to the permissibility of indemnification for an indemnitee's own negligence. First is a concern that a party being indemnified for its own negligence will have less incentive to exercise due care in the performance of its work. *See Jankele v. Texas Co.*, 54 P.2d 425, 427 (Utah 1936) ("Undoubtedly contracts exempting persons from liability for negligence induce a want of care, for the highest incentive to the exercise of due care rests in a consciousness that a failure in this respect will fix liability to make full compensation for any injury resulting from the cause.").

The other rationale for treating indemnification in the construction arena differently from other contexts is a concern that general contractors, because of unequal bargaining power, can compel their subcontractors to accept such an onerous contractual term as one that requires a party to assume liability for the negligence of others. *See Brooks v. Judlau Contracting, Inc.*, 898 N.E.2d 549, 551 (N.Y. 2008) (quoting *Itri Brick & Concrete Corp. v. Aetna Cas. & Sur. Co.*, 680 N.E.2d 1200, 1204 (N.Y. 1997)) ("The Legislature concluded that such 'coercive' bidding requirements unnecessarily increased the cost of construction by limiting the number of contractors able to obtain the necessary hold harmless insurance, and unfairly imposed liability on subcontractors for the negligence of others over whom they had no control. The agreements also needlessly created expensive double coverage for hold harmless or general liability insurance.").

Statutes that limit indemnification in the context of a construction contract usually define what they mean by a "construction" contract. While each case must be examined individually, many of the definitions are similar and along the lines of the following: "contract or agreement relative to the construction, alteration, repair or maintenance of a building, structure, appurtenance and appliance, including moving, demolition and excavating connected therewith." MICH. COMP. LAWS ANN. § 691.991; *see also* MISS. CODE ANN. § 31–5-41 ("[C]ontracts or agreements, for the construction, alteration, repair or maintenance of buildings, structures, highway bridges, viaducts, water, sewer or gas distribution systems, or other work dealing with construction, or for any moving, demolition or excavation connected therewith.").

Despite all such statutes existing to address concerns with the concept of one party to a construction contract being obligated to indemnify another for that party's own negligence, some of these statutes specifically limit the prohibition to instances in which the indemnitee is solely negligent. Other states have adopted broader legislation that prohibits a party from being indemnified for any character of its own negligence—either in whole or in part. Needless to say, this is a very important distinction and one that is evidenced by the fifty-state survey of the issue that follows.

Lastly, it is not unusual that, when an insurer's exposure is tied to its insured's indemnification obligation, the insurer may face additional potential exposure on account of the indemnitee also being an "additional insured" under the indemnitor's general liability policy. While contractual indemnity and additional insured issues are separate, they nonetheless often arise in tandem. This is so because the contract that contains the indemnification obligation may also contain an obligation on the part of the indemnitor to have the indemnitee named as an additional insured under the indemnitor's general liability policy.

If a party is entitled to indemnity under an indemnification agreement, as well as to coverage as an additional insured under the indemnitor's liability policy, it generally should not serve to increase the exposure for the indemnitor's insurer. In general, the coverage afforded to an additional insured creates the same exposure for the insurer that it would have in providing coverage to its named insured for the named insured's contractual obligation to indemnify the additional insured. In other words, the indemnitee either recovers from the insurer *directly*—as an additional insured; or *indirectly*—as the beneficiary of the indemnitor's coverage for its contractual liability. One exception being that, if a defense is owed to an additional insured, the insurer's liability for such defense is likely supplemental to the policy's limits of liability. On the other hand, if an insurer is obligated to provide coverage to its named insured, for the named insured's contractual obligation to pay an indemnitee's defense costs, such defense costs will likely erode the limit of liability.

Where there is a significant difference for insurers, between the obligation to provide coverage to an additional insured, versus coverage to the named insured for its contractual indemnity obligation, is when only one of these two avenues to recovery is available. For example, consider a party who, despite being an indemnitee under an indemnification agreement, even for its own negligence, cannot enforce such right because of a statutory prohibition. In such case, this same party is nonetheless likely entitled to coverage as an additional insured, under the indemnitor's general liability policy. There are few prohibitions against an additional insured being entitled to coverage for its own negligence. *But see* Oregon, *supra*.

Alternatively, a party may be named as an additional insured, but nonetheless denied coverage because its liability does not satisfy the scope of the additional insured endorsement, e.g., the additional insured coverage is limited to ongoing operations (as is often the case), and the liability at issue arises out of completed operations. However, such party may also be an indemnitee under an indemnification agreement—and the scope of such agreement is not limited to ongoing operations. Therefore, despite being denied coverage as an additional insured, the party is now the beneficiary of the indemnitor's general liability coverage for its contractual obligation.

What follows is a survey of the right of an indemnitee to be indemnified for its own negligence in the context of a construction project. Where a state does not have a specific statute addressing indemnification in the construction context, the law generally concerning an indemnitee's right to be indemnified for its own negligence is provided. The full text of the statutes may not be provided below.

50-State Survey: Permissible Scope of Indemnification in Construction Contracts

Alabama: The Supreme Court of Alabama held that an indemnitee may be indemnified for its own negligence provided that the contractual obligation is sufficiently explicit. *Indus. Tile, Inc. v. Stewart*, 388 So. 2d 171, 176 (Ala. 1980) ("[I]f the parties knowingly, evenhandedly, and for valid consideration, intelligently enter into an agreement whereby one party agrees to indemnify the other, including indemnity against the indemnitee's own wrongs, if expressed in clear and unequivocal language, then such agreements will be upheld."). "This Court has stated that an indemnity contract purporting to indemnify for the consequences of the indemnitee's own negligence is unambiguous and, therefore, enforceable when its language specifically refers to the negligence of the indemnitee. This Court, however, has also stated and held that such 'talismanic' or thaumaturgic language is not necessary if the requisite intent is otherwise clear." *Nationwide Mut. Ins. Co. v. Hall*, 643 So. 2d 551, 555 (Ala. 1994). *See also Holcim (US), Inc. v. Ohio Cas. Ins. Co.*, 38 So. 3d 722, 729 (Ala. 2009) ("[I]f two parties knowingly, clearly, and unequivocally enter into an agreement whereby they agree that the respective liability of the parties will be determined by some type of agreed-upon formula, then Alabama law will permit the enforcement of that agreement as written."); *Amerisure Mut. Ins. Co. v. QBE Ins. Corp.*, 2012 U.S. Dist. LEXIS 125811, No. 11-1751 (N.D. Ala. Sept. 5, 2012) ("When one seeks indemnification from another for damages that were caused by his own negligence, strict construction of the indemnity agreement against the contractor is particularly appropriate.") (citation omitted); *Scroggs v. WTI Transp., Inc.*, No. 14-869, 2015 U.S.

Dist. LEXIS 185005 (N.D. Ga. Jan. 13, 2015) ("[U]nder Alabama law, the absence of language in indemnity agreement specifically referring to indemnitee's own negligence is not required for enforcement of agreement.") (noting that, in *Hall*, a "contract in which the indemnitor agreed to 'save . . . harmless from <u>all</u> damage suits and claims arising in connection with said property and from <u>all</u> liability for injuries to persons or property while in, on, or about the premises' unambiguously created a right to indemnity against the indemnitees own negligence"); *Carter v. Youngsville II Hous. LLLP*, No. 16-01496, 2018 U.S. Dist. LEXIS 88493 (W.D. La. May 25, 2018) (addressing Alabama law) (concluding that agreement expressed "in clear and unequivocal language" a right of indemnification for indemnitee's own negligence) ("Page agreed to defend and indemnity Youngsville, and its agent, Morrow Realty, from any claim arising out of or resulting from Page's performance of the subcontracted work, regardless of whether such claim was caused in part by Youngsville or Morrow Realty"); *Gencon Ins. Co. v. St. Paul United Methodist Church*, No. 14-333, 2017 U.S. Dist. LEXIS 217681 (M.D. Ala. April 24, 2017) (concluding that agreement permitted indemnification for indemnitee's own negligence, despite being "simple and broad") ("User [St. Paul] agrees to indemnify and hold [GSC] (or any of its employees, agents, or officers) harmless against claims and liability of any kind (including any attorney's fees and costs) arising out of injury or death to any person or persons or damage to any property occurring, in, upon or about the premises during user's occupancy or use.").

Alaska: Alaska statute prohibits indemnification for an indemnitee's sole negligence: "A provision, clause, covenant, or agreement contained in, collateral to, or affecting a construction contract that purports to indemnify the promisee against liability for damages for (1) death or bodily injury to persons, (2) injury to property, (3) design defects, or (4) other loss, damage or expense arising under (1), (2), or (3) of this section from the sole negligence or willful misconduct of the promisee or the promisee's agents, servants, or independent contractors who are directly responsible to the promisee, is against public policy and is void and unenforceable[.]" ALASKA STAT. § 45.45.900. The statute does not affect the validity of certain insurance contracts or an indemnification agreement regarding the handling, containment, or cleanup of oil or hazardous substances as further defined by statute. *Id.; see also Hoffman Const. Co. of Alaska v. U.S. Fabrication & Erection, Inc.*, 32 P.3d 346, 354 (Alaska 2001) ("AS 45.45.900 only invalidates an indemnity clause if the clause purports to indemnify the indemnitee for the indemnitee's sole negligence."); *Municipality of Anchorage v. Integrated Concepts & Research Corp.*, No. 13-00063, 2016 U.S. Dist.

LEXIS 150176 (D. Alaska Oct. 31, 2016) ("The provision is an indemnification clause that essentially reproduces the indemnification requirement imposed by Alaskan law that mandates that subcontractors be held responsible for losses or damages caused by their *sole* negligence or willful misconduct . . . does not show that the parties carefully allocated the risks of professional negligence. Accordingly, the claim for professional negligence can properly stand.") (emphasis in original).

Arizona: Arizona statute prohibits indemnification for an indemnitee's sole negligence: "A. A covenant, clause or understanding in, collateral to or affecting a construction contract or architect-engineer professional service contract that purports to indemnify, to hold harmless or to defend the promisee from or against liability for loss or damage resulting from the sole negligence of the promisee or the promisee's agents, employees or indemnitee is against the public policy of this state and is void." Ariz. Rev. Stat. § 32–1159. The statute makes exceptions for: a person who, as an accommodation, enters into an agreement with a contractor that permits the contractor to enter on or adjacent to the person's property to perform the construction contract for others; agreements to which the state or a political subdivision of the state is a party, including intergovernmental agreements and agreements governed by sections 34-226 and 41-2586; and agreements entered into by agricultural improvement districts. *Id.; see also James v. Burlington N. Santa Fe Ry. Co.*, 636 F. Supp. 2d 961 (D. Ariz. 2007) (addressing § 32-1159 in detail, as well as anti-indemnity statutes in general and other states' treatment of them) (noting that "limited and intermediate form indemnity clauses in construction contracts may be used in Arizona to shift the risk of loss to an indemnitor even as to claims caused *in part* by the active negligence of the indemnitee, broad form indemnity clauses that purport to shift the entire risk of loss to an indemnitor, even as to liabilities caused by the *sole negligence* of the indemnitee, are against the public policy of this state and void under Arizona's anti-indemnity statute") (emphasis in original); *Cantex Inc. v. Giles Eng'g Assocs.*, No. 1 CA-CV 15-0620, 2017 Ariz. App. Unpub. LEXIS 1742 (Ariz. Ct. App. Nov. 21, 2017) (noting, in a choice of law context, that A.R.S. § 32-1159 "allows parties to a construction contract to include an indemnity agreement purporting to indemnify, hold harmless, or defend the indemnitee so long as it does not purport to do so when the indemnitee is solely negligent".).

Arkansas: The Supreme Court of Arkansas held that an indemnitee may be indemnified for its own negligence provided that the contractual obligation is sufficiently explicit. *See Chevron U.S.A. Inc. v. Murphy Exploration & Prod. Co.*, 151 S.W.3d 306, 310 (Ark. 2004) ("When considering indemnification agreements entered into by prime or general contractors and subcontractors, this court has held that a subcontractor's intention to obligate itself to indemnify a prime contractor for the prime contractor's own negligence must be expressed in clear and unequivocal terms and to the extent that no other meaning can be ascribed. While no particular words are required, the liability of an indemnitor for the negligence of an indemnitee is an extraordinary obligation to assume, and we will not impose it unless the purpose to do so is spelled out in unmistakable terms.") (citation omitted); *see also Thornton Drilling v. Nat'l Union Fire Ins. Co.*, 537 F.3d 943, 945 (8th Cir. 2008) ("Under Arkansas law, an agreement to indemnify is enforceable in accordance with normal contract law principles, except that a promise to indemnify another party for its own negligence must be clear and unequivocal."); *Starboard Holdings, Ltd. v. ABF Freight Systems*, No. 15-22047, 2017 U.S. Dist. LEXIS 18628 (S.D. Fla. Feb. 8, 2017) ("[B]ecause it seems clear that both parties are sophisticated business entities that freely negotiated and entered into the . . . agreement . . . the general rule under Arkansas law [citing *Chevron*] does not apply given the facts presented and the indemnity agreement need not be strictly construed."); *Producers Rice Mill, Inc. v. Rice Hull Speciality Prods.*, 519 S.W.3d 354 (Ark. Ct. App. 2017) ("[M]ere general, broad, and seemingly all-inclusive language is not sufficient to impose liability for an indemnitee's own negligence; to impose such liability, the language must be 'in unmistakable terms' to the extent that no other meaning can be ascribed.") (citing *United Sys. of Ark., Inc. v. Beason & Nalley, Inc.*, 448 S.W.3d 731 (Ark. Ct. App. 2014).

California: California has a complex statutory indemnification scheme. "Except as provided in Sections 2782.1 [indemnity for adjacent property owners that permit access], 2782.2 [indemnity of professional engineers], 2782.5 [agreements as to allocation or limitation of liability for design defects], and 2782.6 [indemnity of professional engineers or geologists with respect to hazardous materials], provisions, clauses, covenants, or agreements contained in, collateral to, or affecting any construction contract and that purport to indemnify the promisee against liability for damages for death or bodily injury to persons, injury to property, or any other loss, damage or expense arising from the sole negligence or willful misconduct of the promisee or the promisee's agents, servants, or independent contractors who are directly responsible to the promisee, or for defects in design furnished by those persons, are against public policy and are void and unenforceable; provided, however, that this section shall not affect the validity of any insurance contract, workers' compensation, or agreement issued by an admitted insurer as defined by the Insurance Code." West's Ann. Cal. Civ. Code § 2782(a). *See also* West's Ann. Cal.

Civ. Code § 2782(d), *et seq.* (placing limitations on indemnification of builders and general contractors, by subcontractors, for construction defects, under residential construction contracts, and amendments, entered into after January 1, 2009, as well as addressing numerous others issues related to claims in this context) (E.g., "unenforceable to the extent the claims arise out of, pertain to, or relate to the negligence of the builder or contractor or the builder's or contractor's other agents, other servants, or other independent contractors who are directly responsible to the builder, or for defects in design furnished by those persons, or to the extent the claims do not arise out of, pertain to, or relate to the scope of work in the written agreement between the parties").

On October 11, 2011, California Governor Brown signed into law West's Ann. Cal. Civ. Code § 2782.05(a), which provides that "provisions, clauses, covenants, and agreements contained in, collateral to, or affecting any construction contract and amendments thereto entered into on or after January 1, 2013, that purport to insure or indemnify, including the cost to defend, a general contractor, construction manager, or other subcontractor, by a subcontractor against liability for claims of death or bodily injury to persons, injury to property, or any other loss, damage, or expense are void and unenforceable to the extent the claims arise out of, pertain to, or relate to the active negligence or willful misconduct of that general contractor, construction manager, or other subcontractor, or their other agents, other servants, or other independent contractors who are responsible to the general contractor, construction manager, or other subcontractor, or for defects in design furnished by those persons, or to the extent the claims do not arise out of the scope of work of the subcontractor pursuant to the construction contract. This section shall not be waived or modified by contractual agreement, act, or omission of the parties. Contractual provisions, clauses, covenants, or agreements not expressly prohibited herein are reserved to the agreement of the parties. This section shall not affect the obligations of an insurance carrier under the holding of *Presley Homes, Inc. v. American States Insurance Company* (2001) 90 Cal.App.4th 571, nor the rights of an insurance carrier under the holding of *Buss v. Superior Court* (1997) 16 Cal.4th 35." The statute contains numerous exceptions and other relevant provisions that are beyond the scope of setting forth here. *See also Crawford v. Weather Shield Mfg. Inc.*, 187 P.3d 424, 442 (Cal. 2008) ("[T]he duty 'to defend' JMP against claims 'founded upon' damage or loss caused by Weather Shield's negligent performance of its work, as set forth in Weather Shield's subcontract, imposed such duties on Weather Shield as soon as a suit was filed against JMP that asserted such claims, and regardless of whether it was ultimately determined that Weather Shield was actually negligent."); *Oltmans Construction Co. v. Bayside Interiors, Inc.*, 10 Cal. App. 5th 355 (2017) (discussing § 2782.05(a)) ("This language [of the contract] plainly implies that Oltmans is entitled to indemnification for a claim that arises out of its negligence that is not active negligence or willful misconduct. What is disputed is whether its active negligence precludes it from recovering any indemnity or only from being indemnified for the portion of its liability based on its own active negligence or intentional misconduct. . . . The indemnity provision in the present case makes unmistakably clear that the parties intended to limit the indemnitee Oltmans' right to indemnification for liability arising out of the scope of the indemnitor Bayside's work only 'to the extent' the claims arose out of Oltmans' active negligence or willful misconduct. Had the parties intended to prohibit Oltmans from obtaining any indemnification if it was actively negligent, that prohibition could have been stated simply and straightforwardly. Rather, the provision limits the right to indemnification only 'to the extent' of Oltmans' active negligence, and no more."); *Aero. Corp. v. W.E. O'Neil Constr. Co.*, No. BC628270, 2018 Cal. Super. LEXIS 3931 (Cal. Super. Ct. Nov. 1, 2018) ("Compounding this misreading of the statute [§ 2782 (a)]; party did not seek indemnity for its sole negligence, or any aspect of its own negligence], KMA argues that if AECOM (or any other subcontractor) were negligent and KMA was not then KMA has no obligation to defend AECOM. This is directly contrary to the holding of *Crawford*. The indemnitor has a duty to defend even if it was later determined not to be negligent."); *Garcia v. Brunton Enters.*, No. BC643161, 2019 Cal. Super. LEXIS 89 (Cal. Super. Ct. Mar. 22, 2019) ("With regard to construction contracts, indemnity provisions are void and unenforceable to the extent the claims arise out of, pertain to, or relate to the active negligence or willful misconduct of the promise (sic).").

Colorado: Colorado statute prohibits indemnification for any character of an indemnitee's own negligence: "Except as otherwise provided in paragraphs (c) and (d) of this subsection (6), any provision in a construction agreement that requires a person to indemnify, insure, or defend in litigation another person against liability for damage arising out of death or bodily injury to persons or damage to property caused by the negligence or fault of the indemnitee or any third party under the control or supervision of the indemnitee is void as against public policy and unenforceable." C.R.S.A. § 13-21-111.5(6)(b). C.R.S.A. § 13-21-111.5 also addresses insurance and the permissible scope of coverage for additional insureds: "(c) The provisions of this subsection (6) shall not affect any provision in a construction agreement that requires a person to indemnify and insure another person against liability for damage, including but not limited to the reimbursement of attorney fees and costs, if provided for by contract or statute, arising out of death or bodily injury to persons or damage to property, but not for any amounts that are greater than that represented by the degree or percentage of negligence or fault attributable to the indemnitor or the indemnitor's agents, representatives, subcontractors, or suppliers. (d)(I) This subsection (6) does not apply to contract clauses that require the indemnitor to purchase, maintain, and carry insurance covering the acts or omissions of the indemnitor, nor shall it apply to contract provisions that require the indemnitor to name the indemnitee as an additional insured on the indemnitor's policy of insurance, but only to the extent that such additional insured coverage provides coverage to the indemnitee for liability due to the acts or omissions of the indemnitor. Any provision in a construction agreement that requires the purchase of additional insured coverage for damage arising out of death or bodily injury to persons or damage to property from any acts or omissions that are not caused by the negligence or fault of the party providing such additional insured coverage is void as against public policy." *See also Sterling Const. Management, LLC v. Steadfast Ins. Co.*, No. 09–02224, 2011 U.S. Dist. LEXIS 99604 (D. Colo. Sept. 6, 2011) ("Thus, as a matter of first impression, this Court would be extremely reluctant to read § 111.5(6)(b) to void an indemnification clause as against public policy without a showing that it was being invoked in the very circumstances that the legislature sought to prevent."); *Pa. Lumbermens Mut. Ins. Co. v. RStart, LLC*, No. 18-00478, 2018 U.S. Dist. LEXIS 166429 (D. Colo. Sept. 27, 2018) (citing *Sterling* and noting that the scope of the indemnity agreement was problematic under the statute, but that the question for the court was whether a party was seeking indemnity for its own negligence); *Cont'l Ins. Co. v. Cintas Corp.*, No 18-00254, 2019 U.S. Dist. LEXIS 167457 (D. Colo. July 12, 2019) ("Having determined that the contract between Arbors and Cintas qualifies as a 'construction agreement,' a provision requiring Arbors to indemnify Cintas for liability arising from Cintas's own negligence is void under Colorado law.").

Connecticut: Connecticut statute prohibits indemnification for any character of an indemnitee's own negligence: "Any covenant, promise, agreement or understanding entered into in connection with or collateral to a contract or agreement relative to the construction, alteration, repair or maintenance of any building, structure or appurtenances thereto including moving, demolition and excavating connected therewith, that purports to indemnify or hold harmless the promisee against liability for damage arising out of bodily injury to persons or damage to property caused by or resulting from the negligence of such promisee, such promisee's agents or employees, is against public policy and void, provided this section shall not affect the validity of any insurance contract, workers' compensation agreement or other agreement issued by a licensed insurer." CONN. GEN. STAT. ANN. § 52–572k(a). *See also Cappello v. Phillips*, No. CV085004470S, 2011 Conn. Super. LEXIS 1371 (Conn. Super. Ct. June 1, 2011) ("While an agreement purporting to hold an owner or a general contractor free from liability for its own negligence undermines the strong public policy of placing and keeping responsibility for maintaining a safe workplace on those parties ... the same cannot be said for an agreement which simply obligates one of the parties to a construction contract to obtain a liability policy insuring the other."); *A & G Contracting v. Design/Build Collaborative, LLC*, No. NNHCV106008755S, 2012 Conn. Super. LEXIS 1975 (Conn. Super. Ct. Aug. 2, 2012) ("Although agreements related to construction contracts that seek to indemnify a party for its own negligence are void under § 52–572k; . . . courts have held that indemnification agreements do not violate § 52–572k where they provide that a subcontractor shall indemnify a contractor for third-party claims to the extent that the injuries claimed arose out of the subcontractor's own conduct."); *Mastrobattisto, Inc. v. Nutmeg Util. Prods.*, No. CV156028626S, 2016 Conn. Super. LEXIS 445 (Conn. Super. Ct. Feb. 23, 2016) (indemnification obligation by the defendant for any defects in the materials *it provided* or work *it performed*) (emphasis in original) ("[T]he indemnification provision does not violate § 52-572k(a) because the provision does not purport to indemnify the plaintiff for injuries caused by its own negligence, but only indemnifies the plaintiff for injuries that arose out of the *defendant's own conduct*.") (emphasis in original); *Brown v. Direct Invest Riverbend Exec. Park, LLC*, No. HHDCV126027418S, 2015 Conn. Super. LEXIS 1931 (Conn. Super. Ct. July 22, 2015) (holding that § 52–572k only applies to construction contracts and the indemnification agreement at issue was enforceable because the parties were "both sophisticated commercial entities, and the hold harmless and indemnity clauses of the services agreement are bargained-for elements of the contract"); *Jackson v. Costco Wholesale Corp.*, No. CV156008167S, 2017 Conn. Super. LEXIS 5192 (Conn. Super. Ct. Dec. 19, 2017) ("Connecticut courts have emphasized the difference between an additional insured and an indemnitee in the context of General Statutes § 52-572k.") (Section "52-572k prohibit[s] clauses purporting to require subcontractors to indemnify and hold harmless general contractors for the general contractor's negligence. The statute says nothing about requiring general contractors to be included as additional insureds."); *Henderson v. Bismark Constr. Co.*, No. FBTCV176062488S, 2019 Conn. Super. LEXIS 1959 (Conn. Super. Ct. July 10, 2019) ("[T]he allegations of the amended complaint fall within the duty to defend provision of the Indemnity Clause and that Section 52-572k, although it would bar any indemnification by A&A for any negligence by OWI, does not bar that duty to defend.") (noting that, while there is no appellate authority on point, every Superior Court decision identified by the court's research has so held).

Delaware: Delaware statute prohibits indemnification for any character of an indemnitee's own negligence: "(a) A covenant, promise, agreement or understanding in, or in connection with or collateral to, a contract or agreement … relative to the construction, alteration, repair or maintenance in the State of a road, highway, driveway, street, bridge or entrance or walkway of any type constructed thereon in the State, and building, structure, appurtenance or appliance in the State, … purporting to indemnify or hold harmless the promisee or indemnitee or others, or their agents, servants and employees, for damages arising from liability for bodily injury or death to persons or damage to property caused partially or solely by, or resulting partially or solely from, or arising partially or solely out of the negligence of such promisee or indemnitee or others than the promisor or indemnitor, or its subcontractors, agents, servants or employees, is against public policy and is void and unenforceable, even where such covenant, promise, agreement or understanding is crystal clear and unambiguous in obligating the promisor or indemnitor to indemnify or hold harmless the promisee or indemnitee from liability resulting from such promisee's or indemnitee's own negligence … . (b) Nothing in subsection (a) of this section shall be construed to void or render unenforceable policies of insurance issued by duly authorized insurance companies and insuring against losses or damages from any causes whatsoever." DEL. CODE ANN. tit. 6, § 2704. *See J. S. Alberici Constr. Co. v. Mid-West Conveyor Co.*, 750 A.2d 518 (Del. 2000) ("Section 2704(a) is clear on its face: a contractual provision requiring one party to indemnify another party for the second party's own negligence, whether sole or partial, is against public policy and is void and unenforceable."); *Pac. Ins. Co. v. Liberty Mut. Ins. Co.*, 956 A.2d 1246, 1258–59 (Del. 2008) (enforcing the insurance "savings provision" of § 2704 (b)); *Menkes v. Saint Joseph Church*, No. 09C-03-289, 2011 Del. Super. LEXIS 141 (Del. Super. Ct. Mar. 18, 2011) ("Under Delaware law, a general contractor in a construction contract cannot assign its liability for its own wrongdoing to a third party. However, the presence of language assigning the general contractor's own liability to another party does not always invalidate the entire indemnification

clause of a contact. Whether an indemnification contract clause remains enforceable depends on whether the offensive language can be stricken from the contract so that the remaining obligation under the contract would be valid under Delaware law.");
Slattery v. Pettinaro Construction Co., No. N12C-11-252, 2015 Del. Super. LEXIS 481 (Del. Super. Ct. Apr. 30, 2015) ("Section 2704(a) relates to the public policy of certain contracts of purported indemnification. There may be a public policy concern where a contractual provision requires one party to indemnify another party for the second party's own negligence. Here, however, the indemnification clause requires Delcard to indemnify Pettinaro only to the extent caused by the negligent acts or omissions of Delcard. . . . Accordingly, 6 Del. C. § 2704 does not void the indemnification clause."); *Wash. House Condo. Ass'n of Owners v. Daystar Sills, Inc.*, No. N15C-01-10, 2018 Del. Super. LEXIS 1316 (Del. Super. Ct. Nov. 13, 2018) (examining an indemnity clause and addressing whether it comes within § 2704); *Del. State Univ. v. Thomas Co.*, No. 15-1144, 2020 U.S. Dist. LEXIS 21680 (D. Del. Nov. 19, 2020) ("[T]he court concludes that § 2704 does not prohibit enforcement of a limitation of liability clause. This conclusion is based on the distinction between indemnity and hold harmless clauses versus limitation of liability clauses, the prior enforcement of a similar limitation of liability clause in Delaware, and the purpose of the § 2704 prohibition of indemnity and hold harmless provisions to promote work place safety by incentivizing the parties to perform their work safely.").

District of Columbia: The District of Columbia Court of Appeals held that an indemnitee may be indemnified for its own negligence provided that the contractual obligation is sufficiently explicit. *See District of Columbia v. Murtaugh*, 728 A.2d 1237, 1245 (D.C. Cir. 1999) ("An indemnity provision … should not be construed to permit an indemnitee to recover for his or her own negligence unless the court is firmly convinced that such an interpretation reflects the intention of the parties. … Where the District expects to shift the ultimate responsibility for its negligence to its contractors, such an intention should be plainly evident from the face of the contract.") (citations and internal quotes omitted); *see also Rivers & Bryan, Inc. v. HBE Corp.*, 628 A.2d 631, 635 (D.C. Cir. 1993) ("In order to find that a party contracted away its own liability by receiving full indemnity therefor, there must be a clear intention to do so that is apparent from the face of the contract."); *Parker v. John Moriarty & Assocs.*, 189 F. Supp. 3d 38 (D.D.C. 2016) ("[T]he Court concludes that the language of the indemnity provision is ambiguous as to whether Strittmatter is obligated to indemnify JMAV for any claims arising out of JMAV's own negligence. Indeed, the Court finds that the provision at issue is distinguishable from those in cases cited by JMAV because it includes a provision specifically requiring that the injury be 'caused by or arise[] in whole or in part, from any negligent or non-negligent act or omission of [Strittmatter] or any of its agents, employees, sub-subcontractors or others.' Instead, the Court finds the provision at issue to be most similar to that considered by the D.C. Court of Appeals in [*District of Columbia v. Royal*, 465 A.2d 367 (D.C. Cir. 1983)], where the court found that it was not plainly evident from the face of the contract that responsibility for the indemnitee's negligence would shift to the indemnitor. Here, the Court finds that the language of the contract, including the provision referencing Strittmatter's conduct, does not clearly reflect the parties' intention to obligate Strittmatter for claims caused by or arising out of JMAV's negligence."); *Parker v. John Moriarty & Assocs.*, 332 F. Supp. 3d 220 (D.D.C. 2018) ("The Court now finds that JMAV similarly has failed to cite any evidence that was not before the Court in *Parker I* [discussed above] to show that JMAV and Strittmatter intended the indemnity provision to cover JMAV's own negligence, if any."); *United States Conf. of Mayors v. Great-West Life & Annuity Ins. Co.*, 288 F. Supp. 3d 4 (D.D.C. 2017) ("While parties are free to enter into indemnification agreements . . . such agreements are narrowly construed by courts so as not to read into [them] any obligations the parties never intended to assume.") (citing *Rivers & Bryan*).

Florida: Florida statute prohibits indemnification for any character of an indemnitee's own negligence unless the contract contains a monetary limitation on the extent of the indemnification that bears a reasonable commercial relationship to the contract and is part of the project specifications or bid documents, if: "Any portion of any agreement or contract for or in connection with, or any guarantee of or in connection with, any construction, alteration, repair, or demolition of a building, structure, appurtenance, or appliance, including moving and excavating associated therewith, between an owner of real property and an architect, engineer, general contractor, subcontractor, sub-subcontractor, or materialman or any combination thereof wherein any party referred to herein promises to indemnify or hold harmless the other party to the agreement, contract, or guarantee for liability for damages to persons or property caused in whole or in part by any act, omission, or default of the indemnitee arising from the contract or its performance, shall be void and unenforceable unless the contract contains a monetary limitation on the extent of the indemnification that bears a reasonable commercial relationship to the contract and is part of the project specifications or bid documents, if any. Notwithstanding the foregoing, the monetary limitation on the extent of the indemnification provided to the owner of real property by any party in privity of contract with such owner shall not be less than $1 million per occurrence, unless otherwise agreed by the parties." FLA.

STAT. ANN. § 725.06 (see complete text of statute for other provisions, such as those relating to public contracts and a prohibition against an indemnitor indemnifying the indemnitee for damages to persons or property caused in whole or in part by any act, omission, or default of a party other than, among others, the indemnitor and any of its contractors, subcontractors, subsubcontractors, materialmen, or agents of any tier or their respective employees). *See also Peninsula II Developers v. Gryphon Construction*, No. 11-16038CA42, 2013 Fla. Cir. LEXIS 14108 (Fla. Cir. Ct. June 3, 2013) ("[T]he Court similarly finds that Sec. 725.06(1) is inapplicable to the subcontract since Peninsula II is not seeking damages for its own negligence. That said, to the extent the statute could apply, a reference to a cap on indemnity is found in section 4.7.1. of the subcontract wherein it states: 'The Subcontractor's obligation to indemnify as set forth herein shall be limited to $1,000,000 (One Million dollars) or as specifically stated in Exhibit E, whichever is greater, per occurrence which sum the parties hereto acknowledge bears a reasonable commercial relationship to this Agreement and shall be deemed part of the project specifications and bid documents.'"); *Griswold Ready Mix Concrete, Inc. v. Tony Reddick, & Pumpco, Inc.*, 134 So. 3d 985 (Fla. Ct. App. 2012) ("The indemnity provision at issue in this case does not contain a dollar limit to Griswold's potential liability. For that reason, it is void and unenforceable as provided in section 725.06."); *Blok Builders, LLC v. Katryniok*, 245 So. 3d 779 (Fla. Ct. App. 2018) (concluding that, for § 725.06(1) to apply, excavation must be associated with the "construction, alteration, repair, or demolition of a building, structure, appurtenance, or appliance") ("The project in this case did not involve such construction. The master contract between BellSouth and Mastec involved the laying and maintenance of utility lines. The contract does not involve a building, structure, appurtenance, or appliance. Therefore, given its plain and ordinary meaning, the statute does not govern the contractual provisions.") (but not deciding the case on the basis that section 725.06 can never apply to a contract with a utility); *Great Divide Ins. Co. v. Amerisure Ins. Co.*, No. 17-14271, 2018 U.S. Dist. LEXIS 41443 (S.D. Fla. Mar. 14, 2018) (concluding that the indemnity clause did not violate § 725.06 to the extent that a party seeks indemnity only for the negligence caused by the indemnitor); *CB Contrs., LLC v. Allens Steel Prods.*, 261 So. 3d 711 (Fla. Ct. App. 2018) ("Because the subject indemnity clauses are only void and unenforcable as to the 'portion' purporting to impose the indemnity obligation for the acts or omissions of Appellant, we conclude that the trial court erred in ruling that the entirety of the clauses are void."). Various versions of the statute have been in effect. Confirm that any case law discussion is of the relevant version.

Georgia: Georgia statute prohibits indemnification for an indemnitee's sole negligence: "A covenant, promise, agreement, or understanding in or in connection with or collateral to a contract or agreement relative to the construction, alteration, repair, or maintenance of a building structure, appurtenances, and appliances, including moving, demolition, and excavating connected therewith, purporting to require that one party to such contract or agreement shall indemnify, hold harmless, insure, or defend the other party to the contract or other named indemnitee, including its, his, or her officers, agents, or employees, against liability or claims for damages, losses, or expenses, including attorney fees, arising out of bodily injury to persons, death, or damage to property caused by or resulting from the sole negligence of the indemnitee, or its, his, or her officers, agents, or employees, is against public policy and void and unenforceable. This subsection shall not affect any obligation under workers' compensation or coverage or insurance specifically relating to workers' compensation, nor shall this subsection apply to any requirement that one party to the contract purchase a project specific insurance policy, including an owner's or contractor's protective insurance, builder's risk insurance, installation coverage, project management protective liability insurance, an owner controlled insurance policy, or a contractor controlled insurance policy." GA. CODE. ANN. § 13–8-2(b); *see also Lanier at McEver, L.P. v. Planners & Eng'rs Collaborative, Inc.*, 663 S.E.2d 240, 243 n.2 (Ga. 2008) ("Parties may avoid violating … § 13–8-2(b) if their agreement also includes an insurance clause which shifts the risk of loss to an insurer, no matter who is at fault."); *Garrett v. Nelson And Affiliates, LLC*, 761 F. Supp. 2d 1312 (M.D. Ala. 2011) (applying Georgia law) ("Instead of relying on particular contractual language to enforce indemnity agreements, Georgia courts require that, when the provisions of the contract which require indemnity and insurance are construed together, the provisions show that the parties intended coverage by insurance.") (citation and internal quotations omitted); *Kennedy Development Co., Inc. v. Camp*, 719 S.E.2d 442 (Ga. 2011) (noting that Georgia courts have consistently construed the statute "more broadly than courts in other jurisdictions have construed analogous statutes") ("As to the second threshold condition, requiring that the provision purport to indemnify the indemnitee for its sole negligence, our precedent is clear that this condition is satisfied by language like that in the Assignment Agreement, to the effect that a party will indemnify and hold harmless the other party as to 'any' or 'all' claims, damages, losses, injuries, or the like arising from the subject of the parties' contractual relationship, 'no matter the origin of the claim or who is at fault.'"); *Nationwide Mut. Ins. Co. v. Architectural Glazing Sys.*, No. 13-01069, 2015

U.S. Dist. LEXIS 188329 (N.D. Ga. Aug. 25, 2015) ("Even if the Court were to find that this contract related to the construction, alteration, repair or maintenance of a building covered by § 13-8-2(b), the contract still would not be void as against public policy. It is well-settled that when a contract includes an insurance clause which shifts risk of loss to an insurer, O.C.G.A. 13-8-2(b) does not apply."); *See US Nitrogen, LLC v. Weatherly, Inc.*, 343 F. Supp. 3d 1354 (N.D. Ga. 2018) (O.C.G.A. 13-8-2(b) not applicable as the agreement did not limit a party's liability to third parties). In 2016 Georgia added subsection (c) to § 13–8-2: "A covenant, promise, agreement, or understanding in or in connection with or collateral to a contract or agreement for engineering, architectural, or land surveying services purporting to require that one party to such contract or agreement shall indemnify, hold harmless, insure, or defend the other party to the contract or other named indemnitee, including its, his, or her officers, agents, or employees, against liability or claims for damages, losses, or expenses, including attorney fees, is against public policy and void and unenforceable, except for indemnification for damages, losses, or expenses to the extent caused by or resulting from the negligence, recklessness, or intentionally wrongful conduct of the indemnitor or other persons employed or utilized by the indemnitor in the performance of the contract. This subsection shall not affect any obligation under workers' compensation or coverage or insurance specifically relating to workers' compensation, nor shall this subsection apply to any requirement that one party to the contract purchase a project specific insurance policy or project specific policy endorsement."

Hawaii: Hawaii statute prohibits indemnification for an indemnitee's sole negligence: "Any covenant, promise, agreement or understanding in, or in connection with or collateral to, a contract or agreement relative to the construction, alteration, repair or maintenance of a building, structure, appurtenance or appliance, including moving, demolition or excavation connected therewith, purporting to indemnify the promisee against liability for bodily injury to persons or damage to property caused by or resulting from the sole negligence or willful misconduct of the promisee, the promisee's agents or employees, or indemnitee, is invalid as against public policy, and is void and unenforceable; provided that this section shall not affect any valid workers' compensation claim under chapter 386 or any other insurance contract or agreement issued by an admitted insurer upon any insurable interest under this code." HAW. REV. STAT. ANN. § 431:10–222; *see also Espaniola v. Cawdrey Mars Joint Venture*, 707 P.2d 365, 370–71 (Haw. 1985) (addressing Hawaii legislature's intent in drafting anti-indemnity statute); *Arthur v. State*, 377 P.3d 26 (Haw. 2016)

("[P]ursuant to HRS § 431:10-222, in the construction industry, a contractor is not contractually liable for the sole negligence or willful misconduct of another, or for the defense thereof, as such contractual requirements would cause higher insurance premiums and greater construction costs, thereby harming Hawaii's economy.") ("[I]f the complaint allegation rule were to apply, it is possible in a case where initial allegations were brought against multiple parties, for example, that a promisor would be compelled to defend a promisee against negligence claims where ultimate liability is attributed solely to the promise. Such a result contravenes HRS § 431:10-222[.] As such, we hold that with respect to a duty to defend in a construction contract, the scope of a promisor's duty to defend is determined at the end of litigation. HRS § 431:10-222 effectively renders coextensive the duties to indemnify and defend in construction contracts.").

Idaho: Idaho statute prohibits indemnification for an indemnitee's sole negligence: "A covenant, promise, agreement or understanding in, or in connection with or collateral to, a contract or agreement relative to the construction, alteration, repair or maintenance of a building, structure, highway, appurtenance and appliance, including moving, demolition and excavating connected therewith, purporting to indemnify the promisee against liability for damages arising out of bodily injury to persons or damage to property caused by or resulting from the sole negligence of the promisee, his agents or employees, or indemnitees, is against public policy and is void and unenforceable." IDAHO CODE ANN. § 29–114; *see also Beitzel v. Orton*, 827 P.2d 1160 (Idaho 1992) ("The indemnification clause does not require Orton to indemnify GTNW, if Beitzel's injuries had been caused solely by GTNW's negligence. To this extent, the clause does not violate I.C. § 29-114.").

Illinois: Illinois statute prohibits indemnification for any character of an indemnitee's own negligence: "With respect to contracts or agreements, either public or private, for the construction, alteration, repair or maintenance of a building, structure, highway bridge, viaducts or other work dealing with construction, or for any moving, demolition or excavation connected therewith, every covenant, promise or agreement to indemnify or hold harmless another person from that person's own negligence is void as against public policy and wholly unenforceable." 740 ILL. COMP. STAT. ANN. 35/1. *See also Camper v. Burnside Const. Co.*, 998 N.E.2d 1264 (Ill. Ct. App. 2013) ("[W]e find that the indemnification clause of the purchase order agreement, which sought to indemnify Welch for 'any and all claims' arising out of the enumerated conduct, was void as against public policy under the Anti–Indemnity Act."); *Halloran & Yauch, Inc. v. Roughneck Concrete Drilling & Sawing Co.*, No. 1–13–1059,

2013 Ill. App. Unpub. LEXIS 2036 (Ill. Ct. App. Sept. 13, 2013) (discussing purpose of Anti–Indemnity Act); *Pekin Ins. Co. v. Designed Equip. Acquisition Corp.*, 63 N.E.3d 242 (Ill. Ct. App. 2016) ("The Act expressly states that it applies to 'contracts or agreements, either public or private, for the construction, alteration, repair or maintenance of a building, structure, highway bridge, viaducts, or other work dealing with construction.' Here, the contract at issue between Abel and Designed is a lease or rental agreement for scaffolding equipment. Both parties admit that the lease does not contain the word 'construction.' However, we have not found any case that states that there is a magic word that must be used in an agreement in order to bring it within the purview of the Act.") ("We, like the trial court, cannot imagine that a lease of scaffolding equipment by a building restoration company can be reasonably interpreted as not being for the 'construction, alteration, repair or maintenance' of a building or structure or 'other work dealing with construction.' Designed is asking this court to render an interpretation of the lease that runs contrary to common sense, and we refuse to do so."); *933 Van Buren Condo. Ass'n v. Van Buren*, 61 N.E.3d 929 (Ill. Ct. App. 2016) ("Because there is nothing in the record to suggest that WVB construed the indemnification provision as relieving it of liability for its own acts or omissions, that paragraph did not extinguish WVB's incentive to exercise due care, and the primary purpose behind the Construction Contract Indemnification for Negligence Act was not implicated. Therefore, we will interpret the contract in a manner that renders the agreement enforceable rather than void."); *State Auto Prop. & Cas. Ins. Co. v. Shores Builders, Inc.*, No. 19-773, 2020 U.S. Dist. LEXIS 183922 (S.D. Ill. Oct. 5, 2020) ("Here, the indemnity provision in the Agreement limits Rock Branch's responsibility to claims 'arising out of, or resulting from, the performance, or failure in performance, of Subcontractor's [Rock Branch] Work ....' Illinois courts have found similar language valid under the Act."); *Wilda v. JLG Indus.*, 470 F. Supp. 3d 770 (N.D. Ill. 2020) ("A contract 'for' construction does not mean a contract 'about,' 'related to,' or 'in connection with' construction. It means a contract to build something.") ("The fact that Area Erectors planned to use the equipment for construction does not change the essential character of the contract. It was a rental agreement, not a construction contract. It does not matter that the accident happened on a construction site, because the 'focus of the statute . . . is 'contracts or agreements,' not accidents.'").

Indiana: Previously, an Indiana statute prohibited indemnification for an indemnitee's sole negligence as follows: "All provisions, clauses, covenants, or agreements contained in, collateral to, or affecting any construction or design contract except those pertaining to highway contracts, which purport to indemnify the promisee against liability for: (1) Death or bodily injury to persons; (2) Injury to property; (3) Design defects; or (4) Any other loss, damage or expense arising under either (1), (2) or (3); from the sole negligence or willful misconduct of the promisee or the promisee's agents, servants or independent contractors who are directly responsible to the promisee, are against public policy and are void and unenforceable." IND. CODE ANN. § 26–2–5–1. An exception is provided for "a construction or design contract if liability insurance normally available within the United States at standard rates cannot be obtained for the facility being constructed or designed because it constitutes a dangerous instrumentality." *Id.* at § 26–2–5–2; *see also Estate of Williams v. S. Indiana Gas and Elec. Co., Inc.*, 551 F. Supp. 2d 751 (S.D. Ind. 2008) (addressing in detail whether an indemnification agreement was void under § 26–2–5–1); *Amerisure Ins. Co. v. Scottsdale Ins. Co.*, 795 F. Supp. 2d 819 (S.D. Ind. 2011), *aff'd on other grounds*, 695 F.3d 632 (7th Cir. 2012) ("Scottsdale is entitled to a determination that the indemnity clause contained in the Subcontract is void and unenforceable because it requires Central Steel to indemnify ISF for ISF's own negligence and violates Indiana Code § 26-2-5-1_which mandates that such agreements are void and unenforceable."); *Wilhelm Constr., Inc. v. Secura Ins.*, No. 49A02-1604, 2017 Ind. App. Unpub. LEXIS 642 (Ind. Ct. App. May 24, 2017) ("A plain reading of the Anti-Indemnity Statute reveals that immediately following the language which would seem to limit application of the statute to the sole negligence of the promisee, the General Assembly inserted the much broader, arguably nearly all-encompassing, language which extends application of the statute to not only the sole negligence of the promisee, but also the sole negligence of promisee's agents, servants, and independent contractors who are directly responsible to the promisee. *See* Ind. Code § 26-2-5-1. Therefore, we believe that the question of 'sole negligence' is not merely limited to Appellants, but also includes the 'sole negligence' of any independent contractors who are directly responsible to Appellants.").

In response to *Wilhelm Constr.*, effective July 1, 2019, sub-paragraph (b)(4) of § 26–2–5–1 now states: "any other loss, damage, or expense arising under subdivision (1), (2), or (3); from sole negligence or willful misconduct of the promisee are against public policy and are void and unenforceable. Sole negligence does not include vicarious liability, imputed negligence, or assumption of a nondelegable duty." In addition, for purposes of contracts entered into on or after July 1, 2019, § 26–2–5–4 was added to Indiana Code to address indemnification in conjunction with contracts pertaining to professional services of several professionals, including design professionals and architects. Refer to the statute for other changes.

Iowa: The Supreme Court of Iowa held that an indemnitee may be indemnified for its own negligence provided that the contractual obligation is sufficiently explicit. *McNally & Nimergood v. Neumann-Kiewit Constructors, Inc.*, 648 N.W.2d 564, 571–72 (Iowa 2002) ("A contract for indemnification is generally subject to the same rules of formation, validity and construction as other contracts. However, we have crafted a special rule of construction for indemnification contracts when the contract is claimed to relieve the indemnitee from liability for its own negligence. This rule provides that indemnification contracts will not be construed to permit an indemnitee to recover for its own negligence unless the intention of the parties is clearly and unambiguously expressed ... . [O]ur rule of construction does not actually require the contract to specifically mention the indemnitee's negligence or fault as long as this intention is otherwise clearly expressed by other words of the agreement.") (citations omitted); *See also Wells Dairy, Inc. v. Am. Indus. Refrigeration, Inc.*, 762 N.W.2d 463, 470 (Iowa 2009) (recognizing that Iowa has an implied contractual indemnity doctrine) ("[A]n implied contractual duty to indemnify may arise from a contractual relationship that lacks an express obligation to indemnify where there are 'independent duties' in the contract to justify the implication. Such 'independent duties' arise in the context of implied contractual indemnity when the contract implies 'a mutual intent to indemnify for liability or loss resulting from a breach of the duty.' In other words, we have found an implied contractual duty to indemnify where the circumstances require that a party to an agreement 'ought to act as if he had made such a promise, even though nobody actually thought of it or used words to express it.'") (citations omitted); *Isakson v. College Square Mall Partners, L.L.C.*, No. 0-624, 2010 Iowa App. LEXIS 1082 (Iowa Ct. App. Sept. 22, 2010) ("[T]o prevail on a contractual indemnity claim, the indemnitee must normally establish that he or she was not negligent. However, there is no rule of construction that requires the indemnitee to prove the indemnitor was negligent."); *Jeffries v. General Cas. Ins. Cos.*, 863 N.W.2d 36 (Iowa Ct. App. 2015) ("This rule provides that indemnification contracts will not be construed to permit an indemnitee to recover for its own negligence unless the intention of the parties is clearly and unambiguously expressed. Thus, indemnification contracts claimed to contain these provisions are construed more strictly than other contracts. Additionally, where an indemnification is not given by one in the insurance business but is given incident to a contract whose main purpose is not indemnification, the indemnity provision must be construed strictly in favor of the indemnitor.").

Kansas: Kansas statute prohibits indemnification for any character of an indemnitee's own negligence: "An indemnification provision in a contract [defined to include construction contract] which requires the promisor to indemnify the promisee for the promisee's negligence or intentional acts or omissions is against public policy and is void and unenforceable." KAN. STAT. ANN. § 16–121(b). Further, "[a] provision in a contract which requires a party to provide liability coverage to another party, as an additional insured, for such other party's own negligence or intentional acts or omissions is against public policy and is void and unenforceable." *Id.* at § 16–121(c). The statute applies to indemnification and additional insured provisions entered into after January 1, 2009 and it does not affect the contractual obligation of a contractor or owner to provide railroad protective insurance or general liability insurance. *Id.* at § 16–121(d)(1). *See Oakes v. Repcon, Inc.,* No. 16-1074, 2017 U.S. Dist. LEXIS 34798 (D. Kan. Mar. 10, 2017) (court unable to determine applicability of § 16–121(b) because of uncertainty whether contract at issue is a "construction contract"); *Sunflower Elec. Power Corp. v. M&S Steel, Inc.,* No. 17-1158, 2018 U.S. Dist. LEXIS 66786 (D. Kan. Apr. 20, 2018) (same).

Kentucky: The Supreme Court of Kentucky held that an indemnitee may be indemnified for its own negligence provided that the contractual obligation is sufficiently explicit. *Fosson v. Ashland Oil & Ref. Co.,* 309 S.W.2d 176, 178 (Ky. 1957) ("[W]hen there is a doubt as to the meaning of an indemnity clause the construction should be against the contention that the contract was meant to indemnify against an indemnitee's own negligence. We have said that every presumption is against such intention. But such clauses are not against public policy and in cases where it is not improbable that a party would undertake such an indemnification of another party we reach a different result.") (citation omitted). More recently, however, the Court of Appeals of Kentucky addressed *Fosson,* and other related Kentucky cases, and held that indemnification provisions for an indemnitee's own negligence are "not against public policy generally, but they are when agreed to by a party in a clearly inferior bargaining position." *Speedway SuperAmerica, LLC v. Erwin,* 250 S.W.3d 339, 344 (Ky. Ct. App. 2008); *see also Martin County Coal Corp. v. Universal Underwriters Ins. Servs., Inc.,* 727 F.3d 589 (6th Cir. 2013) (holding that an indemnity agreement was void as against Kentucky public policy) ("Crum Motor Sales was in a clearly inferior bargaining position in relation to Martin County Coal. . . . At the time of entering into the 1997 indemnification agreement, Martin County Coal was a wholly owned subsidiary of an out-of-state corporation, the A.T. Massey Coal Company, Inc., listed on the New York Stock Exchange. Crum Motor Sales was a nearly insolvent mom-and-pop wholly in-state company with fewer than ten employees. We therefore disagree with Martin County Coal's assertion that Crum Motor Sales 'was a sophisticated business entity.' There was a major disparity in bargaining power between Martin County Coal and Crum Motor Sales."); *Black v. Dixie Consumer Products, LLC*, No. 08-00142, 2014 U.S. Dist. LEXIS 59927 (W.D. Ky. Apr. 30, 2014) ("Under Kentucky law, indemnification provisions that are applied to defend against the indemnitee's own negligence . . . are not against public policy generally, but they are when agreed to by a party in a clearly inferior bargaining position. Where such provisions are negotiated as part of an arm's-length transaction between two business corporations with presumably equal bargaining power, the Kentucky courts have found no compelling reason to disturb their written contract.") (court unable to determine whether one party was a "sophisticated corporate entity" that engaged in arm's length negotiation with Georgia Pacific); *Wilson Equip. Co., LLC v. Motorists Mut. Ins. Co.*, No. 2017-CA-001064, 2018 Ky. App. Unpub. LEXIS 524 (Ky. Ct. App. July 27, 2018) ("Wilson Equipment and Stanley Pipeline are both corporations. The two had done business together for almost thirty years, and the Rental Contract containing the indemnification provision had been utilized for some ten years. The rental agreement plainly states that Stanley Pipeline assumed 'all risks' associated with the rental and use of the equipment. There is nothing in the record before this Court that establishes that Wilson Equipment and Stanley Pipeline were not of equal bargaining power in entering into the Rental Contract. Accordingly, we conclude that the Rental Contract's indemnification provision is valid and unequivocal."); *Live Nation Worldwide, Inc. v. Secura Ins.*, 423 F. Supp. 3d 383 (W.D. Ky. 2019) ("Secura has not put forward any facts that suggest ESG and Live Nation are not sophisticated parties or that the VSA was not negotiated at arm's length. When, as in this case, the exculpatory clause is 'part of an arm's-length transaction between sophisticated parties with equal bargaining power,' the clause will be enforced unless such enforcement violates public policy.").

Louisiana: The Supreme Court of Louisiana held that an indemnitee may be indemnified for its own negligence provided that the contractual obligation is sufficiently explicit. *Berry v. Orleans Parish Sch. Bd.*, 830 So. 2d 283, 205 (La. 2002) ("[A] contract of indemnity whereby the indemnitee is indemnified against the consequences of his own negligence is strictly construed, and such a contract will not be construed to indemnify an indemnitee against losses resulting to him through his own negligent acts unless such an intention is expressed in unequivocal terms."). *See also Reggio v. E.T.I.*, 15 So. 3d 951, 953 (La. 2008) (restating *Berry*); *Scarberry v. Entergy*

Corp., 136 So. 3d 194 (La. Ct. App. 2014) (discussing background of Louisiana law regarding indemnity or hold harmless agreements); *Deville v. Conmaco/Rector L.P.*, 516 Fed. Appx. 296 (5th Cir. 2012) ("Louisiana courts have not held that any certain prescribed language is required to shift liability from one party to another. Rather, the courts look to the contract as a whole."); *Ponder v. SDT Waste & Debris Servs., L.L.C.*, No. 2015 CA 1656, 2017 La. App. LEXIS 1493 (La. Ct. App. Aug. 16, 2017) ("A contract of indemnity will not be construed to indemnify the indemnitee against losses resulting from his own negligence unless such an intention is expressed in unequivocal terms. The established principle supporting the rule is that general words alone, *i.e.*, 'any and all liability,' do not necessarily import an intent to impose an obligation so extraordinary and harsh as to render an indemnitor liable to an indemnitee for damages occasioned by the sole negligence of the latter."); *O'Neal v. Foremost Ins. Co.*, 265 So. 3d 846 (La. Ct. App. 2019) (concluding that indemnification "from any liability for injury on or about the property which may be suffered by any employee, tenant or guest upon the property" was not sufficient to support indemnity for the indemnitee's own negligence); *Couvillion Grp., L.L.C. v. Plaquemines Par. Gov't*, 295 So. 3d 400 (La. 2020) ("Requiring PEC to indemnify Plaquemines for damage related to the work stoppage would result in Plaquemines being indemnified for its sole fault. Use of the phrase 'any and all claims' does not expressly provide indemnity to Plaquemines for its sole negligence, nor does it reflect the required specificity to trigger such indemnity.") (citing *Berry* and *Ponder*). La. Rev. Stat. Ann. § 38:2216(G) provides: "[A]ny provision contained in a public contract, other than a contract of insurance, providing for a hold harmless or indemnity agreement, or both, [f]rom the contractor to the public body [or other public contractors] for damages arising out of injuries or property damage to third parties caused by the negligence of the public body, its employees, or agents [or other public contractors] … is contrary to the public policy of the state, and any and all such provisions in any and all contracts are null and void."

Maine: The Supreme Judicial Court of Maine held that an indemnitee may be indemnified for its own negligence provided that the contractual obligation is sufficiently explicit. *Emery Waterhouse Co. v. Lea*, 467 A.2d 986, 993 (Me. 1983) ("Indemnity clauses to save a party harmless from damages due to negligence may lawfully be inserted in contracts … and such clauses are not against public policy. But, when purportedly requiring indemnification of a party for damage or injury caused by that party's own negligence, such contractual provisions, with virtual unanimity, are looked upon with disfavor by the courts, and are construed strictly against extending the indemnification to include recovery by the indemnitee for his own negligence. It is only where the contract on its face by its very terms clearly and unequivocally reflects a mutual intention on the part of the parties to provide indemnity for loss caused by negligence of the party to be indemnified that liability for such damages will be fastened on the indemnitor, and words of general import will not be read as expressing such an intent and establishing by inference such liability.") (citations omitted); *State Farm Mut. Auto. Ins. Co. v. Koshy*, 995 A.2d 651, 667 (Me. 2010) (calling for "the strict construction of a contract that provides for a party to be indemnified for losses *resulting from that party's own negligence*") (emphasis in original) (citing *Emery*); *McCue v. Enter. Rent-A-Car Co.*, No. 18-30, 2020 Me. Super. LEXIS 73 (Me. Super. Ct. Mar. 4, 2020) ("The court's reading of the cases is that an exculpatory clause seeking to absolve a party from liability for its' own negligence must expressly spell out with the greatest particularity the intent of the parties contractually to extinguish negligence liability. It may very well be that Price and MacKenzie mutually understood and intended to eliminate liability for MacKenzie for its own negligence in 'slip and fall incidents,' but the law requires more than an assumption or inference to that effect. Rather, it must be 'expressly spelled out.'").

Maryland: Maryland statute prohibits indemnification for an indemnitee's sole negligence: "(1) A covenant, promise, agreement, or understanding in, or in connection with or collateral to, a contract or agreement relating to architectural, engineering, inspecting, or surveying services, or the construction, alteration, repair, or maintenance of a building, structure, appurtenance or appliance, including moving, demolition, and excavating connected with those services or that work, purporting to indemnify the promisee against liability for damages arising out of bodily injury to any person or damage to property caused by or resulting from the sole negligence of the promisee or indemnitee, or the agents or employees of the promisee or indemnitee, is against public policy and is void and unenforceable. MD. CODE ANN., CTS. & JUD. PROC. § 5–401(a) (1). *See also Heat & Power Corp. v. Air Prods. & Chems., Inc.*, 578 A.2d 1202, 1206 (Md. 1990) ("Article 13 of the contract required Contractor to indemnify Owner for any liability 'resulting from or arising out of or in connection with the performance of this contract by Contractor ... .' This provision cannot be construed as indemnifying the Owner against its own sole negligence.") (addressing prior version of anti-indemnity statute); *Turner Constr. Co. v. BFPE Int'l, Inc.*, No. 15-368, 2016 U.S. Dist. LEXIS 39161 (D. Md. Mar. 26, 2015) ("If a particular contract provision or sentence can properly be construed as reflecting two agreements, one providing for indemnity if the promisee is solely negligent and one providing for indemnity if the promisee and promisor are concurrently negligent, only the former agreement is voided by the statute.") (quoting *Heat & Power*); *United Nat'l Ins. Co. v. Peninsula Roofing Co.*, No. 16-3548, 2018 U.S. Dist. LEXIS 55881 (D. Md. Mar. 30, 2018) (rejecting insurer's argument that a subrogation waiver is prohibited by § 5-401) ("A subrogation waiver does not indemnify the promisee. Instead, it shifts the risk of loss to the insurance company regardless of which party is at fault."). In 2016 the following provision was added to § 5–401(a): (2) "A covenant, a promise, an agreement, or an understanding in, or in connection with or collateral to, a contract or an agreement relating to architectural, engineering, inspecting, or surveying services, or the construction, alteration, repair, or maintenance of a building, a structure, an appurtenance, or an appliance, including moving, demolition, and excavating connected with those services or that work, purporting to require the promisor or indemnitor to defend or pay the costs of defending the promisee or indemnitee against liability for damages arising out of bodily injury to any person or damage to property caused by or resulting from the sole negligence of the promisee or indemnitee, or the agents or employees of the promisee or indemnitee, is against public policy and is void and unenforceable." Section 5–401(a)(3) provides that (a)(1) and (a)(2) "do not affect the validity of any insurance contract, workers' compensation, any general indemnity agreement required by a surety as a condition of execution of a bond for a construction or other contract, or any other agreement issued by an insurer."

Massachusetts: Massachusetts statute prohibits indemnification by a subcontractor for injury or damage not caused by the subcontractor: "Any provision for or in connection with a contract for construction, reconstruction, installation, alteration, remodeling, repair, demolition or maintenance work, including without limitation, excavation, backfilling or grading, on any building or structure, whether underground or above ground, or on any real property, including without limitation any road, bridge, tunnel, sewer, water or other utility line, which requires a subcontractor to indemnify any party for injury to persons or damage to property not caused by the subcontractor or its employees, agents or subcontractors, shall be void." MASS. GEN. LAWS ANN. ch. 149, § 29C; *see also Spellman v. Shawmut Woodworking & Supply, Inc.*, 840 N.E.2d 47, 52 (Mass. 2006) ("[Section 29C] in no way prohibits contractual indemnity arrangements whereby the subcontractor agrees to assume indemnity obligations for the entire liability when both the subcontractor and the general contractor or owner are causally negligent.") (internal quotation and citations omitted); *Norfolk & Dedham Mut. Fire Ins. Co. v. Morrison*, 924 N.E.2d 260, 268–69 (Mass. 2010) (addressing G.L. ch. 186, § 15 and looking to G.L. ch. 149, § 29C) (described as a similar statute for guidance) ("We agree with the reasoning of these cases that an agreement in a lease that the tenant indemnify or hold harmless the landlord is distinct from an agreement to purchase insurance on the landlord's behalf, which covers the liability of both in the event of a negligently caused injury. The statute seeks to protect a tenant from overreaching by the landlord with respect to maintaining the safety of the leased premises. It does not seek to limit commercial landlords and tenants from negotiating the apportionment of risk through the acquisition of insurance for their mutual protection and the benefit of third parties."); *Hillside FXF, LLC v. Premier Design + Build Group, LLC*, No. SUCV2013-03831, 2016 Mass. Super. LEXIS 814 (Mass. Super. Ct. Dec. 1, 2016) ("General contractors and owners are prohibited by § 29C from receiving indemnity for their sole causal negligence, but § 29C does not proscribe full indemnification when the conduct of the subcontractor is only a partial cause of the injury. Thus, a contractual indemnity arrangement whereby the subcontractor agrees to indemnify the contractor for the entire liability when both the subcontractor and the general contractor or owner are causally negligent, is not prohibited by Section 29C. What is forbidden is shifting that liability to a subcontractor even where it plays no role in causing the damages."); *Silva v. Rochester Bituminous Prods.*, No. 1683 CV 00512, 2018 Mass. Super. LEXIS 71 (Mass. Super. Ct. June 11, 2018) ("Rochester's agreement seeks indemnity from a lawsuit arising from Clover's 'work' and is not limited to circumstances where Rochester is liable as a result of negligence caused by Clover. As such, Rochester's language is overbroad and void under Chapter 149, § 29C.") (noting that "an indemnification provision which requires a subcontractor to indemnify where it has been 'alleged' to be negligent (as opposed to have 'caused' by the subcontractor) is overbroad under the statute"); *Medeiros v. CTA Construction Co.*, No. 17-10330, 2020 U.S. Dist. LEXIS 110441 (D. Mass. Feb. 26, 2020) (Section 29C not applicable to an indemnification provision in a rental agreement to provide a crane and crane operator, but not to perform actual construction work).

Michigan: Michigan statute prohibits indemnification for an indemnitee's sole negligence: "In a contract for the design, construction, alteration, repair, or maintenance of a building, a structure, an appurtenance, an appliance, a highway, road, bridge, water line, sewer line, or other infrastructure, or any other improvement to real property, including moving, demolition and excavating connected therewith, a provision purporting to indemnify the promisee against liability for damages arising out of bodily injury to persons or damage to property caused by or resulting from the sole negligence of the promisee or indemnitee, his agents or employees, is against public policy and is void and unenforceable." MICH. COMP. LAWS ANN. § 691.991(1). *See also Estate Dev. Co. v. Oakland County Road Com'n*, Nos. 291989, 292159, 295968, 2011 Mich. App. LEXIS 587 (Mich. Ct. App. Mar. 24, 2011) ("[U]nder the statute, an indemnitor is not liable for the indemnitee's negligence, unless the indemnitor is also negligent, regardless of contractual language to the contrary.") (citation and internal quotes omitted); *Foldi v. Young Men's Christian Ass'n*, No. 282434 (Mich. Ct. App. Apr. 29, 2009) (indemnitor unable to use statute to void indemnification provision because it could not establish that indemnitee was solely negligent); *Caterpillar Inc. v. R & R Steel Construction Co.*, No. 10-21, 2012 U.S. Dist. LEXIS 21431 (W.D. Mich. Feb. 21, 2012) ("Because the more recent Michigan Court of Appeals cases and the Michigan Supreme Court have favored the interpretation of § 691.991 espoused by Caterpillar, the Court finds that there is no statutory bar prohibiting Caterpillar from seeking full indemnification under the terms of its contract with R&R. Even if a jury finds that Caterpillar bears some responsibility for the accident, the indemnification provisions allow Caterpillar to collect indemnification for all liability arising under the contract so long as the accident is not solely attributable to Caterpillar's negligence."); *Miller-Davis Co. v. Ahrens Const., Inc.*, 848 N.W.2d 95 (Mich. 2014) ("The only legal restriction upon indemnity in the subcontractor context is the prohibition on indemnification against the 'sole negligence' of the contractor, which is not at issue here.") (quoting § 691.991); *Koch v. A.Z.*, 912 N.W.2d 205 (Mich. Ct. App. 2017) (holding that MCL § 691.991(2) – effective March 1, 2013 and related to the extent to which a public entity may require a general contractor or subcontractor to indemnify it -- is subject to prospective application only and, therefore, not applicable to contracts entered into before the effective date).

Minnesota: Minnesota statute prohibits indemnification for any character of an indemnitee's own negligence: "An indemnification agreement contained in, or executed in connection with, a building and construction contract is unenforceable except to the extent that: (1) the underlying injury or damage is attributable to the negligent or otherwise wrongful act or omission, including breach of a specific contractual duty, of the promisor or the promisor's independent contractors, agents, employees, or delegatees; or (2) an owner, a responsible party, or a governmental entity agrees to indemnify a contractor directly or through another contractor with respect to strict liability under environmental laws." MINN. STAT. ANN. § 337.02. *See also Seward Hous. Corp. v. Conroy Bros. Co.*, 573 N.W.2d 364, 366 (Minn. 1998) ("[N]o party can be indemnified when its own negligent acts or omissions are the underlying cause of the injury or damages. This restriction ensures that each party remains responsible for its own negligent actions."). MINN. STAT. ANN. § 337.05 contains several provisions concerning insurance for indemnification obligations. *See Westfield Ins. Co. v. Weis Builders, Inc.*, No. Civ.00-987, 2004 U.S. Dist. LEXIS 13658 (D. Minn. July 1, 2004) ("The Minnesota Supreme Court has interpreted sections 337.02 and 337.05 to uphold a construction contract that required the subcontractor to provide insurance coverage for all damages and injuries, including claims for which the contractor may be or may be claimed to be liable."); *Holmes v. Watson-Forsberg Co.*, 488 N.W.2d 473, 475 (Minn.1992) (determining that even though an indemnification provision may be unenforceable under section 337.02, a promise to purchase insurance to cover any negligent acts by the promisee is valid and enforceable); *Engineering & Const. Innovations, Inc. v. L.H. Bolduc Co., Inc.*, 825 N.W.2d 695 (Minn. 2013) ("Section 337.02 therefore renders unenforceable indemnification agreements in which a party assumes responsibility to pay for damages that are not caused by the party's own wrongful conduct. But in Minn. Stat. § 337.05 (2012), '[t]he legislature has established a narrow exception to the general prohibition of indemnification from the indemnitee's own negligence.' .... Section 337.05 embodies the Legislature's approval of the construction industry's 'practical response to [risk allocation] problems inherent in the performance of a subcontract' whereby 'the parties are free to place the risk of loss upon an insurer by requiring one of the parties to insure against that risk.'"); *Carlson v. Barta*, No. A14-0003, 2014 Minn. App. Unpub. LEXIS 1122 (Minn. Ct. App. Oct. 20, 2014) ("Under the plain language of the statute, Barta and Carlson's contract is not a building and construction contract. The contract is titled 'Timber Sale Contract.' It identifies the seller, the purchaser, the amount purchaser agreed to pay seller, the timber species, the estimated volume, the unit price, and the bid value. The contract in no way describes 'the design, construction, alteration, improvement, repair, or maintenance of real property.'); *Tietz v. United Rentals (N. Am.), Inc.*, No. A13-2284, 2014 Minn. App. Unpub. LEXIS 771 (Minn. Ct. App. July 21, 2014) ("Appellant does not cite to any binding Minnesota case law or statutory authority extending 'building and construction' contracts to encompass an agreement between a party to a construction contract and a remote nonparty for the rental of equipment. The legislature could have included rental equipment in its definition of a building and construction contract if that had been its intent."); *Indep. Sch. Dist. No. 477 v. Midwest Asphalt Corp.*, No. A20-0564, 2020 Minn. App. Unpub. LEXIS 988 (Minn. Ct. App. Dec. 28, 2020) ("We conclude that the language of section 6.3 unambiguously establishes a substantive limit to the extent to which Court Surfaces agreed to indemnify Midwest. The provision appears to track the limit established by section 337.02 so as to ensure that the indemnification agreement is enforceable.").

Mississippi: Mississippi statute prohibits indemnification for any character of an indemnitee's own negligence: "With respect to all public or private contracts or agreements, for the construction, alteration, repair or maintenance of buildings, structures, highway bridges, viaducts, water, sewer or gas distribution systems, or other work dealing with construction, or for any moving, demolition or excavation connected therewith, every covenant, promise and/or agreement contained therein to indemnify or hold harmless another person from that person's own negligence is void as against public policy and wholly unenforceable. This section does not apply to construction bonds or insurance contracts or agreements." MISS. CODE ANN. § 31–5–41; *see also Transocean Enter., Inc. v. Ingalls Shipbuilding, Inc.*, 33 So. 3d 459, 464 (Miss. 2010) ("This statute could reasonably be interpreted as invalidating indemnity or 'hold-harmless' clauses in construction contracts to indemnify another person from that person's own negligence."); *Thrash Commer. Contrs., Inc. v. Terracon Consultants, Inc.*, 889 F. Supp. 2d 868 (S.D. Miss. 2012) ("In the court's opinion, the Mississippi Supreme Court, like most courts, would more likely view a limitation of liability clause as beyond the purview of § 31-5-41. But regardless of how the statute is interpreted, it does not preclude enforcement of the limitation of liability provision in circumstances of this case. That is to say, even if the limitation of liability provision between Thrash and Terracon might be viewed as running afoul of the anti-indemnification statute to the extent it would operate to insulate Terracon from liability, in part, for losses caused by its own negligence, the fact is, Thrash has made no claim against Terracon for negligence. Rather, it has asserted only claims for breach of contract. By its terms, the statute only renders void as against public policy any agreement 'to indemnify or hold harmless another person from that person's own negligence.' It does not purport to invalidate an agreement between contracting parties to limit one party's liability to the other for breach of the contract."); *Deviney Constr. Co. v. Ace Util. Boring & Trenching, LLC*, No. 11-468, 2014 U.S. Dist. LEXIS 88658 (S.D. Miss. June 30, 2014) ("Neither party cites any case law discussing whether the anti-indemnity statute applies to bar a claim seeking only attorney's fees and defense costs, rather than indemnification. And neither party filed a rebuttal in support of its motion, so the Court will deny both Ace's and Deviney's motions on this issue at this time.").

Missouri: Missouri statute prohibits indemnification for any character of an indemnitee's own negligence, subject to exceptions: "1. Except as provided in subsection 2 of this section, in any contract or agreement for public or private construction work, a party's covenant, promise or agreement to indemnify or hold harmless another person from that person's own negligence or wrongdoing is void as against public policy and wholly unenforceable. 2. The provisions of subsection 1 of this section shall not apply to: (1) A party's covenant, promise or agreement to indemnify or hold harmless another person from the party's own negligence or wrongdoing or the negligence or wrongdoing of the party's subcontractors and suppliers of any tier; (2) A party's promise to cause another person or entity to be covered as an insured or additional insured in an insurance contract; ... (8) An agreement containing a party's promise to indemnify, defend or hold harmless another person, if the agreement also requires the party to obtain specified limits of insurance to insure the indemnity obligation and the party had the opportunity to recover the cost of the required insurance in its contract price; provided, however, that in such case the party's liability under the indemnity obligation shall be limited to the coverage and limits of the required insurance." Mo. ANN. STAT. § 434.100. *See also Hertz Equip. Rental Corp. v. Ammon Painting Co.*, No. WD70191, 2009 Mo. App. LEXIS 1131 (Mo. Ct. App. Aug. 4, 2009) ("[T]he appellants point to nothing establishing that indemnification agreements were against public policy before August 28, 1999. And, to strike down this indemnification agreement, which was signed April 1998, would violate section 434.100.4's command that section 434.100 applies only to contracts entered into after August 28, 1999. While indemnification agreements relating to public or private construction work signed after August 28, 1999, are void because they run counter to Missouri public policy, the appellants point to nothing that would make CSC's indemnification agreement void. CSC's indemnification provision is clearly worded and plainly requires Ammon to indemnify CSC for any injuries relating from its use of the equipment. Both CSC and Ammon are sophisticated business entities. The indemnification provision is enforceable.")

Montana: Montana statute prohibits indemnification (or additional insured rights) for any character of an indemnitee's own negligence: "(1) Except as provided in subsections (2) and (3), a construction contract provision that requires one party to the contract to indemnify, hold harmless, insure, or defend the other party to the contract or the other party's officers, employees, or agents for liability, damages, losses, or costs that are caused by the negligence, recklessness, or intentional misconduct of the other party or the other party's officers, employees, or agents is void as against the public policy of this state. (2) A construction contract may contain a provision: (a) requiring one party to the contract to indemnify, hold harmless, or insure the other party to the contract or the other party's officers, employees, or agents for liability, damages, losses, or costs, including but not limited to reasonable attorney fees, only to the extent that the liability, damages, losses, or costs are caused by the negligence, recklessness, or intentional misconduct of a third party or of the indemnifying party or the indemnifying party's officers, employees, or agents; or (b) requiring a party to the contract to purchase a project-specific insurance policy, including but not limited to an owner's and contractor's protective insurance, a project management protective liability insurance, or a builder's risk insurance." MONT. CODE ANN. § 28-2-2111. *See also BNSF Ry. Co. v. Toltz, King, Duvall, Anderson, and Assocs., Inc.*, No. CV 16-24, 2017 U.S. Dist. LEXIS 52148 (D. Mont. Apr. 5, 2017) (addressing various timing issues concerning the applicability of § 28–2-2111, which was enacted on July 1, 2003).

Nebraska: Nebraska statute prohibits indemnification for any character of an indemnitee's own negligence: "In the event that a public or private contract or agreement for the construction, alteration, repair, or maintenance of a building, structure, highway bridge, viaduct, water, sewer, or gas distribution system, or other work dealing with construction or for any moving, demolition, or excavation connected with such construction contains a covenant, promise, agreement, or combination thereof to indemnify or hold harmless another person from such person's own negligence, then such covenant, promise, agreement, or combination thereof shall be void as against public policy and wholly unenforceable. This subsection shall not apply to construction bonds or insurance contracts or agreements." NEB. REV. STAT. ANN. § 25–21,187(1). NEB. REV. STAT. ANN. § 25–21,187(2) addresses protections for architects, engineers and surveyors; *Kuhn v. Wells Fargo Bank of Nebraska, N.A.*, 771 N.W.2d 103, 117 (Neb. 2009) ("Statutes like § 25–21,187(1) are not uncommon, but are generally applied to construction contracts. The purpose of such statutes is to prohibit avoidance by parties to construction contracts of all risks created by their own fault associated with contract performance, to require employers to provide employees with a safe place to work, and to preclude delegating to subcontractors such duty.") (holding that "maintenance of a building," within the meaning of § 25–21,187(1), does not encompass the ordinary activities associated with management of commercial property); *Greis Trucking & Excavating, Inc. v. Union Pac. R.R. Co.*, No. 12CV3160, 2013 U.S. Dist. LEXIS 193501 (D. Neb. May 28, 2013) ("On the present record, the court cannot determine either the scope of the indemnification provision or whether the indemnification provision is void and unenforceable pursuant to Neb. Rev. Stat. § 25-21,187(1). Genuine issues with respect to several underlying facts make it inappropriate for the court to rule as a matter of law at this time. For example, the parties disagree about whether the contact at issue is a construction contract that is governed by the anti-indemnity statute. The type of work that is the subject of the contract is not defined. The contract indicates that the work to be performed under the contract is listed in an attachment, but no document is attached. Also, there are genuine issues of fact with respect to the interplay between the indemnity provision and the insurance procurement provision of the contract. The court cannot determine whether the indemnification provision, in the context of the contract's additional requirement that Greis procure insurance, falls within the statute's exception for 'construction bonds or insurance agreements.'"); *GGA-PC v. Performance Eng'g., Inc.*, No. 16-567, 2017 U.S. Dist. LEXIS 226650 (D. Neb. Dec. 5, 2017) (holding that a limitation of liability clause constitutes an indemnity and is therefore void under § 25-21,187(1)) ("Plaintiff contends that allowing enforcement of this liability provision makes someone other than the defendants bear most of the loss caused by the defendants' negligence. The total alleged loss is $225,000, and if the limitation of liability is upheld, defendants would only be liable for $50,000.").

Nevada: The Supreme Court of Nevada held that an indemnitee may be indemnified for its own negligence provided that the contractual obligation is sufficiently explicit. *Brown Ins. Agency v. Star Ins. Co.*, 237 P.3d 92, 96 (Nev. 2010) ("Where the indemnification clause does not specifically and expressly include indemnity for the indemnitee's own negligence, an indemnification clause 'for any and all liability' will not indemnify the indemnitee's own negligence."). The court rejected what it called the "modern minority rule," which provides that "an indemnity provision 'for any and all liability' means *all* liability, including that arising from the indemnitee's concurrent negligence." *Id.* at 96–97 (citation omitted and emphasis in original). "The rationale behind the minority view is that such indemnity contracts are so common in the modern business world that courts should leave the parties with their bargain for 'any and all liability.'" *Id.* (citations omitted). The court concluded that the majority rule provides clarity and fairness to the parties, while the modern minority rule "allows for too much to be read into the terms of a contract that the parties may not have intended and could substantially benefit one party to the extreme detriment of the other." *Id.* at 97. *See also Reyburn Lawn & Landscape Designers, Inc. v. Plaster Dev. Co.*, 255 P.3d 268, 275 (Nev. 2011) ("According to the indemnity clause at issue here, Plaster must be indemnified for 'any and all' liabilities that aris[e] directly or indirectly out of Reyburn's obligations under the subcontract. Consistent with our holding in *Brown*, we determine that this phrasing does not unequivocally condition Reyburn's duty to indemnify Plaster upon anything other than Reyburn's actions, and it does not explicitly state that Reyburn has to indemnify Plaster for Plaster's own negligence. Because the clause at issue here is not explicit, and because we must strictly construe the indemnity clause's language, [citing *Brown*], we conclude that there must be a showing of negligence on Reyburn's part prior to triggering Reyburn's duty to indemnify Plaster.") (citations and internal quotes omitted) (alteration in original); *United Rentals Hwy. Techs. v. Wells Cargo*, 289 P.3d 221 (Nev. 2012) (holding that the "'to the extent caused' language in an indemnification clause must be strictly construed as limiting an indemnitor's liability to cover the indemnitee's losses only to the extent the injuries were caused by the indemnitor"); *Halpern v. Edge Grp., LLC*, No. 57489, 2013 Nev. Unpub. LEXIS 2007 (Nev. Mar. 21, 2013) ("Here, the indemnity provision requires Halpern to indemnify Edge 'against any and all claims, . . . arising from any claims made by Jeffers Mangels Butler & Marmarro LLP, Alec Glasser, Brian Roche, [and] Roche Group LLC.' Halpern relies on *Brown* and *Reyburn* to argue that this indemnity provision is not sufficiently explicit to provide indemnification for Edge's negligence. Halpern contends that the indemnity provision in its settlement agreement with Edge is of the same broad and general nature as the provisions that this court concluded, in *Brown* and *Reyburn*, were insufficient without an explicit statement of intent to indemnify an indemnitee against its own negligence. We agree and conclude that the indemnity provision here does not explicitly state Halpern's intent to indemnify Edge for its own wrongdoing."); *Demars v. Simco*, No. CV14-02265, 2018 Nev. Dist. LEXIS 1136 (Nev. Dist. Ct. Nov. 8, 2018) ("Nevada law is clear, 'contracts purporting to indemnify a party against its own negligence will only be enforced if they clearly express such an intent and a general provision indemnifying the indemnitee against any and all claims, standing alone, is insufficient.'") (quoting *Reyburn*).

New Hampshire: The Supreme Court of New Hampshire held that an indemnitee may be indemnified for its own negligence provided that the contractual obligation is sufficiently explicit. *Merrimack Sch. Dist. v. Nat'l Sch. Bus Serv.*, 661 A.2d

1197, 1199 (N.H. 1995) ("[I]ndemnity agreements are strictly construed, particularly when they purport to shift responsibility for an individual's own negligence to another. The indemnity provision, however, need not state explicitly the parties' intent to provide indemnity for the negligence of another. Express language is not necessary where the parties' intention to afford protection for another's negligence is clearly evident.") (internal quotation and citation omitted); *see also Kessler v. Gleich*, 13 A.3d 109, 111 (N.H. 2010) (holding that the indemnification provision at issue did not require indemnity for attorney's fees and costs incurred in bringing an action because it did not specify that such fees and costs are recoverable in an action between the parties) ("We align ourselves with those courts that will not infer a party's intention to waive the benefit of the general rule that parties are responsible for their own legal fees unless the intention to do so is unmistakably clear from the language of the promise."); *Penta Corp. v. Town of Newport*, No. 212-2015-CV-00011, 2016 N.H. Super. LEXIS 7 (N.H. Sup. Ct. May 11, 2016) ("[I]indemnity agreements are strictly construed, particularly when they purport to shift responsibility for an individual's own negligence to another. New Hampshire courts apply the general rules of contract interpretation to express indemnity agreements. Courts must look to the parties intent at the time the agreement was made, considering the written agreement, all its provisions, its subject matter, the situation of the parties at the time the agreement was entered into, and the object intended. Courts assign the words and phrases used by the parties the common meaning that would be given to them by a reasonable person.") (citations and internal quotes omitted); *Perry v. SNH Dev.*, No. 2015-00678, 2017 N.H. Super. LEXIS 32 (N.H. Super. Ct. Sept. 13, 2017) (indemnity agreements interpreted in the same manner as contracts generally, except they "are strictly construed, particularly when they purport to shift responsibility for an individual's own negligence to another") (quoting *Merrimack Sch. Dist.*).

New Jersey: New Jersey statute prohibits indemnification for an indemnitee's sole negligence: "A covenant, promise, agreement or understanding in, or in connection with or collateral to a contract, agreement or purchase order, relative to the construction, alteration, repair, maintenance, servicing, or security of a building, structure, highway, railroad, appurtenance and appliance, including moving, demolition, excavating, grading, clearing, site preparation or development of real property connected therewith, purporting to indemnify or hold harmless the promisee against liability for damages arising out of bodily injury to persons or damage to property caused by or resulting from the sole negligence of the promisee, his agents, or employees, is against public policy and is void and unenforceable; provided that this section shall not affect the validity of any insurance contract, workmen's compensation or agreement issued by an authorized insurer." N.J. Stat. Ann. § 2A:40A-1; *see also Twp. of Lakewood v. Epic Mgmt., Inc.*, 2009 N.J. Super. Unpub. LEXIS 1906 (N.J. Super. Ct. App. Div. July 20, 2009) ("[T]here is no essential public policy impediment to an indemnitor undertaking to indemnify the indemnitee in respect of the indemnitee's own negligence. Even in the context of an indemnity agreement in a construction contract, it is not against public policy for the indemnitor to promise to hold harmless the indemnitee for the indemnitee's own negligence as long as the indemnitee is not solely at fault. This principle derives from the judicial recognition that ordinarily the financial responsibility for the risk of injury during the course of a construction project is shifted in any event by the primary parties to their insurance carriers. The impact of the indemnity agreement is therefore, in practical effect, the parties' allocation between themselves of the total required insurance protection for the project. The parties ought to be free to determine how the insurance burdens will be distributed between them and who will pay for specific coverage for specific risks.") (citations and internal quotations omitted); *Shannon v. B.L. England Generating Station*, No. 10–04524, 2013 U.S. Dist. LEXIS 168715 (D.N.J. Nov. 27, 2013) ("[W]here the New Jersey anti-indemnity statute prohibits an owner from seeking indemnification from a contractor for its own negligence absent clear and unequivocal language, it cannot achieve a different result by requiring the contractor to procure insurance for the same indemnity obligation. This would frustrate the public policy underlying the anti-indemnity statute. The aim of the statute is evidently to ensure that an indemnified party continues to have an interest in avoiding accidents. To allow indemnification by insurance would be to accomplish indirectly what is directly prohibited."); *Andalora v. R.D. Mech. Corp.*, 152 A.3d 968 (N.J. Super. App. Div. 2017) ("The clause provided that it was to be construed as broadly as permitted under the 'applicable law.' In New Jersey, the outer limit of such an indemnification clause is set by N.J.S.A. 2A:40A-1, which prohibits indemnification of a party for its sole negligence."); *Melon v. Highview Star Props.*, No. BER-L-6291-15, 2018 N.J. Super. Unpub. LEXIS 3257 (N.J. Super. Ct. Law Div. Aug. 17, 2018) ("The parties here were free to negotiate the allocation of liability, which they did. Highview and Garden State unambiguously agreed Garden State would not be held liable for a finding of negligence on the part of Highview, in accordance with N.J.S.A. 2a:40A-1.").

New Mexico: New Mexico statute prohibits indemnification for any character of an indemnitee's own negligence: "A provision in a construction contract that requires one party to the contract to indemnify, hold harmless, insure or defend the other party to the contract, including the other party's employees or agents, against liability, claims, damages, losses or expenses, including attorney fees, arising out of bodily injury to persons or damage to property caused by or resulting from, in whole or in part, the negligence, act or omission of the indemnitee, its officers, employees or agents, is void, unenforceable and against the public policy of the state." N. M. S. A. 1978, § 56–7-1 A. "A construction contract may contain a provision that, or shall be enforced only to the extent that, it (1) requires one party to the contract to indemnify, hold harmless or insure the other party to the contract, including its officers, employees or agents, against liability, claims, damages, losses or expenses, including attorney fees, only to the extent that the liability, damages, losses or costs are caused by, or arise out of, the acts or omissions of the indemnitor or its officers, employees or agents; or (2) requires a party to the contract to purchase a project-specific insurance policy, including an owner's or contractor's protective insurance, project management protective liability insurance or builder's risk insurance." N. M. S. A. 1978, § 56–7-1 B. "This section does not apply to indemnity of a surety by a principal on any surety bond or to an insurer's obligation to its insureds." N. M. S. A. 1978, § 56–7-1 C. *See also Holguin v. Fulco Oil Servs. L.L.C.*, 245 P.3d 42, 50 (N.M. 2010) ("The indemnity clause in each Service Contract states that the Contractors will indemnify Southern Union against all claims arising out of the performance of the Contractor's work 'caused in whole or in part by any act or omission, including negligence, of the Contractor, … even if it is caused in part by the negligence or omission of any indemnitee.' As we have held above, the last segment of this clause violates Section 56-7-1 (A) by requiring the Contractors to indemnify Southern Union for Southern Union's own negligence, therefore, that provision of the indemnity clause is void and unenforceable. Under Section 56-7-1(B), however, the remainder of the indemnity clause that provides that the Contractors will indemnify Southern Union for claims based on the Contractors' negligence is enforceable."); *United Rentals Northwest, Inc. v. Yearout Mechanical, Inc.*, 237 P.3d 728 (N.M. 2010) (holding that statute's anti-indemnity protections apply to rental contracts for construction equipment because they are contracts "relating to construction.") (containing lengthy discussion of history and purpose of state's anti-indemnity statute); *Safeway, Inc. v. Rooter 2000 Plumbing & Drain SSS*, 368 P.3d 389 (N.M. 2016) ("The indemnification provision in this case is statutorily void and unenforceable because it requires Rooter to indemnify Safeway for Safeway's own negligence. Similarly, as a matter of both law and policy, Rooter should not have to pay for Safeway's legal defense caused by Safeway's own fault where Rooter settled with Plaintiffs for its share of fault."); *First Mercury Ins. Co. v. Cincinnati Ins. Co.*, 14-01052, 2016 U.S. Dist. LEXIS 140970 (D.N.M. Sept. 27, 2016) (addressing in detail the insurance exception to the statute), *aff'd* 882 F.3d 1289 (10th Cir. 2018) ("Because the Subcontract Agreement's provisions requiring High Desert to name Bingham as an additional insured fall within the exception listed in § 56-7-1(B)(2) as a construction contract requiring a party to purchase a project-specific insurance policy, the provisions are valid under New Mexico law. Thus, Bingham is an additional insured under the First Mercury Policy.").

New York: New York statute prohibits indemnification for any character of an indemnitee's own negligence: "1. A covenant, promise, agreement or understanding in, or in connection with or collateral to a contract or agreement relative to the construction, alteration, repair or maintenance of a building, structure, appurtenances and appliances including moving, demolition and excavating connected therewith, purporting to indemnify or hold harmless the promisee against liability for damage arising out of bodily injury to persons or damage to property contributed to, caused by or resulting from the negligence of the promisee, his agents or employees, or indemnitee, whether such negligence be in whole or in part, is against public policy and is void and unenforceable; provided that this section shall not affect the validity of any insurance contract, workers' compensation agreement or other agreement issued by an admitted insurer. This subdivision shall not preclude a promisee requiring indemnification for damages arising out of bodily injury to persons or damage to property caused by or resulting from the negligence of a party other than the promisee, whether or not the promisor is partially negligent." N.Y. GEN. OBLIG. § 5–322.1; *see also Itri Brick & Concrete Corp. v. Aetna Cas. & Sur. Co.*, 680 N.E.2d 1200, 1204 (N.Y. 1997) ("The purpose of this provision [§ 5–322.1] was to prevent a prevalent practice in the construction industry of requiring subcontractors to assume liability by contract for the negligence of others. The Legislature concluded that such 'coercive' bidding requirements unnecessarily increased the cost of construction by limiting the number of contractors able to obtain the necessary hold harmless insurance, and unfairly imposed liability on subcontractors for the negligence of others over whom they had no control. The agreements also needlessly created expensive double coverage for hold harmless or general liability insurance."); *Brooks v. Judlau Contracting, Inc.*, 898 N.E.2d 549, 550 (N.Y. 2008) (holding that Section 5–322.1 allows a general contractor—who has been found to be partially at fault—to enforce an indemnification provision against its subcontractor for that portion of damages attributable to the negligence of the subcontractor, so long as the indemnification provision does not purport to indemnify the general contractor for its own negligence); *Port Parties, Ltd. v. Merchandise Mart Properties, Inc.*, 959 N.Y.S.2d 37 (N.Y. App. Div. 2013) ("In the absence of the insurance policy Merchandise Mart was supposed to obtain, the subject indemnification provision does not have the favorable effect of allocating loss for the purpose of placing the risk on the party with insurance coverage. Relief from the bar against exemption from liability for a party's own negligent acts (General Obligations Law §§ 5-322, 5-322.1, 5-323, 5-325) is granted only where recovery against the negligent party is obviated by the availability of adequate insurance. Since the effect of enforcing the indemnification provision in the instant matter would be to exempt Port Parties from liability for an injury that was concededly caused by its own negligence without the commensurate protection afforded by insurance coverage, the indemnification provision is void and unenforceable."); *Guryev v. Tomchinsky*, 981 N.Y.S.2d 429 (N.Y. App. Div. 2014) ("Tomchinsky's contention that the contractual indemnification clause violated General Obligations Law § 5-322.1 is without merit. The terms of the indemnification clause did not require Tomchinsky to indemnify the Condominium defendants for their own negligence. Moreover, since the Condominium defendants have established their freedom from negligence, the contractual indemnification agreement, as applied, does not run afoul of the proscriptions of General Obligations Law § 5-322.1."); *Clavin v CAP Equip. Leasing Corp.*, No. 4907, 20292/15E, 2017 N.Y. App. Div. LEXIS 8538 (N.Y. App. Div. Dec. 5, 2017) ("The sole potential basis for liability against the contractual indemnitee CAP Rents is for common-law negligence. If CAP Rents was found to be negligent at trial, the indemnification clause would become unenforceable under GOL § 5-322.1, since it would indemnify CAP Rents for its own negligence. Alternatively, if CAP Rents were found not negligent, there would be no basis to seek contractual indemnification. Because there is no outcome that would entitle CAP Rents to contractual indemnification, summary judgment is warranted."); *Fedrich v Granite Bldg. 2, LLC*, 86 N.Y.S.3d 566 (N.Y. App. Div. 2018) ("STAT demonstrated that Granite and Kulka had certain responsibilities with respect to the removal of the construction debris and, thus, that they would not be able to prove themselves free from negligence in the event that the injured plaintiff was successful on his claims against Granite.") (citing § 5-322.1 and *Itri Brick*); *Farrugia v 1440 Broadway Assoc.*, 82 N.Y.S.3d 1 (N.Y. App. Div. 2018)

("[T]he indemnification provision does not run afoul of General Obligations Law § 5-322.1 because the limitation it contains ('To The Fullest Extent Permitted By Law') obligates Harbour to only indemnify the owner to the extent that plaintiff's accident arose out of Harbour's and its contractor's work, except for that percentage of negligence attributable to the owner. Consequently, the owner will not be indemnified for its own negligence."). In general, there is a substantial body of New York case law, particularly from the N.Y. Supreme Court, addressing § 5-322.1.

North Carolina: North Carolina statute prohibits indemnification for any character of an indemnitee's own negligence: "Any promise or agreement in, or in connection with, a contract or agreement relative to the design, planning, construction, alteration, repair or maintenance of a building, structure, highway, road, appurtenance or appliance, including moving, demolition and excavating connected therewith, purporting to indemnify or hold harmless the promisee, the promisee's independent contractors, agents, employees, or indemnitees against liability for damages arising out of bodily injury to persons or damage to property proximately caused by or resulting from the negligence, in whole or in part, of the promisee, its independent contractors, agents, employees, or indemnitees, is against public policy and is void and unenforceable. Nothing contained in this section shall prevent or prohibit a contract, promise or agreement whereby a promisor shall indemnify or hold harmless any promisee or the promisee's independent contractors, agents, employees or indemnitees against liability for damages resulting from the sole negligence of the promisor, its agents or employees. This section shall not affect an insurance contract, workers' compensation, or any other agreement issued by an insurer." N.C. GEN. STAT. § 22B-1; *see also One Beacon Ins. Co. v. United Mech. Corp.*, 700 S.E.2d 121 (N.C. Ct. App. 2010) (addressing § 22B-1) (holding that putative indemnitee failed to allege facts or forecast any evidence to support a finding that the claim for which it sought to be indemnified stemmed from the indemnitor's acts or omissions); *Weaver Cooke Constr., LLC v. Stock Bldg. Supply, LLC*, No. 14-CV-537, 2016 U.S. Dist. LEXIS 109490 (E.D.N.C. Aug. 12, 2016) ("If a phrase or portion of an indemnification provision violates § 22B-1, the offensive language may be redacted and the remaining language enforced."); *New Bern Riverfront Dev., LLC v. Weaver Cooke Constr., LLC*, 09-10340-8, 2018 Bankr. LEXIS 3999 (E.D.N.C. Bkcy. Ct. Dec. 19, 2018) ("Curenton has solidly established that Weaver Cooke bears at least partial responsibility for the very damages for which it would seek indemnity from Curenton. To permit Weaver Cooke to require Curenton to indemnify it for damages for which Weaver Cooke indisputable was partially responsible would ignore both the language and purpose of § 22B-1; indeed, it would be as if the statute, and the public policy it seeks to protect, did not exist.").

For purposes of contracts entered into, amended, or renewed on or after August 1, 2019, § 22B-1 provides as follows: "(a) Provisions in, or in connection with, a construction agreement or design professional agreement purporting to require a promisor to indemnify or hold harmless the promisee, the promisee's independent contractors, agents, employees, or indemnitees against liability for damages arising out of bodily injury to persons or damage to property proximately caused by or resulting from the negligence, in whole or in part, of the promisee, its independent contractors, agents, employees, or indemnitees, is against public policy, void and unenforceable. Nothing contained in this subsection shall prevent or prohibit a contract, promise or agreement whereby a promisor shall indemnify or hold harmless any promisee or the promisee's independent contractors, agents, employees or indemnitees against liability for damages resulting from the sole negligence of the promisor, its agents or employees. (b) Provisions in, or in connection with, a construction agreement or design professional agreement purporting to require a promisor to indemnify or hold harmless the promisee, the promisee's independent contractors, agents, employees, indemnitees, or any other person or entity against losses, damages, or expenses are against public policy, void, and unenforceable unless the fault of the promisor or its derivative parties is a proximate cause of the loss, damage, or expense indemnified."

North Dakota: The Supreme Court of North Dakota held that an indemnitee may be indemnified for its own negligence under certain circumstances. "It is almost universally held that an indemnity agreement will not be interpreted to indemnify a party against the consequences of his own negligence unless that construction is very clearly intended." *Bridston v. Dover Corp.*, 352 N.W.2d 194, 196 (N.D. 1984). Following a review of several Supreme Court of North Dakota decisions, the Eighth Circuit Court of Appeals concluded that "the general rule emerges that when an indemnity agreement contains both hold harmless and insurance provisions, the parties clearly intend that the indemnitee will be indemnified against the consequences of its own negligence." *Myers v. ANR Pipeline Co.*, 959 F.2d 1443, 1448 (8th Cir. 1992) (internal quotation omitted); *see Bridston*, 352 N.W.2d at 196 ("The requirement that the YMCA obtain liability insurance in an amount satisfactory to UND is clearly meant to provide further assurance to UND of indemnity from the YMCA in the event an action is brought against the UND for the negligent acts of either or both UND and YMCA.") (internal quotation omitted); *Chapman v. Hiland Partners GP Holdings, LLC*, 49 F. Supp. 3d 649 (D.N.D. 2014) (examining various contractual language in detail to determine if it satisfies the requirements for a party to be indemnified for its own negligence); *Peterson v. Murex Petro. Corp.*, No. 17-165, 2019 U.S. Dist. LEXIS 149552 (D.N.D. Apr. 10, 2019) (rejecting argument that *Bridston* and *Rupp v. American Crystal Sugar, Co.*, 465 N.W.2d 614 (N.D. 1991) set out requirements "that must be satisfied before a court can conclude that contracting parties have clearly intended to provide indemnity to an indemnitee for its own negligence" when the contractual language at issue "expressly provides for indemnification for the indemnitee's own negligence").

Ohio: Ohio statute prohibits indemnification for any character of an indemnitee's own negligence: "A covenant, promise, agreement, or understanding in, or in connection with or collateral to, a contract or agreement relative to the design, planning, construction, alteration, repair, or maintenance of a building, structure, highway, road, appurtenance, and appliance, including moving, demolition, and excavating connected therewith, pursuant to which contract or agreement the promisee, or its independent contractors, agents or employees has hired the promisor to perform work, purporting to indemnify the promisee, its independent contractors, agents, employees, or indemnities against liability for damages arising out of bodily injury to persons or damage to property initiated or proximately caused by or resulting from the negligence of the promisee, its independent contractors, agents, employees, or indemnities is against public policy and is void. Nothing in this section shall prohibit any person from purchasing insurance from an insurance company authorized to do business in the state of Ohio for his own protection or from purchasing a construction bond." OHIO REV. CODE ANN. 2305.31. *See also Kemmeter v. McDaniel Backhoe Serv.*, 732 N.E.2d 385 (Ohio 2000) ("The public policy at the heart of the statute is to make parties responsible for their own negligence. The statute voids contract terms where a promisee attempts to shift responsibility for its negligence to the promisor. Conversely, a contract term that does not address the indemnification of the promisee's own negligence is not affected by the statute.") ("Whether the contract facially violates R.C. 2305.31 or not, the relevant inquiry in a case under this statute is whether a promisor would be indemnifying a promisee for the promisee's own negligence under the contract. The necessary corollary to a prohibition of indemnifying a promisee's negligence is a prohibition of the indemnification of costs associated with a promisee's *alleged* negligence. If a plaintiff alleges negligence against a promisee, a promisor may not agree to undertake the defense costs the promisee incurs in defending itself against claims regarding its own negligence.") (emphasis in original); *Cleveland v. Vandra Bros. Constr., Inc.*, 948 N.E.2d 1027 (Ohio. Ct. App. 2011) ("In the instant case, the Dawsons' complaint alleges negligence against the city and Vandra. The city's contract with Vandra provides that Vandra shall indemnify, defend, and hold the city harmless against all claims occurring during the performance of the contract. A review of the record reveals that the potholes James hit were existing potholes not caused by Vandra. The city failed to support its motion for summary judgment with any evidence that Vandra's negligence caused the accident. Furthermore, R.C. 2305.31 prohibits the city from seeking indemnification from Vandra for damages caused by or resulting from the city's negligence of the promisee, regardless of whether such negligence is sole or concurrent. Because there is no genuine issue of fact with respect to Vandra's negligence and the indemnification agreement is void, the city's indemnification claim against Vandra must fail.").

Oklahoma: Oklahoma statute addresses indemnification for an indemnitee's own negligence: "Except as provided in subsection C or D of this section, any provision in a construction agreement that requires an entity or that entity's surety or insurer to indemnify, insure, defend or hold harmless another entity against liability for damage arising out of death or bodily injury to persons, or damage to property, which arises out of the negligence or fault of the indemnitee, its agents, representatives, subcontractors, or suppliers, is void and unenforceable as against public policy. C. The provisions of this section do not affect any provision in a construction agreement that requires an entity or that entity's surety or insurer to indemnify another entity against liability for damage arising out of death or bodily injury to persons, or damage to property, but such indemnification shall not exceed any amounts that are greater than that represented by the degree or percentage of negligence or fault attributable to the indemnitor, its agents, representatives, subcontractors, or suppliers. D. This section shall not apply to construction bonds nor to contract clauses which require an entity to purchase a project-specific insurance policy, including owners' and contractors' protective liability insurance, project management protective liability insurance, or builder's risk insurance." 15 Okl. St. Ann. § 221. *See also BITCO Gen. Ins. Corp. v. Wynn Construction Co.*, No. 17-462, 2017 U.S. Dist. LEXIS 127848 (W.D. Okla. Aug. 11, 2017) ("Plaintiff asserts that § 221(B) specifically prohibits and voids any additional insured coverage for Nabholz and any duty to defend Nabholz under plaintiff's insurance contracts issued to Wynn for damages arising out of Nabholz's own negligence or fault. Having reviewed Nabholz's counterclaim, the Court finds that Nabholz has alleged that its damages arise, in part, out of the work or operations performed by Wynn and, thus, is seeking damages based upon Nabholz's alleged vicarious liability for the alleged negligence of Wynn. Because Nabholz alleges that plaintiff's duty to defend arises, in part, out of Wynn's alleged negligence or fault, the Court finds that § 221(B) does not completely bar any duty to defend Nabholz under plaintiff's insurance contracts and that Nabholz's breach of contract and bad faith claims to the extent they are premised upon an alleged breach of a duty to defend should not be dismissed."); *BITCO Gen. Ins. Corp. v. Commerce & Industry Ins. Co.*, No. 15-206, 2017 U.S. Dist. LEXIS 29292 (W.D. Okla. Mar. 7, 2017) ("[T]he Court finds that subsection (C) of Oklahoma's anti-indemnity statute would not apply to BITCO's duty to defend as subsection (C) is specifically limited to indemnity and does not include the duty to defend."); *JP Energy Mktg. v. Commerce & Indus. Ins. Co.*, 412 P.3d 121 (Ok. Ct. Civ. App. 2018) ("The plain language of the statute also prohibits contract provisions requiring the indemnitor to insure another entity for liability arising out of the indemnitee's own negligence. See 15 O.S. § 221(B); This includes agreements that the indemnitor will name the indemnitee as an additional insured in the indemnitor's policy or procure additional insured coverage for the indemnitee.") ("The policy does not cover JP against liability for its own negligence. We hold the agreements to name JP as an additional insured in the IPS-Wilcrest Subcontract and the Navigators insurance contract do not violate § 221(B) nor do they conflict with the provisions and intent of Oklahoma's anti-indemnity statute.").

Oregon: Oregon statute prohibits indemnity for any character of an indemnitee's own negligence (as well as additional insured rights): "(1) Except to the extent provided under subsection (2) of this section, any provision in a construction agreement that requires a person or that person's surety or insurer to indemnify another against liability for damage arising out of death or bodily injury to persons or damage to property caused in whole or in part by the negligence of the indemnitee is void. (2) This section does not affect any provision in a construction agreement that requires a person or that person's surety or insurer to indemnify another against liability for damage arising out of death or bodily injury to persons or damage to property to the extent that the death or bodily injury to persons or damage to property arises out of the fault of the indemnitor, or the fault of the indemnitor's agents, representatives or subcontractors." O.R.S. § 30.140. *See also Walsh Const. Co. v. Mutual of Enumclaw*, 104 P.3d 1146, 1150 (Or. 2005) (agreeing with the decision of the Court of Appeals that "[w]hether the shifting allocation of risk is accomplished directly, *e.g.*, by requiring the subcontractor itself to indemnify the contractor for damages caused by the contractor's own negligence, or indirectly, *e.g.*, by requiring the subcontractor to purchase additional insurance covering the contractor for the contractor's own negligence, the ultimate—and [in this respect] statutorily forbidden—end is the same."); *Cont'l Cas. Ins. Co. v. Zurich Am. Ins. Co.,* 402 Fed. Appx. 174, 177 (9th Cir. 2010) ("Here, the plain language of the contractual procure insurance provision limits coverage to liability arising out of Safway's own negligence. Furthermore, even if the provision could be read as improperly requiring Safway to procure insurance covering the upstream contractors for their own negligence, it can still be enforced to the extent it requires coverage for liability arising out of Safway's own negligence. Accordingly, we conclude that § 30.140 does not void Safway's promise to procure insurance.") (citation omitted); *American Hallmark Ins. Co. of Texas v. American Family Mut. Ins. Co.,* No. 09–976, 2011 U.S. Dist LEXIS 60695 (D. Or. June 6, 2011) ("Or. Rev. Stat. § 30.140 was enacted to prevent 'parties with greater leverage in construction agreements (generally, owners and contractors) from shifting exposure for their own negligence-or the costs of insuring against that exposure-to other parties (generally subcontractors) on a 'take-it-or-leave-it' basis." (quoting *Walsh*); *Sec. Nat'l Ins. Co. v. Sunset Presbyterian Church,* No. A156062, 2017 Ore. App. LEXIS 1501 (Or. Ct. App. Dec. 6, 2017) (holding that an insurance clause in a subcontract can be enforced to the extent it does not contravene § 30.140) ("The unlawful potential of such an insurance or indemnity provision can be excised, while the lawful portion can be enforced. To the extent that the insurance provision of the subcontract requires B&B to secure insurance for potential liability to Andersen for B&B's work, there *is* a 'written contract' that requires B&B to have added Andersen to the SNIC policy.") (citation omitted and emphasis in original); *Probuilders Specialty Ins. Co. v. Phoenix Contr., Inc.,* No. 16-cv-00601, 2017 U.S. Dist. LEXIS 2440 (D. Or. Jan. 2, 2017) ("[T]he Contractors Special Conditions require . . . an independent contractor to agree to indemnify the insured for liability arising from the negligence of the independent contractor. There is no conflict between such an indemnification agreement and Oregon law. Indeed, this sort of agreement is contemplated by the statute[.]"); *Portland GE v. Liberty Mut. Ins. Co.,* 112 F. Supp. 3d 1160 (D. Or. 2015) ("Under *Montara Owners Ass'n. [v. La Noue Dev., LLC*, 353 P.3d 563 (Or. 2015)] Plaintiff's contract with NAES is void to the extent it requires NAES to make Plaintiff an additional insured for damages caused by Plaintiff's own negligence, but the contract remains enforceable to the extent that it requires NAES to make Plaintiff an additional insured for damages caused by NAES's negligence."); *First Mercury Ins. Co. v. Westchester Surplus Lines*

Ins. Co., 731 Fed. Appx. 716 (9th Cir. 2018) (indemnity agreement held to be void under § 30.140) ("The County's suggestion that the Agreement was for the sale of goods points to an irrelevancy as far as this custom-made product for incorporation in the Bridge is concerned. The statute makes no such distinction between goods and services. Nor does the statute provide different provisions for a subcontractor who happens to be more financially stable or successful than the contractor itself. The statute speaks to which entity has the authority over awarding the construction work in question. Here, ZellComp, not Strongwell, was that entity.").

Pennsylvania: The Supreme Court of Pennsylvania held that an indemnitee may be indemnified for its own negligence provided that the contractual obligation is sufficiently explicit. *See Bernotas v. Super Fresh Food Mkts., Inc.*, 863 A.2d 478, 482–83 (Pa. 2004) ("It is well-settled in Pennsylvania that provisions to indemnify for another party's negligence are to be narrowly construed, requiring a clear and unequivocal agreement before a party may transfer its liability to another party. *Ruzzi v. Butler Petroleum Co.*, 588 A.2d 1, 7 (Pa. 1991); *Perry v. Payne*, 66 A. 553 (Pa. 1907). Accordingly, indemnification provisions are given effect only when clearly and explicitly stated in the contract between two parties."). "No inference from words of general import can establish such indemnification." *Ruzzi*, 588 A.2d at 4; *see also Bernotas* at 484 ("[U]nless expressly stated, pass through indemnification clauses violate the long standing policy underlying the rule narrowly construing indemnification provisions. When the provision sought to be 'passed through' involves indemnification for acts of another party's negligence, the theory will not be applied, unless the contract language is clear and specific. Sound public policy requires an unequivocally stated intention to be included in the subcontract for this particular type of provision to pass through from the general contract. The general language of a standard incorporation clause cannot trump the specific language of the subcontract, when the former supports indemnification for negligent acts but the latter is ambiguous regarding the circumstances under which indemnification will occur."); *Lane v. Commonwealth of Pa.*, 954 A.2d 615, 624–25 (Pa. Super. Ct. 2008) ("[W]e conclude that the language of this contract established that Appellee's indemnification obligation does not extend to injuries or claims that bore no relation to its work. The circumstances surrounding this contract support this interpretation. Appellee is not an insurance company and certainly did not intend to assume liability for all injuries occurring at the construction site regardless of whether its work caused those injuries. Indemnity for another party's negligence causing injuries to persons on the construction site would be a hazard so unusual and extraordinary that Appellee cannot be presumed to have assumed such an obligation absent express language in that regard. The *Perry-Ruzzi* principle applies herein") (addressing history of state's indemnification rules); *Burlington Coat Factory of Pa., LLC v. Grace Constr. Mgmt. Co., LLC,* 126 A.3d 1010 (Pa. Super. Ct. 2015) ("Since Appellants drafted a contract with two conflicting indemnity provisions, we will enforce only the narrower of the two and exclude indemnity for the indemnitee's own negligence."); *Horn v. Schappert,* No. 3202 EDA 2013, 2015 Pa. Super. Unpub. LEXIS 1357 (Pa. Super. Ct. May 13, 2015) ("Pennsylvania law governing the interpretation of clauses that relieve a party of liability for his own negligence is well-settled. When interpreting the validity and enforceability of indemnity clauses Pennsylvania law does not recognize as effective an agreement concerning negligent acts unless an express stipulation concerning the indemnitee's negligence was included in the document. This principle requires that parties employ express terms to indicate that the active negligence of the indemnitee will be assumed by the indemnitor. . . . General language purporting to preclude liability arising from 'any and all acts or omissions' (or similar phrases) is insufficient to protect an indemnitee from his own negligence."); *Frederick Mut. Ins. Co. v. Ahatov,* 274 F. Supp. 3d 273 (E.D. Pa. 2017) ("We find that the Builder's Agreement fails to include the required 'clear and unequivocal language' and as such, the indemnity clause can only be read to require Concept to indemnify Dubinsky for liability imposed upon him for Concept's negligence."); *Air Prods. & Chems., Inc. v. P&G Mfg. Co.,* No. 18-4878, 2019 U.S. Dist. LEXIS 168113 (E.D. Pa. Sept. 30, 2019) (*Perry-Ruzzi* rule not applicable to duty to defend aspect of an indemnity agreement) ("It appears that under Pennsylvania law following *Mace* [*v. Atl. Ref. & Mktg. Corp.,* 785 A.2d 491 (Pa. 2001)], a contractual provision in the non-insurance context that includes an indemnification provision that contains a duty to defend is to be interpreted by general contact principles (including those relevant to indemnification claims)."). *See also* 68 PA. CONS. STAT. ANN. § 491 (prohibiting indemnification of an architect, engineer, surveyor, or his agents, servants, or employees arising out of: (1) the preparation or approval of maps, drawings, opinions, reports, surveys, change orders, designs, or specifications or (2) the giving of or the failure to give directions or instructions by the architect, engineer, surveyor, or his agents, servants, or employees provided such giving or failure to give is the primary cause of the damage, claim, loss or expense).

Rhode Island: Rhode Island statute prohibits indemnification for any character of an indemnitee's own negligence: "(a) A covenant, promise, agreement, or understanding in, or in connection with or collateral to, a contract or agreement relative to the design, planning, construction, alteration, repair, or maintenance of a building, structure, highway, road, appurtenance, and appliance … pursuant to which contract or agreement the promisee … has hired the promisor to perform work, purporting to indemnify the promisee … against liability for damages arising out of bodily injury to persons or damage to property proximately caused by or resulting from the negligence of the promisee … is against public policy and is void; provided that this section shall not affect the validity of any insurance contract, worker's compensation agreement, or an agreement issued by an insurer. (b) Nothing in this section shall prohibit any person from purchasing insurance for his or her own protection or from purchasing a construction bond." R.I. GEN. LAWS § 6–34–1; *see also Rodrigues v. DePasquale Bldg. and Realty Co.*, 926 A.2d 616, 623 (R.I. 2007) ("The clear and direct mandate of § 6-34-1 bars the enforcement of that portion of the indemnification clause that attempts to indemnify [the contractor] for any negligence on its part. However, there is nothing in § 6-34-1 that bars [the contractor] from attempting to secure indemnification from [the subcontractor] for claims resulting from negligence on the part of [the subcontractor].") (quoting *Cosentino v. A.F. Lusi Constr. Co.*, 485 A.2d 105, 107 (R.I.1984)).

South Carolina: South Carolina statute prohibits indemnification for an indemnitee's sole negligence: "Notwithstanding any other provision of law, a promise or agreement in connection with the design, planning, construction, alteration, repair or maintenance of a building, structure, highway, road, appurtenance or appliance … purporting to indemnify the promisee … against liability for damages arising out of bodily injury or property damage proximately caused by or resulting from the sole negligence of the promisee … is against public policy and unenforceable. Nothing contained in this section shall affect a promise or agreement whereby the promisor shall indemnify or hold harmless the promisee … against liability for damages resulting from the negligence, in whole or in part, of the promisor, its agents or employees. The provisions of this section shall not affect any insurance contract or workers' compensation agreements; nor shall it apply to any electric utility, electric cooperative, common carriers by rail and their corporate affiliates or the South Carolina Public Service Authority." S.C. CODE ANN. § 32–2–10; *see also Standard Pac. of the Carolinas, LLC v. Amerisure Ins. Co.*, No. 10-1620, 2011 U.S. Dist. LEXIS 963 (D.S.C. Jan. 5, 2011), *rev'd on other grounds*, 500 Fed. Appx. 237 (4th Cir. 2012) ("This section does not apply to insurance contracts. The plaintiff alleges that this [construction] agreement is an 'insured contract,' making the code section inapplicable. Although no South Carolina cases interpret § 32-2-10 and the agreement discusses the insurance policy the contractor is required to obtain, the agreement was not issued by a licensed insurer and does not likely fit the definition of an 'insurance contract' as contemplated by the statute."); *D.R. Horton, Inc. v. Builders FirstSource - Southeast Grp., LLC*, 810 S.E.2d 41 (S.C. Ct. App. 2018) ("The indemnification agreement in this case purports to require BFS to indemnify D.R. Horton for its own negligence in violation of section 32-2-10. Because the agreement violates the statute, we cannot require BFS to pay for damages caused by D.R.").

South Dakota: South Dakota statute prohibits indemnification for an indemnitee's sole negligence: "A covenant, promise, agreement or understanding in, or in connection with or collateral to, a contract or agreement relative to the construction, alteration, repair or maintenance of a building, structure, appurtenance and appliance, including moving, demolition and excavating connected therewith, purporting to indemnify the promisee against liability for damages arising out of bodily injury to persons or damage to property caused by or resulting from the sole negligence of the promisee, his agents or employees, or indemnitee, is against the policy of the law and is void and unenforceable." S.D. CODIFIED LAWS § 56–3-18; *see also id.* at §§ 56–3-16 and 56–3-17 (limiting the obligations of a contractor for the liability of an architect or engineer); *Chicago & North Western Transp. Co. v. V & R Sawmill, Inc.*, 501 F. Supp. 278 (D.S.D. 1980) ("The situation which was not present in [*Becker v. Central Tel. & Utilities Corp.*, 365 F. Supp. 984 (D.S.D. 1973)]-indemnification by an innocent indemnitor for the sole negligence of the indemnitee-is present in this case. The only negligence upon which an award to Houk could be based is the negligence of Plaintiff. Therefore, S.D.C.L. 56-3-18 would appear to render the indemnification agreement void in this case.").

Tennessee: Tennessee statute prohibits indemnification for an indemnitee's sole negligence: "A covenant promise, agreement or understanding in or in connection with or collateral to a contract or agreement relative to the construction, alteration, repair or maintenance of a building, structure, appurtenance and appliance, including moving, demolition and excavating connected therewith, purporting to indemnify or hold harmless the promisee against liability for damages arising out of bodily injury to persons or damage to property caused by or resulting from the sole negligence of the promisee, the promisee's agents or employees, or indemnitee, is against public policy and is void and unenforceable." TENN. CODE ANN. § 62–6-123; *see also Armoneit v. Elliott Crane Serv., Inc.*, 65 S.W.3d 623, 632 (Tenn. Ct. App. 2001) ("[T]he mere existence of insurance coverage is not enough to save the indemnity provision. Pursuant to Tenn. Code Ann. § 62-6-123, the indemnity provision in Elliott Crane's standard rental agreement is void in its entirety as contrary to public policy."); *Rentenbach Constructors, Inc. v. Bowen*, No. E2000-1213-COA-R3-CV, 2000 Tenn. App. LEXIS 747 (Tenn. Ct. App. Nov. 13, 2000) (holding that indemnity exception for 'sole gross negligence' by the promisee meant that sole simple negligence was not so excepted; therefore, because agreement expressed a clear intent to indemnify for loss occasioned by promisee's sole simple negligence, it was void and unenforceable under § T.C.A. 62-6-123); *Am. Guar. & Liab. Ins. Co. v. Norfolk S. Ry. Co.*, 278 F. Supp. 3d 1025 (E.D. Tenn. 2017) (holding that § 62-6-123 does not apply to contracts for maintenance of railroad crossings or insurance contracts; thus statute inapplicable to whether party can be indemnified for its own negligence as an additional insured); *Trimboli v. Maxim Crane Works, L.P.*, No. 18-00346, 2020 U.S. Dist. LEXIS 36465 (M.D. Tenn. Mar. 3, 2020) ("The Old Hickory Bridge project involved the alteration of a structure—namely, the removal of the unused natural gas pipeline from the bridge—or, if one chooses to characterize it differently, the demolition of the pipeline. An equipment and services agreement related to such a project is well within the plain language of [§ 62–6-123].").

Texas: The Supreme Court of Texas held that an indemnitee may be indemnified for its own negligence provided that the contractual obligation is sufficiently explicit. See *Ethyl Corp. v. Daniel Constr. Co.*, 725 S.W.2d 705, 707–08 (Tex. 1987) (rejecting the clear and unequivocal test in favor of the express negligence doctrine, which provides that parties seeking to indemnify the indemnitee from the consequences of its own negligence must express that intent in specific terms within the four corners of the contract); *see also Cabo Const., Inc. v. R S Clark Const., Inc.*, 227 S.W.3d 314, 317 (Tex. Ct. App. 2007) (holding that, in addition to the express negligence doctrine, a party seeking to be indemnified for its own negligence must also satisfy the conspicuousness requirement, which mandates that the contract language appear in larger type or contrasting colors, or otherwise call attention to itself) (citing *Storage & Processors, Inc. v. Reyes*, 134 S.W.3d 190, 192 (Tex. 2004)) ("However, if both contracting parties have actual knowledge of the plan's terms, an agreement can be enforced even if the fair notice requirements were not satisfied."); *Enron Corp. Sav. Plan v. Hewitt Assocs., L.L.C.*, 611 F. Supp. 2d 654, 674 (S.D. Tex. 2009) ("[W]e are convinced that the requirement of fair notice—both elements, i.e., express negligence and conspicuousness—is irrelevant in the face of Dominion's actual knowledge of the subject provisions of the Contract.") (quoting *Cleere Drilling Co. v. Dominion Exploration & Prod., Inc.*, 351 F.3d 642, 647 (5th Cir. 2003)); *Hamblin v. Lamont*, 433

S.W.3d 51 (Tex. Ct. App. 2013) ("Under the express negligence doctrine, parties seeking to indemnify the indemnitee from the consequences of its own negligence must express that intent in specific terms. Under the doctrine of express negligence, the intent of the parties must be specifically stated within the four corners of the contract.") (discussing *Ethyl*); *Blankenship v. Spectra Energy Corp.*, No. 13–12–00546, 2013 Tex. App. LEXIS 10169 (Tex. Ct. App. Aug. 15, 2013) (noting that "conspicuous" is defined in Texas Business and Commerce Code § 1.201(b)(10) as a term "so written, displayed, or presented that a reasonable person against which it is to operate ought to have noticed it" and the statute provides examples of conspicuous terms); *Safeway, Inc. v. PDX, Inc.*, 676 Fed. Appx. 229 (5th Cir. 2017) ("We have previously stressed that 'broad statements of indemnity' are insufficient to satisfy the express negligence rule. In fact, Texas courts have held insufficient even clauses that provide indemnification 'from and against all claims, damages, losses, and expenses' '[t]o the fullest extent permitted by law.' Moreover, where the intent to indemnify a party for its own negligence can be gleaned from a contract only by implication or deduction, the agreement is not enforceable.") ("Although both the Supreme Court of Texas and our court have suggested that there may be an actual knowledge exception to the express negligence rule, neither has so held. Intermediate courts in Texas are split on the question. We do note that an actual knowledge exception appears inconsistent with the express negligence rule's extremely limited text-based inquiry."); *MEMC Pasadena, Inc. v. Goodgames Indus. Solutions, LLC*, 143 F. Supp. 3d 570 (S.D. Tex. 2015) ("In discussing conspicuousness, the Supreme Court of Texas has held that language in capital headings, language in contrasting type or color, and language in an extremely short document, such as a telegram, is conspicuous. Indemnity provisions not hidden under a separate heading or surrounded by unrelated terms may also be conspicuous. However, provisions located on the back of a work order in a series of numbered paragraphs without headings or contrasting type are not conspicuous. Here, the indemnity provision is identified with a heading in capital letters and appears in a separately numbered paragraph without unrelated terms in it. Accordingly, the Court finds that Section 10 is conspicuous.") (citations omitted); TEX. CIV. PRAC. & REM. CODE ANN. § 130.002 (precluding indemnification in various situations involving registered architects and licensed engineers); *Safeway, Inc. v. PDX, Inc.*, 676 Fed. Appx. 229 (5th Cir. 2017) ("There is no doubt that an indemnitor's actual knowledge of its obligation obviates the need for a court to consider conspicuousness under Texas law.") ("[T]o the extent there is an actual knowledge exception to the express negligence rule, such knowledge must be of the fact that the indemnitee's negligence or strict liability is included in the indemnity obligation . . . [T]he purpose of the express negligence rule is to confirm that those on the hook for another party's negligence are fully aware of the extent of that obligation; an understanding merely that there is *some* obligation is not a valid alternative. Accordingly, Safeway's purported knowledge is no substitute for compliance with the express negligence doctrine.") (emphasis in original); *Pioneer Energy Servs. Corp. v. Burlington Ins. Co.*, No. 14-18-00879, 2020 Tex. App. LEXIS 8528 (Tex. Ct. App. Oct. 29, 2020) ("[W]hen faced with provisions in which the express-negligence test bars indemnity for some claims but not others, we have enforced the indemnity provision for claims within the provision's coverage while barring indemnity for claims outside its coverage.") (addressing satisfaction of conspicuousness test when some factors are in favor of it and other factors are against it).

Utah: Utah statute prohibits indemnification for any character of an indemnitee's own negligence, except for that of an owner in certain circumstances: "(2) Except as provided in Subsection (3), an indemnification provision in a construction contract is against public policy and is void and unenforceable. (3) When an indemnification provision is included in a contract related to a construction project between an owner and party listed in Subsection (1)(a) [construction manager; general contractor; subcontractor; sub-subcontractor; supplier; or any combination of the foregoing], in any action for damages described in Subsection (1)(b)(i) [bodily injury to a person; damage to property; or economic loss], the fault of the owner shall be apportioned among the parties listed in Subsection (1)(a) pro rata based on the proportional share of fault of each of the parties listed in Subsection (1)(a), if: (a) the damages are caused in part by the owner; and (b) the cause of the damages defined in Subsection (1)(b)(i) did not arise at the time and during the phase of the project when the owner was operating as a party defined in Subsection (1)(a)." UTAH CODE ANN. § 13–8-1; *see also Meadow Valley Contractors, Inc. v. Transcon. Ins. Co.*, 27 P.3d 594, 598 (Utah. Ct. App. 2001) ("[T]he insurance provision of the subcontract agreement requires BT Gallegos to procure insurance and to name Meadow Valley as an additional insured. The provision does not, however, require BT Gallegos to personally insure or indemnify Meadow Valley for liability arising out of Meadow Valley's own negligence. Therefore, the insurance provision of the subcontract agreement does not violate section 13–8–1.").

Vermont: The Supreme Court of Vermont held that an indemnitee may be indemnified for its own negligence provided that the contractual obligation is sufficiently explicit. *See Tateosian v. State of Vermont*, 945 A.2d 833, 841 (Vt. 2007) ("[W]e adopt the general rule that an indemnity clause covers the sole negligence of the indemnitee only where it clearly expresses that intent."); *see also Hamelin v. Simpson Paper Co.*, 702 A.2d 86, 88 (Vt. 1997) (finding that the indemnitee could be indemnified because such arrangement was explicitly contemplated in the agreement); *Southwick v. City of Rutland*, 35 A.3d 113 (Vt. 2011) (addressing *Tateosian* and *Hamelin* and holding that an indemnity agreement was unambiguous and sufficiently expressed in terms to enable a party to be indemnified for its own negligence); *Hemond v. Frontier Communs. of Am.*, 122 A.3d 1205 (Vt. 2015) ("[W]e conclude that the indemnity clause in this case is enforceable. Unlike *Tateosian*, where there was a disparity in bargaining power, the agreement in this case was made between two parties in an arm's-length transaction. Further, the language expresses an intent to cover injuries and damages that occur as a result of either party's negligence.") ("In *Southwick*, the contract provision required one defendant, the Vermont Swim Association (VSA), to indemnify the City of Rutland for 'all claims for bodily injury or property damage arising from or out of the presence of [VSA] ... or [VSA]'s activities,' and we concluded that it was deliberately broad enough to cover all injuries and damages that might occur — as a result of either party's negligence.").

Virginia: Virginia statute prohibits indemnification for any character of an indemnitee's own negligence: "Any provision contained in any contract relating to the construction, alteration, repair or maintenance of a building, structure or appurtenance thereto, including moving, demolition and excavation connected therewith, or any provision contained in any contract relating to the construction of projects other than buildings by which the contractor performing such work purports to indemnify or hold harmless another party to the contract against liability for damage arising out of bodily injury to persons or damage to property suffered in the course of performance of the contract, caused by or resulting solely from the negligence of such other party or his agents or employees, is against public policy and is void and unenforceable. This section applies to such contracts between contractors and any public body, as defined in § 2.2–4301. This section shall not affect the validity of any insurance contract, workers' compensation, or any agreement issued by an admitted insurer." Va. Code Ann. § 11–4.1 (2009); *see also* Va. Code Ann. § 11-4.4 (addressing the enforceability of indemnification provisions in private and public contracts with design professionals). In *Uniwest Const., Inc. v. Amtech Elevator Servs., Inc.*, 699 S.E.2d 223 (Va. 2010), the Supreme

Court of Virginia interpreted § 11–4.1 to prohibit indemnification for any character of an indemnitee's own negligence. The court held: "Because the phrases 'caused by' and 'resulting solely from' are disjunctive in the statute, it voids any indemnification provision that reaches damage caused by the negligence of the indemnitee, even if the damage does not result solely from the negligence of the indemnitee. Thus, the issue is not whether an indemnification provision is written so broadly that it encompasses the negligence of parties in addition to the indemnitee. Rather, the issue is whether the provision is so broad that it indemnifies the indemnitee from its own negligence." *Id.* at 230. While the court's opinion was subsequently withdrawn in part, it did not include its interpretation of § 11–4.1. *Uniwest Const., Inc. v. Amtech Elevator Servs., Inc.*, 714 S.E.2d 560 (Va. 2011). *See also Supchak v. Fuller Const. Corp.*, No. CL10–1999, 2013 Va. Cir. LEXIS 75 (Va. Cir. Ct. July 12, 2013) ("[I]n this case, it appears that Fuller is attempting to indemnify itself for its own negligence in Section 7 of the Subcontract with Westcon and Article 4.6.1 of the Subcontract with G & B. The language in the indemnification clause in *Uniwest* and the subject provisions here is almost identical. Like in *Uniwest*, the subject provisions require the indemnitor to indemnify the indemnitee regardless of whether the indemnitee's own negligence caused the claim. The language of Section 7 and Article 4.6.1 reaches beyond the negligence of other parties and indemnifies Fuller. As such, the subject provisions violate Va. Code Ann. § 11–4 .1 and are void."); *Allstate Ins. Co. v. Structures Design/Build, LLC*, No. 15-00354, 2016 U.S. Dist. LEXIS 34349 (W.D. Va. Mar. 17, 2016) ("The disputed language in the subcontract provides that the 'Subcontractor agrees to save, indemnify and hold Contractor harmless against any and all liability, claims, judgments, or demands, ... including losses arising from indemnitee's own negligence, active or passive[.]' The court believes that the plain language in this provision clearly requires PJ Little to indemnify Structures, even for claims arising solely from Structures' own negligence. Because Virginia law voids any provision that reaches damage caused by the negligence of the indemnitee, even if the damage does not result solely from the negligence of the indemnitee, the court concludes that this language in the subcontract conflicts with the public policy expressed in § 11-4.1 and is void."); *RSC Equip. Rental, Inc. v. Cincinnati Ins. Co.*, 54 F. Supp. 3d 480 (W.D. Va. 2014) (concluding that § 11–4.1 not applicable because the contract at issue was a rental agreement and not a construction contract); *Travelers Indem. Co. v. Lessard Design, Inc.*, 321 F. Supp. 3d 631 (E.D. Va. 2018) (indemnification provision that required contractor to indemnify owner for owner's sole negligence void pursuant to § 11-4.1; based on *Uniwest*, clause must be invalidated in its entirety); *Hellas Constr., Inc. v. Bayside Concrete, Inc.*, No. 18-553, 2019 U.S. Dist. LEXIS 234348 (E.D. Va. Mar. 12, 2019) ("Here, the plain meaning of the indemnification subparagraphs exclude indemnification for Hellas' sole negligence; they do not exclude indemnification for Hellas' *contributory* negligence. Because the Subcontract may cover any degree of negligence by Hellas, it is void under Va. Code § 11-4.1.") (emphasis in original).

Washington: Washington statute prohibits indemnification for any character of an indemnitee's own negligence: "(1) A covenant, promise, agreement or understanding in, or in connection with or collateral to, a contract or agreement relative to the construction, alteration, repair, addition to, subtraction from, improvement to, or maintenance of, any building, highway, road, railroad, excavation, or other structure, project, development, or improvement attached to real estate, including moving and demolition in connection therewith, a contract or agreement for architectural, landscape architectural, engineering, or land surveying services, or a motor carrier transportation contract, purporting to indemnify, including the duty and cost to defend, against liability for damages arising out of such services or out of bodily injury to persons or damage to property: (a) Caused by or resulting from the sole negligence of the indemnitee, his agents or employees is against public policy and is void and unenforceable; (b) Caused by or resulting from the concurrent negligence of (i) the indemnitee or the indemnitee's agents or employees, and (ii) the indemnitor or the indemnitor's agents or employees, is valid and enforceable only to the extent of the indemnitor's negligence and only if the agreement specifically and expressly provides therefor, and may waive the indemnitor's immunity under industrial insurance, Title 51 RCW, only if the agreement specifically and expressly provides therefor and the waiver was mutually negotiated by the parties. This subsection applies to agreements entered into after June 11, 1986." Wash. Rev. Code Ann. § 4.24.115. *See Millican v. N.A. Degerstrom, Inc.*, 313 P.3d 1215 (Wash. Ct. App. 2013) (noting that, under § 4.24.115, a subcontractor is only permitted to indemnify the general contractor to the extent of the subcontractor's negligence).

West Virginia: West Virginia statute prohibits indemnification for an indemnitee's sole negligence: "A covenant, promise, agreement or understanding in or in connection with or collateral to a contract or agreement entered into on or after the effective date of this section, relative to the construction, alteration, repair, addition to, subtraction from, improvement to or maintenance of any building, highway, road, railroad, water, sewer, electrical or gas distribution system, excavation or other structure, project, development or improvement attached to real estate, including moving and demolition in connection therewith, purporting to indemnify against liability for damages arising out of bodily injury to persons or damage to property caused by or resulting from the sole negligence of the indemnitee, his agents or employees is against public policy and is void and unenforceable and no action shall be maintained thereon. This section does not apply to construction bonds or insurance contracts or agreements." W. VA. CODE ANN. § 55–8-14. However, indemnification for an indemnitee's sole negligence is permitted if it can be "inferred from the contract that there was a proper agreement to purchase insurance for the benefit of all concerned." *Dalton v. Childress Serv. Corp.*, 432 S.E.2d 98, 101 (W. Va. 1993) ("It would be silly for us to hold a broad indemnity clause, even if it included the magic words 'sole negligence,' void on its face just because of the remote possibility that it *might* indemnify an indemnitee against his sole negligence under circumstances where there was not a properly purchased insurance fund under a valid clause allocating risks and requiring insurance coverage. A more rational interpretation of *W.Va.Code* 55-8-14 [1975] is that this section requires courts to void a broad indemnity agreement *only:* (1) if the indemnitee is found by the trier-of-fact to be solely (100 percent) negligent in causing the accident; and (2) it cannot be inferred from the contract that there was a proper agreement to purchase insurance for the benefit of all concerned. In this way, the harm that the Legislature wanted to guard against in *W.Va.Code* 55-8-14 [1975] can be prevented without undermining the valid liability and insurance concerns of people doing business in West Virginia.") (emphasis in original). *See also Kruis v. Allmine Paving, LLC*, No. 13-25, 2013 U.S. Dist. LEXIS 145432 (N.D. W.Va. Oct 8, 2013) ("[E]ven assuming West Virginia Code § 55-8-14 applies to this Agreement, it does not void 'a broad indemnity clause that specifically exempt[s] the 'sole negligence' of the indemnitee.'" (quoting *Dalton*); *Elk Run Coal Co. v. Canopius US Ins., Inc.*, 775 S.E.2d 65 (W. Va. 2015) ("The H & D Agreement between Elk Run and Medford clearly included an agreement to purchase insurance for the benefit of all concerned; therefore, even under *Dalton*, the agreement is not void and unenforceable.") (discussing § 55-8-14).

Wisconsin: The Supreme Court of Wisconsin held that an indemnitee may be indemnified for its own negligence provided that the contractual obligation is sufficiently explicit. *See Deminsky v. Arlington Plastics Mach.*, 657 N.W.2d 411, 420–21 (Wis. 2003) ("[A]greements to indemnify a party against its own negligence must be strictly construed, but so long as that standard is met, such agreements are valid."). The *Deminsky* Court held that the agreement must satisfy the conspicuous standard set forth in Wis. Stat. Ann. § 401.201(10) ("conspicuous" was subsequently amended by statute to mean "with reference to a term, means so written, displayed or presented that a reasonable person against which it is to operate ought to have noticed it. Whether a term is 'conspicuous' or not is a decision for the court. Conspicuous terms include any of the following: (1) A heading in capitals equal to or greater in size than the surrounding text, or in contrasting type, font, or color to the surrounding text of the same or lesser size. (2) Language in the body of a record or display in larger type than the surrounding text, or in contrasting type, font, or color to the surrounding text of the same size, or set off from surrounding text of the same size by symbols or other marks that call attention to the language." Wis. Stat. Ann. § 401.201(2)(f)). *See also Colleran v. Wildes*, 886 N.W.2d 592 (Wis. Ct. App. 2016) ("The law in Wisconsin is skeptical of liability-shifting provisions which attempt to protect a party against its own negligence, however, parties are not prohibited from agreeing to such provisions. Indeed, our supreme court has held that indemnity contracts in which parties agree to indemnify the indemnitee for the indemnitee's own negligence are to be strictly construed.") (quoting *Deminsky*); *Am. Family Mut. Ins. Co. v. Cintas Corp. No. 2*, 375 Wis. 2d 797 (Wis. Ct. App. 2017) ("This line of cases explicitly holds that where a provision to purchase insurance is combined with a provision to indemnify and hold harmless the indemnitee, those provisions show the clear intent of the parties to indemnify the indemnitee for its own negligence. We, therefore, conclude that the language in the contract between Cintas and Becker requiring Becker to obtain insurance and to defend, indemnify, and hold Cintas harmless, clearly expresses the intent of the parties that Becker would defend and indemnify and hold Cintas harmless for any claims against Cintas, including for its own negligence. Additionally, we hold that the purpose and unmistakable intent of the parties in entering into the agreement with these terms was for no other reason than to indemnify Cintas for its own negligent acts."). The Wisconsin Supreme Court, in *Am. Family Mut. Ins. Co. v. Cintas Corp. No. 2*, 914 N.W.2d 76 (Wis. 2017), concluded that Ohio law in fact governed the indemnity agreement and affirmed the decision of the Court of Appeals, but on different grounds.

Wyoming: The Supreme Court of Wyoming held that an indemnitee may be indemnified for its own negligence provided that the contractual obligation is sufficiently explicit. *Wyoming Johnson, Inc. v. Stag Indus.*, 662 P.2d 96, 99 (Wyo. 1983) ("Generally, contracts exculpating one from the consequences of his own acts are looked upon with disfavor by the courts. Therefore, an agreement for indemnity is construed strictly against the indemnitee, particularly when the indemnitee was the drafter of the instrument. If the indemnitee means to throw the loss upon the indemnitor for a fault in which he himself individually shares, he must express that purpose beyond any peradventure of doubt. The test is whether the contract language specifically focuses attention on the fact that by the agreement the indemnitor was assuming liability for indemnitee's own negligence.") (citations omitted). *See also Morrow v. Xanterra Parks & Resorts*, 925 F. Supp. 2d 1231 (D. Wyo. 2013) ("[C]ontracts purporting to indemnify a party against its own negligence will only be enforced if they clearly express such an intent, and a general provision indemnifying the indemnitee against any and all claims, standing alone, is not sufficient. [M]ere general, broad, and seemingly all-inclusive language is not sufficient to impose liability for an indemnitee's own negligence. The AOR agreement does not specifically focus attention on the fact that by the agreement Mr. Morrow was assuming liability for Xanterra's own negligence and thus the AOR agreement's indemnity provision does not pass the test for enforceability under Wyoming law.") (discussing *Stag*) (internal quotations omitted); *Union Pac. R. Co. v. Caballo Coal Co.*, 246 P.3d 867, 872 (Wyo. 2011) ("Under the terms of their agreement, CCC was obligated to indemnify UP for any loss, damages, etc. arising from the operation of the trains over the tracks 'to the extent that they result from any negligence or wrongful act or omission of CCC's officers, employees or agents.' This type of provision, which grounds the right to indemnification upon the indemnitor's negligence, is common. By contrast, there are indemnification agreements where the indemnitor agrees to indemnify the indemnitee for all losses, regardless of fault. Provisions of this sort that exculpate the indemnitee from the consequences of his own negligence are disfavored by the courts and strictly construed. *See, e.g., Wyoming Johnson, Inc. v. Stag Industries, Inc., 662 P.2d 96, 99 (Wyo.1983).* UP's and CCC's agreement did not include an all-inclusive right to indemnification and allowed for indemnification only when the indemnitor's negligence, wrongful act or omission resulted in the indemnitee's loss. It is not, therefore, the sort of indemnification provision to which the rule of strict construction applies."). Wyo. Stat. Ann. § 30–1-131 prohibits indemnification for the sole or concurrent negligence of the indemnitee in any agreement pertaining to any well for oil, gas, or water, or mine for any mineral, but shall not affect the validity of any insurance contract or any benefit conferred by worker's compensation. *See Pennant Service Co., Inc. v. True Oil Co., LLC*, 249 P.3d 698 (Wyo. 2011) ("An agreement containing a provision violative of the anti-indemnity statute is not void and unenforceable in total, but only to the extent that it violates the statute. Further, indemnification is not prohibited except for the indemnitee's own negligence.");

Kaiser-Francis Oil Co. v. Noble Casing, Inc., No. 16-00309, 2017 U.S. Dist. LEXIS 71618 (D. Wyo. May 10, 2017) (addressing § 30–1-131 in detail); *Lexington Ins. Co. v. Precision Drilling Co., L.P.*, 830 F.3d 1219 (10th Cir. 2016) (Gorsuch, J.) (addressing § 30–1-131 in detail); *Casper Inn, LLC v. Superior Builders, Inc.*, No. 16-11, 2017 U.S. Dist. LEXIS 214269 (D. Wyo. July 17, 2017) ("In giving the express language of the Contract its plain and ordinary meaning each party is responsible for damages caused by its own actions or inactions. The Contract's failure to address the issue of comparative liability or comparative indemnity, however, renders the Court unable to make a finding that one party is responsible to indemnify the other in light of the Laundreauxs' allegations against all parties. Taking the Laundreauxs' allegations in conjunction with the express terms of the Contract each party is to address the allegations made against it directly and there is no indemnity when there are allegations of concurrent fault."); *Ground Eng'g Consultants v. DePatco Inc.*, No. 17-082, 2018 U.S. Dist. LEXIS 234200 (D. Wyo. Aug. 14, 2018) ("The plain words of the indemnity provision thus preclude indemnification for Ground. Ground is not explicitly included in the indemnity provision, and therefore is not a party DePatco agreed to indemnify.").

CHAPTER

14

Qualified Pollution Exclusion

As Oliver Wendell Holmes famously observed, a page of history is worth a volume of logic, an aphorism worth remembering when dealing with claims that may (or may not) be classified as pollution claims and consequently may or may not be covered under the standard commercial general liability policy.

The commercial general liability (CGL) policy was the result of insurance industry efforts during the 1930s to improve the basic liability insurance product to make it more attractive to businesses seeking insurance protection as part of their approach to risk management and was formally established during the 1940s. There is a 1941 version of the CGL policy, but the 1943 version was the first to be widely sold. Other major revisions occurred in 1955, 1966, 1973, and 1986—with still further versions following, this time more frequently and with less significant changes. Prior to the CGL, businesses typically had to consider purchasing separate insurance for their various exposures.

The CGL was sold as one-stop shopping for general liability protection (and was even called the "comprehensive" general liability policy until the name was changed in 1986 to reduce the risk that courts would seize on this to broaden the coverage insurers thought they were selling) and contained the now famous insuring agreement that the insurer would pay "all sums that the insured becomes legally obligated to pay as damages" because of "bodily injury" or "property damage" covered by the insurance. *See generally* JEFFREY W. STEMPEL, STEMPEL ON INSURANCE CONTRACTS § 14.01 (3d ed. 2006 & Supp. 2014); BARRY R. OSTRAGER & THOMAS R. NEWMAN, HANDBOOK ON INSURANCE COVERAGE DISPUTES Ch. 7 (16th ed. 2012); EUGENE ANDERSON, JORDAN STANZLER, & LORELIE S. MASTERS, INSURANCE COVERAGE LITIGATION CH. I (2d ed. 2004).

Under the CGL as interpreted by most courts, anything for which the policyholder might be liable was covered (or at least potentially covered for purposes of triggering the duty to defend) unless it was specifically excluded. In addition, most courts apply the general rule of contract law that exclusions are strictly construed against the insurer and that the insurer bears the burden of persuasion to show that an exclusion applies. The net effect was to require that claims against a policyholder involving pollution-related liability (e.g., an oil spill, toxic waste disposal, smokestack emissions) would likely be found to be covered.

Reacting to this, the Insurance Services Office (ISO) developed and issued in 1970 a pollution exclusion now generally referred to as the "qualified pollution exclusion," so named in retrospect because it was replaced in 1986 by today's "absolute" and "total" pollution exclusions (*see* Ch. 15, *infra*). After its issuance in 1970, the qualified pollution exclusion was widely used and became part of the 1973 CGL form. During its roughly fifteen-year reign, the qualified exclusion became the focus of considerable coverage litigation, with courts dividing almost in half between the meaning proffered by policyholders and that proffered by insurers.[1]

The 1970 exclusion is qualified in that, while it bars coverage for pollution, coverage is reinstated by an exception to the exclusion if the discharge of the pollutant in question was "sudden and accidental"—words that have been at the heart of the coverage disputes involving the exclusion. It should also be noted that, under the ground rules of insurance contract interpretation, if the insurer demonstrates the applicability of an exclusion, a policyholder seeking to restore coverage bears the burden of persuasion as to the applicability of the exception it is trying to invoke. STEMPEL ON INSURANCE CONTRACTS §§ 2.06; 4.04. Consequently, litigation over the qualified pollution exclusion involved a process where typically the policyholder would tender defense of a liability claim, the insurer would argue that the claim involved the release of pollution, and the policyholder would in turn argue that the alleged pollution discharge was sudden and accidental. The qualified pollution exclusion contained in the 1973 CGL form stated that the insurance policy did not apply to "bodily injury" or "property damage" arising out of the discharge, dispersal, release or escape of smoke, vapors, soot, fumes, acids, alkalis, toxic chemicals, liquids or gases, waste materials or other irritants, contaminants or pollutants into or upon land, the atmosphere or any watercourse or body of water; but this exclusion did not apply if such discharge, dispersal, release, or escape was sudden and accidental.

In most cases involving the exclusion, there was no dispute that a claim alleged liability stemming from the release of chemical pollutants. The battleground between insurers and policyholders was whether the pollution claim might nonetheless be covered because the discharge of the chemicals in question had been "sudden and

---

1 There were, of course, versions of the qualified pollution exclusion used in policies sold prior to 1970. But the ISO issuance of the widely used 1970 form made the qualified pollution exclusion effectively part of the standard CGL policy.

accidental." Insurers took the position that only an abrupt discharge met the language of the exception restoring coverage while policyholders argued that a discharge that had been gradual but unintended satisfied the exception and mandated coverage. In addition, policyholders argued that where they did not intentionally cause harmful pollution, they should be covered while insurers argued that the critical question was whether the discharge was intended even if bad consequences from the discharge were unforeseen.

Insurers focused on the voluntariness of the release of chemicals. Policyholders focused on whether there was intent to injure. Insurers argued that a "sudden" release must also be an abrupt or swift release—a so-called "temporal" element. Policyholders noted that the term "sudden" is in many dictionaries defined as merely "unexpected" rather than fast and that there should be coverage because of the standard axiom that ambiguous language is construed against the insurer/contract drafter, particularly if it is contained in an exclusion. Insurers argued that policyholders had the burden to prove the clarity of the term "sudden" since it was part of an exception to an exclusion and that the dictionary definition of sudden-as-unexpected was not the common understanding of the word. And on and on.

Faced with these arguments, some courts ruled for policyholders based on the ambiguity argument and the dictionary entry (sometimes listed as the first or preferred meaning) that "sudden" means "unexpected" as well as "abrupt." Other courts took the view that the common use of the word "sudden" implied speed or abruptness and was insufficiently ambiguous to invoke the *contra proferentem* rule that ambiguities be construed against the drafter of unclear or problematic language. STEMPEL ON INSURANCE CONTRACTS § 4.08. In addition, courts siding with insurers often noted that construing sudden to mean merely unexpected would make "sudden" a mere synonym for "accidental." This would make the words "sudden and accidental" redundant, violating the general rule that each term in a contract is to be given effect.

Typical of the pro-policyholder view of the qualified pollution exclusion is *Claussen v. Aetna Casualty & Surety Co.*, 380 S.E.2d 686 (Ga. 1989), in which the Supreme Court of Georgia viewed the word "sudden" as sufficiently ambiguous that it could reasonably mean that an unexpected discharge (or even unexpected harm) was not within the scope of the exclusion, which must be strictly construed to avoid unfairly depriving the policyholder of coverage. The court explained that, while it is difficult to think of "sudden" without a temporal connotation (such as, a sudden flash, a sudden burst of speed, or a sudden bang), "even in its popular usage, 'sudden' does not usually describe the duration of an event, but rather its unexpectedness: a sudden storm, a sudden turn in the road, sudden death … . Thus, it appears that 'sudden' has more than one reasonable meaning. And, under the pertinent rule of construction the meaning favoring the insured must be applied, that is, 'unexpected.'" *Id.* at 688.

In making this determination, the Supreme Court of Georgia was responding to a certified question from the Eleventh Circuit Court of Appeals, which was reviewing a federal trial court's determination that the unambiguous meaning of sudden meant abrupt or swift. Not only were different states dividing over the qualified pollution exclusion, but federal and state judges were disagreeing over the meaning of the words in the exclusion and their application.

Representative of the pro-insurer view of the qualified pollution exclusion is *Dimmitt Chevrolet, Inc. v. Southeastern Fidelity Insurance Corp.*, 636 So. 2d 700 (Fla. 1993), in which the Supreme Court of Florida read the language literally to focus on the nature of the discharge rather than the nature of the alleged injury or the policyholder's state of mind. Notwithstanding the dictionary definitions of "sudden" as "unexpected," *Dimmitt* held that the plain and ordinary meaning of "sudden" carried a temporal dimension and that any other view would needlessly make the word "accidental" redundant. The court concluded that, while the word "sudden" can connote a sense of the unexpected, it is not standing alone in the pollution exclusion, but, rather, is an integral part of the conjunctive phrase "sudden and accidental." *Id.* at 704. "The term accidental is generally understood to mean unexpected or unintended. Therefore, to construe sudden also to mean unintended and unexpected would render the words sudden *and* accidental entirely redundant … . The very use of the words 'sudden *and* accidental' reveal [*sic*] a clear intent to define the words differently, stating two separate requirements. Reading 'sudden' in its context … the inescapable conclusion is that 'sudden,' even if including the concept of unexpectedness, also adds an additional element. … This additional element is the temporal meaning of sudden, i.e., abruptness or brevity." *Id.*

In so holding, the *Dimmitt* Court reversed its decision of six months earlier in the same case, ruling for the insurer in response to a motion for rehearing. Not only were state courts (even neighboring state courts) and federal courts disagreeing with each other over the meaning of the qualified pollution exclusion, here the same court was disagreeing with itself.

The division and uncertainty of this state of affairs, as well as the size of the claims that insurers were forced to cover in states rendering pro-policyholder construction of the qualified pollution exclusion, prompted insurers to revise the exclusion—adopting the "absolute pollution exclusion" in the 1986 CGL form, an exclusion that remains commonly in use in CGL forms (or, by endorsement, an even broader "total pollution exclusion").

Although the qualified pollution exclusion was in essence abolished more than twenty-five years ago, there remain potential claims involving pre-1986 policies or claims still in the litigation pipeline because of the nature of occurrence-based CGL policies, which can be triggered by injurious events afflicting claimants years in the past. In addition, some customized CGL policies or other types of liability policies such as environmental impairment may continue to use the sudden-and-accidental discharge language of the qualified pollution exclusion. The phrase is also used in the CGL form's "impaired property" exclusion and some first-party property policies. Consequently, the precedents established in the various states regarding the qualified pollution exclusion would logically continue to apply to any similarly worded pollution language or for purposes of interpreting the phrase "sudden and accidental" as used in other policy language.

50-State Survey: Qualified Pollution Exclusion

Alabama: The Supreme Court of Alabama stated that "[b]ecause the 'judicial construction placed upon particular words or phrases made prior to the issuance of a policy employing them will be presumed to have been the construction intended to be adopted by the parties,' we hold that the 'sudden and accidental' exception to the pollution exclusion clause provides coverage when the 'discharge, dispersal, release or escape' of contaminants into the environment was unexpected and unintended." *Ala. Plating Co. v. U.S. Fid. & Guar. Co.*, 690 So. 2d 331, 336 (Ala. 1996) (noting that courts had, prior to the decision, uniformly interpreted the term "sudden and accidental" to mean that the damage had to be unintended or unexpected for the provision to apply and therefore insurance contracts provided coverage for gradual events) (contamination from a plant that had permission to discharge treated water into a waterway not subject to exclusion). The court held that the term "sudden" was sufficiently ambiguous such that it could be construed to provide coverage where a policyholder gradually released material that allegedly caused injury to a third party's person or property. *Id.; see also Porterfield v. Audubon Indem. Co.*, 856 So. 2d 789, 800–01 (Ala. 2002) (restating the holding of *Alabama Plating* after engaging in a lengthy discussion of its reasoning, in a case involving coverage under an absolute pollution exclusion for lead paint exposures).

Alaska: No instructive authority. *See Whittier Props. Inc. v. Alaska Nat'l Ins. Co.*, 185 P.3d 84, 89 (Alaska 2008) (noting that courts interpreting Alaska law have declined to interpret the meaning of the phrase "sudden and accidental") (citing *Sauer v. Home Indem. Co.*, 841 P.2d 176 (Alaska 1992) and *MAPCO Alaska Petroleum, Inc. v. Cent. Nat'l Ins. Co. of Omaha*, 795 F. Supp. 941 (D. Alaska 1991)).

Arizona: The Ninth Circuit Court of Appeals held that, under Arizona law, "the 'sudden and accidental' exception 'unmistakably connotes a temporal quality.'" *Smith v. Hughes Aircraft Co.*, 22 F.3d 1432, 1437 (9th Cir. 1993) (applying Arizona law). The court reasoned that otherwise "sudden" would simply be a synonym for "accidental" and the temporal brevity furthered public policy by excluding deliberate indifference on the part of a polluting insured. *Id.* The court of appeals affirmed the district court's decision to reject the insured's attempt to "break down its long-term waste practices into temporal components in order to find coverage," for claims resulting from the contamination of drinking water through the discharge of TCE into unlined ponds, as "the evidence unequivocally demonstrates that the pollution was gradual." *Id.* at 1438; *see also Nucor Corp. v. Emp'rs Ins. Co. of Wausau*, Nos. 1 CA-CV 10-0174, 1 CA-CV 10-0454, 2012 Ariz. App. LEXIS 187 (Ariz. Ct. App. Nov. 23, 2012) (citing *Smith* for the contention that "Arizona law holds that the 'sudden and accidental' exception 'connotes a temporal quality'"); *Maricopa Cnty. v. Ariz. Prop. & Cas. Ins. Guar. Fund*, No. 2 CA-CV 98-0076, 2000 Ariz. App. Unpub. LEXIS 6 (Ariz. Ct. App. Apr. 27, 2000) (concluding that the "sudden and accidental" exception to the pollution exclusion is "reasonably susceptible" to different interpretations) (noting that "substantial authority supports both insurance carriers and policyholders on the issues relating to the exception" and discussing the outcomes of both in detail); *Nammo Talley Inc. v. Allstate Ins. Co.*, 99 F. Supp. 3d 999 (Ariz. 2015) ("This Court is therefore bound to follow Circuit precedent and interpret 'sudden and material' (sic) as having a temporal meaning. As Talley has offered neither fact nor legal argument suggesting that its injuries were the result of a 'sudden' event, the Court will grant summary judgment in Allstate's favor.") (rejecting argument that holding from *Hughes* is not applicable).

Arkansas: In *Murphy Oil USA, Inc. v. Unigard Security Insurance Co.*, 61 S.W.3d 807 (Ark. 2001), the Supreme Court of Arkansas held that insurers must defend because the pollution exclusion could be read in two ways and any doubt must be resolved in favor of the insured. "Murphy Oil and ESLIC cross swords over whether the 'sudden happening' refers to the initial spill in 1970 or to the alleged damage caused by the subsequent migration of the contaminants. . . . [W]e believe the language can be legitimately read either way." *Id* at 814-15 (noting opinion of the Pennsylvania Supreme Court, in *Sunbeam Corp. v. Liberty Mut. Ins. Co.*, 781 A.2d 1189, 1195 (Pa. 2001), that "proof of custom in the insurance industry may indicate that the 'sudden and accidental' exception … meant 'unexpected' and 'unintended' and not a requirement of abruptness"). The *Murphy Oil* Court stated that "[t]ruthfully, the [qualified] Pollution Exclusion and its exception could be read either as Murphy Oil interprets it or in accordance with Unigard's reading. The test, however, is whether the mere possibility of coverage exists in this case." *Murphy Oil USA, Inc.*, 61 S.W.3d at 815. "Moreover, the doctrine of *contra preferentum* would lead towards an interpretation of the exception favorable to Murphy Oil." *Id.* Although arising in the broader context of the duty to defend, *Murphy Oil* appears to reject the argument that the term "sudden" must always clearly mean "abrupt."

California: The California Court of Appeal held that "[t]he sudden and accidental exception to the pollution exclusion refers to the discharge of pollutants. 'Sudden' has a temporal element and does not mean a gradual or continuous discharge. 'Accidental' means an unexpected or unintended *discharge*, not unexpected or unintended *damage*." *Standun, Inc. v. Fireman's Fund Ins. Co.*, 73 Cal. Rptr. 2d 116, 120 (Cal. Ct. App. 1998) (emphasis in original). In *State v. Allstate Insurance Co.*, 201 P.3d 1147, 1156 (Cal. 2009), the Supreme Court of California cited *Standun* for the proposition that the sudden and accidental pollution exclusion means an unexpected discharge, not simply unexpected damage. The court held that, in a case like the one at hand, involving deposit of waste material into an evaporating pond, "the initial deposit of wastes [is] not a polluting event subject to the policy exclusion," rather the claim of liability is directed at "the subsequent escape of chemicals from the [insured's] ponds into the surrounding soils and groundwater, making that the relevant set of polluting events." *Id.* at 1157. "Our holding does not extend indemnity to situations where the policyholder can do no more than speculate that some polluting events may have occurred suddenly and accidentally, or where sudden and accidental events have contributed only trivially to the property damage from pollution … . Only if the insured can identify particular sudden and accidental events and prove they contributed substantially to causing indivisible property damage for which the insured bore liability is the insurer obliged to indemnify its insured for the entirety of the damages." *Id.* at 1168; *see also Brown v. Mid-Century Ins. Co.*, 156 Cal. Rptr. 3d 56 (Cal. Ct. App. 2013) (finding pipe's gradual and continuous release of water over a month did not qualify as "sudden" under a homeowners' policy); *Nicholson v. Allstate Ins. Co.*, 979 F. Supp. 2d 1054 (E.D. Cal. 2013) (citing *ACL Techs., Inc. v.*

Northbrook Prop. & Cas. Ins. Co., 22 Cal. Rptr. 2d 206 (Cal. Ct. App. 1993) for the contention that interpreting "sudden and accidental" requires defining the terms independently, "giving [sudden] a meaning with a temporal aspect – immediacy, quickness or abruptness – that does not allow it to cover events, such as happened in this case – that occurred gradually"); *Associated Indem. Corp. v. Argonaut Ins. Co.*, No. 254858, 2015 Cal. App. Unpub. LEXIS 4762 (Cal. Ct. App. July 7, 2015) ("The evidence that Twin Palms occupied the relevant parcel of land for part of the policy period, and that its business involved sandblasting and powdercoating, does not eliminate the possibility of a sudden and accidental polluting event. For example, there is no undisputed evidence about who or what occupied Parcel 18 for the balance of the policy period (January 17, 1986, to September 1986) and what activities were conducted there during that period. Also, Argonaut does not explain why sandblasting and powdercoating could not involve sudden and accidental discharges of pollutants, in addition to the expected discharges when Twin Palms engaged in its normal business operations."); *County of Stanislaus v. Travelers Indem. Co.*, 142 F. Supp. 3d 1065 (E.D. Cal. 2015) (evidentiary issues prevented the insured from establishing the possibility of a sudden and accidental discharge); *Miller Martial Deduction Trust v. Estate of Dubois*, No.16-01883, 2018 U.S. Dist. LEXIS 111348 (E.D. Cal. Jul. 2, 2018) (taking issue with expert's conclusions that releases were sudden and accidental and stating that insured must do more than speculate that some polluting events may have occurred suddenly or accidentally).

Colorado: The Supreme Court of Colorado held that "[a]lthough 'sudden' can reasonably be defined to mean abrupt or immediate, it can also reasonably be defined to mean unexpected and unintended. Since the term 'sudden' is susceptible to more than one reasonable definition, the term is ambiguous, and we therefore construe the phrase 'sudden and accidental' against the insurer to mean unexpected and unintended." *Hecla Mining Co. v. N.H. Ins. Co.*, 811 P.2d 1083, 1092 (Colo. 1991) ("If we were to construe 'sudden and accidental' to have a solely temporal connotation, the result would be inconsistent definitions within the CGL policies. In the portion of the policies defining occurrence, accident is defined to include 'continuous or repeated exposure to conditions, which result in bodily injury or property damage, neither expected nor intended from the standpoint of the insured.' If 'sudden' were to be given a temporal connotation of abrupt or immediate, then the phrase 'sudden and accidental discharge' would mean: an abrupt or immediate, and continuous or repeated discharge. The phrase 'sudden and accidental' thus becomes inherently contradictory and meaningless.") (involving claims for environmental damaged caused by insured's mining operations); *see also Cotter Corp. v. Am. Empire Surplus Lines Ins. Co.*, 90 P.3d 814, 821 (Colo. 2004) (applying the definition of "sudden and accidental" from *Hecla* in the context of claims for bodily injury and property damage caused by seepage from insured's mill); *Pub. Serv. Co. of Colo. v. Wallis & Co.*, 986 P.2d 924, 933 (Colo. 1999) ("[W]e construe the phrase 'sudden, unintended and unexpected' in the London pollution exclusion clause to mean 'unprepared for, unintended and unexpected.'"); *Mock v. Allstate Ins. Co.*, 340 F. Supp. 3d 1087 (D. Colo. 2018) (distinguishing *Hecla* and concluding that "policy language indicating that the insurance covers 'sudden and direct physical loss to property' [in homeowner's policy] means loss which was brought about in a short time, not loss which occurred over time) (explaining that *Hecla* was based on the court seeking to "avoid inconsistency between the policy's definition of 'occurrence' and the use of the phrase 'sudden and accidental' in the pollution exclusion").

Connecticut: The Supreme Court of Connecticut held that "the term 'sudden' requires that the release in question occurs abruptly or within a short amount of time." *Buell Indus., Inc. v. Greater N.Y. Mut. Ins. Co.*, 791 A.2d 489, 496 (Conn. 2002) (recognizing that the meaning of the sudden and accidental pollution exclusion was an issue of first impression in Connecticut, but acknowledging that lower courts in the state had interpreted "sudden" to embrace a temporal element). The court explained that its conclusion was dictated by the juxtaposition of the word "accidental" with the word "sudden:" "The very use of the words sudden and accidental … reveal a clear intent to define the words differently, stating two separate requirements. Reading sudden in its context, … the inescapable conclusion is that sudden, even if including the concept of unexpectedness, also adds an additional element because unexpectedness is already expressed by accident[al]. This additional element is the temporal meaning of sudden, i.e., abruptness or brevity. To define sudden as meaning only unexpected or unintended, and therefore as a mere restatement of accidental, would render the suddenness requirement mere surplusage." *Id.* (citation and quotation omitted) (finding that the leak of toxins into groundwater occurring over a period of years could not be considered "sudden"); *see also R.T. Vanderbilt Co. v. Cont'l Cas. Co.*, 870 A.2d 1048, 1060 (Conn. 2005) (recognizing *Buell Industries* holding in defining "sudden" in a sudden and accidental pollution exclusion as containing a temporal meaning); *Schilberg Integrated Metals Corp. v. Cont'l Cas. Co.*, 819 A.2d 773, 781–82 (Conn. 2003) (applying the definition of "sudden and accidental" from *Buell Industries* in the context of pollution caused by insured's recycling of metal wires); *PCS Phosphate Co. v. Am. Home Assur. Co.*,

No. 14-99, 2016 U.S. Dist. LEXIS 41432 (E.D.N.C. Mar. 29, 2016) (applying Connecticut law and stating, in an evidentiary case, that "[a] sudden and accidental release of contaminants at another location does not fall within the ambit of the underlying actions and thus cannot possibly give rise to a duty to defend or to indemnify or contribute costs."); *Hyde v. Allstate Ins. Co.*, No. 18-00031, 2018 U.S. Dist. LEXIS 204835 (D. Conn. Dec. 4, 2018) (applying *Buell* to interpretation of property policy that provides coverage for "sudden and accidental direct physical loss to property" for a claim for impairment to the structural integrity of basement walls due to defective concrete) ("[T]he Hydes acknowledge that the concrete decay and deterioration itself was gradual, and not sudden, but claim that the incremental development of the broader damage may have included sudden events, such as shifting, bulging, or cracking. These allegations do not serve to plausibly place the Hydes' claimed loss within coverage of the Policies []."); *Carney v. Allstate Ins. Co.*, No. 16-00592, 2018 U.S. Dist. LEXIS 161401 (D. Conn. Sept. 20, 2018) ("The Court does not find Plaintiff's invocation of sudden 'release events' in an attempt to surmount the 'sudden' requirement credible or convincing. Plaintiff's claimed loss isn't a micro-event, or a series of micro-events, it is the gradual deterioration of the basement walls."). [There have been a plethora of decisions, within the past few years, from Connecticut state and federal courts, addressing "sudden and accidental" in the context of coverage for the deterioration of basement walls, as at issue in *Hyde* and *Carney*.]

Delaware: The Supreme Court of Delaware held "that the term 'sudden,' as used in [a sudden and accidental] provision, clearly and unambiguously includes a temporal element synonymous with 'abrupt.'" *E.I. du Pont de Nemours & Co. v. Allstate Ins. Co.*, 693 A.2d 1059, 1061 (Del. 1997); *see also Hercules, Inc. v. AIU Ins. Co.*, 784 A.2d 481, 496 (Del. 2001) (holding that the qualified pollution exclusion at issue barred "coverage for pollution unless" caused by a 'sudden, unexpected and unintended' happening and that "[b]ecause the jury did not find that the property damage for which [insured] was found liable was the result of a 'sudden' or 'abrupt' event, coverage was barred") (applying the exclusion in the context of soil and groundwater contamination caused by the leakage of dioxin).

District of Columbia: A New York Federal Court, looking to New York and Maryland law for guidance on D.C. law, held that "sudden" has a temporal element and that "normal business operations" can "cause accidental damage." *Certain Underwriters at Lloyd's v. AMTRAK*, 2017 U.S. Dist. LEXIS 154584, No. 14-4717 (E.D.N.Y. Sept. 21, 2017). "[S]uch accidents are at the very heart of liability insurance.

A company may intentionally transport cargo containers as part of its business operations, but it is still possible that one of its employees might unintentionally load a container in such a way that it falls and causes damage in transit. . . . [T]he Court reads the record in this case to suggest that the contamination at Sunnyside Yard came from inadvertent spills during fueling and storage operations, not an intentional release of hazardous waste." *Id.* at *11-12.

Florida: The Supreme Court of Florida held that "[t]he use of the word 'sudden' can connote a sense of the unexpected. However, rather than standing alone in the pollution exclusion clause, it is an integral part of the conjunctive phrase 'sudden and accidental.' The term accidental is generally understood to mean unexpected or unintended. Therefore, to construe sudden also to mean unintended and unexpected would render the words sudden *and* accidental entirely redundant. ... The very use of the words 'sudden *and* accidental' reveal [*sic*] a clear intent to define the words differently, stating two separate requirements. Reading 'sudden' in its context ... the inescapable conclusion is that 'sudden,' even if including the concept of unexpectedness, also adds an additional element. ... This additional element is the temporal meaning of sudden, i.e., abruptness or brevity." *Dimmitt Chevrolet, Inc. v. S.E. Fid. Ins. Corp.*, 636 So. 2d 700, 704 (Fla. 1993) (emphasis in original) (involving leakage from a petroleum tank); *see also Liberty Mut. Ins. Co. v. Lone Star Indus., Inc.*, 661 So. 2d 1218, 1220 (Fla. Dist. Ct. App. 1995) (holding that an expected and intentional release of contaminants over a period of years could not be "sudden and accidental" under *Dimmitt*); *Cont'l Cas. Co. v. City of Jacksonville*, No. 09-14559, 2010 U.S. App. LEXIS 13035 (11th Cir. June 24, 2010) (applying Florida law) (determining that insurer would not be required to indemnify insured even if insured were not a polluter because the policy's provision focused on whether pollution had actually occurred rather than "who caused the pollution"), *aff'g* 654 F. Supp. 2d 1338, 1344–45 (M.D. Fla. 2009) (holding that *Dimmett* remains good law and maintaining that "sudden and accidental" unambiguously means "immediate or abrupt").

Georgia: The Supreme Court of Georgia held that "the [sudden and accidental] pollution exclusion clause is capable of more than one reasonable interpretation [and therefore] ... must ... be construed in favor of the insured to mean 'unexpected and unintended.'" *Claussen v. Aetna Cas. & Sur. Co.*, 380 S.E.2d 686, 690 (Ga. 1989) (involving contamination caused by the release of hazardous substances into a landfill owned by the insured). The court explained that, while it is difficult to think of "sudden" without a temporal connotation (such as, a sudden flash, a sudden burst of speed or a sudden bang), "even in its popular usage, 'sudden' does not usually describe the duration of an event, but rather its unexpectedness: a sudden storm, a sudden turn in the road, sudden death. ... Thus, it appears that 'sudden' has more than one reasonable meaning. And, under the pertinent rule of construction the meaning favoring the insured must be applied, that is, 'unexpected.'" *Id.* at 688, *answer to certified question conformed to* 888 F.2d 747 (11th Cir. 1989) (holding that "sudden and accidental" means "unexpected and unintended" and noting insurance industry adopted pollution exclusion "to exclude only intentional polluters"), *remanded to* 754 F. Supp. 1576 (S.D. Ga. 1990) ("The term ['sudden and accidental'] means 'unexpected and unintended' from the point of view of the insured.").

Hawaii: Courts speculating. *See Pac. Emp'rs Ins. Co. v. Servco Pac., Inc.*, 273 F. Supp. 2d 1149, 1157–58 (D. Haw. 2003) (recognizing that the meaning of the "sudden and accidental" pollution exclusion was an open issue under Hawaii law) (holding that, on account of such legal ambiguity regarding the meaning of the exclusion, there was a potential for coverage under Hawaii law and the insurer was obligated to defend); *see also Sentinel Ins. Co. v. Fire Ins. Co. of Haw.*, 875 P.2d 894, 916 (Haw. 1994) (addressing the evolution of the CGL policy for purposes of resolving trigger of coverage and noting that, while "accident" suggested an intent to cover only sudden, unexpected, but identifiable events, the "occurrence" approach expressly provided that an occurrence included any injury or damage that resulted, not only from an accident, but also from injurious exposure over an extended period); *U.S. Fire Ins. Co. v. Estate of Campbell*, No. 11-00006, 2011 U.S. Dist. LEXIS 149854 (D. Haw. Dec. 29, 2011) (finding that "the applicability of the qualified pollution exclusion turns on the interpretation of the word 'sudden'"). The District Court of Hawaii predicted "that, if the Hawai'i Supreme Court determined that the 'unexpected and unintended' definition of 'sudden' was in accord with Campbell Estate's reasonable expectations, the supreme court would hold that the term is ambiguous and construe it against U.S. Fire. Thus, the supreme court would apply that definition even though it arguably renders the term 'accidental' superfluous, contrary to the general rules of contract interpretation." *Id.*

Idaho: The Supreme Court of Idaho concluded that the phrase "sudden and accidental" in a qualified pollution exclusion was not ambiguous and refers to an unexpected, unintentional incident that occurs over a short period of time. *N. Pac. Ins. Co. v. Mai*, 939 P.2d 570, 572 (Idaho 1997) (involving environmental contamination of a landfill caused by automobile oil waste). The court explained: "'Sudden' is defined as 'happening or coming unexpectedly ... changing angle or character all at once … marked by or manifesting abruptness or haste … made or brought about in a short time.' It is not reasonable to interpret 'sudden' to include an event that occurs over anything other than a short period of time. Therefore, it is not ambiguous. 'Accidental' is a derivative of 'accident,' which this Court has said has a settled legal meaning in the context of other insurance policies. This meaning is an unintentional happening, an event that is unusual and not expected." *Id.* (citations omitted) (alteration in original). "The trial court interpreted the exclusion as excluding only those occurrences that are neither expected nor intended from the viewpoint of the insured. Although this may be an appropriate interpretation of 'accidental,' we conclude it does not create ambiguity in the exception." *Id.* at 573.

Illinois: The Supreme Court of Illinois held "that the term 'sudden' in the pollution exclusion exception … is ambiguous and … construe[d] it in favor of the insured to mean unexpected or unintended." *Outboard Marine Corp. v. Liberty Mut. Ins. Co.*, 607 N.E.2d 1204, 1220 (Ill. 1992) (finding that the insurer was required to defend its insured for claim involving the gradual discharge of pollutants into Lake Michigan). The court explained: "The pollution exclusion exception retriggers coverage for toxic releases which are 'sudden and accidental.' The policies define 'accident' to include 'continuous or repeated exposure to conditions.' … [A]n accidental release or discharge would include, according to the policy, a gradual release or a 'continuous or repeated' release. To construe 'sudden' to mean 'abrupt' results in a contradiction if one accepts the insurers' own definition of the term 'accident.' Such a construction would result in the pollution exclusion exception clause retriggering coverage for toxic releases which are 'abrupt' *and* gradual or 'continuous or repeated' releases. Clearly, under such a construction this clause would be rendered absurd. However, if 'sudden' means unexpected or unintended, as it is defined by numerous dictionaries, the clause retriggers coverage for unexpected or unintended releases which are exactly the type of uncertainties or risks that an insured would want to insure against." *Id.* at 1219 (citations omitted) (emphasis in original); *see also Keystone Consol. Indus., Inc. v. Emp'rs Ins. Co. of Wausau*, 470 F. Supp. 2d 873, 887 (C.D. Ill. 2007) (citing *Outboard Marine* for the proposition that, under Illinois law, "sudden" means "unexpected or unintended," and addressing the exclusion in the context of environmental contamination from the operation of insured's wire mill); *United States v. Clark*, No. 08-CV-4158, 2010 U.S. Dist. LEXIS 85775 (N.D. Ill. Aug. 19, 2010) (holding that insurers had a duty to defend policyholder in case involving EPA cleanup of hazardous materials because there was no indication that the materials were released intentionally) (determining that Illinois law is "clear" that a qualified pollution exclusion "permits coverage for unintended and unexpected environmental contamination" even when contamination is not abrupt); *Velsicol Chem., LLC v. Westchester Fire Ins. Co.*, No. 15-2534, 2017 U.S. Dist. LEXIS 144698 (N.D. Ill. Sept. 7, 2017) ("[I]f the spills or releases were routine and ordinary parts of the business then they cannot be labeled unexpected.") (examining witness testimony of environmental spills and concluding that, "whether spills or leaks were accidental or routine and ordinary parts of the business is a disputed question of material fact.").

Indiana: The Supreme Court of Indiana held that the interpretation of "sudden" in the qualified pollution exclusion was ambiguous and therefore would be interpreted in favor of the insured. *Am. States Ins. Co. v. Kiger*, 662 N.E.2d 945, 948 (Ind. 1996) (addressing contamination from an underground storage tank at a gas station). The court held that "sudden" could be understood to mean "unexpected." *Id.* "When the insurance industry itself has offered differing interpretations of the same language, [a court] must assume that the insured understood the coverage in the more expansive way." *Id.* (examining the drafting history of the exclusion); *see also Seymour Mfg. Co. v. Commercial Union Ins. Co.*, 665 N.E.2d 891, 892 (Ind. 1996) (noting similarities to *Kiger* and holding that "'sudden and accidental' and 'pollutant' in liability coverage policy construed against the insurer in favor of coverage for EPA action to recover environment cleanup and other costs"); *CONRAIL v. Ace Prop. & Cas. Ins. Co.*, No. 02638, 2013 Phila. Ct. Com. Pl. LEXIS 461 (Pa. Ct. Com. Pl. 2013) (applying Indiana law) (involving policy coverage for clean-up costs arising from environmental contamination at various railroad sites) (discussing the evolving definitions of the terms "sudden" and "accidental").

Iowa: The Supreme Court of Iowa held that the phrase "sudden and accidental," in the context of the qualified pollution exclusion, is comprised of two parts: "sudden," which constitutes a "temporal element," and "accidental," which is "an unexpected and unintended event." *Iowa Comprehensive Petroleum Underground Storage Tank Fund Bd. v. Farmland Mut. Ins. Co.*, 568 N.W.2d 815, 818 (Iowa 1997). The court rejected the argument that "sudden" meant only unforeseen or unexpected, reasoning that such an interpretation "would render either the term 'accidental' or 'sudden' redundant; they would mean virtually the same." *Id.* at 819 (contamination caused by leaks from an underground storage tank, taking place over at least a ten-year period, could not be considered "sudden" under the policy); *see also Hydrite Chem. Co. v. Aetna Cas. & Sur. Co.*, No. 02–0111, 2005 Iowa App. LEXIS 280 (Iowa Ct. App. Apr. 13, 2005) (finding there existed a genuine issue of material fact "whether the contamination was sudden, or was a result of leakage over a long period of time"); *National Surety Corp. v. Westlake Investments LLC*, 880 N.W.2d 724 (Iowa 2016) ("Applying the same logic [of *Comprehensive Petroleum*], we conclude that in the context of a modern standard-form CGL policy containing an exclusion precluding coverage for property damage 'expected or intended from the standpoint of the insured,' the term 'accident' means 'an unexpected and unintended event.'")

Kansas: The Court of Appeals of Kansas held "that the term 'sudden and accidental' should be given a temporal meaning, that it is unambiguous, and that the meaning of the word 'sudden' combines both the elements of without notice or warning and quick or brief in time." *Farm Bureau Mut. Ins. Co., Inc. v. Laudick*, 859 P.2d 410, 412 (Kan. Ct. App. 1993) (involving a leak over a long period of time from a gas station's underground storage tank). "[W]e are persuaded that 'sudden' possesses a temporal element, generally connoting an event that begins abruptly or without prior notice or warning, but the duration of the event—whether it lasts an instant, a week, or a month—is not necessarily relevant to whether the inception of the event is sudden." *Id.* at 414 (citation omitted); *see also U.S. Fid. & Guar. Co. v. Morrison Grain Co., Inc.*, 999 F.2d 489, 493 (10th Cir. 1993) (applying Kansas law) ("If the discharge of pollutants is brief or short, unexpected or unanticipated, not gradual or sustained, and not intended or expected, then the 'sudden and accidental' exception applies."); *Coffeyville Res. Ref. & Mktg., LLC v. Liberty Surplus Ins. Corp.*, 714 F. Supp. 2d 1119 (D. Kan. 2010) (addressing the release of a large amount of crude oil from policyholder's oil refinery where discharge occasioned by consequences of flooding, carrying oil residue into neighboring city) (reviewing Kansas precedent requiring that discharge and duration of pollution be abrupt to fall within exception to qualified pollution exclusion and finding that coverage was owed given that the "uncontroverted facts show[ed] that the release of crude oil from the [Insured's] refinery was 'abrupt and neither expected nor intended by the Insured' within the meaning" of the policy).

Kentucky: The Sixth Circuit Court of Appeals, applying Kentucky law, held that it was not "possible to define 'sudden' without reference to a temporal element that joins together conceptually the immediate and the unexpected." *U.S. Fid. & Guar. Co. v. Star Fire Coals, Inc.*, 856 F.2d 31, 34 (6th Cir. 1988) (applying Kentucky law). "We believe that the phrase 'sudden and accidental' is not a synonym for 'unexpected and unintended,' and that it should not be defined by reference to whether the accident or damages were expected … . 'Sudden' in its common usage, means 'happening without previous notice or with very brief notice,' while 'accidental' means 'occurring sometimes with unfortunate results by chance alone.' The meaning of these terms is clear and should not be twisted simply to provide insurance coverage when the courts deem it desirable." *Id.* at 34–35 (citations omitted) (holding that it was impossible to characterize the discharge of coal dust, on a regular ongoing basis over a seven- to eight-year period, as "sudden"); *see also Transamerica Ins. Co. v. Duro Bag Mfg. Co.*, 50 F.3d 370, 373 (6th Cir. 1995) (declining to certify the question to the Supreme Court of Kentucky given that, in the court's opinion, settled issues of contract interpretation resolved the issue of the exclusion's meaning) ("We see no meaningful distinction between *Star Fire Coals* and the present case. In both cases, the insured had deliberately discharged waste over a period of years. Accordingly, defendant cannot claim the protection of the 'sudden and accidental' language, and the District Court correctly concluded that the pollution exclusion clause bars coverage in this case.").

Louisiana: The Louisiana Court of Appeal stated that "the [sudden and accidental] exception is not implicated merely because the damages may have been accidental, in the sense that they were unexpected or unintended. What is relevant is whether the insured expected or intended the discharge or release." *Grefer v. Travelers Ins. Co.*, 919 So. 2d 758, 772 (La. Ct. App. 2005) (discussing the qualified pollution exclusion in the course of addressing the applicability of a total pollution exclusion to claims for property damage caused by naturally occurring radioactive material from a pipe-cleaning process); *see also Costanza v. Allstate Ins. Co.*, No. 02-1492 Section "K" (4), 2005 U.S. Dist LEXIS 36607 (E.D. La. Oct 26, 2005) (denying insurer's summary judgment motion in finding that "whether water filtration and mold growth that remains invisible to a homeowner is considered 'sudden' or 'accidental' must be left for trial"); *In re Chinese Manufactured Drywall Prods. Liab. Litig.*, 759 F. Supp. 2d 822, 834 (E.D. La. 2010) (addressing the terms "sudden" and "accidental" in the context of homeowners's insurance) (explaining that "it appears that the critical phrase 'sudden and accidental' means an event which is either abrupt (though expected), or unexpected" and that "the event must occur from an unknown cause or be an unusual result of a known cause"); *Primm v. State Farm Fire & Cas. Co.*, 426 So. 2d 356, 360 (La. Ct. App. 1983) ("The term 'sudden and accidental'... signifies an event which is unexpected, unforeseen and abrupt.").

Maine: The First Circuit Court of Appeals predicted that Maine would likely join the jurisdictions that accord "sudden" its unambiguous, plain, and commonly accepted meaning of temporally abrupt. *A. Johnson & Co. v. Aetna Cas. & Sur. Co.*,

933 F.2d 66, 72 (1st Cir. 1991) (applying Maine law) (addressing the exclusion in the context of the disposal of waste at a hazardous waste site). The court reached its decision based on *Travelers Indem. Co. v. Dingwell*, 414 A.2d 220 (Me. 1980), in which the Maine Supreme Judicial Court concluded that only the initial release—and not the behavior of the pollutants in the environment after the initial release—is "relevant to the 'sudden and accidental' inquiry." *Id.*; *see also Barrett Paving Materials, Inc. v. Cont'l Ins. Co.*, 488 F.3d 59, 63–64 (1st Cir. 2007) (applying Maine law) (failing to clarify the meaning or application of the qualified pollution exclusion, but distinguishing *A. Johnson*) (relying on *Dingwell*, to find that the "sudden and accidental" pollution exclusion did not preclude a duty to defend) (concluding that, unlike in *A. Johnson*, where the allegations involved an alleged polluter's regular business activity over an extended period of time, the allegations at issue did not specify how the pollutants may have been released from the facility into the soil or the sewers, i.e., suddenly and accidentally, or through routine operations) (involving the discharge of pollutants from a manufactured gas plant); *Prime Tanning Co. v. Liberty Mut. Ins. Co.*, 750 F. Supp. 2d 198, 212 (D. Me. 2010) (finding that insurer had no duty to defend where insured used tannery byproducts as "fertilizer" resulting in contamination because the "fertilizer" was deliberately used for its intended purpose over a period of twenty-five years) ("[S]preading fertilizer is a traditional environmental risk, regardless of whether it was properly composed and handled"; but the court's focus regarding the meaning of "sudden" was based on Missouri law).

Maryland: The Court of Appeals of Maryland held that "the language of [the qualified pollution] exclusion provides coverage only for pollution which is both sudden *and* accidental. It does not apply to gradual pollution carried out on an ongoing basis during the course of business. The notion of giving a temporal aspect to the terms 'sudden and accidental' and excluding coverage for gradual pollution has been embraced by numerous other jurisdictions … We agree with the numerous cases holding that allegations of longstanding business activities resulting in pollution do not constitute allegations of 'sudden and accidental' pollution." *Am. Motorists Ins. Co. v. ARTRA Grp., Inc.*, 659 A.2d 1295, 1308–10 (Md. 1995) (emphasis in original). The court embraced those decisions that rejected the insured's attempt to break down its long-term waste practices into temporal components in order to find coverage where the evidence unequivocally demonstrated that the pollution was gradual. *Id.* (holding that the exclusion applied to claims involving the release of hazardous chemicals over a long period of time from an insured's paint manufacturing facility). *See also Indus. Enters., Inc. v. Penn Am. Ins. Co.*, 637 F.3d

481, 490 (4th Cir. 2011) (applying Maryland law) (holding that insurer had no duty to defend under a CGL policy for policyholder's violations of the Comprehensive Environmental Response, Compensation, and Liability Act because such a violation does not amount to property damage), *rev'g Indus. Enters., Inc. v. Penn Am. Ins. Co.*, No. RDB-07–2239, 2008 U.S. Dist. LEXIS 67657 (D. Md. Sept. 2, 2008), a case noted in the first edition of General Liability Insurance Coverage: Key Issues in Every State that had implied a more policyholder-friendly construction of the qualified exclusion by stating that "under Maryland law, pollution that is both temporally isolated and unintended is covered because it meets the 'sudden and accidental' exception to the pollution exclusion. Pollution that accumulates gradually, even if unintended, is not covered."); *Bentz v. Mut. Fire, Marine & Inland Ins. Co.*, 575 A.2d 795 (Md. App. 1990) (finding that the contamination arising from the pesticide sprayed on the customer's house was "sudden" and "accidental" so as to fall within the exception to pollution exclusion in the exterminator's liability policy).

Massachusetts: The Supreme Judicial Court of Massachusetts held that "[f]or the word 'sudden' to have any significant purpose, and not to be surplusage when used generally in conjunction with the word 'accidental,' it must have a temporal aspect to its meaning, and not just the sense of something unexpected. We hold, therefore, that when used in describing a release of pollutants, 'sudden" in conjunction with 'accidental' has a temporal element." *Lumberman's Mut. Cas. Co. v. Belleville Indus., Inc.*, 555 N.E.2d 568, 572 (Mass. 1990) (addressing the exclusion in the context of PCB pollution of a harbor arising out of the manufacture of electrical capacitors); *see also Liberty Mut. Ins., Co. v. SCA Servs., Inc.*, 588 N.E.2d 1346, 1349 (Mass. 1992) (citing *Lumberman's* in rejecting "sudden" to mean "unexpected") (holding that releases caused by crushing and emptying barrels were not sudden and accidental, even though each individual release was abrupt because the discharge operations continued over a span of months); *House of Clean, Inc. v. St. Paul Fire & Marine Ins. Co., Inc.*, 705 F. Supp. 2d 102, 108 (D. Mass. 2010) ("Under Massachusetts law, 'sudden' carries a temporal element requiring an abrupt, non-gradual release. As a result, there is no duty to defend where the complaints arise out of routine business practices or activities.") (citing *Belleville Indus.*); *House of Clean, Inc. v. St. Paul Fire & Marine Ins. Co.*, 775 F. Supp. 2d 302, 312–13 (D. Mass. 2011) ("The basement floodings were sudden and accidental events but the storage of PCE powder in the cardboard boxes in [insured's] basement was an intentional and regular business practice. ... [T]he Court concludes that the first time[insured's] basement flooded, the release of PCE qualified as 'sudden and accidental,' but thereafter [insured's] continued practice of storing PCE ... was intentional and the resulting pollution was not accidental."); *Century Indem. Co. v. Liberty Mut. Ins. Co.*, 708 F. Supp. 2d 202, 211–13 (D.R.I. 2010) (applying Massachusetts law) (addressing whether there were sufficient allegations of a "sudden and accidental" release to trigger a duty to defend); *Acadia Ins. Co. v. Cunningham*, 771 F. Supp. 2d 172, 183 (D. Mass. 2011) (citing *Lumberman's* with favor and reasoning that "[t]o avoid a construction that renders language superfluous, sudden as well as accidental should each have meaning") (finding that insurer may have duty to defend in case of unexpected water damage) (court construed meaning of "sudden," but not in context of pollution discharge); *Unifirst Corp. v. Liberty Mut. Ins.* Co., No. 08–4300-BLS2, 2011 Mass. Super. LEXIS 16 (Mass. Super. Ct. Feb. 15, 2011) (holding that, although dry cleaner "routinely" discharged chlorinated solvents into neighboring ground, insurer was not entitled to summary judgment because a jury could reasonably find that substantial portions of the damage resulted from alternative, accidental releases); *Narragansett Elec. Co. v. Am. Home Assur. Co.*, 921 F. Supp. 2d 166, 181-182 (S.D.N.Y. 2013) (applying Massachusetts law) (citing *SCA Services* as "constru[ing] the term 'sudden' in the 'sudden and accidental' exception to have a temporal element, such that 'only an abrupt discharge or release of pollutants falls within the exception'") ("[U]nder Massachusetts law, releases occurring over extended periods of time as part of the insured's regular business activities are not sudden and accidental, absent additional facts."); *OneBeacon America Insurance Company v. Narragansett Electric Company*, 57 N.E.3d 18 (Mass. 2016) ("On the undisputed facts, the release of pollutants at the J.M. Mills landfill cannot be characterized as sudden and accidental, as that term is construed under Massachusetts law, and so does not fall within the exception to the pollution exclusion of the relevant policies.") (landfill received contaminated waste from the insured); *Plaistow Project, LLC v. Ace Prop. & Cas. Ins. Co.*, No. 16-11385, 2018 U.S. Dist. LEXIS 155965 (D. Mass. Sep. 13, 2018) ("[T]he dry cleaning machines would circulate perchlorethlene to perform their dry cleaning function. On no more than six occasions between 1971 and the early 1980s, after customers cleaned items that were not permitted to be placed in the machines, the 'button-trap' clogged, and perchlorethlene spilled and puddled on the floor. Accepting this affidavit as true for purposes of summary judgment, these releases occurred suddenly, not gradually, and thus were 'sudden' for purposes of the exception.").

Michigan: The Supreme Court of Michigan "conclude[d] that when considered in its plain and easily understood sense, 'sudden' is defined with a 'temporal element that joins together conceptually the immediate and the unexpected.' The common, everyday understanding of the term 'sudden' is 'happening, coming, made or done quickly, without warning or unexpectedly; abrupt.' 'Accidental' means '[o]ccurring unexpectedly and unintentionally; by chance.' ... [W]e find that the terms 'sudden' and 'accidental' used in the pollution-exclusion clause are unambiguous." *Upjohn Co. v. N.H. Ins. Co.*, 476 N.W.2d 392, 397–98 (Mich. 1991) ("[W]e conclude that the release of material from tank FA-129 could not possibly be considered 'sudden' because the release of by-product from tank FA-129 was not unexpected by [the insured].") (citation omitted) (addressing applicability of the exclusion to releases of chemical by-products from a pharmaceutical company's underground storage tank); *see also Aero-Motive Co. v. Great Am. Ins.*, 302 F. Supp. 2d 738, 745 (W.D. Mich. 2003) ("The 'sudden and accidental' clause is phrased in the conjunctive, if ... the releases were not sudden, it is not necessary to determine whether they were accidental.") ("[T]he [c]ourt concluded that all fires after the first were foreseeable and thus could not have been accidental."); *S. Macomb Disposal Auth. v. Nat'l Sur. Corp.*, 608 N.W.2d 814, 818 (Mich. Ct. App. 2000) (finding that the initial leakage from underneath a landfill site, not the secondary migration which contaminated surrounding groundwater, was the relevant event for the purpose of determining whether the qualified pollution exclusion applied); *Arco Indus. Corp. v. Am. Motorists Ins. Co.*, 594 N.W.2d 61, 66 (Mich. Ct. App. 1998) (finding that incidents of discharge, such as a bucket tipping or a drum being punctured, possessed the temporal element that "sudden" requires); *Bronson v. Am. States Ins. Co.*, 546 N.W.2d 702, 706 (Mich. Ct. App. 1996) (involving the release of contaminants at an industrial area, occurring over decades during which an insured intentionally and continuously collected toxic wastes in lagoons, while on notice that the lagoons were the source of groundwater pollution, was not unexpected and could not be "sudden and accidental.").

Minnesota: The Supreme Court of Minnesota held that in the context of the qualified pollution exclusion "'sudden and accidental' modifies 'discharge [etc.].' It refers not to the placement of waste in a particular place but to the discharge or escape of the waste from that place. The word 'sudden' is used in tandem with the word 'accidental,' and 'accidental' in liability insurance parlance means unexpected or unintended; thus to construe 'sudden' to mean 'unexpected' is to create a redundancy. It seems incongruous, too, to think of a leakage or seepage that occurs over many years as happening suddenly ... . [H]ere ... the term 'sudden' is used to indicate the opposite of gradual. Consequently, we hold that the 'sudden and accidental' exception to the pollution exclusion does not apply to asbestos fibers released gradually over time from the insured's product." *Bd. of Regents of Univ. of*

Minn. v. Royal Ins. Co. of Am., 517 N.W.2d 888, 892 (Minn. 1994); *Midwest Family Mut. Ins. Co. v. Wolters*, 831 N.W.2d 628, 638 (Minn. 2013) (discussing *Board of Regents* at length and "[a]pplying the plain-meaning approach of … *Board of Regents*" in the context of the absolute pollution exclusion policy, as a matter of first impression); *accord Tinucci v. Allstate Ins. Co.*, 487 F. Supp. 2d 1058 (D. Minn. 2007); *see also Anderson v. Minn. Ins. Guar. Ass'n*, 534 N.W.2d 706, 709 (Minn. 1995) ("[A] CGL policy with a pollution exclusion clause affords no coverage for a waste disposal site which gradually over time pollutes an area. On the other hand, if an explosion sends chemical fumes over a residential area, or an oil truck overturns and spills oil into a marsh, these would be sudden and accidental happenings, so that the exclusion would not apply and there would be insurance coverage."); *Westling Mfg. Co., Inc. v. W. Nat'l Mut. Ins. Co.*, 581 N.W.2d 39, 46 (Minn. Ct. App. 1998) (concluding that it was reasonable for the jury to find that abrupt spill of contaminants that eventually leaked into the groundwater was sufficiently "sudden" for the exclusion exception to apply); *Wakefield Pork, Inc. v. Ram Mut. Ins. Co.*, 731 N.W.2d 154, 162 (Minn. Ct. App. 2007) (applying the *Westling* definition of "sudden" and concluding that "regardless of whether manure is an 'agricultural chemical,' the escape of pollution in this case was not covered by the 'accidental-spillage' provision of the policy because it was not a 'sudden or abrupt and accidental or unexpected' discharge").

Mississippi: A Mississippi District Court held that "sudden and accidental as used in the language of the pollution exclusion should be accorded its plain and ordinary meaning, i.e., without notice and by chance, so as to exclude routine and repeated discharges." *U.S. Fid. & Guar. Co. v. T.K. Stanley, Inc.*, 764 F. Supp. 81, 84–85 (S.D. Miss. 1991) (addressing the exclusion in the context of the emission of hydrogen sulfide gas from a salt water disposal facility); *see also U.S. Fid. & Guar. Co. v. B & B Oil Well Serv., Inc.*, 910 F. Supp. 1172, 1182 (S.D. Miss. 1995) ("[T]he exception is not implicated merely because the damages may have been accidental, in the sense that they were unexpected or unintended. What is relevant is whether the insured expected or intended the discharge or release.").

Missouri: The Eighth Circuit Court of Appeals, applying Missouri law, held that "[t]he term 'sudden,' … 'when considered in its plain and easily understood sense, … is defined with a temporal element that joins together conceptually the immediate and the unexpected.' Indeed, assigning meaning to both 'sudden' and 'accidental' eliminates any perceived ambiguity … . Because 'accidental' includes the unexpected, however, 'sudden' must mean abrupt. To hold otherwise would render the word 'sudden' superfluous." *Aetna Cas. & Sur. Co. v. Gen. Dynamics Corp.*,

968 F.2d 707, 710 (8th Cir. 1992) (applying Missouri law) (addressing the exclusion in the context of claims against the insured for environmental contamination at several sites); *see also Charter Oil Co. v. Am. Emp'rs Ins. Co.*, 69 F.3d 1160 (D.C. Cir. 1995) (applying Missouri law) (discussing *General Dynamics* at length and the consistency of the *General Dynamics* Court's interpretation of "sudden and accidental" with other circuit courts) ("sudden" means "abrupt" as used in "sudden and accidental" exception to pollution exclusion); *Trans World Airlines, Inc. v. Assoc. Aviation Underwriters*, 58 S.W.3d 609, 622–23 (Mo. Ct. App. 2001) (citing *Gen. Dynamics* for the proposition that "sudden" must include a temporal element such that it is abrupt, immediate, and unexpected, but concluding it was a moot point since the discharge at issue—deliberate disposal of waste—could not be considered "accidental"); *Kirk v. Schaeffler Group USA, Inc.*, No. 13-5032, 2015 U.S. Dist. LEXIS 5954 (W.D. Mo. Jan. 20, 2015) (discussing the protracted litigation in *Liberty Mut. Ins. Co. v. Fag Bearings Corp.*, including the Eight Circuit's opinion at 153 F.3d 919 (8th Cir. 1998) that affirmed the District Court's opinion that certain releases were long term and gradual, and, therefore, not sudden, as defined in *Gen. Dynamics*, nor were they accidental because the insured did not do enough to prevent a continuous occurrence of TCE releases).

Montana: The Supreme Court of Montana "h[e]ld that in the context of the phrase 'sudden and accidental,' the word 'sudden,' even if it includes the concept of unexpectedness, also encompasses a temporal element, because unexpectedness is already expressed by the word 'accidental.'" *Sokoloski v. Am. W. Ins. Co.*, 980 P.2d 1043, 1045 (Mont. 1999) (addressing coverage under a homeowner's policy for damage to walls and other property caused by soot from the prolonged burning of candles during the holiday season) ("While time is relative and a geologist might speak of sudden events occurring over hundreds or even thousands of years and an astrophysicist may speak in terms of millions of years, most people and institutions measure time in much more finite terms. So must the courts. In the context of the coverage of smoke damage by a homeowner's insurance policy, the Court determines that 'sudden' connotes a sense of immediacy, which is measured in seconds, minutes and might be stretched to hours, but not weeks. Therefore, the Court rules the gradual accumulation of soot and smoke over a 4–5 week period is not 'sudden and accidental' for purposes of policy coverage."); *see also Travelers Cas. & Sur. Co. v. Ribilmmunochem Research, Inc.*, 108 P.3d 469, 476 (Mont. 2005) ("[I]n order for the word 'sudden' to have significant purpose, and not to be surplusage when used generally in conjunction with the word 'accidental,' it must have a temporal aspect to its meaning, and not merely a sense of something unexpected.") (specifically extending *Sokoloski*'s holding to the qualified pollution exclusion in a general liability policy).

Nebraska: The Supreme Court of Nebraska concluded, following a comprehensive survey of the issue nationally, that "[s]ince the 'sudden and accidental' exception to the pollution exclusion clause is expressed in the conjunctive, both requirements must be met for the exception to become operative." *Dutton-Lainson Co. v. Cont'l Ins. Co.*, 716 N.W.2d 87, 97 (Neb. 2006). "[U]nder the terms of the policy at issue, an event occurring over a period of time is not sudden. The language of an insurance policy should be considered in accordance with what a reasonable person in the position of the insured would have understood it to mean." *Id.* at 99. The court concluded that this means that "the term 'sudden,' as found in the context of the qualified pollution exclusion, … refer[s] to the objectively temporally abrupt release of pollutants into the environment." *Id.* (addressing the applicability of the exclusion to property damage caused by the deposit of drums containing degreaser solvent into a landfill over a course of years); *see also Bituminous Cas. Corp. v. Aaron Ferer & Sons Co.*, No. 4:06CV3128, 2007 U.S. Dist. LEXIS 51427 (D. Neb. July 16, 2007) (relying on *Dutton-Lainson* and holding that "[b]ecause the [insureds] have presented no evidence tending to show that the release of hazardous substances at the Site was sudden and accidental, [the insurer] is entitled to the entry of summary judgment"); *Kaiser v. Allstate Indem. Co.*, 949 N.W.2d 787 (Neb. 2020) (addressing *Dutton-Lainson* in the context of a property policy exclusion for vandalism, with an exception for "sudden and accidental direct physical loss caused by fire resulting from vandalism") ("[A]n event occurring over a period of time is not sudden. Thus, just as we held in *Dutton-Lainson* that pollution occurring over 37 years was not sudden, we now also hold that a property loss from methamphetamine vapor and residue occurring by indoor methamphetamine use or production over a period of months or more is not sudden.").

Nevada: No instructive authority. *But see Century Sur. Co. v. Casino W., Inc.*, No. 60622, 2014 Nev. LEXIS 50 (Nev. May 29, 2014) (holding that absolute pollution exclusion did not bar coverage for injuries from carbon monoxide exposure when four people died while sleeping in a motel room directly above a pool heater). *Casino West* reflects considerable influence of the ambiguity and reasonable expectations principles in Nevada, particularly where an exclusion (rather than a coverage grant or condition) is the term in dispute. *See also Crystal Bay Gen. v. Aetna Cas. & Sur. Co.*, 959 F.2d 239 (9th Cir. 1992) (affirming in part and reversing in part the District

Court of Nevada's decision in *Crystal Bay Gen. Imp. Dist. v. Aetna Cas. & Sur. Co.*, 713 F. Supp. 1371 (D. Nev. 1989)) ("The district court's implicit finding that the [sewage] spill constituted an 'occurrence' within the meaning of the [CGL] policy was not clearly erroneous. There was evidence that the spill was a sudden event that [Crystal Bay] neither 'expected' nor 'intended.'").

New Hampshire: The Supreme Court of New Hampshire addressed a policy provision that afforded coverage when an insured suffered loss or damage to livestock that was caused by sudden and accidental damage from artificially generated electrical current and held, following an examination of qualified pollution exclusion decisions, that "defining 'sudden' to include unexpected events does not strip the word of its independent meaning and significance. While it is certainly possible to read the term 'accidental' to include unexpected events, the joint use of the words 'sudden and accidental' serves distinct purposes not accomplished by either word standing alone ... . '[S]udden' is not to be construed as synonymous with 'instantaneous.' ... [S]uch an interpretation suggests that the term 'sudden and accidental' is at least reasonably susceptible to an interpretation consistent with 'unexpected and unintended.' ... [E]ven if the word 'sudden' is given the temporal connotation the defendant advances, in this policy it is not clear if in order to be covered the *onset* of damages must occur 'suddenly' or if the *aggregate* damage must occur 'suddenly.' [T]he term 'sudden and accidental' is, at the very least, not 'so clear as to create no ambiguity which might affect the insured's reasonable expectations.' ... We ... construe 'sudden and accidental' in such a way as to provide coverage to the insured on the basis that the phrase includes events that are 'unexpected and unintended.'" *Hudson v. Farm Family Mut. Ins. Co.*, 697 A.2d 501, 504 (N.H. 1997) (emphasis in original); *see also EnergyNorth Natural Gas, Inc. v. Am. Home Assur. Co.*, No. 99–502-JD, 2003 U.S. Dist. LEXIS 12665 (D.N.H. July 17, 2003) (following *Hudson* and holding that the pollution exclusion did not apply to claims for the discharge of manufactured gas plant waste over a long period of time because the exclusion's exception for "seepage, pollution or contamination ... caused by a sudden, unintended and unexpected happening during the period of this Insurance" was satisfied).

New Jersey: The Supreme Court of New Jersey stated that "[a]lthough the word 'sudden' is hardly susceptible of precise definition, and is undefined in those CGL policies that include the standard pollution-exclusion clause, we are persuaded that 'sudden' possesses a temporal element, generally connoting an event that begins abruptly or without prior notice or warning, but the duration of the event—whether it lasts an instant, a week, or a month—is not necessarily relevant to whether the inception of the event is sudden." *Morton Int'l, Inc. v. Gen. Accident Ins. Co.*, 629 A.2d 831, 847 (N.J. 1993) (addressing the exclusion in the context of claims for property damage at a mercury processing plant). However, the court went on to hold that, on account of misrepresentations made by insurers to state regulators, concerning the scope of the qualified pollution exclusion, it would be "construed to provide coverage identical with that provided under the prior occurrence-based policy, except that the clause will be interpreted to preclude coverage in cases in which the *insured* intentionally discharges a known pollutant, irrespective of whether the resulting property damage was intended or expected." *Id.* at 875; *see also Gen. Ceramics Inc. v. Fireman's Funds Ins. Cos.*, 66 F.3d 647, 652 (3d Cir. 1995) (applying New Jersey law) (citing *Morton* in finding that "the unintended discharge of pollutants is covered under the 'sudden and accidental' exception even when the discharge was gradual and not 'abrupt'"); *Benjamin v. State Farm Ins. Co.*, No. 15-4123, 2017 U.S. Dist. LEXIS 131078 (D.N.J. Aug. 17, 2017) (citing *Morton* in finding that an insurer must establish that the insured intentionally discharged a known pollutant in order for the pollution exclusion to apply); *Cooper Indus., LLC v. Emplrs. Ins. of Wausau*, No. L-9284-11, 2017 N.J. Super. Unpub. LEXIS 3239 (N.J. Super. Ct. Law Div. Oct. 16, 2017 ("As to the pollution exclusion, this defense requires the Insurers to prove that Edison 'intentionally discharge[d] a known pollutant.' (quoting *Morton*) ("The Insurers also have not convinced this Court that, even if the substances were released and known to be pollutants, that they were released in such quantities that an individual in the early twentieth century would have believed they were likely to cause environmental harm. The evidence also indicates that when a potential problem was identified at Silver Lake, the Storage Battery plant there typically took swift and effective action to stop pollution. All these issues considered together would seem to preclude the application of the pollution exclusion in this case."); *Schoneboom v. Allstate N.J. Ins. Co.*, No. A-1472-18T2, 2020 N.J. Super. Unpub. LEXIS 547 (N.J. Super. Ct. App. Div. Mar. 19, 2020) (discussing New Jersey law in detail) ("Allstate never supported its motion with evidence that plaintiff was negligent by failing to maintain the oil tank. To the contrary, the evidence on summary judgment revealed that plaintiff continually employed professionals to service the tank and she followed their recommendations. Allstate provided no suggestion as to what more plaintiff could have done under the circumstances. Moreover, there was no evidence that *at its inception*, the leak did not begin suddenly. The fact that it lasted for years did not make it anything less than 'sudden and accidental.'") (emphasis in original).

New Mexico: The Supreme Court of New Mexico, as a matter of first impression, held that "the term 'sudden,' in the Policies' pollution exclusion, means 'unexpected,' rather than indicating a temporal limitation on the occurrence." *United Nuclear Corp. v. Allstate Ins. Co.*, 285 P.3d 644, 656 (N.M. 2012), *rev'g* 252 P.3d 798 (N.M. Ct. App. 2011) (finding "the meaning of the term 'sudden' as used in the Policies is ambiguous" and noting that ambiguities must be construed in the insured's favor) (addressing environmental damage caused by radioactive material discharged by the mining company). The court rejected the analysis in *Mesa Oil Co. v. Insurance Co. of North America*, 123 F.3d 1333, 1340 (10th Cir. 1997) (applying New Mexico law), which found that "[t]he word 'sudden' clearly expresses a meaning of quickness or abruptness, particularly in light of the fact that it would be entirely redundant when paired with the word 'accidental' if it merely meant 'unexpected.'" According to the *United Nuclear* Court, "*Mesa Oil's* holding that 'sudden' clearly means 'abrupt' was premised on two [erroneous] assumptions ... , and thus provided inadequate support for the district court's and the Court of Appeals' reliance on that case." *United Nuclear Corp.*, 285 P.3d at 652. The court noted the frequency of dictionary definitions equating "sudden" with "unexpected," as well as the drafting history of the exclusion, which suggested that it was not a substantial change in prior coverage, which had generally included pollution-related injury that was unintentional. *Id.* at 651–52. In addition, the court invoked the approach of protecting the reasonable expectations of the policyholder as well as the ambiguity doctrine. *See id.* at 653 ("[The] conspicuous division among courts on the meaning of the term 'sudden' is another indication that the term may be reasonably susceptible to two distinct interpretations.").

New York: The Court of Appeals of New York held that "eliminating the temporal aspect from the meaning of sudden in the exception to the pollution coverage exclusion would render the sudden and accidental contingencies of the exception unavoidably redundant for unintended pollutant discharges. This redundancy is removed by including within the meaning of *sudden* in the pollution exclusion exception its temporal quality, as a discharge of the pollutant *abruptly, precipitantly or brought about in a short time* ... . The focus in determining whether the temporally sudden *discharge* requirement is met, for the purpose of nullifying the pollution coverage exclusion, is on the initial release of the pollutant, not on the length of time the discharge remains undiscovered, nor the length of time that damage to the environment continued as a result of the discharge, nor on the timespan of the eventual dispersal of the discharged pollutant in the environment."

Northville Indus. Corp. v. Nat'l Union Fire Ins. Co. of Pittsburgh, 679 N.E.2d 1044, 1047–48 (N.Y. 1997) (emphasis in original) (quotations and citations omitted) (addressing the exclusion in the context of the release of gasoline from storage tanks over a period of years); *see also Md. Cas. Co. v. Cont'l Cas. Co.*, 332 F.3d 145, 151 (2d Cir. 2003) (applying New York law) (citing to *Northville* in finding that "New York law interprets the phrase 'sudden and accidental' as having a temporal component, requiring that a discharge be both 'sudden' and 'accidental' in order to fall within the exception") (affirming the district court's summary judgment decision in favor of Continental based on the conclusion that gradual pollution is not within the "sudden and accidental" exception); *Flynn v. Allstate Indem. Co.*, No. 08–30417, 2009 N.Y. Misc. LEXIS 862 (N.Y. City Ct. Mar. 24, 2009) ("[T]here can be little doubt that the initial discharge of waste oil was 'sudden and accidental.' … The fact that the discharge was not readily discoverable and, thus, continued for a period of time, through no fault of the insured, should not move an otherwise covered occurrence within the rather shadowy perimeter of the exclusion."); *Emerson Enters., LLC v. Kenneth Crosby, LLC*, 768 F. Supp. 2d 484 (W.D.N.Y. 2011) (finding, though not focused on qualified exclusions per se, that insurer had no duty to indemnify where pollution resulted from intentional and systematic discharge of waste, despite insured's lack of intentions to pollute) (holding that "coverage for any contamination caused by the overflow of the dry well is clearly and unambiguously excluded by the [insurer's] policy" even if, as the insured alleged, the overflow was caused by rain or melting snow) (citing *Agway, Inc. v. Travelers Indem. Co.*, No. 93-CV-557, 1993 U.S. Dist. LEXIS 21092 (N.D.N.Y. Dec. 6, 1993)) ("[T]here is no reasonable way to construe intended disposal as an unintentional discharge, despite the fact that subsequent contamination may not have been intended or expected."), *aff'd sub nom. Emerson Enters., LLC v. Hartford Accident & Indem. Co.*, No. 12-4287, 2013 U.S. App. LEXIS 18436 (2d Cir. Sept. 5, 2013) (applying New York law) ("New York law, construing this type of pollution exclusion, has held that the unintended consequences of intentional discharges are not 'accidental.'"); *Travelers Indem. Co. v. Northrop Grumman Corp.*, No. 12 Civ. 3040 (KBF), 2014 U.S. Dist. LEXIS 33058 (S.D.N.Y. Mar. 13, 2014) (holding that the discharges of chemicals during certain time period were neither sudden nor accidental, precluding coverage) ("New York courts have repeatedly held that the 'sudden and accidental' pollution exclusion is 'unambiguously plain and operative.' … Discharges that occur over a period of time are, definitionally, not 'sudden.' … [New York] [c]ase law has interpreted 'accidental' as meaning neither intentional nor purposeful. The law is clear that 'accidental' includes an incident occurring 'by chance.'"); *Iannucci v. Allstate Ins. Co.*, 354 F. Supp. 3d 125 (N.D.N.Y. 2018) (addressing "sudden and accidental" in the context of coverage for a roof collapse).

North Carolina: The Supreme Court of North Carolina held that "sudden" has a temporal element. *Waste Mgmt. of Carolinas, Inc. v. Peerless Ins. Co.*, 340 S.E.2d 374, 383 (N.C. 1986). "[T]he focus of the 'pollution exclusion' is *not* upon intention, expectation, or even foresight. Rather, the exclusion clause is concerned less with the accidental nature of the occurrence than with the nature of the damage. The exclusion limits the insurer's liability for accidental events by excluding damage caused by the gradual release, escape, discharge, or dispersal of irritants, contaminants, or pollutants. The focus of the exclusion is not upon the release but upon the fact that it pollutes or contaminates. When courts consider the release alone to be the key to the pollution exclusion clause, the sudden and accidental exception can be bootstrapped onto almost any allegations that do not specify a gradual release or emission." *Id.* at 380–81 (emphasis in original) (addressing exclusion in the context of claims for contamination caused by dumping hazardous materials at a landfill over the course of several years); *see also Home Indem. Co. v. Hoechst Celanese Corp.*, 494 S.E.2d 774, 783 (N.C. Ct. App. 1998) (following *Waste Management* and holding that leaks and spills that occurred on regular or sporadic basis during day-to-day operations at manufacturing plant were not sudden).

North Dakota: No instructive authority. *But see Ind. Lumbermens Ins. Co. v. PrimeWood, Inc.*, No. A3–97–23, 1999 U.S. Dist. LEXIS 23490 (D.N.D Jan. 8, 1999) (addressing the exception to the "impaired property" exclusion for damages that result from the loss of use of other property not physically damaged that is caused by *sudden and accidental* physical damage to the insured's products after they have been put to their intended use) (interpreting "sudden and accidental" to mean "unexpected and unintended" and holding that the exception to the "impaired property" exclusion applied to claims against a cabinet manufacturer for the premature yellowing of cabinet doors).

Ohio: The Supreme Court of Ohio "h[e]ld that the word 'sudden' in the exception is *not* synonymous with the word 'unexpected' in the typical definition of 'occurrence'; instead, the word also has a *temporal* aspect." *Hybud Equip. Corp. v. Sphere Drake Ins. Co.*, 597 N.E.2d 1096, 1102 (Ohio 1992) (emphasis in original). The court gave three reasons for its conclusion: "First, … the word 'sudden,' … is not ambiguous … . As it is most commonly used, 'sudden' means happening quickly, abruptly, or without prior notice. … Second, … unless 'sudden' is interpreted to have a temporal aspect, the word does not add anything to the phrase 'sudden and accidental.' … Third, if 'sudden' were interpreted to be synonymous with 'unexpected,' then the entire pollution exclusion would not serve the purpose for which it was clearly included … . [T]he pollution exclusion would exclude only bodily injury or property damage that was already excluded by the common definition of 'occurrence.'" *Id.* (addressing the pollution exclusion in the context of environmental damage caused by the disposal of waste); *see also Emp'rs. Ins. of Wausau v. Amcast Indus. Corp*, 709 N.E.2d 932, 933 (Ohio Ct. App. 1998) (concluding "that Amcast's disposal of foundry sand as part of its normal and routine operations, rather than the release of contaminants from the foundry sand when it is mixed with tar-plant waste, is the polluting activity that is subjected to the pollution-exclusion exception contained in the insurers' polices and that this polluting activity was not sudden and accidental…"); *Goodrich Corp. v. Commercial Union Ins. Co.*, Nos. 23585, 23586, 2008 Ohio App. LEXIS 2716 (Ohio Ct. App. June 30, 2008) (finding that the insured had "established to the jury that it had sustained damages due to sudden and accidental releases of [contaminants] into the groundwater").

Oklahoma: The Supreme Court of Oklahoma held that "[t]he ordinary and popular meaning of 'sudden' necessarily includes an element of time. Decisions finding ambiguity have focused on technical distinctions crafted by lawyers rather than the ordinary understanding of the word. A finding of ambiguity requires that the term 'sudden' be lifted from its context in the policy and scrutinized so closely that any plain meaning is no longer discernable." *Kerr-McGee Corp. v. Admiral Ins. Co.*, 905 P.2d 760, 763 (Okla. 1995). The court reasoned that defining "sudden" to mean "unexpected or unintended" would make the term "mere surplusage" as the word "accidental" embraces this meaning. *Id.* at 764. "Clearly, the ordinary meaning of 'sudden' cannot describe the gradual routine disposal of industrial waste that occurred over a number of years." *Id.*; *see also Macklanburg-Duncan Co. v. Aetna Cas. & Sur. Co.*, 71 F.3d 1526, 1537 (10th Cir. 1995) (applying Oklahoma law) (disposal of hazardous waste pursuant to long-term, routine, disposal practices were clearly not "sudden" within the meaning ascribed by *Kerr-McGee*); *Stanley v. Farmers Ins. Co.*, No. 05-622-M, 2006 U.S. Dist. LEXIS 79974 (W.D. Okla. Oct. 25, 2006) (citing *Kerr-McGee* as dictating the meaning of the sudden and accidental discharge of water exception to a faulty workmanship exclusion in a homeowner's policy); *Fossil Creek Energy Corp. v. Cook's Oilfield Servs.*, 242 P.3d 537, 544 (Okla. Civ. App. 2010) (denying summary judgment based on an issue of disputed fact as to whether the leakage from the mud pit was "sudden and accidental").

Oregon: The Supreme Court of Oregon held that "the phrase 'sudden and accidental' could be synonymous with the phrase 'unintended and unexpected.'" *St. Paul Fire & Marine Ins. Co. v. McCormick & Baxter Creosoting*, 923 P.2d 1200, 1217 (Ore. 1996). The court rejected the insurers' argument that such a reading of the phrase "sudden and accidental" renders it redundant. *Id.* (rejecting the insurers' argument that an unintended event is always an unexpected event and concluding that not every unintended event (or result) necessarily is unexpected). The court was also persuaded by the fact that, before the phrase "sudden and accidental" was incorporated into pollution exclusions, it had been used in numerous "machinery and boiler" policies where it had been routinely interpreted to mean "unintended and unexpected." *Id.* (finding that environmental contamination caused by the leaching of chemicals from wood treatment plants was sudden and accidental within the meaning of the exclusion). *But see Precision Castparts Corp. v. Hartford Acc. & Indem. Co.*, No. 04–1699, 2008 U.S. Dist. LEXIS 46361 (D. Ore. June 12, 2008) (distinguishing *McCormick & Baxter* and holding that the discharge of thorium into the city sewer was expected and intended and, thus, not "sudden and accidental"); *see also Emp'rs Ins. of Wausau, A Mut. Co. v. Tektronix, Inc.*, 156 P.3d 105, 119 (Ore. Ct. App. 2007) (engaging in lengthy discussion of which party bears the burden of providing the "sudden and accidental" exception before concluding that it rests with the insured); *Siltronic Corp. v. Emplrs. Ins. Co.*, No. 11-0193, 2018 U.S. Dist. LEXIS 126184 (D. Ore. July 19, 2018) (finding the qualified pollution exclusion "ambiguous as to whether the 'sudden and accidental' nature of the 'discharge, dispersal, release or escape' is to be determined from the perspective of the insured or the original polluter") (construing the provision against the insurer and holding that the "insured's perspective is the relevant measure for whether a 'discharge, dispersal, release or escape' was 'sudden and accidental'"). The Supreme Court of Oregon has also held that the terms "sudden, unexpected and unintended" and "sudden, unexpected and unintentional," when used in the context of a pollution exclusion, "have the same legal meaning that we ascribed to the term 'sudden and accidental' in the policies at issue in *McCormick & Baxter Creosoting.*" *Allianz Global Risks US Ins. Co. v. Ace Prop. & Cas. Ins. Co.*, 483 P.3d 1124 (Ore. 2021).

Pennsylvania: The Supreme Court of Pennsylvania, addressing the issue at the state court equivalent stage of a Rule 12(b)(6) motion, held that, because of the special usage of the term "sudden and accidental" in the insurance industry, an insured can establish coverage under a general liability policy, which includes a qualified pollution exclusion, whether the contamination be gradual or abrupt "so long as it was unexpected and unintended." *Sunbeam Corp. v. Liberty Mut. Ins. Co.*, 781 A.2d 1189, 1195 (Pa. 2001). The court also endorsed the so-called regulatory estoppel argument: "[H]aving represented to the insurance department, a regulatory agency, that the new language in the 1970 policies—'sudden and accidental'—did not involve a significant decrease in coverage from the prior language, the insurance industry will not be heard to assert the opposite position when claims are made by the insured policyholders." *Id.* at 1192–93 (addressing the exclusion in the context of environmental pollution caused by manufacturers); *see also Bituminous Cas. Corp. v. Hems*, No. 06-1047, 2007 U.S. Dist. LEXIS 38429 (E.D. Pa. May 3, 2007) ("In *Sunbeam Corp.* … the Supreme Court of Pennsylvania held that the meaning of the 'sudden and accidental' exception to the standard pollution exclusion clause included in insurance liability policies should be interpreted based on the custom and usage of terms in the industry. The *Sunbeam* court concluded that the exception applies to both gradual and abrupt pollution or contamination as long as it is unexpected and unintended."); *Chemetron Invs., Inc. v. Fid & Cas. Co. of N.Y.*, 886 F. Supp. 1194, 1197 (W.D. Pa. 1994) (explaining that under Pennsylvania law, "the exception for 'sudden and accidental' discharges applies only to discharges that are abrupt and last a short time"); *Wiseman Oil Co., v. TIG Insurance Co.*, No. 011-1011, 2013 U.S. Dist. LEXIS 14747 (W.D. Pa. Jan. 22, 2013) (addressing *Sunbeam* and regulatory estoppel in detail); *Wehrenberg v. Metro. Prop. & Cas. Ins. Co.*, 715 Fed. Appx. 209 (3d Cir. 2017) (discussing *Sunbeam* in the context of a non-pollution claim under a property policy) ("Here, the evidence in the record reflects that the demolition of the property happened over a time span of about a month, a period of time that, as the District Court observed, cannot itself be considered 'abrupt.' But even if the initial physical damage could be considered 'abrupt,' the record evidence shows that after Wehrenberg learned of the damage in June 2012, he authorized Hyman to continue working on the property, at least to the extent of sheetrock being hung, which Wehrenberg himself then characterized as 'remodeling.' Under these circumstances, we cannot say that the damage to the property was either 'sudden' or 'accidental,' much less 'sudden and accidental,' as required under the Policy."); *Doherty v. Allstate Indem. Co.*, No. 15-05165, 2017 U.S. Dist. LEXIS 52795 (E.D. Pa. Apr. 6, 2017) (discussing *Sunbeam* in the context of a non-pollution claim under a property policy) ("Doherty must therefore adduce evidence that the losses were sudden and accidental in order to satisfy the 'burden of proving facts that bring [her] claim within the policy's affirmative grant of coverage.' Pennsylvania courts have held that 'accidental' means something that is unexpected and unintended (as opposed to foreseeable or certain to occur) while 'sudden' connotes an additional temporal element of abruptness or brevity. . . . The requirement that losses be 'sudden and accidental' thus contains both an accidental element and a temporal, sudden element, each of which must be established independently.").

Rhode Island: The Supreme Court of Rhode Island held that the word "sudden" "bars coverage for the intentional or reckless polluter but provides coverage to the insured that makes a good-faith effort to contain and to neutralize toxic waste but, nonetheless, still experiences unexpected and unintended releases of toxic chemicals that cause damage. Thus, coverage will be provided when the contamination was unexpected from the insured's standpoint: that is, when the insured reasonably believed that the waste-disposal methods in question were safe. The insured must show that it had no reason to expect the unintended damage and that it undertook reasonable efforts to contain the waste safely. In other words, a manufacturer that uses state-of-the-art technology, adheres to state and federal environmental regulations, and regularly inspects, evaluates, and upgrades its waste-containment system in accordance with advances in available technology should reap the benefits of coverage under our construction of this type of pollution-exclusion clause. But one that knowingly or recklessly disposes of waste without the necessary and advisable precautions will forfeit coverage under this clause." *Textron, Inc. v. Aetna Cas. & Sur. Co.*, 754 A.2d 742, 750 (R.I. 2000) (addressing hazardous waste generated during the insured's long-term use of a manufacturing facility in the context of exceptions to pollution exclusions for "sudden and accidental" discharges and "seepage, pollution or contamination ... caused by a sudden, unintended and unexpected happening during the period of this Insurance"); *see also St. Paul Fire & Marine Ins. Co. v. Warwick Dyeing Corp.*, 26 F.3d 1195, 1201 (1st Cir. 1994) (applying Rhode Island law) (finding "that the term 'sudden and accidental,' means, at the very least, 'unintended and unexpected'" and "intentional and expected discharges of pollutants are not covered under policies with the standard pollution exclusion") (addressing environmental contamination caused by the insured's expected and intended disposal of hazardous waste into landfills); *Travelers Cas. & Sur. Co. v. Providence Wash. Ins. Co., Inc.*, 685 F.3d 22, 33 (1st Cir. 2012) (applying Rhode Island law) (noting *Textron* for the contention that the pollution exclusion bars cover for the intentional or reckless polluter); *Nunez v. Merrimack Mut. Fire Ins. Co.*, 88 A.3d 1146, 1148 (R.I. 2014) (property policy) ("[A]ssuming *arguendo* that we were to adopt the plaintiffs' interpretation of *Textron* and determine that the loss was 'sudden and accidental' from their perspective, the damage would nevertheless remain uncovered under the policy. The plain language of the policy protects against loss caused by the '[s]udden and accidental tearing apart, cracking, burning or bulging of a steam or hot water heating system.' The plaintiffs, however, failed to present any evidence indicating that the loss was due to such a tearing apart, cracking, burning or bulging.").

South Carolina: The Supreme Court of South Carolina held that the term "sudden" is ambiguous and susceptible of more than one reasonable interpretation, and, therefore, construing the ambiguity, as it must, in favor of the insured, "sudden" is to be interpreted as "unexpected." *Greenville Cnty. v. Ins. Reserve Fund, a Div. of S.C. Budget & Control Bd.*, 443 S.E.2d 552, 553 (S.C. 1994) (addressing the exclusion in the context of claims by landowners, against a county, for inverse condemnation of their property caused by the county's maintenance of a landfill over the course of many years); *see also Helena Chem. Co. v. Allianz Underwriters Ins. Co.*, 594 S.E.2d 455, 460 (S.C. 2004) ("[T]his Court [in *Greenville*] specifically held that the term 'sudden' is to be interpreted as 'unexpected.' Consequently, we must determine whether the discharge, release, or escape of the pesticide was unexpected and accidental.") (holding that contamination at various sites was caused by the insured's routine business operations and was, therefore, not unexpected and accidental and did not fall within the exception to the pollution exclusion); *Graf v. Allstate Ins. Co.*, No. 2:06-cv-1045-CWH, 2006 U.S. Dist. LEXIS 94908 (D.S.C. Jan. 25, 2007) (citing *Greenville* for the proposition that "sudden" means "unexpected") ("The record does not show that the plaintiffs expected or intended their home to suffer from moisture intrusion. Nor does the record show that the plaintiffs expected or intended that the builder would defectively install the stucco exterior on their home. Therefore, the damage to the plaintiffs' house was sudden [within the context of a homeowner's policy providing coverage for "sudden and accidental physical loss to the property"].").; *Ross Dev. Corp. v. Fireman's Fund Ins. Co.*, 910 F. Supp. 2d 828, 833 (D.S.C. 2012) (holding that under the policy's qualified pollution exclusion, "sudden and accidental" clearly and unambiguously refers to the release of pollutants and not to any resulting property damage). "The South Carolina Supreme Court has held that 'sudden' contains no temporal limitation and means only 'unexpected.'" *Id.* (citing *Greenville*). "The South Carolina Supreme Court has also held that 'property damage caused by pollution arising from ordinary business operations is not covered' in a policy containing qualified pollution exclusion because such pollution cannot be said to be 'unexpected and accidental.'" *Ross Dev. Corp.*, 910 F. Supp. 2d at 833 (citing *Helena Chemical*) (finding that whether Ross's placement of pyrite slag occurred during "routine business operations" was irrelevant because the court found it intentional), *aff'd sub nom. Ross Dev. Corp. v. PCS Nitrogen Inc.*, No. 12-1189, 2013 U.S. App. LEXIS 5748 (4th Cir. Mar. 22, 2013) (applying South Carolina law) (holding that "because no party disputes the fact that Ross *intentionally* used pyrite slag as fill material (i.e., discharged waste) on the site, the 'sudden and accidental' exception to the qualified pollution exclusion does not apply") (emphasis in original); *S.C. Ins. Reserve Fund v. East Richland County Pub. Serv.*, 789 S.E. 2d 63 (Ct. App. S.C. 2016) ("We hold the releases of the odors here were not accidental and unexpected, thus, the exception does not apply. Brazell testified the air release valve was essential to the operation of the sewer line because it prevented the lines from exploding. Brazell also stated the District was aware that when the sewer pumps turned on, they would force air containing hydrogen sulfide into the environment. Although Brazell stated it was impossible to know when the pumps would turn on during a given day, he also acknowledged the pumps usually turned on several times a day. Accordingly, the District's knowledge that the pumps would turn on occasionally is sufficient to demonstrate that the releasing of the odors was not only expected, it was a necessary function of the line's normal operations.").

South Dakota: The Supreme Court of South Dakota, following a comprehensive survey of the issue nationally, held that "[f]rom our review of the divergent cases, we are persuaded by those courts finding 'sudden and accidental' unambiguous. Recognizing that 'sudden' has multiple dictionary definitions, we construe 'sudden' in the context of 'sudden and accidental' as used in this insurance contract. Such interpretation leads us to deduce that 'sudden' has a temporal meaning. To conclude otherwise effectively eliminates the word 'sudden' from the policy. It is our duty to construe an insurance contract according to its plain meaning." *Demaray v. De Smet Farm Mut. Ins. Co.*, 801 N.W.2d 284, 289 (S.D. 2011). "No language in the Alvine complaint arguably supported a cause of action for a 'sudden and accidental' discharge of pollutants. 'Intermittently' cannot be construed to mean abrupt or immediate. The complaint clearly made claims against Demaray and Hagemann for 'past and continuing' and 'repeated' discharges that 'will continue.' There is no immediacy or abruptness with a discharge that is intermittent, repeated, and likely to continue." *Id.* at 290. "The majority of courts decline to microanalyze an insured's long-term, routine disposal of pollutants in order to find discrete sudden and accidental polluting events." *Id.* (citations, quotations, and alterations omitted).

Tennessee: The Court of Appeals of Tennessee held "that the proper interpretation of the term 'sudden' necessarily includes a temporal element ... .

We find that the usual, natural, and ordinary meaning of 'sudden' is 'abrupt'—the opposite of 'gradual,' 'routine,' or 'continuous.'" *Drexel Chem. Co. v. Bituminous Ins. Co.*, 933 S.W.2d 471, 477 (Tenn. Ct. App. 1996). "When discharges of pollution occur on a regular, ongoing basis over a lengthy period of time as a normal part of an operation, such discharges are not 'sudden' within the meaning of the pollution exclusion clause. However, where the damage is caused by a 'few discrete polluting events, each of which was short in duration and accidental in nature,' the discharge will fall within the 'sudden and accidental' exception to the pollution exclusion and, therefore, the insurer will be liable for coverage under the policy." *Id.* (addressing contamination from numerous spills and leaks that occurred in the regular operation of a chemical mixing company's facility over course of several years); *see also U.S. Fid. & Guar. Co. v. Murray Ohio Mfg. Co.*, 693 F. Supp. 617 (M.D. Tenn. 1988), *aff'd*, 875 F.2d 868 (6th Cir. 1989) (applying Tennessee law) (defining the phrase "sudden and accidental" as "occurring both unexpectedly and relatively quickly in time") (addressing unintentional waste leakage occurring over a span of six years in the context of a duty to defend and finding such pollution was not "sudden"); *Sulphuric Acid Trading Co., Inc. v. Greenwich Ins. Co.*, 211 S.W.3d 243, 250 n.3 (Tenn. Ct. App. 2006) (explaining *Drexel* in the context of addressing the absolute pollution exclusion); *Interstate Packaging Co. v. Century Indem. Co.*, No. 3:11-cv-00589, 2012 U.S. Dist. LEXIS 35416 (M.D. Tenn. Mar. 14, 2012) (holding that the policy exclusions barred coverage for damages arising from the insured's intentional disposal of contaminated waste for economic reasons) (finding that the polluting events must meet both "sudden and accidental" requirements independently to fall within the exception).

    Texas: The Court of Appeals of Texas, after noting that only Texas federal courts had addressed the issue (and holding that "sudden" has a temporal element), held that "[t]he term 'sudden' has several recognized meanings, among which are 'unexpected' and 'unintended.' To determine its meaning in this case, the term must be read within the context of the policy. To read the word 'sudden' in the pollution exclusion to mean only unexpected and unintended would make it redundant of the word 'accidental.' The term 'accidental' already encompasses the concepts of being unexpected and unintended. In contrast, common usage of the term 'sudden' includes a temporal aspect." *Mesa Operating Co. v. Cal. Union Ins. Co.*, 986 S.W.2d 749, 755 (Tex. Ct. App. 1999) (addressing the exclusion in the context of claims for damages caused by salt water that leaked from a well into an aquifer over the course of several years); *see also St. Paul Surplus Lines Ins. Co. v. Geo Pipe Co.*, 25 S.W.3d

900, 904 (Tex. Ct. App. 2000) (following *Mesa* and holding that the sudden and accidental physical damage exception to the "impaired property" exclusion did not apply to a hole in oil well tubing, which was caused by corrosion of a weld, because corrosion is physical damage that is incremental or gradual); *Gulf Metals Indus., Inc. v. Chi. Ins. Co.*, 993 S.W.2d 800, 807 (Tex. Ct. App. 1999) ("[T]he word 'sudden' clearly and unambiguously imparts a sense of temporal urgency."); *Alpert v. Riley*, 274 S.W.3d 277, 288 (Tex. Ct. App. 2008) (noting the reasoning behind *Gulf Metals'* interpretation of "sudden" as having a temporal meaning because "accidental" describes an unforeseen or unexpected event and ascribing the same meaning to "sudden" would render the terms redundant); *SnyderGeneral Corp. v. Cont'l Ins.Co.*, 133 F.3d 373, 377 (5th Cir. 1998) (applying Texas law) (affirming the district court's grant of summary judgment for the insurer) (finding that since the insured expected the waste to discharge into the environment, the discharge was not "accidental"); *Longhorn Gasket & Supply Co. v. United States Fire Ins. Co.*, No. 15-41625, 2017 U.S. App. LEXIS 15706 (5th Cir. Aug. 18, 2017) (holding that, while the case law is mixed, asbestos constitutes a pollutant, and then shifting burden to the insured to attempt to prove that the sudden and accidental exception applies).

Utah: The Supreme Court of Utah held "that the language [of the qualified pollution exclusion] is unambiguous and that the term 'sudden' contains a temporal element, such as being abrupt or quick, and the term 'accidental' means something akin to unintended or unexpected. … The courts adopting this view have reasoned that the term 'sudden' includes an element of 'immediacy,' 'quickness,' or 'abruptness,' because the contrary reading would render the word 'accidental' (which clearly means unexpected) redundant." *Sharon Steel Corp. v. Aetna Cas. & Sur. Co.*, 931 P.2d 127, 135 (Utah 1997). "[I]f the releases were part of the overall business operations, then even if some of the releases viewed individually may have been 'sudden,' this does not alter the conclusion that the overall pattern of discharges was not 'sudden and accidental.'" *Id.* at 136 (citation and internal quotes omitted) (finding that the "sudden and accidental" exception did not restore coverage for the release of toxic material from tailings from the insured's ore milling operations); *see also Hartford Accident & Indem. Co. v. U.S. Fid. & Guar. Co.*, 962 F.2d 1484, 1488 (10th Cir. 1992) (applying Utah law) (interpreting "sudden and accidental" to mean "temporally abrupt" and "unexpected or unintended," while construing the two terms as separate, conditional requirements for coverage); *Wheeler v. Allstate Ins. Co.*, No. 15-4159, 2017 U.S. App. LEXIS 7954 (10th Cir. May 4, 2017) (discussing "sudden and accidental" in the context of an exclusion's exception for "the sudden and accidental escape of water or steam from a plumbing…system").

Vermont: No instructive authority. *But see Maska U.S., Inc. v. Kansa Gen. Ins. Co.*, 198 F.3d 74 (2nd Cir. 1999) (applying Vermont law) (addressing evidence that since 1970, when liability insurers began including pollution exclusions in their policies, the Vermont Department of Banking Insurance disapproved such policies based on its determination that the exclusions were unfair and discriminatory and inconsistent with the public's expectation of coverage under a general liability policy).

Virginia: A Virginia District Court, after noting the absence of a Supreme Court of Virginia decision interpreting the "sudden and accidental" pollution exclusion, predicted that a Virginia court would find that "[t]he sounder interpretation of the phrase 'sudden and accidental,' and the one adopted by the majority of jurisdictions, is that the phrase means both unexpected and unintended *and* quick or abrupt. This interpretation is the most accurate because it gives effect to both words in the phrase." *Morrow Corp. v. Harleysville Mut. Ins. Co.*, 101 F. Supp. 2d 422, 431 (E.D. Va. 2000) (emphasis in original) (addressing the pollution exclusion in the context of environmental property damage caused by the release of perchloroethylene in the insured's dry-cleaning business); *see also Asbestos Removal Corp. of Am., Inc. v. Guar. Nat. Ins. Co.*, 846 F. Supp. 33, 35 (E.D. Va. 1994), *aff'd*, 48 F.3d 1215 (4th Cir. 1995) (applying Virginia law) (defining "sudden" pollution as pollution which occurs "abruptly, instantly, or within a very short time") (involving pollution arising from the deliberate and continuous disposal, storage, and handling of toxic material over a number of years).

Washington: The Supreme Court of Washington, after finding the qualified pollution exclusion language to be ambiguous, held that "'sudden and accidental' means 'unexpected and unintended.' That is, for injury or damage to be covered under the occurrence clause, it must be neither expected nor intended. Gradual polluting events may fall within the occurrence clause provided they result in unexpected and unintended damage." *Queen City Farms, Inc. v. Cent. Nat. Ins. Co. of Omaha*, 882 P.2d 703, 723 (Wash. 1994) (en banc), *dissenting opinion amended by* 891 P.2d 718 (Wash. 1995) (noting that, because insurance policies often use words with similar meanings (i.e., "discharge, dispersal, release or escape"), "sudden and accidental" could mean unexpected and unintended) (discussing at length that representations were made by insurers to state insurance regulators that the pollution exclusion was intended to exclude coverage for intentional polluters and clarify the "occurrence" clause) (holding that toxic chemicals leaking out of a waste pit was "sudden and accidental"); *see also Time Oil Co. v. Cigna Prop. & Cas. Ins. Co.*, 743 F. Supp. 1400, 1408 (W.D. Wash. 1990) (holding that the term "sudden" in the context of the "sudden and accidental" pollution exclusion clause means "unforeseen and unexpected"); *Am. Nat'l Fire Ins. Co. v. B & L Trucking & Constr. Co.*, 951 P.2d 250, 255 (Wash. 1998) (citing *Queen City* for the meaning of "sudden and accidental"); *Reichhold Chems., Inc. v. Hartford Accident & Indem. Co.*, 750 A.2d 1051, 1054 (Conn. 2000) (applying Washington law) (citing to *Queen City* for the meaning of "sudden and accidental" in the context of pollution coverage) (holding that Washington law interprets "sudden and accidental" as "unexpected and unintended"); *Teck Metals, Ltd. v. Certain Underwriters at Lloyd's London*, 735 F. Supp. 2d 1246, 1250 (E.D. Wash. 2010) (finding that "the term 'sudden' [in the qualified pollution exclusion] does not contain a temporal element"); *Babai v. Allstate Ins. Co.*, No. 12-1518, 2014 U.S. Dist. LEXIS 189114 (W.D. Wash. Oct. 8, 2014) (discussing "sudden and accidental" in the context of policy requiring "a sudden and accidental direct physical loss"); *Port of Longview v. Arrowood Indem. Co.*, No. 46651-6, 2016 Wash. App. LEXIS 3100 (Wash. Ct. App. Dec. 21, 2016) (discussing *Queen City Farms*) ("[T]he exclusion does not apply if the *discharge or release* of contaminants is unexpected or unintended. Further, if contaminants are deposited in a place of containment, the relevant release is the escape of contaminants from that place into the environment.") (emphasis in original).

West Virginia: The Supreme Court of Appeals of West Virginia held that "the policies issued by [the insurer] covered pollution damage, even if it resulted over a period of time and was gradual, so long as it was not expected or intended." *Joy Techs., Inc. v. Liberty Mut. Ins.*, 421 S.E.2d 493, 500 (W. Va. 1992). The court's decision was based, in part, on the fact that "the insurance group representing [the insurer] unambiguously and officially represented to the West Virginia Insurance Commission that the exclusion in question did not alter coverage under the policies involved, coverage which included the injuries in the present case." *Id.* at 499–500 (addressing the qualified pollution exclusion in the context of contamination caused by PCBs used to clean mining equipment).

Wisconsin: The Supreme Court of Wisconsin concluded "that the phrase 'sudden and accidental,' contained in the pollution exclusion clause, means unexpected and unintended damages." *Just v. Land Reclamation, Ltd.*, 456 N.W.2d 570, 573 (Wis. 1990) (finding the phrase "sudden and accidental" ambiguous) (reasoning that the ambiguous phrase requires the court "to apply the interpretation favoring the insured" and "reject[ing] the insurers argument that the phrase 'sudden and accidental' has only a temporal meaning within the exclusionary clause"). "This conclusion comports with substantial evidence indicating that the insurance industry itself originally intended the phrase to be construed as 'unexpected and unintended.' This court may examine extrinsic evidence as an aid to determining the meaning of contract language when an insurance contract is ambiguous." *Id.* (addressing the exclusion in the context of environmental damage caused by discharges from a landfill); *see also Sharp v. Vick*, 670 N.W.2d 557 (Wis. Ct. App. 2003) (citing *Just* for the meaning of "sudden and accidental" in a homeowner's policy and concluding that the exception to the pollution exclusion applied because the insureds did not expect or intend the bodily injuries caused by their improper maintenance of a water well); *Biller v. Farmers Ins. Exch.*, 821 N.W.2d 413 (Wis. Ct. App. 2012) (property policy) (distinguishing *Just* because the policy language specified that, for coverage to exist, "the 'sudden and accidental' discharge must be exactly that"); *Enbridge Energy Co. v. Dane Cty.*, 929 N.W.2d 572 (Wis. 2019) (distinguishing *Just*, when interpreting "sudden" in the context of Wis. Stat. § 59.70(25), which precludes a county from requiring additional insurance from a hazardous liquid pipeline operator that has comprehensive general liability insurance with coverage for "sudden and accidental" pollution liability) (concluding that "sudden" has a temporal meaning, "such as something happening quickly, abruptly, or immediately," to avoid surplusage, if "sudden" meant "unexpected and unintended").

Wyoming: The Supreme Court of Wyoming held the "the words 'sudden and accidental' encompass a temporal aspect that requires the occurrence of an event to happen abruptly, without any significant notice and unexpectedly." *Sinclair Oil Corp. v. Republic Ins. Co.*, 929 P.2d 535, 543 (Wyo. 1996). "The exception to the exclusion clauses does not preserve coverage for gradual and unintentional discharges of pollutants unless such discharge is caused by a 'sudden and accidental' event as we have defined that phrase." *Id.* (addressing the exclusion in the context of damages from the insured's refinery operations); *see also Gainsco Ins. Co. v. Amoco Prod. Co.*, 53 P.3d 1051, 1062 (Wyo. 2002) (citing *Sinclair* in the context of addressing the total pollution exclusion).

CHAPTER
15

"Absolute" Pollution Exclusion

As discussed in the previous chapter, commercial general liability insurance policies have for some time sought to exclude coverage for pollution. The 1973 commercial general liability (CGL) form contained the qualified pollution exclusion addressed in the prior chapter. Under this exclusion, pollution-related claims were generally not covered unless the discharge of the pollutant was "sudden and accidental." Insurers interpreted this language to mean that the discharge must be both unintentional and abrupt if there was to be coverage. However, approximately half the states disagreed and found it sufficient to establish coverage if the discharge (or sometimes even the damage from the discharge) was unintentional, no matter how extended or ongoing the time period of the discharge. As the previous chapter illustrates, litigation over the meaning of "sudden and accidental" was abundant.

Reacting to this situation, the insurance industry replaced the qualified pollution exclusion with an "absolute" pollution exclusion that became part of the 1986 CGL form. Under the absolute pollution exclusion, the CGL policy clearly provides that it does not cover Superfund-style government-mandated cleanup and also states, more generally, that the policy does not cover bodily injury or property damage "arising out of the actual, alleged or threatened discharge, dispersal, seepage, migration, release or escape of 'pollutants,'" provided that such discharge, dispersal, etc. was of waste or from various specifically described premises, subject to certain exceptions. *See* INS. SERVS. OFFICE INC., COMMERCIAL GENERAL LIABILITY COVERAGE FORM, No. CG 00011185, § I2f (1984).

"Pollutants" are defined as

> any solid, liquid, gaseous or thermal irritant or contaminant, including smoke, vapor, soot, fumes, acids, alkalis, chemicals and waste. Waste includes materials to be recycled, reconditioned or reclaimed.

Id.

While the absolute pollution exclusion has undergone changes between the 1986 and later forms, its general purpose has remained the same—eliminate the "sudden and accidental" exception that had generated so much litigation over the scope of the qualified pollution exclusion.

Despite the breadth of the absolute pollution exclusion that is contained in the Insurance Services Office (ISO) CGL form, it is not unusual for insurers to replace it with an endorsement that is even broader in scope. This modified version is often referred to as the "total" pollution exclusion. While the absolute pollution exclusion requires that the discharge, dispersal, etc. of "pollutants" be of waste or from certain specifically described premises, the total pollution exclusion, as its name implies, does not contain this qualification. One commonly used total pollution exclusion provides as follows:

This insurance does not apply to:

f.   Pollution

(1) "Bodily injury" or "property damage" which would not have oc-curred in whole or part but for the actual, alleged or threatened discharge, dispersal, seepage, migration, release or escape of "pol-lutants" at any time.

(2) Any loss, cost or expense arising out of any:

(a) Request, demand, order or statutory or regulatory requirement that any Insured or others test for, monitor, clean up, remove, contain, treat, detoxify or neutralize, or in any way respond to, or assess the effects of "pollutants"; or

(b) Claim or suit by or on behalf of a governmental authority for damages because of testing for, monitoring, cleaning up, remov-ing, containing, treating, detoxifying or neutralizing, or in any way responding to, or assessing the effects of, "pollutants".

INS. SERVS. OFFICE PROPS., INC., TOTAL POLLUTION EXCLUSION ENDORSEMENT, No. CG 21 49 09 99 (1998).

For purposes of the issue discussed in this chapter, the absolute and total pollution exclusions are considered equivalent and are sometimes referred to herein as simply the pollution exclusion.

Although adoption of the absolute pollution exclusion was supposed to end the split in the states that had surrounded the qualified pollution exclusion, this proved not to be the case. While all courts have consistently applied the pollution exclusion to bar coverage for suits against a CGL policyholder involving traditional "smokestack" or "dumping" pollution, courts have divided over whether the exclusion, despite its broad language, applies to any claim involving a chemical or irritant—in other words, any hazardous substance.

Liability insurers have been aggressive and rather successful in some states invoking the exclusion to deny claims involving any hazardous substance, such as carbon monoxide poisoning due to faulty furnace repair, injuries from paint or adhesive fumes, bug or lawn spraying, and even to drifting smoke—all claims that many policyholders contend do not meet the commonsense definition of a pollution claim. In other states, courts have refused to give the absolute exclusion such a broad and literal (policyholders would say "hyperliteral") reading if this results in no coverage for liability claims that were noncontroversially viewed as within the scope of general liability policy coverage prior to 1986. Where the claim is one ordinarily arising out of the appropriate everyday activity of a commercial policyholder (faulty repair, negligent maintenance of a job site, poor performance) rather than due to polluting conduct per se, these courts tend to find the claim outside the scope of the pollution exclusion. *See W. Alliance Ins. Co. v. Gill,* 686 N.E.2d 997, 1000 (Mass. 1997) ("A reasonable policyholder might well understand carbon monoxide is a pollutant when it is emitted in an industrial or environmental setting, but would not reasonably characterize carbon monoxide emitted from a malfunctioning or improperly operated restaurant oven as pollution.") (citation and quotation omitted).

As the following survey of the issue demonstrates, in some states there are precedents that are inconsistent or at least in tension, requiring counsel and claims professionals to make distinctions that place a claim within one or another line of cases (see, for example, in Washington (discussed below) a claim involving chemical fumes from waterproofing was excluded but a spurting gasoline claim was not).

The basic divide is one of whether the pollution exclusion clause is interpreted in a highly textual, broad, literal manner to apply to liability arising out of or related to the discharge of any hazardous substance (the pro-insurer position, at least in the most common factual scenarios leading to dispute) or whether the exclusion is construed in a more functional manner focusing on the intent, purpose, and goal of the exclusion (the pro-policyholder position in most cases).[1] The divide between the courts regarding application of the pollution exclusion is also frequently described as a difference over whether the exclusion applies only to what is historically regarded as a pollution claim, such as hazardous waste or industrial pollution, often referred to as "traditional environmental pollution," or whether the exclusion, based on a broad linguistic reading, makes it applicable to claims involving any hazardous substance. *Compare Reed v. Auto-Owners Ins. Co.*, 667 S.E.2d 90, 92 (Ga. 2008) (holding that the pollution exclusion precluded coverage for a carbon monoxide claim as nothing in the text of the exclusion supported a reading that it was "limited to what is commonly or traditionally considered environmental pollution") *with Am. States Ins. Co. v. Koloms*, 687 N.E.2d 72, 79 (Ill. 1997) (holding that the pollution exclusion did not preclude coverage for a carbon monoxide claim) ("[W]e agree with those courts which have restricted the exclusion's otherwise potentially limitless application to only those hazards traditionally associated with environmental pollution. We find support for our decision in the drafting history of the exclusion, which reveals an intent on the part of the insurance industry to so limit the clause.").

Pro-policyholder courts on this issue are also more likely to emphasize that the pollution exclusion is an exclusion, which under the ground rules of insurance policy construction requires the insurer to shoulder the burden of persuasion to demonstrate that the exclusion clearly applies to the claim at issue. In addition,

---

1 Insurer counsel will, of course, contend that the purpose of the pollution exclusion was indeed to bar coverage for any case that involved the discharge of a chemical. The available drafting history of the exclusion and the background of its adoption, however, appear to be to the contrary—at least to one of the authors. Jeffrey W. Stempel, *Reason and Pollution: Correctly Construing the "Absolute" Exclusion in Context and in Accord with Its Purpose and Party Expectation*, 34 TORT & INS. L.J. 1 (1998); Jeffrey W. Stempel, *Unreason in Action: A Case Study in the Wrong Approach to Construing the Liability Insurance Pollution Exclusion*, 50 FLA. L. REV. 463 (1998). *But see* William P. Shelley & Richard C. Mason, *Appl i cation of the Absolute Pollution Exclusion to Toxic Tort Claims: Will Courts Choose Policy Co n struction or Deconstruction?*, 33 TORT & INS. L.J. 749 (1998) (taking opposite view and supporting insurer position on breadth of pollution exclusion). *See also Apana v. TIG Ins. Co.*, 574 F.3d 679 (9th Cir. 2009) (characterizing divide in judicial decisions as between those looking at the literal text of the exclusion versus those that consider the reasonable expectations of the policyholder); *MacKinnon v. Truck Ins. Exch.*, 73 P.3d 1205, 1208–09 (Cal. 2003) (explaining division of authority).

the general rule of contract construction in most states is that exclusions are to be narrowly construed and that policy language operating in the nature of an exclusion (e.g., narrow definitional language) should be strictly construed. Further, all states subscribe in some form to the *contra proferentem* principle in which ambiguous contract language is construed against the drafter, which is usually the insurer in most coverage disputes. *See Am. States Ins. Co. v. Kiger*, 662 N.E.2d 945, 949 (Ind. 1996) ("[S]ince the term 'pollutant' does not obviously include gasoline and, accordingly, is ambiguous, we once again must construe the language against the insurer who drafted it.").

Policyholder counsel also contend that the exclusion was not designed to read out from historical CGL coverage claims that do not involve widespread injury impacting the underwriting and risk pooling attending the CGL. Under this view, a carbon monoxide poisoning claim involving a house or parts of an apartment building would not be excluded, although a tanker truck explosion blanketing an entire neighborhood would fall within the exclusion because the nature and magnitude of the injury and claim are different.

As one court described the litigation over the pollution exclusion: "[T]here exists not just a split of authority, but an absolute fragmentation of authority." *Porterfield v. Audubon Indem. Co.*, 856 So. 2d 789, 800 (Ala. 2002). Another put it this way: "[T]here is a smorgasbord of authority offering a varying range of views and analyses [of the traditional versus non-traditional issue]." *TerraMatrix, Inc. v. U.S. Fire Ins. Co.*, 939 P.2d 483, 488 (Colo. App. 1997). Speaking of smorgasbords, *see Greengrass, Inc. v. Lumbermans Mut. Cas. Co.*, No. 09 Civ. 7697, 2010 U.S. Dist. LEXIS 76781 (S.D.N.Y. July 27, 2010), *aff'd*, 2011 U.S. App. LEXIS 22442 (2nd Cir. Nov. 4, 2011) (holding that the absolute pollution exclusion did not preclude coverage for odors emanating from the "Sturgeon King's" delicatessen) (noting that, according to Zagat's restaurant guide, "The smells alone are worth the price of admission.").

The following is a state-by-state listing of each state's dominant approach and key precedents. As always, some care is involved in reviewing the survey. Some precedents have obvious pro-insurer or pro-policyholder consequences but may be quite fact-specific. For example, a court may declare that the pollution exclusion is unambiguous in applying it to a clear case of traditional pollution. If a different case arises involving a less traditional pollution claim, the court may not be so confident in the exclusion's clarity. Similarly, a court may refuse to apply the exclusion to something like carbon monoxide poisoning of a camping family due to a malfunctioning space heater but be more willing to bar coverage if the carbon monoxide drifts to an adjoining campsite and causes injury there. Simply put, when it comes to the applicability of the pollution exclusion, facts can matter as much as the court's position on the fundamental divide between insurers and policyholder over the scope of the exclusion.

50-State Survey: "Absolute" Pollution Exclusion

Alabama: The Supreme Court of Alabama, despite concluding that lead paint qualifies as a "pollutant" under the terms of the pollution exclusion, went on to hold that the exclusion did not apply to preclude coverage because "a reasonably prudent insured might have concluded in 1991 that the presence of lead-paint flakes, chips, and/or dust in a residential apartment would not qualify as a discharge, dispersal, release, or escape of a pollutant." *Porterfield v. Audubon Indem. Co.*, 856 So. 2d 789, 805 (Ala. 2002) (noting also that more than sixty pollution exclusion cases were decided by courts during nine months case was pending); *see also Essex Ins. Co. v. Avondale Mills, Inc.*, 639 So. 2d 1339, 1342 (Ala. 1994) (finding a worker's exposure to asbestos released into "the environs of the building" during its dismantling was not a sufficient release into atmosphere to make exclusion applicable); *Scottsdale Ins. Co. v. American Safety Indem. Co.*, No. 1:10-cv-WS-N, 2010 U.S. Dist. LEXIS 144547 (S.D. Ala. Nov. 10, 2010) (unpublished, Dkt. 45, Ex. 1) (refusing to apply exclusion to suit seeking damages from builder for corrosive effects of Chinese drywall on ground that pollution exclusion limited to situations where policyholder contemporaneously performing operations; no application after builder has completed operations and left site prior to drywall problems); *QBE Ins. Corp. v. Estes Heating & Air Conditioning, Inc.*, No. 10-456, 2012 U.S. Dist. LEXIS 16159 (S.D. Ala. Feb. 8, 2012) (finding pollution exclusion precluded coverage for claims against HVAC system installer whose HVAC system exacerbated and proximately caused bodily injury and property damage related to Chinese drywall); *Pennsylvania Nat. Mut. Cas. Ins. Co. v. Snead Door, LLC*, No. 4:12-CV-3731, 2013 U.S. Dist. LEXIS 18535 (N.D. Ala. Feb. 12, 2013) (holding that pollution exclusion barred coverage for Chinese drywall supplier that did not install drywall or otherwise construct home); *Federated Mut. Ins. Co. v. Abston Petroleum, Inc.*, 967 So. 2d 705, 713 (Ala. 2007) (finding the pollution exclusion precluded coverage for gas that leaked from underground lines of aboveground tanks) ("We hold that gasoline, although not a pollutant when properly used for the purposes for which it is intended, is clearly a pollutant when it leaks into the soil from underground lines or tanks or when fumes from such a leak are so dangerous that a business must be closed, as was the case here ... . Because we conclude that gasoline is clearly a pollutant as that term is used in the policy, any argument that the pollution-exclusion clause is ambiguous cannot be supported."); *Evanston Ins. Co. v. J&J Cable Constr., LLC*, No. 15-506, 2016 U.S. Dist. LEXIS 129371 (M.D. Ala. Sept. 22, 2016) ("[B]ecause *Porterfield* directs courts to look at previous Alabama Supreme Court interpretations of the pollution exclusion, and because *Armstrong* [*United States Fidelity & Guaranty Co. v. Armstrong*, 479 So. 2d 1164 (Ala. 1985)] found as a matter of law that sewage is not a pollutant under the qualified pollution-exclusion, a reasonably prudent person would understand 'pollutant' not to include sewage under the facts of this case.").

In *Maxine Furs, Inc. v. Auto-Owners Ins. Co.*, No. 10-13547, 2011 U.S. App. LEXIS 6706 (11th Cir. Mar. 31, 2011), the Eleventh Circuit, applying Alabama law, determined that no coverage was owed where a business owner's fur coats and related products were soiled by the smell of curry, which had been absorbed through a shared air duct with a neighboring Indian food restaurant, as the court found that curry aroma is a contaminant excluded under the pollution exception within the owner's first-party property policy. The court stated that "[a] contaminant is something that 'soil[s], stain[s], corrupts[s] or infect[s] by contact or association [quoting WEBSTER'S THIRD NEW INT'L DICTIONARY]. [W]hat happened here is that the curry aroma soiled Maxine's furs. Otherwise, they would not have needed cleaning. We do not think that a reasonable person could conclude otherwise. Accordingly, we conclude that curry aroma is a pollutant under the policy."

Stempel needed blood pressure medication after Maniloff alerted him to this case, but calmed down a bit because it was a first-party property case and as a federal court decision does not directly set Alabama law. The *Maxine Furs* court ignores the drafting intent and overall purpose of the policy favoring a textual approach, but then interprets the exclusion broadly—which violates the textual interpretation rule calling for strict narrow construction of exclusions, with the burden of persuasively showing clarity placed upon the insurer. If curry were within the common concept of "pollution," the EPA would presumably be shutting down Indian restaurants throughout America. By the court's reasoning, we would have the same result if local juvenile delinquents snuck into Maxine's at night to smoke where their parents would not find them or if there was smoke damage from a fire (absent a specific textual exception to the pollution exclusion). [Maniloff: Jeff has *still* not stopped talking about THAT "curry" case.]

Alaska: The Supreme Court of Alaska held that the language of the pollution exclusion was unambiguous and applied it to preclude coverage for gasoline that leaked from a broken fill pipe connected to an underground storage tank. *Whittier Props., Inc. v. Ala. Nat'l Ins. Co.*, 185 P.3d 84, 89–92 (Alaska 2008). In this case of first impression the court "conclude[d] that the better-reasoned approach is the one advocated by [the insurer] and adopted by the majority of courts that have reviewed a pollution exclusion identical or markedly similar to the clause [here]. We hold that there is no ambiguity because, even though gasoline that is in the UST is a 'product' for purposes of other parts of the insurance policy, when the gasoline escapes or reaches a location where it is no longer a useful product it is fairly considered a pollutant." *Id.* at 90–91.

Arizona: The Court of Appeals of Arizona held that the pollution exclusion did not bar coverage for a claim for injury to a professional golfer, who ingested bacteria-contaminated drinking water at the policyholder's golf course, because the plain meaning of "pollutant does not include bacteria." *Keggi v. Northbrook Prop. & Cas. Ins. Co.*, 13 P.3d 785, 790 (Ariz. Ct. App. 2000). The court "decline[d] to interpret the term 'pollutants' so broadly as to include 'bacteria,' and thereby to negate coverage in this case, especially where there was no evidence that the contamination of the water with the bacteria was caused by traditional environmental pollution [which the court determined was the insurance industry's purpose in creating the absolute pollution exclusion]." *Id.* at 792. Arizona federal courts have addressed the issue more recently. *See Saba v. Occidental Fire & Cas. Co.*, No. 14-00377, 2014 U.S. Dist. LEXIS 174169 (D. Ariz. Dec. 16, 2014) ("In this case, the carbon monoxide was not a pre-existing substance; it was produced by the negligent installation of the water heater itself and did not result from any efforts at environmental cleanup. This takes the case out of any 'traditional environmental pollution-related claims,' and thus Arizona public policy as interpreted by the *Keggi* court prevents this Court from giving the pollution exclusion the interpretation requested by Occidental. Further, the transaction as a whole, the insuring of a plumbing business, calls into question a broader application of the pollution exclusion than would arise in 'traditional environmental pollution-related claims.' In the present case, activities such as the installation of plumbing devices were contemplated by the policies. The scope of interpretation requested by Occidental would seemingly eviscerate coverage."); *Nat'l Fire Ins. Co. v. James River Ins.*, 162 F. Supp. 3d 898 (D. Ariz. 2016) ("After careful consideration, the Court concludes that the Policy's clause operates to exclude coverage for traditional environmental pollution claims, and does not exclude the property damage caused by Hydrogen Sulfide gas created by Quik Flush's faulty pipe installation."); *Starr Surplus Lines Ins. Co. v. Star Roofing, Inc.*, No. 18-0641, 2019 Ariz. App. Unpub. LEXIS 1196 (Ariz. Ct. App. Oct. 31, 2019) (underlying plaintiff suffered injuries as a result of being overcome by breathing fumes released from the insured's roofing work) ("After considering the Arizona public policy limitations on pollution exclusions as comprehensively analyzed in *Keggi*, pollution exclusions are intended to cover traditional environmental pollution claims and not the bodily injuries allegedly suffered by Delarosa as a result of Star Roofing's alleged negligence in the installation of the commercial building's roof."); *London Bridge Resort LLC v. Ill. Union Ins. Co.*, No. 20-08109, 2020 U.S. Dist. LEXIS 227816 (D. Ariz. Dec. 4, 2020) (using the reasoning of *Keggi* to interpret the scope of coverage under a pollution liability policy) ("The Court has little trouble concluding that no plausible interpretation of 'traditional environmental pollution' includes a virus outbreak [Covid-19].").

Arkansas: The Supreme Court of Arkansas held that the pollution exclusion did not apply to a claim arising out of a sewer system backup in a mobile home park. *Minerva Enter., Inc. v. Bituminous Cas. Corp.*, 851 S.W.2d 403, 406 (Ark. 1993). The court found that "the pollution exclusion in the case before us is, at least, ambiguous. It is not clear from the language of the policy that the single back-up of a septic tank in a mobile home park is necessarily the kind of damage the clause was intended to exclude." *Id.* "[T]he term 'waste' must be considered within the context of the entire list, all of which are pollutants related to industrial waste." *Id.*; *see also State Auto Prop. & Cas. Ins. Co. v. Ark. Dept. of Envtl. Quality*, 258 S.W.3d 736, 742–43 (Ark. 2007) (rejecting the insurer's argument that *Minerva* was wrongly decided, but reversing summary judgment granted to insured because fact finder failed to consider extrinsic evidence to decide whether release of gasoline from storage tanks was "persistent industrial pollution" that exclusion was meant to preclude); *Scottsdale Ins. Co. v. Morrow Valley Co., LLC*, 411 S.W.3d 184 (Ark. 2012) (citing *Minerva* and *Ark. Dept. of Envtl. Quality* and holding that the pollution exclusion was ambiguous and did not apply to claim against poultry farmer because definition of "gases, smoke, dust, fumes, odors, and particulates" as pollutants was susceptible to more than one reasonable interpretation); *Universal Cas. Co. v. Triple Transport, Inc.*, No. 4:08CV01822BSM, 2009 U.S. Dist. LEXIS 59358 (E.D. Ark. July 13, 2009) (finding fact question whether water containing hydrocarbons, reserve pit water, and drilling mud or oil were "pollutants"); *Tyson Foods, Inc. v. Allstate Ins. Co.*, No. 09C07087, 2011 Del. Super. LEXIS 379 (Del. Super. Ct. Aug. 31, 2011) (applying Arkansas law) (holding that the pollution exclusion did not preclude coverage for contamination of surface water, ground water and drinking water caused by discharge of poultry waste).

California: The Supreme Court of California, seeking to avoid "absurd results," refused to apply the language of the absolute pollution exclusion literally and broadly, holding that the scope of the pollution exclusion would be limited "to injuries arising from events commonly thought of as pollution, i.e., environmental pollution." *MacKinnon v. Truck Ins. Exch.*, 73 P.3d 1205, 1216 (Cal. 2003) (holding that the pollution exclusion did not apply to preclude from coverage claims resulting from exposure to insecticide). The court recognized that "terms such as 'commonly thought of as pollution,' or 'environmental pollution,' are not paragons of precision, and further clarification may be required." *Id.* at 1217; *see also Griffin Dewatering Corp. v. N. Ins. Co. of N.Y.*, 97 Cal. Rptr. 3d 568, 589–90 (Cal. Ct. App. 2009) (finding that the "*MacKinnon* decision [was] the appropriate way to determine the reasonableness of the insurer's coverage determination" under the absolute pollution exclusion where the injury-causing event was the flow of raw sewage flowing from a sewer line under construction by the insured); *Johnson v. Clarendon Nat. Ins. Co.*, No. G039659, 2009 Cal. App. Unpub. LEXIS 972 (Cal. Ct. App. Feb. 4, 2009) (analyzing *MacKinnon* and holding that the pollution exclusion did not preclude coverage for mold). *Compare SEMX Corp. v. Fed. Ins. Co.*, 398 F. Supp. 2d 1103 (S.D. Cal. 2005) (concluding that, because the injury-causing event [the release of ammonia gases into the air] was a one-time release, and not the result of the insured's normal operations, the pollution exclusion did not apply to preclude coverage) *with Garamendi v. Golden Eagle Ins. Co.*, 25 Cal. Rptr. 3d 642 (Cal. Ct. App. 2005) (holding that the pollution exclusion applied to preclude coverage for claims for injuries caused by the repeated long-term exposure to silica dust). *See also Am. Cas. Co. of Reading, PA v. Miller*, 71 Cal. Rptr. 3d 571, 582 (Cal. Ct. App. 2008) (holding that release of chemicals into sewer by furniture-stripping business was environmental pollution and therefore within absolute pollution exclusion); *Ruffin Road Venture Lot IV v. Travelers Prop. Cas. Co.*, No. 10-CV-11, 2011 U.S. Dist. LEXIS 66095 (S.D. Cal. June 20, 2011) (discussing a pollution inclusionary provision, but analogizing it to a pollution exclusion provision and determining that dirt did not fall under policy's "pollutant" definition that was "drawn almost word-for-word from the so called absolute pollution exclusion") (declaring that "the policy's definition of 'pollutant' is most naturally understood as a reference to traditional environmental pollution"); *Villa Los Alamos Homeowners Ass'n v. State Farm General Ins. Co.*, 130

Cal. Rptr. 3d 374 (Cal. Ct. App. 2011) (holding that *MacKinnon's* interpretation of the pollution exclusion applies to first party property policies and that the release of asbestos during the scraping of a popcorn ceiling in a residential unit constituted environmental pollution); *Nicholson v. Allstate Ins. Co.*, 979 F. Supp. 2d 1054 (E.D. Cal. 2013) (citing *MacKinnon* and declining to classify bat guano as a pollutant because an insured could not be reasonably expected to believe policy precluded coverage for bat infestation); *EFK Investments, LLC v. Peerless Ins. Co.*, No. 13-5910, 2014 U.S. Dist. LEXIS 137864 (N.D. Cal. Sept. 26, 2014) ("In determining whether an injury arises from events commonly regarded as 'environmental pollution,' post-*MacKinnon* cases have looked to evidence such as: whether the insured knew of the presence of the pollutant; how widespread was the dissemination of the pollutant; whether the pollutant is one that is regulated by state and federal environmental laws; whether handling of the alleged pollutant is regulated or controlled; and, relatedly, whether the nature of the pollutant is such that a reasonable insured would understand that any release would be harmful."); *Essex Walnut Owner L.P. v. Aspen Specialty Ins. Co.*, 335 F. Supp. 3d 1146 (N.D. Cal. 2018) (applying *MacKinnon* to determine the extent of coverage under a pollution policy's insuring agreement) ("[T]he basic teaching of *MacKinnon* - namely, that 'pollutant' should be understood to mean something that is commonly thought of as pollution, i.e., environmental pollution — logically applies even in the context of the case at bar."); *Kingsley Management Corp. v. Occidental Fire & Cas.*, 441 F. Supp. 3d 1016 (S.D. Cal. 2020) ("In light of this historical analysis provided in *MacKinnon*, the Court is inclined to agree with Plaintiffs in that Coverage B's pollution exclusion was intended to exclude the acts of persistent polluters and the Court would therefore be expanding the historical intent of the pollution exclusion clause by including the acts of parties that did not engage in any act of pollution."); *Crosby Estate at Rancho Sante Fe Master Ass'n v. Ironshore Specialty Ins. Co.*, No. 19-2369, 2020 U.S. Dist. LEXIS 205411 (S.D. Cal. Nov. 3, 2020) (holding that the pollution exclusion did not preclude coverage for allegations that residents of a homeowners' association honked their horns while passing over a neighboring association's speedbumps because "[a]lthough the Policy defines pollutants to include 'any noise,' the term 'any noise' is not to be read literally and in isolation, but must be construed in the context of how it is used in the policy, i.e., defining 'pollutant'").

Colorado: The Colorado Court of Appeals, noting that there is a "smorgasbord of authority" offering a varying range of views and analyses of the traditional versus non-traditional issue, aligned itself with the jurisdictions that have concluded that the plain language of the pollution exclusion is not limited solely to environmental or industrial contexts and held that "the pollution exclusion clause is unambiguous when applied to ammonia vapors, that ammonia constitutes a pollutant under the pollution exclusion clause, and that movement of the ammonia vapors within the office building air duct or ventilation system constituted a 'discharge, dispersal … release, or escape' within the meaning of the pollution exclusion." *TerraMatrix, Inc. v. U.S. Fire Ins. Co.*, 939 P.2d 483, 488 (Colo. Ct. App. 1997) (alteration in original); *see also New Salida Ditch Co., Inc. v. United Fire & Cas. Co.*, No. 08-cv-00391, 2009 U.S. Dist. LEXIS 118377 (D. Colo. Dec. 18, 2009) (*affirmed New Salida Ditch Co. v. United Fire & Cas. Ins. Co.*, 400 Fed. Appx. 338 (10th Cir. 2010) (finding claims arising out of the discharge of soil, sand, dirt, rocks, and sediment into a river to be precluded by the pollution exclusion); *Allstate Ins. Co. v. Von Metzger*, No. 10-CV-00863-PAB-CBS, 2011 U.S. Dist. LEXIS 19741 (D. Colo. Feb. 28, 2011) ("Colorado courts addressing absolute pollution exclusions determine whether the exclusion is ambiguous by examining how it would apply to the facts and circumstances of the particular case") (finding that insurer had no duty to defend policyholder for damages caused by oil and other toxins in soil of housing development because policyholders were on notice of the pollution on property and exclusion's wording, which differed from the standard CGL language, suggested insurer's intent to avoid coverage for builder's failure to clean up or disclose pollution to buyers) (finding that exclusion did not even require discharge of pollutant but was applicable whenever pollution was "cause" of injury); *Mt. States Mut. Cas. Co. v. Roinestad*, 296 P.3d 1020 (Colo. 2013) (holding that pollution exclusion applied to cooking oil and grease that had been poured down a sewer drain—where two men suffered injuries from breathing hydrogen sulfide fumes—because volume of grease discharged created dangerous buildup of toxic gas above amount of hydrogen sulfide naturally found in sewers) (determining that pollution exclusion was not limited to traditional pollutants); *Figuli v. State Farm Mut. Fire & Cas.*, 304 P.3d 595 (Colo. Ct. App. 2012) (stating that raw sewage was unambiguously a pollutant as used in the pollution exclusion).

Connecticut: The Supreme Court of Connecticut held that the leakage of contaminants and hazardous substances into soil and water, at a site where the insured removed insulation from copper wire, fell squarely within the pollution exclusion. *Schilberg Integrated Metals Corp. v. Continental Cas. Co.*, 819 A.2d 773, 785 (Conn. 2003) (holding that *Heyman Assocs. No. 1 v. Ins. Co. of the State of Pa.*, 653 A.2d 122 (Conn. 1995) did not adopt the approach that the exclusion does not apply when pollution occurs in the course of the insured's central business activity); *see also Heyman Assocs.*, 653 A.2d at 122 (holding that exclusion precluded coverage for fuel oil released into a harbor). *But see Danbury Ins. Co. v. Novella*, 727 A.2d 279, 285 (Conn. Super. Ct. 1998) (distinguishing *Heyman Assocs.* and finding exclusion inapplicable, as ambiguous, in case involving lead paint chipping and flaking off interior and exterior walls of insured's rental unit) ("Although *Heyman* did not expressly adopt an 'environmental' reading of pollution exclusion clauses, its underlying facts, where fuel oil spilled or released into a waterway caused environmental damage, present a classic case of environmental pollution."); *Nat'l Grange Mut. Ins. Co. v. Caraker*, No. CV030070715, 2006 Conn. Super. LEXIS 815 (Conn. Super. Ct. Feb. 28 2006) ("The exclusion clause is … ambiguous with respect to whether asbestos released as described in the complaint can be properly classified as a pollutant."); *R.T. Vanderbilt Co., Inc. v. Hartford Accident & Indem. Co.*, 156 A.3d 539 (Conn. Ct. App. 2017)("The question whether a pollution exclusion clause in a comprehensive general liability policy bars coverage for claims arising from exposure to toxic substances such as asbestos in indoor environments and/ or in the course of their intended use is one of first impression for Connecticut's appellate courts. Recognizing that the question is a close one, over which our sister courts are sharply divided, we conclude that the pollution exclusions bar coverage only when the exposure arises from traditional environmental pollution, such as when the dumping of waste materials containing asbestos causes asbestos fibers to migrate onto neighboring properties or into the natural environment.") ("We agree with our sister courts that this drafting history makes abundantly clear that the insurance industry drafted the pollution exclusion in 1970 to address new liabilities that had arisen in conjunction with the advent of the modern environmental regulatory system in the 1960s, and that the exclusion was intended to bar coverage only for liabilities arising out of traditional environmental pollution such as the intentional dumping of hazardous waste and other toxic materials into the natural environment. The clause was never intended to apply to situations in which a commercial or industrial product is discovered to pose health threats to individuals who manufacture, apply, or are otherwise exposed to it in the ordinary course of business.") (*aff'd* 216 A.3d 629 (Conn. 2019)) (adopting the Appellate Court's "thorough and well reasoned opinion" regarding the applicability of the pollution exclusion); *Wayland v. Atl. Mut. Cas. Co.*, No. X03CV116026748S, 2015 Conn. Super. LEXIS 2022 (July 29, 2015) ("Anyone with even a superficial knowledge of what carbon monoxide is—a colorless, odorless, potentially deadly gas which comes from engines which run on gasoline—cannot honestly argue that it is not a pollutant.") ("This court therefore rejects plaintiff's argument that her failure to warn and/or inspect claims are not precluded by the Total Pollution Exclusion.").

Delaware: The Superior Court of Delaware held that "it is appropriate to apply the total pollution exclusion outside of situations involving 'traditional' environmental and industrial pollution." *Farm Family Cas. Co. v. Cumberland Ins. Co., Inc.*, No. k11C-07-006, 2013 Del. Super. LEXIS 427 (Del. Super. Ct. Oct. 2, 2013) (finding that lead paint was a pollutant and a contaminant under the total pollution exclusion, and, therefore, coverage was precluded in lead poisoning claim resulting from negligent residential lead paint abatement process). Other Delaware courts that have addressed the pollution exclusion have done so applying the law of another state.

District of Columbia: After a lengthy discussion on the history of pollution exclusions, the Circuit Court of Appeals for the District of Columbia held that pollution exclusions are limited to pollution of natural environments, particularly for the types of pollution regulated by federal environmental law. *Richardson v. Nationwide Mut. Ins. Co.*, 826 A.2d 310 (D.C. Cir. 2003) (concluding that security guard's inhalation of carbon monoxide fumes from an apartment house furnace did not fall within the absolute pollution exclusion) (vacated due to settlement after grant of rehearing en banc).

Florida: The Supreme Court of Florida held that the pollution exclusion precluded coverage for claims for bodily injury and loss of income arising out of a blueprint machine that was knocked over in an office and emitted ammonia fumes. *Deni Assocs. of Fla., Inc. v. State Farm Fire & Cas. Ins. Co.*, 711 So. 2d 1135, 1141 (Fla. 1998). The court rejected various arguments that the pollution exclusion was ambiguous and only excluded environmental or industrial pollution. *Id.* at 1138–39; *see also Fogg v. Fla. Farm Bureau Mut. Ins. Co.*, 711 So. 2d 1135, 1141 (Fla. 1998) (companion case to *Deni*) (holding that the pollution exclusion precluded coverage for bodily injury claims by bystanders who were negligently sprayed with a chemical by a crop-dusting plane); *First Specialty Ins. v. GRS Mgmt.*, No. 08–81356, 2009 U.S. Dist. LEXIS 72708 (S.D. Fla. Aug. 17, 2009) (involving a claim arising out of ingestion of swimming pool water tainted by viral contaminants subject to pollution exclusion); *Chestnut Assocs. v. Assurance Co. of Am.*, No. 8:13-CV-1755-T-17TBM, 2014 U.S. Dist. LEXIS 59278 (M.D. Fla. Apr. 29, 2014) (holding that ejaculate which contaminated swimming pool constituted pollutant and, therefore, pollution exclusion precluded coverage); *Nova Cas. Co. v. Waserstein*, 424 F. Supp. 2d 1325, 1334 (S.D. Fla. 2006) (holding that the pollution exclusion applied to preclude coverage for personal injury claims filed by workers in a building who alleged that they were harmed when the building owner/insured failed to keep the air and surfaces in the building free of various organisms and allergens); *Phila. Indem. Ins. Co. v. Yachtsman's Inn Condominium Assoc., Inc.*, 595 F. Supp. 2d 1319, 1325 (S.D. Fla. 2009) (finding pollution exclusion unambiguously applied to claims for exposure to battery acid, raw sewage, and feces); *Mt. Hawley Ins. Co. v. Dania Distrib. Ctr.*, 513 Fed. Appx. 890 (11th Cir. 2013) (determining that insurer had no duty to defend where numerous pollutants were released into ground during construction operations, which caused injury to homeowners and construction workers); *JB Recycling Group, Inc. v. Landmark Am. Ins. Co.*, No. 11-23695, 2012 U.S. Dist. LEXIS 115042 (S.D. Fla. Aug. 15, 2012) (holding that fuel and operating fluids released onto property when mulching excavator caught fire constituted pollutants and triggered the pollution exclusion); *Gen. Fidelity v. Foster*, No. 09-80743, 2011 U.S. Dist. LEXIS 103618 (S.D. Fla. Mar. 24, 2011) (unpublished opinion) (determining that "the compounds released by the elemental sulfur and strontium [in the gypsum drywall] are pollutants within the meaning of the policy and the Pollution Exclusion does apply"); *Granite State Ins. Co. v. American Bldg. Materials, Inc.*, 504 Fed. Appx. 815 (11th Cir. 2013) (holding that damages from Chinese drywall were excluded from coverage under plain language of the pollution exclusion); *CDC Builders, Inc. v. Amerisure Mut. Ins. Co.*, No. 10-21678, 2011 U.S. Dist. LEXIS 114509 (S.D. Fla. Aug. 16, 2011) (determining that pollution exclusion applied to damages from Chinese drywall); *Colony Ins. Co. v. Total Contracting & Roofing, Inc.*, No. 10-23091 (S.D. Fla. Oct. 18, 2011) (following *CDC Builders* regarding Chinese drywall); *First Specialty Ins. Corp. v. Milton Const. Co.*, No. 12-20116, 2012 U.S. Dist. LEXIS 97972 (S.D. Fla. July 16, 2012) (holding that damages which resulted from Chinese drywall, including "rapid sulfidation" to personal property, fell under the pollution exclusion); *Am. Home Assur. Co. v. Arrow Terminals, Inc.*, No. 8:11-cv-1278-T-30, 2012 U.S. Dist. LEXIS 65610 (M.D. Fla. May 8, 2013) (holding that "into or upon land, the atmosphere, or any watercourse or body of water" language limits the pollution exclusion to outdoor environmental contamination so exclusion did not apply to damage caused by interior Chinese drywall; *In re FEMA Trailer Formaldehyde Prod. Liab. Litig.*, No. 07-1873, 2011 U.S. Dist. LEXIS 7083 (E.D. La. Jan. 25, 2011) (applying Florida law) (holding that formaldehyde fumes constituted pollutant under total pollution exclusion and precluded insured from coverage); *Rockhill Ins. Co. v. Coyote Land Co.*, No. 3:09cv556, 2011 U.S. Dist. LEXIS 11040 (N.D. Fla. Feb. 4, 2011) (finding that insurer had no duty to defend insured after insured was sued for "damages relating to the emanation of hydrogen sulfide gas from [insured's] landfill" because hydrogen sulfide, is "a hazardous air pollutant" that fell under the policy's pollution exclusion); *Markel Intern. Ins. Co., Ltd. v. Florida West Covered RV & Boat Storage, LLC*, No. 11–11511, 2011 U.S. App. LEXIS 16552 (11th Cir. Aug. 11, 2011) (applying Florida law) (millings from roadwork, that mixed with flood water, constituted a "pollutant" within the meaning of the absolute pollution exclusion) (claim for bacterial infection); *Maxum Indem. Co. v. Fla. Constr. Servs.*, 59 F. Supp. 3d 1382 (M.D. Fla. 2014) ("As the Eleventh Circuit and many other courts have held, and as Defendants do not dispute, carbon monoxide is a pollutant."); *Evanston Ins. Co. v. Haven S. Beach, LLC*, 152 F. Supp. 3d 1370 (S.D. Fla. 2015) (holding that "[t]he allegations in the Underlying Complaint clearly support a finding that Haven poured forth the liquid nitrogen, a 'pollutant', into Mrs. Kaufman's beverage. Accordingly, the Pollution Exclusion applies and bars coverage for the Kaufman's claims."). *But see WPC Indus. Contractors Ltd. v. Amerisure Mut. Ins. Co.*, 660 F. Supp. 2d 1341, 1348 (D. Fla. 2009) (holding that the pollution exclusion did not apply—but on the basis that the exclusion's specific terms were not satisfied); *Westport Ins. Corp. v. VN Hotel Group, LLC*, 513 Fed. Appx. 927 (11th Cir. 2013) (concluding that legionella bacteria did not qualify as a pollutant because it was (1) not an irritant or contaminant, and (2) not a "solid, liquid, gaseous, or thermal" substance); *Colony Ins. Co. v. Great Am. Alliance Ins. Co.*, 317 F. Supp. 3d 1181 (S.D. Fla. 2018) (carbon monoxide is a pollutant and exception to exclusion not applicable as carbon monoxide did not originate from A/C ducts or vents but merely traveled through them); *AIX Specialty Ins. Co. v. Williams-Panton*, No. 18-62553, 2019 U.S. Dist. LEXIS 35026 (S.D. Fla. Mar. 4, 2019) (pollution exclusion applied to personal injury caused by inhaling toxic fumes, from oil-based paint, that recirculated through a building's air condition unit); *BBG Design Build v. Southern Owners Inc. Co.*, 820 Fed. Appx. 962 (11th Cir. 2020) (pollution exclusion "clearly encompasses" construction debris, such as "fiberglass particulates and other bits of dust in the air as a result of construction work-which caused irritation to . . . lungs, eyes, and skin when it contaminated the air . . . breathed"); *Capitol Specialty Ins. Corp. v. West View Apartments*, No. 20-22476, 2021 U.S. Dist. LEXIS 97241 (S.D. Fla. April 15, 2021) ("According to the underlying state court complaint, West View's employees poured acid through the wrong vent, which unfortunately caused serious injuries to Crespo and Lopez. These allegations are essentially that someone discharged or released liquid acid, which caused bodily injury. Accordingly, the Court finds that the pollution exclusion applies, and Capitol has no duty to defend West View in the state court action.") (rejecting argument that "pouring" did not satisfy the exclusion's discharge or dispersal, i.e., "movement," requirement).

Georgia: The Supreme Court of Georgia held that the pollution exclusion unambiguously precluded coverage for a carbon monoxide leak in an insured landlord's rental property because it qualified as a "pollutant." *Reed v. Auto-Owners Ins. Co.*, 667 S.E.2d 90, 92 (Ga. 2008). "As all parties recognize, the question thus narrows to whether carbon monoxide gas is a 'pollutant'—i.e., matter, in any state, acting as an 'irritant or contaminant,' including 'fumes.' We need not consult a plethora of dictionaries and statutes to conclude that it is." *Id.* The court concluded that nothing in the text of the pollution exclusion supported a reading that it was "limited to what is commonly or traditionally considered environmental pollution." *Id.* In *Ga. Farm. Bureau Mut. Ins. Co. v. Smith*, 784 S.E.2d 422 (Ga. 2016), the Supreme Court of Georgia held that "[u]nder the broad definition contained in Chupp's policy, we conclude that lead present in paint unambiguously qualifies as a pollutant and that the plain language of the policy's pollution exclusion clause thus excludes Smith's claims against Chupp from coverage." *See also Truitt Oil & Gas Co. v. Ranger Ins. Co.*, 498 S.E.2d 572, 574 (Ga. Ct. App. 1998) (holding pollution exclusion applicable to claim arising out of gasoline leak from storage container, rendering neighbor's real property inaccessible, because of road closure due to cleanup); *Scottsdale Ins. Co. v. Pursley*, 487 Fed. Appx. 508 (11th Cir. 2012) (following *Reed* and holding that carbon monoxide was a pollutant which triggered pollution exclusion); *Racetrac Petroleum, Inc. v. Ace American Ins. Co.*, 841 F. Supp. 2d 1286 (N.D. Ga. 2011) (holding that benzene, which is typically found in unleaded gasoline in small amounts, was a pollutant under the pollution exclusion, and it did not make a difference whether injuries resulted from exposure to highly concentrated amounts or typical concentration found in gasoline), *affirmed* 2011 U.S. App. LEXIS 22455 (11th Cir. Nov. 3, 2011) (concluding that the claims came within the scope of the pollution exclusion and also agreeing with the district court that the pollution exclusion did not "violate Georgia public policy since the liability insurance policies at issue are primarily intended to provide Racetrac with coverage for the countless other risks associated with operating convenience stores"); *Evanston Ins. Co. v. Sandersville R.R. Co.*, No. 5:15-247, 2016 U.S. Dist. LEXIS 134162 (M.D. Ga. Sept. 29, 2016) (following a detailed analysis of Georgia law addressing the pollution exclusion, court held that the exclusion precluded coverage for injuries caused by welding fumes). *But see Barrett v. Nat'l Union Fire Ins. Co. of Pittsburgh*, 696 S.E.2d 326, 330 (Ga. Ct. App. 2010) (declining to follow *Reed* because the allegations of the complaint indicated that the release of natural gas, standing alone, did not cause the underlying plaintiff's injuries) (distinguishing cases where the presence of the pollutant, following its release, dispersal, or seepage was the "but-for" cause of the plaintiff's injury); *Minkoff v. Action Remediation, Inc.*, No. 559/06, 2010 N.Y. Misc. LEXIS 4857 (N.Y. Sup. Ct. Sept. 30, 2010) (applying Georgia law) (concluding that damages resulting from the use of a bleach and Sporicidin mix in mold remediation were not precluded from coverage under policy's pollution exclusion because, as standard supplies in the cleaning business, "a reasonable insured would expect the chemicals released by the mix of bleach and Sporicidin … to be covered by the CPL") (noting that a pollution exclusion including such chemicals "would raise public policy issues"); *Centro Dev. Corp. v. Cent. Mut. Ins. Co.*, 720 Fed. Appx. 1004 (11th Cir. 2018) (storm water qualifies as a pollutant); *Recyc Sys. Southeast, LLC v. Farmland Mut. Ins. Co.*, No. 17-225, 2018 U.S. Dist. LEXIS 82248 (M.D. Ga. May 16, 2018) (pollution exclusion applied to noxious odors from a holding pond containing nutrient-rich water disposed of by poultry plants); *Evanston Ins. Co. v. Xytex Tissue Servs., LLC*, 378 F. Supp. 3d 1267 (S.D. Ga. 2019) ("[W]hen bodily injury results from the migration, release, or escape of lead-based paint or carbon monoxide, the substances unambiguously meet the definition for 'pollutant.' The same cannot be said for nitrogen."); *Associated Indem. Corp. v. Hughes*, No. 18-00201, 2019 U.S. Dist. LEXIS 111883 (N.D. Ga. Apr. 25, 2019) (storm water, even when uncontaminated, is a "pollutant"); *Sullivan v. Everett Cash Mut. Ins. Co.*, No. 18-00207, 2019 U.S. Dist. LEXIS 141628 (N.D. Ga. Apr. 17, 2019) (concluding that airborne particulates and dust "fall well within the definition of 'pollutant'") ("The phrase 'any solid . . . irritant or contaminant' plainly includes dust and any other particles emitted by a poultry plant, even if those substances are not explicitly listed in the Policy."); *Evanston Ins. Co. v. Sandersville R.R.*, 761 Fed. Appx. 940 (11th Cir. 2019) (pollution exclusion applied to injury from inhaling welding fumes which contained iron particles) ("[W]elding fumes unambiguously qualify as an 'irritant or contaminant,' including . . . fumes."); *Century Cmtys. of Ga. v. Selective Way Ins. Co.*, No. 18-5267, 2019 U.S. Dist. LEXIS 224489 (N.D. Ga. Oct. 25, 2019) (pollution exclusion applied to property damage caused by "water runoff, sediment, silt, and other pollutants"); *Lang v. FCCI Ins. Co.*, No. 19-3902, 2021 U.S. Dist. LEXIS 73764 (N.D. Ga. Mar. 30, 2021) (dust from construction work qualified as a pollutant) ("[D]ust is inescapably and unambiguously a 'pollutant,' i.e., an 'irritant or contaminant' under the circumstances here where Plaintiff has alleged that the dust, whether due to its accumulation or otherwise, caused Mr. Love's difficulty breathing and ultimate ICU visit").

Hawaii: A Hawaii District Court held that the pollution exclusion precluded coverage to a plumbing company, for claims arising out of its use of an extremely strong drain cleaner at a Wal-Mart store, which generated "noxious fumes" injuring a store employee. *Apana v. TIG Ins. Co.*, 504 F. Supp. 2d 998, 1006 (D. Haw. 2007). "Nothing in the language of the Total Pollution Exclusion Endorsement references or even impliedly limits the clause to instances of traditional environmental pollution or requires that the pollution cover an extended area." *Id.* On appeal, the Ninth Circuit certified the "traditional" versus "non-traditional" issue to the Supreme Court of Hawaii. *Apana v. TIG Ins. Co.*, 574 F.3d 679 (9th Cir. 2009). The case was subsequently dismissed by the parties. *Apana v. TIG Ins. Co.*, No. 29942, 2010 Haw. LEXIS 53 (Haw. April 7, 2010); *see also Allstate Ins. Co. v. Leong*, No. 09–00217, 2010 U.S. Dist. LEXIS 46277 (D. Haw. May 11, 2010) (finding that pollution exclusion was not applicable to sewage flow that damaged a neighbor's retaining wall) ("Even if the court assumes that the sewer pipe leaked waste materials or other irritants, contaminants or pollutants, it is unclear whether the damage to the retaining wall was *caused* by 'waste materials or other irritants, contaminants or pollutants.") (citation omitted from original); *Nautilis Ins. Co. v. Hawk Transp. Serv., LLC*, CV. No. 10-00605, 2011 U.S. Dist. LEXIS 65663 (D. Haw. June 20, 2011) (noting that Hawaii has not definitively decided whether to read total pollution exclusions as only applying to traditional environmental pollutants or more broadly to encompass any hazardous substance) (declining to determine which pollution exclusion interpretation to apply because "even applying the more liberal test— *i.e.* the test which limits the exclusion to situations involving traditional environmental pollution—[the insurer] is entitled to summary judgment because the [hazardous solid waste] pollutants alleged to have been dispersed in the Underlying Suit involve traditional environmental pollution") (citations omitted from original); *Nautilus Ins. Co. v. SER Trucking, Inc.*, No. 11-00172, 2011 U.S. Dist. LEXIS 138288 (D. Haw. Nov. 8, 2011) (concluding that the pollution exclusion barred coverage for damages from dumping solid waste consisting of "waste tires, partially buried tires, concrete rubble greater than eight inches in diameter, and partially buried re-bar"); *Charter Oak Fire Ins. Co. v. Endurance American Specialty Ins. Co.*, 40 F. Supp. 3d 1296 (D. Haw. 2014) (pollution exclusion did not preclude coverage for individuals killed by an explosion that occurred when seized fireworks were being destroyed); *Allen v. Scottsdale Ins. Co.*, 307 F. Supp. 2d 1170 (D. Haw. 2004) ("Considering the Hawaii legislative and administrative materials that discuss 'fugitive dust' and the existing case law pertaining to the applicability of pollution exclusion clauses to dust, this court concludes that the exclusion clause at issue in this case is not ambiguous. Furthermore, this court determines that fugitive dust is a pollutant.").

Idaho: An Idaho district court held that the pollution exclusion precluded coverage for claims for damages caused by tailings (an unwanted by-product of a manufacturing process) from mining operations. *Monarch Greenback, LLC v. Monticello Ins. Co.*, 118 F. Supp. 2d 1068, 1080 (D. Idaho 1999). "[N]ot only are mine tailings within the pollution exclusion's definition of 'pollutant,' but also the 'hazardous substances' found within the tailings clearly constitute an 'irritant' or 'contaminant' and are 'pollutants.'" *Id.*; *see also Esterovich v. City of Kellogg*, 80 P.3d 1040, 1042 (Idaho 2003) (addressing a procedural issue, unrelated to the pollution exclusion, Supreme Court of Idaho noted that the trial court had found that the exclusion did not preclude coverage for injury caused by exposure to smoke used to test a city's sewer system).

Illinois: The Supreme Court of Illinois held that the pollution exclusion did not preclude coverage for claims arising out of carbon monoxide emitted from a building's furnace. *Am. States Ins. Co. v. Koloms*, 687 N.E.2d 72, 79 (Ill. 1997). "[W]e agree with those courts which have restricted the exclusion's otherwise potentially limitless application to only those hazards traditionally associated with environmental pollution. We find support for our decision in the drafting history of the exclusion, which reveals an intent on the part of the insurance industry to so limit the clause." *Id.*; *see also Conn. Specialty Ins. Co. v. Loop Paper Recycling, Inc.*, 824 N.E.2d 1125, 1138 (Ill. App. Ct. 2005) (holding that the exclusion focuses on traditional environmental pollution and for it to apply "the pollutant must actually spill beyond the insured's premises and into the environment"); *Pekin Ins. Co. v. Pharmasyn, Inc.*, No. 2-10-1000, 2011 Ill. App. Unpub. LEXIS 2540 (Ill. App. Ct. 2011) (holding that claims of injury from harmful fumes that escaped into common areas and neighboring properties resulting from production of organic compounds were excluded from coverage under the pollution exclusion); *Kim v. State Farm Fire & Cas. Co.*, 728 N.E.2d 530, 536 (Ill. App. Ct. 2000) (holding that, under *Koloms*, since the release of "perc" [dry cleaning chemical] did constitute traditional environmental pollution, the pollution exclusion applied to bar coverage); *Country Mut. Ins. Co. v. Hilltop View*, LLC, 998 N.E.2d 950 (Ill. App. Ct. 2013) (determining that swine waste odors were not "traditional environmental pollution"); *Scottsdale Indem. Co. v. Vill. of Crestwood*, 673 F.3d 715 (7th Cir. 2012) (Posner, J.) (holding that the pollution exclusion precluded coverage for claims alleging village delivered contaminated tap water to residents) (rejecting "traditional environmental pollution" formula of evaluation and replacing it with the "adverse self-selection" formula, which focuses on the cause or likelihood of pollution, as opposed to the nature of the pollutant, and how this likelihood of pollution affects the insurer's business); *Village of Crestwood v. Ironshore Specialty Ins. Co.*, 986 N.E.2d 678 (Ill. App. Ct. 2013) (citing *Koloms* and holding that pollution exclusion "did not provide coverage for claims asserting village knowingly mixed contaminated water into municipal water supply"); *Pacific Employers Ins. Co. v. Clean Harbors Environmental Services, Inc.*, No. 08 C 2180, 2010 U.S. Dist. LEXIS 10668 (N.D. Ill. Feb. 4, 2010) ("That a personal injury was caused by chemicals does not remove it from the intended scope of the policy based on the pollution exclusion language before this Court. This is so even if the chemicals are classified as contaminant or irritants and the accident was caused by their escape or release[.] … In the context of the facts of this case, [Plaintiff] Lopez sustained injuries during his day-to-day duties. That those injuries were sustained from the chemicals in drums he was hauling does not place the claim within the pollution exclusion."); *Erie Ins. Exchange v. Imperial Marble Corp.*, 957 N.E.2d 1214 (Ill. App. Ct. 2011) (insured manufactured marble vanities and countertops that created odorous emissions that insured was authorized to emit under an Illinois EPA permit) ("The policy's pollution exclusion is arguably ambiguous as to whether the emission of hazardous materials in levels permitted by an IEPA permit constitute traditional environmental pollution excluded under the policy."); *Indem. Ins. Co. of N. Am. v. Silver Creek Pig, Inc.*, No. 13-1440, 2015 U.S. Dist. LEXIS 57201 (D. Ill. Feb. 13, 2015) ("The court finds that, in this instance, manure, along with the smells associated with it, would not be 'traditional environmental pollution' necessary to trigger application of the pollution exclusion."); *Country Mut. Ins. Co. v. Bible Pork, Inc.*, 42 N.E.3d 958 (Ill. App. Ct. Nov. 20, 2015) (holding pollution exclusion not applicable to pollution caused by hog farming because it is not traditional); *PQ Corp. v. Lexington Ins. Co.*, No. 13-3482, 2016 U.S. Dist. LEXIS 99088 (N.D. Ill. July 29, 2016), *aff'd on other grounds*, 2017 U.S. App. LEXIS 11457 (7th Cir. June 27, 2017) ("Lexington points to no evidence that the formaldehyde vapors PQ believes contaminated its products ever escaped into the land, atmosphere, or water around the Double D facility. The damage, as far as may be gleaned from the record, was contained to the warehouse itself. This was not 'traditional' pollution under Illinois law, and so falls outside the bounds of the pollution exclusion here."); *Westfield Ins. Co. v. Indem. Ins. Co. of N. Am.*, 423 F. Supp. 3d 534 (C.D. Ill. 2019) (concluding that "the Illinois Supreme Court would agree with the *Hilltop View* decision that odors, in and of themselves, are not traditional types of pollution").

Indiana: The Supreme Court of Indiana held that the pollution exclusion did not preclude coverage for claims for damages caused by the discharge of petroleum from an underground storage tank at a gas station. *Am. States Ins. Co. v. Kiger*, 662 N.E.2d 945, 949 (Ind. 1996). "[S]ince the term 'pollutant' does not obviously include gasoline and, accordingly, is ambiguous, we once again must construe the language against the insurer who drafted it." *Id.* The court also described it as an "oddity" and "strange" that an insurance company would sell a "garage policy" to a gas station "when that policy specifically excluded the major source of potential liability." *Id.* at 948. *See also Indiana Farm Bureau Ins. Co. v. Harleysville Ins. Co.*, 965 N.E.2d 62 (Ind. Ct. App. 2012) (following *Kiger* and reaffirming that because a "garage policy" did not mention gasoline, it was deemed ambiguous, and therefore, the pollution exclusion did not apply); *Freidline v. Shelby Ins. Co.*, 774 N.E.2d 37, 42 (Ind. 2002) (pollution exclusion not applicable to bodily injury claims arising from fumes inhaled during carpet installation); *Great Lakes Chem. Corp. v. Int'l Surplus Lines Ins. Co.*, 638 N.E.2d 847, 851 (Ind. Ct. App. 1994) (concluding that, while damages were environmental, the pollution exclusion was not applicable because claims were in the nature of products liability); *Nat'l Union Fire Ins. Co of Pittsburgh v. Standard Fusee Corp.*, 917 N.E.2d 170, 185 (Ind. Ct. App. 2009) (finding the pollution exclusion ambiguous and unenforceable for claims for perchlorate that leaked from a flare production facility) (reversed and remanded by Supreme Court of Indiana on Dec. 29, 2010 after ruling that Maryland law applied to dispute, 940 N.E.2d 810 (Ind. 2011)); *State Auto. Mut. Ins. Co. v. Flexdar, Inc.*, 964 N.E.2d 845 (Ind. 2012) (holding that the pollution exclusion clause—deemed ambiguous—must be construed against insurer, which, therefore, obligates insurer to pay for cleanup costs caused by industrial solvent trichloroethylene) ("Indiana decisions have been consistent in recognizing the requirement that language of a pollution exclusion be explicit."); *State Auto. Ins. Co. v. DMY Realty Co., LLP*, 977 N.E.2d 411 (Ind. Ct. App. 2012) (holding that the pollution exclusion was ambiguous and insurer could not deny coverage for soil damage caused from dry cleaning chemicals). *But see W. Bend Mut. Ins. Co. v. U.S. Fid. & Guar. Co.*, 598 F.3d 918, 922–23 (7th Cir. 2010) (applying Indiana law) (finding the pollution exclusion precluded coverage for claims arising from leaks in gasoline storage tanks and noting that the pollution exclusion, as drafted, specifically eradicated the ambiguities on which *Kiger* rested); *St. Paul Fire & Marine Ins. Co. v. City of Kokomo*, No. 13-01573, 2015 U.S. Dist. LEXIS 82465 (S. D. Ind. June 25,

2015) (a pollution exclusion that "generally incorporates eleven federal laws; the environmental title of the Indiana Code; any amendments to any of those laws; and any list, regulation, or rule issued or promulgated by a federal governmental authority or an Indiana state or local governmental authority . . . is insufficient to comply with Indiana's stringent standard that an insurance policy 'specify what falls within its pollution exclusion.'"); *Old Republic Ins. Co. v. Gary/Chi. Int'l Airport Auth.*, No. 15-281, 2016 U.S. Dist. LEXIS 96361 (N.D. Ind. July 25, 2016) (concluding that "the Indiana Supreme Court would determine that Old Republic's failure to be more specific (by its use of the broad terms 'pollution' and 'contamination' without more) renders its pollution exclusion ambiguous"); *Atl. Cas. Ins. Co. v. Garcia*, 227 F. Supp. 3d 990 (N.D. Ind. 2017) (declining to rule on whether the pollution exclusion applied as coverage was preluded on another basis) (issue whether a pollution exclusion that applies to all material for which a Material Safety Data Sheet is required under federal, state, or local law – which are for all chemicals deemed "hazardous" by OSHA – "is enough to satisfy the Indiana Supreme Court's stringent standards with respect to pollution exclusions"); *Greene v. Will*, 349 F. Supp. 3d 849 (N.D. Ind. 2019) (deeming the terms "waste," "chemicals," and "fumes" to be inherently ambiguous) (not ruling on pollution exclusion – "an evolving area of the law, subject to differing interpretations" -- as other bases existed to grant insurer's motion for summary judgment).

Iowa: The Supreme Court of Iowa held that the pollution exclusion barred coverage for a claim involving the death of a worker at a hog confinement facility due to carbon monoxide that was released from a propane power washer in a restroom. *Bituminous Cas. Corp. v. Sand Livestock Systems, Inc.*, 728 N.W.2d 216, 222 (Iowa 2007). "We agree with Bituminous that carbon monoxide falls within the extremely broad language of the policies' definition of 'pollutants.' It is difficult to say the exclusions are 'fairly susceptible to two interpretations,' which is required for us to find the exclusions ambiguous." *Id.* at 221. "The plain language in the exclusions encompasses the injury at issue here because carbon monoxide is a gaseous irritant or contaminant, which was released from the propane power washer." *Id.* at 222.

Kansas: The Tenth Circuit Court of Appeals certified the following question to the Supreme Court of Kansas: "If the definition of a 'pollutant' in the exclusion clause is ambiguous [first Certified Question], and must, therefore, be construed in a light most favorable to the insured, is a mist of anhydrous ammonia fertilizer released from a plow during farm fertilizing operations nonetheless a 'pollutant' under the exclusion clause, such that the liability claim for injuries caused by exposure to that mist is not covered?" *Union Ins. Co. v. Mendoza*, 374 Fed. Appx. 796, 797 (10th Cir. 2010) (noting that, while the interpretation of the pollution exclusion has been considered by two Kansas Court of Appeals decisions, they differ from earlier interpretations of Kansas law by two federal district courts). After initially accepting the certification, the Kansas Supreme Court later dismissed, taking the position that guidance from the state's high court was no longer necessary. In response, the Tenth Circuit ruled for the insurer. *See Union Ins. Co. v. Mendoza*, 405 Fed. Appx. 270, 275–76 (10th Cir. 2010) (concluding that summary judgment for insurer was appropriate where claimant was exposed to mist of anhydrous ammonia fertilizer and suffered injuries resulting from the chemical irritant after it was sprayed on land adjacent to her construction job) (noting that chemical's application for use as fertilizer did not change court's determination that it fell within the policy definition of pollutant). The Kansas cases noted by the Tenth Circuit in its certification would appear to be in conflict. *Compare Regent Ins. Co. v. Holmes*, 835 F. Supp. 579, 581–82 (D. Kan. 1993) (holding that pollutant definition in exclusion was ambiguous without definition of terms irritant and contaminant) and *Westchester Fire Ins. Co. v. City of Pittsburg*, 794 F. Supp. 353, 355 (D. Kan. 1992) (determining pollution exclusion to be so broad and imprecise as to be ambiguous) *with Atlantic Avenue Assocs. v. Central Solutions, Inc.*, 24 P.3d 188, 189–92 (Kan. Ct. App. 2001) (finding no ambiguity in pollution exclusion as applied to preclude coverage for claim by property owner that concrete floor was damaged by corrosive material leaking from containment drums stored on property) and *Crescent Oil Co. v. Federated Mut. Ins. Co.*, 888 P.2d 869, 870, 871–73 (Kan. Ct. App. 1995) (concluding that the language of exclusion was not ambiguous as applied to underground storage tank leaking gasoline from service station property onto adjoining property).

But in *Gerdes v. American Family Mutual Insurance Co.*, 713 F. Supp. 2d 1290 (D. Kan. 2010), the federal trial court found sufficient commonality and guidance from these cases to hold that the pollution exclusion barred coverage under a first-party property policy for fire damage to a home when the fire also created and spread pollution from mercury that had been stored in the home (the insured was a former dentist who—we are not making this up—had "2 tablespoons of mercury stored in the basement of the Home" albeit "in a heavy duty plastic 'hiker's' bottle with water over it, as he was trained in dental school" although there was apparently no lesson about getting rid of toxic material after you retire).

Regardless of the merits of these decisions regarding the pollution exclusion itself, we see *Gerdes* as simply a case that "chose" one approach rather than the conflicting approach reflected in other Kansas cases, and we are puzzled by the reluctance of the Kansas Supreme Court to make a definitive statement about the proper application of the exclusion. But reading the tea leaves between the lines (and braving a cliché or two), it seems clear that Kansas cases have taken an increasingly receptive approach to application of the exclusion. For example, the *Gerdes* court could have reasonably ruled that the home in question was destroyed by a garden variety fire (covered) and that the additional chemical damage from the mercury released in the fire did not convert the matter to a pollution claim. Similarly, the *Mendoza* case could have reasonably ruled that misdirected spraying of fertilizer more or less directly on a third party was more like standard issue negligence (covered) than the type of widespread, long-tail degradation that prompted use of the absolute pollution exclusion.

By making the decisions they did, these federal courts made a choice among conflicting approaches and precedents, as did the Kansas Supreme Court by ducking the issue. Policyholder counsel might also complain that *Crescent Oil* involved traditional environmental pollution (a gas tank leak) while the seepage at issue in *Atlantic Avenue* was a more standard pollution claim than either the misdirected spraying of *Mendoza* or the home fire in *Gerdes* and that a finding of no ambiguity for the exclusion in the state court cases does not necessarily mean the exclusion was unambiguous in the more nuanced federal court cases. But overall, it appears that Kansas is a state tending pro-insurer in its application of the pollution exclusion.

Kentucky: The Court of Appeals of Kentucky held that the pollution exclusion did not apply to claims for bodily injury arising out of a carbon monoxide leak from a boiler used by a dry cleaner. *Motorists Mut. Ins. Co. v. RSJ, Inc.*, 926 S.W.2d 679, 681–82 (Ky. Ct. App. 1996) (examining drafting history of the exclusion and continued use of environmental law terminology). "[W]e are convinced that an ordinary business person would not apprehend the provision as excluding coverage for the type of damage incurred through an unexpected leak in a vent pipe." *Id.* at 682. *But see Sunny Ridge Enters., Inc. v. Fireman's Fund Ins. Co.*, 132 F. Supp. 2d 525, 527 (E.D. Ky. 2001) (holding that pollution exclusion precluded coverage for damage caused by nuclear material that was released by a monitoring gauge that was destroyed during the melting of scrap metal); *Certain Underwriters at Lloyd's v. NFC Mining Inc.*, No. 10-5232, 2011 U.S. App. LEXIS 11924 (6th Cir. June 9, 2011) (holding that damages caused by coal dust were excluded even though insured believed these damages would be covered) (noting that, even if belief had been reasonable, under Kentucky law, plain language of exclusion precludes resorting to reasonable expectations doctrine); *Grizzly Processing LLC v. Wausau Underwriters Ins. Co.*, No. 7:08–226, 2010 U.S. Dist. LEXIS 22477 (E.D. Ky. Mar. 11, 2010) (excluding coverage for claims alleging bodily injury resulting from the contamination of residences with coal dust because coal dust constituted pollutant under policy); *Certain Underwriters at Lloyd's v. Abundance Coal, Inc.*, No. 2009-CA-001283-MR, 2011 Ky. App. LEXIS 116 (Ky. Ct. App. June 24, 2011) (refusing to definitely conclude that coal dust and debris were excluded under absolute pollution exclusion and noting that "the dust at issue here is not a pollutant if it does not cause the irritation, contamination, negative health or environmental effects, or other types of harm contemplated in the insurance agreement"); *Hardy Oil Co., Inc. v. Nationwide Agribusiness Ins. Co.*, No. 5:11-00075, 2013 U.S. Dist. LEXIS 4760 (E.D. Ky. Jan. 11, 2013) (citing *Abundance Coal* and holding that removal of water and soil polluted with diesel fuel, which led to a government-ordered cleanup, was type of classic environmental catastrophe that the pollution exclusion sought to exclude), *affirmed on other grounds* 2014 U.S. App. LEXIS 18405 (6th Cir. Sept. 22, 2014); *Travelers Property Casualty Co. of Am. v. Begley Co.*, No. 13-199; 2014 U.S. Dist. LEXIS 132168 (E.D. Ky. Sept. 18, 2014) ("Tetrachloroethylene is the type of substance commonly classified as a pollutant and its leakage into the environment, drawing the involvement of a government agency seeking investigation and remediation, is the type of situation commonly covered by the total pollution exclusion."); *Barber v. Arch Ins. Co.*, 494 F. Supp. 3d 450 (W.D. Ky. 2020) (concluding that coal dust, confined inside a coal mine, is a "pollutant," despite that it is located where it is supposed to be).

Louisiana: The Supreme Court of Louisiana held that the pollution exclusion did not preclude coverage for claims for hydrocarbons in a parish water system. *Doerr v. Mobil Oil Corp.*, 774 So. 2d 119, 136 (La. 2000). "[W]e find that the proper interpretation of the pollution exclusion in this case is that the exclusion was designed to exclude coverage for environmental pollution only and not for all interactions with irritants or contaminants of any kind." *Id.* "The applicability of a total pollution exclusion in any given case must necessarily turn on several considerations: (1) Whether the insured is a 'polluter' within the meaning of the exclusion; (2) Whether the injury-causing substance is a 'pollutant' within the meaning of the exclusion; and (3) Whether there was a 'discharge, dispersal, seepage, migration, release or escape' of a pollutant by the insured within the meaning of the policy." *Id.* at 135. The *Doerr* Court set out numerous factors to be examined for purposes of determining if these criteria have been met. *Id.* at

135–36; *see also State Farm Fire & Cas. Co. v. M.L.T. Constr. Co., Inc.*, 849 So. 2d 762, 771 (La. Ct. App. 2003) (finding that workplace exposure to mold and mildew from ongoing roof work not subject to pollution exclusion); *Finger v. Audubon Ins. Co.*, No. 09–8071 (La. Civ. Dist. Ct., Orleans Parish, Mar. 23, 2010) (order granting motions) (finding pollution exclusion inapplicable in Chinese drywall litigation because, based on *Doerr* and a 1997 advisory letter from the Louisiana Department of Insurance, the exclusion was never intended to apply to residential homeowner's claims for damage caused by substandard building materials); *Aspen Ins. UK, Ltd. v. Dune Energy, Inc.*, 400 Fed. Appx. 960, 963 (5th Cir. 2010) (applying Louisiana law) (specifically designated under 5th Cir. R. 47.5 as "not precedent except under the limited circumstances set forth in 5th Cir. R. 47.5.4) (determining that oil leakage falls within "seepage and pollution" exclusion of policy and is clearly the type of claim insurers intended to exclude from CGL coverage); *Lodwick, L.L.C. v. Chevron U.S.A., Inc.*, 126 So. 3d 544 (La. Ct. App. 2013) (concluding that damages to neighboring properties due to oil and gas production and exploration activities were not covered because they fell under pollution exclusion); *Bridger Lake, LLC v. Seneca Ins. Co., Inc.*, No. 11-0342, 2014 U.S. Dist. LEXIS 27703 (W.D. La. Mar. 3, 2014) (holding that pollution exclusion precluded coverage for damages resulting from rupture of underground pipe carrying crude oil); *Marcelle v. Southern Fidelity Ins. Co.*, 954 F. Supp. 2d 429 (E.D. La. 2013) (holding that bat guano and its odor was clearly a "waste" or "contaminant," and the pollution exclusion unambiguously applied); *Hanover Ins. Co. v. Superior Labor Servs.*, No. 16-2490, 2016 U.S. Dist. LEXIS 162480 (E.D. La. Nov. 23, 2016) (pollution exclusion not applicable to silica because insurer could not answer all three *Doerr* factors in the affirmative); *Meridian Chems., LLC v. Torque Logistics, LLC*, No. 18-002, 2018 U.S. Dist. LEXIS 167372 (M.D. La. Sep. 27, 2018) (applying *Doerr* factors and concluding that the pollution exclusion precluded coverage for Black Liquor Soap); *Evanston Ins. Co. v. Riceland Petroleum Co.*, 369 F. Supp. 3d 673 (W.D. La. 2019) (applying *Doerr* factors and concluding that the pollution exclusion precluded coverage for contamination of property, from oil and gas facilities, from the improper disposal of oilfield waste in unlined earthen pits); *Apollo Energy, LLC v. Certain Underwriters at Lloyd's, London*, 387 F. Supp. 3d 663 (M.D. La. 2019) (applying *Doerr* factors and concluding that the pollution exclusion precluded coverage for an oil spill); *Kan. City. S. Ry. Co. v. Wood Energy Grp. Inc.*, 289 So. 3d 671 (La. Ct. App. 2020) ("Samples taken of the soil there also revealed the presence of arsenic and various semivolatile organic compounds. Undoubtedly the property damage originated from the 'discharge, dispersal, seepage, migration, release, or escape of pollutants[.]'"); *United Specialty Ins. Co. v. Sandhill Prod. Inc.*, No. 20-163, 2021 U.S. Dist. LEXIS 51454 (W.D. La. Mar. 17, 2021) (applying *Doerr* factors and concluding that the pollution exclusion precluded coverage for contamination of a property due to "oil and gas exploration and production activities"); La. *Dep't of Envtl. Quality v. Tidewater Landfill LLC*, No. 2020-0334, 2021 La. App. LEXIS 391 (La. Ct. App. Mar. 24, 2021) (applying *Doerr* factors and determining that pollution exclusion did not preclude coverage for cost associated with closing a landfill)) ("[I]f the LDEQ was seeking costs to clean or repair the adjacent waters and property into which the landfill's solid waste is infiltrating or damages from the infiltration, the repairs and damages sought would be 'effects' caused by the 'pollutant' waste. Thus, the LDEQ's claims would be excluded under the Primary Policy. However, the closure of the landfill itself cannot conclusively be said to be an 'effect' of a pollutant.").

Maine: The First Circuit Court of Appeals, applying Maine law, held that the pollution exclusion did not preclude coverage for claims arising out of exposure to fumes from roofing products at a job site. *Nautilus, Inc. v. Jabar*, 188 F.3d 27, 31 (1st Cir. 1999). "[T]he total pollution exclusion clause is ambiguous as applied to the … claims because an ordinarily intelligent insured could reasonably interpret the pollution exclusion clause as applying only to environmental pollution." *Id.* at 30; *see also Boise Cascade Corp. v. Reliance Nat'l Indem. Co.*, 99 F. Supp. 2d 87, 102 (D. Me. 2000) (following *Jabar* and holding that the pollution exclusion did not preclude coverage for claims for bodily injury caused by exposure to chlorine gas). *But see Prime Tanning Co., Inc. v. Liberty Mut. Ins. Co.*, 750 F. Supp. 2d 198, 213 (D. Me. 2010) (apparently applying Maine law but also discussing Missouri law without clear choice of law decision) (finding that no duty to defend was owed in action seeking damages caused by disposal of tanning byproducts and sludge) (determining that hazardous products such as these are "pollutants" within the meaning of the exclusion even if euphemistically described as "fertilizer" by insured).

Maryland: The Court of Appeals of Maryland held that the pollution exclusion did not preclude coverage for claims for bodily injuries caused by exposure to manganese welding fumes. *Clendenin Bros., Inc., v. U.S. Fire Ins. Co.*, 889 A.2d 387, 395 (Md. 2006). "Without some limiting principle, the pollution exclusion clause would extend far beyond its intended scope, and lead to some absurd results." *Id.* at 396; *see also Sullins v. Allstate Ins. Co.*, 667 A.2d 617, 624 (Md. 1995) (holding that the pollution exclusion was ambiguous and did not apply in the context of lead paint). "We conclude that an insured could reasonably have understood the provision at issue to exclude coverage for injury caused by certain forms of industrial pollution, but not coverage for injury allegedly caused by the presence of leaded materials in a private residence. There simply is no language in the exclusion provision from which to infer that the provision was drafted with a view toward limiting liability for lead paint-related injury." *Id.* at 620; *Clipper Mill Fed., LLC v. Cincinnati Ins. Co.*, No. JFM-10-1647, 2010 U.S. Dist. LEXIS 112172 (D. Md. Oct. 20, 2010) (concluding that insurer has duty to defend for bodily injuries caused by airborne toxic fumes because of enumerated exception within policy pollution exclusion for bodily injury claims to persons on premises where injury was "caused by inadequate ventilation of vapors," claimant was first exposed to vapors during policy period, and claimant received diagnosis or treatment from physician within one year of exposure); *Chubb Customs Ins. Co. v. Standard Fusee Corp.*, 2 N.E.3d 752 (Ind. App. Ct. 2014) (applying Maryland law) (holding that perchlorate contamination from manufacturing marine signal/safety flares amounted to traditional environmental pollutant, which fell within pollution exclusion); *Travelers Indem. Co. v. MTS Transp., LLC*, No. 11-01567, 2012 U.S. Dist. LEXIS 127847 (W.D. Pa. Sept. 7, 2012) (applying Maryland law) (concluding pollution exclusion was ambiguous as applied to petroleum asphalt roadway spill); *Brownlee v. Liberty Mut. Fire Ins. Co.*, 175 A.3d 697 (Md. App. Ct. 2017) (answering certified question) ("We conclude that the application of Georgia's interpretation of the pollution exclusion contained in the Liberty Mutual insurance policies does not violate Maryland's public policy. Absent a legislative affirmation that pollution exclusion clauses are against public policy, we decline to declare that Georgia's law violates Maryland's public policy. Therefore, Georgia's interpretation of the pollution exclusion clause governs here."); *Allstate Ins. Co. v. Rochkind*, 381 F. Supp. 3d 488 (D. Md. 2019) ("Unlike the exclusion in *Sullins*, and akin to the expansive definition of pollutants in *Clipper Mill*, the exclusion here expressly incorporates '[l]ead in any form' into the coverage exclusion."); *Unitrin Auto & Home Ins. Co. v. Karp*, 481 F. Supp. 3d 514 (D. Md. 2020) (determining, following lengthy review of Maryland law, that the pollution exclusion was ambiguous with respect to home heating oil).

Massachusetts: The Supreme Judicial Court of Massachusetts held that the pollution exclusion did not preclude coverage for a claim by a restaurant patron for carbon monoxide poisoning arising out of a tandoori oven located in the restaurant's poorly ventilated kitchen. *W. Alliance Ins. Co. v. Gill*, 686 N.E.2d 997, 1000 (Mass. 1997). The pollution exclusion "should not reflexively be applied to accidents arising during the course of normal business activities simply because they

involve a 'discharge, dispersal, release or escape' of an 'irritant or contaminant.'"
Id. at 999. "A reasonable policyholder might well understand carbon monoxide is
a pollutant when it is emitted in an industrial or environmental setting, but would
not reasonably characterize carbon monoxide emitted from a malfunctioning
or improperly operated restaurant oven as pollution." *Id.* at 1000 (citation and
quotation omitted). The *Gill* Court rested its decision, in part, on *Atlantic Mutual
Insurance Co. v. McFadden*, 595 N.E.2d 762, 764 (Mass. 1992), which held that
the pollution exclusion did not apply to claims for exposure to lead paint in a
residential setting. *But see McGregor v. Allamerica Ins. Co.*, 868 N.E.2d 1225, 1228
(Mass. 2007) (finding pollution exclusion precluded coverage for home heating
oil spill) (distinguishing *Gill* and *McFadden* because they "rested primarily on the
observation that the harm at issue was not caused by the kind of release that an
ordinary insured would understand as pollution. By contrast, spilled oil is a classic
example of pollution, and a reasonable insured would understand oil leaking into the
ground to be a pollutant.") ("The location of an oil spill at a residence, rather than
an industrial or manufacturing site, does not automatically alter the classification
of spilled oil as a pollutant."); *United Specialty Ins. Co. v. Weisberg*, No. 2010-02318,
2011 Mass. Super. LEXIS 312 (Mass. Super. Ct. Dec. 28, 2011) (holding that
pollution exclusion precluded coverage for oil seepage resulting from disabled
heating system unless future case finds that vandalism exception applies). *See also
Nascimento v. Preferred Mut. Ins. Co.*, 513 F.3d 273, 279 (1st Cir. 2008) (applying
Massachusetts law) (finding that insurer had no duty to defend government cleanup
claim arising out of discharge of oil); *Maestranzi Bros., Inc. v. Am. Employers' Ins.
Co.*, No. 2005-1856B, 2010 Mass. Super. LEXIS 65 (Mass. Super. Ct. Apr. 9, 2010)
(using pro rata approach to determine covered damages where policyholder's actions
were covered by different policies, some containing absolute pollution exclusion
clauses precluding coverage and some containing qualified exclusion clauses (*see*
Chapter 14) under which coverage was available); *Granite State Ins. Co. v. American
Bldg. Materials, Inc.*, No. 8:10-1542-T-24, 2011 U.S. Dist. LEXIS 139455 (M.D.
Fla. Dec. 5, 2011) (applying Massachusetts law) (holding that pollution exclusion
was unambiguous and precluded coverage for Chinese drywall claims); *Arrowood
Indem. Co. v. Oxford Cleaners & Tailors, LLC*, No. 13-12298, 2014 U.S. Dist. LEXIS
113734 (D. Mass. Aug. 15, 2014) ("[I]n light of the policy's pollution exclusion and
the personal injury provision's delineated application to intentional torts, the term
'wrongful entry' is not reasonably susceptible of an interpretation that would cover
the unintentional migration of contaminants like PCE. An objectively reasonable

insured would have expected the pollution exclusion to bar coverage for D&D's suit against Oxford, and would not have anticipated coverage of that same claim by the personal injury provision."); *Scottsdale Ins. Co. v. MRH Indian Enters. LLC*, No. 19-11878, 2020 U.S. Dist. LEXIS 114472 (D. Mass. Jun. 30, 2020) (reciting Massachusetts law addressing the pollution exclusion and declining to address, on jurisdictional grounds, whether odors from a composting facility are "pollution").

Michigan: The Court of Appeals of Michigan held that there was a genuine issue of material fact whether the pollution exclusion precluded coverage for claims for injuries caused by exposure to a sanitizing agent used by an air-duct cleaning service. *Hastings Mut. Ins. Co. v. Safety King, Inc.*, 778 N.W.2d 275, 282 (Mich. Ct. App. 2009). "[The insurer] did not prove that triclosan is an irritant or contaminant. Rather, the evidence set forth by [the insured] showed that triclosan was supposed to be where it was located, i.e., in ductwork, and that it is *not* generally expected to cause injurious or harmful effects to people." *Id.* at 280. *But see McKusick v. Travelers Indem. Co.*, 632 N.W.2d 525, 531 (Mich. Ct. App. 2001) (concluding that the pollution exclusion precluded coverage for injuries caused by release of chemicals from a high-pressure hose delivery system) ("There are no exceptions to the exclusion and no limitations regarding its scope, including the location or other characteristics of the discharge. Although we recognize that other jurisdictions have considered the terms 'discharge,' 'dispersal,' 'release,' and 'escape' to be environmental terms of art, thus requiring the pollutant to cause traditional environmental pollution before the exclusion is applicable, we cannot judicially engraft such limitation."); *Arch Ins. Co. v. Commercial Steel Treating Corp.*, No. 11-15535, 2013 U.S. Dist. LEXIS 121574 (E.D. Mich. Aug. 27, 2013) (holding that pollution exclusion expressly applied to criminal charges of violating Air Use Permit by operating damaged smoke stack without scrubber, releasing sulfuric acid vapors into air); *McGuirk Sand & Gravel, Inc. v. Meridian Mut. Ins. Co.*, 559 N.W.2d 93, 98 (Mich. Ct. App. 1996) (concluding that the pollution exclusion precluded coverage for claims for damage caused by noncombustible water contaminated with petroleum, even though it was determined to be safe enough for disposal in city's wastewater system); *Lymtal Int'l, Inc. v. Chubb Custom Ins. Co.*, No. CIV-10-0688, 2011 U.S. Dist. LEXIS 15153 (W.D. Okla. Feb. 15, 2011) (applying Michigan law) (determining that insured-manufacturer of industrial coating comprised of numerous chemicals was entitled to conduct discovery to determine if latent ambiguity—an ambiguity where "there is an ambiguity concerning the identity of the intended beneficiary of a promise in a contract"—existed in the policy to preempt pollution exclusion because insured met burden to demonstrate that pollution exclusion could potentially "eviscerate[ ] coverage for the sole product" of insured manufacturers) (citations omitted from original); *Hastings Mut. Ins. Co. v. Mosher Dolan Cataldo & Kelly, Inc.*, No. 296791, 2014 Mich. App. LEXIS 138 (Mich. Ct. App. Jan. 23, 2014) (holding that "absence of language including mold specifically, or naturally-occurring biological contaminants generally, in the definition of pollutant, supports...[the] argument that...mold damage claim is not excluded by pollution exclusion"), *reversed* 856 N.W.2d 550 (Mich. 2014) (noting that Court of Appeals erred in holding that insurer did not have a duty to defend because the fungi exclusion only precluded coverage for some of the claims); *Secura Ins. v. DTE Gas Services*, No. 14–10401, 2014 U.S. LEXIS 171339 (E.D. Mich. Dec. 11, 2014) (citing *McKusick*) ("The Michigan Court of Appeals has made clear that pollution exclusions are not limited to traditional environmental pollution."); *Decker Mfg. Corp. v. Travelers Indem. Co.*, No. 1:13-820, 2015 U.S. Dist. LEXIS 12169 (W.D. Mich. Feb. 3, 2015) ("The Court is satisfied that Decker's placement of its waste in the Landfill is equivalent to the placement of waste in a container, and that, under the facts of this case, the Michigan Supreme Court would apply the container approach used in *Kent County [v. Home Ins. Co.*, 551 N.W.2d 424 (Mich. Ct. App. 1996)] and *South Macomb [Disposal Auth. v. Am. Ins. Co.*, 572 N.W.2d 686 (Mich. Ct. App. 1997)]. Under this approach, the relevant discharge is the discharge from the Landfill into the environment rather than the placement of waste into the Landfill."); *Hobson v. Indian Harbor Ins. Co.*, No. 316714, 2015 Mich. App. LEXIS 486 (Mich. Ct. App. Mar. 10, 2015) ("In this case, plaintiffs' allegedly suffered injuries because of the negligence on the part of the insured that resulted in a fire. Plaintiffs did not allege injuries that were caused in whole or in part by the discharge, dispersal, release, seepage, migration or escape of a pollutant. Defendant's contention that the pollutant was the basis for plaintiff's claim is inaccurate. Plaintiffs were allegedly injured by (sic) when the fire and smoke engulfed them. It did not pollute them."); *Hous. Enter. Ins. Co. v. Hope Park Homes Ltd.*, 446 F. Supp. 3d 229 (E.D. Mich. 2020) ("It is undisputed in this case that the concentration of carbon monoxide in Underlying Plaintiffs' home was noxious and rendered the air unfit for use by the introduction of unwholesome or undesirable elements—here, the carbon monoxide itself. As a matter of law, carbon monoxide therefore falls within the 'pollution exclusion' in Plaintiff's Policy.") ("There is no language in the pollution exclusion requiring that a pollutant be man-made, and Michigan law would not permit the Court to 'engraft' such a requirement.").

Minnesota: The Supreme Court of Minnesota found that "carbon monoxide released from a negligently installed boiler is a 'pollutant' that is subject to the absolute pollution exclusion." *Midwest Family Mut. Ins. Co. v. Wolters*, 831 N.W.2d 628 (Minn. 2013) (noting that the pollution exclusion did not "use language descriptive of the natural environment only," and therefore, "the exclusion applies to indoor carbon monoxide"). The Court of Appeals of Minnesota held that the pollution exclusion precluded coverage for claims brought by homeowners against neighboring hog farm for emitting manure odors. *Wakefield Pork, Inc. v. RAM Mut. Ins. Co.*, 731 N.W.2d 154, 160 (Minn. Ct. App. 2007). The court concluded that the plain language of the exclusion precluded coverage for harm from the gases, hydrogen sulfide, and noxious and offensive odors that emanated from the insured's pig farm. *Id.* The court distinguished the Supreme Court of Minnesota's decision in *Board of Regents v. Royal Insurance Co.*, 517 N.W.2d 888 (Minn. 1994), which held that the pollution exclusion did not preclude coverage for the release of asbestos that originated from inside a building and "did not address a situation where contaminants were released 'into the atmosphere' from neighboring land and then contaminated or polluted air inside a building." *Id.* at 161; *see also Cont'l Cas. Co v. Advance Terrazzo & Tile Co., Ins.*, 462 F.3d 1002, 1009 (8th Cir. 2006) (applying Minnesota law) (finding pollution exclusion precluded coverage for claims arising out of exposure to carbon monoxide, which is an "irritant" as stated in exclusion); *Auto-Owners Inc. Co. v. Hanson*, 588 N.W.2d 777, 779–81 (Minn. Ct. App. 1999) (concluding that lead paint was a "pollutant" within the terms of the pollution exclusion and chipping and flaking of paint was a "discharge, dispersal or release"); *League of Minn. Cities Ins. Trust v. City of Coon Rapids*, 446 N.W.2d 419, 422 (Minn. Ct. App. 1989) (finding that the pollution exclusion precluded coverage for claims by ice rink patrons exposed to nitrogen dioxide, a toxic by-product of a Zamboni ice-cleaning machine, that had built up in an arena); *Brouse v. Nationwide Agribusiness Ins. Co.*, No. 14-1729, 2015 Minn. App. Unpub. LEXIS 727 (Minn. Ct. App. July 27, 2015) ("As in *Wakefield Pork*, appellants' allegations regarding 'offensive and noxious odors' fall within the plain language of the absolute pollution exclusions in Dairy Dozen's insurance policies.") ("Flies and other insects meet the plain-meaning definition of 'contaminant' because they impaired appellants' use and enjoyment of their properties by making them 'impure or unclean.'); *Travelers Prop. Cas. Co. of Am. v. Klick*, No. 15-2403, 2016 U.S. Dist. LEXIS 139752 (D. Minn. Oct. 6, 2016) ("Here, the Pollution Exclusion precludes coverage for injury arising out of the release of pollutants into 'atmosphere.' Accordingly, under *Board of*

Regents and *Wakefield Pork*—which both involved exclusions for pollutants released into 'atmosphere'—the Pollution Exclusion applies when the pollutant at issue is released directly into ambient or outdoor air, even if the pollutant indirectly affects air inside an enclosed structure. Conversely, the Pollution Exclusion does not apply when the pollutant is released directly into air inside an enclosed structure such as a house or other building.") (*aff'd* 2017 U.S. App. LEXIS 15017 (8th Cir. Aug. 14, 2017)) (further discussion of the existence of a release into the atmosphere (boat's wheelhouse) despite the initial release into the engine compartment); *Restaurant Recycling, LLC v. New Fashion Pork, LLP*, No. 17-7, 2017 U.S. Dist. LEXIS 109755 (D. Minn. July 14, 2017) (fat products used to produce feed for swine were contained with lasalocid -- medication regulated by the FDA used in chicken and turkey feed, but not approved for use in swine -- causing serious health problems in swine) (rejecting the argument that that the pollution exclusion did not apply because lasalocid "can be administered to swine and other animals at safe levels and, therefore, is not a contaminant") (also rejecting the argument that the contaminants were not dispersed because they were never separated from the fat product), *aff'd* 922 F.3d 414 (8th Cir. 2019) ("Even if lasalocid were not a pollutant, the complaint did not allege that lasalocid by itself caused or would have caused all of the damage; to the contrary, New Fashion Pork alleged that both lasalocid and lascadoil were unsafe for consumption by animals, and that fat product contaminated with both substances caused serious health issues for its swine."); *Owners Ins. Co v. McPherson Minn. Lake Mut. Ins. Co.*, No. 81-17-847, 2018 Minn. Dist. LEXIS 214 (Minn. Dist. Ct. June 19, 2018) (concluding that "methane is not a 'pollutant' as it relates to the Owners Policy" because it is neither a "contaminant" nor a "pollutant"); *Seifert v. IMT Ins. Co.*, No. 20-1102, 2020 U.S. Dist. LEXIS 192121 (D. Minn. Oct. 16, 2020) ("[Insurer's] attempt to place the coronavirus in the same category of pollutants as 'smoke, vapor, soot, fumes, acids, alkalis, chemicals, and waste' is unavailing.").

Mississippi: The Fifth Circuit Court of Appeals held that the pollution exclusion precluded coverage for claims for injuries arising out of a hypersensitive plaintiff's exposure to paint and glue fumes released during the painting of a residence. *Am. States Ins. Co. v. Nethery*, 79 F.3d 473, 478 (5th Cir. 1996) (applying Mississippi law). "An irritant is a substance that produces a *particular* effect, not one that generally or probably causes such effects. The paint and glue fumes that irritated Nethery satisfy both the dictionary definition and the policy exclusion of irritants." *Id.* at 476 (emphasis in original); *see also Am. States Ins. Co., v. F.H.S., Inc.*, 843 F. Supp. 187, 189 (S.D. Miss. 1994) (concluding that the pollution exclusion precluded coverage for injuries caused by an ammonia leak from a pressure relief valve of a refrigeration system); *Eott Energy Pipeline, L.P. v. Hattiesburg Speedway, Inc.*, 303 F. Supp. 2d 819, 825 (S.D. Miss. 2004) (concluding that the pollution exclusion precluded coverage for costs of cleaning up oil spill, complying with regulatory authorities and oil lost in spill, but that the exclusion did not preclude coverage for the repair of a pipeline or lost profits because they were not caused by the release of a pollutant, but, rather, a motor grader blade striking a pipeline); *Lopez v. Shelter Ins. Co.*, No. 4:10CV55, 2011 U.S. Dist. LEXIS 63948 (S.D. Miss. June 16, 2011) (using same rationale as cases involving pollution exclusions to determine that insured was precluded from coverage because contamination exclusion was applicable to damages resulting from Chinese drywall's emission of sulfur gases); *Bishop v. Alfa Mut. Ins. Co.*, No. 4:10CV49, 2011 U.S. Dist. LEXIS 64149 (S.D. Miss. June 16, 2011) (same); *Prestige Props. v. Nat'l Builders & Contrs. Ins. Co.*, No. 1:12CV205, 2013 U.S. Dist. LEXIS 146738 (S.D. Miss. Oct. 10, 2013) (holding that pollution exclusion barred coverage for damages resulting from Chinese drywall); *Grain Dealers Mut. Ins. Co. v. Cooley*, No. 16-39, 2017 U.S. Dist. LEXIS 217770 (S.D. Miss. Mar. 30, 2017) (finding the majority view to be more persuasive, "particularly when other courts applying Mississippi law have reached a similar conclusion," and concluding that gasoline is a pollutant under the Pollution Exclusions) ("It is a rare substance indeed that is always a pollutant; the most noxious of materials have their appropriate and non polluting uses.") (*rev'd on other grounds*, 734 Fed. Appx. 223 (5th Cir. 2018)); *Burroughs Diesel, Inc. v. Travelers Indem. Co. of America*, No. 18-48, 2019 U.S. Dist. LEXIS 225361 (S.D. Miss. Nov. 1, 2019) ("Plaintiff claims that hydrochloric acid released or discharged on a neighboring property migrated to its property, causing damage. The policy's definition of 'pollutants' specifically includes 'acids.' Therefore, HCl is a 'pollutant' as defined by the policy, and the pollution exclusion applies - barring the application of any exception.") (addressing various property policy exceptions) (*aff'd* 817 Fed. Appx. 2 (5th Cir. 2020)) (upholding the district court's decision that "BDI failed to prove that an exception to the policy's pollution exclusion applies").

Missouri: The Missouri Court of Appeals held that the pollution exclusion did not preclude coverage for property damage claims arising from the release of 2,000 gallons of gasoline from a storage tank at a service station. *Hocker Oil Co., Inc. v. Barker-Phillips-Jackson, Inc.*, 997 S.W.2d 510 (Mo. Ct. App. 1999). "Hocker is in the business of transporting, selling and storing gasoline on a daily basis. Gasoline is not a pollutant in its eyes. Gasoline is the product it sells. Gasoline belongs in the environment in which Hocker routinely works ... . [I]n that environment, gasoline is not a pollutant. Hocker was entitled to characterize gasoline in a manner consistent with its daily activities absent specific policy language to the contrary. [The insurer's] failure to identify 'gasoline' as a pollutant in its pollution exclusion resulted in uncertainty and indistinctness. The policy was, therefore, ambiguous as to whether gasoline was a pollutant for purposes of the exclusion." *Id.* at 518 (citing to *Kiger's* observation [*see* Indiana] that it would be an oddity for an insurance company to sell a liability policy to a gas station that would specifically exclude that insured's major source of liability); *see also Heringer v. Am. Family Mut. Ins. Co.*, 140 S.W.3d 100, 104–06 (Mo. Ct. App. 2004) (pollution exclusion precluded coverage for claim for exposure to lead paint) (distinguishing *Hocker* because lead was specifically and unambiguously defined in the policy as a pollutant) (rejecting insured's argument that the pollution exclusion is only applicable to traditional environmental pollution); *Hartford Accident & Indem. Co. v. Doe Run Resources Corp.*, No. 4:08-CV-1687, 2010 U.S. Dist. LEXIS 40608 (E.D. Mo. Apr. 26, 2010) (concluding that it could not state, as a matter of law, that lead was a pollutant within the meaning of the pollution exclusion, as insured's lead claims went beyond smelter emissions); *American Western Home Ins. Co. v. Utopia Acquisition L.P.*, No. 08-0419, 2009 U.S. Dist. LEXIS 23219 (W.D. Mo. Mar. 24, 2009) (pollution exclusion applied to "airborne contaminants and/or irritants") ("[*Hocker Oil*] rested on the unique facts of that particular case; particularly, the oddity of having a policy issued to a gas station exclude coverage for spilled gasoline on the basis that gasoline was a pollutant. Under Missouri law, the term 'pollutant' is not limited to traditional environmental pollutants or situations, and the pollution exclusion is not limited to so-called 'environmental pollution.'"); *Doe Run Resources Corp. v. Lexington Ins. Co.*, 719 F.3d 876 (8th Cir. 2013) (holding that pollution exclusion applied to claims of tortious release of lead and other chemicals, but did not apply to claims concerning distribution of these hazardous materials or alleging insured made hazardous materials open to public without posting warning signs); *Doe Run Resources Corp. v. Lexington Ins. Co.*, 719 F.3d 868 (8th Cir. 2013) (concluding that release of lead and other hazardous materials from mine and mill work fell under pollution exclusion, and deletion of broader lead exclusion did not create ambiguity or negate application of pollution exclusion); *United Fire & Cas. Co. v. Titan Contractors Serv., Inc.*, 751 F.3d 880 (8th Cir. 2014) (concluding that TIAH, a chemical concrete sealant used by insured-contractors, constituted a pollutant); *American Nat. Property & Cas. Co. v. Wyatt*, 400 S.W.3d 417 (Mo. Ct. App. 2013) (holding that the pollution exclusion was ambiguous and did not preclude coverage for injuries from carbon monoxide emitted from car accidentally left running in garage); *Williams v. Emplrs. Mut. Cas. Co.*, 845 F.3d 891 (8th Cir. 2017) ("[T]he pollution exclusion in each policy bars coverage for bodily injury or property damage alleged to have resulted from the presence of Radium or alpha particles in Autumn Hills' water supply.").

In *Doe Run Res. Corp. v. Am. Guar. & Liab. Ins.*, No. SC96107, 2017 Mo. LEXIS 488 (Mo. Oct. 31, 2017) the Supreme Court of Missouri addressed an issue of first impression: "[W]hether an insurance policy's general pollution exclusion bars defense coverage of a toxic tort claim arising from alleged industrial pollution." *Id.* at *6-7. At issue was coverage for bodily injuries sustained by individuals who were exposed to toxic emissions – lead, arsenic, cadmium and sulfer dioxide -- from Doe Run's metallurgical industrial complex. The court held: "[P]laintiffs allege toxic chemicals are present in the air, water, and surrounding environment and these toxic chemicals are harmful to the individuals who breathe them. These claims certainly allege the existence of an irritant or contaminant under the ordinary meanings of the words; these emissions could be understood to both 'produce irritation' and 'corrupt' the breathable air, making it 'unfit for use.' Accordingly, the toxic emissions expelled from Doe Run's facilities are unequivocally a pollutant under the plain meaning of the term." *Id.* at *10. The court distinguished *Hocker Oil*, noting that "the Reid lawsuits make absolutely no allegation of any injury caused by Doe Run's business products. Indeed, each of the selected quotations cited by Doe Run in its brief omits the actual alleged cause of injury: toxic releases emanating from Doe Run's metallurgical facility." *Id.* at *13. "Because these toxic lead byproducts are not Doe Run's business commodities, *Hocker Oil* does not apply." *Id.* at *15. *See also Zurich Am. Ins. Co. v. Ins. Co. of N. Am.*, 392 F. Supp. 3d 992 (E.D. Mo. 2019) (holding, following lengthy discussion of Missouri law, that "asbestos unambiguously falls within the exclusion's definition of 'contaminants,' 'irritants,' and 'pollutants,' and the policy is not rendered ambiguous as a matter of law merely because asbestos is not explicitly listed in the exclusion") (addressing "sudden and accidental" pollution exclusion).

Montana: The Supreme Court of Montana held that the pollution exclusion precluded coverage for diesel fuel that leaked from an underground tank at a gas station. *Mont. Petroleum Tank Release Compensation Bd. v. Crumleys, Inc.*, 174 P.3d 948, 959 (Mont. 2008). "[W]e conclude that most consumers would consider diesel a pollutant when it leaks into the ground and contaminates soil and groundwater. As the Supreme Court recognized, even a valuable and useful product can become a pollutant when it contaminates a natural resource." *Id.* (referring to *U.S. v. Standard Oil Co.*, 384 U.S. 224 (1966)). That diesel is a pollutant "is evidenced by both the clear language of the policy, and by the obvious hazards diesel fuel poses to community health and safety once it has leaked into the soil." *Id. See also Dick Anderson Constr. v. Nat'l Fire Ins. Co.*, No. CV 10-35-BU-RFC-CSO, 2011 U.S. Dist. LEXIS 29274 (D. Mont. Feb. 4, 2011) (determining that insurer was required to defend policyholder in case where sewer lift station leaked and contaminated the underlying plaintiff's well because the insurer failed to prove lift station was a "waste facility," as required under policy's pollution exclusion); *Palmer v. Northland Cas. Co.*, No. 15-58, 2016 U.S. Dist. LEXIS 138556 (D. Mont. Oct. 5, 2016) ("Whereas it was questionable whether the oil company's wrongful injection of a diluted mix into the oil pipeline was the kind of 'contamination' contemplated by the pollution exclusion in *Enron [Oil Trading & Transp. Co. v. Walbrook Ins. Co., Ltd.*, 132 F.3d 526 (9th Cir. 1997)], here, it is unequivocally clear that injury caused by the release of hydrocarbon vapors is the kind of 'bodily injury' the Oil/Gas Exclusion excludes."); *Swank Enters. v. United Fire & Cas Co.*, No. 19-179, 2020 U.S. Dist. LEXIS 61255 (D. Mont. Apr. 7, 2020) (pollution exclusion precluded coverage for bodily injuries caused by exposure to epoxies because the term "pollutants," which included "chemicals," "unambiguously includes the epoxies used at the Project site").

Nebraska: The Supreme Court of Nebraska held that the pollution exclusion precluded coverage for claims for contamination of food stored in a warehouse due to fumes from a floor sealant. *Cincinnati Ins. Co. v. Becker Warehouse, Inc.*, 635 N.W.2d 112, 120 (Neb. 2001). "We conclude that as a matter of law, [the insurer's] pollution exclusion, though quite broad, is unambiguous. The language of the policy does not specifically limit excluded claims to traditional environmental damage; nor does the pollution exclusion purport to limit materials that qualify as pollutants to those that cause traditional environmental damage." *Id.; see also Harleysville Ins. Group v. Omaha Gas Appliance Co.*, 772 N.W.2d 88, 95–96 (Neb. 2009) (involving claims for carbon monoxide poisoning, due to faulty repair of a gas boiler, which the parties agreed were precluded from coverage by the pollution exclusion) (rejecting argument that an umbrella policy's pollution exclusion only precluded coverage for strict liability pollution claims, but not pollution-related injuries caused by negligence); *Ferrell v. State Farm Ins. Co.*, No. A-01–637, 2003 Neb. App. LEXIS 123 (Neb. Ct. App. May 13, 2003) (following *Becker Warehouse* and holding that coverage for injuries caused by exposure to mercury in an apartment was precluded by the pollution exclusion); *State Farm Fire & Cas. Co. v. Dantzler*, 852 N.W.2d 918

(Neb. 2014) (parties did not dispute that lead-based paint was a pollutant under the pollution exclusion and "[r]egardless of how the lead-based paint is separated from the painted surface or what form it takes once it is separated, an individual's exposure to and absorption of that lead-based paint results from the 'discharge, dispersal, spill, release or escape' of a pollutant"); *Church Mut. Ins. Co. v. Clay Center Christian Church*, 746 F.3d 375 (8th Cir. 2014) (holding that pollution exclusion precluded coverage for injuries resulting from exposure to carbon monoxide); *Topp's Mech., Inc. v. Kinsale Ins. Co.*, 374 F. Supp. 3d 813 (D. Neb. 2019) (finding the argument that a pollution exclusion, which precludes coverage for "any liability from [b]odily injury . . . arising out of the . . . discharge, dispersal, seepage, migration, release or escape of pollutants," applied to any liability arising out of the alleged escape of any pollutants persuasive, as it is consistent with Nebraska's broad interpretation of pollution exclusions) (pollution exclusion precluded coverage for bodily injury caused by ammonia gas release).

Nevada: The Supreme Court of Nevada held that the pollution exclusion did not bar coverage for injuries from carbon monoxide exposure when four people died while sleeping in a motel room directly above a pool heater. *Century Sur. Co. v. Casino West, Inc.*, No. 60622, 2014 Nev. LEXIS 50 (Nev. May 29, 2014) (reviewing the pollution exclusion landscape nationally and interpreting its application to traditional and non-traditional pollutants) (concluding that pollution exclusion was ambiguous and susceptible to multiple interpretations, and noting, "[t]o demonstrate that the absolute pollution exclusion applies to nontraditional indoor pollutants, an insurer must plainly state that the exclusion is not limited to traditional environmental pollution").

New Hampshire: The Supreme Court of New Hampshire held that the pollution exclusion did not preclude coverage for claims for injury to a child for lead poisoning on account of exposure to paint carried on his father's clothing from his workplace. *Weaver v. Royal Ins. Co.*, 674 A.2d 975, 978 (N.H. 1996). "Because there are two reasonable interpretations of the policy language, we conclude that the pollution exclusion is ambiguous." *Id.* at 978; *see also Titan Holdings Syndicate v. City of Keene*, 898 F.2d 265, 268 (1st Cir. 1990) (applying New Hampshire law) ("Excessive noise and light may be 'irritants,' but they are not *solid, liquid, gaseous or thermal* irritants. Nor are they generally thought of as similar to smoke, vapor, soot, fumes, acids, alkalis, chemicals or waste, the illustrative terms used in the policy definition."); *EnergyNorth Nat. Gas, Inc. v. Am. Home Assurance Co.*, No. Civ. 99–502-JD, 2003 U.S. Dist. LEXIS 12665 (D.N.H. July 16, 2003) (concluding that

Weaver was not controlling because the pollution at issue (manufactured gas plant waste) was clearly environmental); *Mellin v. N. Sec. Ins. Co.*, 115 A.3d 799 (N.H. 2015) ("Although an insured may have reasonably understood that the pollution exclusion clause precluded coverage for damages resulting from odors emanating from large-scale farms, waste-processing facilities, or other industrial settings, these circumstances are distinguishable from those before us, which involve an odor created in a private residence by common domestic animals. . . . In addition, although Northern emphasizes that the plaintiffs referred to the cat urine odor as 'a chemical smell similar to ammonia,' we do not believe that the reference to 'ammonia' in this context triggers the pollution exclusion clause.").

New Jersey: The Supreme Court of New Jersey held that the pollution exclusion should be read to apply "to injury or property damage arising from activity commonly thought of as traditional environmental pollution," or more specifically pollution resulting from "environmental catastrophe related to intentional industrial pollution." *Nav-Its, Inc. v. Selective Ins. Co. of Am.*, 869 A.2d 929, 937 (N.J. 2005) (addressing the exclusion in the context of exposure to toxic fumes in a floor coating/ sealant operation). "[W]e are confident that the history of the pollution-exclusion clause in its various forms demonstrates that its purpose was to have a broad exclusion for traditional environmentally related damages." *Id.* at 936–37; *see also Baughman v. U.S. Liab. Ins. Co.*, 662 F. Supp. 2d 386, 399 (D.N.J. 2009) (holding that exposure to mercury at daycare center occupying a former thermometer manufacturing facility was not traditional environmental pollution because it was indoors, and therefore not excluded by the pollution exclusion) (relying on other jurisdictions' "conclusion that traditional environmental pollution does not include exposure to toxic materials released indoors" and determining that pollution exclusion "thus does not include mercury contamination in Kiddie Kollege [daycare facility]"); *Merchants Ins. Co. of N.H., Inc. v. Hessler*, No. COV/03–5857, 2005 U.S. Dist. LEXIS 18173 (D.N.J. Aug. 18, 2005) (holding that the pollution exclusion did not apply to bodily injury and property damage resulting from exposure to lead paint); *Spartan Oil Co. v. New Jersey Property Liability Ins. Guar. Ass'n*, No. A-5156-10T2, N.J. Super. Unpub. LEXIS 1290 (N.J. Super. Ct. App. Div. June 8, 2012) (application of pollution exclusion to heating oil spill hinged on meaning of "delivered" or "finally delivered" as used in exclusion); *Woodcliff Lake Bd. of Educ. v. Zurich Am. Ins. Co.*, No. A-5772-11T3, 2013 N.J. Super. Unpub. LEXIS 2041 (N.J. Super. Ct. App. Div. Aug. 14, 2013) (holding that coverage for damages resulting from asbestos abatement was precluded under property policy's pollution exclusion and vandalism exception did not apply); *Herz v.*

141 Bloomfield Ave. Corp., No. A-2954-13T2, 2015 N.J. Super. Unpub. LEXIS 1274 (N.J. Super. Ct. App. Div. June 1, 2015) ("'Pollutants' is defined in the policy as including 'waste,' which would encompass the type of discharge expected from a faulty septic system. Because the Verona Inn was shut down as the result of a threatened discharge of 'pollutants,' under the CGL policy exclusion, there is no coverage."); *Castoro & Co. v. Hartford Accident & Indem. Co.*, No. 14-1305, 2016 U.S. Dist. LEXIS 134686 (D.N.J. Sept. 29, 2016) (despite observing that, under *Nav-Its*, the pollution exclusion is limited to traditional environmental pollution, the court held that, according to *Nav-Its*, even when a pollution exclusion's language does not require intent, "New Jersey public policy requires intent to avoid unregulated and sweeping elimination of pollution-caused damage coverage.") (applying an intent requirement from *Morton International* (*see* New Jersey, chapter 14, involving the qualified pollution exclusion); *Benjamin v. State Farm Ins. Co.*, No. 15-4123, 2017 U.S. Dist. LEXIS 131078 (D.N.J. Aug. 17, 2017) (discussing and following *Castoro*) ("Given the applicability of the pollution exclusion only in a context involving 'traditional environmental pollution' under *Nav-Its* and the failure of Clarendon to allege (let alone demonstrate the existence of evidence from which a reasonable fact-finder could find) that Plaintiffs intended to pollute the Property, the Court declines to grant summary judgment at this time on the grounds that the Pollution Exclusion applies."); *Birch v. Hanover Ins. Co.*, No. 2490-19, 2021 N.J. Super. Unpub. LEXIS 453 (N.J. Super. Ct. App. Div. Mar. 19, 2021) (pollution exclusion did not apply to the explosion of a homeowner's propane tank because it did not qualify as "a traditional 'industrial pollution' event").

New Mexico: No instructive authority.

New York: The Court of Appeals of New York held that the pollution exclusion did not preclude coverage for a bodily injury claim arising out of paint or solvent fumes discharged during painting and stripping work performed by the insured. *Belt Painting Corp. v. TIG Ins. Co.*, 795 N.E.2d 15, 21 (N.Y. 2003). "Were we to adopt [the insurer's] interpretation, under the language of this exclusion any 'chemical,' or indeed, any 'material to be recycled,' that could 'irritate' person or property would be a 'pollutant.' We are reluctant to adopt an interpretation that would infinitely enlarge the scope of the term 'pollutants,' and seemingly contradict both a 'common speech' understanding of the relevant terms and the reasonable expectations of a businessperson." *Id.* at 20. "Even if the paint or solvent fumes are within the definition of 'pollutant,' the exclusion applies only if the underlying injury is caused by 'discharge, dispersal, seepage, migration, release or escape' of the fumes. It cannot be said that this language unambiguously applies to ordinary paint or solvent fumes that drifted a short distance from the area of the insured's intended use and allegedly caused inhalation injuries to a bystander." *Id. Accord, Greengrass, Inc. v. Lumbermans Mut. Cas. Co.*, No. 09 Civ. 7697, 2010 U.S. Dist. LEXIS 76781 (S.D.N.Y. July 27, 2010) (insurer owed duty to defend in claim involving odors from fish served at insured restaurant because food odors were not a pollutant but a byproduct integral to operation of restaurant) (noting that owner reasonably expected liability insurance protection for such claims), *aff'd*, 2011 U.S. App. LEXIS 22442 (2nd Cir. Nov. 4, 2011) (rejecting the insurer's argument that the pollution exclusion applied on the basis that, under the New York City Administrative Code, restaurant odors, in sufficiently detectable quantities, may constitute "air contaminants"). *But see Maxine Furs, Inc. v. Auto-Owners Ins. Co.* (*see* Alabama) (determining that curry aroma was pollutant). *See also Great American Restoration Services, Inc. v. Scottsdale Ins. Co.*, 911 N.Y.S.2d 142, 146 (N.Y. App. Div. 2010) ("Scottsdale's interpretation of the pollution exclusion presents an ambiguity which must be resolved against it. Although asbestos may be a thermal irritant, the term 'asbestos' is not specifically included within the definition of a 'pollutant' as defined under the terms of the policy. Moreover, Scottsdale's position that damages from asbestos are excluded under the pollution exclusion would render the specific asbestos exclusion meaningless, in violation of settled canons of construction.") (also concluding that the asbestos exclusion did not apply because, although it stated that no coverage is provided for property damage arising out of the "removal," "disposal," or "use" of asbestos, it did not preclude coverage for damages arising out of the unknowing or accidental release or dispersal of asbestos); *Broome County v. The Travelers Indem. Co.*, 125 A.D.3d 1241 (N.Y. App. Div. 2015) (first-party property) (applying pollution exclusion to silica and distinguishing *Belt Painting*); *Cincinnati Ins. Co. v. Roy's Plumbing, Inc.*, No. 16-2511, 2017 U.S. App. LEXIS 9729 (2nd Cir. May 31, 2017) ("New York courts, however, limit the reach of pollution exclusions to those cases where the damages alleged are truly environmental in nature, or where the underlying complaint alleges damages resulting from what can accurately be described as the pollution of the environment.") (applying the pollution exclusion to sewage); *National Union Fire Ins. Co. of Pittsburgh, PA v. Burlington Ins. Co.*, No. 155114/2013, 2018 N.Y. Misc. LEXIS 1503 (N.Y. Sup. Ct. Apr. 27, 2018) (not addressing whether World Trade Center emissions are properly considered "classic" or "traditional" environmental pollution as the claimants asserted independent claims that were not covered by the pollution exclusion); *Weitsman & Son of Scranton v. Hartford Fire Ins. Co.*, No. 16-0780, 2018

U.S. Dist. LEXIS 22970 (N.D.N.Y. Feb. 13, 2018) (pollution exclusion applied to "a white cloud of chlorine gas large enough to travel outdoors to two adjoining properties and trap and engulf five people (including an automobile) there") (concluding case is "factually distinguishable from the gaseous substances in the other two New York cases relied on by Plaintiffs, which involved (1) a spray of sulfuric acid that remains on a property and affects only one person, or (2) some paint and solvent fumes that remain in an office building and bother one person").

North Carolina: The Court of Appeals of North Carolina held that the pollution exclusion did not preclude coverage for claims for damage to chicken that was contaminated by the insured's resurfacing of the floors in a chicken processing facility. *W. Am. Ins. Co. v. Tufco Flooring East, Inc.*, 409 S.E.2d 692, 699 (N.C. Ct. App. 1991) (overruled on other grounds in *Gaston County Dyeing Mach. Co. v. Northfield Ins. Co.*, 524 S.E.2d 558 (N.C. 2000)). "In light of the language of the [insurer's] policy and [insured's] reasonable belief that damages accidentally arising from its normal business activities would not be excluded, we agree that the pollution exclusion clause in the [insured's] policy applies only to discharges into the environment and not to the non-environmental damage that led to [plaintiff's] claim against [insured]." *Id.* at 700; *see also Auto-Owners Ins. Co. v. Potter*, 105 Fed. App'x 484, 497 (4th Cir. 2004) (applying North Carolina law) (following *Tufco* and holding that, to the extent claims were for traditional environmental damage, the pollution exclusion precluded coverage for injury and damage arising out of a housing developer's provision of contaminated well water); *Federal Ins. Co. v. Southern Lithoplate, Inc.*, 7 F. Supp. 3d 579(E.D.N.C. Mar. 14, 2014) (citing *Tufco* and holding that pollution exclusion applied to groundwater contamination from disposal of hazardous chemicals related to production of lithographic plates and other photography products) ("The central business activity exception [*Tufco*] cannot be read so broadly that it eviscerates the pollution exclusion in every case in which an insured uses a pollutant in the course of its central business activity."); *Pennsylvania Nat. Mut. Cas. Ins. Co. v. Robin Hood Container Express, Inc.*, No. 5:08-CV-531, 2010 U.S. Dist. LEXIS 58891 (E.D.N.C. June 14, 2010) (determining that insurer, on account of policy's pollution exclusion, had no duty to defend insured after insured had been "joined as a third party defendant in a lawsuit for environmental clean-up costs … under CERCLA" at site where insured "operated [ ] a container drop yard" that had been originally contaminated by a fertilizer plant in operation twenty-five years ago); *United Nat. Ins. Co. v. Horton Sales Development Corp.*, No. 1:11-00028, 2012 U.S. Dist. LEXIS 176772 (W.D. N.C. Dec. 13, 2013) (holding that pollution exclusion applied broadly and precluded coverage for pollution clean-up costs which development corporation owed third party); *New NGC, Inc. v. ACE Am. Ins. Co.*, 105 F. Supp. 3d 552 (W.D.N.C. 2015) (discussing *Tufco* in great detail and concluding that the pollution exclusion applied to preclude coverage for corrosion of metal pipes and electrical wiring, deterioration of air condition coils, melting of insulation and bodily injury in the form of respiratory ailments and allergy-like symptoms, all from exposure to defective drywall); *Colony Ins. Co. v. Buckeye Fire Equip. Co.*, No. 19-00534, 2020 U.S. Dist. LEXIS 194709 (W.D.N.C. Oct. 20, 2020) (appeal pending) (applying *Tufco*, to a "Hazardous Materials" exclusion, akin to a pollution exclusion, and concluding that it did not preclude coverage for bodily injury caused by exposure to fire suppressing foam containing PFOA and PFOS, as it was not traditional environmental pollution).

North Dakota: In *Hiland Partners GP Holdings, LLC v. Nat'l Union Fire Ins. Co.*, 847 F.3d 594 (8th Cir. 2017), the Eighth Circuit, applying North Dakota law, held that the pollution exclusion applied because "[c]ondensate [a saleable byproduct that results from the processing of gas and hydrocarbon products] is…a contaminant because flammable, volatile, and explosive liquid and gas has the ability to soil, stain, corrupt, or infect the environment." The court noted that its "conclusion is in accord with the bulk of the case authority which holds that oil, gasoline, and other petroleum products are toxic by nature and therefore they constitute a contaminant when released into the environment." The court rejected the insured's argument that "even if condensate has the inherent properties of a contaminant, it does not fall within the policy's definition of a contaminant because the condensate caused harm in a manner other than by contamination."

Ohio: The Supreme Court of Ohio held that the pollution exclusion was not applicable to a claim for bodily injury caused by exposure to carbon monoxide from a faulty heater in an apartment. *Andersen v. Highland House Co.*, 757 N.E.2d 329, 334 (Ohio 2001). "Based on the history and original purposes for the pollution exclusion, it was reasonable for [the insureds] to believe that the policies purchased for their multiunit complex would not exclude claims for injuries due to carbon monoxide leaks." *Id.* at 333; *see also Bosserman Aviation Equip., Inc. v. U.S. Liab. Ins. Co.*, 915 N.E.2d 687, 696 (Ohio Ct. App. 2009) (following *Andersen* and holding that pollution exclusion did not preclude coverage for exposure to harmful chemical agents contained in aircraft fuel while reconditioning and repairing aircraft-refueling equipment) ("[A] pollution-exclusion clause of this nature does not apply to an exposure to toxic chemicals confined within an employee's work area, as there is no discharge, dispersal, release, or escape of pollutants."); *Citizens Ins. v. Lanly Co.*, Nos. 1:07 CV 241, 1:07 CV 467, 1:07 CV 469, 2007 U.S. Dist. LEXIS 78557 (N.D. Ohio Oct. 23, 2007) (addressing confusion over the pollution exclusion created by *Andersen*).

In *HoneyBaked Foods, Inc. v. Affiliated FM Ins. Co.*, No. 3:08CV01686, 2011 U.S. Dist. LEXIS 27289 (N.D. Ohio Mar. 4, 2011), a case addressing a first-party property policy, involving ham and turkey contaminated by listeria monocytogenes bacteria, the court certified the following question to the Supreme Court of Ohio: "In light of [*Anderson v. Highland House*], does the reasonable–expectations doctrine apply … so that coverage, which otherwise would be excluded under the terms and conditions of the policy, is afforded, provided that the trier of fact determines that the insured reasonably expected, when purchasing the policy, that the policy would cover the loss at issue?" The *HoneyBaked* court found the language of the exclusion clear but noted that the policyholder stated that "it reasonably believed that the all-risk policy would cover spoliation of its product during processing," which would make coverage illusory and unfairly surprising if the exclusion were read literally to treat bacterial contamination as pollution because the bacteria is a "contaminant." However, the Ohio high court declined to accept the certified question. *See HoneyBaked Foods, Inc. v. Affiliated FM Ins. Co.*, 947 N.E.2d 681 (Ohio 2011). *See also Mesa Underwriters Specialty Ins. Co. v. Myers*, No. 14-2201, 2016 U.S. Dist. LEXIS 108444 (N.D. Ohio Aug. 16, 2016) ("It is undisputed that the sealant is 'harmful or fatal if swallowed,' that its manufacturer urges 'immediate' action in the event of a spill, and that Myers and his crew donned protective gear when applying the sealant. It is also undisputed that the pollutant escaped from or seeped off the roof and flowed into Lake Erie. And there is no dispute that the damages Sireco seeks are the costs it incurred cleaning up the sealant that made its way into the lake.") (holding that pollution exclusion applies); *JTO, Inc. v. Travelers Indem. Co. of Am.*, No. 16-648, 2017 U.S. Dist. LEXIS 38033 (N.D. Ohio Mar. 16, 2017) ("Clearly, the United States' and State of Ohio's Complaints against JTO are exactly the kind of environmental actions that fall within the raison d'etre of the absolute pollution exclusion. Furthermore, Plaintiff cannot plausibly argue that under the definitions of dredge and fill in both the Clean Water Act and Ohio statute that they are anything but 'contaminants' under the plain language of the policies."); *Graftech International, Ltd. v. Pacific Employers Insurance Co.*, No. 105258, 2017 Ohio App. LEXIS 5814 (Ohio Ct. App. Dec. 28, 2017) (distinguishing *Anderson* and holding that pollution exclusion precluded coverage for bodily injury sustained by employees from exposure to fumes or particles from the burning of coal-tar pitch in a smelting plant) ("The circumstances here do not raise the same concerns addressed in *Anderson*. The alleged toxic exposure in this case occurred in an industrial setting that would be a prime example of a 'traditional' case of environmental pollution."); *R.W. Beckett Corp. v. Allianz Global Corp. & Specialty SE*, No. 19-428, 2020 U.S. Dist. LEXIS 72253 (N.D. Ohio Apr. 24, 2020) (concluding that asbestos exposure involved a "discharge, dispersal, release, or escape of an 'irritant,' 'contaminant,' or 'pollutant,'" but pollution exclusion not applicable as "the parties intended 'atmosphere' to mean the air in the external environment and not the air in a residential basement or otherwise enclosed within a structure"); *Hartford Accident & Indem. Co. v. FFP Holdings LLC*, No. 15-377, 2020 U.S. Dist. LEXIS 178110 (N.D. Ohio Sept. 28, 2020) (concluding, without analysis, that the pollution exclusion applied to environmental contamination, after determining that Ohio law, and not Indiana, governed).

Oklahoma: The Supreme Court of Oklahoma held that the pollution exclusion precluded coverage for claims for injuries caused by exposure to lead paint by patients in a hospital's dialysis unit. *Bituminous Cas. Corp. v. Cowen Constr., Inc.*, 55 P.3d 1030, 1035 (Okla. 2002). "Nowhere in the policy's lexicon is there language employed which would sustain finding—as suggested by the insured—the pollution exclusion clause only excluded from coverage that bodily injury and/or property damage which occurred when the general 'environment' was damaged by the insured's acts." *Id.* at 1034. However, the court noted that the pollution exclusion at issue was an endorsement that applied, in part, to "Bodily injury or property damage arising out of the actual, alleged or threatened discharge, dispersal, release or escape of pollutants." *Id.* at 1031 n.1. The Oklahoma high court stated that the policy's original pollution exclusion, couched in geographic terms, could be read to support a finding that an "environmental" limitation exists as to its scope. *Id.* at 1034. *See also Markel Ins. Co., Inc. v. Burns*, No. CIV-09-185-SPS, 2011 U.S. Dist. LEXIS 39188 (E.D. Okla. Apr. 8, 2011) (invoking *Bituminous* to deny coverage and duty to defend where policyholder released large quantities of pesticide into city water supply); *Certain Underwriters at Lloyd's London v. B3, Inc.*, 262 P.3d 397 (Okla. Civ. Ct. App. 2011) (holding that sewage constituted a "pollutant" and pollution exclusion precluded coverage for property damage claims which resulted from wastewater treatment plant's disposal of sewage); *Above It All Roofing & Constr., Inc. v. Sec. Nat'l Ins. Co.*, 285 F. Supp. 3d 1224 (N.D. Okla. 2018) (concluding that asbestos qualifies as both an "irritant" or "contaminant," and, therefore, is a "pollutant") (rejecting the argument that the pollution exclusion could not apply as the policy had an asbestos exclusion); *MJH Props. LLC v. Westchester Surplus Lines Ins. Co.*, 814 Fed. Appx. 421 (10th Cir. 2020) ("Although the Oklahoma Supreme Court did not address these specific substances in *Bituminous* [Essentria IC3, piperonyl butoxide, and permethrins], it interpreted a nearly identical total pollution exclusion provision broadly to include non-environmental pollutants.").

Oregon: The Court of Appeals of Oregon held that the pollution exclusion precluded coverage—but in the context of claims for property damage that was clearly caused by traditional environmental pollution. *Martin v. State Farm Fire & Cas. Co.*, 932 P.2d 1207, 1212 (Or. Ct. App. 1997) (involving petroleum contamination from underground petroleum tanks); *see also Larsen Oil Co. v. Federated Serv. Ins. Co.*, 859 F. Supp. 434, 438 (D. Or. 1994) (holding that the pollution exclusion unambiguously applied to claims for damage caused by the discharge of heating oil into a home, notwithstanding that the insured did not cause the discharge), *aff'd* 70 F.3d 1279 (9th Cir. 1995) ("The pollution exclusion contains no condition or qualification; it simply does not require that the insured discharge the pollutant."); *Goritsan v. Nautilus Ins. Co.*, No. 10-CV-433-HU, 2010 U.S. Dist. LEXIS 141508 (D. Or. Nov. 15, 2010) (declaring that further discovery was necessary, but noting that insurer may have a duty to defend policyholder after irritating liquid damaged property because artful pleading speaks of injury from "flow" of liquid rather than its toxicity) (objections to magistrate's order denied in *Goritsan v. Nautilus Ins. Co.*, No. 10-CV-433-HU, 2011 U.S. Dist. LEXIS 16890 (D. Or. Feb. 17, 2011)); *Colony Ins. Co. v. Victory Constr. LLC*, No. 16-00457, 2017 U.S. Dist. LEXIS 34368 (D. Or. Mar. 9, 2017) ("This Court predicts that the Oregon Supreme Court's analysis would be similar to the analysis of the Iowa Supreme Court. As in *Bituminous [Cas. Corp. v. Sand Livestock Systems, Inc.*, 728 N.W.2d 216 (Iowa 2007)], this Court does not even get to the point of considering the exclusion's drafting history, multiple reasonable interpretations of the policy, or the policyholder's reasonable expectations, because the plain meaning of the words 'irritant' and 'contaminant' resolve the case. This Court must follow the interpretative framework set out by the Oregon Supreme Court.") (addressing bodily injury caused by exposure to carbon monoxide).

Pennsylvania: The Supreme Court of Pennsylvania held that the pollution exclusion precluded coverage for a bodily injury claim arising out of fumes emitted from a concrete sealer. *Madison Constr. Co. v. Harleysville Mut. Ins. Co.*, 735 A.2d 100, 110 (Pa. 1999). The court concluded that the definition of "pollutant" clearly and unambiguously encompassed the cement sealing agent and rejected the argument that the policy's definition of "pollutant" is so broad that virtually any substance, including many useful and necessary products, could be said to come within its scope. *Id.* at 606–07. "[G]uided by the principle that ambiguity (or the lack thereof) is to be determined by reference to a particular set of facts, we focus on the specific product at issue." *Id.* at 607. *See also Wagner v. Erie Ins. Co.*, 801 A.2d 1226, 1232–33 (Pa. Super. Ct. 2002), *affirmed* 847 A.2d 1274 (Pa. 2004) (holding that the pollution exclusion precluded coverage for a claim for damages caused by gasoline that leaked into soil from an underground line at a gas station); *Jaskula v. Essex Ins. Co.*, 900 A.2d 931, 934 (Pa. Super. Ct. 2006) (finding that the pollution exclusion precluded coverage for response costs when an insured cut an oil line in the course of waterproofing a basement); *Heri Krupa, Inc. v. Tower Group Cos.*, No. 12-4386, 2013 U.S. Dist. LEXIS 37495 (E.D. Pa. Mar. 18, 2013) (concluding that diesel fuel constituted a pollutant, and pollution exclusion precluded coverage for lost business income when company shut down to perform remediation and restoration for diesel fuel spill); *Matcon Diamond, Inc. v. Penn Nat'l Ins. Co.*, 815 A.2d 1109, 1114 (Pa. Super. Ct. 2003) (pollution exclusion precluded coverage for claims arising out of the release of carbon monoxide); *Travelers Prop. Cas. Co. of Am. v. Chubb Custom Ins. Co.*, 864 F. Supp. 2d 301 (E.D. Pa. 2012) (holding that pollution exclusion precluded coverage for damage due to noxious odors and contaminated wastewater from pig excrement); *Hussey Copper, Ltd. v. Royal Ins. Co.*, 391 Fed. Appx. 207 (3d Cir. 2010) (applying exclusion to preclude coverage for contamination of a retention pond by lead-coated copper roofing panels and rejecting policyholder argument that statements by insurance industry to state regulators in connection with move from qualified to absolute pollution exclusion created "regulatory estoppel" against insurer). *But see Lititz Mut. Ins. Co. v. Steeley*, 785 A.2d 975, 981–82 (Pa. 2001) (holding that lead paint is a "pollutant," but exclusion not applicable because the process by which it degrades and became available for ingestion and inhalation does not involve a "discharge," "dispersal," "release," or "escape"); *Whitmore v. Liberty Mut. Fire Ins. Co.*, No. 07–5162, 2008 U.S. Dist. LEXIS 76049 (E.D. Pa. Sept. 30, 2008) (finding that pollution exclusion, under first-party policy, did not preclude coverage for claim for property damage caused by heating oil that spilled during delivery to an above-ground storage tank because it remained in the basement and did not contaminate the environment); *Westchester Fire Ins. Co. v. Treesdale, Inc.*, No. 2:05cv1523, 2008 U.S. Dist. LEXIS 37232 (W.D. Pa. May 2, 2008) (following *Lititz*) ("[T]he state of the law on the question of whether asbestos is a pollutant is unresolved. However, the Court need not resolve that difficult issue in this case because, as Defendants note, both policies require that the pollutant be dispersed in one of several defined ways to fall within the exclusion. Plaintiffs have not argued, much less demonstrated, that the manner in which the asbestos 'moved' in the Underlying Claims meets any of these defined ways."); *Mines Safety Appliances Co. v. AIU Ins. Co.*, No. N10C-07-241, 2016 Del. Super. LEXIS 64 (Del. Super. Ct. Jan. 22, 2016) (applying Pennsylvania law and distinguishing *Madison Construction*) ("The miners were exposed to toxic substances in a place where the dust was reasonably expected to be. The dust was a necessary bi-product of the activity for which MSA's safety equipment was designed to be used. The dust did not result in injury caused by what is commonly understood to be environmental contamination, for which coverage would be excluded. Rather, this is a case about coverage for injuries caused by an allegedly defective product designed to counter the effects of exposure to dangerous materials."); *Netherlands Ins. Co. v. Butler Area Sch. Dist.*, No. 17-341, 2017 U.S. Dist. LEXIS 89073 (W.D. Pa. June 9, 2017) ("Although there is no directly applicable factual scenario, both the Supreme Court of Pennsylvania and the Superior Court of Pennsylvania have ruled that standard pollution exclusion language like that contained in the Policies at issue does not apply to a substance such as lead that is a component of a product that degrades over time rendering the substance incrementally bioavailable. These findings are similar to the facts, as here, where lead and copper are essentially components of the water system at Summit Elementary, which have degraded over time, thereby allegedly rendering the lead and copper bioavailable.") (following *Lititz*); *Atlantic Casualty Ins. Co. v. Zymblosky*, No. 1167, 2017 Pa. Super. Unpub. LEXIS 2701 (Pa. Super. Ct. July 17, 2017) (affirming, without discussing, trial court's decision that bodily injury, caused by chlorine gas released into the air, was a pollutant within the pollution exclusion) (also addressing whether pollution exclusion rendered the coverage illusory); *Foremost Ins. Co. v. Rodriguez*, No. 19-360, 2019 U.S. Dist. LEXIS 115205 (E.D. Pa. Jul. 11, 2019) ("Although carbon monoxide is not expressly included in the policy's definition of pollutant, 'Pennsylvania courts . . . routinely find substances not expressly included in the provision to be pollutants.' . . . Courts have interpreted similar pollution exclusion provisions and concluded that carbon monoxide is unambiguously a pollutant."); *Barg v. Encompass Home & Auto Ins. Co.*, No. 16-6049, 2018 U.S. Dist. LEXIS 8951 (E.D. Pa. Jan. 19, 2018) (holding that heating oil is a contaminant because it interfered with the use of concrete, building materials and soil) (declining to follow *Whitmore v. Liberty Mut.* because it "was decided on summary judgment on a record that did not contain 'any product report, expert opinion, or other source of information to show or even argue that home heating oil [was] a 'pollutant' within the policy's pollution exclusion.'"); *Ben Weitsman & Son of Scranton, LLC v. Hartford Fire Ins. Co.*, No. 16-0780, 2018 U.S. Dist. LEXIS 22970 (N.D.N.Y. Feb. 13, 2018) (applying Pennsylvania law and holding that the pollutant exclusion applied) ("[C]hlorine is a chemical. Even if chlorine were not a chemical, chlorine is clearly an 'irritant.'"); *Allegheny Ludlum, LLC v. Liberty Mut. Ins. Co.*, 487 F. Supp. 3d 350 (W.D. Pa. 2020) (pollution exclusion precluded coverage for bodily injury caused by exposure to welding fumes containing hexavalent chromium, a toxic substance under federal statutory and regulatory standards); *Biela v. Westfield Ins. Co.*, No. 19-4383, 2021 U.S. Dist. LEXIS 9011 (E.D. Pa. Jan. 19, 2021) (heating oil a pollutant) (declining to follow *Whitmore* as an environmental consultant took samples at the property and the results revealed several substances identified as pollutants by federal law and regulation).

Rhode Island: A Rhode Island District Court addressed the applicability of the pollution exclusion in the following context: "With respect to Lot 192, the Complaint alleges that Poulton 'installed and/or maintained one or more PVC pipes and other drains and conduits . . . that unreasonably direct drainage of surface water and sediment directly onto [the Farm's property].' In addition, the Complaint alleges that '[t]he unreasonable drainage of surface water and erosion onto [the Farm's property] has irreparably altered the water table' and that 'engineers halted the installation [of a drain] to avoid the dispersion and direct drainage of effluent into the drain's fresh water stream outlet.' Basically, the damage alleged is from water and effluent drained on to the Farm's property from Poulton's property." *Geovera Specialty Ins. Co. v. Poulton*, No. 16-432, 2017 U.S. Dist. LEXIS 165539 (D.R.I. Sept. 26, 2017). The court held that the pollution exclusion was not applicable: "Neither surface water nor effluent are explicitly included in the policy's definition of pollutant. While 'waste' can certainly mean effluent in some contexts, it is not clear that the definition of pollution here would include effluent. When a policy's terms are capable of more than one reasonable meaning, then the policy is strictly construed in favor of the insured and against the insurer." *Id.* at *16. *See also Picerne-Military Housing, LLC v. Am. Int'l Specialty Lines Ins. Co.*, 650 F. Supp. 2d 135, 139–40 (D.R.I. 2009) (addressing whether buried construction and demolition debris was a "Pollution Condition" under a Pollution Legal Liability policy and noting that it was a twist on an oft-litigated issue: "[I]n the usual course the question of what constitutes a pollutant arises out of a general liability insurer's attempt to enforce a pollution exclusion. In that context, the insurer urges a broad reading of the exclusion while the insured presses for a narrow interpretation to afford greater coverage. Here, things are backwards. [The insurer's] pollution liability policy insures (in language mirroring the standard definition used by virtually all carriers in this context) that which most commercial general liability policies seek to exclude."). Despite being "backwards," the court's analysis—which cites to pollution exclusion decisions nationally for guidance—may be useful in the pollution exclusion context. *See also Dutchman Dental, LLC v. Providence Mut. Fire Ins. Co.*, No. KC-2016-1281, 2020 R.I. Super. LEXIS 23 (R.I. Super. Ct. Mar. 11, 2020) ("[T]he Court does not believe that either party seriously questions whether home heating oil, released from holding into a building, is a pollutant. Several laws of this state consider expelled oil to be a pollutant, and RIDEM imposes civil penalties when oil is not handled properly. The nearby jurisdictions of Massachusetts, Connecticut, New Hampshire, and Maine have also concluded that oil was a pollutant under similar circumstances. Thus, this Court concludes that oil is a pollutant under the Policy.") (addressing pollution exclusion under property policy and deciding issue based on causation aspect of exclusion).

South Carolina: The Fourth Circuit Court of Appeals held that the pollution exclusion did not apply to preclude coverage for claims for bodily injury caused by exposure to paint fumes, vapor, dust, and other residue from the insured's painting operations. *NGM Ins. Co. v. Carolina's Power Wash & Painting, LLC*, 407 Fed. Appx. 653, 655 (4th Cir. 2011) (applying South Carolina law). The court discussed the nationwide split of authority and concluded that, because the pollution exclusion is subject to more than one reasonable interpretation, it creates an ambiguity, and, therefore, must be construed liberally in favor of the insured and strictly against the insurer. *See also Ross Development Corp. v. PCS Nitrogen Inc.*, 526 Fed. Appx. 299 (4th Cir. 2013) (holding that pollution exclusion barred coverage for damages resulting from lead and arsenic found in pyrite slag, a byproduct of phosphate fertilizer production).

South Dakota: The Supreme Court of South Dakota held that the pollution exclusion applied to preclude coverage for claims arising out of excessive dust emissions from a cement plant. *S.D. State Cement Plant Comm'n v. Wausau Underwriters Ins. Co.*, 616 N.W.2d 397, 406 (S.D. 2000). "Because the causes of action in the complaint are based upon alleged 'contamination,' assuming that the allegations that [the insured] caused contamination are true, no coverage would apply and [the insurer] would not have a duty to defend because the causes of action in the complaint all clearly fall within the definition of pollution in the pollution exclusion clause." *Id.* at 407. The court rejected the trial court's determination that a broad construction of the pollution exclusion would render it meaningless on the basis that any substance could conceivably irritate or contaminate. *Id.* at 406.

Tennessee: The Court of Appeals of Tennessee held that the pollution exclusion precluded coverage for a claim for injury caused when a tanker truck spewed 1,800 gallons of sulphuric acid on an employee of a loading company's subcontractor. *Sulphuric Acid Trading Co., Inc. v. Greenwich Ins. Co.*, 211 S.W.3d 243, 254 (Tenn. Ct. App. 2006). After addressing the split of authority nationally on the "traditional" versus "non-traditional" issue, the court concluded that "the facts of this case are such that we do not need to decide with which side Tennessee should be aligned … . It would defy logic to hold that the discharge of 1,800 gallons of sulphuric acid into the environment was anything other than environmental pollution. We hold that these facts demonstrate the type of 'classic environmental pollution' that would trigger the Absolute Pollution Exclusion under *either* of the two lines of reasoning adopted by the various states. While the facts before us do involve an employee injured in the course and scope of his employment, we must look at the big picture and cannot ignore the fact that the injury occurred during an event resulting in substantial environmental pollution. As applied to the facts of the instant case, we agree with the trial court that the Absolute Pollution Exclusion is not ambiguous. As to which of the two diverse lines of cases should be adopted in Tennessee, that decision must await another day and another case." *Id.* at 253–54; *see also* State Auto. Mut. Ins. Co. v. Frazier's Flooring, Inc., No. 3:08-CV-178, 2009 U.S. Dist. LEXIS 20884 (E.D. Tenn. March 13, 2009) (declining to exercise jurisdiction in a declaratory judgment action because the pollution exclusion is an unsettled question under Tennessee law) (discussing *Sulphuric Acid Trading* and federal decisions) ("Though there are two federal courts that have considered the interpretation of pollution exclusion clauses under Tennessee law, they are of little help to the Court here. Both cases, after stating that the issue is unsettled in Tennessee, apply the standard rules of contract interpretation under Tennessee law but, nevertheless, they reach opposite conclusions."); *Certain Underwriters at Lloyd's v. Alkabsh*, No. 09-2711, 2011 U.S. Dist. LEXIS 26593 (W.D. Tenn. Mar. 15, 2011) (determining that gasoline, which leaked from underground storage tank at convenience store, constituted pollutant under total pollution exclusion and precluded insured from coverage under policy).

Texas: The Supreme Court of Texas held that the pollution exclusion precluded coverage for claims arising out of a large cloud of hydrofluoric acid caused by an accident at an oil refinery. *Nat'l Union Fire Ins. Co. v. CBI Indus.*, 907 S.W.2d 517,

521–22 (Tex. 1995). The court held that, because "the contract language is not fairly susceptible of more than one legal meaning or construction, however, extrinsic evidence is inadmissible to contradict or vary the meaning of the explicit language of the parties' written agreement. In this case, the policies unequivocally deny coverage for damage resulting from pollutants, however the damage is caused." *Id.* (citations omitted); *see also Nautilus Ins. Co. v. Country Oaks Apartments Ltd.*, 566 F.3d 452, 458 (5th Cir. 2009) (applying Texas law) (concluding that the pollution exclusion precluded coverage for claims for emission of carbon monoxide from a furnace into an apartment); *Acadia Ins. Co. v. Jacob and Martin, Ltd.*, No. 4:13-cv-798 (N.D. Tex. May 28, 2014) (holding that insurer would not have to provide coverage for employee's death which allegedly resulted from asphyxia due to methane gas inhalation after he opened a manhole and released toxic fumes as more investigation was necessary to determine if employee asphyxiated from methane gas or other substance). *But see Clarendon America Ins. Co. v. Bay, Inc.*, 10 F. Supp. 2d 736, 744 (S.D. Tex. 1998) (concluding that bodily injury caused when plaintiffs' skin touched wet cement and concrete, while the cement and its ingredients were in the cement's intended container or location, did not satisfy the "discharge, dispersal, seepage, migration, release or escape" requirement of the pollution exclusion). *RLI Ins. Co. v. Gonzalez*, 411 Fed. Appx. 696 (5th Cir. 2011) (applying Texas law) (concluding that insurer had no duty to indemnify policyholder for injuries caused by silica exposure because silica dust is an air contaminant clearly within the meaning of "all contaminants"); *Nat'l Union Fire Ins. Co. of Pittsburgh, PA v. Continental Carbon Co.*, 517 Fed. Appx. 269 (5th Cir. 2013) (affirming lower court decision that pollution exclusion barred coverage for claims of harm from exposure to dust and particulate pollution discharged during production of furnace grade carbon black in pelletized form, which was used in tires and other rubber and plastic goods); *Texas Molecular Ltd. Partnership v. American Intern. Specialty Lines Ins. Co.*, 424 Fed. Appx. 354 (5th Cir. 2011) (affirming decision that pollution exclusion barred coverage for claims of employees' deaths from exposure to lethal amounts of hydrogen sulfide while working at hazardous waste underground injection wells); *Dallas Nat'l Ins. Co. v. Sabic Ams., Inc.*, No. 01-08-00758-CV, 2011 Tex. App. LEXIS 1741 (Tex. Ct. App. Mar. 10, 2011) (holding that insurer had to reimburse policyholder's defense costs where groundwater was contaminated by methyl tertiary butyl ether because the policy excluded costs arising out of government environmental regulations, not private causes of action); *Lapolla Indus., Inc. v. Aspen Specialty Ins. Co.*, No. 13-4436-cv, 2014 U.S. App. LEXIS 9199 (2d Cir. May 19, 2014) (applying Texas law) (affirming decision that pollution exclusion precluded coverage for claims of damages from "off-gassing" of hazardous compounds and toxins after spray foam application); *Burlington Ins. Co. v. JC Instride, Inc.*, 30 F. Supp. 3d 587 (S.D. Tex. 2014) (rejecting application of the pollution exclusion based on no dispersal) ("Malone alleges that he entered the mud tank, and while inside the tank came into direct contact with the caustic materials. Malone does not allege that the caustic component of or in the mud was dispersed or emitted."); *BMS Enters. v. Gen. Star Indem. Co.*, No. 14-3375, 2015 U.S. Dist. LEXIS 34637 (S.D.N.Y. Mar. 11, 2015) (applying Texas law) ("Any injury to claimants in the Disaster Site Litigation stems from dust, debris, or other toxins were first discharged, dispersed, and/or released from the site of the World Trade Center collapse. That is sufficient under Texas law to invoke the Pollution Exclusion in the General Star Policy."); *Tow v. Gemini Ins. Corp.*, No. 12-36187, 2015 Bankr. LEXIS 3463 (S.D. Tex. Oct. 9, 2015) ("Comeaux's complaint alleges the discharge of a variety of harmful substances in the form of dangerous and toxic fumes. He states that he suffered injuries as a result of exposure to these fumes, and injuries to his back sustained while seeking to escape the fumes. These fumes qualify as contamination of the air by discharge of harmful substances, and are therefore pollution for the purposes of the policy exclusion."); *In re Liquidation of Legion Indem. Co.*, 44 N.E.3d 1170 (Ill. App. Ct. 2015) (applying Texas law) ("[M]old and fungi are not remotely similar to bat guano and a reasonable person would not necessarily understand mold to match any of the Exclusion terms in the same clear and unambiguous manner that 'waste' included bat guano."); *Shaw v. Liberty Mut. Fire Ins. Co.*, No. 15-686, 2016 U.S. Dist. LEXIS 17626 (M.D. Fla. Feb. 12, 2016) (applying Texas law) ("The Shaws' injuries arose out of the migration of carbon monoxide, a pollutant, from the parking garage to their room, on account of improperly maintained systems, and the failure to utilize appropriate detection equipment. Thus, the pollution exclusion applies, even if the other failures identified by the Shaws contributed to their injuries.") (also rejecting insureds' argument that regulatory estoppel precluded application of pollution exclusion); *United Fire & Cas. Co. v. Condeb, L.P.*, No. 14-150, 2016 U.S. Dist. LEXIS 35253 (E.D. Tex. Feb. 22, 2016) ("Considering the mothballs and mothball fumes are 'pollutants' and further considering Defendants have not presented a reasonable interpretation for why the 'Total Pollution Exclusion Endorsement' would not apply to the allegations contained in Ms. Chriestenson's underlying petition, the 'Total Pollution Exclusion Endorsement' applies. This exclusion is unambiguous."); *Longhorn Gasket & Supply Co. v. United States Fire Ins. Co.*, 698 Fed. Appx. 774 (5th Cir. 2017) ("The pollution exclusion in U.S. Fire's excess policies is broad, and applies generally to 'irritants, contaminants, and pollutants.' Though the case law is mixed, we conclude, under the plain language of the policy exclusion, that asbestos constitutes a pollutant and an irritant."); *Great Am. Ins. Co. v. Ace Am. Ins. Co.*, 325 F. Supp. 3d 719 (N.D. Tex. 2018) (pollution exclusion precluded coverage for property damage caused by rock fines, which were "clearly waste material generated in the rock crushing process") (noting that the rock fines "became irritants or contaminants when they were discharged and dispersed where they did not belong"); *HLT Props. LLC v. Evanston Ins. Co.*, 388 F. Supp. 3d 718 (W.D. Tex. 2019) ("costs for cleaning up lead-containing sand piles are excluded by the total pollution exclusion"); *E. Concrete Materials, Inc. v. Ace Am. Ins. Co.*, 948 F.3d 289 (5th Cir. 2020) (holding that rock fines that rendered creek unfit for trout and other species were a contaminant) ("[T]he rock fines posed no threat to drinking water, nor to anyone who would use the area for fishing nor to the fish that they might catch. But when we look at the effects on the overall ecosystem, rock fines are contaminants."); *Canal Indem. Co. v. Caljet*, 485 F. Supp. 3d 813 (S.D. Tex. 2020) ("[E]ven if the Court were to assume that benzene is a pollutant in this situation, the bodily injury was allegedly caused by direct exposure to gasoline, not by the discharge, dispersal, seepage, migration, release, or escape of benzene—as required by the Pollution Exclusions.").

Utah: A Utah District Court held that the pollution exclusion did not preclude coverage for injuries caused by the release of a hydrocarbon vapor cloud that led to an explosion and fire during the unloading of waste. *United Nat'l Ins. Co. v. Int'l Petroleum & Exploration*, No. 2:04-CV-00631, 2007 U.S. Dist. LEXIS 93429 (D. Utah Dec. 20, 2007). The court examined the "traditional" versus "non-traditional" debate and concluded that, because of two possible interpretations, the exclusion is ambiguous. "Under [the insurer's] literal construction of the pollution exclusion, the exclusion would apply to potentially limitless circumstances and would, accordingly, severely limit [the insured's] coverage under the Policy." *See also Headwaters Resources, Inc. v. Illinois Union Ins. Co.*, 770 F.3d 885 (10th Cir. 2014) ("In the end, the fact that coverage may be excluded for regular business activities and projects does not shortcut our analysis, and we have frequently concluded that the routine commercial activities of the insured can occasion application of a CGL policy's pollution exclusion to bar coverage under Utah law.") (citing cases).

Vermont: The Supreme Court of Vermont, following a lengthy discussion of the history of the pollution exclusion and the two approaches taken by courts nationally – exclusion bars coverage for all injuries caused by pollutants or only those injuries caused by traditional environmental pollution – held that the exclusion applied to preclude coverage for bodily injuries caused by exposure to a spray-foam insulation installed by the insured at a school. *Cincinnati Specialty Underwriters Ins. Co. v. Energy Wise Homes, Inc.*, 120 A.3d 1160 (Vt. 2015). The typical definition of "pollutants" was expanded to include "that which has been recognized in industry or government to be harmful or toxic to persons, property or the environment, . . . " *Id.* at 1162. The court held: "There appears to be no dispute that the airborne chemicals and residues at issue 'ha[ve] been recognized in industry or government to be harmful or toxic to persons, property or the environment.' Insurer cites numerous authorities in support of this contention, and defendants do not argue otherwise. These toxic chemicals allegedly became airborne, and were inhaled, as a result of Energy Wise's application of spray-foam insulation. This represents a 'dispersal' or 'release' of such chemicals under a common-sense reading of those terms." *Id.* at 1167. The court noted, however, that its holding was of a "limited nature." "[T]the Vermont Department of Financial Regulation requires all insurers issuing liability policies in Vermont to *provide* coverage for pollution by endorsement unless the Department approves a 'Consent to Rate' application. Thus, our decision today applies only to surplus lines insurers." *Id.* at 1168. (emphasis in original). [*See Uhler v. Poulos Ins.*, No. 104-2-16, 2017 Vt. Super. LEXIS 392 (Vt. Super. Ct. July 25, 2017) for a discussion of *Energy Wise* in the context of a subsequent pollution exclusion-related broker malpractice case.] In *Whitney v. Mut. Ins. Co.*, 135 A.3d 272 (Vt. 2015), the Vermont high court addressed the applicability of a pollution exclusion, in a homeowner's policy, to a claim for damage to property caused by the spraying of a pesticide for bed bugs. The court noted that the homeowner's policy was not subject to any state regulation that required a pollution endorsement or prohibited a pollution exclusion. *Id.* at 275. The court made two observations about it just-decided decision in *Cincinnati*: (1) "We concluded that we did not have to address whether the standard 'absolute pollution exclusion' would have excluded the risk of bodily injury from the spray foam insulation that caused harm to the plaintiff because the language in the policy in *Cincinnati* was even broader than the standard 'absolute pollution exclusion.'" *Id.* at 274. "The main lesson of *Cincinnati* for our purposes is that pollution exclusions are not presumed, as a class, to be ambiguous or to be limited in their application to traditional environmental pollution. They should be construed in the same way as any other insurance contract provision. Our goal in interpreting an insurance policy, like our goal in interpreting any contract, is to ascertain and carry out the parties' intentions. Therefore, we interpret policy language according to its plain, ordinary and popular meaning." *Id.* at 274-75. The court held that the pollution exclusion precluded coverage: "The undisputed facts are that chlorpyrifos is: toxic to humans; can cause nausea, dizziness, confusion, and at very high exposures, respiratory paralysis and death; and is banned for residential use. Triple A's use of chlorpyrifos in the Whitneys' home violated EPA regulations, and federal and state law. . . . We do not find it hard to conclude that, in the context of this case, the terms 'irritant,' 'contaminant,' and 'pollutant' plainly and unambiguously encompass the chlorpyrifos sprayed 'corner to corner, wall to wall' throughout the Whitneys' home. As we have previously noted, we cannot deny the insurer the benefit of unambiguous provisions inserted into the policy for its benefit." *Id.* at 276.

Virginia: The Supreme Court of Virginia held that the pollution exclusion precluded coverage for claims by 214 women for miscarriages arising out of contamination by trihalomethanes of a city's water supply. *City of Chesapeake v. States Self-Insurers Risk Retention Group, Inc.*, 628 S.E.2d 539, 541 (Va. 2006). The court declined the parties' request to examine how other jurisdictions have resolved similar disputes because the plain language of the policy provided the answer. *Id.* at 541–42; *see also Firemen's Ins. Co. of Wash., D.C. v. Kline & Son Cement Repair, Inc.*, 474 F. Supp. 2d 779, 798–99 (E.D. Va. 2007) (holding, following a comprehensive review of the issue, that the pollution exclusion precluded coverage for personal injury claim arising from inhalation of vapors following the insured's application of epoxy sealant to a concrete warehouse floor); *PBM Nutritionals, LLC v. Lexington Ins. Co.*, 724 S.E.2d 707 (Va. 2012) (citing *City of Chesapeake* and holding that pollution exclusion precluded coverage for loss of infant formula product when formula became contaminated with high levels of melamine from faulty production system); *TRAVCO Ins. Co. v. Ward*, 715 F. Supp. 2d. 699, 716 (E.D. Va. 2010), *affirmed* 504 Fed. Appx. 251 (4th Cir. 2013) (following *City of Chesapeake* and *Kline* and holding that the pollution exclusion precluded coverage, under a homeowner's policy, for damage to the insured's residence caused by toxic gases released by Chinese drywall). *See also Nationwide Mut. Ins. Co. v. Boyd Corp.*, No. 3:09-CV-211, 2010 U.S. Dist. LEXIS 5438 (E.D. Va. Jan. 25, 2010) ("[A] reasonable person would not classify flood waters alone as pollutants."); *Builders Mut. Ins. Co. v. Half Court Press, L.L.C.*, No. 6:09-cv-00046, 2010 U.S. Dist. LEXIS 78727 (W.D. Va. Aug. 3, 2010) (holding that insurer was not excused from duty to defend where damage caused by water (a non-pollutant) and other sediment); *Mount Vernon Fire Ins. Co. v. Adamson*, No. 3:09cv817-HEH, 2010 U.S. Dist. LEXIS 106758 (E.D. Va. Sept. 15, 2010) (finding that mold was excluded by policy) (specific mold exclusion as well as pollution exclusion diminishes precedential value of this case); *Builders Mut. Ins. Co. v. Parallel Design & Dev.*, No. 4:10cv68, 2011 U.S. Dist. LEXIS 55279 (E.D. Va. May 13, 2011) (holding that pollution exclusion did not preclude coverage for insured where defective drywall allegedly emitted sulfide gases and toxic chemicals because the court, without a clear explanation of the term "pollutant" in the policy, could not determine whether pollution exclusion applied to only traditional pollutants or included substances that cause indoor harm); *Proto v. The Futura Group, L.L.C.*, No. CL09-2455, 2011 Va. Cir. LEXIS 253 (2nd Cir. May 6, 2011) (applying Virginia law) (unpublished opinion) ("The language of the pollution exclusion is not ambiguous and its plain meaning encompasses the sulfur-dioxide 'released' and 'discharged' by the Chinese drywall."); *Nationwide Mut. Ins. Co. v. The Overlook, LLC*, 785 F. Supp. 2d 502 (E.D. Va. 2011) (finding that insured real estate developer was not entitled to coverage, where drywall used in construction of townhouses allegedly emitted sulfide gases, because definition of "pollutant" in pollution exclusion "does not apply solely to traditional environmental pollution," and, thus, included sulfide gas); *Evanston Ins. Co. v. Germano*, 514 Fed. Appx. 362 (4th Cir. 2013) (affirming that sulfuric gases released from Chinese drywall were pollutants); *Dragas Management Corp. v. Hanover Ins. Co.*, 798 F. Supp. 2d 766 (E.D. Va. 2011) (concluding that pollution exclusion was not ambiguous and the reduced sulfur gases released from Chinese drywall were pollutants); *Allied Prop. & Cas. Ins. Co. v. Zenith Aviation, Inc.*, 336 F. Supp. 3d 607 (E.D. Va. 2018) ("Given the Policy's definition of a 'pollutant,' concrete dust is clearly a pollutant since it can undoubtedly function as both an 'irritant' and a 'contaminant.'") (Zenith's alleged losses, by its own description, resulted from the concrete dust's deleterious effect on its inventory and machinery.") (addressing the issue under a first-party policy and concluding that the pollution exclusion was not applicable for causation reasons).

Washington: The Supreme Court of Washington held that the pollution exclusion precluded coverage for claims for injuries suffered by a tenant when fumes from a waterproofing material being applied to her apartment building entered her unit. *Quadrant Corp. v. Am. States Ins. Co.*, 110 P.3d 733, 743 (Wash. 2005). The *Quadrant* Court distinguished *Kent Farms, Inc. v. Zurich Insurance Co.*, 998 P.2d 292 (Wash. 2000) on the basis that the "*Kent Farms* court distinguished between cases in which the substance at issue was polluting at the time of the injury and cases in which the offending substance's toxic character was not central to the injury." *Id.* at 742. The *Kent Farms* court had held that the underlying plaintiff "was not polluted by diesel fuel. It struck him; it engulfed him; it choked him. It did not pollute him. Most importantly, the fuel was not acting as a 'pollutant' when it struck him any more than it would have been acting as a 'pollutant' if it had been in a barrel that rolled over him, or if it had been lying quietly on the steps waiting to trip him." *Kent Farms*, 998 P.2d at 295. The *Quadrant* court concluded that *Kent Farms*'s discussion of traditional environmental harms was limited by the facts of that case. *Quadrant*, 110 P.3d at 743. *See also Western Nat. Assur. Co. v. Maxcare of Washington, Inc.*, No. 67952-0-I, 2012 Wash. App. LEXIS 2933 (Wash. Ct. App. Dec. 24, 2012) (following *Quadrant Corp.* and concluding that pollution exclusion precluded coverage for use of toxic and potentially toxic chemicals (including household cleaners) while repairing smoke damage); *Oregon Mut. Ins. Co. v. Seattle Collision Center, Inc.*, No. C08-1670JLR, 2009 U.S. Dist. LEXIS 85632 (W.D. Wash. Sept. 18, 2009) (addressing *Quadrant* and *Kent Farm's*) (pollution exclusion precludes coverage for environmental property damage caused by the release of perc and its degradation compounds); *Oregon Mut. Ins. Co. v. American States Ins. Co.*, 403 Fed. Appx. 249, 251 (9th Cir. Nov. 16, 2010) (holding that no potential for coverage and no duty to defend exist where "allegations arise solely out of violations of [state toxic substance control act] and only claim past and future remedial action costs associated with traditional environmental pollution") ("[Pollution exclusion] as interpreted under Washington law, clearly and unambiguously exclude liability for such traditional environmental harms.") (determining that exclusion was doubly applicable because case involved claim for government-ordered remediation as well as traditional environmental pollution).

The Washington Supreme Court's decision in *Xia v. ProBuilders Specialty Inc. Co., RRG*, 400 P.3d 1234 (Wash. 2017) took an approach to the pollution exclusion that no Washington court, or any court nationally, had ever taken. The court held that, despite carbon monoxide being a pollutant, the pollution exclusion did not apply to injuries caused by exposure to it. The court reached this conclusion based on the so-called "efficient proximate cause" rule. The court determined that the efficient proximate cause of the injuries was the negligent installation of a hot water heater. Because that was a covered occurrence, that set in motion a causal chain, that led to discharging toxic levels of carbon monoxide, being an excluded peril, the pollution exclusion was not applicable. In *Dolsen Cos. v. Bedivere Ins. Co.*, No. 16-3141, 2017 U.S. Dist. LEXIS 151057 (E.D. Wash. Sept. 11, 2017), the first post-*Zia* decision, the District Court held that the pollution exclusion applied to preclude coverage for the seepage of a farm's untreated manure into groundwater. The court concluded that the claim came within *Quadrant* and declined to apply *Zia* as a basis to find the exclusion inapplicable: "It was the inadequate storage of the manure that caused the seepage—and the negligent construction is necessarily intertwined with the storage. This very occurrence is explicitly excluded by the terms of the policy, which excludes from coverage the seepage of pollutants stored or processed as waste. There is no other occurrence beside the act intimately tied with the storing of manure—the polluting event." *Id.* at *22-23.

West Virginia: A West Virginia District Court held that the pollution exclusion precluded coverage for claims for property damage caused by coal tar left by a coal fuel generation plant. *Supertane Gas Corp. v. Aetna Cas & Sur. Co.*, No. 92CV14, 1994 U.S. Dist. LEXIS 21602 (N.D. W.Va. Sept. 27, 1994). "Although the Court did not find a West Virginia case on the absolute pollution exclusion, the Court is persuaded that West Virginia would find such an exclusion, as presented here, to be unambiguous." *Id.* at *10. *See also Gemini Ins. Co. v. Sirnaik, LLC*, No. 18-00424, 2019 U.S. Dist. LEXIS 74094 (S.D. W.Va. May 2, 2019) (pollution exclusion precluded coverage for a warehouse fire which caused the release of toxic and/or chemical smoke, soot, pollutants, air contaminants, odors, gases, fumes, particulate matter, ash, toxic water run-off and other harmful "fallout material").

Wisconsin: The Supreme Court of Wisconsin held that the pollution exclusion did not preclude coverage for claims arising out of inadequately ventilated carbon dioxide from breathing. *Donaldson v. Urban Land Interests, Inc.*, 564 N.W.2d 728, 732 (Wis. 1997). The court held that "the pollution exclusion clause does not plainly and clearly alert a reasonable insured that coverage is denied for personal injury claims that have their genesis in activities as fundamental as human respiration." *Id. But see Peace v. Nw. Nat'l Ins. Co.*, 596 N.W.2d 429, 440 (Wis. 1999) ("[W]e conclude that the pollution exclusion clause … excludes bodily injury from the ingestion of lead in paint that chips, flakes, or breaks down into dust or fumes. When the 'pollutant' lead—once contained—begins to disperse, discharge, or escape from the containment of the painted surface, it falls within the plain language of the pollution exclusion clause."). *See also Lagone v. Am. Family Mut. Ins. Co.*, 731 N.W.2d 334, 339 (Wis. Ct. App. 2007) ("Because the *Peace* and *Donaldson* courts applied a reasonable expectations test to the same policy language but reached different conclusions, it is important to consider the facts in each case.") (holding that carbon monoxide is more analogous to *Donaldson* and not a pollutant); *Hirschhorn v. Auto-Owners Ins.*, 809 N.W.2d 529 (Wis. 2012) (finding that bat guano was a pollutant under homeowners policy containing absolute pollution exclusion, and insureds' "alleged loss resulted from the 'discharge, release, escape, seepage, migration or dispersal' of bat guano"); *Wilson Mut. Ins. Co. v. Falk*, 857 N.W.2d 156 (Wis. 2014) (holding that pollution exclusion unambiguously excluded coverage for well contamination caused by the seepage of cow manure); *Preisler v. Gen. Cas. Ins. Co.*, 857 N.W.2d 136 (Wis. 2014) (holding that a "reasonable insured would understand that decomposing septage is a 'contaminant' and therefore, a 'pollutant' as defined in the policies when it has decomposed and seeps into a water supply."); *Connors v. Zurich Am. Ins. Co.*, 872 N.W.2d 109 (Wis. Ct. App. 2015) ("[W]hile coverage would not be available if the policy here contained the standard pollution exclusion, one reasonable interpretation of the included substances categories is that they involve products or byproducts that would be expected to be used in, or result from the operation of, certain commercial or industrial operations, and that would not include mist- or vapor-borne bacteria. We conclude that the specifically identified substances provision is susceptible to more than one interpretation by a reasonable insured, and therefore is ambiguous."); *Advanced Waste Servs. v. United Milwaukee Scrap, LLC*, 863 N.W.2d 634 (Wis. Ct. App. 2015) (rejecting the argument that the pollution exclusion did not apply on the basis that the insured did not disperse the pollutant; noting that, in *Hirschhorn*, the insureds did not directly disperse the pollutant, but, rather, the bats did); *Ramos v. Charter Oak Fire Ins. Co.*, 871 N.W.2d 866 (Wis. Ct. App. 2015) ("For the reasons we explain in *Connors*, we conclude that the pollution exclusion applicable here is ambiguous on the question of whether the bacteria are 'pollutants' in the context of the occurrence alleged. The exclusion is ambiguous in this context because the bacteria are not obviously in the nature of the commercial or industrial products or byproducts specified in the pollution exclusion, and therefore a reasonable insured could expect coverage."); *Foley v. Wis. Mut. Ins. Co.*, No. 2017AP545, 2018 Wisc. App. LEXIS 261 (Wis. Ct. App. Mar. 1, 2018) (deeming trichothecene - which is "highly toxic to humans" – released from stachybotrys mold to be a "contaminant" and, therefore, a "pollutant").

Wyoming: The Supreme Court of Wyoming aligned itself with those jurisdictions that have held that the pollution exclusion is limited to the concept of environmental pollution. *Gainsco Ins. Co. v. Amoco Prod. Co.*, 53 P.3d 1051, 1066 (Wyo. 2002) (holding that the pollution exclusion did not preclude coverage for bodily injury caused by exposure to poisonous hydrogen sulfide gas while emptying a vacuum truck in an oil field). Responding to the conflict in authority, the court considered the original purpose of the pollution exclusion—response to federal and state legislation mandating responsibility for the cleanup costs of environmental pollution—and concluded that the current version of the exclusion has the same purpose. *Id.* at 1066.

CHAPTER
16

Trigger-of-Coverage for Latent Injury and Damage Claims

The insuring agreement of Part A of the commercial general liability policy affords coverage for "bodily injury" and "property damage" (*see, e.g.*, Ins. Servs. Office, Inc., Commercial General Liability Coverage Form, No. CG 00010413, § I1a (2012)), *provided* such injury or damage occurs "during the policy period." ISO Form, CG 00010413 at § I1b2.

In most general liability claim scenarios it is obvious whether the "bodily injury" or "property damage" was sustained by the underlying claimant *during the policy period.* For example, if a customer slips on a banana peel and suffers a broken arm while on the premises of an insured-supermarket, it is quite easy to determine if this injury, occurring on a date certain, was during the policy period. The same goes for "property damage" in most cases. Take an insured–boiler manufacturer whose product explodes and causes fire damage. There is little chance of a dispute over the date of such damage and whether it was during the policy period.

While this "timing" issue will be a non-issue in most claims, there exists a category of claims where the answer to the question, whether "bodily injury" or "property damage" occurred "during the policy period," is as challenging and contentious as a wayward banana peel claim is simple.

These vexing claims are ones in which bodily injury or property damage is caused by exposure to hazardous substances—most often bodily injury on account of exposure to asbestos and property damage on account of exposure to hazardous waste or other industrial pollution. In these situations, the injuries often evolve slowly. It could be years between the time that a person is exposed to asbestos and a disease is diagnosed. Likewise, it could be a long time between a property's exposure to hazardous waste and the day that its damaged condition is discovered.

These types of claims are known by various names, such as latent injury or damage, delayed manifestation, continuous injury or damage, or long-tail (referred to collectively as latent injury or damage claims). The message that all of these labels convey is that the claim involves injury or damage that may have been taking place for years—before anyone knew it. In other words, the injury or damage was latent.

What's at issue in the latent claims context is whether each policy on the risk during this lengthy period when unknown injury or damage was taking place is obligated to provide coverage for the loss that is eventually discovered.

Coverage for latent injury and damage claims has been aggressively and abundantly litigated for the past three decades. And no wonder. Considering the massive financial exposure faced by insureds targeted in asbestos bodily injury and environmental property damage claims, their ability to potentially tap multiple years of policies to respond to these behemoth losses was critical to their fiscal well-being (not to mention for creating adequate funds to compensate the underlying claimants for their injuries). It also served as a means to obtain coverage under policies that were on the risk prior to insurers' adoption of pollution and asbestos exclusions.

For example, an insured sued in the 1990s, by thousands of claimants that were exposed to its asbestos-containing product that was placed in the stream of commerce in 1950, stood to receive coverage under forty-plus years of insurance for some of these claims. This is a far cry from the potential alternative—coverage being limited to the one policy on the risk at the time that each claimant was diagnosed with an asbestos-caused injury. Tens of millions, and sometimes hundreds of millions, of dollars were at stake.

While the bulk of the litigation concerning coverage for latent injuries and damages involved asbestos and hazardous waste, it was not always so limited. Disputes also arose over which, and how many, policies were obligated to provide coverage for latent injuries caused by exposure to pharmaceuticals, medical devices, noise that resulted in hearing loss, Agent Orange, and others.

In addition to coverage litigation over latent injuries and damages being aggressive and abundant, it was also frequently multi-party. By definition, if a policyholder is pursuing coverage under policies that were on the risk for twenty, thirty, or forty years, not to mention excess policies, there is likely a need to name numerous insurers (perhaps a dozen and sometimes many more) as defendants. With so much at stake and so many parties involved, litigation over latent injury and damage claims often proceeded at a glacial pace.

As is often the case with burgeoning insurance coverage issues, courts responded to the novelty of latent injury and damage claims by identifying various schools of thought that provided answers and then determined which of these options to adopt for themselves. These schools of thought become known as "trigger of coverage" theories. While the term "trigger of coverage," or just "trigger" for short, is almost universally used in the latent claims context, the term appears nowhere in a commercial general liability policy. This is a point that was not lost on many courts. *See Atchison, Topeka & Santa Fe Ry. Co. v. Stonewall Ins. Co.*, 71 P.3d 1097, 1125 (Kan. 2003) ("Insurance policies do not refer to a trigger or trigger of coverage. Those terms are labels for the event or events that under the terms of the insurance policy determines whether a policy must respond to a claim in a given set of circumstances.") (citation omitted). Perhaps courts felt the need to clarify this point lest parties would be reading *and re-reading* their commercial general liability (CGL) policies in search of a term that they would never find.

In general, five trigger theories emerged. Numerous courts, including state high courts, have spilled a lot of ink describing these methods in detail before announcing which one they adopt. These various trigger methods are as follows.

1. *Manifestation Trigger*: "[T]he date of loss is assigned to the policy period when property damage or actual damage [or bodily injury] is discovered, becomes known to the insured or a third party, or should have reasonably been discovered." *EnergyNorth Natural Gas, Inc. v. Certain Underwriters at Lloyd's*, 848 A.2d 715, 718 (N.H. 2004) (citation and internal quotes omitted). The manifestation trigger, which, by definition, limits coverage to a single policy year, was often advocated by insurers. However, it is the clear minority view. *See Associated Aviation Underwriters v. Wood*, 98 P.3d 572, 599 (Ariz. Ct. App. 2004).

One common reason for judicial rejection of the manifestation trigger was that "[in] most cases … a manifestation rule would reduce coverage: insurers would refuse to write new insurance for the insured when it became apparent that the period of manifestations, and hence a flood of claims, was approaching. The insured would be left without coverage for victims whose diseases were not yet manifested." *Owens Illinois, Inc. v. United Ins. Co.*, 650 A.2d 974, 981 (N.J. 1994). It has also been observed that "[n]othing in the language of the policies requires that the claimed property damage be discovered or manifested during the policy period. The inquiry instead, is whether the property damage, as defined in the policies, 'occurred' within the policy period and within the meaning of the word 'occurrence.'" *Trustees of Tufts Univ. v. Commercial Union Ins. Co.*, 616 N.E.2d 68, 74 (Mass. 1993).

2. *Exposure Trigger*: "[T]he exposure theory provides that coverage is triggered by the mere exposure to the harmful conditions during the policy period." *Cole v. Celotex Corp.*, 599 So. 2d 1058, 1076 (La. 1992). The exposure trigger has been justified on the basis that "each inhalation of asbestos fibers [does not] result[] in bodily injury, but rather every asbestos-related injury results from inhalation of

asbestos fibers. Because such inhalation can occur only upon exposure to asbestos, and because it is impossible practically to determine the point at which the fibers actually imbed themselves in the victim's lungs, to equate exposure to asbestos with 'bodily injury' caused by the inhalation of the asbestos is the 'superior interpretation of the contract provisions.'" *Commercial Union Ins. Co. v. Sepco Corp.*, 765 F.2d 1543, 1546 (11th Cir. 1985) (applying Alabama law) (quoting *Ins. Co. of N. Am v. Forty-Eight Insulations, Inc.*, 633 F.2d 1212, 1223 (6th Cir. 1980)).

The exposure theory has also been adopted on the basis that it "honors the contracting parties' intent by providing for consistency between the insured's tort liability and the insurer's coverage: 'The contracting parties would expect coverage to parallel the theory of liability.'" *Cole*, 599 So. 2d at 1077 (La. 1992) (quoting *Forty-Eight Insulations*, 633 F.2d at 1219 (6th Cir. 1980)).

3. *Injury-in-Fact Trigger*: "[C]overage is first triggered at that point in time at which an actual injury can be shown, retrospectively, to have been first suffered. This rationale places the injury-in-fact somewhere between the exposure, which is considered the initiating cause of the disease or bodily injury, and the manifestation of symptoms, which, logically, is only possible when an injury already exists." *Montrose Chem. Corp. v. Admiral Ins. Co.*, 913 P.2d 878, 894 (Cal. 1995). The injury-in-fact trigger is sometimes referred to as an "actual injury" trigger. Adoption of the injury-in-fact trigger is often justified on the basis that it is truest to the policy language. *See Gelman Sciences, Inc. v. Fid. & Cas. Co. of N.Y.*, 572 N.W.2d 617, 623 (Mich. 1998), *overruled on other grounds by Wilkie v. Auto-Owners Ins. Co.*, 664 N.W.2d 776, 786 (Mich. 2003) ("[A]ccording to the policies' explicit terms, actual injury must occur during the time the policy is in effect in order to be indemnifiable, i.e., the policies dictate an injury-in-fact approach"). As discussed below, injury-in-fact can often be synonymous with a continuous trigger.

4. *Continuous Trigger*: "[T]he injury occurs continuously from exposure until manifestation." *Gelman Sciences, Inc. v. Fid. & Cas. Co. of N.Y.*, 572 N.W.2d 617, 621 (Mich. 1998), *overruled on other grounds by Wilkie v. Auto-Owners Ins. Co.*, 664 N.W.2d 776, 786 (Mich. 2003). The continuous trigger (also sometimes called the "multiple" or "triple" trigger) is premised on the notion that, even after a claimant (or property) is no longer *directly* exposed to a hazardous substance, the injury sustained upon initial exposure remains ongoing. In other words, the claimant is sustaining so-called "exposure in residence" (of their body). *See J.H. France Refractories Co. v. Allstate Ins. Co.*, 626 A.2d 502, 507 (Pa. 1993) ("The medical evidence in this case unequivocally establishes that injuries occur during the development of asbestosis

immediately upon exposure, and that the injuries continue to occur even after exposure ends during the progression of the disease right up until the time that increasing incapacitation results in manifestation as a recognizable disease. If any of these phases of the pathogenesis occurs during the policy period, the insurer is obligated to indemnify [the insured] under the terms of the policy.").

The continuous trigger traces its origin to *Keene Corp. v. Ins. Co. of N. Am.*, 667 F.2d 1034 (D.C. Cir. 1981). The District of Columbia Court of Appeals examined the exposure and manifestation trigger theories and concluded that each one was appropriate, but not exclusive, for purposes of determining which policies were obligated to provide coverage for asbestos bodily injuries: "[I]nhalation exposure, exposure in residence, and manifestation all trigger coverage under the policies. We interpret 'bodily injury' to mean any part of the single injurious process that asbestos-related diseases entail." *Id.* at 1047.

In addition to the medical etiology of asbestos bodily injury, the *Keene* court also rested its decision on Keene's reasonable expectations:

> When Keene purchased the policies, it could have reasonably expected that it was free of the risk of becoming liable for injuries of which it could not have been aware prior to its purchase of insurance. There is no doubt that these losses would be covered if the diseases at issue developed spontaneously upon inhalation. Inhalation of asbestos is an "occurrence" that causes injury for which Keene may be held liable. The possibility that the insurers may not be liable arises solely because there is a period of time between the point at which the injurious process began and the point at which injury manifests itself.

Id. at 1046.

Support for the continuous trigger has also been found in the drafting history of the commercial general liability (CGL) policy:

> [T]he drafters of the standard occurrence-based CGL policy, and the experts advising the industry regarding its interpretation when formulated in 1966, contemplated that the policy would afford liability coverage for all property damage or injury occurring during the policy period resulting from an accident, or from injurious exposure to conditions. Nothing in the policy language purports to exclude damage or injury of a continuous or

progressively deteriorating nature, as long as it occurs during the policy period.

Montrose, 913 P.2d at 892 (Cal. 1995).

At least one court has concluded that "the continuous trigger theory is a legal fiction permitting the law to posit that many repeated small events occurring over a period of decades are actually only one ongoing occurrence. In cases where property damage is continuous and gradual and results from many events happening over a long period of time, it makes sense to adopt this legal fiction for the purposes of determining what policies have been triggered." *Pub. Serv. Co. of Colo. v. Wallis & Cos.*, 986 P.2d 924, 939 (Colo. 1999).

Given the significant difficulty of determining when an injury-in-fact or actual injury occurred in the context of asbestos bodily injury and environmental property damage, it is likely to be the case that, as a practical matter, an injury-in-fact trigger and continuous trigger are one and the same. For example, in *N. States Power Co. v. Fid. & Cas. Co. of N.Y.*, 523 N.W.2d 657 (Minn. 1994), the Supreme Court of Minnesota adopted a presumption that, where damages occurred over multiple policy periods, such damages were continuous from the point of the first damage to the point of discovery. Then "[a] party wishing to show that no appreciable damage occurred during a triggered policy period bears the burden of proving that fact." *Id.* at 664.

5. *Double Trigger*: While not discussed in many of the decisions that review the various trigger schools of thought, another method, sometimes called the "double" trigger, has been employed, albeit not frequently. Under this method, injury occurs at the time of exposure and manifestation but not necessarily during the period in between. *See Zurich Ins. Co. v. Raymark Indus., Inc.*, 514 N.E.2d 150, 160–61 (Ill. 1987). The theory behind the double trigger is a rejection of the continuous trigger's concept that, even after a claimant (or property) is no longer *directly* exposed to a hazardous substance, the injury sustained upon initial exposure remains ongoing "in residence." "The [*Raymark*] Court explicitly rejected the notion that 'those who ultimately manifest an asbestos-related disease necessarily sustained bodily injury between the time when they were no longer exposed to asbestos and the time when their disease manifested itself.'" *John Crane, Inc. v. Admiral Ins. Co.*, No. 04CH8266 (Ill. Cir. Ct. Apr. 12, 2006) (quoting *Raymark*).

Much has been written by courts over the various trigger-of-coverage options that exist for deciding which policies are obligated to provide coverage for latent injury and damage claims. Most judges authoring these opinions are quick to discuss the various named trigger theories and then select one to apply. Other courts have proceeded more cautiously, concluding that the trigger-of-coverage labels may not be as neat and tidy as they seem. *See Plantation Pipe Line Co. v. Cont'l Cas. Co.*, No. 1:03-CV-2811-WBH, 2006 U.S. Dist. LEXIS 100761 (N.D. Ga. Sept. 25, 2006) ("In its present analysis, the Court consciously avoids using a particular label in resolving the present trigger issue, instead focusing on the actual language and analysis in these cases. Neither the district courts nor the parties can agree about the appropriate verbiage for the different trigger theories, however, it is the substance, not the name that controls.").

Courts have also declined to immediately adopt a prenamed trigger theory on the basis that, while convenient, it may come at the expense of the facts and policy language:

> In reviewing several trigger cases from other jurisdictions, we think it apparent that some courts too quickly label the "trigger theory" they are supposedly applying without carefully considering the factual distinctions, or lack thereof, between exposure, injury in fact, and manifestation. Even more troubling, some courts are too hasty in applying a particular trigger without carefully considering the relevant policy language. We must not forget that the issue presented today is fundamentally a question of insurance contract interpretation.

Gelman Sciences, 572 N.W.2d at 622 (Mich. 1998), *overruled on other grounds by Wilkie v. Auto-Owners Ins. Co.*, 664 N.W.2d 776, 786 (Mich. 2003).

Despite their differences, the various trigger theories that have been debated and adopted over the years share a common trait: they generally result in multiple policies (in some manner) being obligated to provide coverage for latent injury and damage claims. The one theory that would have prevented this—manifestation—was resoundingly rejected. Needless to say, the adoption of trigger theories that resulted in more than a single policy year being obligated to provide coverage caused a significant increase in insurers' liability for asbestos and environmental claims. Indeed, the continuous trigger has been justified on the basis of its ability to maximize coverage. *See Owens Illinois*, 650 A.2d at 981 (N.J. 1994).

Once a court determines that multiple policy years are obligated to provide coverage for latent injury or damage, the focus often shifts to determining how much of such total damage must be borne by each insurer that issued one or more of the triggered policies. Like trigger, this issue, usually called "allocation," has been the subject of contentious, abundant, and slow-moving multi-party litigation over the past three decades. Allocation is the subject of Chapter 18.

50-State Survey: Trigger-of-Coverage for Latent Injury and Damage Claims

Alabama: The Court of Appeals for the Eleventh Circuit held that an exposure trigger applied to claims for bodily injury resulting from exposure to asbestos. *Commercial Union Ins. Co. v. Sepco Corp.*, 765 F.2d 1543, 1545–46 (11th Cir. 1985) (applying Alabama law). "[E]very asbestos-related injury results from inhalation of asbestos fibers. Because such inhalation can occur only upon exposure to asbestos, and because it is impossible practically to determine the point at which the fibers actually imbed themselves in the victim's lungs, to equate exposure to asbestos with 'bodily injury' caused by the inhalation of the asbestos is the 'superior interpretation of the contract provisions.'" *Id.* at 1546 (quoting *Ins. Co. of N. Am v. Forty-Eight Insulations, Inc.*, 633 F.2d 1212, 1223 (6th Cir. 1980)). More recently, in *Alabama Gas Corp. v. Travelers Cas. and Sur. Co.*, 990 F. Supp. 2d 1163 (N.D. Ala. 2014) an Alabama District Court held that "in light of Alabama law and the relevant policy language, the court finds Alabama applies an injury in fact requirement for indemnity under a policy of insurance." (addressing the various trigger theories and case law nationally applying each one) (*affirmed* at 568 Fed. Appx. 837 (11th Cir. 2014)).

Alaska: An Alaska District Court held that an exposure trigger applied to claims for environmental property damage and that coverage was triggered when groundwater was exposed to contaminants. *Mapco Alaska Petroleum, Inc. v. Cent. Nat'l Ins. Co. of Omaha*, 795 F. Supp. 941, 948 (D. Alaska 1991). "In light of the Alaska Supreme Court's general concurrence with California insurance law, coverage should be triggered by exposure to contaminants rather than by manifestation of the damage." *Id.*

Arizona: The Court of Appeals of Arizona held that a continuous trigger applied to claims for bodily injury caused by exposure to water from an aquifer that was contaminated by TCE used at an aircraft-cleaning facility. *Associated Aviation Underwriters v. Wood*, 98 P.3d 572, 602 (Ariz. Ct. App. 2004). "Under the particular facts of this case, we interpret 'bodily injury' to include the cellular damage caused by TCE exposure *and*, even after exposure has ceased, the continuing injurious process initiated thereby. In other words, both exposure and exposure-in-residence occurring during the policy period will trigger insurance coverage. In addition, the policy clearly is also triggered if 'disease' manifests itself during the policy period." *Id.* (emphasis in original).

Arkansas: No instructive authority.

California: The Supreme Court of California held that a continuous trigger applied to claims for bodily injury and property damage resulting from the insured's disposal of hazardous waste. *Montrose Chem. Corp. v. Admiral Ins. Co.*, 913 P.2d 878, 904 (Cal. 1995). "Under this trigger of coverage theory, bodily injuries and property damage that are continuous or progressively deteriorating throughout successive policy periods are covered by all policies in effect during those periods." *Id.* at 894. *See also Armstrong World Indus., Inc. v. Atena Cas. & Sur. Co.*, 45 Cal. App. 4th 1, 47 (Cal. Ct. App. 1996) (applying the continuous trigger theory in the context of asbestos-related bodily injury) ("[T]he trial court's factual findings here, made after consideration of extensive medical testimony, amply support the conclusion that injury actually occurs upon exposure and continues until death."). In *State v. Continental Ins. Co.*, 281 P.3d 1000 (Cal. 2012), the Supreme Court of California addressed *Montrose* and stated that, there "we held that in the context of a third party liability policy property damage that is continuous or progressively deteriorating throughout several policy periods is potentially covered by all policies in effect during those periods." *Id.* at 1005. The *Continental* Court observed that "the term 'trigger of coverage' does not appear in the language of the CGL insurance policies here, it is a term of convenience used to describe that which, under the specific terms of an insurance policy, must happen in the policy period in order for the *potential* of coverage to arise. The issue is largely one of timing—what must take place *within the policy's effective dates* for the potential of coverage to be 'triggered?'" *Id.* (emphasis in original). *See also Compass Ins. Co. v. Univ. Mech. & Eng'g Contrs., Inc.*, No. 14-04295, 2016 U.S. Dist. LEXIS 39624 (N.D. Cal. Mar. 25, 2016) (noting that, in *State v. Continental*, "the California Supreme Court recently re-affirmed the vitality of the analogous 'continuous trigger' rule to 'long-tail' injuries like those caused by asbestos") (rejecting the insurer's argument that, to trigger coverage for an asbestos bodily injury claim, exposure to asbestos and injury must both happen within the policy period) ("That the 'Policy Period, Territory' clause says occurrences must happen during the policy period is of no moment. The clause does not define 'occurrence' and is, at best, ambiguous in that it does not clearly 'limit coverage to those claims in which the causal acts took place during the policy period.'"); *Fluor Corp. v. Superior Court*, 354 P.3d 302 (Cal. 2015) (addressing California's continuous trigger case law, in the context of interpreting the term "loss," for purposes of interpreting a statute addressing assignment of policy rights); *Montrose Chemical Corp. of California v. Superior Court*, 460 P.3d 1201 (Cal. 2020) ("There is no requirement that ... the conditions giving rise to the damage or injury ... themselves occur within the policy period in order for potential liability coverage to arise. Extending this logic to the continuous injury context, we held that bodily injury and property damage which is continuous or progressively deteriorating throughout several policy periods is potentially covered by all policies in effect during those periods. This principle is also known as the 'continuous injury trigger of coverage.'" (reiterating rule adopted in earlier *Montrose* decision).

Colorado: The Supreme Court of Colorado held that a continuous trigger applied to claims for environmental property damage at waste sites. *Pub. Serv. Co. of Colo. v. Wallis & Cos.*, 986 P.2d 924, 939 (Colo. 1999). "We note that the continuous trigger theory is a legal fiction permitting the law to posit that many repeated small events occurring over a period of decades are actually only one ongoing occurrence. In cases where property damage is continuous and gradual and results from many events happening over a long period of time, it makes sense to adopt this legal fiction for the purposes of determining what policies have been triggered." *Id.*

Connecticut: In *R.T. Vanderbilt Co. v. Hartford Accident & Indem. Co.*, 156 A.3d 539 (Conn. Ct. App. 2017), the Appellate Court of Connecticut, following a lengthy analysis, adopted "the continuous trigger theory, under which every policy in effect, beginning at the time of initial asbestos exposure and extending through the latency period and up to the manifestation of asbestos related disease, is on the risk for defense and liability costs." The court explained its decision as follows: "We believe that continuous trigger best accounts for the progressive nature of asbestos related diseases, as both the layperson and at least some subset of medical professionals would consider the tissue damage and other harms imposed throughout the development of asbestosis and asbestos related cancers to constitute personal or bodily injuries as defined in the standard form commercial general liability policy. We also believe that continuous trigger represents the fairest and most efficient means of resolving and administering complex, multiclaimant asbestos litigation such as the present case." The court also noted that, in *Security Ins. Co. of Hartford v. Lumbermens Mut. Cas. Co.*, 826 A.2d 107 (Conn. 2003), the Supreme Court did not "establish continuous trigger or any other trigger theory as the law of Connecticut." The Connecticut Supreme Court affirmed, adopting the opinion of the appeals court. 216 A.3d 629, 637 (Conn. 2019). *See also Steadfast Ins. Co. v. Purdue Frederick*

Co., No. X08CV020191697S, 2006 Conn. Super. LEXIS 1970 (Conn. Super. Ct. May 18, 2006) (associating *Security Ins.*'s allocation methodology with the triggering of multiple insurance policies) (declining to adopt a continuous trigger in the context of claims for bodily injury resulting from the ingestion of the insured's pharmaceutical product OxyContin). "Injuries … [in environmental contamination cases] usually evolve slowly, and thus it is difficult to define the date on which an occurrence triggers liability for insurance purposes. Many years may pass from the time a toxin enters the body until the time the toxin's presence manifests itself in the form of a disease." (citation and quotation omitted). "There is no contention that this case involves 'long latency loss claims' or a 'continuous trigger' situation."

Delaware: The Delaware Superior Court held that "Delaware law supports the imposition of a continuous trigger." *E. I. du Pont de Nemours & Co. v. Admiral Ins. Co.*, No. 89C-AU-99, 1995 Del. Super. LEXIS 631 (Del. Super. Ct. Oct. 27, 1995). Following a review of the various trigger theories, the court explained: "The policy reasoning underlying continuous trigger fits logically within the context of contamination of soil and groundwater over a period of years. Since … the process of contamination had indisputably been ongoing for decades, the continuous trigger should apply." *See also Hercules, Inc. v. AIU Ins. Co.*, 784 A.2d 481, 492 (Del. Super. Ct. 2001) (citing *du Pont* for the proposition that Delaware has adopted the continuous trigger theory and applying it for purposes of addressing allocation for environmental property damage); *Viking Pump, Inc. v. Century Indem. Co.*, 2 A.3d 76 (Del. Ch. Ct. 2009) (applying New York law) (*see* New York, *infra.*); *Rite Aid Corp. v. ACE Am. Ins. Co.*, No. 19-04-150, 2020 Del. Super. LEXIS 2797 (Del. Super. Ct. Sept. 22, 2020) (applying both Pennsylvania and Delaware's shared legal principles) (concluding that personal injury related to "opioid abuse and opioid used disorder would plainly fall into the category of a 'latent injury' because, similar to asbestosis or mesothelioma, 'such injuries may not manifest themselves until a considerable time after the initial exposure causing injury occurs'" and therefore, the application of a multiple trigger theory was appropriate) (*appeal granted* 2020 Del. LEXIS 435 (Del. Dec. 1, 2020)).

District of Columbia: The District of Columbia Court of Appeals adopted a continuous trigger for purposes of asbestos bodily injury claims. *Keene Corp. v. Ins. Co. of N. Am.*, 667 F.2d 1034 (D.C. Cir. 1981). The court examined the exposure and manifestation trigger theories and concluded that each one was appropriate, but not exclusive, for purposes of determining which policies were obligated to provide coverage: "[I]nhalation exposure, exposure in residence, and manifestation all trigger coverage under the policies. We interpret 'bodily injury' to mean any part of the single injurious process that asbestos-related diseases entail." *Id.* at 1047; *see also Independent Petrochemical Corp. v. Aetna Cas. & Sur. Co.*, 654 F. Supp. 1334, 1343 (D.D.C. 1986) (noting that *Keene* considered the laws of Delaware, New York, District of Columbia, Pennsylvania, Connecticut, and Massachusetts and rested its analysis on principles of insurance law common to all of those jurisdictions); *Young Women's Christian Association of the National Capital Area, Inc. v. Allstate Ins. Co. of Canada*, 275 F.3d 1145, 1150 (D.C. Cir. 2002) (noting that the District of Columbia applies a continuous trigger to occurrence based policies where the damage can be characterized as continuous or progressive).

Florida: A Florida District Court applied an injury-in-fact trigger to claims for environmental property damage. *CSX Transp., Inc. v. Admiral Ins. Co.*, No. 93–132, 1996 U.S. Dist. LEXIS 17125 (M.D. Fla. Nov. 6, 1996). The parties agreed that the "injury in fact" trigger should be applied, despite the court's observation that there was substantial authority suggesting that the multiple or continuous trigger theory would be applied in the circumstances of this case. Nonetheless, "in view of the parties' substantial agreement upon application of the injury in fact theory, coupled with the fact that, as a practical matter, the two theories appear to be functionally equivalent in these circumstances, the Court will adopt the injury in fact trigger of coverage."

Georgia: A Georgia District Court, following a survey of several prior Georgia federal court decisions, held that coverage was triggered for environmental property damage that occurred within the effective dates of the policy periods, regardless of when the damage was discovered. *Plantation Pipe Line Co. v. Cont'l Cas. Co.*, No. 03-2811, 2006 U.S. Dist. LEXIS 100761 (N.D. Ga. Sept. 25, 2006); *see also Briggs & Stratton Corp. v. Royal Globe Ins. Co.*, 64 F. Supp. 2d 1346, 1350 (M.D. Ga. 1999) (holding that an exposure trigger applied to environmental property damage resulting from the discharge of untreated waste water) ("It is not disputed that during the Transcontinental policy period PMI used the chemical materials it purchased from B & S in its electroplating operations, and that as a result of those electroplating operations waste waters containing chemical substances originating with B & S were discharged onto the property, damaging it."); *Boardman Petroleum, Inc. v. Federated Mut. Ins. Co.*, 498 S.E.2d 492, 493–94 (Ga. 1998) (failing to answer a certified question from the Eleventh Circuit Court of Appeals asking which trigger-of-coverage theory applies in Georgia due to the court's resolution of another issue as dispositive); *Columbia Cas. Co. v. Plantation Pipe Line Co.*, 790 S.E.2d 645 (Ga.

Ct. App. 2016) ("Even if this Court were inclined to adopt the continuous trigger theory, application of this theory is premised on the assumption that the Columbia policy contains language that limits coverage to property damage that takes place during the policy period. But, unlike more contemporary standard CGL policies, the Columbia policy and the provisions of the Lexington policy that it expressly incorporates do *not* provide that the policy applies only to property damage that occurs during the policy period.") (emphasis in original) ("[W]e are presented with a policy that by its plain terms covers property damage caused by an occurrence, provided the occurrence takes pace during the policy period."); *Travelers Prop. Cas. Co. of Am. v. Cont'l Cas. Co.*, 226 F. Supp. 3d 1359 (N.D. Ga. 2017) (noting that the court in *Columbia Cas. Co. v. Plantation* refused to adopt the "continuous trigger" "because the policy at issue did not provide that it applied to property damage that occurred during the policy period but required only that the occurrence had taken place during the policy period").

Hawaii: In *Sentinel Ins. Co., Ltd. v. First Ins. Co. of Haw., Ltd.*, 875 P.2d 894, 915 (Haw. 1994) the Supreme Court of Hawaii adopted an injury-in-fact trigger in the context of a claim for construction defects. While the case involved construction defects, the court reached its decision based upon a review of cases nationally involving environmental property damage and toxic torts. *Id.* at 914–17. Further, the court noted that "[t]he injury-in-fact trigger is … true to the terms of the CGL policy and suitable for any type of injury." *Id.* at 917. *See also Association of Apartment Owners of Imperial Plaza v. Fireman's Fund Ins. Co.*, 939 F. Supp. 2d 1059 (D. Hawaii 2013) ("Plaintiff demonstrates that damage to the Property occurred— namely in the form of water carrying arsenic into the concrete slab, which resulted in accumulated arsenic that required abatement. Plaintiff also establishes that the water infiltration occurred progressively over time as a continuous and indivisible process of injury. *Id. See Sentinel*, 76 Hawai'i at 301, 875 P.2d 894 (holding that continuous injury trigger would apply if insurance company could not identify with reasonable certainty which damages occurred during the policy period because the loss caused by water infiltration into the building progressed continuously).") (addressing all-risks property policy).

Idaho: An Idaho District Court noted that "Idaho has a 'trigger' rule similar to Texas's 'injury in fact' approach. *Millers Mut. Fire Ins. Co. of Texas v. Ed Bailey, Inc.*, 647 P.2d 1249, 1251 (Idaho 1982) (noting that an 'occurrence' is said to have taken place at the time the policy holder was 'actually damaged')." *See also State of Idaho v. Bunker Hill Co.*, 647 F. Supp. 1064, 1070 (D. Idaho 1986) (addressing the various trigger-of-coverage theories and holding that, under the circumstances of the case, the court did not need to adopt a trigger method because the language of the policies was clear and unambiguous that the environmental property damage for which insurance was provided must occur during the policy period).

Illinois: The Supreme Court of Illinois held that, for purposes of claims for bodily injury caused by exposure to asbestos, coverage is triggered under the policies on the risk when the person is exposed to asbestos, on the date of manifestation of a disease and at the time of a disordered, weakened, or unsound condition before the clinical manifestation of a disease. *Zurich Ins. Co. v. Raymark Indus., Inc.*, 514 N.E.2d 150, 160–61 (Ill. 1987). "The [*Raymark*] Court explicitly rejected the notion that 'those who ultimately manifest an asbestos-related disease necessarily sustained bodily injury between the time when they were no longer exposed to asbestos and the time when their disease manifested itself.'" *John Crane, Inc. v. Admiral Ins. Co.*, No. 04CH8266 (Ill. Cir. Ct. Apr. 12, 2006) (quoting *Raymark* at 161); *see also Outboard Marine Corp. v. Liberty Mut. Ins. Co.*, 670 N.E.2d 740, 748 (Ill. Ct. App. 1996) (adopting a continuous trigger for purposes of environmental property damage); *John Crane, Inc. v. Admiral Ins. Co.*, 991 N.E.2d 474 (Ill. Ct. App. 2013) (discussing *Zurich v. Raymark*) ("Our supreme court found no continuing bodily injury from the time 'exposure to asbestos ends and the time an asbestos-related disease becomes diagnosable.' No new evidence presented before the trial court below challenged this finding in *Zurich*. Once our supreme court has declared the law with respect to an issue, this court must follow that law, as only the supreme court has authority to overrule or modify its own decisions. We therefore decline CNA's invitation to revisit this issue.").

Indiana: The Supreme Court of Indiana held that a multiple trigger theory applied to claims for bodily injury caused by the ingestion of DES and that "each insurer on the risk between the ingestion of DES and the manifestation of a DES-related illness is liable to the insured for indemnification." *Eli Lilly and Co. v. Home Ins. Co.*, 482 N.E.2d 467, 471 (Ind. 1985); *see also Travelers Cas. & Surety Co. v. U. S. Filter Corp.*, 895 N.E.2d 1172, 1179 (Ind. 2008) (favorably citing *Eli Lilly* for its adoption of the multiple trigger interpretation of occurrence-based policies in the delayed manifestation context); *PSI Energy, Inc. v. Home Ins. Co.*, 801 N.E.2d 705, 733 (Ind. Ct. App. 2004) ("We agree with the Insurers that our courts are required to apply the 'injury-in-fact' trigger of coverage approach.") (citing *Allstate Ins. Co. v. Dana Corp.*, 759 N.E.2d 1049, 1060–61 (Ind. 2001) (considering coverage for cleanup costs associated with environmental contamination from insured's manufactured gas plants); *Wolf Lake Terminals, Inc. v. Mutual Marine Ins. Co.*, 433 F. Supp. 2d 933, 948 (N.D. Ind. 2005) (holding that an "injury in fact" trigger applies in the context of coverage for environmental property damage); *Thomson Inc. v. Insurance Co. of North America*, 11 N.E.3d 982 (Ind. Ct. App. 2014) ("Because our supreme court in *Lilly* specifically cited *Eagle–Picher's* manifestation theory in its trigger analysis and held that manifestation is the end point of the continuous trigger, we are unwilling to depart from *Eagle–Picher's* definition of manifestation.") (defining manifestation as the date when disease was capable of diagnosis).

Iowa: No instructive authority.

Kansas: The Supreme Court of Kansas held that a continuous trigger applied to claims for bodily injury caused by noise-induced hearing loss. *Atchison, Topeka & Santa Fe Ry. Co. v. Stonewall Ins. Co.*, 71 P.3d 1097, 1125–26 (Kan. 2003). "The unprotected employees have been subjected to excessive noise levels for a continuous period of time. It is part of the single injurious process which resulted in hearing impairment. Santa Fe's failure to protect the claimants is the occurrence which gives rise to the injury." *Id.* at 1126; *see also Cessna Aircraft Co. v. Hartford Acc. & Indem. Co.*, 900 F. Supp. 1489, 1503 (D. Kan. 1995) ("[A]pplication of the 'injury-in-fact' trigger is more consistent with the language of the … policies, especially where, as here, the contamination is alleged to have occurred in particular policy periods and to have continued through many policy periods.").

Kentucky: A Kentucky District Court, noting that no Kentucky court had ever adopted a specific trigger theory, declined to do so as such task was better left to the Supreme Court of Kentucky. *Eckstein v. Cincinnati Ins. Co.*, No. 505CV043M, 2005 U.S. Dist. LEXIS 27957 (W.D. Ky. Nov. 14, 2005) (addressing coverage for a residence damaged by mold); *see also Acuity Ins. Co. v. Higdon's Sheet Metal & Supply Co.*, No. 3:06-CV-162-H, 2007 U.S. Dist. LEXIS 24997 (W.D. Ky. Apr. 3, 2007) ("Although some states have adopted a coverage trigger theory to establish the date of loss for determining when coverage is triggered … Kentucky has not done so. Instead, coverage is determined by examining the terms of the policies at issue.").

Louisiana: The Supreme Court of Louisiana held that an exposure trigger applied to claims for bodily injury caused by exposure to asbestos. *Cole v. Celotex Corp.*, 599 So. 2d 1058, 1076 (La. 1992). The court rested its decision on the fact that the exposure theory comports with a literal construction of the policy language, maximizes coverage, and honors the contracting parties' intent by providing consistency between the insured's tort liability and the insurer's coverage. *Id.* at 1076–77; *see also Grefer v. Travelers Ins. Co.*, 919 So. 2d 758, 765–66 (La.

Ct. App. 2005) (citing *Cole* for the proposition that an exposure trigger applies to claims for environmental property damage) (court rejected a manifestation trigger and the argument that the exposure trigger only applies to bodily injury/latent disease cases); *Am. Guarantee & Liability Ins. Co. v. Anco Insulation, Inc.*, No. Civ.A.02–987A1, 2005 U.S. Dist. LEXIS 48924 (M.D. La. July 29, 2005) ("*Cole* and its progeny demonstrate that Louisiana law has expressly rejected the application of the triple-trigger theory and consistently applied the exposure theory when determining the date of accrual of a claim resulting from long-term exposure to latent, disease-producing substances such as asbestos."); *S. Silica of Louisiana, Inc. v. Louisiana Ins. Guar. Ass'n*, 979 So. 2d 460, 465 (La. 2008) ("One of the most perplexing issues that arises in long-latency occupational disease cases involves the determination of when a cause of action for tort liability accrues, since insidious diseases, such as silicosis, are typically characterized by a lengthy latency period, and consequently, a lengthy temporal separation between the alleged tortious conduct and the appearance of injury. In *Cole v. Celotex Corporation*, 599 So. 2d 1058, 1065 (La. 1992), this court adopted the significant exposure theory for purposes of establishing the applicable trigger for insurance coverage."); *Clarendon Am. Ins. Co. v. S. States Plumbing, Inc.*, No. 09–1974, 2011 U.S. Dist. LEXIS 30485 (W.D. La. March 23, 2011) ("Louisiana courts apply the exposure theory to bodily injury resulting from long-latency occupational disease. *See S. Silica of La., Inc. v. La. Ins. Guar. Ass'n*, 979 So. 2d 460, 464 (La. 2008). Under the exposure theory, the bodily injury is deemed to occur when the exposure to the harmful conditions occurred."); *Marshall v. Air Liquide-Big Three, Inc.*, 107 So. 3d 13 (La. Ct. App. 2012) (citing *Cole* and stating that it was "undisputed that the 'exposure theory' applies to this case."); *Arceneaux v. Amstar Corp.*, 200 So. 3d 277 (La. 2016) (addressing allocation of defense costs for latent injury claims (workplace hearing loss) and explaining *Cole*: "Under the exposure theory, the 'occurrence' that triggers coverage under an insurance policy is the plaintiff's exposure to harmful conditions within the policy period. Such a theory was adopted to establish when coverage was triggered in cases that involved diseases when there is a 'lengthy temporal separation between the alleged tortious conduct and the appearance of injury.'"); *Coleman v. Anco Insulations, Inc.*, No. 15-821, 2017 U.S. Dist. LEXIS 69749 (M.D. La. May 8, 2017) (rejecting the argument that, based on *Cole*, post-employment policies can be triggered, for asbestos bodily injury, on account of a continuing duty to warn); *Houston Specialty Ins. Co. v. Ascension Insulation & Supply, Inc.*, No. 17-1010, 2018 U.S. Dist. LEXIS 134996 (W.D. La. Aug. 7, 2018) (applying *Cole* to claims for bodily injury, caused by exposure to moisture during a home remodeling and concluding that summary judgment was not warranted as it was "not possible to confirm, from the petition alone, the dates the children were allegedly exposed").

Maine: No instructive authority. *But see Citizens Communications Co. v. American Home Assur. Co.*, No. Civ. A. CV-02–237, 2004 Me. Super. LEXIS 28 (Me. Super. Ct. Feb. 19, 2004) (not addressing the issue, but noting, in the context of a claim involving environmental property damage, that "[m]ost courts now employ the 'continuous trigger,' by triggering any policy on the risk at any time the continuing loss occurred, and requiring the insurers of those triggered policies to either prepare to defend or to prepare to pay up to its policy limits").

Maryland: The Court of Appeals of Maryland held that "*at a minimum, coverage under the policy to provide a defense and indemnification of the insured is triggered upon exposure to the insured's asbestos products during the policy period by a person who suffers bodily injury as a result of that exposure." Lloyd E. Mitchell, Inc. v. Md. Cas. Co.*, 595 A.2d 469, 478 (Md. 1991) (emphasis added); *see also National Union Fire Ins. Co. of Pittsburgh, PA v. Porter Hayden Co.*, 331 B.R. 652, 661 (D. Md. 2005) (noting that the *Mitchell* Court cited with approval cases adopting not only an exposure trigger, but also injury-in-fact and continuous triggers, thereby precluding the court from concluding that *Mitchell* compels, or even supports, the argument that it adopted an "exposure-only" trigger); *Md. Cas. Co. v. Hanson*, 902 A.2d 152, 170 (Md. Ct. App. 2006) ("[T]he law in Maryland is that, in cases such as [those involving] proof of repeated exposure to lead, which, in turn, results in lead-based poisoning injuries that continue for several years with continuous exposure, the continuous injury or injury-in-fact trigger is applicable and thus triggers insurance coverage during all applicable policy periods.") (relying on *Riley v. United Services Auto. Ass'n*, 871 A.2d 599 (Md. Ct. App. 2005)); *Harford County v. Harford Mut. Ins. Co.*, 610 A.2d 286, 294–95 (Md. 1992) (holding that, for purposes of environmental property damage, policies on the risk earlier than discovery or manifestation of damage can be triggered); *Mayor & City Council of Balt. v. Utica Mut. Ins. Co.*, 802 A.2d 1070, 1100 (Md. Ct. App. 2002) (holding that a continuous trigger applied to claims for asbestos in buildings); *Pennsylvania Nat. Mut. Cas. Ins. Co. v. Attsgood Realty*, No. JFM-09-2650, 2010 U.S. Dist. LEXIS 75549 (D. Md. July 27, 2010) ("In a lead paint case such as this, Maryland follows the 'continuous trigger' rule.") (citing *Hanson* and *Utica Mut.*); *National Union Fire Ins. Co. of Pittsburgh, Pa. v. Porter Hayden Co.*, No. 03–3414, 2014 U.S. Dist. LEXIS 114 (D. Md. Jan. 2, 2014) ("Pursuant to the 'continuous trigger theory,' insurance coverage for asbestos-related bodily injury claims is triggered 'from the date of initial exposure [to asbestos fibers] to the date of manifestation [of asbestos-related disease].'") (quoting *Porter Hayden*, *supra*); *Pa. Nat'l Mut. Cas. Ins. Co. v. Jacob Dackman & Sons, LLC*, No. RDB-16-2640, 2017 U.S. Dist. LEXIS 148907 (D. Md. Sept. 14, 2017) (undertaking factual analysis to determine beginning and end trigger dates in a claim for exposure to lead in a residential setting); *Allstate Ins. Co. v. Blue*, No. 18-1199, 2019 U.S. Dist. LEXIS 9481 (D. Md. Jan. 18, 2019) ("Under the continuous trigger rule, repeated exposure to lead, which, in turn, results in lead-based poisoning injuries that continue for several years with continuous exposure triggers insurance coverage during all applicable policy periods."). In *Rossello v. Zurich Am. Ins. Co.*, 226 A.3d 444 (Md. 2020), the Court of Appeals of Maryland examined the state's trigger of coverage law in detail and noted that "Maryland's appellate courts have thus made clear that in extended exposure cases, continuous or progressive damage will constitute an 'occurrence' within the policy period that the asbestos remains present. In other words, a policy period is triggered when actual injury occurs and progressive injury can therefore trigger multiple policy periods." *Id.* at 111. The court added a cautionary note concerning trigger: "Although this discussion has referred to various trigger theories by name, we must stress that courts and litigants should be careful when referring to such delineated theories. The nomenclature and reference of specific trigger models 'can be deceiving,' because a court must apply policy language to the factual context before it." *Id.* at 112.

Massachusetts: The Supreme Judicial Court of Massachusetts held that, under policies that provided coverage for an occurrence during the policy period, an exposure trigger applied to claims for bodily injury caused by exposure to asbestos. *A.W. Chesterton Co. v. Mass. Insurers Insolvency Fund*, 838 N.E.2d 1237, 1251–52 (Mass. 2005). It was stipulated that, under policies that did not require an occurrence during the policy period, a continuous trigger applied. *Id.* at 1251; *see also Rubenstein v. Royal Ins. Co. of Am.*, 694 N.E.2d 381, 387 (Mass. Ct. App. 1998) (addressing trigger of coverage for environmental property damage and noting that the language of the particular policy controlled and the focus of inquiry was whether property damage occurred within the policy period); *Keyspan New England, LLC v. Hanover Ins. Co.*, Nos. 93–01458, 04–01855, 2008 Mass. Super. LEXIS 326 (Mass. Super. Ct. Aug. 14, 2008) (holding that coverage for environmental property damage was triggered if damage happened within the policy period); *Boston Gas Co. v. Century Indem. Co.*, 910 N.E.2d 290, 301 (Mass. 2009) (noting that, in *Trustees of Tufts Univ. v. Commercial Union Ins. Co.*, 616 N.E.2d 68 (Mass. 1993), the Massachusetts high court rejected the manifestation trigger, for purposes of environmental contamination, and the court has not yet had occasion to adopt one of the other trigger theories in such context) (not addressing the issue because it was not before the court); *Graphic Arts Mut. Ins. Co. v. D.N. Lukens, Inc.*, No. 11–10460, 2013 U.S. Dist. LEXIS 75201 (D. Mass. May 29, 2013) (noting that "[o]ne issue that *Boston Gas* left undecided was when a progressive injury first occurs") (examining all trigger theories and adopting the continuous trigger).

Michigan: The Supreme Court of Michigan held that an injury-in-fact trigger applied to claims for environmental property damage caused by seepage from a wastewater pond. *Gelman Sciences, Inc. v. Fid. & Cas. Co. of N.Y.*, 572 N.W.2d 617, 623 (Mich. 1998), *overruled on other grounds by Wilkie v. Auto-Owners Ins. Co.*, 664 N.W.2d 776, 786 (Mich. 2003). "[A]ccording to the policies' explicit terms, actual injury must occur during the time the policy is in effect in order to be indemnifiable, i.e., the policies dictate an injury-in-fact approach. The manifestation trigger simply is not supported by the policy language." *Id.*; *see also Wolverine World Wide, Inc. v. Liberty Mut. Ins. Co.*, No. 260330, 2007 Mich. App. LEXIS 657 (Mich. Ct. App. Mar. 8, 2007) (citing *Gelman* as establishing that Michigan uses an injury-in-fact trigger and applying it in the context of contamination related to the insured's disposal of toxic sludge from its tannery operations); *Continental Cas. Co. v. Indian Head Industries, Inc.*, No. 05–73918, 2012 U.S. Dist. LEXIS 51555 (E.D. Mich. Apr. 12, 2012) (court discussed *Gelman* and the parties agreed that the "injury in fact" trigger applied in a claim involving asbestos bodily injury) (*aff'd* 666 Fed. Appx. 456 (6th Cir. 2016)).

Minnesota: The Supreme Court of Minnesota applied an injury-in-fact trigger to claims for property damage resulting from the insured's coal-tar gasification plant operations. *N. States Power Co. v. Fid. & Cas. Co. of N.Y.*, 523 N.W.2d 657, 662–63 (Minn. 1994). "Where, as in this case, the damages occurred over multiple policy periods, the trial court should presume that the damages were continuous from the point of the first damage to the point of discovery or cleanup. A party wishing to show that no appreciable damage occurred during a triggered policy period bears the burden of proving that fact." *Id.* at 664; *see also In re Silicone Implant Ins. Coverage Litigation*, 667 N.W.2d 405, 417 (Minn. 2003) (holding that an injury-in-fact trigger applied to claims for bodily injury caused by silicone-gel breast implants) ("[B]ecause damage occurred at or about the time of implantation, we conclude that the policies were triggered at or about the time of implantation."); *Tony Eiden Co. v. State Auto Property and Cas. Ins. Co.*, No. A07–2222, 2009 Minn. App. Unpub. LEXIS 149 (Minn. Ct. App. Jan. 26, 2009) (addressing Minnesota case law applying an injury-in-fact trigger).

Mississippi: No instructive authority. For guidance, *see* discussion in Chapter 17.

Missouri: Missouri law appears unsettled concerning which trigger theory applies. *See United States v. Conservation Chem. Co.*, 653 F. Supp. 152, 197 (W.D. Mo. 1986) ("[T]he Special Master finds that Missouri tends to follow the injury in fact analysis to actually determine or discover when an injury occurred. But there may be circumstances where the Missouri courts will look to the exposure and manifestation theories to determine when the injury occurred.") (addressing coverage for environmental damage resulting from the operation of the insured's chemical waste disposal facility); *see also Nationwide Ins. Co. v. Central Missouri Elec. Cooperative, Inc.*, 278 F.3d 742, 747 (8th Cir. 2001) ("It is not entirely clear which of these [trigger] approaches is appropriate under Missouri law. Although we have previously predicted that Missouri would apply an exposure theory of damages, *Continental Ins. Co. v. Northeastern Pharm. & Chem. Co., Inc.*, 842 F.2d 977, 984 (8th Cir. 1988) (en banc), an argument can be made that an injury in fact approach is more appropriate. *Shaver*, 817 S.W.2d at 657 (coverage triggered 'when the complaining party was actually damaged.')"); *Independent Petrochem. Corp. v. Aetna Cas. Insur. Co.*, 672 F. Supp. 1, 3 (D.D.C. 1986) (applying Missouri law) ("Because we conclude that the obligations of both insurers are triggered under either theory of liability, we need not determine which method is required under Missouri law.").

Montana: No instructive authority. For guidance, *see* discussion in Chapter 17.

Nebraska: No instructive authority. For guidance, *see Kaapa Ethanol, L.L.C. v. Affiliated FM Ins. Co.*, No. 7:05CV5010, 2008 U.S. Dist. LEXIS 61515 (D. Neb. July 29, 2008), *rev'd on other grounds*, 2011 U.S. App. LEXIS 22158 (8th Cir. Nov. 3, 2011) addressed in Chapter 17. *See also Dutton-Lainson Co. v. Continental Ins. Co.*, 778 N.W.2d 433, 445 (Neb. 2010) (while not specifically addressing trigger of coverage, the court's analysis of allocation was undertaken based on a continuous trigger) ("[T]he total amount of the property damage should be allocated to the various policies in proportion to the period of time each was on the risk. If, for example, contamination occurred over a period of 10 years, 1/10th of the damage would be allocable to the period of time that a policy in force for 1 year was on the risk and 3/10ths of the damage would be allocable to the period of time a 3-year policy was in force.") (quoting *Northern States Power Co. v. Fidelity & Cas. Co. of N.Y.*, 523 N.W.2d 657, 664 (Minn. 1994)).

Nevada: No instructive authority. For guidance, *see* discussion in Chapter 17.

New Hampshire: The Supreme Court of New Hampshire held that, under policies that required property damage during the policy period, an injury-in-fact trigger applied to claims for property damage caused by the insured's manufactured gas plant operations. *EnergyNorth Natural Gas, Inc. v. Certain Underwriters at Lloyd's*, 848 A.2d 715, 721–22 (N.H. 2004) (*EnergyNorth I*). "The language of these three policies unambiguously distinguishes between the causative event—an accident or continuous or repeated exposure to conditions—and the resulting property damage. It is the property damage that must occur during the policy period, and 'which results' from the accident or 'continuous or repeated exposure to conditions.'" *Id.* at 721. With respect to policies that covered liability for accidents occurring during the policy period and those that applied to occurrences happening during the policy period, the court adopted an exposure trigger. *Id.* at 724–25; *see also EnergyNorth Natural Gas, Inc. v. Certain Underwriters at Lloyd's*, 934 A.2d 517 (N.H. 2007) (summarizing *EnergyNorth I*).

New Jersey: The Supreme Court of New Jersey held that a continuous trigger applied to claims for bodily injury and property damage caused by exposure to asbestos. *Owens Illinois, Inc. v. United Ins. Co.*, 650 A.2d 974, 995 (N.J. 1994). "[T]hat when progressive indivisible injury or damage results from exposure to injurious conditions for which civil liability may be imposed, courts may reasonably treat the progressive injury or damage as an occurrence within each of the years of a CGL policy." *Id.* More recently, in *Continental Ins. Co. v. Honeywell International, Inc.*, 188 A.3d 297 (N.J. 2018), the Supreme Court of New Jersey, in the context of an allocation/choice of law decision, declined to accept a dissenting Justice's invitation to "address alterations to the continuous-trigger concept as it was originally fashioned, and to the *Owens-Illinois* allocation paradigm, in order to promote social policy regarding tort law." *Id.* at 324. *See also Quincy Mut. Fire Ins. Co. v. Borough of Bellmawr*, 799 A.2d 499, 514 (N.J. 2002) (applying the continuous trigger to claims for environmental property damage) ("exposure relating to the Borough's initial depositing of toxic waste into the Landfill is the first trigger of coverage under the continuous trigger theory and constitutes an 'occurrence.'"); *Polarome Intern., Inc. v. Greenwich Ins. Co.*, 961 A.2d 29, 44–45 (N.J. Super. Ct. App. Div. 2008) (holding that policies issued after manifestation of injury were not obligated to provide coverage) ("[T]he last pull of the trigger occurs with the initial manifestation of a toxic-tort personal injury. Upon initial manifestation, the 'scientific uncertainties' that led to adoption of the continuous-trigger approach no longer exist.") (citation omitted); *Farmers Mut. Fire Ins. Co. of Salem v. New Jersey Property-Liability Ins. Guar. Assoc.*, 74 A.3d 860 (N.J. 2013) ("Insurance carriers have been on notice that in long-tail, continuous-trigger cases involving indivisible injury *Owens–Illinois* would not be the last word. As such, the application of the *Owens–Illinois* allocation scheme has been a work in progress from the very beginning.") (*see* Chapter 18; Allocation); *Potomac Ins. Co. of Illinois v. Pennsylvania Mfrs.' Ass'n Ins. Co.*, 73 A.3d 465 (N.J. 2013) (explaining *Owens-Illinois* and operation of continuous trigger); *Castoro & Co. v. Hartford Accident & Indem. Co.*, No. 14-1305, 2016 U.S. Dist. LEXIS 134686 (D.N.J. Sept. 29, 2016) ("In its reply, Plaintiff argues that test borings of the site 'demonstrat[ed] differing debris at differing locations horizontally and vertically,' and 'at varying depths.' Again, however, Plaintiff does not argue or allege that the contamination itself could be separated into distinct injuries. . . . Thus, Plaintiff concedes that the *damage* is indivisible, and alleges only that each *input* is distinct and divisible. The continuous-trigger theory, therefore, applies."); *Mid-Monmouth Realty Assocs. v. Metallurgical Indus.*, No. A-0237-14T2, 2017 N.J. Super. Unpub. LEXIS 993 (N.J. Super. Ct. App. Div. Apr. 21, 2017) ("In environmental contamination cases, the initial discharge of contaminants is an occurrence that triggers coverage. There is no need to determine precisely when the groundwater became contaminated because, as our Supreme Court stated, '[w]e prefer to adopt a rule that takes into consideration the impossibility under certain circumstances of establishing exactly when the groundwater contamination began[.]'") (quoting *Quincy Mutual*) (holding that property damage took place during each policy period between 1971 and 1986 where first discharge of contaminants into the ground began in 1967); *Cooper Indus., LLC v. Emplrs. Ins. of Wausau*, No. L-9284-11, 2017 N.J. Super. Unpub. LEXIS 3239 (N.J. Super. Ct. App. Div. Oct. 16, 2017) ("The Glen Ridge Plant ceased operating in 1910, and Cooper's predecessor sold the West Orange Plant in 1960. The Contaminants for which Cooper may be held responsible are alleged to have remained present at the Lower Passaic since that time. As the Policies cover a period from February 28, 1959 to March 1, 1986; each Policy terms therefore appears to be triggered here."); *Mid-Monmouth Realty Assoc. v. Metallurgical Industries*, A-0237-14T2, 2017 N.J. Super. Unpub. LEXIS 993 (N.J. Super. Ct. App. Div. April 21, 2017) (policies issued between 1971 and 1986 triggered, based on continuous trigger, when wastewater was disposed since 1967 and waste materials, contaminated with heavy metals and other chemicals, as early as 1981).

New Mexico: A New Mexico District Court rejected the application of a continuous trigger for damages caused when the roof of an underground cavern, caused by the insured's solution mining of salt, collapsed. *Mid-Continent Cas. Co. v. I&W, Inc.*, 86 F. Supp. 3d 1280 (D.N.M. 2015). "[T]he Court agrees with Plaintiff that the cases cited by Defendants [supporting a continuous trigger] are sufficiently distinguishable to foreclose reliance on those cases. For example, the property damage in *EnergyNorth* [*see* New Hampshire] involved the leaking of hazardous contaminants onto a site over time and the migration of those contaminants through the soil causing continuous injury to the property. The case at bar is not an environmental contamination case. Here, there is no evidence concerning exactly what damage took place during any policy period. Because Defendants in this case cannot establish when any such 'loss' occurred, the analytical framework of a 'continuous injury' theory is inappropriate, and there is no support for a finding that coverage is triggered across all the policies that were issued to I & W." *Id.* at 1290. *See also Leafland Group-II, Montgomery Towers Ltd. Partnership v. Ins. Co. of N. Am.*, 881 P.2d 26, 28–29 (N.M. 1994) (involving diminution in the value of an apartment building resulting from the presence of asbestos and holding that first-party insurer did not owe coverage because its policy was not triggered). The court reasoned that "the underlying problem causing the diminution in property value—the use of asbestos in constructing the buildings—was present long before [the insured] acquired the property. The presence of asbestos had, in effect, already diminished the value of the property before [the insured] purchased the property and bought insurance from [the insurer], even though the presence of asbestos remained undetected for some time after [the insured] bought the property. In other words, the diminution in property value was discovered, but not caused, during the time the policy was in effect. Because the claimed loss occurred prior to the time the insurance was purchased, 'the concept of risk that is inherent in all policies of insurance is lacking.'" *Id.* at 29 (citation omitted).

New York: The Second Circuit Court of Appeals held in *Stonewall Ins. Co. v. Asbestos Claims Mgmt. Corp.*, 73 F.3d 1178 (2d Cir. 1994) that "the medical evidence regarding the carcinogenic mechanisms of asbestos sufficiently establishes an insidious disease process involving billions of cellular mutations that constitute injuries. The jury could reasonably have concluded that these mutations occurred in a continuous sequence from initial exposure to the manifestation of the clinical diseases known as lung cancer and mesothelioma. Based on this evidence, the jury found that, for asbestos-induced cancer claims, CU's policies (the only ones at issue in the jury trial) are triggered from the date of first exposure to the date of death or claim, whichever is earlier. We will not disturb this finding." *Id.* at 1198-99. "[C]ontinual progression of a disease process into successive policy years is not excluded from the definition of 'bodily injury' contained in these policies, nor from the concept of 'injury-in-fact,' and the jury and the District Court were entitled to credit the testimony of NGC's experts regarding the timing and nature of the injuries involved in asbestosis and pleural plaques." *Id.* at 1998. *See also Cont'l Cas. Co. v. Employers Ins. Co. of Wausau*, 871 N.Y.S.2d 48, 62 (N.Y. App. Div. 2008) (noting that, in *Cont'l Cas. Co. v. Rapid-American Corp.*, 609 N.E.2d 506 (N.Y. 1993), the Court of Appeals of New York "declined to subscribe to an exposure theory … and instead appeared to approve of injury-in-fact as a trigger for coverage") (addressing asbestos bodily injury claims); *Viking Pump, Inc. v. Century Indem. Co.*, 2 A.3d 76, 110 (Del. Ch. Ct. 2009) (applying New York law) ("New York law … generally holds that an occurrence-based policy is triggered up on an 'injury-in-fact' to a tort plaintiff. In other words, where contract language … indicates that an 'occurrence' is 'injurious exposure to conditions, which results in personal injury,' then the injury-in-fact theory dictates that the plaintiff's exposure to asbestos attributable to the insured during the policy period triggers the policy. Indeed, the operative language of the … Policies basically tracks the injury-in-fact theory. New York courts have generally found that a plaintiff who proves that she suffered compensable damage as a result of asbestos exposure is injured during all periods of material exposure and therefore that any policy is triggered if it was in existence when the exposure occurred."), *aff'd in part and rev'd in part* 148 A.3d 633 (Del. 2016) ("We agree with Warren that the Superior Court's application of an 'exposure' trigger is inconsistent with New York law. We also reject the Excess Insurers' contention that Warren is essentially seeking a 'continuous trigger' as opposed to New York's operative injury-in-fact trigger. Plaintiffs did not rely on a presumption that asbestos-related injuries take place from exposure through manifestation. Rather, they presented to the jury expert medical testimony that the cellular and molecular damage that leads to asbestos-related disease is a continuous process that is triggered after there is an injury-in-fact, *i.e.*, the claimant's first significant exposure to asbestos."); *Fulton Boiler Works, Inc. v. American Motorists Ins. Co.*, 828 F. Supp. 2d 481 (N.D.N.Y. 2011) ("Generally, a comprehensive general liability policy is triggered by an injury-in-fact during the policy period. In other words, where the evidence establishes a progressive bodily disease [e.g. asbestosis, pleural plaques, or cancer], with injury-in-fact recurring throughout the disease process, all policies in effect at any time during that process are triggered. Indeed, New York recognizes that whenever the facts show injury during a relevant policy period, the policy applies, even though injury was also shown to have occurred in an earlier period covered by a prior policy.") (quotations and citations from *Stonewall Ins. Co. v. Asbestos Claims Mgmt. Corp.*, 73 F.3d 1178 (2d Cir. 1994) omitted); *Pac. Emplrs. Ins. Co. v. Troy Belting & Supply Co.*, No. 11-912,

2015 U.S, Dist. LEXIS 130681 (N.D.N.Y. Sept. 29, 2015) (accepting that date of first exposure to asbestos is the date that triggers coverage); *Mineweaser v. One Beacon Ins. Co.*, No. 14-0585A, 2018 U.S. Dist. LEXIS 91203 (W.D.N.Y. May 30, 2018) (applying injury-in-fact trigger and rejecting argument that plaintiffs' injuries "were not diagnosed and did not, therefore, accrue, during the policy periods"); *Danaher Corp. v. Travelers Indem. Co.*, 414 F. Supp. 3d 436 (S.D.N.Y. 2019) (declaring itself bound to follow *Stonewall*) ("[T]he Court holds that a triggering injury in fact for the Underlying Claims may be found as early as the time of first exposure to asbestos or silica, and may continue progressively through the claimant's death or the date of filing the claim, whichever occurs earlier."); *Carrier Corp. v. Allstate Ins. Co.*, 187 A.D.3d 1616 (N.Y. App. Div. Oct. 9, 2020) (noting that "the applicable test in determining what event constitutes personal injury sufficient to trigger coverage is injury-in-fact, 'which rests on when the injury, sickness, disease or disability actually began'") (finding a triable issue of fact as to whether asbestos-related injury began upon first exposure).

North Carolina: The North Carolina Court of Appeals held that an exposure trigger was appropriate in instances where it is difficult "to ascribe a 'date certain' or 'single event'" to the harm suffered. *Radiator Specialty Co. v. Arrowood Indem. Co.*, 850 S.E.2d 624 (N.C. Ct. App. 2020). The *Radiator* court noted that, pursuant to *Gaston County Dyeing Mach. Co. v. Northfield Ins. Co.*, 524 S.E.2d 558 (N.C. 2000), an injury-in-fact trigger of coverage would apply where "an injury-in-fact occurs on a date certain and all subsequent damages flow from the single event," but noted that *Imperial Cas. and Indem. Co. v. Radiator Specialty Co.*, 862 F. Supp. 1437 (E.D.N.C. 1994), *aff'd* 67 F.3d 534 (4th Cir. 1995) was more persuasive in the context of latent injuries. "*Imperial Casualty* is not binding upon this Court. And we acknowledge that *Gaston* is the law of North Carolina according to our Supreme Court. But *Gaston* concerned a very different set of facts — it dealt with liability resulting from a ruptured pressure vessel, a discrete event that occurred on a date certain. Injury resulting from benzene or asbestos exposure is neither discrete nor so certain. Reading the contract language and interpreting it by its terms, it seems clear that a 'bodily injury' is something caused by an 'occurrence,' which can include exposure. As such, we hold that the trial court's ruling, that coverage was triggered by exposure, was not inconsistent with the terms of the insurance policies. We, therefore, hold that the trial court did not err in applying an exposure theory of coverage instead of injury-in-fact." *See also Hutchinson v. Nationwide Mut. Fire Ins. Co.*, 594 S.E.2d 61 (N.C. Ct. App. 2004) and *Harleysville*

Mut. Ins. Co. v. Hartford Cas. Ins. Co., 90 F. Supp. 3d 526 (E.D.N.C. 2015) addressed in Chapter 17.

North Dakota: No instructive authority. For guidance, *see Grinnell Mut. Reinsurance Co. v. Thies*, 755 N.W.2d 852 (N.D. 2008) addressed in Chapter 17.

Ohio: An Ohio trial court held that a continuous trigger applied to claims for bodily injury caused by exposure to asbestos. *Owens-Corning Fiberglas Corp. v. Am. Centennial Ins. Co.*, 660 N.E.2d 770, 788 (Ohio Com. Pl. 1995) ("This court, therefore, is not concerned with the distinction that all persons exposed to asbestos do not experience malignant diseases as a result of such exposure. This information does not change the fact that in every instance of asbestos exposure there is immediate injury which continues, with some degree of severity, throughout a person's life."); *see also Goodyear Tire & Rubber Co. v. Aetna Cas. & Sur. Co.*, 769 N.E.2d 835, 841 (Ohio 2002) (discussing continuous trigger principles in the context of adopting an allocation methodology) ("When a continuous occurrence of environmental pollution triggers claims under multiple primary insurance policies, the insured is entitled to secure coverage from a single policy of its choice that covers 'all sums' incurred as damages 'during the policy period,' subject to that policy's limit of coverage."); *Lincoln Elec. Co. v. St. Paul Fire and Marine Ins. Co.*, 210 F.3d 672, 690, n.24 (6th Cir. 2000) (applying Ohio law) (adopting a "flexible continuing trigger," for purposes of asbestos bodily injury claims, which presumes a continuous trigger but allows evidence of injury-in-fact to rebut such presumption and constrict the trigger period); *Pennsylvania Gen. Ins. Co. v. Park-Ohio Indus.*, 930 N.E.2d 800, 808 (Ohio 2010) (discussing continuous trigger principles in the context of allocation) ("When loss or damage occurs over time and involves multiple insurance-policy periods and multiple insurers, a claim may be made by the targeted insurer against a nontargeted insurer with applicable insurance policies for contribution."); *William Powell Co. v. OneBeacon Ins. Co.*, No. C-130681, 2014 Ohio App. LEXIS 2959 (Ohio Ct. App. July 9, 2014) (discussing *Goodyear* and continuous trigger principles in the context of allocation) (*aff'd in part and rev'd in part* 75 N.E.3d 909 (Ohio Ct. App. 2016) but not addressing trigger); *Exel Direct, Inc. v. Nautilus Ins. Co.*, 314 F. Supp. 3d 885 (S.D. Ohio 2018) (rejecting insured's effort to apply a continuous trigger) ("Here, the claimed 'property damage' is the fire damage—not merely ongoing lint accumulation. In other words, had the underlying complaints asserted damage to the dryer, Nautilus may have been obligated to defend and indemnify as to the impairment of the dryer."); *Nat'l Sure. Corp. v. Bedivere Ins. Co.*, 17-3455, 2019 U.S. Dist. LEXIS 109386 (N.D. Ill. July 1, 2019) (concluding that an Ohio court would apply a continuous trigger theory to asbestos exposure because "the Ohio Supreme Court endorsed the reasoning of a continuous trigger without explicitly saying so in *Goodyear*" and "[s]ubsequent Ohio Court of Appeals decisions have interpreted *Goodyear* to endorse the continuous trigger theory in latent injury cases").

Oklahoma: No instructive authority. For guidance, *see* discussion in Chapter 17.

Oregon: The Supreme Court of Oregon held that an injury-in-fact trigger applied to claims for environmental property damage caused by the insured's wood-treatment operations. *St. Paul Fire & Marine Ins. Co., Inc. v. McCormick & Baxter Creosoting Co.*, 923 P.2d 1200, 1210 (Or. 1996). "The policies do not make coverage contingent on the time when the property damage was discovered or on the time when the insured's liability became fixed." *Id.* at 1211; *see also Sierra Pac. Inv. Co. v. Unigard Sec. Ins. Co.*, No. 03–366-AS (D. Or. Nov. 17, 2003) (addressing *McCormick & Baxter* in the context of claims for environmental property damage).

Pennsylvania: The Supreme Court of Pennsylvania held that a continuous trigger applied to claims for bodily injury caused by exposure to asbestos. *J.H. France Refractories Co. v. Allstate Ins. Co.*, 626 A.2d 502, 506 (Pa. 1993). The court held that "[t]he medical evidence in this case unequivocally establishes that injuries occur during the development of asbestosis immediately upon exposure, and that the injuries continue to occur even after exposure ends during the progression of the disease right up until the time that increasing incapacitation results in manifestation as a recognizable disease. If any of these phases of the pathogenesis occurs during the policy period, the insurer is obligated to indemnify [the insured] under the terms of the policy." *Id.* at 507. The court determined that all phases of the disease process independently meet the policy definition of "bodily injury." *Id.*; *see also Koppers Co., Inc. v. Aetna Cas. and Sur. Co.*, 98 F.3d 1440, 1445–46 (3rd Cir. 1996) (applying Pa. law) (not adopting a trigger theory but holding that a jury instruction that allowed for a continuous trigger, even if erroneous, was harmless error because the insured introduced uncontroverted evidence that the property damage (mostly groundwater contamination through leaching) was continuous, progressive, and indivisible throughout the relevant policy periods, as well as evidence that the causes of the contamination (e.g., leaks, drips, spills, or disposals) existed at each site during each policy period); *Titeflex Corp. v. National Union Fire Ins. Co. of Pittsburgh, PA*, 88 A.3d 970 (Pa. Super. Ct. 2014) ("Our Supreme Court has thus far adopted the 'multiple trigger' theory to determine the occurrence of injury for insurance coverage purposes only in cases involving toxic torts."); *General Refractories Co. v.*

First State Ins. Co., No. 04-3509, 2015 U.S. Dist. LEXIS 69727 (E.D. Pa. May 29, 2015) (declining to distinguish *J.H. France* on the basis that the policy there was triggered by "bodily injury" during the policy period and the policies here were triggered by "an accident or occurrence during the policy period.").

In *Pennsylvania National Ins. Co. v. St. John*, 106 A.3d 1 (Pa. 2014), the Pennsylvania Supreme Court discussed the scope of *J.H. France*: "[W]hile the multiple trigger theory of liability appropriated the reasonable expectations of the insured in *J.H. France* [asbestos], the circumstances of the damage to Appellants' dairy herd, coupled with the language of the Penn National policies does not warrant its application herein. Our holding in *J.H. France* remains an exception to the general rule under Pennsylvania jurisprudence that the first manifestation rule governs a trigger of coverage analysis for policies containing standard CGL language. We therefore find *J.H. France* distinguishable and decline to apply the multiple trigger theory of liability to determine coverage under the Penn National policies for the damages sustained by Appellants' dairy herd." *Id.* at 23. *See also Pa. Mfrs. Ass'n Ins. Co. v. Johnson Matthey, Inc.*, 160 A.3d 285 (Pa. Commw. 2017) (concluding that the court in *St. John* did not limit *J.H. France* to asbestos or bodily injury claims) ("Rather, the Court held that the justification for the multiple trigger of coverage was not the peculiar nature of asbestos disease, but the long latency of the claim for which coverage was sought.") ("Contrary to Insurer's characterizations, neither the Supreme Court's rejection of a multiple trigger of coverage in *St. John* nor the Court's reasoning in that opinion suggests that *J.H. France Refractories Co.* is inapplicable to property damage coverage for undetected environmental contamination."); *Armstrong World Indus. v. Ace Prop. & Cas. Co.*, No. CI-12-06271, 2020 Pa. Dist. & Cnty. Dec. LEXIS 1012 (Pa. C.C.P. (Lancaster Cty.) Mar. 9, 2020) ("Though deciding that case law in Pennsylvania recognizes a continuous trigger in environmental pollution cases, discovery may still reveal that the contamination did not occur prior to the policy periods of a defendant particularly given the disputed facts raised regarding OU-1. Accordingly, the court stops short of declaring which policies at issue have been triggered until discovery is complete."); *Rite Aid Corp. v. ACE Am. Ins. Co.*, No. 19-04-150, 2020 Del. Super. LEXIS 2797 (Del. Super. Ct. Sept. 22, 2020) (applying both Pennsylvania and Delaware's shared legal principles) (concluding that personal injury related to "opioid abuse and opioid used disorder would plainly fall into the category of a 'latent injury' because, similar to asbestosis or mesothelioma, 'such injuries may not manifest themselves until a considerable time after the initial exposure causing injury occurs'" and therefore, the application of a multiple trigger theory was appropriate) (*appeal granted* 2020 Del. LEXIS 435 (Del. Dec. 1, 2020)).

Rhode Island: The Supreme Court of Rhode Island held that a manifestation trigger applied to claims for property damage resulting from groundwater contamination at the insured's aerospace equipment manufacturing facility. *Textron, Inc. v. Aetna Cas. & Sur. Co.*, 754 A.2d 742, 746 (R.I. 2000). "Property damage triggers coverage under this type of comprehensive general-liability-insurance policy when the damage (1) manifests itself, (2) is discovered or, (3) in the exercise of reasonable diligence is discoverable." *Id.* "The third trigger of [this] test does not force a manufacturer to 'go around looking to find out if he's contaminating anything.' … it simply addresses the problem of latent injury (such as asbestos poisoning) or latent damage (such as groundwater contamination), when the injury or damage, although covered by the policy, is not immediately discernible or occurs after an unexpected event sets in motion a series of incidents that eventually results in the manifestation of the damage." *Id.* (citation omitted); *see also CPC Int'l, Inc., v. Northbrook Excess & Surplus Ins. Co.*, 668 A.2d 647, 649 (R.I. 1995) (same); *Truk-Away of R.I., Inc. v. Aetna Cas. & Sur. Co.*, 723 A.2d 309, 313 (R.I. 1999) (same); *Emhart Indus., Inc. v. Century Indem. Co.*, 559 F.3d 57, 79 (1st Cir. 2009) ("Even if this so-called 'considered dicta' supported the use of a 'continuous trigger' standard, Emhart would still have to distinguish *CPC*, which is the definitive ruling with respect to triggers of coverage for 'occurrence'-based policies."); *Textron-Wheatfield*, 754 A.2d at 745–46 (reiterating *CPC* discoverability standard); *Travelers Cas. & Sur. Co., Inc. v. Providence Washington Ins. Co., Inc.*, 685 F.3d 22 (1st Cir. 2012) ("It is not necessarily certain that the Rhode Island Supreme Court has put to rest the continuous trigger test in the environmental context. *See Textron–Gastonia*, 723 A.2d at 1141 ('Because we conclude that liability under the policy may be established by one of the recognized *CPC* tests, we need not address the continuous trigger-of-coverage standard.')"); *Textron, Inc. v. Travelers Cas. & Sur. Co.*, No. PB-2012-1371, 2017 R.I. Super. LEXIS 130 (R.I. Super. Ct. Aug. 10, 2017) ("As a last salvo, Travelers argues that this Court should apply the manifestation trigger-of coverage rule. [discussion of *CPC* omitted] However, even assuming arguendo that such a rule applied in this case, under the pleadings test, only a potential for coverage is required. As belabored above, nothing in the complaints in Exhibits 1 through 7 negates Travelers' duty to defend. The complaints contain factual allegations that potentially fall under Travelers' insurance policies; nothing more is needed to trigger the duty to defend.").

South Carolina: The Fourth Circuit Court of Appeals held that an injury-in-fact trigger applied to claims for property damage caused by the insured's leaking underground gasoline storage system. *Spartan Petroleum Co., Inc. v. Federated Mut. Ins. Co.*, 162 F.3d 805, 810–11 (4th Cir. 1998) (applying South Carolina law). "[T]he injury-in-fact trigger requires an insured to demonstrate that during the policy period an injury, caused by the underlying 'occurrence,' occurred to the property that is the subject of the underlying third-party action. Once an injury-in-fact has triggered coverage as to *that* property, coverage is triggered continuously thereafter to allow coverage under all policies in effect from the time of injury-in-fact during the progressive damage to that property." *Id.* at 811 (citation and internal quotes omitted) (emphasis in original); *State Nat'l Ins. Co. v. Eastwood Constr., LLC*, No. 16-2607, 2017 U.S. Dist. LEXIS 226348 (D.S.C. Apr. 18, 2017) ("In this case, the underlying complaint alleges that there has been significant damage due to water intrusion, but does not provide a date when the property damage began or whether it has ended. Therefore, it is plausible that State National may have a duty to defend because its coverage may be triggered under South Carolina's modified continuous trigger or North Carolina's continuous trigger."). For additional guidance, *see* discussion in Chapter 17.

South Dakota: No instructive authority. For guidance, *see* discussion in Chapter 17.

Tennessee: No instructive authority. *But see In re Edge*, 60 B.R. 690 (M.D. Tenn. 1986). The Bankruptcy Court for the Middle District of Tennessee addressed whether a claim against a debtor-dentist, for pre-petition malpractice, arose post-petition as the injuries were discovered at that time. *Id.* at 691. In reaching its decision, the court looked for guidance to cases addressing trigger of coverage for asbestos bodily injury. *Id.* at 700–02. The court was persuaded by the Sixth Circuit's decision in *Ins. Co. of N. Am v. Forty-Eight Insulations, Inc.*, 633 F.2d 1212 (6th Cir. 1980), adopting an exposure trigger. *Id.* at 700–01. "Though we are not here interpreting the language of a contract, the analysis in *Forty-Eight Insulations* is compelling: The policies that guide interpretation of the Bankruptcy Code are served by the conclusion that a claim arises at the time of the negligent act, notwithstanding that access to other courts or the running of a statute of limitation may be timed from some other point in the relationship between tortfeasor and victim. This same logic forms the Sixth Circuit's holding in *Forty-Eight Insulations*." *Id.* at 701.

Texas: In *Don's Bldg. Supply, Inc. v. OneBeacon Ins. Co.*, 267 S.W.3d 20 (Tex. 2008), discussed in Chapter 17, the Supreme Court of Texas adopted an actual injury or injury-in-fact trigger for purposes of construction defect claims. The nature of the court's opinion, however, suggests that it is likely to be closely examined by future courts addressing trigger of coverage for environmental claims. The *Don's Bldg.* Court also concluded: "[W]e stress that we do not attempt to fashion a universally applicable 'rule' for determining when an insurer's duty to defend a claim is triggered under an insurance policy, as such determinations should be driven by the contract language—language that obviously may vary from policy to policy." *Id.* at 30; *see also Allstate Ins. Co. v. Hunter*, 242 S.W.3d 137 (Tex. Ct. App. 2007) (noting that Texas courts have adopted various trigger theories for different types of claims).

Utah: A Utah District Court held that an injury-in-fact trigger applied to claims for environmental pollution caused by the insured's waste oil disposal. *Quaker State Minit-Lube, Inc. v. Fireman's Fund Ins. Co.*, 868 F. Supp. 1278, 1304 (D. Utah 1994). "Using an actual injury trigger, an 'occurrence' for purposes of CGL insurance policy coverage took place each time hazardous waste such as drain oil was discharged onto the Ekotek Site property and, by definition, inflicted 'property damage' at that site. … Where releases resulting in contamination are continuing, 'injuries-in-fact' triggering coverage are also continuing." *Id.* (citations omitted). However, the court also noted that the "manifestation" trigger "may provide a meaningful starting point in a case of hidden, gradual, and probably underground hazardous waste contamination," but the site at issue did not present such a case. *Id. See also One Beacon American Ins. Co. v. Huntsman Polymers Corp.*, 276 P.3d 1156 (Utah Ct. App. 2012) ("Although One Beacon presents *Sharon Steel Corp. v. Aetna Casualty & Surety Co.*, 931 P.2d 127 (Utah 1997), as 'neatly deal[ing] with the issue[ ]' of 'what coverage trigger is used in a continuous injury case,' it eventually clarifies that 'choice of a trigger theory was not an issue on appeal' in *Sharon Steel* because 'one of the insurers in that case[ ] settled the [coverage] issue with the insured using a continuous trigger analysis,' which the appellant did not contest. Thus, although *Sharon Steel* may be instructive on how to allocate defense and indemnity costs among multiple insurers, it is not helpful in determining whether Utah law favors application of the continuous trigger theory or the exposure trigger theory.") (concluding that Texas law applied).

Vermont: The Supreme Court of Vermont held that a continuous trigger applied to claims for environmental property damage caused by the depositing of debris from a waste hauling business. *Towns v. N. Sec. Ins. Co.*, 964 A.2d 1150, 1165 (Vt. 2008). The court observed that a condition of coverage was that it applied only to bodily injury or property damage "which occur[ed] during the policy period" and the policy contained no other conditions or language stating that such damage must also be discovered or manifested during the policy period. *Id.* at 1163. "[T]o [apply a manifestation trigger] would in effect transform the typically more expensive occurrence-based policy into a cheaper claims-made policy, a form of coverage specifically designed to limit the insurer's risk by restricting coverage to claims made during the policy period *'without regard to the timing of the damage or injury.'" Id.* at 1164 (emphasis in original and citation omitted). *See also Bradford Oil Co., Inc. v. Stonington Ins. Co.,* 54 A.3d 983 (Vt. 2011) (discussing *Towns* in the context of allocation) ("Under the continuous-trigger test, any insurance carrier who insured the risk during the period from the point the property was first exposed to the migration of hazardous chemicals into the soil and groundwater to the point where the migration ceased is liable in some amount. Thus, the injury is deemed to have 'occurred' at each and every point of time at which there was a contributing contamination.").

Virginia: No instructive authority. *See Morrow Corp. v. Harleysville Mut. Ins. Co.,* 110 F. Supp. 2d 441, 448 (E.D. Va. 2000) (recognizing that "[t]he Supreme Court of Virginia has not yet signaled which of these [trigger-of-coverage] approaches it will adopt, or, indeed, whether it will adopt some other approach to determining what triggers pollution coverage under occurrence-based CGL policies") (not selecting a trigger theory because the policy at issue specifically stated that it provided coverage for a "pollution occurrence at the time the property damage first manifests itself").

Washington: Trigger of coverage for latent injury claims has been limited to decisions from Washington District Courts. *See Skinner Corp. v. Fireman's Fund Ins. Co.,* No. C95–995WD, 1996 U.S. Dist. LEXIS 9321 (W.D. Wash. Apr. 3, 1996) ("Washington has adopted the 'continuous trigger rule' for insurance coverage in cases involving undiscovered, progressively worsening conditions causing injury or damage. Under the continuous trigger rule, every policy in force throughout the injury-causing process is triggered.") (involving claims for bodily injury caused by exposure to asbestos); *Weyerhaeuser Co. v. Fireman's Fund Ins. Co.,* No. C06–1189MJP, 2007 U.S. Dist. LEXIS 92521 (W.D. Wash. Dec. 17, 2007) ("Washington has adopted the continuous trigger rule for insurance coverage in cases involving undiscovered, progressively worsening conditions causing injury or damage.") (involving claims for bodily injury caused by exposure to asbestos); *Time Oil Co. v. Cigna Prop. & Cas. Ins. Co.,* 743 F. Supp. 1400, 1417 (W.D. Wash. 1990) (parties agreed that Washington has adopted a continuous trigger) (involving claims for contamination of groundwater); *Cadet Mfg. Co. v. American Ins. Co.,* No. C04–5411,

2006 U.S. Dist. LEXIS 51241 (W.D. Wash. July 26, 2006) (noting that Washington has adopted the continuous trigger or continuous damage trigger for determining insurance coverage for ongoing environmental contamination).

West Virginia: A West Virginia Circuit Court held that a continuous trigger applied to claims for property damage resulting from contamination of soil and groundwater arising out of the insured's operations. *Wheeling Pittsburgh Corp. v. Am. Ins. Co.*, No. 93-C-340 (W.Va. Cir. Ct. Oct. 18, 2003). "It is undisputed that the issue presented [to] the Court is one of first impression within this jurisdiction inasmuch as the West Virginia Supreme Court of Appeals has never addressed the issue of when insurance coverage is triggered within the context of environmental claims." The court went on to examine case law from other jurisdictions addressing trigger theories and ultimately adopted the continuous trigger. Applying a similar rationale as the Supreme Court of California in *Montrose Chem. Corp. v. Admiral Ins. Co.*, 913 P.2d 878 (Cal. 1995), the court concluded that "the present action involves allegations of a continuous, indivisible injurious process resulting from Wheeling Pittsburgh's operations and culminating in environmental property damage." *See also State Auto Pro. & Cas. Ins. Co. v. H.E.Neumann Co.*, No. 14-19679, 2016 U.S. Dist. LEXIS 130172 (S.D.W.V. Sept. 23, 2016) (following extensive analysis, court found that "in applying West Virginia substantive law—the manifestation theory is the appropriate approach for the timing-of-coverage issue relating to the latent-disease allegations in the Underlying Litigation. As such, Francis's 'bodily injury' [caused by workplace exposure to various chemicals] triggered coverage at the time his illness manifested.") (*vacated by* 2017 U.S. Dist. LEXIS 66099 (S.D.W.Va. Mar. 17, 2017) as a condition of the parties' settlement); *Westfield Ins. Co. v. Sistersville Tank Works, Inc.*, 484 F. Supp. 3d 283 (N.D.W.Va. 2020) (predicting that the Supreme Court of Appeals of West Virginia would apply a continuous or multiple trigger of coverage in the context of latent bodily injuries) (noting that there "does not appear to be any substantive state-level case law directly discussing trigger of coverage application in the context of latent bodily injuries arising from exposures to hazardous substances like those alleged in the pending state-court cases underlying this matter").

Wisconsin: The Court of Appeals of Wisconsin held that a continuous trigger applied to claims for environmental property damage caused by contamination at the insured's dump. *Society Ins. Co. v. Town of Franklin*, 607 N.W.2d 342, 348 (Wis. Ct. App. 2000) (citing *Wis. Elec. Power Co. v. Cal. Union Ins. Co.*, 419 N.W.2d 255 (Wis. Ct. App. 1987)). "[P]olicies in effect from the time the contamination began up until its remediation are all triggered." *Id.*; *see also Plastics Eng'g Co. v. Liberty Mut.*

Ins. Co., 759 N.W.2d 613, 623 (Wis. 2009) (acknowledging *Society's* holding that the continuous trigger theory applies in Wisconsin); *Westport Ins. Corp. v. Appleton Papers Inc.*, 787 N.W.2d 894, 917 (Wis. Ct. App. 2010) ("The jury found 'there was "property damage" under the policies occurring in the Lower Fox River and Green Bay' during each of the policy years. This finding meant that the Insurers' responsibility was continuously triggered in each year."); *W.D. Hoard & Sons Co. v. Scharine Group, Inc.*, 342 Wis.2d 249 (Wis. Ct. App. 2012) (acknowledging continuous trigger as the law but holding that it did not apply under the facts at issue) ("There was no manure in the basin, and thus no possible damage by manure seepage, until after the policy period had ended. Accordingly, Hoard presents no reason for why the continuous trigger theory creates coverage."); *Strauss v. Chubb Indem. Ins. Co.*, 771 F.3d 1026 (7th Cir. 2014) ("Because Wisconsin consistently bases its decisions regarding coverage disputes solely on the language contained in the policies, regardless of whether the disputed policy is for first-party or third-party liability, we consider the language of the policy in dispute rather than rely on a general theory that would apply regardless of policy language. We therefore review the Policy as it was written and in the context of current Wisconsin law, which does not require the application of any single trigger theory to first-party policies.") (addressing time of an occurrence under a first-party policy and holding that "given the Chubb Defendants' definition of 'occurrence,' which includes 'continuous or repeated exposure,' the parties 'contemplated a long-lasting occurrence' that could give rise to a loss 'over an extended period of time'").

Wyoming: No instructive authority.

CHAPTER
17

Trigger-of-Coverage for Construction Defects and Non-Latent Injury and Damage Claims

Claims for coverage for latent bodily injury and property damage caused by exposure to hazardous substances—most notably asbestos and hazardous waste—have been the subject of contentious litigation over the past three decades. In general, at the center of these disputes is the fact that such injuries often evolve slowly. It could be years between the time that a person is exposed to asbestos and a disease is diagnosed. Likewise, it could be a long time between a property's exposure to hazardous waste and the day that its damaged condition is discovered. In other words, the claim involves injury or damage that may have been taking place for years—before anyone knew it.

This scenario gave rise to questions whether such latent injury or damage satisfied the requirement of the insuring agreement for Part A of the commercial general liability policy that, while coverage is available for "bodily injury" and "property damage" (*see, e.g.,* INS. SERVS. OFFICE, INC., COMMERCIAL GENERAL LIABILITY COVERAGE FORM, No. CG 00010413, § I1a (2012)), such injury or damage must occur "during the policy period." ISO FORM, CG 00010413 at § I1b2. If so, coverage would be owed under multiple years of policies for latent injury and damage claims. In general, policyholders succeeded in this area by convincing courts to adopt one of several theories that allowed for the triggering of multiple years of coverage.

This issue—commonly referred to as "trigger of coverage"—is discussed in Chapter 16. Readers that are new to the trigger issue are recommended to review the introduction to Chapter 16 as the concepts discussed therein are the building blocks for this chapter.

Trigger of coverage disputes, however, are no longer limited to the asbestos and hazardous waste arenas. The adoption of various theories that obligated multiple years of policies to provide coverage for asbestos bodily injury and environmental property damage had an enormous impact on the amount of coverage available for such claims. So it should come as no surprise that efforts have been made by policyholders to apply these limits-increasing theories to claims outside the rubric of traditional toxic tort and hazardous waste. Most notably, policyholders have sought to apply the continuous or injury in fact trigger to the surfeit of construction defect claims. Just as they did with asbestos bodily injury and environmental property damage claims, insurers have been arguing for the adoption of the manifestation trigger.

While insurers fared poorly in their efforts to have courts apply a manifestation trigger to claims for asbestos bodily injury and environmental property damage, they have had a slightly better showing when the subject at hand has been construction defects. *See Korossy v. Sunrise Homes, Inc.*, 653 So. 2d 1215, 1226 (La. Ct. App. 1995) ("We find the manifestation theory should be applied in this case. The differential settlement resulted from each home's continuous or repeated exposure to the injurious conditions over a course of time, but the effects of the excessive settlement did not become 'damage' until it was discovered by the homeowners.").

But just as in the case of asbestos bodily injury and environmental property damage, the continuous and injury in fact triggers have enjoyed much success in coverage litigation for construction defects. *See Don's Bldg. Supply, Inc. v. OneBeacon Ins. Co.*, 267 S.W.3d 20, 24 (Tex. 2008). "[P]roperty damage occurred when a home that is the subject of an underlying suit suffered wood rot or other physical damage. The date that the physical damage is or could have been discovered is irrelevant under the policy." *Id.* "This policy links coverage to damage, not damage detection." *Id.* at 29. "The policy asks when damage happened, not whether it was manifest, patent, visible, apparent, obvious, perceptible, discovered, discoverable, capable of detection, or anything similar." *Id.* at 30; *see also Sentinel Ins. Co., Ltd. v. First Ins. Co. of Hawaii, Ltd.*, 875 P.2d 894, 917–18 (Hawaii 1994). "The injury-in-fact trigger is … true to the terms of the CGL policy and suitable for any type of injury." *Id.* at 917. The court concluded that all policies issued to a contractor, that were on the risk from shortly after completion of an apartment complex in 1981, to settlement of the underlying action in 1988, were potentially obligated to provide coverage. *Id.* at 918. The court also held that, if an insurer cannot establish with reasonable certainty which damages occurred during its policy period, then the continuous trigger would apply. *Id.*

In recent years, trigger of coverage disputes, especially in construction defect cases, have taken-on a new focus. In general, courts historically adopted the continuous trigger by concluding that the policy requirement, that *"bodily injury" or "property damage" must occur during the policy period*, is more open-ended than insurers had intended. Insurers intended by this requirement that "bodily injury" or "property damage" must be discovered or become evident during the policy period. Many courts, however, failed to see that qualification in the policy language. Dissatisfaction with such decisions caused insurers to take a different tack—adopting policy provisions that were designed to qualify and more specifically pin-point when "bodily injury" or "property damage" must take place for it to be covered. In essence, insurers have attempted to limit courts' discretion over trigger of coverage and take back control of the issue.

Insurers have used two principal methods in commercial general liability policies in an attempt to regain control in trigger disputes–Insurance Services Office's "Montrose Endorsement" and a variety of manuscript endorsements, in one form or another, that are generally referred to by such names as First Manifestation Endorsement, Claims in Progress Exclusion, Discovered Injury or Damage Exclusion or Prior Damages Exclusion (collectively "First Manifestation Endorsements").

The "Montrose Endorsement" is the insurance industry's response to its dissatisfaction with the Supreme Court of California's decision in *Montrose Chemical Corp. v. Admiral Ins. Co.*, 913 P.2d 878 (Cal. 1995). In a nutshell, *Montrose* permitted a party to purchase a liability insurance policy to cover property damage that the insured knew existed at the time of the purchase, so long as the insured's *liability* for such property damage was still contingent and not a certainty. Indeed, the Supreme Court of California seemed willing to go so far as to permit coverage under a policy purchased even *after* the insured was sued, so long as the insured's liability was in any degree contingent. *Id.* at 906. Not content with the *Montrose* Court's finding of coverage for what ISO considered to be known losses, the organization introduced an endorsement in 1999, followed by incorporation of the endorsement's language into the October 2001 edition of its CGL form (CG 00 01), that amended the policy's insuring agreement. The Montrose Endorsement does not eliminate the fundamental requirement of the Insuring Agreement that "bodily injury" or "property damage" must occur during the policy period. However, it qualifies that requirement by stating that, prior to the policy period, no insured knew that the "bodily injury" or "property damage" had occurred, in whole or in part. Further, if an insured knew, prior to the policy period, that the "bodily injury" or "property damage" had occurred, then any continuation, change or resumption of such "bodily injury" or "property damage," during or after the policy period, will be deemed to have been known prior to the policy period. In essence, by operation of these provisions, the policy on the risk at the time that the insured first obtains knowledge of "bodily injury" or "property damage" becomes the last policy that can be triggered. The Montrose Endorsement does not eliminate the continuous trigger by any means. It is still in play for all policies on the risk during the period of progressive "bodily injury" or "property damage" so long as the insured was not aware of it. But by addressing "known loss" as it does, the endorsement serves to establish an end-date to the continuous trigger for progressive injury or damage.

First Manifestation Endorsements vary in their language and scope, but are essentially designed to preclude coverage for "bodily injury" or "property damage" that took place before the policy period, *even if the insured did not know that injury or damage had taken place* and even if the injury or damage was continuous or progressive. In essence, coverage is limited to "bodily injury" or "property damage" that first takes place during the policy period. While the Montrose Endorsement similarly precludes coverage for "bodily injury" or "property damage" that took place prior to the policy period, the insured must have been aware of its existence for coverage to be denied. Precluding coverage for "bodily injury" or "property damage" that took place prior to the policy period, but was not known by the insured to exist, was not ISO's principal concern when drafting the Montrose Endorsement.[1] This may be why some insurers were not content with the Montrose Endorsement—seeing it as too limited in scope—and, instead, went out on their own and drafted broader First Manifestation and similar Endorsements.

In general, the fundamental purpose of these policy provisions is the same—tie trigger of coverage to something more specific than the unqualified requirement that "bodily injury" or "property damage" must occur during the policy period. This chapter does not address cases involving Montrose and First Manifestation Endorsements. First Manifestation Endorsements vary in their policy language and decisions addressing both types of endorsements are extremely fact-driven. Unlike cases that decide fundamental principles of coverage law, cases that address

---

1 "Introduction of Various New and Revised Commercial General Liability Endorsements," ISO Commercial General Liability Forms Filing GL-99-O99FO, at 3 ("From a coverage standpoint, there is a clear distinction between, on one hand, the injury or damage which has occurred and which, prior to the inception of the policy period, is known by the insured to have occurred, and, on the other hand, injury or damage which has yet to occur or which is occurring but is not yet known to the insured at the inception of the policy period. We have serious concerns with court decisions which have held an insurer responsible for defense and/or indemnity of an insured in cases where the insured knew, prior to the inception of the policy period, that injury or damage had occurred or had begun to take place.").

Montrose and First Manifestation Endorsements, because of their uniqueness, are more difficult to apply to future disputes.

In addition to construction defects, efforts have been made by policyholders, in a host of other claim scenarios, to obtain coverage under multiple policies on the basis that injury or damage was continuous. The issue also arises in the context of policyholders attempting to advocate for bodily injury or property damage taking place at a certain time—on account of a lack of coverage during the period when the insurer maintains that such injury or damage took place. As the following fifty-state survey of the issue demonstrates, the facts of these claims differ widely. For this reason there is no consensus that can describe the results of these efforts.

Chapter 16 addressed trigger of coverage for claims involving toxic torts and environmental property damage. This chapter addresses trigger of coverage for claims for (1) construction defects; (2) random scenarios in which efforts have been made by policyholders to establish that more than one general liability policy is obligated to provide coverage for ongoing, but unknown, bodily injury or property damage; and (3) bodily injury or property damage taking place at a time that the insurer maintains there was no policy in place. When reviewing this issue, reference should be made to Chapter 16 and the manner in which the relevant state responded to trigger arguments in the toxic tort and environmental property damage arenas. It is possible that the court, confronted with a trigger argument in a less traditional context, will look for guidance from traditional claims.

50-State Survey: Trigger of Coverage for Construction Defects and Non-Latent Injury and Damage Claims

Alabama: The Supreme Court of Alabama held that "as a general rule the time of an 'occurrence' of an accident within the meaning of an indemnity policy is not the time the wrongful act is committed but the time the complaining party was actually damaged." *Am. States Ins. Co. v. Martin*, 662 So. 2d 245, 250 (Ala. 1995) (citation and quotation omitted). The court concluded that mental anguish sustained by investors that lost money in a real estate business was not covered because such "bodily injury" was not experienced until after the policies expired. *Id.* The court observed that, under the terms of the policy, "an injury, and not an occurrence that causes injury, must fall within the policy period for it to be covered." *Id.* The court rejected the argument that the policies should be triggered because the incidents that led to the mental anguish occurred during the policy periods. *Id.; see also Assurance Co. of Am. v. Admiral Ins. Co.*, No. 10–0117, 2011 U.S. Dist. LEXIS 54498 (S.D. Ala. May 18,

2011) (applying rule from *Martin* to construction defect) ("Based on the evidence submitted by the parties, the court finds that Scottsdale has not met its summary judgment obligation on this issue. There are clearly questions of fact as to when Welch was actually damaged with respect to the defects listed in his complaint in the underlying lawsuit. As an example, there is a clear dispute as to when any actual damage from any settlement of the house occurred. There is also a dispute about when the water damage around the French doors was first manifested. According to Welch's 'rough guess,' it was between October 1998 and October 1999. On the other hand, one of the expert witnesses in the Welch lawsuit testified that, judging by the nature and extent of the damage, such damage must have begun to occur within one year of completion of the house. There are simply no definitive dates from which a conclusion about a date of occurrence can be drawn. For the remainder of the alleged defects, there is no evidence of record about any date of occurrence."); *Cincinnati Ins. Co. v. Amerisure Ins. Co.*, 11–0271, 2012 U.S. Dist. LEXIS 129953 (S.D. Ala. Sept. 12, 2012) (citing *Martin* and *Admiral*) ("Where, as here, faulty construction work results in gradual deterioration of the property, if an 'occurrence' were deemed to have happened the instant that deterioration began, then the occurrence would be the wrongful act itself, since the deterioration commenced immediately thereafter. So, through its extraordinarily expansive notion of when a complaining party is actually damaged, Cincinnati would have the manifestation rule collapse into a wrongful-act rule. There is no support in Alabama case law for usurping and undermining *Warwick* [446 So. 2d 1021 (Ala. 1984)] in this manner."); *Auto-Owners Ins. Co. v. Wier-Wright Enters.*, No. 15-1118, 2017 U.S. Dist. LEXIS 37477 (N.D. Ala. Mar. 16, 2017) ("[T]he damage to the Bells' home and personal property did not manifest until February of 2013, *after* the Wier-Wright policy expired. Thus, according to the *Cincinnati Insurance Co.* decision and the Alabama law upon which it is founded, the damage did not 'occur' until February of 2013, even though the root cause of the damage allegedly was faulty construction that was completed in 2011, and even though the Bells first noticed the roof leaks in 2011.") (emphasis in original) (addressing *Cincinnati v. Amerisure* in detail); *Evanston Ins. Co. v. J&J Cable Constr., LLC*, No. 15-506, 2016 U.S. Dist. LEXIS 129371 (M.D. Ala. Sept. 22, 2016) (addressing when bodily injury and property damage took place on account of sewage back-up into a home); *Essex Ins. Co. v. J & J Masonry LLC*, No. 14-2138, 2015 U.S. Dist. LEXIS 42336 (N.D. Ala. Apr. 1, 2015) (citing *Warwick* and describing Alabama as applying a "manifestation of damages rule for determining when an insurance policy's defense and coverage obligations are triggered.");

Barton v. Nationwide Mut. Fire Ins. Co., No. 17-618, 2020 U.S. Dist. LEXIS 25943 (N.D. Ala. Feb. 14, 2020) ("Alabama law is clear that, in determining the timing of an 'occurrence' for insurance coverage purposes, the relevant inquiry is when the property damage took place, not when the underlying work was performed.") (quoting *Cincinnati Insurance Co.); Owners Ins. Co. v. GTR, Inc.*, 461 F. Supp. 3d 1190 (M.D. Ala. 2020) ("[T]he policy issued to GTR clearly states that it only covers bodily injury or property damage that 'occurs during the policy period.' . . . Thus, the fact that GTR performed the repair work within the policy period is not dispositive as to whether the Goodens' alleged damages occurred within the policy period.") (citing *Martin*).

Alaska: The Supreme Court of Alaska held that no coverage was owed under a liability policy issued to a garage where such policy was no longer on the risk at the time that a truck—on which the garage had previously performed brake service—was involved in an accident that killed and injured several people. *Makarka v. Great Am. Ins. Co.*, 14 P.3d 964, 969 (Alaska 2000). The court noted that the policy limited coverage to bodily injury occurring during the policy period. *Id.* at 968. "This language cannot reasonably be read as a reference to negligent acts that predate the occurrence of injury." *Id.* Therefore, the policy on the risk at the time that the garage performed the faulty brake servicing was not obligated to provide coverage. *Id.* at 968–69.

Arizona: The Court of Appeals of Arizona held that, in the context of a construction defect claim, coverage is owed for ongoing property damage that occurs during the policy period even if other similar damage preceded that damage. *Lennar Corp. v. Auto-Owners Ins. Co.*, 151 P.3d 538, 549 (Ariz. Ct. App. 2007). At issue were policies on the risk *after* the property damage manifested. *Id.* at 548. The court rejected the insurers' argument that all of the property damage should be deemed to have occurred when the first property damage manifested itself. *Id.* at 548. The appeals court declined to address the insurers' "known loss" argument because, since the issue was not raised in the trial court, there were insufficient facts for the court to evaluate. *Id.* at 549; *see also Am. Family Mut. Ins. Co. v. Spectre West Builders Corp.*, No. CV09-968, 2011 U.S. Dist. LEXIS 11328 (D. Ariz. Feb. 4, 2011) ("The Court also finds sufficient evidence that the damage occurred during the policy periods. The nature of an occurrence policy is to provide coverage for all occurrences during a policy period, including incremental damage. *Lennar, 151 P.3d at 548–49.* Insurers must provide coverage for ongoing property damage. *Id.* American Family insured Spectre at various times from July of 1999 to September of 2008 under commercial general liability policies. Construction of the MVVs took place between 2004 and 2006. Spectre turned the condos over to the Association in May of 2006, and the Association instituted the Arbitration in May of 2008, after finding numerous defects. The Court finds sufficient evidence that ongoing and incremental property damage occurred during the policy periods, specifically at least the policies in effect from February 8, 2006 to April 8, 2006 and August 15, 2007 to August 15, 2008."); *Teufel v. Am. Family Mut. Ins. Co.*, No. 1 CA-CV 15-0736, 2017 Ariz. App. Unpub. LEXIS 558 (Ct. App. Ariz. May 9, 2017) ("Cetotor did not allege that the policy-period rockslides caused any physical damage, either abrupt or incremental, during the policy period. At most, the allegations of policy-period rockslides support an inference of faulty workmanship -- which, by itself, is not covered under the policy. According to Cetotor's amended complaint, the faulty workmanship did not result in property damage until after the policy's cancellation. Specifically, Cetotor alleged that a rockslide deposited rocks against the residence in November 2011 and August 2012. Because Cetotor's physical-damages claims were limited to post-policy-period events, the action did not implicate American's duty to defend under the Longlook Policy.") (*aff'd* and *rev'd* on other issues 419 P.3d 546 (Ariz. 2018)); *Nat'l Fire Ins. Co. v. James River Ins.*, 162 F. Supp. 3d 898 (D. Ariz. 2016) ("Arizona case law makes evident that an 'occurrence' is the point at which damage materialized. Therefore, under the Policy, the coverage was not triggered by the faulty work that Quik Flush performed between August 26, 2007, and May 30, 2007, when installation caused the 'dip in the pipe' that led to leaking Hydrogen Sulfide gas. Rather, the 'occurrence' is the point at which the *Knuth* tenants were injured or damaged. . . . Accordingly, the occurrence that triggered coverage was EJ's first encounter with Hydrogen Sulfide gas 'in early October 2007,' within the Policy's coverage period."); *757BD, LLC v. Nat'l Union Fire Ins. Co.*, 804 Fed. Appx. 592 (9th Cir. 2020) ("[E]ven if damages caused by the alleged misrepresentation and breach of fiduciary duty could somehow be construed as 'property damage,' that damage occurred before the policy's effective date and there is no coverage.").

Arkansas: An Arkansas District Court held that "[t]he generally accepted rule is that the time of the occurrence of an accident within the meaning of an indemnity policy is not the time when the wrongful act was committed, but the time when the complaining party was actually damaged. ... It is immaterial when the event which caused the injury took place; the deciding factor is when the injury occurred." *Valiant Ins. Co. v. Hamilton Funeral Serv. Ctrs.*, 926 F. Supp. 127, 129 (W.D. Ark. 1996) (citations omitted). Accordingly, no coverage was owed to a funeral home under a policy that was off the risk at the time that relatives discovered the condition of an exhumed body due to leakage of the casket and vault. *Id.*

California: The California Court of Appeal adopted a continuous trigger in the context of a construction defect claim. *Pepperell v. Scottsdale Ins. Co.*, 62 Cal. App. 4th 1045 (1998). Following a lengthy discussion of *Montrose Chemical Corp. v. Admiral Ins. Co.*, 913 P.2d 878 (Cal. 1995), the court held "in light of the terms of the standard occurrence-based CGL policy, the allegations of the Nila complaint regarding the construction defects and the continuing or progressive damage caused by those defects, the 'continuous injury' trigger of coverage must be applied as a matter of law." *Id.* at 1051. The court rejected Scottsdale's argument that there was no property damage during its policy period as the insurance contract ended on May 31, 1989 and the house did not leak until March 1991. "The argument rests on the invalid proposition that the damage must be *manifested* within the policy period. The *Montrose II* court definitively rejected that proposition." *Id.* at 1052 (emphasis in original). "Nila's complaint alleged defective design and construction involving virtually every part of the home-inter alia, a defective foundation which resulted in 'splitting and cracking of walls, floors, and ceilings throughout the Residence'; a defective landscaping and drainage system 'weakening and undermining … the support and foundation for the Residence, as well as leaking and moisture seepage'; a defective roof design and construction leading to numerous leaks throughout the home; defectively designed, constructed and installed retaining walls and backfill 'leading to loss of support and leaking of the Residence'; not to mention smaller details such as flashing, caulking, weatherproofing, window installation, painting and plastering. The complaint further alleged the latent and hidden defects 'were not discovered … until on or about March 8, 1991, when [they] began to manifest themselves to varying degrees.' The clear implication of the complaint is that there existed—at least *potentially*—a covered event, i.e., a continuing and progressively deteriorating process which began with defective design and construction admittedly *within* the pertinent policy period. That being the case, unless there are exculpatory facts, such as policy exclusions on the duty to defend or the ultimate issue of coverage, or meritorious affirmative defenses to coverage which might be available to the insurer (facts which do not affirmatively appear in the record before us), Scottsdale had a duty to defend Pepperell." *Id.* at 1054–55 (emphasis in original); *see also Acceptance Ins. Co. v. American Safety Risk Retention Group, Inc.*, No. 08cv1057, 2011 U.S. Dist. LEXIS 88101 (S.D. Cal. Aug. 9, 2011) (noting that, while *Pepperell* adopted a continuous trigger, the court concluded that it was a disputed issue of fact whether the property damage at issue was in fact continuous) ("While it is generally possible for property damage to be a later manifestation of damage which was already in the process of occurring, this is not necessarily so. Defendants have provided no evidence to show or even suggest that this was the case here. They base their argument on the general proposition that because some construction defects were present at the Project as of the policy inception dates, all of the subsequently manifested damage was already in the process of occurring as of the policy inception dates. This unsupported assertion is not sufficient."); *Grimsley v. Mid-Century Ins. Co.*, No. A126347, 2011 Cal. App. Unpub. LEXIS 875 (Cal. Ct. App. Feb. 2, 2011) (declining to apply the *Montrose* continuous trigger to an automobile accident—"a demonstrably single event or occurrence, with immediate manifest damages"); *Stonelight Tile, Inc. v. California Ins. Guarantee Assn.*, 150 Cal. App. 4th 19, 35 (2007) (discussing *Montrose* at length and holding that, because a tile manufacturer's injury from dust, emitted by a recycler, was continuous over multiple liability policy periods, all such policies were triggered, even though one insurer specifically covered the recycler's "tub grinding" which allegedly caused different type of damage by generating dust); *Garriott Crop Dusting Company v. Superior Court*, 270 Cal. Rptr. 678, 682 (Cal. Ct. App. 1990) (policy can be triggered even if the claimant did not yet own the damaged property during the policy period) ("Nowhere do the policies say to whom that property must belong, save that it must not belong to the insured. In other words, the policies themselves do not expressly require that the eventual claimant own the property at the time the property is damaged for coverage to ensue; they merely require that the damage, the 'physical injury to … tangible property,' take place during the policy period."); *Standard Fire Ins. Co. v. Spectrum Community Ass'n*, 46 Cal. Rptr.3d 804 (Cal. Ct. App. 2006) (following *Garriott*); *St. Paul Fire & Marine Ins. Co. v. Vadnais Corp.*, 582 Fed. Appx. 759 (9th Cir. 2014) ("Under the 'continuous injury' trigger of coverage, a duty to defend can arise based on allegations of defective construction and subsequent ongoing deterioration, even though damages are not manifested until years later, because there could potentially have existed a covered event during the policy period.") (citing *Pepperell*); *McCracken v. Arch Specialty Ins. Co.*, No. 14–03088, 2014 U.S. Dist. LEXIS 85285 (C.D. Cal. June 23, 2014) (citing *Pepperell* and holding that insurer's "reliance on the date that the Plaintiffs first noticed the water damage as the first instance of damage is misplaced."); *McMillin Management Services, L.P. v. Financial Pacific Ins. Co.*, No. D069814, 2017 Cal. App. LEXIS 1000 (Cal. Ct. App. Nov. 14, 2017) ("Coverage for property damage under an occurrence based CGL policy, such as the policies in this case, is deemed 'to occur over the entire process of the continuing injury,' and not simply when the damage is discovered or becomes manifest.") (citing *Pepperell*); *Pulte Home Corp. v. American Safety Indemnity Co.*, 14 Cal. App. 5th 1086 (2017) ("Where insuring agreements provide coverage for property damage occurring during the policy periods, a construction defect complaint alleging progressive damage gives rise to the potential that there existed—at least potentially—a covered event, i.e., a continuing and progressively deteriorating process which began with defective design and construction … within the pertinent policy period."); *First Mercury Ins. Co. v. Kinsale Ins. Co.*, No. 18-00071, 2018 U.S. Dist. LEXIS 142073 (N.D. Calif. Aug. 21, 2018) ("First Mercury's argument rests on the assumption that the Sluskys observed the paint discoloration at the same time when it first occurred. But there remains the possibility that the paint discoloration occurred earlier. As with 'improper piling of dirt against [a] building' that results in dry rot damage or a crack in a swimming pool that eventually leads to leakage, it is possible that here the occurrence of the paint damage began far earlier than when the Sluskys first observed it.") (citing *Pepperell*); *Interstate Fire & Cas. Ins. Co. v. First Specialty Ins. Co.*, 482 F. Supp. 3d 1060 (E.D. Calif. 2020) ("[T]he 'property damage' could theoretically occur during construction of the home, or after completion of the home but before close of escrow, or even after close of escrow.") (citing *Pepperell*).

Colorado: The Court of Appeals of Colorado rejected a manifestation trigger and adopted an exposure trigger in the context of a claim for corrosion of a roof constructed by the insured. *Am. Employer's Ins. Co. v. Pinkard Constr. Co.*, 806 P.2d 954, 956 (Colo. Ct. App. 1990). "Although predominantly applied in asbestos cases involving progressive bodily injury, the exposure theory has been applied to cases dealing with property damage of the continuous and progressive type." *Id.* "Here, the damage slowly progressed. And, although not immediately apparent, the evidence shows that progressive and continuous deterioration of the roof infected the integrity of the structure causing actual property damage during the respective policy periods." *Id.; see also American Family Mut. Ins. Co. v. Teamcorp., Inc.*, 659 F. Supp. 2d 1115, 1131-32 (D. Colo. 2009) (following *Pinkard*) ("In this case, however, the complaint does not specify when the property damage actually occurred or when the Hubbells were actually damaged by the Teamcorp Defendants' actions. … Further, the complaint can be construed to allege ongoing property damage. Once the infrastructure was sited incorrectly and the uninhabitable structure impeded the use of the lot for its intended purpose, those conditions continued to exist and had to be corrected."); *Hoang v. Assurance Co. of Am.*, 149 P.3d 798 (Colo. 2007) (following *Garriott, see* California).

Connecticut: The Supreme Court of Connecticut agreed with one insurer's argument that another insurer's policies were triggered based on property damage caused by "continuing and progressive water intrusion" that commenced after construction was completed. *Travelers Cas. and Sur. Co. of America v. Netherlands Ins. Co.*, 95 A.3d 1031 (Conn. 2014) ("We conclude that the underlying complaint alleges property damage that triggered Netherlands' duty to defend Lombardo. Netherlands' policies covered periods from August 31, 2000 until June 30, 2006. Although the construction of the law library was completed in 1996, the problems began in the 'months and years' that followed the state's occupancy on January 31, 1996, and the 'water intrusion proved to be continuing and progressive' into the 2000s, when the 'state retained forensic engineers to investigate the full extent and likely causes of the problem.' Thus, the property damage alleged in the underlying complaint—however broadly worded—extended into Netherlands' policy periods."). *See also R.T. Vanderbilt Co. v. Hartford Accident & Indem. Co.*, 156 A.3d 539 (Conn. Ct. App. 2017) ("The [*Netherlands*] court did not explain why it appeared to conflate two distinct trigger theories—injury-in-fact and continuous trigger—nor did it purport to adopt, or provide any rationale for adopting, one theory or the other as the law of Connecticut. Accordingly, we believe that the most reasonable interpretation of the *Netherlands* decision is that our Supreme Court merely (1) upheld the trial court's use of an injury-in-fact trigger theory as reasonable under the specific facts of that case and (2) recognized that the application of an injury-in-fact trigger by the trial court in Netherlands was not inconsistent with the application of a continuous trigger theory by the trial court in Security [*Ins. Co. of Hartford v. Lumbermens Mut. Cas. Co.*, 826 A.2d 107 (Conn. 2003)].") (appeal granted, 171 A.3d 63 (Conn. 2017)). The Connecticut Supreme Court affirmed, adopting the opinion of the appeals court. 216 A.3d 629, 637 (Conn. 2019). *See also Oliveira v. Safeco Ins. Co. of Am.*, No. 18-338, 2019 U.S. Dist. LEXIS 147256 (D. Conn. Aug. 29, 2019) ("But unlike cases involving gradual environmental contamination or gradual progression of a disease, coverage for defective concrete foundation cases is not triggered until there is a 'collapse'—that is, until the point when the structure of the home became substantially impaired.")

Delaware: A Delaware trial court held that an injury-in-fact trigger applied to a claim under a homeowners policy for progressive damage to an insured's home. *See Carlozzi v. Fid. & Cas. Co.*, No. 99C-03–083JRS, 2001 Del. Super. LEXIS 228 (Del. Sup. Ct. May 3, 2001). "Regardless of the cause of the water saturation, it is undisputed in the record that water saturation caused the foundation of the home to settle which resulted in damage to the home over an extended period of time. This extended period of time reached into the 1997 Policy period. Thus, the ongoing water damage was part of 'a series of related events ... [which] ... cause[d] ... property damage during the policy period ...' In other words, since progressive damage occurred during the 1997 Policy period, the 1997 Policy provides coverage unless the loss is otherwise excluded." (alteration in original). While *Carlozzi* involved coverage under a homeowner's policy, the policy language at issue, as well as the court's rationale for its decision, suggests that it would apply in the context of determining trigger of coverage for a construction defect claim under a general liability policy.

District of Columbia: The District of Columbia Court of Appeals held that a continuous trigger applied, in the context of a construction defect claim, where the damage could be characterized as being continuous or progressive. *Young Women's Christian Ass'n of the National Capital Area, Inc. v. Allstate Ins. Co. of Canada*, 275 F.3d 1145, 1150 (D.C. Cir. 2002). The court distinguished *Wrecking Corp. of Am. v. Ins. Co. of N. Am.*, 574 A.2d 1348 (D.C. Cir. 1990), which adopted a manifestation trigger, but also recognized an exception to this general rule when the damage to property can be characterized as continuous or progressive. *Id.* at 1154. "Unlike in *Wrecking*, in which there was no evidence that the property damage was of a 'continuous and progressive' nature, the evidence of Beer's negligence establishes that the corrosion caused by the exposure to excessive chloride ions was of a continuous and progressive nature. As such, this evidence suffices to bring the instant case within the exception recognized in *Wrecking*. Accordingly, as under Ontario law, District of Columbia law applies the continuous trigger where the damage is of a continuous nature. Furthermore, to the extent the language of the policies is ambiguous, District of Columbia law interprets ambiguities against the insurers." *Id. See also Hartford Financial Services Group, Inc. v. Hand*, 30 A.3d 180 (D.C. Cir. 2011) ("Issues about the time of loss or occurrence of loss are frequent topics of analysis in the insurance case law. In the context of insurance policies covering the risk of physical injury to property, the general rule is that a compensable injury occurs when actual damage to property is discovered by the insurance beneficiary.") (citing *Wrecking* and also noting that "a limited exception exists where the damage can be characterized as being continuous or progressive").

Florida: The Eleventh Circuit Court of Appeals rejected a manifestation trigger and adopted an injury-in-fact trigger for purposes of damage caused by construction defects. *Trizec Props., Inc. v. Biltmore Constr. Co.*, 767 F.2d 810, 813 (11th Cir. 1985) (applying Florida law). "It is the damage itself which must occur during the policy period for coverage to be effective. Here, the actual date that the damage occurred is not expressly alleged, but the language of the complaint, 'at least marginally and by reasonable implication,' could be construed to allege that the damage (cracking and leaking of roof deck with resultant rusting) may have begun to occur immediately after installation, 1971 to 1975, and continued gradually thereafter over a period of time." *Id.* (citation and quotation admitted). *But see Harris Specialty Chems., Inc. v. U.S. Fire Ins. Co.*, No. 3:98-CV-351-J-20B, 2000 U.S. Dist. LEXIS 22596 (M.D. Fla. July 7, 2000) (court applied a manifestation trigger to claims for discoloration of the exterior of buildings that took place about three to five years after a water sealant was applied); *Mid-Continent Cas. Co. v. Frank Casserino Construction, Inc.*, No. 6:09-cv-1065, 2010 U.S. Dist. LEXIS 59636 (M.D. Fla. June 16, 2010) (construction defect) ("In Florida … coverage under a CGL policy is triggered when property damage manifests itself, not when the negligent act or omission giving rise to the damage occurs.") (citing cases, including *Harris Specialty*, and noting that *Trizec* involved duty to defend and that the *Trizec* Court concluded that it did not need to address whether damage must manifest itself before coverage is triggered); *Arnett v. Mid-Continent Cas. Co.*, No. 08-2373, 2010 U.S. Dist. LEXIS 71666 (M.D. Fla. July 16, 2010) (addressing fact issues over the time that property damage caused by faulty construction manifested); *Mid-Continent Cas. Co. v. Siena Home Corp.*, No. 5:08–CV–385, 2011 U.S. Dist. LEXIS 79132 (M.D. Fla. July 8, 2011) ("[T]he 'manifestation' of the 'occurrence' of property damage, for purposes of determining coverage of the Mid–Continent policies in this case, is the time that such damage was discernable and reasonably discoverable either because it was open and obvious or upon a prudent engineering investigation, and not the time of actual discovery where the two circumstances come about in sequence at different times."); *Voeller Const., Inc. v. Southern-Owners Ins. Co.*, No. 13–3169, 2014 U.S. Dist. LEXIS 61862 (M.D. Fla. May 5, 2014) (noting that "Florida Supreme Court has yet to issue an opinion on which 'trigger of coverage' theory should apply under Florida law, and there is disagreement among the trial courts in Florida and district courts in the Middle District of Florida as to which theory governs") (choosing to follow *Trizec* and holding that, "because the allegations in the Association's complaint suggest that physical damage occurred at some point after the buildings were completed in 2007 and before KEG's inspection of the property in July 2010," policies during this period were triggered); *Trovillion Const. & Development, Inc. v. Mid-Continent Cas. Co.*, No. 12–914, 2014 U.S. Dist. LEXIS 6265 (M.D. Fla. Jan. 17, 2014) (discussing

Florida's trigger case law and following *Axis Surplus Ins. Co. v. Contravest Const. Co.*, 921 F. Supp. 2d 1338 (M.D. Fla. 2012) (and *Trizec*) which held that injury-in-fact trigger applies to occurrence policies); *St. Paul Fire & Marine Ins. Co. v. Cypress Fairway Condo. Ass'n*, 114 F. Supp. 3d 1231 (M.D. Fla. 2015) ("[T]here is some debate between the parties about which occurrence trigger theory, injury-in-fact or manifestation, is applicable. The Court is persuaded that the injury-in-fact rule is the appropriate trigger for coverage, thus the relevant question is whether there is record evidence that shows the damage occurred during the policy period."); *Carithers v. Mid-Continent Cas. Co.*, 782 F.3d 1240 (11th Cir. 2015) (agreeing with analysis in *Trizec* but limiting holding to the facts of this case and expressing "no opinion on what the trigger should be where it is difficult (or impossible) to determine when the property was damaged. We only hold that the district court did not err in applying the injury-in-fact trigger in this case."). In *N. River Ins. Co. v. Broward County Sheriff's Office*, 428 F. Supp. 2d 1284, 1290 (S.D. Fla. 2006), the court concluded that the policy on the risk at the time of arrest and incarceration—being when the underlying plaintiff was actually harmed—is triggered for purposes of malicious prosecution. *Id.* However, the court was clear in distinguishing its decision from *Trizec Prop.* on the basis of the different factual underpinnings: "[T]he multiple trigger theory has been adopted in very limited circumstances, such as asbestosis, where the injuries caused by exposure do not manifest themselves until a substantial time after the exposure causing the injury." *Id.* at 1291 (citation omitted); *BITCO Nat'l Ins. Co. v. Old Dominion Ins. Co.*, 379 F. Supp. 3d 1230 (N.D. Fla. 2019) (noting that, while the Florida Supreme Court has not addressed the trigger issue, the Eleventh Circuit has [*Trizec* and *Carithers*] and finding that injury-in-fact is the appropriate approach); *Southern-Owners Ins. Co. v. Wentworth Constr. Co., LLC*, No. 15-80789, 2019 U.S. Dist. LEXIS 229662 (S.D. Fla. Dec. 10, 2019) ("The underlying complaint is silent as to the timing or discovery of the damage. However, because it is undisputed that at least some stucco work transpired during the policy period, the Court is compelled to consider that the underlying complaint 'at least marginally and by reasonable implication,'. . . could be construed to allege that the damage . . . may have begun to occur immediately after installation."); *Auto-Owners Ins. Co. v. Envtl. House Wrap, Inc.*, No. 17-817, 2019 U.S. Dist. LEXIS 115898 (M.D. Fla. July 12, 2019) ("[I]n the absence of controlling (or persuasive) authority suggesting that the Court should apply the manifestation trigger (or some other test) to determine whether the alleged damages occurred during ongoing operations in the instant case, the Court will apply the injury-in-fact trigger.").

Georgia: A Georgia District Court held that a continuous trigger applied to claims against an exterminator for property damage caused by termites. *Arrow Exterminators, Inc. v. Zurich Am. Ins. Co.*, 136 F. Supp. 2d 1340, 1349 (N.D. Ga. 2001). By so concluding, policies off the risk before the damage was discovered were nonetheless obligated to provide coverage because the damage occurred before the policies expired. *Id. See also Ameristeel Corp. v. Employers Mut. Cas. Co.*, No. 96-85 HL, 2005 U.S. Dist. LEXIS 15715 (M.D. Ga. July 26, 2005) ("Although Georgia courts have not ruled on the question, federal district courts in all three of Georgia's districts have applied Georgia law to 'occurrence' policies with similar terms to hold that exposure during dates of coverage to conditions that result in property damage constitutes an 'occurrence' within the meaning of these insurance contracts.") (citations and quotation omitted); *Lee v. Universal Underwriters Ins. Co.*, 2014 U.S. Dist. LEXIS 192471, 12-3540 (N.D. Ga. June 25, 2014) ("The admission of liability included an admission that the dealership negligently repaired Darris Lee's Ford Expedition on June 1, 2005. The negligent repair of the vehicle is the occurrence. As a result of the negligent repair of the vehicle, the physical condition of the vehicle continually deteriorated causing the automobile crash on December 11, 2008. Therefore, the injuries to Darris Lee and Harold Brenner arose out of continuous or repeated exposure to substantially the same general conditions—the negligent repair of the vehicle and the resulting deterioration to the vehicle.") (*aff'd* 642 Fed. Appx. 969 (11th Cir. 2016)) ("Here, we thus construe the ambiguous policy language against Universal and conclude that the policy covered the 'occurrence' of the negligent repair that took place during the coverage period, even though the injury did not manifest until after the coverage period. We affirm the district court's grant of summary judgment to the Claimants.").

Hawaii: The Supreme Court of Hawaii held that an injury-in-fact trigger applied to a claim for property damage caused by construction defects. *Sentinel Ins. Co., Ltd. v. First Ins. Co. of Hawaii, Ltd.*, 875 P.2d 894, 917–18 (Hawaii 1994). "The injury-in-fact trigger is … true to the terms of the CGL policy and suitable for any type of injury." *Id.* at 917. The court concluded that all policies issued to a contractor, that were on the risk from shortly after completion of an apartment complex in 1981, to settlement of the underlying action in 1988, were potentially obligated to provide coverage. *Id.* at 918. The court also held that, if an insurer cannot establish with reasonable certainty which damages occurred during its policy period, then the continuous trigger would apply. *Id. See also C. Brewer and Co., Ltd. v. Industrial Indem. Co.*, No. 28958, 2013 Haw. App. LEXIS 472 (Hawaii Ct. App. Aug. 7, 2013) (addressing *Sentinel's* trigger analysis in detail and applying it to various fact-specific claim scenarios at issue). [As an aside, *C. Brewer* went to the Hawaii Supreme Court and the court interpreted a "Designated Premises Endorsement" to mean that, if the insured's headquarters are a designated premise, a policy provides coverage for injury or damage at a non-designated premise, if the negligent corporate decision, leading to the injury or damage, was made at the corporate headquarters. *See* 347 P.3d 163 (Hawaii 2015). In response to the decision, ISO announced in a September 26, 2016 Circular that it was making state filings to revise its Limitation of Coverage to Designated Premises or Project endorsements to attempt to preclude the rule adopted in *C. Brewer*. *See* ISO form CG 21 44 04 17.]

Idaho: The Supreme Court of Idaho held that, for purposes of various claims arising out of a wrongful conviction, the occurrence took place when the resulting injury first manifested itself, which was at the time of arrest, charging, or prosecution (depending on the claim). *Idaho Counties Risk Mgmt. Program Underwriters v. Northland Ins. Cos.*, 205 P.3d 1220, 1225–26 (Idaho 2009). Thus, no coverage was owed to a municipality under policies issued to it several years after these events took place. *Id.* at 1228. Notwithstanding that the underlying plaintiff alleged "continuing torts," the court observed that "[r]eliance on the commencement of the statute of limitation is not dispositive in determining when a tort occurs for insurance purposes. Statutes of limitation and triggering dates for insurance purposes serve distinct functions and reflect different policy concerns." *Id.* at 1226. While the court used the term "manifestation," at issue was the availability of coverage for injury that allegedly took place *after* such manifestation. *See also Bingham Mechanical, Inc. v. CNA Ins. Co.*, 2014 U.S. Dist. LEXIS 46028, 10-00342 (D. Idaho Mar. 31, 2014) (addressing the timing of property damage, in the context of construction defect coverage, but for purposes of addressing a "Known or Continuing Injury or Damage" endorsement).

Illinois: The Appellate Court of Illinois rejected a discovery trigger and adopted a continuous trigger for purposes of claims involving asbestos in buildings. *U.S. Gypsum Co. v. Admiral Ins. Co.*, 643 N.E.2d 1226, 1255–56 (Ill. App. Ct. 1994). "Our decision is consistent with the basic principles announced in *Zurich* [*Ins. Co. v. Raymark Indus., Inc.*, 514 N.E.2d 150 (Ill. 1987)] and *Wilkin* [*U.S. Fidelity & Guar. Co. v. Wilkin Insulation Co.*, 578 N.E.2d 926 (Ill. 1991)]. The supreme court's use of a triple trigger in *Zurich* recognizes that multiple policy periods can be triggered by the evolving nature of an illness resulting from the exposure to asbestos. Similarly, our application of a continuous trigger recognizes that the property damage that results from the release of asbestos fibers and the reentrainment of asbestos fibers is a continuing process which necessarily occurs over multiple policy periods. The *Zurich* decision looks beyond the discreet event of the manifestation of the disease as the sole trigger. Similarly, the seductive appeal of a single discovery trigger must bow to the policy language as well as to the empirical realities and other general equitable considerations of reasonableness and fairness." *Id.* at 1257. *See also Secura Ins. Co. v. Plumb*, No. 13-04054, 2014 U.S. Dist. LEXIS 125261 (C.D. Ill. Sept. 8, 2014) ("[T]he [*Zurich Insurance v. Raymark*] court noted that merely inhaling asbestos fibers injures lung tissue. The circumstances of this case are not analogous. Superior's policy defines 'property damage' in pertinent part as physical injury to tangible property. This definition provides no terminology that, as in *Zurich Insurance*, can be interpreted to mean that a preliminary vulnerable condition prior to actual breakdown suffices to constitute physical injury. Moreover, unlike asbestos, a defective foundation is not necessarily injurious immediately upon installation."); *Frankenmuth Mut. Ins. Co. v. Hodsco Construction, Inc.*, 191 F. Supp. 3d 863 (N.D. Ill. 2016) ("The complaint alleges that the Tower Crossing homes were constructed in 2002 and 2003, that the Policy Period ran until December 31, 2003, and that Hodsco's work was deficiently discharged in a manner that allowed water to fall inside the homes, plausibly from 2003 until its discovery in 2005. The complaint also states that the defects caused mold growth within the interior spaces of the homes. The Court finds that these allegations are sufficient to require Frankenmuth to defend Hodsco in the State Court Litigation, unless a policy exclusion applies."); *St. Paul Fire & Marine Ins. Co. v. City of Waukegan*, 82 N.E.3d 823 (Ill. Ct. App. 2017) (addressing trigger of coverage for a variety of claims arising out of a wrongful conviction, a subject which has been extensively litigated in Illinois); *TIG Ins. Co. v. City of Elkhart*, 122 F. Supp. 3d 795 (N.D. Ind. 2015) for a discussion of changes in Illinois law on the subject of trigger of coverage for claims arising out of wrongful conviction); *Sanders v. Ill. Union Ins. Co.*, 157 N.E.3d 463 (Ill. 2019) (coverage for an underlying malicious prosecution claim was triggered when wrongfully convicted individual was maliciously prosecuted) ("[W]e conclude that the word offense in the insurance policy refers to the wrongful conduct underlying the malicious prosecution. In so ruling, we consider both the meaning of the word offense and the contractual requirement that the offense must both happen and take place during the policy period. A malicious prosecution neither happens nor takes place upon exoneration.") ("Our focus remains on the provisions of this contract. Yet it has not escaped our notice that most courts that have considered this issue also have ruled that a malicious prosecution for insurance purposes occurs at the commencement of the prosecution.") (numerous Illinois citations omitted).

Indiana: An Indiana District Court held that property damage took place from the time that defective concrete was poured through the time at which a third party discovered or was notified of the damage to its property and had an opportunity to prevent further damage from the defective concrete. *Irving Materials, Inc. v. Zurich Am. Ins. Co.*, No. 03-361, 2007 U.S. Dist. LEXIS 98914 (S.D. Ind. Mar. 30, 2007). "[Insured's] expert determined that the distress produced by the alkali carbonate reactivity in the coarse aggregate provided … resulted in the property damage that occurred and was occurring during the September 1999 to September 2001 time period. This damage was not limited to the concrete itself but collaterally as well from the shoving, buckling, or crushing of adjacent materials, structures, and joints." *Id.* (citation omitted). *See also Grange Mut. Cas. Co. v. West Bend Mut. Ins. Co.*, 946 N.E.2d 593, 596 (Ind. Ct. App. 2011) ("[W]e agree that the time of the damage, as opposed to the time of the alleged negligent conduct that caused the damage, is the triggering event. We do not agree, however, that no damage occurred during West Bend's policy period to trigger coverage under its policy with McCurdy. Although the damages resulting from McCurdy's negligence became apparent only after they evolved over time, some damage clearly resulted when the drain pipe was fractured, which was within West Bend's policy period."); *TIG Ins. Co. v. City of Elkhart*, 122 F. Supp. 3d 795 (N.D. Ind. 2015) (holding that trigger of coverage, for malicious prosecution, is the date that a person was wrongfully charged) (court noted that it was "comfortable with this conclusion despite the existence of Indiana cases applying a multiple trigger approach in other contexts" and distinguishing malicious prosecution from asbestos bodily injury claims).

Iowa: An Iowa District Court applied an actual injury trigger in the context of claims for property damage caused by the insured's defective windows. *Liberty Mut. Ins. Co. v. Pella Corp.*, 631 F. Supp. 2d 1134, 1135 (S.D. Iowa 2009), *aff'd in part and rev'd in part on other grounds*, 650 F.3d 1161 (8th Cir. 2011). "Under Iowa law, property damage is deemed to occur at the time that the underlying claimant sustained or allegedly sustained any injury or damage. Successive policies may be triggered as long as the factual allegations contained in the underlying complaint permit a finding of continuing damage." *Id.* at 1134–35 (citation omitted); *see also Genesis Ins. Co. v. City of Council Bluffs*, 677 F.3d 806 (8th Cir. 2012) (noting that, even though the Iowa Supreme Court has not decided when, for insurance coverage purposes, the tort of malicious prosecution occurs, the majority rule nationally is that it occurs when the underlying criminal charges are filed and predicting that the Iowa Supreme Court would adopt this rule); *Chicago Ins. Co. v. City of Council Bluffs*, 713 F.3d 963 (8th Cir. 2013) (following *Genesis*); *Sickler v. Auto Owners Ins. Co.*, 871 N.W.2d 521 (Iowa. Ct. App. 2015) ("While the insured, Toad's Repair, negligently overhauled Sickler's truck engine while the Auto Owners policy was in force, Sickler did not incur property damage or loss of use of his property until the engine failure in December 2011, after the policy had expired. Because the Auto Owners policy explicitly required the damages to occur within the policy period, we find no coverage.") (citing decisions from other jurisdictions relied upon for support); *National Sur. Corp. v. Westlake Invs., LLC*, 872 N.W.2d 409 (Iowa Ct. App. 2015) ("The evidence is replete with testimony and exhibits regarding problems with the complex both during and after the policy period. Several experts emphasized that the winter 2003-2004 as the critical time period in which the damage was done, and that the damage at Westlake existed by June 30, 2004. In other words, problems surfaced before the sale closed in November 2003, but continued for years after that time because they were not properly fixed or prevented. . . . We conclude the evidence showed Westlake incurred property damage and loss of use continuously since the occurrence causing the damages. And although the water penetration was realized in some units and given some amount of attention during the policy period, it was not resolved.") (*aff'd on other grounds* 880 N.W.2d 724 (Iowa 2016)); *Van Der Weide v. Cincinnati Ins. Co.*, No. C14-4100, 2017 U.S. Dist. LEXIS 4469 (N.D. Iowa Jan. 12, 2017) ("[U]nder Iowa law both the date of the discovery of damage and the date of the negligent act giving rise to the damage are irrelevant when an occurrence policy is at issue. Instead, the relevant inquiry is whether damage was sustained during the policy period. Here . . . Cincinnati was put on notice, no later than May 5, 2014, of Van Der Weide's allegation the home started to sustain damage almost immediately after substantial completion, during the policy period. In other words, Cincinnati became aware, while the state court case was pending, of a potential 'occurrence' that would have triggered an obligation to indemnify Bouma.").

Kansas: No instructive authority.

Kentucky: A Kentucky District Court suggested that an actual injury trigger may apply in the context of coverage for a construction defect claim. *Generali U.S. Branch v. Nat'l Trust Ins. Co.*, No. 5:07-CV-139, 2009 U.S. Dist. LEXIS 76890 (W.D. Ky. Aug. 27, 2009). For purposes of allocation, the court observed that there was some evidence that damage to a house was "ongoing and continuous through several policy periods." While the court did not undertake allocation, it was because it was not convinced that the damage was not divisible or allocable between the policy periods. *See also Acuity Ins. Co. v. Higdon's Sheet Metal & Supply Co.*, No. 06-162-H, 2007 U.S. Dist. LEXIS 24997 (W.D. Ky. Apr. 3, 2007) ("Although some states have adopted a coverage trigger theory to establish the date of loss for determining when coverage is triggered … Kentucky has not done so. Instead, coverage is determined by examining the terms of the policies at issue."); *St. Paul Guardian Ins. Co. v. City of Newport*, 804 Fed. Appx. 379 (6th Cir. 2020) ("We take the policies at face value. They provide coverage for injury that 'happens while the agreement is in effect' and is 'caused by . . . [m]alicious prosecution.' As the district court noted, 'every day he spent in prison, Mr. Virgil suffered from injury; obviously, wrongful imprisonment and the resultant physical and dignitary harms that accompany such confinement represent[] a continuous and ongoing injury.' Those injuries were caused by the malicious prosecution and were continuous, that is, they happened repeatedly, during the relevant coverage period. We conclude that these injuries are covered by the policy language as that language would be used and understood by the common person, and at a minimum, we cannot say that these injuries are clearly *not* covered.") (emphasis in original).

Louisiana: The Court of Appeal of Louisiana held that a manifestation trigger applied to termite infestation because the effects of such infestation "did not become 'damage' until it was discovered by the homeowners." *James Pest Control, Inc. v. Scottsdale Ins. Co.*, 765 So. 2d 485, 491 (La. Ct. App. 2000) (following *Korossy v. Sunrise Homes, Inc.*, 653 So. 2d 1215 (La. Ct. App. 1995) which adopted a manifestation trigger for property damage caused by construction defect). "[T]he application of manifestation theory eliminates the difficult factual issue of determining when a hidden property damage actually occurs, a proof problem that is not as difficult in asbestos cases when the dates of injurious exposure to a substance can usually be determined." *Id.; see also Oxner v. Montgomery*, 794 So. 2d 86, 93 (La. Ct. App. 2001) (following *Korossy* and *James Pest Control* and holding that a manifestation trigger applied to property damage caused by construction defect); *Clarendon America Ins. Co. v. Southern States Plumbing, Inc.*, 830 F. Supp. 2d 544 (E.D. La. 2011) ("Louisiana courts apply the 'manifestation theory' to determine when property damage occurs."). *But see Mangerchine v. Reaves*, 63 So. 3d 1049, 1058 (La. Ct. App. 2011) ("A review of Louisiana jurisprudence involving third-party claims for construction defects under commercial general liability (CGL) policies shows that the manifestation theory is the most generally-accepted trigger theory for such claims. (citations omitted) But the issue is far from settled in Louisiana, and there is considerable inconsistency in the jurisprudence involving damage claims arising from construction defects under CGL policies. In short, the manifestation theory has not been uniformly adopted in such cases as a bright line rule."); *Eagle Pipe and Supply, Inc. v. Amerada Hess Corp.*, 79 So. 3d 246 (La. 2011) (noting that Louisiana cases "interpreting whether an 'occurrence' occurs during a policy period of insurance coverage have considered both the exposure theory and the manifestation theory"); *Colville Plumbing & Irr., Inc. v. Century Sur. Co.*, No. 12–1444, 2013 U.S. Dist. LEXIS 1665 (W.D. La. Jan. 3, 2013) ("While the Louisiana Supreme Court has not specifically adopted either theory in the context of construction defects [exposure or manifestation], the clear weight of authority in more recent cases considers defects in construction that result in damage subsequent to completion to be accidents and occurrences when they manifest themselves.") (citing cases); *Landry v. Williamson*, No. 2014 CA 12015, La. App. Unpub. LEXIS 213 (La. Ct. App. May 1, 2015) ("In the instant case, the Burkarts purchased the subject property on August 28, 2002, and moved into the home on September 5, 2002. Thereafter, the Burkarts first noticed water leaking into the home on September 26, 2002. The Burkarts did not become aware that the leaks, and subsequent damage, were the result of the absence of a secondary water barrier until 2004. It is undisputed that all of these events transpired *after* the Scottsdale policy expired on August 1, 2002. Accordingly, because the property damage did not manifest until after the expiration of Scottsdale's policy, the Burkarts' alleged property damage did not occur 'during the policy period.'") (emphasis in original) (citing numerous cases in support of Louisiana's adoption of a manifestation trigger for construction defect claims); *Mann v. Tim Clark Constr., LLC*, 273 So. 3d 397 (La. Ct. App. 2019) (rejecting exposure trigger and adopting manifestation trigger in the context of construction defect); *M&R Drywall, Inc. v. MAPP Constr., LLC*, 280 So. 3d 260 (La. Ct. App. 2019) (construction defect) ("[T]he clear weight of authority in more recent cases adopts the manifestation theory."); *Anderson v. Laborde Constr. Indus., LLC*, No. 2019 CA 0356, 2020 La. App. LEXIS 425 (La. Ct. App. March 12, 2020) ("In the case of third-party claims for construction defects under commercial general liability (CGL) policies, Louisiana courts have generally applied the manifestation trigger theory for such claims.").

Maine: A Maine District Court held that a manifestation trigger applied to damage to a large industrial paper dryer designed and built by the insured. *Honeycomb Sys., Inc. v. Admiral Ins. Co.*, 567 F. Supp. 1400, 1405 (D. Me. 1983). "The general rule is that an occurrence happens when the injurious effects of the occurrence become 'apparent,' or 'manifest themselves.'" *Id.* However, more recently, a Vermont

District Court, applying Maine law, held that Maine would adopt an injury-in-fact and continuous trigger standard to determine when property damage caused by construction defect occurred. *Travelers Indem. Co. v. Acadia Ins. Co.*, No. 1:08-CV-92, 2009 U.S. Dist. LEXIS 40252 (D. Vt. May 8, 2009). "[U]nder Maine law, coverage for progressive property damage is triggered under a standard occurrence-based CGL policy when property damage occurs (without regard to when it becomes manifest), and continuously thereafter while the damage is ongoing." The court distinguished *Honeycomb Systems* on the basis that, unlike construction defect, that case "did not present a factual situation in which property suffered an injury that went unnoticed until the injury progressed to an advanced stage over time." *See also Hawkesworth v. Nationwide Mut. Ins. Co.*, No. 2:10–232, 2011 U.S. Dist. LEXIS 66016 (D. Me. June 21, 2011) ("The record before the Court contains evidence that the infamous foyer leak was first repaired during the coverage period. The need for this 2002 repair work is in line with Haskell's expert testimony that the construction defects would have resulted in water penetration 'almost immediately.' In short, the Court is satisfied that Plaintiffs have met their burden of creating a triable issue of fact as to property damage during the coverage period.").

Maryland: No instructive authority.

Massachusetts: A Massachusetts trial court held that an injury-in-fact trigger applied to a claim against a gun manufacturer, whose employee stole handgun components, assembled the guns, and sold them on the black market, one of which ended up in the hands of a drug-dealer who used it to injure one person and kill another. *Hernandez v. Scottsdale Ins. Co.*, No. 050758D, 2009 Mass. Super. LEXIS 201 (Mass. Super. Ct. Aug. 6, 2009). After examining various trigger theories, the court held that "[i]n this case, a jury could find that the occurrence comprised a host of negligent acts taking place over the course of nine months. Yet the appropriate trigger of coverage in these circumstances is the injury-in-fact theory, which implicates only the policy period during which injuries or damages can be proven." Therefore, only the policy on the risk at the time that the underlying plaintiffs were shot was obligated to provide coverage. *See also Certain Interested Underwriters at Lloyds of London v. Boston Group Dev., Inc.*, No. 011885, 2002 Mass. Super. LEXIS 72 (Mass. Super. Ct. Feb. 26, 2002) (addressing differences in trigger of coverage between environmental and nonenvironmental claims) (*aff'd* 2003 Mass. App. LEXIS 1190 (Mass. Ct. App. Nov. 4, 2003)); *Sarsfield v. Great Am. Ins. Co. of N.Y.*, No. 07-11026, 2011 (D. Mass. June 3, 2011) (rejecting use of a continuous trigger in a wrongful imprisonment claim because its rationale is not well-suited to a situation where the injury is evident from the outset and first occurred prior to the inception of coverage); *Billings v. Commerce Ins. Co.*, 936 N.E.2d 408, 413 (Mass. 2010) ("We also reject Billings's suggestion that malicious prosecution be treated as a continuing tort for the duration of the underlying litigation, and that an 'occurrence' under the policy continues from the date the underlying malicious complaint was filed until the termination of that underlying litigation. A malicious prosecution is not a tort where it is difficult to ascertain when the injurious effects of the tortious conduct first become manifest; any reasonable person recognizes that the injury occurs on the filing."); *Creamer v. Arbella Insurance Group*, 120 N.E.3d 1239 (Mass. Ct. App. 2019) ("[T]he underlying complaint established that the release of the oil occurred during the sellers' ownership of the property. The 'property damage itself' thus occurred while the policy was in effect. This was sufficient to trigger coverage under the policy, regardless of whether the property damage was 'disclosed or manifested during the policy period.'").

Michigan: The Sixth Circuit Court of Appeals, applying Michigan law, adopted an injury-in-fact trigger for purposes of property damage caused by the insured's defective wood chips used at playgrounds. *Newby Intern., Inc. v. Nautilus Ins. Co.*, 112 Fed. App'x 397, 402 (6th Cir. 2004) (applying Michigan law). "Under the injury-in-fact approach, the operative date is the date upon which the wood chips supplied by PMI damaged the property of another, and not the date upon which the School District discovered the damage." *Id.* (relying on *Gelman Scis., Inc. v. Fid. & Cas. Co. of N.Y.*, 572 N.W.2d 617 (Mich. 1998), *overruled on other grounds by Wilkie v. Auto-Owners Ins. Co.*, 664 N.W.2d 776 (Mich. 2003)); *Les Stanford Cadillac, Inc. v. Cincinnati Ins. Co.*, No. 12-15630, 2015 U.S. Dist. LEXIS 40063 (E.D. Mich. Mar. 30, 2015) ("The terms of the CGL unambiguously provide coverage for property damage that occurs during the policy period, which was May 1, 2004, to May 1, 2007. Defendant claims the defects occurred in 2012, when Plaintiff first observed the defects. Plaintiff has provided a report from a Certified Special Inspector, Rochelle C. Jaffe, indicating that the defects existed from the time of installation, and a report from Fuller, the manufacturer of the adhesive used to install the tile, indicating that the cause of the defects was improper adhesive techniques and installation. Based on the information Plaintiff has provided, whether the damage occurred during the policy period is a genuine issue of material fact.") (*vacated on stipulation of the parties*, 2015 U.S. Dist. LEXIS 84428 (E.D. Mich. May 29, 2015)); *Zack v. Clock*, No. 343732, 2019 Mich. App. LEXIS 2939 (Mich. Ct. App. June 11, 2019) ("[T]he policy at issue clearly and unambiguously provides coverage only if it is caused by an occurrence that took place in the coverage territory *and* the bodily injury or property damage 'occurs during the policy period.'") (emphasis in original) ("Because plaintiffs did not learn that their son's ashes were not, in fact, buried until after the policy coverage had ended, they did not suffer their emotional, mental and physical injuries resulting from that negligent act until after the policy had terminated.").

Minnesota: The Supreme Court of Minnesota held that an "actual injury" or "injury-in-fact" trigger applied for purposes of damage caused by construction defects. *Wooddale Builders, Inc. v. Md. Cas. Co.*, 722 N.W.2d 283, 292 (Minn. 2006). "Under this rule, a liability policy is 'triggered' if the complaining party (here, the homeowner) is actually damaged during the policy period, regardless of when the underlying negligent act occurred. Thus, an insurer is on the risk with respect to a particular home if, during the period of one of its policies, there is property damage to that home—provided the damage results from a covered occurrence." *Id.* (citation omitted). *See also Donnelly Bros. Constr. Co., Inc. v. State Auto Prop. & Cas. Co.*, 759 N.W.2d 651, 656 (Minn. Ct. App. 2009) ("Minnesota applies an 'actual-injury' rule to determine whether insurance coverage has been triggered by an occurrence. To trigger a policy, the insured must show that some damage occurred during the policy period.") (citation and quotation omitted) (involving construction defects); *Tony Eiden Co. v. State Auto Property and Cas. Ins. Co.*, No. A07-2222, 2009 Minn. App. Unpub. LEXIS 149 (Minn. Ct. App. Jan. 26, 2009) ("In its detailed and comprehensive findings of fact, the district court found that property damage occurred when the house became affected by 'wood rot' and 'deterioration,' which the district court found was caused by 'repeated water intrusion and continued exposure to moisture and temperature conditions conducive to fungi growth.' The district court found that it is 'not possible to determine the extent of property damage occurring at any particular time, or in any particular year' but that 'it is more likely than not that th[e] rotting process began, at least to some degree, within the first year or two after construction.'"); *Sand Companies, Inc. v. Gorham Housing Partners III, LLP*, No. A10-113, 2010 Minn. App. Unpub. LEXIS 1212 (Minn. Ct. App. Dec. 21, 2010) (construction defect) (following *Wooddale Builders* and applying an "actual injury" trigger, such that a liability policy is triggered if the complaining party is actually damaged during the policy period, regardless of when the underlying negligent act occurred); *Diocese of Duluth v. Liberty Mutual Group*, 565 B.R. 914 (D. Minn. 2017) (addressing coverage for sexual abuse claims and examining Minnesota's adoption of the actual injury trigger in a host of claims contexts); *Thumper Pond Resort, LLC v. Stock Bldg. Supply Midwest, LLC*, No. A18-1935, 2019 Minn. App. Unpub. LEXIS

1136 (Minn. Ct. App. Dec. 9, 2019) (coverage for "property damage" caused by an "occurrence" during the policy period) ("'occurrence' within the meaning of an occurrence policy is not the time when the wrongful act was committed but the time when the complaining party was actually injured"). ("The occurrence-based CGL policy issued by Integrity to Gorski did not provide for limitless coverage, but rather for things amounting to an 'occurrence' during the policy period. The 2015 roof collapse occurred nearly ten years after the end of the policy period.").

Mississippi: A Mississippi District Court, after reviewing various trigger theories, predicted that the Supreme Court of Mississippi would apply the continuous trigger to a claim for construction defects. *Essex Ins. Co. v. Massey Land & Timber, LLC*, No. 04 -102, 2006 U.S. Dist. LEXIS 36748 (S.D. Miss. May 22, 2006). The court concluded that, notwithstanding that certain dirt work performed by the insured, at a residential subdivision, was completed in August or September 1999, a policy on the risk in December 2000, when damage was reported, was obligated to provide coverage. *See also Maxum Indem. Co. v. Wilson*, 707 F. Supp. 2d 683, 685 (S.D. Miss. 2010) ("There is neither allegation nor proof that the subject building sustained any tangible, physical injury during the policy period, and the loss for which Southern Specialty Foods demands recovery, and hence for which Wilson seeks indemnity, is the loss that was sustained when the subject building collapsed in 2008. Thus, since the only tangible, physical injury or loss of use of the building occurred when it collapsed, after ASIC's policy had expired, there is no coverage under the ASIC policy for the loss."); *Travelers Indem. Co. v. Forrest County*, 206 F. Supp. 3d 1216 (S.D. Miss. 2016) (addressing coverage for wrongful conviction) ("Mississippi does not apply a blanket rule that an injury or occurrence always happens at a specific point in time, such as manifestation. Rather, Mississippi law requires that the insurance policy be construed as written when plain and unambiguous, and that it be read 'most favorably' to the policyholder."); *Travelers Indem. Co. v. Mitchell*, 925 F.3d 236 (5th Cir. 2019) (addressing coverage for wrongful conviction and examining case law nationally) ("Travelers and Scottsdale ask us to hold that that insurance coverage be triggered by a single moment of wrongful conduct, or a single moment of injury—even when the policy's terms do not. If insurers want that result, they know how to bargain for it. Like the insurers in many of the cases cited by Travelers and Scottsdale, four insurers won summary judgments in this case because they wrote policies requiring that the wrongful act occur during the policy period.").

Missouri: The Supreme Court of Missouri held that an occurrence policy "covers cases of progressive injury where the cause of the damage is present during the policy period but the damage is not apparent until after the policy period." *D.R. Sherry Construction, Ltd. v. Am. Family Mut. Ins. Co.*, 316 S.W.3d 899, 905 (Mo. 2010) (coverage owed to a general contractor under a policy on the risk at the time of construction notwithstanding that foundation and drywall cracking did not manifest until after the policy period had expired). The insured-contractor succeeded in arguing that coverage was owed because "the damage began during the policy period and was progressive from that point forward. [The insured's] progressive damage theory was premised on allegations that unanticipated and repeated exposure to poor soil conditions under the house, beginning during the policy period, caused the house to settle out of level, which caused property damage to the house's foundation." *Id.* at 904–05. A Missouri District Court held that, for purposes of a claim for conspiracy to deprive a person of a fair trial, the triggering date for coverage is that on which the conspiring first took place. *Am. States Preferred Ins. Co. v. McKinley*, No. 07–0584CV, 2009 U.S. Dist. LEXIS 35784 (W.D. Mo. Apr. 28, 2009). The court based its decision on *Hampton v. Carter Enterprises, Inc.*, 238 S.W.3d 170 (Mo. Ct. App. 2007), where the Missouri Court of Appeals, while noting the continuing nature of conduct constituting malicious prosecution, concluded that the "triggering date for coverage should be limited to the date on which the party first continued the malicious prosecution." *Id.* (quoting *Hampton*, 238 S.W.3d at 177). "The *Hampton* court noted that the offense of malicious prosecution is committed with the institution of the underlying prosecution—the point at which the judicial process is maliciously invoked without probable cause, causing the victim's injury." *Id.*; *see also Owners Ins. Co. v. Warren Funeral Chapel, Inc.*, No. 2:10–cv–4182, 2011 U.S. Dist. LEXIS 71926 (W.D. Mo. July 5, 2011) ("Here, the only damages alleged in the *Johnson* action are the physical and emotional sickness caused by the realization that Johnson's decedent's body was mistreated. Such damages could not have occurred until Defendant Johnson was aware of the mistreatment of her decedent's body. It is uncontroverted that Johnson did not realize that her decedent's body had been mistreated before Board inspectors searched Warren Funeral Chapel on July 11, 2008. Based on the evidence submitted in this case, a reasonable juror could not conclude that any alleged emotional distress or sickness due to the Warren Defendants' violation of the right of sepulcher occurred before July 11, 2008."); *Kretsinger Real Estate Co. v. Amerisure Ins. Co.*, 498 S.W.3d 506 (Mo. Ct. App. 2016) (concluding that property damage took place when defective concrete was installed and not when crumbling, cracking and deterioration of a parking lot manifested itself); *Republic-Vanguard Ins.*

Co. v. Cent. State Holdings, LLC, No. 16-1616, 2018 U.S. Dist. LEXIS 221354 (E.D. Mo. Dec. 3, 2018) ("The parties' respective arguments as to whether the claimed damages, i.e. the fire damage, arose during the policy period hinge on whether or not the theory of 'progressive damage' applies to the facts here. Under Missouri law, 'occurrence-type' policies, like the Policy in this case, cover cases of progressive damage 'where the cause of the damage is present during the policy period but the damage is not apparent until after the policy period.' (*D.R. Sherry*). Progressive damage applies where loss begins during a policy period and continues until the damage is discovered.") (insufficient evidence to establish, as a matter of law, that fire damage was progressive); *Argonaut Great Cent. Ins. Co. v. Lincoln Cty.,* 952 F.3d 992 (8th Cir. 2020) (addressing timing issues for purposes of coverage for malicious prosecution-related claims).

Montana: The Supreme Court of Montana adopted an actual injury trigger for purposes of damage caused by construction defect. *Swank Enters., Inc. v. All Purpose Servs., Ltd.,* 154 P.3d 52, 56 (Mont. 2007). The court concluded that the improper application of paint to tanks at a water treatment plant constituted physical injury at the time of such application. *Id.* Accordingly, the policy on the risk at the time of application was triggered. In so holding, however, the court noted that "the fact that the discovery or diagnosis of the problem did not occur until after the 1997 policy period is of no consequence. A 'physical injury' can occur even though the injury is not 'diagnosable,' 'compensable,' or manifest during the policy period as long as it can be determined, even retroactively, that some injury did occur during the policy period." *Id.* (citing *In re Silicone Implant Litig.,* 667 N.W.2d 405, 415 (Minn. 2003)) (quotations omitted). *See also Truck Insurance Exchange v. O'Mailia,* 343 P.3d 1183 (Mont. 2015) ("[T]here is no evidence that physical injury—and thus property damage—was sustained during the policy period. Even if exposure to excessively high temperatures created a generally harmful condition during the policy period, the existence of that condition did not result in property damage occurring during the policy period, and thus did not constitute an 'occurrence' as defined by the policy."); *Northland Cas. Co. v. Mulroy,* 357 F. Supp. 3d 1045 (D. Mont. 2019) ("The use of untreated logs created the conditions for a later beetle infestation, but the complained-of damage did not occur until Mulroy had to remediate and/or replace portions of the structures.") (relying on *O'Mailia*) (*rev'd on other grounds,* 713 Fed. Appx. 713 (9th Cir. 2019)).

Nebraska: A Nebraska District Court rejected a manifestation trigger and adopted an injury-in-fact trigger for a claim under a first-party property policy for process liquid tanks that were damaged due to ongoing settlement of unstable soil beneath the tanks. *Kaapa Ethanol, L.L.C. v. Affiliated FM Ins., Co.*, No. 05-5010, 2008 U.S. Dist. LEXIS 61515 (D. Neb. July 29, 2008), *rev'd on other grounds*, 660 F.3d 299 (8th Cir. 2011) ("[T]he rule in the vast majority of the courts to have addressed the issue, is that coverage is triggered from the date of the first latent injury/damage and continues to be triggered at least until the date the injury/damage first becomes manifest. Since coverage is triggered in the event of an injury/damage during the policy period, the foregoing rule merely comports with the express terms of the policy. The same rule should be applied in interpreting similar policy language, whether the claim is for first party or third party coverage." *Id.* at *89. "[I]f faced with the question, Nebraska would adhere to the 'injury-in-fact' trigger and hold that in first party property insurance cases, coverage for property loss or damage that has progressed over time occurs when the damage commenced, not merely when it was discovered." *Id.* at *91.

Nevada: The Supreme Court of Nevada held that a manifestation trigger applied to a first-party property policy for purposes of cracks in the walls of a residence that occurred during several policy periods but were not discovered until a later policy was in effect. *Jackson v. State Farm Fire & Cas. Co.*, 835 P.2d 786, 789 (Nev. 1992). The court distinguished progressive property damage from asbestos cases and adopted the reasoning of *Prudential-LMI Com. Insurance v. Superior Court*, 798 P.2d 1230 (Cal. 1990) that, "[b]efore the manifestation, the loss is a mere contingency whereby the insured has not yet suffered a compensable loss." *Id.*; *see also United National Ins. Co. v. Frontier Ins. Co., Inc.*, 99 P.3d 1153, 1157 (Nev. 2004) (holding that policy on the risk at the time that a hotel marquee sign was negligently installed was not obligated to provide coverage for its collapse that occurred after the policy expired) ("[R]eading the word 'occurrence' and the phrase 'property damage' together, we conclude that the policy language is unambiguous and requires that tangible, physical injury must occur during the CGL policy period for coverage to be triggered under either prong of the definition."). In *Day Construction Co. v. Clarendon American Ins. Co.*, 459 F. Supp. 2d 1039, 1045–46 (D. Nev. 2006), the court noted that the Supreme Court of Nevada had never squarely addressed which trigger of coverage theory applied to liability policies. The court discussed *Jackson* and ultimately concluded that it need not predict which theory the Nevada high court might adopt because the policy at issue required "both the 'property damage' and an 'occurrence' giving rise to the property damage to occur within the Policy period. In addition, the Policy explicitly contracts out of the continuous exposure theory by way of the 'deemer' provision, wherein Clarendon avoids liability for property damage arising prior to the inception of, but continuing into, its Policy term." *Id.* at 1046. *See also National Fire & Marine*

Ins. Co. v. Redland Ins. Co., No. 13–00144, 2014 U.S. Dist. LEXIS 107382 (D. Nev. Aug. 5, 2014) ("[T]he timing of a construction defect does not necessarily correlate with the timing of the property damage. The construction defects, which must have existed at the time the projects were completed, ultimately gave rise to the property damage at issue in the Underlying Action. However, the fact that some residences were completed during the relevant policy periods is not sufficient to impose a duty to defend. Similarly, the fact that Southwest Carpentry may have constructed the residences negligently or in a defective manner during the relevant policy periods is not sufficient to impose a duty to defend. Rather, the duty to defend is only triggered when there is an 'occurrence' or a physical manifestation of 'property damage' during the relevant policy period.") ("[W]hether the property damage was in fact 'discovered' during or after Defendants' policy coverage periods is irrelevant at this juncture. Indeed, the date on which a homeowner discovers the damage does not necessarily correlate with the date on which the damage occurred. Under Defendants' policies, the duty to defend is triggered by the occurrence of property damage, not the discovery of property damage."); *Fed. Ins. Co. v. Coast Converters, Inc.*, 339 P.3d 1281 (Nev. 2014) (addressing first-party policy) ("In *Jackson v. State Farm Fire & Casualty Co.*, this court adopted the so-called 'manifestation rule.' Under the 'manifestation rule,' an insurer is only liable under an insurance policy if the policy was in effect when the loss became manifest. A loss becomes manifest at the 'point in time when appreciable damage occurs and is or should be known to the insured, such that a reasonable insured would be aware that his notification duty under the policy has been triggered.'").

New Hampshire: A New Hampshire District Court applied an injury-in-fact trigger to a claim for damages caused by the negligent construction of extraction and injection wells at a Superfund site. *MACTEC Eng'g & Consulting, Inc. v. OneBeacon Ins. Co.*, No. 06-466, 2007 U.S. Dist. LEXIS 58374 (D.N.H. Aug. 8, 2007) (citing *EnergyNorth Natural Gas, Inc. v. Underwriters at Lloyd's, London*, 150 N.H. 828, 836 (2004)). Nonetheless, the court concluded that only a single policy was triggered because it was the only one on the risk at the time that the property damage was occurring.

New Jersey: The Superior Court of New Jersey, Appellate Division, declined to automatically apply a continuous trigger to claims for damages caused by the incorporation of defective fire-retardant plywood into roofing systems of residential construction. *Aetna Cas. & Sur. Co. v. Ply Gem Indus., Inc.*, 778 A.2d 1132, 1146 (N.J. Super. Ct. App. Div. 2001). "[A]ll that is evident from the pleadings and documents in this record with respect to the Maryland complaints is that the FRTP which Hoover manufactured, and upon which these suits against Hoover are based, was installed within the policy periods and caused damage to other property at some point in time. There is no allegation as to when the property damage occurred and thus, no way to determine, without more, whether the allegations of property damage caused by the insured's product were covered claims because they occurred during the policy periods." *Id.* "At least in the absence of more proofs, we reject the theory that the 'continuous trigger' or 'progressive damage' theory requires us to conclude there was 'property damage' upon installation." *Id.*; *see also Crivelli v. Selective Ins. Co. of Am.*, No. 4358–02, 2005 N.J. Super. Unpub. LEXIS 703 (N.J. Super. Ct. App. Div. Sept. 27, 2005) (holding that no coverage was owed under a policy on the risk after negligent installation of a roof because there was no evidence of ongoing or progressive injury or damage commencing at the time of installation); *Langan Engineering and Environmental Services, Inc. v. Greenwich Ins. Co.*, No. 07-2983, 2008 U.S. Dist. LEXIS 99614 (D.N.J. Dec. 8, 2008) (concluding that continuous trigger is limited to asbestos, toxic torts and environmental contamination and holding that policy on the risk prior to a wall collapse was not triggered, even though complaint alleged that "property damage, consisting of the continuous movement, deterioration, increasing cracks, and developing bulges in the wall, was apparent … years before the collapse of the wall."); *Selective Way Ins. Co. v. Arthur J. Ogren, Inc.*, 2010 N.J. Super. Unpub. LEXIS 2979 (N.J. Super. Ct. App. Div. Dec. 13, 2010) (not deciding if the continuous trigger applied to a construction defect claim because, even if it did, no coverage would be owed under a policy that was issued two years after property damage manifested) (applying *Polarome's* conclusion that the "last pull of the trigger" is manifestation) (*see* New Jersey, Chapter 16); *Memorial Properties, LLC v. Zurich American Ins. Co.*, 46 A.3d 525 (N.J. 2012) ("[T]he actual damage to the party asserting the claim, not the wrongful act that precipitated that damage, triggers the 'occurrence.'") ("[T]he 'occurrence' relating to the New Jersey and New York plaintiffs' causes of action took place when they learned of the harvesting of their decedents' body parts in 2006, not in 2003 when that harvesting took place."); *Gutierrez v. Travelers Property and Cas. Co. of America, Inc.*, 2013 N.J. Super. Unpub. LEXIS 277 (N.J. Super. Ct. App. Div. Feb. 6, 2013) ("[T]he actual, cognizable damage to plaintiffs' property occurred after the renovations were completed and the 'severe cracking, shifting and other major deficiencies began to develop.' Because the 'occurrence' here was well after April 1, 2002, there was no covered property loss during the policy period."); *Air Master & Cooling, Inc. v. Selective Ins.*

Co. of Am., 171 A.3d 214 (N.J. Super. Ct. App. Div. 2017) (adopting continuous trigger for purposes of construction defect and concluding that the "last pull" of the continuous trigger is the time of "essential" manifestation of injury) ("In the present insurance context involving the 'essential' manifestation of an injury, we regard the term to connote the revelation of the inherent nature and scope of that injury. On one end of the spectrum, manifestation cannot be merely tentative. . . . Nor must the manifestation be definitive or comprehensive. . . The critical term 'essential,' as used in this coverage context, should be understood and applied consistent with such concepts."); *Travelers Lloyds Ins. Co. v. Rigid Global Bldgs., LLC*, No. 18-5814, 2020 U.S. Dist. LEXIS 25759 (D.N.J. Feb. 13, 2020) ("Applying that reasoning here [of *Air Master & Cooling*], the Court is satisfied that Rigid is not entitled to coverage under a continuous trigger theory. '[P]roperty damage must, in fact, occur before an insurer's liability on a CGL policy can be invoked under the 'continuous trigger' theory.' Here, all of the damages attributed to Rigid in the Grand Slam Action relate to the 2014 partial roof collapse. Indeed, Grand Slam offered absolutely no proofs of damages from 2009 to 2011—the Travelers Policy Periods.") ("Moreover, even if the Court accepts that the 2009-2011 leaks were an occurrence that started the continuous trigger, the analysis does not end there. The next step [is] to determine what damage occurred during each of the triggered policy periods in order to calculate the extent of each policy's exposure. The wholesale lack of any damages from the Travelers Policy Periods defeats Grand Slam's arguments for coverage. Said differently, the fact that no damages can even be allocated to the Travelers Policy Periods demonstrates that there is no basis for coverage.").

New Mexico: No instructive authority.

New York: The Supreme Court of New York, Appellate Division, held that an insurer that issued a policy that was on the risk on the date that a criminal prosecution was terminated in favor of the accused was not obligated to provide coverage for a malicious prosecution claim. *Newfane v. General Star Nat. Ins. Co.*, 784 N.Y.S.2d 787, 791 (N.Y. App. Div. 2004). The court held that malicious prosecution was deemed to have occurred on the date that the criminal prosecution was instituted without probable cause (here, more than a decade before the relevant policy was issued). *Id.* at 793; *see also MRI Broadway Rental, Inc. v. U.S. Mineral Products Co.*, 704 N.E.2d 550, 553 (N.Y. 1998) (characterizing its decision in *Sturges Mfg. Co. v. Utica Mut. Ins. Co.*, 332 N.E.2d 319 (N.Y. 1975) as adopting the installation date as the time of injury-in-fact when a defective component product is integrated into a larger product) (defective ski straps used in the manufacture of ski bindings); *Maryland Cas. Co. v. W.R. Grace and Co.*, 23 F.3d 617, 627 (2nd Cir. 1993) (applying New

York law) (applying the injury-in-fact trigger from *Cont'l Cas. Co. v. Rapid-American Corp.*, 609 N.E.2d 506 (N.Y. 1993) and holding that claims for asbestos in buildings trigger the policy on the risk at the time of installation of asbestos—regardless of whether it had been discovered by the building owner); *Maxum Indem. Co. v. A One Testing Labs., Inc.*, 150 F. Supp. 3d 278 (S.D.N.Y. 2015) ("When faulty workmanship in building materials is the gravamen of an allegation of property damage, under an injury-in-fact analysis, the injury may be said to occur at the time of installation.") ("Unlike a gas leak or a progressive disease, A-1's alleged failure to properly inspect B&V's work and recognize its deficiency is not a continuous occurrence creating new injuries in fact at different points in time. Instead, the damage, if any, was sustained at the time of A-1's alleged breach. In light of the 'injury-in-fact' rule in New York law and the explicit provisions of the insurance contract that established when certain property damage could be said to occur, it is apparent that even if the allegations in the UAC were otherwise covered they would fall outside of the policy period."); *Welliver McGuire, Inc. v. Ace Am. Ins. Co.*, No. 17-06040, 2019 U.S. Dist. LEXIS 159047 (W.D.N.Y. Sept. 16, 2019) (discussing *A One Testing* and insured's inability to prove that property damage occurred during the policy period).

North Carolina: The Supreme Court of North Carolina held that "where the date of the injury-in-fact can be known with certainty, the insurance policy or policies on the risk on that date are triggered." *Gaston County Dyeing Mach. Co. v. Northfield Ins. Co.*, 524 S.E.2d 558, 564 (N.C. 2000) (overruling *W. Am. Ins. Co. v. Tufco Flooring East, Inc.*, 409 S.E.2d 692 (N.C. Ct. App. 1991) to the extent that it purported to establish a bright-line rule that property damage occurs "for insurance purposes" at the time of manifestation or on the date of discovery). The court specifically declined to adopt the "continuous" or "multiple trigger" theory and concluded that, notwithstanding that the rupture of a pressure vessel caused ensuing property damage that continued over time, contaminating multiple dye lots and extending over two policy periods, because the injury-in-fact occurred on a date certain, only the policies on the risk on the date of the injury-causing event were triggered. *Id.* at 565; *see also Hutchinson v. Nationwide Mut. Fire Ins. Co.*, 594 S.E.2d 61, 64 (N.C. Ct. App. 2004) ("Assuming *arguendo* that the damage was caused by the continual entry of water, if it can be determined with certainty that the entry of water was caused by faulty construction pre-dating insurance coverage, defendants are not liable for plaintiffs' damages."); *Alliance Mut. Ins. Co. v. Guilford Ins. Co.*, 711 S.E.2d 207, *4 (N.C. Ct. App. 2011) (table) ("[T]he PEX water supply line was improperly installed in 2004, and this improper installation ultimately caused the leak which caused the property damage. However, this is not a case of a continual leak which began in 2004 and was not discovered until December 2006; the leak began in 2006. The 'property damage' thus did not occur, or begin to occur, until December 2006. Therefore, no portion of the property damage caused by the leak 'occur[ed] during the policy period' as required by Defendant's policy which had ended on 21 February 2005.") (discussing *Hutchinson*); *Builders Mut. Ins. Co. v. Mitchell*, 709 S.E.2d 528 (N.C. Ct. App. 2011) (examining whether the facts alleged permitted a determination to be made, pursuant to *Gaston County's* "known with certainty" standard, when water damage to a defectively built home took place); *Erie Ins. Exchange v. Builders Mut. Ins. Co.*, 742 S.E.2d 803 (N.C. App. 2013) (lengthy discussion of trigger of coverage under North Carolina law reflecting its complexity and fact-based nature) (distinguishing cases "in which property damage occurred over an extended period of time, although the condition causing such damage was not discovered until after substantial property damage had already occurred") ("[I]n the present case, according to the allegations of the Hardison Action complaint, TPD Builder and its subcontractors negligently altered the slope and constructed an inadequate retaining wall, and this faulty construction ultimately caused the slope collapse that resulted in the property damage to the Hardisons' property. Nonetheless, all property damage alleged in the Hardison Action relates to the single occurrence of the slope collapse that occurred during defendant's policy period."); *Harleysville Mut. Ins. Co. v. Hartford Cas. Ins. Co.*, 90 F. Supp. 3d 526 (E.D.N.C. 2015) (lengthy discussion of trigger of coverage under North Carolina law reflecting its complexity and fact-based nature) ("Applying the reasoning of *Gaston* to the contrasting circumstances of the present case leads to the conclusion the court has adopted here. When, as in this case, the alleged accidents that cause the injuries-in-fact occur on dates that are not certain, there are possible multiple occurrences. Thus, all policies on the risk on the possible dates of those injury-causing events are triggered. Such an approach remains consistent with *Gaston* because it still look[s] to the cause of the property damage, e.g., the dates the roofs failed and water intruded, rather than the ultimate 'effect' of such water intrusion, e.g., manifestation of rotten structural elements or mold. The key difference leading to a multiple trigger of coverage rather than single trigger of coverage, is that the dates of the injuries-in-fact are inherently uncertain and cannot be established as a single trigger of coverage.") (holding that, under the "multiple trigger of coverage test," "each of the insurance companies in the present action had a duty to defend and share equally in defense costs in the underlying lawsuits, where their policies were in effect within the time frame between the date any building allegedly first was completed through the date of the lawsuits"); *State Nat'l Ins. Co. v. Eastwood Constr., LLC*, No. 16-2607, 2017 U.S. Dist. LEXIS 226348 (D.S.C. April 18, 2017) ("The court agrees with the *Hartford* [*Harleysville v. Hartford*] court's analysis. Thus, the court finds that, where the initial date of property damage is not known, as in this case, the North Carolina Supreme Court would likely apply a continuous trigger and all policies in effect from the date of the event causing the property damage until the damage ceases will be triggered.").

North Dakota: The Supreme Court of North Dakota held that the liability policy on the risk at the time that the complaining party was "actually damaged" is obligated to provide coverage. *Grinnell Mut. Reinsurance Co. v. Thies*, 755 N.W.2d 852, 859 (N.D. 2008). The court concluded that homeowner's (liability) policies issued to the seller of a home were not obligated to provide coverage for a claim brought by the purchaser for mold damage that had existed prior to the sale but was not discovered until after the sale and the seller's policies had expired. *Id.* at 854. The policy's definition of "occurrence" required "property damage" "during the policy period." *Id.* at 856. The court concluded that such language supported a conclusion that the occurrence happened when the complaining party was actually damaged, rather than when any mold may have accumulated. *Id.* at 859. The *Grinnell* Court followed its decision in *Friendship Homes, Inc. v. Am. States Ins. Cos.*, 450 N.W.2d 778 (N.D. 1990), which held that, in the context of a third-party claim, policy language that requires damage to "occur during the policy period" means when the complaining party was actually injured. *Id.* at 859 (citing *Friendship Homes* at 779–80).

Ohio: The Court of Appeals of Ohio held that a continuous trigger applied to property damage caused by construction defect. *Westfield Ins. Co. v. Milwaukee Ins. Co.*, No. CA2004–12–298, 2005 Ohio App. LEXIS 4255 (Ohio Ct. App. Sept. 12, 2005). "[T]here is no requirement that the damage 'manifest' itself during the policy period. Rather, it is the damage itself which must occur during the policy period for coverage to be effective." *Id.* (citation and quotation omitted); *accord Plum v. W. Am. Ins. Co.*, No. C-050115, 2006 Ohio App. LEXIS 387 (Ohio Ct. App. Feb. 3, 2006). However, in *Fidelity & Guaranty Ins. Underwriters, Inc. v. Nationwide Tanks, Inc.*, No. C-1–03–843, 2006 U.S. Dist. LEXIS 9854 (S.D. Ohio Feb. 22, 2006), the court declined to apply a continuous trigger to damage caused when an above-ground storage tank ruptured. "While damage to the tank itself from corrosion may have occurred continuously, including during the policy period, the injuries … alleged in the underlying case did not involve long-term exposure or delayed manifestation injuries. The injuries here occurred in one fell swoop, well outside the policy period, when the tank burst on March 3, 2000." *See also Lightening Rod Mut. Ins. Co. v. Southworth*, 55 N.E.3d 1174 (Ohio Ct. App. 2016) (addressing trigger of coverage in the context of a Montrose endorsement, but citing *Westfield* and *Plum* for the proposition that the continuous trigger applies to trigger coverage issued prior to the date of discovery or manifestation of the property damage) (*appeal accepted*, 67 N.E.3d 823 (Ohio 2017) and *dismissed as having been improvidently accepted*, 86 N.E.3d 274 (Ohio 2017), with a dissenting opinion addressing trigger); *Exel Direct, Inc. v. Nautilus Ins. Co.*, 314 F. Supp. 3d 885 (S.D. Ohio 2018) ("[T]his case is not analogous to cases (citations omitted) in which courts have concluded that property damage occurring after a coverage period elapsed was covered because it was the consequence of ongoing and continuous property damage that occurred during an initial negligent act within the policy period. In each of those cases, the relevant damage inarguably occurred within the policy period, even though it may have manifested later. *See, e.g., Plum v. W. Am. Ins. Co.* . . . . Here, the claimed 'property damage' is the fire damage—not merely ongoing lint accumulation. In other words, had the underlying complaints asserted damage to the dryer, Nautilus may have been obligated to defend and indemnify as to the impairment of the dryer. But they did not, so coverage under the policy was not implicated.").

Oklahoma: No instructive authority. *See Bituminous Cas. Corp. v. Cowen Constr., Inc.*, 55 P.3d 1030, 1032 (Okla. 2002) (concluding that there was no need to reach a certified question that sought the appropriate trigger of coverage for claims against a contractor, for negligent construction of a venting system in a dialysis unit of a hospital, that caused lead poisoning of patients); *see also Ball v. Wilshire Ins. Co.*, 184 P.3d 463, 465 n.8 (Okla. 2007) (recognizing that, in *Cowen*, the Supreme Court of Oklahoma declined to answer one of two certified questions where response to one disposed of the case).

Oregon: The Supreme Court of Oregon relied on *St. Paul Fire v. McCormick & Baxter Creosoting*, 923 P.2d 1200 (1996) (addressing trigger of coverage for environmental property damage (see Chapter 16)) to address coverage for construction defects. *FountainCourt Homeowners' Association v. FountainCourt Development*, 380 P.3d 916 (Or. 2016). "AFM does not seriously dispute that there was proof that *some* property damage did occur during the time its policies were in effect. Indeed, both parties provided expert opinion that supported that conclusion. Rather, AFM's position has been that, because FountainCourt had the burden of demonstrating an 'occurrence' during the policy period, it necessarily was required to demonstrate the amount of damage that occurred during the policy period. That position is inconsistent with our holding in *St. Paul Fire*, and it appears to be at odds with the provision in the policies indicating that property damage not known to the insured prior to the policy period '*includes any continuation*, change or resumption of that 'bodily injury' or 'property damage' *after the end of the policy period.*' In sum, no genuine issue of material fact needed to be resolved at the garnishment proceeding concerning whether at least some property damage occurred when the AFM policies were in effect. The court correctly rejected, as a matter of law, AFM's arguments that FountainCourt was required to prove the precise amount of damages that occurred during the policy period in order to demonstrate that there had been an 'occurrence' that triggered coverage under the policies." *Id.* at 929. An Oregon District Court held that an injury-in-fact trigger applied to property damage caused by construction defect. *MW Builders, Inc. v. Safeco Ins. Co. of Am.*, No. CV 02–1578, 2009 U.S. Dist. LEXIS 35487 (D. Or. Jan. 28, 2009). "Based on the uncontroverted evidence in the record, the court finds that the property damage to the Hotel began after its substantial completion in June 1997, and continued through 2000. ... Oregon law finds coverage under a CGL policy for property damage that occurs during a policy period. Accordingly, coverage under each ... policy in effect from June 1997, until September 2000, has been triggered." *See also California Ins. Co. v. Stimson Lumber Co.*, No. 01–514, 2004 U.S. Dist. LEXIS 10098 (D. Or. May 26, 2004) (applying injury-in-fact trigger in the context of claims for property damage caused by the insured's defective siding); *Shilo Inn v. Maryland Cas. Co.*, 404 Fed. Appx. 230 (9th Cir. 2010) (applying Oregon law) ("Shilo's reliance on *St. Paul* [*Fire & Marine Ins. Co., Inc. v. McCormick & Baxter Creosoting Co.*, 923 P.2d 1200 (Or. 1996)] (*see* Chapter 16) is misplaced. In *St. Paul*, the Oregon Supreme Court held that coverage is triggered by the occurrence of property damage, defined here as physical injury to tangible property, even if the damage is not discovered until later. ... *St. Paul* did not hold that mere installation of a defective product, without resulting physical injury to property during the policy period, triggers coverage."); *Frost v. Northern Ins. Co. of N.Y.*, No. 09-1276, 2011 U.S. Dist. LEXIS 16898 (D. Or. Feb. 17, 2011) ("[P]laintiff seeks recovery of damages awarded for the resulting water damages and water intrusion, not for damages to the waterproof membrane. Regardless of the alleged damage to the deck topping, no facts presented by plaintiff suggest that the resulting property damage of water intrusion and water damage occurred within the policy period ending on November 13, 2004—particularly when it is undisputed that plaintiff observed no water intrusion until late 2005. I would have to assume, based on speculative probability, that such damage occurred within one week after West Coast's faulty workmanship. The court cannot take such a leap."); *Charter Oak Fire Ins. Co. v. Interstate Mechanical, Inc.*, 958 F. Supp. 2d 1188 (D. Or. 2013) ("Courts in Oregon construe nearly identical language in CGL policies to require that actual injury must occur during the policy period in order to trigger a policy's coverage. Under this so-called 'actual injury' theory of triggering insurance coverage, coverage exists under every policy that was in effect during the time periods in which *damage to property actually occurred*, even if the damage was discovered long after it began.") (citations and internal quotes omitted) (emphasis in original) (*vacated on stipulation of the parties*, 2014 U.S. Dist. LEXIS 183970 (D. Or. Jan. 6, 2014)).

Pennsylvania: The Superior Court of Pennsylvania adopted a manifestation trigger for purposes of a medical malpractice claim. *D'Auria v. Zurich Ins. Co.*, 507 A.2d 857, 862 (Pa. Super. Ct. 1986) (holding that the policy on the risk at the time that renal failure manifested was triggered and not policies on the risk while the patient was negligently treated by the physician); *see also Peerless Ins. Co. v. Brooks Sys. Corp.*, 617 F. Supp. 2d 348, 357–58 (E.D. Pa. 2008) (following *D'Auria* and predicting that the Supreme Court of Pennsylvania would adopt a manifestation trigger for purposes of a construction defect claim); *Consulting Eng'rs, Inc. v. Ins. Co. of N. Am.*, 710 A.2d 82, 88 (Pa. Super. Ct. 1998) (adopting a manifestation trigger for purposes of Wrongful Use of Civil Proceedings). "Here, we are not faced with a situation where the injuries, occasioned by the tort, lay dormant for extended periods. When the allegedly wrongful suit is filed, the injuries caused by the tort- humiliation, damage to reputation, suspense, physical hardship and legal expenses- manifest themselves and become evident to a reasonable defendant and, by implication, to the initiator of the wrongful proceedings." *Id.* at 87–88; *Coregis Ins. Co. v. City of Harrisburg*, No. 1:03-CV-920, 2006 U.S. Dist. LEXIS 20340 (M.D. Pa. Mar. 30, 2006) (following *Consulting Engineers* and adopting a manifestation trigger for purposes of malicious prosecution); *Sapa Extrusions, Inc. v. Liberty Mut. Ins. Co.*, No. 13–2827, 2014 U.S. Dist. LEXIS 109221 (M.D. Pa. Aug. 7, 2014) ("Pennsylvania has generally adopted a manifest trigger when dealing with damages that spring from a singular event. Under that theory, an injury 'occurs' when damages stemming from the negligent act first manifest in a way that would put a reasonable person on notice of such an injury."); *Titeflex Corp. v. National Union Fire Ins. Co. of Pittsburgh, PA*, 88 A.3d 970 (Pa. Super. Ct. 2014) ("Our Supreme Court has thus far adopted the 'multiple trigger' theory to determine the occurrence of injury for insurance coverage purposes only in cases involving toxic torts."). That Pennsylvania applies a manifestation trigger, outside the context of asbestos bodily injury, was made clear in *Pennsylvania National Ins. Co. v. St. John*, 106 A.3d 1 (Pa. 2014): "[W]hile the multiple trigger theory of liability appropriated the reasonable expectations of the insured in *J.H. France* [asbestos bodily injury, see chapter 16], the circumstances of the damage to Appellants' dairy herd, coupled with the language of the Penn National policies does not warrant its application herein. Our holding in *J.H. France* remains an exception to the general rule under Pennsylvania jurisprudence that the first manifestation rule governs a trigger of coverage analysis for policies containing standard CGL language. We therefore find *J.H. France* distinguishable and decline to apply the multiple trigger theory of liability to determine coverage under the Penn National policies for the damages sustained by Appellants' dairy herd." *Id.* at 23; *Berkley Specialty Ins. Co. v. Masterforce Constr. Corp.*, No. 19-01162, 2021 U.S. Dist. LEXIS 14006 (M.D. Pa. Jan. 26, 2021) (analyzing trigger of coverage, for a construction defect claim, under five different trigger theories: wrongful act, exposure, first manifestation, continuous or multiple and injury in fact).

Rhode Island: A Rhode Island trial court adopted an actual injury trigger for purposes of "bodily injury" (and mental injury) claims by adoptive parents, against an adoption agency, for withholding medical and family history information from them concerning an adopted child. *Travelers Indem. Co. v. Children's Friend & Serv., Inc.*, No. PC98–2187, 2005 R.I. Super. LEXIS 175 (R.I. Super. Ct. Dec. 1, 2005). The court concluded that "bodily injury" may have been sustained during the period of six policies issued to the adoption agency that were on the risk subsequent to the date of the adoption. The court rejected the insurer's argument that the injury could not have been sustained later than the date of adoption because that was when "the parents were denied the opportunity to make a meaningful decision about whether to adopt a child and as a result have taken on an economic (and emotional) obligation to rear a child whom they might not have adopted had they been fully informed."

South Carolina: In *Crossmann Communities of N.C., Inc. v. Harleysville Mut. Ins. Co.*, 717 S.E.2d 589 (S.C. 2011), the Supreme Court of South Carolina restated its holding in *Joe Harden Builders, Inc. v. Aetna Cas. & Sur. Co.*, 486 S.E.2d 89 (S.C. 1997) that "adopted a modified continuous trigger theory for determining when coverage is triggered under a standard occurrence policy. 'Under this theory, coverage is triggered whenever the damage can be shown in fact to have first occurred, even if it is before the damage became apparent, and the policy in effect at the time of the injury-in-fact covers all the ensuing damages.' ... Coverage is also triggered under every policy applicable thereafter." (quoting *Joe Harden Builders* at 91). "This theory covers instances where an insured may be able to prove in retrospect that damage occurred during the policy period even though damage was not yet manifested at the time." *Joe Harden Builders*, 486 S.E.2d at 91 (addressing coverage for cracks to a brick wall). The *Crossmann* Court also overruled *Century Indemnity Co. v. Golden Hills Builders, Inc.*, 561 S.E.2d 355 (S.C. 2002) and adopted "time on risk" allocation. *See* Chapter 18. *See also Pharmacists Mut. Ins. Co. v. Scyster*, 232 Fed. App'x 217, 226 (4th Cir. 2007) (following *Joe Harden Builders* and holding that coverage was owed under a pharmacist's professional liability policy for patients who received injections of a drug compounded by a pharmacist prior to the policy's effective date but who suffered symptoms and were diagnosed with meningitis during the policy period); *Ross Development Corp. v. Fireman's Fund Ins. Co.*, 910 F. Supp. 2d 828 (D.S.C. 2012) (holding that a "1963 fire could trigger coverage only if it continued to cause new property damage during one or more of the policy periods between 1972 and 1992") (citing *Crossmann Communities*) (*aff'd* at 526 Fed. Appx. 299 (4th Cir. 2013)); *State Nat'l Ins. Co. v. Eastwood Constr., LLC*, No. 16-2607, 2017 U.S. Dist. LEXIS 226348 (D.S.C. Apr. 18, 2017) ("All insurance policies which provide coverage at any time during the progressive property damage are triggered under South Carolina's modified continuous trigger.").

South Dakota: A South Dakota District Court held that a complaint filed by a city, against an architectural firm, for negligence in the performance of services related to the construction of a waste treatment facility, did not cause damage to the city until the facility was turned over to it. *Kirkham, Michael & Assocs., Inc. v. Travelers Indem. Co.*, 361 F. Supp. 189, 193 (D.S.D. 1973), *aff'd* 493 F.2d 475 (8th Cir. 1974). While the court noted that the architect's conduct may have constituted a continuous course of wrongful acts of negligence, it held that "[i]t is the damage incurred by 'accident' that triggers the policies' coverage, not the preceding wrongful acts." *Id.* "Prior to the facility being turned over to the City for possession and operation the City never sustained any *actual* damages." *Id.* (emphasis in original). *See also AMCO Insurance Co. v. Employers Mut. Cas. Co.*, 845 N.W.2d 918 (S.D. 2014) (holding that an exclusion for "property damage" that "commenced or which is alleged to have occurred, prior to the inception or effective date of this policy," whether the damage is "known, unknown, or should have been known" by the insured, did not violate public policy).

Tennessee: The Court of Appeals of Tennessee held that no coverage was owed under policies that were on the risk at the time when an insured negligently constructed a tennis court that subsequently caused a retaining wall on the perimeter of the court to collapse. *State Auto Mut. Ins. Co. v. Shelby Mut. Ins. Co.*, No. C.A. 1162, 1988 Tenn. App. LEXIS 412 (Tenn. Ct. App. June 30, 1988). "We hold that coverage of property damage caused by an occurrence as defined in the policy is limited to damage occurring during the policy period. The negligence of Playrite in constructing the tennis court was not an 'occurrence'; rather, it was the collapse of the wall that constituted an 'occurrence' under appellant's policy." Therefore, no coverage was owed under a policy that expired two years prior to the collapse of the wall.

Texas: The Supreme Court of Texas rejected a manifestation trigger and adopted an actual injury or injury-in-fact trigger for purposes of construction defect claims. *Don's Bldg. Supply, Inc. v. OneBeacon Ins. Co.*, 267 S.W.3d 20, 24 (Tex. 2008). "[P]roperty damage occurred when a home that is the subject of an underlying suit suffered wood rot or other physical damage. The date that the physical damage is or could have been discovered is irrelevant under the policy." *Id.* "This policy links coverage to damage, not damage detection." *Id.* at 29. "The policy asks when damage happened, not whether it was manifest, patent, visible, apparent, obvious, perceptible, discovered, discoverable, capable of detection, or anything similar." *Id.* at 30; *see also Pine Oak Builders, Inc. v. Great Am. Lloyds Ins. Co.*, 279 S.W.3d 650, 653 (Tex. 2009) ("'[T]he key date is when injury happens, not when someone happens upon it'—that is, the focus should be on 'when damage comes to pass, not when damage comes to light.'") (quoting *Don's Bldg. Supply*, 267 S.W.3d at 22); *Mid-Continent Cas. Co. v. Academy Development, Inc.*, No. H-08-21, 2010 U.S. Dist. LEXIS 87637 (S.D. Tex. Aug. 24, 2010) (applying the "actual injury" rule adopted in *Don's Building* to damage to lake-front homes caused by defectively constructed lake walls); *VRV Development L.P. v. Mid-Continent Cas. Co.*, 630 F.3d 451, 458 (5th Cir. 2011) ("'[P]roperty damage' does not necessarily 'occur' at the first link in the causal chain of events giving rise to that property damage. Nearly all property damage will be traceable back to earlier events, but this is not the nature of our inquiry. As the Texas Supreme Court has instructed, we must focus on the time of the 'actual physical damage' to the property, and not the time of the 'negligent conduct' or the 'process … that later results in' the damage.") (quoting *Don's Building*); *Vines-Herrin Custom Homes, LLC v. Great American Lloyds Ins. Co.*, No. 15-00230, 2016 Tex. App. LEXIS 9407 (Tex. Ct. App. Aug. 25, 2016) ("[W]e disagree with the Insurers that the trial court's findings of fact, with respect to when Cerullo noticed visible property damages, shows the trial court disregarded *Don's Building* and applied the 'manifestation rule' rather than the 'actual injury rule.' In fact, in *Don's Building*, the supreme court expressly recognized that when damages are not latent (i.e. are visible) the actual injury rule and the manifestation rule are, for all practical purposes, the same. *See Don›s Bldg.*, 267 S.W.3d at 26 (actual injury rule and manifestation rules 'diverge' when damages are latent). We further conclude the evidence is legally sufficient to support the trial court's findings that property damages occurred during Mid-Continent's policy periods. At trial, Cerullo testified he noticed cracks in ceilings, his windows begin to bow, and his ceilings beginning to sag during Mid-Continent's policy periods."); *United States Metals, Inc. v. Liberty Mutual Group, Inc.*, 490 S.W.3d 20 (Tex. 2015) (citing *Don's Bldg.*) ("Since a defective product that causes damage is not an occurrence until the damage actually happens, it would be inconsistent to now find that a defective product that does *not* cause damage is nevertheless an occurrence at the time of incorporation."); *Gonzalez v. Mid-Continent Cas. Co.*, 969 F.3d 554 (5th Cir. 2020) (insured, during policy period, hammered nails through electrical wires while installing siding, which resulted in a fire that took place after last policy expired) ("[Petition] alleges that the 2016 fire 'relates back to [the] construction and/or installation of siding' in 2013. That is, the theory of the Petition in the Underlying Litigation is that the pierced wires were latent fire hazards—like the latent water damage in *Don's Building*. Though Hamilton did not know about the wire damage until 2016 when the fire broke out, Don's Building says that the date the damage is discovered is 'irrelevant.'") (dissenting opinion: "I would hold that the actual physical damage to Hamilton's house occurred when the fire broke out, not when the alleged negligent hammering happened."). Other Texas state and federal courts have addressed *Don's Building* and applied it to the particular construction defect scenarios before it. *See Indian Harbor Ins. Co. v. KB Lone Star, Inc.*, No. 11–1846, 2012 U.S. Dist. LEXIS 125694 (S.D. Tex. Sept. 5, 2012); *Mid-Continent Cas. Co. v. Castagna*, 410 S.W.3d 445 (Tex. Ct. App. 2013); *Feaster v. Mid-Continent Cas. Co.*, No. 13-3220, 2014 U.S. Dist. LEXIS 164457 (S.D. Tex. Nov. 24, 2014); *Crownover v. Mid-Continent Cas. Co.*, 772 F.3d 197 (5th Cir. 2014); *Lyda Swinerton Builders, Inc. v. Okla. Sur. Co.*, 903 F.3d 435 (5th Cir. 2018).

Utah: No instructive authority. *But see Chapman Construction, LC v. Cincinnati Ins. Co.*, No. 15-172, 2015 U.S. Dist. LEXIS 180878 (D. Utah Sept. 22, 2015) (policy provision - no coverage owed for damage that is known by the insured to have occurred in whole or in part prior to the policy period) ("Even if the court were to consider the extrinsic evidence presented by Cincinnati that Chapman knew of some damage to the condominium project prior to the Cincinnati policy period, Cincinnati has failed to demonstrate that *none* of the allegations in the underlying action is *potentially* covered. Cincinnati has provided some evidence that Chapman knew of concrete damage as early as May 2009, approximately two months prior to the inception of the Cincinnati policy. However, Cincinnati has failed to demonstrate that Chapman was aware of *all* of the damage alleged in the underlying action prior to the Cincinnati policy period. For example, Cincinnati has failed to show that Chapman was aware of damage to handrails, water damage, mold, or failing soffits, all of which were alleged in the underlying action. The Cincinnati policy language, which excludes from coverage 'property damage' that Chapman knew 'had occurred or had begun to occur, in whole or in part' prior to the policy period, cannot fairly be said to exclude from coverage damage that is different in kind from the damage of which Chapman was made aware.") (emphasis in original); *National Union Fire Ins. Co. v. CML Metals Corp.*, No. 12-00934, 2015 U.S. Dist. LEXIS 105873 (D. Utah Aug. 11, 2015) (addressing the time of construction-related property damage under first-party policies).

Vermont: No instructive authority. *See City of Burlington v. Hartford Steam Boiler Inspection & Ins. Co.*, 190 F. Supp. 2d 663, 679 n.13 (D. Vt. 2002) ("In finding that no 'accident' occurred during the policy period, the Court does not adopt or endorse any particular insurance coverage 'trigger theory,' but instead follows what the HIC Boiler Policy itself defines as the trigger.") (addressing first-party property coverage for defective welds in a boiler); *Citizens Ins. Co. of Am. v. Vt. Sch. Bd. Ins. Trust, Inc.*, No. 333-6-19, 2020 Vt. Super. LEXIS 28 (Vt. Super. Ct. Feb. 6, 2020) (refusing to apply a continuous trigger analysis in an assault case) (noting that "[w]hile the Vermont Supreme Court has applied the continuous trigger test in the specialized context of environmental pollution" it has never done so in the case of ordinary personal injuries").

Virginia: No instructive authority. *See Sting Sec., Inc. v. First Mercury Syndicate, Inc.*, 791 F. Supp. 555 (D. Md. 1992) (applying Virginia law) ("[W]here the substance of the complaint concerns economic damage arising from a contractual relationship, the occurrence takes place when the injuries first manifest themselves.") (citation and quotation omitted). Despite the court's adoption of the "manifestation" label, the decision addressed an insurer's obligation to provide coverage under policies issued *after* the date that defects in a security guard scheduling system became evident. *See also Ind. Lumbermens Mut. Ins. Co. v. Timber Treatment Techs., LLC*, No. 16-692, 2017 U.S. Dist. LEXIS 206868 (E.D. Va. Oct. 25, 2017) ("Neither of the aforementioned claims alleged specifically that the purchases or the damages occurred before or on April 15, 2011 [date policies expired]. However, such clarity is not necessary in Virginia insurance law, as these incomplete claims could still result in coverage if, upon development of the facts, the TimberSIL purchases turned out to be before April 15, 2011. Therefore, the damages alleged by Ms. Goodwin and Ms. Myers, while incomplete as to whether they fell within the policy period, are sufficient for coverage under Virginia law.") (involving a wood product, primarily used to construct decks, infused with glass to be long-lasting and resistant to rot, decay and termites).

Washington: The Court of Appeals of Washington adopted a continuous trigger for purposes of property damage caused by negligent construction. *Gruol Constr. Co., Inc. v. Ins. Co. of N. Am.*, 524 P.2d 427, 430 (Wash. Ct. App. 1974). At issue was coverage for damage to a building caused by dry rot which resulted from dirt having been piled against the box sills of the building by backfilling during construction. *Id.* at 429. "Here, the resulting damage was continuous; coverage was properly imposed under the language of the policy on INA and Northwestern Mutual even though the initial negligent act (the defective backfilling) took place within the period of Safeco's policy coverage." *Id.* at 430; *see also Walla Walla College v. Ohio Cas. Ins. Co.*, 204 P.3d 961, 965 (Wash. Ct. App. 2009) (distinguishing *Gruol* and holding that property damage resulted when an improperly installed underground gasoline storage tank ruptured and not at the time of installation, since insured sought coverage for property damage for contamination from the leak, not for damage to the tank itself); *N. American Specialty Ins. Co. v. Bjorn G. Olson Bldg., Inc.*, No. C07-5583, 2009 U.S. Dist. LEXIS 61673 (W.D. Wash. July 16, 2009) (construction defect) ("Washington has adopted the continuous trigger rule for insurance coverage in cases involving undiscovered, progressively worsening conditions causing injury or damage. Thus, when an insured, who is insured by multiple insurers, is responsible for damages that occurred over several policy periods, every policy in force throughout the injury-causing process is triggered and the insurers are jointly and severally liable for the entire amount, minus deductibles, of the loss.") (citing *Gruol*); *Certain Underwriters at Lloyd's London v. Valiant Ins. Co.*, 229 P.3d 930, 933 (Wash. Ct. App. 2010) (following *Gruol*) ("The dry rot caused damage continuously, and therefore was held to be an occurrence covered by all three policies."); *American States Ins. Co. v. Century Sur. Co.*, No. 65046-7-I, 2011 Wash. App. LEXIS 2576 (Wash. Ct. App. Oct. 31, 2011) ("Under the 'continuous trigger' rule, every policy spanning the period during which property damage progresses is liable for all damages attributable to the occurrence.") (citing *Gruol*); *Greenlake Condo. Ass'n v. Allstate Ins. Co.*, No. C14-1860, 2015 U.S. Dist. LEXIS 184729 (W.D. Wash. Dec. 23, 2015) (noting that various decisions "all point to the application of *Gruol* in a first-party insurance context"); *Sunwood Condo. Ass'n v. Travelers Cas. Ins. Co. of Am.*, No. C16-1012, 2017 U.S. Dist. LEXIS 189892 (W.D. Wash. Nov. 16, 2017) (applying *Gruol* to a first-party policy that provides coverage for "loss or damage commencing during the policy period") ("The Court finds the continuous trigger rule may be applied here, but a jury must determine whether the Association's loss was progressive and incremental, with new loss commencing and damage worsening during NSC's policy period.").

West Virginia: A West Virginia District Court adopted a manifestation trigger for purposes of property damage caused by negligent construction. *Simpson-Littman Construction, Inc. v. Erie Ins. Prop. & Cas. Ins. Co.*, No. 3:09-0240, 2010 U.S. Dist. LEXIS 95378 (S.D.W.Va. Sept. 13, 2010). At issue was coverage for structural defects to a home caused by faulty construction of its foundation. The court adopted a manifestation trigger: "According to the plain language of the policy, property damage that occurs as a result of physical injury or destruction is deemed to have occurred at the time of the physical injury that caused the damage. In other words, the date on which the property damage is deemed to have occurred is the date of the actual injury (i.e., the date the cracks appeared in the interior walls of the home, in the brick exterior, or in the block and foundation). This finding is consistent with the language of [the] Policy[.]" *See also Westfield Ins. Co. v. Mitchell*, 22 F. Supp. 3d 619 (S.D.W.Va. 2014) ("It does not appear that the Supreme Court of Appeals of West Virginia has ever determined whether the damage in a negligence claim occurs at the time of the alleged negligence or at the time damages from the alleged negligence results. However, looking at similar language in another policy, this court previously found that 'the date on which the property damage is deemed to have occurred is the date of the actual injury[.]'") (quoting *Simpson-Littman*).

Wisconsin: The Supreme Court of Wisconsin held that a continuous trigger applied to property damage caused by construction defect. *Am. Family Mut. Ins. Co. v. Am. Girl, Inc.*, 673 N.W.2d 65, 84 (Wis. 2004). "Settlement had reached eight inches by the spring of 1995, when the first policy was still in force, and continued throughout 1996 and into 1997, by which time it was approaching one foot. Accordingly, under the continuous trigger holdings of *Society Insurance* [*Co. v. Town of Franklin*, 607 N.W.2d 342 (Wis. Ct. App. 2000) (environmental property damage)] and *Wisconsin Electric* [*Power Co. v. Cal. Union Ins. Co.*, 419 N.W.2d 255

(Wis. Ct. App. 1987) (stray voltage from power supply causing injury to cows)] the policies for the years 1994–95, 1995–96, and 1996–97 cover this loss." *Id.; see also The Selmer Company v. Selective Ins. Co. of S.C.*, No. 2010AP1835, 2011 Wisc. App. LEXIS 722 (Wis. Ct. App. Sept. 8, 2011) (addressing trigger of coverage for construction defect and distinguishing between policies that require an occurrence or accident during the policy period and those that are triggered by property damage during the policy period); *Thompson v. State Farm Fire & Cas. Co.*, 944 N.W.2d 364 (Wash. Ct. App. 2020) (addressing coverage for bodily injury occurring after policies expired, caused by a collapsed deck negligently built years earlier and during the insurer's policy period) ("[W]e conclude the Wilson Mutual policies unambiguously state that they do not provide coverage for bodily injury that occurred outside the policy period. Here, the bodily injury underlying the Thompsons' claims occurred approximately three years after Wilson Mutual's last policy period expired.")

Wyoming: No instructive authority.

CHAPTER
18

Allocation of Latent Injury and Damage Claims

Shane R. Heskin[1]

The method of allocating damages for latent bodily injury and property damage claims, sometimes called long-tail or continuous injury or damage claims, is a critical and determinative question of law that may substantially impact the amount of an insurance company's liability under a commercial general liability (CGL) policy. The two most common types of claims presenting this allocation question are asbestos bodily injury and environmental property damage.

Two principal approaches have been developed over the years by courts confronting the question. The growing majority of jurisdictions has adopted the pro rata method, where, in its purest form, damages are allocated evenly among all years in which bodily injury or property damage has occurred.[2] To take a simple

---

1   Shane Heskin is a partner at White and Williams LLP in Philadelphia. This chapter is dedicated to the memory of Guy A. Cellucci, whose contributions were invaluable to both this chapter and the development of the Massachusetts allocation law discussed herein. Messrs. Cellucci and Heskin served as trial counsel in *Boston Gas Co. v. Century Indem. Co.*, 910 N.E.2d. 290 (Mass. 2009), and successfully advocated the insurer's position on allocation before the Massachusetts Supreme Judicial Court. The author expresses his appreciation to the following White and Williams colleagues for their assistance with the preparation of this chapter: Patricia Santelle, Paul Briganti, Sara Tilitz, Adam Berardi, Craig O'Neill, Sara Mirsky and Austin Moody.

2   *See Rossello v. Zurich Am. Ins. Co.*, 226 A.3d 444, 451 (Md. 2020); *Keyspan Gas E. Corp. v. Munich Reins. Am., Inc.*, 96 N.E.3d 209 (N.Y. 2018); *Arceneaux v. Amstar Corp.*, 200 So.3d 277 (La. 2016); *Ohio Cas. Ins. Co. v. Unigard Ins. Co.*, 268 P.3d 180 (Utah 2012); *Crossmann Communities of North Carolina, Inc. v. Harleysville Mutual Insurance Co.*, 717 S.E.2d 589 (S.C. 2011); *Dutton-Lainson Co. v. Cont'l Ins. Co.*, 778 N.W.2d 433, 445 (Neb. 2010); *Boston Gas Co. v. Century Indemnity Co.*, 910 N.E.2d 290 (Mass. 2009); *Towns v. N. Sec. Ins. Co.*, 964 A.2d 1150, 1162-66 (Vt. 2008); *S. Silica of La., Inc. v. La. Ins. Guar. Ass'n*, 979 So. 2d 460 (La. 2008); *EnergyNorth Nat. Gas, Inc. v. Certain Underwriters at Lloyd's*, 934 A.2d 517, 524-27 (N.H. 2007); *Aetna Cas. & Sur. Co. v. Cmwlth.*, 179 S.W.3d 830 (Ky. 2005); *Sec. Ins. Co. of Hartford v. Lumbermens Mut. Cas. Co.*, 826 A.2d 107, 117-18 (Conn. 2003); *Atchison, Topeka & Santa Fe*

example, if bodily injury or property damage spanned ten years, a policyholder electing to purchase insurance only for one of those years, and consciously deciding to "go bare" for the remaining nine years, would be able to recover only 10 percent of the loss.

A minority of antiquated state high court decisions, however, has adopted the joint-and-several, sometimes called the "all sums" or "pick-and-spike" method, whereby any one policy year is answerable up to its full policy limits for all losses resulting from all years in which bodily injury or property damage has occurred.[3] Under this approach, it does not matter how many years the policyholder chose to "go bare" or how few years the insurer assumed risk. Returning to the ten-year hypothetical, the policyholder can collapse all ten years of continuous bodily injury or property damage into a single year of its choosing. In other words, the policyholder purchasing only one year of coverage is treated the same as the policyholder purchasing ten years of continuous coverage.

Advocates of pro rata allocation argue that proration of damages is required by the policy language limiting coverage to property damage occurring *during* the policy period. Pro rata allocation honors this plain limitation of coverage by *approximating* the "quantum of bodily injury or property damage" occurring during the policy period when the facts do not permit a more precise determination of the *actual* "quantum of bodily injury or property damage" occurring during each policy period. It is also consistent with the widely followed maxim that an insurance policy must be read as a whole without placing undue emphasis on one provision (all sums) over another (during the policy period limitation). This interpretation

---

Ry. Co. v. Stonewall Ins. Co., 71 P.3d 1097 (Kan. 2003); *Liberty Mut. Ins. Co. v. Wheelwright Trucking Co.*, 851 So. 2d 466 (Ala. 2002); *Consol. Edison Co. v. Allstate Ins. Co.*, 98 N.Y.2d 208 (N.Y. 2002); *Pub. Serv. Co. of Colo. v. Wallis & Cos.*, 986 P.2d 924, 938-39 (Colo. 1999); *Hoang v. Assur. Co. of Am.*, 149 P.3d 798 (Colo. 2007); *Domtar, Inc. v. Niagara Fire Ins. Co.*, 563 N.W.2d 724, 732-33 (Minn. 1997); *Sharon Steel Corp. v. Aetna Cas. & Sur. Co.*, 931 P.2d 127, 142 (Utah 1997); *N. States Power Co. v. Fid. & Cas. Co. of N.Y.*, 523 N.W.2d 657, 662 (Minn. 1994); *Owens-Ill., Inc. v. United Ins. Co.*, 650 A.2d 974, 980 (N.J. 1994); *see also Sentinel Ins. Co. v. First Ins. Co.*, 875 P.2d 894 (Haw. 1994).

3   *See, e.g., Lennar Corp. v. Markel Am. Ins. Co.*, 413 S.W.3d 750 (Tex. 2013); *State of California v. Continental Insurance Co.*, 281 P.3d 1000 (Cal. 2012); *Plastics Eng'g Co. v. Liberty Mut. Ins. Co.*, 759 N.W.2d 613 (Wis. 2009); *Goodyear Tire & Rubber Co. v. Aetna Casualty & Surety Co.*, 769 N.E.2d 835 (Ohio 2002); *Allstate Ins. Co. v. Dana Corp.*, 759 N.E.2d 1049 (Ind. 2001); *Am. Nat'l Fire Ins. Co. v. B & L Trucking & Constr. Co.*, 951 P.2d 250 (Wash. 1998); *J.H. France Refractories Co. v. Allstate Ins. Co.*, 626 A.2d 502 (Pa. 1993); *Hercules Inc. v. AIU Ins. Co.*, 784 A.2d 481 (Del. 2001); *Zurich Ins. Co. v. Raymark Indus., Inc.*, 514 N.E.2d 150 (Ill. 1987).

is further supported by the reasonable expectations of the parties as many courts have observed that "[n]o reasonable policyholder could have expected that a single one-year policy would cover all losses caused by [bodily injury] or toxic industrial wastes released into the environment over the course of several decades." *Boston Gas Co. v. Century Indem. Co.*, 910 N.E.2d 290, 309 (Mass. 2009). Public policy considerations also dictate proration. Among other things, "the pro rata method promotes judicial efficiency, engenders stability in the insurance market, provides incentive for responsible commercial behavior, and produces an equitable result."

Conversely, proponents of the "all sums" method argue that the insurer's promise to pay "all sums" trumps the policy language limiting coverage to the bodily injury or property damage that occurs during the policy period. In addition, "all sums" proponents argue that the "other insurance" and number of occurrence clauses contemplate coverage for occurrences that continue both before and after the policy period.

Advocates for pro rata would counter that this interpretation confuses the concepts of concurrent coverage with successive coverage and the number of limits with scope of coverage. Pro rata advocates would also be quick to note that those decisions adopting "all sums" frequently solicit passionate dissents, while no state high court decision adopting pro rata has ever invoked a single dissent.

As discussed in the fifty-state survey that follows, the majority of state high courts expressly rejecting the "all sums" method, in favor of pro rata allocation, include Alabama, Colorado, Connecticut, Hawaii, Kansas, Kentucky, Louisiana, Maryland, Massachusetts, Minnesota, Nebraska, New Jersey, New Hampshire, South Carolina, Utah, and Vermont. Numerous other appellate courts nationwide—including the Second, Third, Fourth, Fifth, Sixth, Seventh, Eighth, and Eleventh Circuit Courts of Appeals—also have rejected the joint-and-several, "all sums" method, in favor of pro rata allocation. The minority of state high courts applying the joint-and-several, "all sums" approach, in some form or another, include California, Delaware, Illinois, Ohio, Pennsylvania, Texas, Washington, Wisconsin, and arguably, Indiana.

Importantly, and as is discussed in more detail below, the New York Court of Appeals ruled in *In the Matter of Viking Pump, Inc.*, 27 N.Y.3d 244 (2016), that when policies contain non-cumulation clauses, "all sums" allocation will apply. This decision announced a limited exception to New York's previously broad implementation of pro rata allocation. In the context of the specific policies at issue in *Viking Pump*, the Court of Appeals narrowly held that "it would be inconsistent with the language of the non-cumulation clauses to use pro rata allocation . . . ." *Id.* at 261.

As with *Viking Pump*, many "all sums" decisions are limited based on the case-specific facts or policy language at issue. For example, in previous editions of this chapter, we highlighted this issue in the unpublished decision of *Ashland Inc. v. Aetna Casualty*, Civ. A. No. 5:98–00340-JMH, Slip Op. (E.D. Ky. May 2, 2006). In *Ashland*, the U.S. District Court for the Eastern District of Kentucky required the policyholder to exhaust all *prior* coverage before tapping excess coverage in subsequent years based on the non-cumulation clause of the policies at issue. In construing this provision, the court held that this "condition applies broadly to 'any other excess policy' that covers the same loss ... prior to the inception date of the ... Policies." Thus, because the amount available under the policyholder's prior available insurance exceeded the limits of the excess policies at issue, the court concluded that "liability appears to be reduced to zero." *Id.* at 12. The court further reasoned that "[t]he all sums approach does not override such a provision, which appears to have been written specifically to address the type of situation at issue here, namely, the allocation of long-term exposure over multiple policy periods. [The Policyholder] is indeed entitled to select any applicable policy, but that selection cannot be made to grant coverage where none exists, any more than the *pro rata* approach can be used to limit the coverage that an insured has bargained for." *Id.* at 13.

Courts have long employed this kind of detailed analysis of specific provisions like the non-cumulation clause, which makes the Court of Appeals' decision in *Viking Pump* less of a sea change to allocation law than it might first seem. The narrowness of the *Viking Pump* decision also mirrors the decision by the Massachusetts Appeals Court in *Chicago Bridge & Iron Co. v. Certain Underwriters at Lloyd's, London*, 797 N.E.2d 434 (Mass. App. Ct. 2003), which was decided under Illinois law. The policies at issue in *Chicago Bridge* also contained a non-cumulation clause, and the court held that "all sums" allocation was proper because the provision "would be superfluous had the drafter intended that damages would be allocated among insurers based on their respective time on the risk." *Id.* at 441. *But see Boston Gas Co. v. Century Indem. Co.*, 910 N.E.2d 290, 311 (Mass. 2009) (acknowledging *Chicago Bridge* but holding that in the absence of a non-cumulation provision, "pro rata allocation is ... consistent with the policy language").

Even those states within the same general allocation camp, however, may vary on the application of that method. The three prevailing pro rata approaches are (1) pro rata, time-on-the-risk, (2) pro rata, available coverage block, and (3) pro rata, by limits and years. Under the "time-on-the-risk" method, loss is assigned in proportion to the amount of time that a carrier's policies were in effect (the numerator) as a percentage of the total period of time in which injury occurred (the denominator). Thus, in the ten-year scenario discussed earlier, if total damages are $100 million, each year is allocated $10 million. A primary insurer in any one of those years with limits of $1 million, for example, is thus responsible for its full limits; the next $9 million then flows to the excess layer in that same year. And if no excess insurance is available above the primary layer of $1 million, the policyholder is responsible for the remaining $9 million.

Significantly, under a pure time-on-the-risk approach, it makes no difference if insurance was "unavailable" in certain years. As the Massachusetts Supreme Judicial Court explained:

> [T]he unavailability exception "effectively provides insurance where insurers made the calculated decision not to assume risk and not to accept premiums. In effect, because the policyholder could not buy insurance, it is treated as though it did by passing those uninsurable losses to insured periods." This would not be equitable to insurers if the insured purchased coverage for only a few years where there was protracted damage.

Boston Gas, 910 N.E.2d at 297 n.11; *see also Crossmann Cmtys. of N.C. v. Harleysville Mut. Ins. Co.*, 717 S.E.2d 589, 602 n.16 (S.C. 2011).

In order to maximize insurance recovery for the policyholder, however, some courts limit the allocation period to the available coverage block. *See, e.g., Stonewall Ins. Co. v. Asbestos Claims Mgmt. Corp.*, 73 F.3d 1178, 1203 (2d Cir. 1995); *Fulton Boiler Works, Inc. v. Am. Motorists Ins. Co.*, 828 F. Supp. 2d 481, 494 (N.D.N.Y. 2011). This exception often leads to the question of whether insurance was in fact available for the covered risk at issue or whether the policyholder consciously elected to "go bare." It also raises the question of who has the burden of proving availability or unavailability. *See, e.g., St. Paul Mercury Ins. Co. v. Northern States Power Co.*, No. A07-1775, 2009 Minn. App. Unpub. LEXIS 977 (Minn. Ct. App. Aug. 25, 2009). Again, using the ten-year hypothetical, if it is established that insurance was available for only five years, and damages remain at $100 million, each policy year would be allocated $20 million based on the coverage block approach to "unavailability." Those endorsing pro rata allocation view this judicially created exception—to pro rata in its pure form—as unfair because the policyholder collects $50 million stemming from property damage for which it paid no premiums, and the insurers collectively pay an additional $50 million for property damage occurring in years they did not insure and for which they received no premium.

The most complicated of the pro rata approaches, however, commingles available coverage years and limits. The purported intent is to reflect the "risk transfer" assumed by the policyholder and its insurers in each insurable year of the loss. This approach was first recognized by the New Jersey Supreme Court in *Owens-Illinois, Inc. v. United Ins. Co.*, 650 A.2d 974 (N.J. 1994) and was most recently adopted by the New Hampshire Supreme Court in *Energy North Natural Gas, Inc. v. Certain Underwriters at Lloyd's*, 934 A.2d 518 (N.H. 2007). Again using the ten-year scenario for illustration, if the insured purchased $10 million of insurance in each of the first nine years for a total of $90 million, and $110 million of insurance in the very last year, the insured in the last year of coverage is responsible for 55 percent of the total loss based on its weighted share of the overall coverage block ($110 million out of a total $200 million). The remaining 45 percent of the total loss is spread evenly (5 percent in each year) among years one through nine based on the remaining weighted share of the overall coverage block (cumulatively $90 million out of a total $200 million). Thus, if total damages were $100 million, $55 million would be allocated to the last year, and $5 million would be allocated each of the remaining nine years for a cumulative total of $45 million.

Of course, the simplistic example used here does not often occur in practice, where there are frequently many other considerations in play. In addition to dealing with potentially overlapping and incongruous coverage layers resulting from stub policies, insolvencies, prior impairments, exhaustion, self-insured retentions, aggregates, or term limits, application of this method requires the additional consideration of whether the policyholder purchased sufficient insurance in each year. In other words, the policyholder can also "go bare" for a certain portion of the risk by underinsuring in any particular year or years. Given these innumerable complexities, courts often appoint special "allocation" masters to assist them with determining each party's appropriate allocation.

The "all sums" approach also presents similar variations that can greatly impact a targeted insurer's exposure. The principal point of distinction is how to deal with so called "reallocation." The issue of reallocation arises when a targeted insurer pays more than its equitable share of a loss in relation to the policyholder's other available coverage. In this situation, the targeted insurer is often forced to seek contribution from the policyholder's other available insurers or is left to obtain a judgment credit or setoff due to the settlement of other carriers on the same risk. Those who believe that the "all sums" approach to allocation is inherently inequitable to begin with usually view reallocation as a cause for further inequity.

The most equitable approach to reallocation is the "apportioned share setoff" method recognized by the Third Circuit Court of Appeals in applying Pennsylvania law. *See Koppers Co., Inc. v. Aetna Cas. & Sur. Co.*, 98 F.3d 1440 (3d. Cir. 1996). Under this method, a targeted insurer may receive a judgment setoff based on the proportionate share of risk assumed by all settling insurers covering the same loss. The end result of this approach is similar to the pro rata, coverage block approach discussed above, but with some potential further inequities. Using the most basic ten-year example, if the targeted insurer covered five years of the $100 million loss and the settling carriers covered the remaining five years of the loss, the targeted insurer would receive a $50 million setoff for the settlement payments received by these carriers—regardless of the *actual* amount paid. Proponents of this approach say that it discourages collusion among parties while appropriately shifting the risk of settling too low on the policyholder. Of course, opponents of the approach argue it discourages settlement for the very same reason.

Theoretically, under this basic example, the targeted insurer is no better off or no worse off than under a pure pro rata, time-on-the-risk approach. But more often than not, the realities of long-tail, continuous injury claims present coverage blocks and coverage questions that are far from basic. The above scenario may lead to further inequity, for example, if the policyholder purchased insurance from a low-rated insurer that later becomes insolvent. The question then arises whether to shift an equitable portion of these insolvent shares to the settled carriers through a setoff or whether to force the remaining carriers to bear the full burden of all insolvent shares. The same question arises if the insured consciously decided to "go bare" for a portion of the risk. Because the principles of setoff and contribution are rooted in equity, the answer is often fact dependent and may vary based on the unique equities of the case.

An alternative to the "apportioned share setoff" method is the *pro tanto* method, which provides a dollar-for-dollar credit based on the *actual* settlement amount paid. Detractors of this more common approach, however, see it as being riddled with even more inequities. Among its many flaws, they would say, is that it places the risk of settling too low on the nonsettling insurer, a nonparticipant to the transaction. It further places the burden of proving the actual settlement amount on the nonsettling insurer, which was not privy to settlement discussions. Disclosure of those settlement details is also hindered by the public policy considerations of encouraging settlement and safeguarding settlement negotiations. This method also encourages collusion by allowing the policyholder to disguise the actual consideration or actual sum given in settlement. The most common mechanism of disguising the actual settlement amount is by including a release for other claims or by providing a broader release than the claim really at issue. In environmental cases, this is easily accomplished by including other sites not at issue or by including a release for potential future bodily injury or natural resource claims that have not been (and never expect to be) asserted. As one court put it in criticizing this approach: "Of course, quantifying the unquantifiable and allocating what is not yet able to be allocated is an impossible task, but it is one the Supreme Court has assigned to insurers ... as an incentive for them to settle their claims. The Supreme Court has stated the law, and we are obliged to follow it." *Puget Sound Energy v. Certain Underwriters at Lloyd's, London*, 138 P.3d 1068, 1077 (Wash. Ct. App. 2006).

Another approach is horizontal exhaustion. This approach is unique to California and Illinois. *See, e.g., Kajima Constr. Servs., Inc. v. St. Paul Fire & Marine Ins. Co.*, 879 N.E.2d 305 (Ill. 2007); *Community Redev. Agency of City of Los Angeles v. Aetna Cas. & Sur. Co.*, 57 Cal. Rptr. 2d 755 (Cal. Ct. App. 1996). Under this approach, the policyholder must exhaust all applicable primary coverage before it taps an excess carrier for defense or indemnity. The rationale behind this approach is that excess coverage is fundamentally different from primary insurance both with respect to the risk assumed and the premiums accepted. As recognized by the Illinois Supreme Court, permitting "vertical exhaustion" would allow the policyholder to

> effectively manipulate the source of its recovery, avoiding the difficulties encountered as the result of its purchase of fronting insurance and the liquidation of some of its insurers. This would permit [the policyholder] to pursue coverage from certain excess insurers at the exclusion of others. Such a practice would blur the distinction between primary and excess insurance, and would allow certain primary insurers to escape unscathed when they would otherwise bear the initial burden of providing indemnification.

Kajima, 879 N.E.2d at 106–07.

A similar approach has been recognized under Ohio law, but with greater implications. In *GenCorp*, the Sixth Circuit affirmed the district court's holding that the policyholder had elected pro rata allocation by its own to decision to settle with all of its primary insurers. *GenCorp, Inc. v. AIU Ins. Co.*, 297 F. Supp. 2d 995 (N.D.

Ohio 2003), *aff 'd per curium*, 2005 U.S. App. LEXIS (6th Cir. 2005). While the district court recognized the policyholder's right to seek indemnity from any one of its insurers under Ohio law, its decision to settle with *all* of its primary insurers eliminated each of the excess carriers' right to seek contribution. Having elected to allocate its liability over the broadest allocation period possible and having eliminated the only protection afforded to an overpaying insurer, the district court therefore did not permit the policyholder to subsequently "allocate its liability to one policy or to one policy year because this would be contrary to the settlements reached." *Id.* at 1007–08.

A policyholder's recovery may also be limited under "all sums" when anti-stacking principles or noncumulation clauses of certain policies are strictly applied. Anti-stacking is the principle that a policyholder may select a single year in which to recover its loss but no more. This prohibition against stacking of limits was first recognized by the seminal "all sums" decision of *Keene Corp. v. Insurance Co. of North America*, 667 F.2d 1034 (D.C. Cir. 1981), *cert. denied*, 455 U.S. 1007 (1982), reasoning that the "principle of indemnity implicit in the policies requires that successive policies cover single asbestos-related injuries. That principle, however, does not require that [the policyholder] be entitled to 'stack' applicable policies' limits of liability." *Id.* at 1049; *but see State v. Continental Ins. Co.*, 281 P. 3d 1000, 1009 (Cal. 2012) ("[A]bsent antistacking provisions, statutes that forbid stacking, or judicial intervention, standard policy language permits stacking."); OREGON REV. STAT. § 465.480(2)(d) (prohibiting enforcement of non-cumulation clauses in context of long-tail environmental claims, but permitting such clauses to be considered as "a factor . . . in the allocation of contribution claims between insurers"). Certain noncumulation clauses, however, may permit stacking but limit the order in which the policyholder may recover. *See, e.g., Liberty Mut. Ins. Co. v. Treesdale, Inc.*, 418 F.3d 330 (3d Cir. 2005); *but see Spaulding Composites Co. v. Aetna Cas. & Sur. Co.*, 819 A.2d 410 (N.J. 2003) (finding noncumulation clause an unenforceable escape clause), *Greene, Tweed & Co. v. Hartford Accident & Indem. Co.*, Civ. A. No. 03-3637, 2006 U.S. Dist. LEXIS 21447 (E.D. Pa. Apr. 21, 2006) (same).

50-State Survey: Allocation of Latent Injury and Damage Claims

Alabama: *See Liberty Mut. Ins. Co. v. Wheelwright Trucking Co.*, 851 So. 2d 466 (Ala. 2002) (applying both Alabama and Georgia law) (affirming pro rata allocation by trial court and adopting reasoning of *Olin Corp. v. Insurance Co. of North America*, 221

F.3d 307 (2d Cir. 2000) for exhaustion of self-insured retentions). *See also Commercial Union Ins. Co. v. Sepco Corp.*, 918 F.2d 920, 924 (11th Cir. 1990) (applying Alabama law and affirming the district court's decision to apply the pro rata approach to allocate liability among insurers for bodily injury from exposure to asbestos); *see also Liberty Mut. Ins. Co. v. Wheelwright Trucking Co., Inc.*, 851 So. 2d 466, 487 (Ala. 2002) (citing with approval *Olin Corp. v. Ins. Co. of N. Am.*, 221 F.3d 307 (2d Cir. 2000) and holding that policyholder responsible for separate SIR under each triggered policy under Georgia law).

Alaska: No instructive authority. *But see Mapco Express, Inc. v. American International. Specialty Lines Ins. Co.*, No. 3AN-95-8309 (Alaska Super. July 31, 1998) (rejecting horizontal exhaustion).

Arizona: In *City of Phoenix v. First State Ins. Co.*, No. CV-15-00511, 2016 U.S. Dist. LEXIS 119024 (D. Ariz. Sept. 2, 2016), an Arizona federal district court held that both indemnity and defense costs in an asbestos bodily injury case should be allocated pro rata, time-on-the-risk over 26 years of exposure. Although the district court acknowledged that "Arizona cases are silent on the issue," it declined to certify the question to the Arizona Supreme Court on the grounds that the allocation "question is not dispositive, as other grounds [for summary judgment] independently govern this case." *Id.* at *32. Nevertheless, the district court stated that the allocation "question is not very difficult," and provided detailed reasoning as to why the pro rata allocation method is "fair," "efficient," and "consistent with the [insured's] reasonable expectations." *Id.* at *33-40. It should be noted, however, that the policies at issue did not contain "all sums" language and only obligated the insurers to reimburse defense costs rather than provide for a "duty to defend." The decision was affirmed but the court did not need to reach the issue of pro rata allocation. *City of Phoenix v. First State Ins. Co.*, 727 F. App'x 296 (9th Cir. 2018); *see also Berkshire Hathaway Specialty Ins. Co. v. City of Phoenix*, No. 16-01083, 2016 U.S. Dist. LEXIS 156234 (D. Ariz. Nov. 10, 2016) (following *City of Phoenix v. First State Ins. Co.*, and concluding that an excess policy would not be implicated under pro rata allocation).

Arkansas: In an unpublished decision, an Arkansas trial court applied "all sums" to an environmental property damage claim involving three separate oils spills. *Murphy Oil USA, Inc. v. United States Fid. & Guar. Co.*, No. 91–439–2 (Ark. Cir. Ct. Feb. 21, 1995), reprinted in 9 Mealey's Ins. Litig. Rep. No. 19, § I (Mar. 21, 1995).

California: The Supreme Court of California adopted the "all sums" method of allocation, with respect to defense costs, in the context of claims for environmental property damage. *Aerojet-Gen. Corp. v. Transport Indem. Co.*, 948 P.2d 909 (Cal. 1998). Later, in *State of California v. Continental Insurance Co.*, 281 P.3d 1000, 1003 (Cal. 2012) (also known as *Stringfellow*), the high court was faced with non-standard, fact-specific language in the "Insuring Agreement" that it found did not expressly limit coverage to property damage occurring during the policy period. Instead, this limitation appeared solely in the definition of occurrence. *Id.* at 1003 (Cal. 2012). Interpreting this non-standard policy language, the high court held that indemnity costs incurred in the environmental property damage context are allocable jointly-and-severally, and that the policyholder is permitted to stack the limits of all triggered policies across all policy periods. *Id.* at 1008-09; *see also Fluor Corp. v. Superior Court*, 354 P.3d 302, 330 (Cal. 2015) (applying *Stringfellow* in asbestos context); *Compass Ins. Co. v. Univ. Mech. & Eng'g Contrs., Inc.*, No. 14-cv-04295, 2016 U.S. Dist. LEXIS 39624 (N. D. Cal. Mar. 25, 2016). Given the high court's reliance on the absence of this limiting language in the "Insuring Agreement," an argument may be made that a different result is required under policies expressly incorporating the "during the policy period" limitation within the "Insuring Agreement." *See, e.g., Kaiser Cement & Gypsum Corp. v. Ins. Co. of State of Pa.*, 155 Cal. Rptr. 3d 283 (Cal. Ct. App. 2013), *rehearing denied* (May 1, 2013) (holding that, based on policy language at issue, stacking was not permitted under *State v. Cont'l*); *Ins. Co. of the Pa. v. San Bernardino*, No. CV-16-0128, 2017 U.S. Dist. LEXIS 45031 (C.D. Cal. Mar. 8, 2017) (holding that stacking was not permitted pursuant to the policies' non-cumulation clause). More recently, the California Supreme Court in *Montrose Chemical Corp. v. Superior Court*, 460 P.3d 1201 (Cal. 2020), held that the excess policies at issue only required "vertical exhaustion," such that the insured was entitled to access available excess coverage under any excess policy once it had exhausted directly underlying excess policies for the same policy period. The court rejected the "horizontal exhaustion" approach urged by the excess insurers, under which the insured would have been able to access an excess policy only after it had exhausted other policies with lower attachment points from every policy period in which the environmental damage resulting in liability occurred. The court concluded that the various "other insurance" clauses in the policies were not specific to other lower-layer insurance and did not "clearly specify whether a rule of horizontal or vertical exhaustion applies here." *Id.* at 1212.

Colorado: The Supreme Court of Colorado adopted the pro rata, time-on-the-risk method of allocation for the environmental cleanup costs of remediating soil and groundwater contamination. *Pub. Serv. Co. v. Wallis & Cos.*, 986 P.2d 924,

334 General Liability Insurance Coverage

939 (Colo. 1999). In expressly rejecting the "all sums" approach with respect to indemnity, the court reasoned: "We do not believe that these policy provisions can reasonably be read to mean that one single-year policy out of dozens of triggered policies must indemnify the insured's liability for the total amount of pollution caused by events over a period of decades, including events that happened both before and after the policy period." *Id.* at 939. Accordingly, the court held that "where property damage is gradual, long-term, and indivisible, the trial court should make a reasonable estimate of the portion of the 'occurrence' that is fairly attributable to each year by dividing the total amount of liability by the number of years at issue." *Id.* at 940. The *Public Service* Court explained further, however, that the "trial court should then allocate liability according to each policy-year, taking into account primary and excess coverage, SIRs, policy limits, and other insurance on the risk." *Id.* The consideration of policy limits should not be confused with the *Owens-Illinois* approach (*see* New Jersey) where allocation is weighted toward years with higher policy limits. Rather, the consideration of policy limits comes into play only where there is concurrent coverage in the same year and coverage layer. *Id.* at 941–42; *see also Travelers Indem. Co. of Am. v. AAA Waterproofing, Inc.*, No. 10CV02826, 2014 U.S. Dist. LEXIS 6334 (D. Colo. Jan. 17, 2014) (holding in construction defect context that defense costs were subject to allocation by equal shares, and finding allocation based on policy limits unworkable where numerous subcontractors had not purchased applicable insurance); *D.R. Horton, Inc. Denver v. Mountain States Mut. Cas. Co.*, No. 12–cv–01080, 2013 U.S. Dist. LEXIS 167233 (D. Colo. Nov. 25, 2013) ("[W]here more than one insurer has a duty to defend, but an insurer believes it has paid a disproportionate share of the defense costs, the respective shares ultimately to be borne by each triggered policy can be determined in litigation among the insurers if they cannot resolve the apportionment by agreement."); *Probuild Holdings, Inc. v. Granite State Ins. Co.*, No. 10-378 (D. Colo. Jan. 3, 2011) (recognizing in context of Chinese drywall bodily injury and property damage claims that Colorado law permits apportionment of defense costs when policies cover successive and overlapping periods); *Hoang v. Monterra Homes (Powderhorn) LLC* (Colo. Ct. App. 2005), *rev'd on other grounds*, 149 P.3d 748 (Colo. 2007) (applying pro rata allocation approach in the context of claims for environmental property damage); *Globe Indem. Co. v. Travelers Indem. Co. of Ill.*, 98 P.3d 971, 974 (Colo. Ct. App. 2004) (holding pro rata not appropriate where damages can be traced to a single clear event, in this case, a landslide); *Twin City Fire Ins. Co. v. Am. Cas. Co.*, No. 14-cv-02401, 2016 U.S. Dist. LEXIS 89930 (D. Colo. May 25, 2016) (applying

pro rata "time-on-the-risk" allocation method to construction defect case involving policies containing "anti-stacking" provisions and policies which expressly provided coverage for "any continuation, change or resumption of … 'property damage' after the end of the policy period."); *Certain Underwriters at Lloyd's v. Hartford Accident & Indem. Co.*, No. 18-01896, 2019 U.S. Dist. LEXIS 130976 (D. Colo. Aug. 5, 2019) ("This Court is not currently persuaded that a TOR [time-on-the-risk] method of allocation is appropriate because the time the 'risk' arose is not specified by the EPA, and because the parties dispute which Underwriters policies are implicated.. . . Moreover, courts have held that the allocation of defense costs is a matter to be worked out among the insurers and, if they cannot do so, then by a court.").

Connecticut: The Supreme Court of Connecticut adopted the pro rata time-on-the-risk method of allocation, with respect to both defense and indemnity, in the context of claims for bodily injury resulting from inhalation of asbestos. *Sec. Ins. Co. of Hartford v. Lumbermens Mut. Cas. Co.*, 826 A.2d 107 (Conn. 2003). In applying this approach, the court held that the policyholder must bear its own equitable share for uninsured periods "not only because [the policyholder] … *chose* to forgo insurance, but also because [the insurer] never contracted to pay for defense [or indemnity] costs arising outside of its policy period." *Id.* at 126. The court further held that equity dictates that the policyholder bear the burden of establishing coverage during missing policy periods as the policyholder "is the party which could have prevented the loss or destruction of the policies" and thus "through its own actions or inactions … has put itself in the position of being, in essence, uninsured for a substantial period of time." *Id.* In an inter-insurer contribution dispute, the court held that, under the continuous trigger, defense costs relating to an underlying construction defect claim were allocable over the entire period during which damage caused by water intrusion had occurred. *Travelers Cas. & Sur. Co. of Am. v. Netherlands Ins. Co.*, 95 A.3d 1031 (Conn. 2014). Relying on *Security Insurance*, a Connecticut appellate court adopted the "unavailability" exception to pro rata allocation, agreeing with the policyholder that damages and defense costs should not be allocated to any period in which insurance was unavailable, which in the case of asbestos claims is principally the period after 1985-86 when asbestos exclusions came into common use. *R.T. Vanderbilt Co., Inc. v. Hartford Accident & Indem. Co.*, 156 A.3d 539 (Conn. Ct. App. 2017) (*appeal granted*, 171 A.3d 63 (Conn. 2017)). The court also found that the policyholder will bear the burden of proving that it was unable to obtain asbestos coverage prior to 1986 (when such insurance was generally available), but insurers will bear the burden to prove that coverage for asbestos liabilities was available to the policyholder after that date. However, the court recognized that, in certain circumstances, there can be an "equitable exception" to the "unavailability" rule if the insured continued to manufacture products containing asbestos after 1986 with the knowledge that such products were hazardous and uninsurable. Finally, the court held that the excess insurers were not allowed to challenge the exhaustion of the limits of certain primary policies under a cost-sharing agreement predating *Security Insurance* because, although the agreement used an allocation methodology that was not entirely consistent with the pro rata approach, it was reasonable and entered into in good faith. The Connecticut Supreme Court affirmed the appellate court's decision in *Vanderbilt* and adopted the appellate court's opinion as the proper statement of Connecticut law concerning these issues. 216 A.3d 629 (Conn. 2019).

Delaware: Delaware is widely assumed to be an "all sums" jurisdiction based on the Delaware Supreme Court's decision in *Hercules Inc. v. AIU Ins. Co.*, 784 A.2d 481 (Del. 2001), which involved environmental property damage. This assumption, however, is arguably incorrect. Most notably, the policy in *Hercules* included a nonstandard continuation of coverage clause extending coverage beyond the policy period in the case of continuing damage. *Id.* at 493. In combination with the "all sums" language, the court did not reach any equitable considerations, concluding simply that the two clauses could not be reconciled with pro rata allocation. *Id.* at 494 n.46. In an earlier case, involving different policy language, continuous property damage, and substantial SIRs, the Delaware Superior Court applied a modified pro rata, time-on-the-risk method in *E.I. du Pont de Nemours & Co. v. Admiral Ins. Co.*, No. 89C-AU-99, 1995 Del. Super. LEXIS 488 (Del. Super. Ct. Oct. 27, 1995). The court concluded that "all sums" is inconsistent with the presumption that damage occurred at a constant, continuous rate from the inception of the environmental damage. *Id.* Other allocation cases decided under Delaware law have sided with "all sums" allocation, distinguishing their facts from those of *du Pont*. *See, e.g., Hercules*, 784 A.2d at 492–94 (rejecting equitable considerations based on continuation clause); *Am. Guar. & Liab. Ins. Co. v. Intel Corp.*, No. 09C-01–170-JOH, 2009 Del. Super. LEXIS 309 (Del. Super. Ct. July 24, 2009) ("[T]he Supreme Court in Hercules, adopted an 'all-sums' liability approach, it seemed to criticize such a modified pro rate allocation. But it did so, in part, based on a particular provision in the policy at issue in that case."); *E.I. DuPont de Nemours & Co. v. Allstate Ins. Co.*, 879 A.2d 929, 939–41 (Del. Super. Ct. 2004) (rejecting equitable considerations because property damage was divisible); *Stonewall Ins. Co. v. E.I. du Pont de Nemours & Co.*, 996 A.2d 1254, 1259 n.12 (Del. 2010) (noting that insurer did not appeal application of "all sums" allocation and affirming lower court's interpretation of non-cumulation clause); *Motors Liquidation Co., DIP Lenders Trust v. Allianz Ins. Co.*, No. N11C-12-022, 2013 Del. Super. LEXIS 605 (Del. Super. Ct. Dec. 31, 2013) ("Delaware generally applies 'all sum,' a joint and several liability approach to allocation.").

District of Columbia: In *Keene Corp. v. Ins. Co. of N. Am.*, 667 F.2d 1034 (D.C. Cir. 1981), *cert. denied*, 455 U.S. 1007 (1982), the U.S. Court of Appeals for the District of Columbia held that, once a policy is triggered, the insurer is liable up to the full policy limit, subject to "other insurance" clauses. *See id.* at 1047–48. The court reasoned: "[E]ach policy has a built-in trigger of coverage. Once triggered, each policy covers [the insured]'s liability. There is nothing in the policies that provides for a reduction of the insurer's liability if an injury occurs only in part during a policy period." *Id.* at 1048. After concluding that each insurer owed an independent duty to provide full indemnification, and noting that the duty to defend is broader than the duty to indemnify, the court held that each insurer was fully liable for the insured's defense costs. *See id.* at 1050. However, in *Certain Underwriters at Lloyd's v. Nat'l R.R. Passenger Corp.*, No. 14-4717, 2017 U.S. Dist. LEXIS 131681 (E.D.N.Y. Aug. 17, 2017), the federal court for the Eastern District of New York rejected *Keene's* prediction that the District of Columbia would apply "all sums" allocation in an action for coverage for environmental cleanup. The court held that, in addition to the fact that "pro rata" allocation is the law of New York, "whose courts would predict unsettled D.C. law to be similar to their own — and Maryland — whose courts the D.C. Court of Appeals often relies on — the "pro rata" approach has, in the Court's view, the simple advantage of being more persuasive." *Id.* at *26. The court further noted that, in the years since the *Keene* decision, "pro rata" has become the clear majority rule. *Id.* at *25. The court therefore concluded that "the D.C. Court of Appeals would follow the 'pro rata' approach in this case." *Id.* at *27.

Florida: *See CSX Transp. v. Admiral Ins. Co.*, No. 93-132, 1996 U.S. Dist. LEXIS 17125 (M.D. Fla. Nov. 6, 1996) (following "all sums" rationale of *Keene* based on then existing belief that "all sums" allocation was the majority rule).

Georgia: A Georgia trial court adopted the pro rata, time-on-the-risk approach in an asbestos case in *Nat'l Serv. Indus., Inc. v. St. Paul Guardian Ins. Co.*, No. 2004 CV 83960 (Ga. Super. Ct. 2005, reprinted in 19 Mealey's Ins. Litig. Rep. No. 30, Section E (June 14, 2005)). More recently, the federal court for the Southern District of New York predicted that under well-established principles of Georgia contract interpretation, pro rata allocation would apply to asbestos claims. *Liberty Mut. Ins. Co. v. Fairbanks Co.*, 170 F. Supp. 3d 634 (S.D.N.Y. 2016). *But see Ameristeel*

Corp. v. Employers Mut. Cas. Co., No. 7:96-CV-85-HL, 2005 U.S. Dist. LEXIS 15715 (M.D. Ga. July 26, 2005) (recognizing that Georgia courts have failed to address the allocation issue, but observing: "Although Georgia law on the issue of allocation is scant, well established principles of contract interpretation support applying a pro rata approach."); *Columbia Cas. Co. v. Plantation Pipe Line Co.*, 790 S.E.2d 645 (Ga. Ct. App. 2016) (declining to reach the issue of allocation, but noting that "one weakness of horizontal allocation strategies . . . is that they implicitly read a pro rata allocation clause into the CGL policies, contrary to the general rule that pro rata clauses, which serve to limit an insurer's indemnity obligation to an insured, are typically considered exclusionary provisions and, as such, should not be imputed into an insurance contract."). *see also Liberty Mut. Ins. Co. v. Wheelwright Trucking Co., Inc.*, 851 So. 2d 466, 487 (Ala. 2002) (applying Georgia law and holding that policyholder would be responsible for separate SIR under each triggered policy); *see also Travelers Prop. Cas. Co. of Am. v. Cont'l Cas. Co.*, 226 F. Supp. 3d 1359 (N.D. Ga. 2017).

Hawaii: The Supreme Court of Hawaii's decision in, *Sentinel Ins. Co. v. First Ins. Co. of Hawaii*, 875 P.2d 894 (Haw. 1994), is often cited by both policyholders and insurers as supporting both the pro rata time-on-the-risk and "all sums" methods of allocation. The decision, in fact, adopts neither approach. While a contribution case, the decision is instructive because the court adopted an injury-in-fact trigger and held that where the amount of damages cannot be accurately attributed to any particular year, damages should be shared by successive insurers on a time-on-the-risk basis. *Id.* at 915. The decision, however, did not answer the threshold question of whether the policyholder may first seek "all sums" from any one of its available insurers as this issue was not before the court.

Idaho: The U.S. District Court for the District of Idaho has suggested, but not held, that Idaho is likely to adopt the pro rata approach to allocation, noting that a "growing plurality of states have already done so, recognizing the logic and fairness inherent in the approach." *See Huntsman Advanced Materials, LLC v. OneBeacon Am. Ins. Co.*, No. 08-CV-00229, 2011 U.S. Dist. LEXIS 81672 (D. Idaho July 21, 2011). The district court, however, refused to explicitly hold that Idaho is likely to adopt the pro rata approach because the case was to be reassigned to a new district court judge and the court was concerned that deciding the law of the case as it relates to allocation would "bind the hands of the trial judge going forward." *Id.* The successor judge held that the insurer was jointly and severally liable for defense costs, relying on policy language stating "that [the insurer] must defend all suits and pay all its expenses in doing so." *Huntsman Advanced Materials LLC v. OneBeacon Am. Ins. Co.*, No. 08-CV-00229, 2012 U.S. Dist. LEXIS 19053 (D. Idaho Feb. 13, 2012).

Illinois: In the context of an asbestos claim, the Supreme Court of Illinois applied "all sums" allocation in *Zurich Ins. Co. v. Raymark Indus., Inc.*, 514 N.E.2d 150 (Ill. 1987). Although this "all sums" holding is still applied in asbestos cases, *see Ill. Tool Works Inc. v. Travelers Cas. & Sur. Co.*, 26 N.E.3d 421, 429 (Ill. 2015), *John Crane, Inc. v. Admiral Ins. Co.*, 991 N.E.2d 474, 491 (Ill. App. Ct. 2013), *Caterpillar, Inc. v. Century Indem. Co.*, No. 3-06-0161, 2007 Ill. App. LEXIS 2274 (Ill. App. Ct. Feb. 2, 2007), it has been distinguished by numerous Illinois appellate courts in other types of cases based on the specific policy language at issue and the unique "triple trigger" applied in asbestos cases under Illinois law. This distinction was recognized in *Varlen Corp. v. Nat'l Union Fire Ins. Co. of Pittsburgh, Pa.*, No. 09-CV-7915, 2011 U.S. Dist. LEXIS 93029 (N.D. Ill. Aug. 17, 2011), where an Illinois federal court declined to extend *Raymark Industries* to the environmental property damage context because the Illinois Supreme Court has not addressed allocation in that context. *See also Vedder v. Continental Western Ins. Co.*, 978 N.E.2d 1111 (Ill. Ct. App. 2012) (holding in auto coverage context that "all sums" ruling in *Raymark* did not permit driver to select excess policy instead of primary policy to provide defense because, unlike primary and excess policies at issue, primary policies at issue in *Raymark* imposed independent defense obligations on insurers); *Fed. Ins. Co. v. Binney & Smith, Inc.*, 913 N.E.2d 43, 54 (Ill. App. Ct. 2009) (holding that advertising injury claims should be allocated on a pro rata, time-on-the-risk basis in the absence of evidence showing actual extent of damages in each year); *AAA Disposal Sys., Inc. v. Aetna Cas. & Sur. Co.*, 821 N.E.2d 1278, 1289 (Ill. App. Ct. 2005) (allocating environmental property damage claim on a pro rata, coverage block basis); *Ill. Cent. R.R. Co. v. Accident & Cas. Co. of Winterthur*, 739 N.E.2d 1049, 1062 (Ill. App. Ct. 2000) (allocating employment discrimination claims on a pro rata, time-on-the-risk basis); *Mo. Pac. R.R. Co. v. Int'l. Ins. Co.*, 679 N.E.2d 801, 806 (Ill. App. Ct. 1997) (allocating hearing loss claims on a pro rata, time-on-the-risk basis); *Outboard Marine Corp. v. Liberty Mut. Ins. Co.*, 670 N.E.2d 740, 750 (Ill. App. Ct. 1996) (allocating environmental property damage claim on pro rata, time-on-the-risk basis). A distinction must also be noted with respect to the Massachusetts Appeals Court decision in *Chicago Bridge & Iron Co. v. Certain Underwriters at Lloyd's, London*, 797 N.E.2d 434 (Mass. App. Ct. 2003), which was decided under Illinois law. As recognized by the Massachusetts high court in *Boston Gas*, *infra*, the unique policy language involved expressly provided that the policy would provide coverage for *continuing* bodily injury or property damage *after* "termination of this policy ... without payment of additional premium." *Boston Gas*, 910 N.E.2d at 304, n.30. *But see Benoy Motor Sales, Inc. v. Universal Underwriters Ins. Co.*, 679 N.E.2d 414 (Ill. App. Ct. 1997) (applying "all sums" based on deemer clause of policies).

Indiana: The Indiana Supreme Court's decision in, *Allstate Ins. Co. v. Dana Corp.*, 759 N.E.2d 1049 (Ind. 2001), is often cited by policyholders as adopting the "all sums" method of allocation. But in *Federated Rural Elec. Ins. Exch. v. Nat'l Farmers Union Prop. & Cas. Co.*, 805 N.E.2d 456, 466 (Ind. Ct. App. 2004), *vacated on procedural grounds*, 816 N.E.2d 1157 (Ind. 2004), the court stated that "the determination ... that Allstate was liable for 'all sums' up to policy limits under the language of its policies was not a final adjudication of the amount Allstate had to pay Dana. The parties err when they attempt to extract from *Dana I* and *Dana II* an 'all sums' rule and apply it out of context." Accordingly, the Indiana Court of Appeals concluded that the *Dana* decision "did not establish an 'all sums' rule to be applied in other contexts ... [and] that other coverage and equitable principles may affect the ultimate amount payable in that case." *Id.*; *accord Irving Materials, Inc. v. Zurich Am. Ins. Co.*, No. 1:03-CV-361, 2007 (S.D. Ind. Mar. 30, 2007), *recons. denied*, 2008 U.S. Dist. LEXIS 18692 (S.D. Ind. Mar. 10, 2008). In another case, the court reaffirmed that the "all sums" method should not be applied reflexively and the pro rata method governed under policies that expressly provided coverage for "those sums" that the insured becomes liable to pay for injury or damage that "occurs during the policy period." *Thomson Inc. v. Ins. Co. of N. Am.*, 11 N.E.3d 982, 1020-21 (Ind. Ct. App. 2014), *cert. denied* 33 N.E.3d 1039 (Ind. 2015); *accord Trinity Homes LLC v. Ohio Cas. Ins. Co.*, 864 F. Supp. 2d 744, 759 (S.D. Ind. 2012) (same); *Thomson, Inc. v. Am. Guar. & Liab. Ins. Co.*, No. 49D07-0807, 2016 Ind. Super. LEXIS 2, at *6-7 (Ind. Sup. Ct. Apr. 18, 2016) ("Under Indiana law, unless policy language expressly mandates pro rata allocation, joint and several allocation will prevail, whereby the policyholder can choose which triggered policies will indemnify it.").

Iowa: An Iowa trial court held that "a pro rata allocation of coverage is the appropriate manner in which to treat damage which occurs in such a way that a precise starting point cannot be determined and which stretches over successive policy periods." *MidAm. Energy Co. v. Certain Underwriters at Lloyd's London*, No. CL 107142, slip op. at 3 (Iowa Dist. Ct. Apr. 13, 2011). The court rejected the insured's argument that the allocation should exclude years in which coverage was unavailable. The court reasoned that, just as the adoption of an "all sums" approach "would disproportionately allocate coverage to a single year of coverage when allocation assumes damage over an extended period of time, so too does an 'unavailability' exception disproportionately allocate damage to insurers for periods of time when no coverage was agreed to or bargained for." *Id.* at 6. *See also MidAmerican Energy Co. v. Certain Underwriters*, No. CL 107142, 2010 Iowa Dist. LEXIS 2 (Iowa Dist. Ct. Dec. 27, 2010) ("The court therefore holds that where, as is alleged here, a single, continuous occurrence takes place over a period of time covering multiple, successive policies of insurance, any damages which are proved shall be allocated proportionately among those insurers found to be on the risk, based on the policy periods and limits of liability in question.").

In *Pella Corp. v. Liberty Mut. Ins. Co.*, 244 F. Supp. 3d 931 (S.D. Iowa 2017), the court held that defense and indemnity costs arising from underlying construction defect claims against a window manufacturer were subject to pro-rata allocation. The CGL policies at issue provided coverage for "those sums . . . that the insured becomes legally obligated to pay as damages because of 'bodily injury' or 'property damage' to which this . . . insurance applies," and that the "insurance applies only to 'bodily injury' or 'property damage' which occurs during the policy period." Although it acknowledged that *MidAmerican* was "well-crafted and persuasive," the *Pella* court concluded that the decision was "of only modest value in predicting how the Iowa Supreme Court would rule." *Id.* at 942. After considering cases from other jurisdictions, the *Pella* court held that "the meaning of the phrase 'during the policy period' is clear and weighs heavily in favor of an interpretation that the CGL Policies call for pro rata allocation." *Id.* at 946. The court rejected the insured's argument that the presence of non-cumulation provisions in the policies supported "all sums" allocation, reasoning that the non-cumulation provisions "contemplate[d] one occurrence causing damage during multiple policy periods as a condition precedent for application of the Provisions' limitation on coverage" and did not "serve as an expansion of coverage (negating the temporal limitation in the coverage provision) for all damages occurring at any time, regardless of insurer." *Id.* at 947.

Kansas: The Supreme Court of Kansas held that, in the context of claims for noise-induced hearing loss, where damages cannot be measured and allocated to particular policy periods, a pro rata, time-on-the-risk method of allocation should be used. *Atchison, Topeka & Santa Fe Ry. Co. v. Stonewall Ins. Co.*, 71 P.3d 1097, 1133 (Kan. 2003). The court concluded that an allocation based on joint and several liability would contradict the fundamental insurance agreement to indemnify the insured for injuries during a specified policy period. *Id.* at 1134; *see also ACE Prop. & Cas. Ins. Co. v. Superior Boiler Works, Inc.*, 504 F. Supp. 2d 1154, 1159 (D. Kan. 2007) (following *Atchison* and holding that summary judgment on allocation was precluded because the key issue to be resolved was whether there existed a single continuous occurrence resulting in unallocable loss implicating successive policy periods).

Kentucky: The Supreme Court of Kentucky adopted the pro rata, time-on-the-risk method of allocation in the context of claims for damage from nuclear waste disposal where damage is not divisible or allocable during and between policy periods. *Aetna Cas. & Sur. Co. v. Commonwealth*, 179 S.W.3d 830 (Ky. 2005); *see also Liberty Mut. Fire Ins. Co. v. Harper Indus., Inc.*, No. 5:05-cv-243-R, 2007 U.S. Dist. LEXIS 10753 (W.D. Ky. Feb. 12, 2007) (holding that the "insurers shall be responsible for their individual and proportionate share of defense costs ... based on a pro rata basis" in the context of claims resulting from construction defects); *Aetna Cas. & Sur. Co. v. Nuclear Eng'g Co.*, No. 200-CA-00114-MR, 2002 Ky. App. LEXIS 451 (Ky. Ct. App. Mar. 8, 2002)).

A Kentucky federal court predicted that a Kentucky state court would hold that defense costs are subject to pro-rata-by-time allocation. *Ky. League of Cities Ins. Servs. Ass'n v. Argonaut Great Cent. Ins. Co.*, No. 5:11-CV-00187, 2013 U.S. Dist. LEXIS 2663, at *11 (W.D. Ky. Jan. 7, 2013) (citing *Ins. Co. of N. Am. v. Forty-Eight Insulations, Inc.*, 633 F.2d 1212 (6th Cir. 1980), *modified* 657 F.2d 814 (6th Cir. 1981), *cert. denied* 454 U.S. 1109 (1981)). In a later case, however, the same court deferred to a Kentucky state court to decide whether pro-rata or "all sums" allocation applied to defense (and apparently indemnity). *Bevidere Ins. Co. v. Triangle Enters.*, No. 3:16-00339, 2017 U.S. Dist. LEXIS 21761, at *22 (W.D. Ky. Feb. 15, 2017).

Louisiana: The Supreme Court of Louisiana endorsed pro rata allocation by holding that solvent insurers were not required to "fill the gap" left by an insolvent carrier and thereby pay more than their pro rata share of damages incurred in connection with silicosis-related bodily injuries. *S. Silica of La., Inc. v. La. Ins. Guar. Ass'n*, 979 So. 2d 460, 466 (La. 2008). In affirming the appellate court on different grounds, the Supreme Court expressly noted that the trial court's finding that solvent insurers were required to "fill the gap" was "contrary to the proration of insurance coverage that is a component of the significant exposure test in long latency disease cases." *Id.* at 466; *see also Cole v. Celotex Corp.*, 599 So. 2d 1058, 1080 (La. 1992) (allocating damages over all triggered policies in asbestos case); *Norfolk S. Corp. v. Cal. Union Ins. Co.*, 859 So. 2d 201, 208 (La. Ct. App. 2003) (allocating "by the total number of years that contaminating activities took place to obtain a judgment amount per year"); *Porter v. Am. Optical Corp.*, 641 F.2d 1128, 1145 (5th Cir. 1981) (recognizing that, under Louisiana law, insurance coverage is prorated among all carriers for cumulative injuries, like that in the case at hand involving exposure to asbestos).

In *Arceneaux v. Amstar Corp.*, 200 So. 3d 277 (La. 2016), which was a dispute over coverage for hearing-loss claims, the Supreme Court of Louisiana extended pro-rata allocation to defense costs based on policy language that limited coverage to bodily injury occurring during the policy period. *Id.* at 285. It noted that, "[a]cross the country in cases where 'it has been determined that the insured is self-insured for part of the coverage period, the weight of authority is that the insured must bear a pro rata share of the defense costs.'" *Id.* (quoting Barry R. Ostrager & Thomas R. Newman, Handbook on Insurance Coverage Disputes, § 6.02(a)(2) (17th ed. 2014)). The court concluded that, even under the broader duty-to-defend standard, the insured could not reasonably expect that the insurer would be liable for losses that occurred outside the policy period. *Id.* The court nevertheless noted that "[t]he manner in which defense costs are to be allocated may need to be determined on a case by case basis, according to the precise language of the insurance contract at issue." *Id.* at 286. *See also Jeter v. Ameron Int'l Corp.*, 2021 La. App. LEXIS 991, *21-22 (La. Ct. App. June 23, 2021) (following *Arceneaux* and applying pro-rata allocation to defense costs in context of asbestos-related bodily injury claim). In *Jeter*, the Louisiana Court of Appeals declined to adopt the "unavailability exception" to pro-rata allocation, explaining that it had been "explicitly evaluated and rejected" in *Arceneaux* and that allocation to uninsured periods is appropriate not only where the insured chose to "go bare" but also where the uninsured periods result from insurer insolvency and a failure to prove the existence of alleged policies. *Id.* at *23-25.

Maine: No instructive authority.

Maryland: In *Rossello v. Zurich Am. Ins. Co.*, the Court of Appeals of Maryland, the state's highest court, adopted the pro rata time-on-the-risk method of allocation in the context of claims for bodily injury resulting from long-term and continuous exposure to asbestos. 226 A.3d 444 (Md. 2020). The *Rossello* court cited favorably to *Mayor & City Council of Balt. v. Utica Mut. Ins. Co.*, 802 A.2d 1070 (Md. Ct. Spec. App. 2002), *app. dismissed*, 821 A.2d 369 (Md. 2003), in which the Court of Special Appeals of Maryland had recognized the "poor fit" between the all sums approach and long-term injuries under the language of CGL policies. *Rossello*, 226 A.3d at 120. The *Rossello* court found that pro rata allocation, by contrast, was "unmistakably consistent with the language of standard CGL policies." *Id.* at 119. It further emphasized that the pro rata approach serves important public policy objectives because of its ease of administration, efficiency and consistency with the parties' reasonable expectations, and that, unlike the equitable result under pro rata allocation, the joint and several approach creates a "false equivalence" between an insured who purchased coverage continuously for many years and an insured who purchased only one year of coverage. *Id.* at 121-22. In addition, the court held that, if an insured decides not to purchase (as opposed to being unable to purchase) insurance for a certain period, it will be liable for a prorated share corresponding to that period. *Id.* at 122-23; *see also Riley v. United Servs. Auto. Assoc.*, 871 A.2d 599 (Md. Ct. Spec. App. 2005), *aff'd on other grounds*, 899 A.2d 819 (Md. 2006) (endorsing pro rata, time-on-the-risk to lead bodily injury claims where damages could not be determined in any particular year); *Pa. Nat'l Mut. Cas. Ins. Co. v. Roberts*, 668 F.3d 106 (4th Cir. 2012); *In re Wallace & Gale Co.*, 385 F.3d 820 (4th Cir. 2004) (applying pro rata allocation in the asbestos context); *Gen. Ins. Co. of Am. v. Walter E. Campbell Co.*, 107 F. Supp. 3d 466, 470-72 (D. Md. 2015) (applying pro-rata allocation to asbestos-related bodily injury claims and declining to certify allocation question to Maryland Court of Appeals).

Shortly before *Rossello* was decided, the Court of Special Appeals, in the context of lead paint-related personal injury claims, reaffirmed its adoption of the pro rata allocation approach, reasoning that "[a]n insurer cannot be required to indemnify its insured for an obligation that the insurer did not contractually agree to assume." *Pa. Nat'l Mut. Cas. Ins. Co. v. Jeffers*, 223 A.3d 1146, 1157 (Md. Ct. Spec. App. 2020); *see also Robinson v. CX Reinsurance Co.*, No. 1888, 2019 Md. App. LEXIS 879 (Md. Spec. Ct. App. Oct. 15, 2019) (declining to overrule *Utica*). *Accord Allstate Ins. Co. v. Jam #32 Corp.*, No. ELH-17-3293, 2019 U.S. Dist. LEXIS 76667, at *19-21 (D. Md. May 7, 2019) (finding pro rata allocation applicable in context of lead paint-related claims); *Allstate Ins. Co. v. Rochkind*, 381 F. Supp. 3d 488, 503 (D. Md. 2019) (declining, in light of "unambiguous case law" favoring pro rata allocation, to certify to Maryland Court of Appeals question whether pro rata method or all sums method applied in context of claims alleging continuous exposure to lead); *Allstate Ins. Co. v. N-4, Inc.*, No. ELH-17-2980, 2018 U.S. Dist. LEXIS 180437, 2018 WL 5234885 (D. Md. Oct. 22, 2018) (same).

In *Jeffers*, the court explained that the pro rata methodology requires identifying a numerator, "representing the time on the risk," and a denominator, "representing the period in which the injured person suffered bodily injury." *Jeffers*, 223 A.3d at 1156. The court found that, in a lead exposure case, bodily injury is suffered, and therefore the denominator period runs, from the date of the first elevated blood lead level (BLL) to the last BLL. *Id.* at 1158-59. *Accord Pa. Nat'l Mut. Cas. Ins. Co. v. Fishkind*, No. JKB-20-0947, 2021 U.S. Dist. LEXIS 100232, at *14 (D. Md. May 25, 2021) (calculating denominator to begin at injured child's birth and end at last elevated BLL); *Pa. Nat'l Mut. Cas. Ins. Co. v. Attsgood Realty*, No. JFM-09-2650, 2010 U.S. Dist. LEXIS 75549 (D. Md. July 2, 2010), *rev'd on other grounds*, 668 F.3d 106 (4th Cir. 2012) ("Maryland's pro rata allocation rule applies not only in cases involving multiple insurers but also involving a single insurer who has insured the subject premises for only a portion of the time during which a plaintiff was exposed to hazardous material."); *see also Pa. Nat'l Mut. Cas. Ins. Co. v. Kirson*, No. TDC-18-3275, 2021 U.S. Dist. LEXIS 49223, at *16 (D. Md. Mar. 16, 2021) (calculating numerator to equal insurer's time on risk between claimant-tenant's arrival at lead-contaminated property and landlord-insured's sale of property where policy limited coverage to delineated properties owned, rented or occupied by insured); *Pa. Nat'l Mut. Cas. Ins. Co. v. Jacob Dackman & Sons, LLC*, No. RDB-16-2640, 2017 U.S. Dist. LEXIS 148907, at *11 (D. Md. Sep. 14, 2017) (rejecting insured-landlord's argument that allocation period should extend past date on which claimant-tenant had vacated lead-contaminated property, reasoning that, although claimant continued to be harmed by lead present in his blood, there was "no evidence of an independent source [of lead] triggering [the claimant]'s injuries").

In *Nat'l Union Fire Ins. Co. v. Porter Hayden Co.*, Nos. CCB-03-3414, CCB-03-3408, 2014 U.S. Dist. LEXIS 114 (D. Md. Jan. 2, 2014), the court held that, absent explicit policy language to the contrary, an excess policy may be triggered when the underlying primary insurer's proportionate share of coverage has been exhausted. The court agreed that Maryland has adopted horizontal exhaustion, but disagreed with the excess insurers' interpretation that the entire primary layer had to be exhausted before their policies would be reached. The court concluded that its interpretation "avoids the problem of requiring an insurer to pay more than its pro rata share." *Id.* at *13; *see also Nat'l Union Fire Ins. Co. v. Porter Hayden Co.*, No. CCB-03-3408, 2014 U.S. Dist. LEXIS 43296, at *13 (D. Md. Mar. 31, 2014) (granting motion to exclude opinions of excess insurers' allocation expert that were based on interpretation of horizontal exhaustion rule previously rejected by court).

In *Gen. Ins. Co. of Am. v. Walter E. Campbell Co.*, No. 12-3307, 2016 U.S. Dist. LEXIS 62842 (D. Md. May 12, 2016), the court, which (as noted above) previously had held that pro-rata allocation applied under Maryland law, issued a number of related rulings in the context of asbestos-related bodily injury claims. Granting the insured's motion for voluntary dismissal of a settled insurer, the court held, among other things, that the insured was obligate to stand in the shoes of a settled insurer and participate on a pro-rata basis to the same extent as the settled insurer would have been obligated to participate under Maryland law. Granting a motion for partial summary judgment filed by non-settled insurers, the court held: (1) the allocation period for indemnity would be the date of a claimant's first exposure to the insured's asbestos product through the date on which the claimant's asbestos-related disease first manifested, exclusive of any periods for which the insured established that insurance for asbestos claims was commercially unavailable to it for procurement; and (2) the insured would be required to pay the pro-rata shares of any judgment or settlement not allocable to the non-settled insurers, including indemnity allocable to any period for which: (a) the insurance procured by the insured has been exhausted; (b) the insurance procured by the insured was issued by one or more insurers that are insolvent; (c) the insurance procured by the insured was issued by an insurer with whom the insured had reached a settlement; and (d) the insured failed to procure insurance, unless the insured established that insurance for asbestos claims was commercially unavailable to it for procurement during that period.

Massachusetts: The Supreme Judicial Court of Massachusetts adopted the pro rata, time-on-the-risk method of allocation in the context of claims for costs of cleanup of oil and tar contamination. *Boston Gas Co. v. Century Indem. Co.,* 910 N.E.2d. 290, 306 (Mass. 2009). In holding that damages should be allocated over all years in which property damage occurred, the Massachusetts high court recognized that the pro rata approach addresses a problem of proof where "it is both scientifically and administratively impossible to allocate to each policy the liability for injuries occurring only within its policy period." *Id.* at 301. The court, therefore, did not foreclose the application of an "injury-in-fact" allocation where the evidence permits a more accurate "estimation of the quantum of property damage" occurring during the policy period. *Id.* at 316. The high court also rejected the "unavailability" exception—noting that it "effectively provides insurance where insurers made the calculated decision not to assume risk and not to accept premiums." *Id.* at 315. The court, however, permitted the policyholder to prorate the amount of its self-insured retention on the same basis as the liability apportioned to each policy period. Thus, if pollution occurred "over the course of a decade, then one-tenth of the total cleanup cost would be apportioned to each policy year, and the [policyholder] would be responsible for one-tenth of the applicable self-insured retention for each year." *Id.* at 316; *see also Crosby Valve, LLC v. OneBeacon Am. Ins. Co.,* 2018 Mass. Super.

LEXIS 271 (Mass. Super. Ct. Oct. 31, 2018) (stating in asbestos coverage action that "[the] pro rata approach is the methodology the SJC has held must be followed in allocating losses in long tail clams . . . where fact-based allocation among different insurers is not feasible"); *OneBeacon Am. Ins. Co. v. Narragansett Elec. Co.* 57 N.E.3d 18, 25 (Mass. App. Ct. 2016) (remanding to trial court to determine allocation of damages on pro-rata basis under *Boston Gas*); *Mass. Ins. Insolvency Fund v. Med. Liab. Ins. Co.,* No. SUCV200805660, 2014 Mass. Super. LEXIS 51 (Mass. Super. Ct. Feb. 3, 2014) (holding that fact-based allocation in medical malpractice context was impossible and, therefore, pro rata allocation applied under *Boston Gas*); *New England Insulation Co., Inc. v. Liberty Mut. Ins. Co.,* 988 N.E.2d 450 (Mass. App. Ct. 2013), *appeal denied,* 991 N.E.2d 188 (Mass. 2013) (finding "no persuasive reason why the pro rata method articulated in *Boston Gas* should not control" and applying pro rata, time-on-the-risk allocation in the asbestos context); *Boston Gas Co. v. Century Indem. Co.,* 708 F.3d 254, 261 (1st Cir. 2013) (applying Massachusetts law) (upholding time-on-the-risk allocation where fact-based allocation was impossible based on evidence presented at trial); *Plaistow Project, LLC v. ACE Prop. & Cas. Ins. Co.,* No. 16-11385-IT, 2018 U.S. Dist. LEXIS 156438, at *43 (D. Mass. May 17, 2018) (recognizing that pro-rata allocation "is only appropriate if facts cannot be developed to determine damages more precisely," but declining to rule on allocation issues as a matter of law because of fact questions); *Graphic Arts Mut. Ins. Co. v. D.N. Lukens, Inc.,* No. 11-cv-10460, 2013 U.S. Dist. LEXIS 75201(D. Mass. May 29, 2013) (applying continuous trigger to asbestos claims and allocating liability on the basis of the period of time that each insurer's policies were in effect); *Peabody Essex Museum, Inc. v. U.S. Fire Ins. Co.,* No. 06-11209-NMG, 2012 U.S. Dist. LEXIS 99474 (D. Mass. Jul. 18, 2012), *aff'd, Peabody Essex Museum, Inc. v. U.S. Fire Ins. Co.,* 802 F.3d 39, 56 (1st Cir. 2015) (upholding pro rata allocation of indemnity and refusing to distinguish between insured and uninsured periods in allocating loss).

In an earlier decision in the *Peabody Essex* litigation, the U.S. District Court for the District of Massachusetts considered whether defense costs should be subject to pro-rata allocation under *Boston Gas. See Peabody Essex Museum, Inc. v. U.S. Fire Ins. Co.,* 2010 U.S. Dist. LEXIS 106275 (D. Mass. Sept. 30, 2010). The court initially acknowledged that "some of the policy rationales for dividing indemnity costs, such as limiting insurance premiums and providing incentives to maintain insurance, arguably apply to defense costs as well." *Id.* at *46. The court nevertheless proceeded to rely on the so-called "in for a penny, in for a pound rule," by which courts have held that where a litigation involves both covered and uncovered claims, the duty to defend extends to the entirety of the litigation, even if the defense of covered claims provides a collateral benefit to uncovered claims. *Id.* at *46-48. On appeal, the First Circuit affirmed this ruling, reasoning that Massachusetts precedent provides for a "broad and formidable contractual duty to defend that heavily favors insureds and that stands apart from indemnity obligations." *Peabody Essex Museum, Inc. v. U.S. Fire Ins. Co.*, 802 F.3d 39, 56 (1st Cir. 2015). The First Circuit further explained that its view was further "narrowed" by *Boston Gas*, in which "the SJC carefully circumscribed its decision to the indemnity allocation questions that were before it." *Id.* (As noted above, the First Circuit also affirmed the district court's ruling on allocation of indemnity.) A New York federal court, predicting Massachusetts law, held that where a primary policy imposed a duty to defend for "any suit" that sought damages, the insurer was jointly and severally liable for the insured's underlying defense costs. *Narragansett Elec. Co. v. Am. Home. Assur. Co.*, 999 F. Supp. 2d 511 (S.D.N.Y. 2014), *rev'd and vacated on other grounds*, 667 Fed. Appx. 8 (2d Cir. Jun. 23, 2016).

Michigan: The Supreme Court of Michigan has not taken a definitive position on allocation in continuous injury cases, however, the Sixth Circuit, along with numerous appellate courts and district courts, have applied the pro rata, time-on-the-risk approach under Michigan law. In *Gelman Sci., Inc. v. Fid. & Cas. Co. of N.Y.*, the Michigan Supreme Court commented on allocation in dicta, reinforcing consideration of the particular language of the policy at issue, and the availability of equitable means where the policyholder cannot meet its burden of showing how much damage occurred in each year. 572 N.W.2d 617, 622–25 (Mich. 1998). Two cases decided by the Michigan Court of Appeals have reached different results on different facts. In *Arco Indus. Corp. v. American Motorists Ins. Co.*, the time-on-the-risk method was adopted to apportion pollution remediation costs among successive insurers for continuous property damage to which an injury-in-fact trigger of coverage had been applied. 594 N.W.2d 61, 69–70 (Mich. Ct. App. 1998), *aff'd without opinion* 617 N.W.2d 330 (Mich. 2000) (emphasizing the policy language stating that coverage applies to damage and injury taking place "during the policy period."). *Accord Motors Liquidation Co., DIP Lenders Trust v. Allianz Ins. Co.*, No. N11C-12-022, 2013 Del. Super. LEXIS 605 (Del. Super. Ct. Dec. 31, 2013), *aff'd*, 191 A.3d 1109 (Del. 2018) (predicting, based on *Arco Industries*, the Michigan Supreme Court "would likely not follow 'all sums'" and finding conflict between Michigan and Delaware law regarding allocation methodology). Conversely, in an unpublished opinion, the Court of Appeals adopted the "all sums" approach based on distinctions in policy language in *Dow Corning Corp. v. Continental Cas. Co.*, Nos. 200143–200154, 1999 Mich. App. LEXIS 2920 (Mich. Ct. App. Oct. 12, 1999). Most significantly, the *Dow Corning* Court highlighted unique language contained in the continuation clause of the policy, like in *Chicago Bridge* and *Hercules, supra*, extending coverage beyond the policy period in the case of continuing damage. Numerous courts have since distinguished *Dow Corning* or held that the Michigan Supreme Court would instead adopt the pro rata time-on-the-risk method of allocation, as applied in *Arco Indus. See, e.g., Decker Mfg. Corp. v. Travelers Indem. Co.*, No. 1:13–820, 2015 U.S. Dist. LEXIS 12169, at *37-38 (W.D. Mich. Feb. 3, 2015) (finding *Dow Corning* inapposite because policies at issue did not contain continuing coverage clause and pro-rata allocation was "consistent with the policy language"); *Stryker Corp. v. Nat'l Union Fire Ins. Co.*, No. 4:01-CV-157, 2005 U.S. Dist. LEXIS 13113 (W.D. Mich. July 1, 2005); *see also Cont'l Cas. Co. v. Indian Head Indus., Inc.*, No. 05–73918, 2010 U.S. Dist. LEXIS 3170 (E.D. Mich. Jan. 15, 2010) (highlighting that *Dow Corning* has limited precedential value, as an unpublished opinion, and because the Michigan Supreme Court affirmed *Arco* eight months *after* the *Dow Corning* opinion was issued); *Wolverine World Wide, Inc. v. Liberty Mut. Ins. Co.*, No. 260330, 2007 Mich. App. LEXIS 657 (Mich. Ct. App. Mar. 8, 2007); *Century Indem. Co. v. Aero-Motive Co.*, 318 F. Supp. 2d 530, 544–45 (W.D. Mich. 2003) (allocating defense costs according to time-on-the-risk method); *Alticor, Inc. v. Nat'l Union Fire Ins. Co. of Pa.*, 916 F. Supp. 2d 813, 832 (W.D. Mich. 2013) ("Michigan courts and the Sixth Circuit have applied the pro rata, or time-on-the-risk, method for allocating damages and costs for situations involving consecutively issued insurance policies."); *City of Sterling Heights v. United Nat'l Ins. Co.*, 319 F. App'x 357, 361–62 (6th Cir. 2009) (holding time-on-the-risk was proper way to allocate indemnity for claims alleging misconduct of city officials); *Cont'l Cas. Co. v. Indian Head Indus.*, 666 F. App'x 456 (6th Cir. 2016) (finding that the policy language limits liability to injuries during the policy period and precludes coverage of those that continued after the policy ended, and therefore the pro rata method of allocation applied); *Livonia Pub. Sch. v. Selective Ins. Co.*, No. 16–10324, 2020 U.S. Dist. LEXIS 125845, at *8-11 (E.D. Mich. July 17, 2020) (concluding that, under "clear" Michigan law, time-on-the-risk allocation applied to defense and indemnity costs arising out of claims alleging "pattern of abuse" of school students resulting in indivisible injuries over two policy periods); *Cont'l Ins. Co. v. Honeywell Int'l, Inc.*, 188 A.3d 297, 313 (N.J. 2018) (recognizing that Michigan follows pro-rata, time-on-the-risk approach to allocation in continuous injury cases, but ultimately finding

New Jersey law applicable). Other distinctions made are that the insurer agreed to cover "those sums" not "all sums"; coverage was provided during the policy period only, not before or after; pro rata, time-on-the-risk is consistent with the "injury-in-fact" trigger of coverage adopted in *Gelman*; and there is an inherent simplicity and predictability with the pro rata, time-on-the-risk allocation method. *See, e.g.,* *Stryker*, (addressing distinctions); *Cont'l Cas. Co. v. Indian Head Indus.*, 2010 U.S. Dist. LEXIS 3170 (E.D. Mich. 2010) (same).

Minnesota: The Supreme Court of Minnesota was the first state high court to adopt the pro rata, time-on-the-risk method of allocation. *See N. States Power Co. v. Fid. & Cas. Co. of N.Y.*, 523 N.W.2d 657, 664 (Minn. 1994) (addressing claims for property damage due to soil and groundwater contamination), and *Domtar, Inc. v. Niagara Fire Ins. Co.*, 563 N.W.2d 724, 733–34 (Minn. 1997) (involving claims for costs associated with cleanup of environmental pollution). The Supreme Court of Minnesota later adopted an "unavailability" exception in *Wooddale Builders, Inc. v. Maryland Cas. Co.*, 722 N.W.2d 283, 297–98 (Minn. 2006). The court reasoned that this exception holds the insured responsible for only those risks that it elected to assume, while eliminating any windfall that would result if the insured received a benefit of insurance coverage that it had deliberately declined to purchase. *Id.* at 297. The insured has the burden of demonstrating "unavailability." *Id.*; *see also St. Paul Mercury Ins. Co. v. N. States Power Co.*, No. A07–1775, 2009 Minn. App. Unpub. LEXIS 977 (Minn. Ct. App. Aug. 25, 2009) (holding insured failed to demonstrate that insurance was unavailable simply because claim may not be covered under earlier accident-based policies; rather the issue is "whether the coverage for the particular risk was generally available in the market place"). The Minnesota Supreme Court held in *Cargill, Inc. v. ACE Am. Ins. Co.*, 784 N.W.2d 341 (Minn. 2010), that an insurer honoring its duty to defend is entitled to contribution from other insurers on the risk on an "equal shares" basis, expressly overruling its prior decision in *Iowa National Mutual Ins. Co. v. Universal Underwriters Ins. Co.*, 150 N.W.2d 233 (Minn. 1967). A Minnesota federal court has interpreted state law precedent to mean that solvent insurers *do not* have to "fill the gap" left by insolvent insurers because doing so "would effectively force insurers to underwrite an insured's other insurance purchasing decisions, becoming a guarantor of all companies." *H.B. Fuller Co. v. U.S. Fire Ins. Co.*, No. 09-2827, 2011 U.S. Dist. LEXIS 77896 (D. Minn. July 18, 2011). The federal court declined to certify the issue to the Minnesota Supreme Court, finding that "the Supreme Court has enumerated various principles which, in conjunction with precedent in other jurisdictions and public policy, allow the [federal] Court to determine the issue[.]" A Minnesota federal court, however, also held that "an insured who chooses to go without coverage for a period of time must bear the portion of the total damages that is allocated to that period of time... But an insured who is involuntarily self-insured is not required to bear the damages allocated to periods of self-insurance." *Land O' Lakes, Inc. v. Employers Mut. Liab. Ins. Co. of Wisc.*, 846 F. Supp. 2d 1007, 1038 (D. Minn. 2012), *aff'd*, 728 F.3d 822 (8th Cir. 2013); *see also Soo Line R.R. Co. v. Travelers Indem. Co.*, No. 18-1989, 2019 U.S. Dist. LEXIS 90279 (D. Minn. May 30, 2019) (explaining basis why the insured must answer an interrogatory seeking information relevant to issues of allocation for claims involving environmental contamination).

Mississippi: In *EMJ Corp. v. Hudson Specialty Ins. Co.*, 833 F.3d 544, 551-56 (5th Cir. 2016), the Fifth Circuit, applying Mississippi law, found that the "other insurance" clauses in two excess carriers' policies were "mutually repugnant." *Id.* (citing *Allstate Ins. Co. v. Chi Ins. Co.*, 676 So. 2d 271, 275 (Miss. 1996)). Therefore, the "other insurance" clauses canceled each other out and the policies required pro rata contribution. *Id.*

Missouri: Although Missouri law is unsettled on the issue of allocation, at least two intermediate appellate decisions support pro rata allocation. *See Cont'l Cas. Co. v. Med. Protective Co.*, 859 S.W.2d 789, 792 (Mo. Ct. App. 1993) ("Where the loss is caused not by a single event but by a series of cumulative acts or omissions, we believe the fair method of apportioning the loss among consecutive insurers is by application of the 'exposure theory' utilized in cases of progressive disease such as asbestosis.") (citing *Ins. Co. of N. Am. v. Forty-Eight Insulations, Inc.*, 633 F.2d 1212 (6th Cir. 1980)); *Nationwide Ins. Co. v. Cent. Mo. Elec. Co-op., Inc.*, 278 F.3d 742, 748 (8th Cir. 2001) (applying Missouri law and holding "time-on-the-risk analysis was appropriate."). *But see Viacom, Inc. v. Transit Cas. Co.*, No. WD-628564, 2004 Mo. App. LEXIS 292 (Mo. Ct. App. 2004) (applying Pennsylvania law but noting that Missouri law would reach the same result); *Monsanto Co. v. C.E. Heath Comp. & Liab. Ins. Co.*, 652 A.2d 30 (Del. 1995) (applying Missouri law and holding that Missouri is an "all sums" state based on *Tinsley v. Aetna Ins. Co. of Hartford*, 205 S.W. 78 (Mo. Ct. App. 1918)).

A Missouri trial court noted that Missouri courts have not specifically addressed the allocation issue, but have applied a pro rata, "time-on-the-risk" approach in other contexts. *Mallinckrodt Inc., et al. v. Cont'l Ins. Co.*, No. 05CC-001214 (St. Louis County, Nov. 9, 2012) (citing *Cont'l Cas. Co., supra; Nationwide Ins. Co., supra*). Accordingly, the court held that Missouri would apply the pro rata method of allocation of damages in the continuous pollution context because the pro rata approach "recognizes the inherent difficulty of proving the exact amount of timing and damages under these facts" and "emphasizes that insurers are on the risk for only a specified period of time." *Id.* at 3. In contrast, the court recognized that the "all sums" approach "does not take into account that a given insurer is likely to pay for damages incurred outside of its policy period" and "places an inordinate amount of power in the hands of the insured by allowing the insured to choose the policy period in which to recover." *Id.*

By contrast, the Missouri Court of Appeals concluded that an "all sums" rather than "pro rata" approach should be applied to allocate damages where specific policy language obligates an insurer "to indemnify the insured for *all sums* which the Assured shall be obliged to pay by reason of the liability . . . for damages . . . on account of property damage, caused by or arising out of each occurrence happening during the policy period." *Doe Run Resources, Corp. v. Certain Underwriters at Lloyd's London*, 400 S.W.3d 463, 475 (Mo. Ct. App. 2013). Notably, in a footnote, the court stated that its decision did "not reach the issue of whether Missouri law requires an all sums approach or a pro rata approach as the plain language of the policies governs here." *Id.* at 474 n. 8. Similarly, in *Nooter Corp. v. Allianz Underwriters Ins. Co.*, the Missouri Court of Appeals focused on the language of the excess insurers' policies and again applied "all sums." 536 S.W.3d 251 (Mo. Ct. App. 2017). The *Nooter* court observed that the policies at issue "operate in a very similar manner to the language analyzed in *Doe Run*." *Id.* at 266, citing *Doe Run, supra.* The *Nooter* court then applied vertical exhaustion, finding the policies' "other insurance" clauses ambiguous, and noting that method is "conceptually consistent" with "all sums" allocation. *Id.* at *271.

More recently, in the context of environmental property damage claims, the Court of Appeals found "all sums" allocation applicable under policy language similar to the language analyzed in *Nooter*. *Northrop Grumman Guidance & Elecs. Co. v. Emplrs. Ins. Co. of Wausau*, 612 S.W.3d 1, 15 (Mo. Ct. App. 2020). The Court of Appeals nevertheless recognized that "[a]llocation does not create legal liability (i.e., impose coverage) for divisible property damage where the fact-finder determined none existed." *Id.* at 18. The court concluded that, because the jury had found one of the insurers liable for property damage in only one of the several areas of the site at issue, and had declined to find that all property damage across the site was "indivisible or commingled," the trial court properly limited the insurer's indemnity obligation to the one area. *Id.* at 18. The Court of Appeals also found no error in the admission of testimony from the insurer's expert concerning a scientifically recognized methodology to determine to a reasonable degree of scientific certainty the relative percentage of groundwater contamination attributable to each site area. Disagreeing with the policyholder that the testimony was irrelevant under all sums allocation, the court explained that "this evidence was not 'allocation' evidence, but rather permissible 'divisibility' evidence presented to show that no covered property damage occurred during the insurers' policy periods." *Id.* (citing *State of Cal. v. Allstate Ins. Co.*, 201 P.3d 1147, 1166-67 (Cal. 2009)).

In *Zurich Am. Ins. Co. v. Ins. Co. of N. Am.*, No. 14-1112, 2018 U.S. Dist. LEXIS 77061 (E.D. Mo. May 8, 2018), a Missouri federal district court, following *Nooter*, held that an insurer that had settled an underlying asbestos-related bodily injury claim against its insured was responsible for the full amount of settlement and could not reduce its liability through a contribution claim against the insured, but could seek contribution from any other triggered insurers. *Id.* at *14-16. In a later decision, the court ruled that the targeted insurer could not obtain contribution from another insurer also on the risk when the claimant was exposed to asbestos because the pollution exclusion in that insurer's policy applied to the claim and relieved it of any indemnity obligation. *Zurich Am. Ins. Co. v. Ins. Co. of N. Am.*, 392 F. Supp. 3d 992, 1005-06 (E.D. Mo. 2019).

Montana: In *U.S. Fid. & Guar. Co. v. Continental Ins. Co.*, No. 04-29, 2010 U.S. Dist. LEXIS 110680 (D. Mont. Oct. 18, 2010), a Montana federal district court noted that the Montana Supreme Court would "likely … adopt joint and several liability for defense costs" but ruling that, even under pro rata allocation, it would not prorate to the insured years during which pollution insurance was unavailable due to the absolute pollution exclusion. *But see NorthWestern Corp. v. AEGIS*, No. 07-1174 (S.D. Cir. Ct. July 29, 2010), *reprinted in* 24–37 Mealey's Litig. Rep.: Insurance (Aug. 4, 2010) (applying the "all sums" method of allocation under Montana law). *In Nat'l Indem. Co. v. State*, No. DA 19-0533, 2020 Mont. LEXIS 2444 (Mont. Oct. 13, 2020), the Montana high court ruled that the insured could not argue that pro-rata allocation was inapplicable because of unavailability due to its failure to raise the issue below.

Nebraska: The Supreme Court of Nebraska adopted the pro rata, time-on-the-risk method of allocation in the context of claims for environmental property damage. *Dutton-Lainson Co. v. Cont'l Ins. Co.*, 778 N.W.2d 433 (Neb. 2010). The court concluded that, based on the policy language, the insured could not assert joint-and-several liability without proving the amount of damages that occurred during the period of coverage provided by each insurer. *Id.* at 444–45.

Nevada: In *Evanston Ins. Co. v. Western Cmty. Ins. Co.*, the court looked to California law to analyze the insurer's duty to contribute to an insured's defense by another insurer. 2016 U.S. Dist. LEXIS 50888 (D. Nev. April 15, 2016). The court concluded "that allocation according to 'time on the risk' would be most equitable and 'accomplish substantial justice' among the parties." *Id.* at *10 (citations omitted) (indicating one insurer was on the risk for 59 days, whereas the other insurer was on the risk for 1460 days). However, the District of Nevada court, noting that "[t]here is no fixed rule for allocating costs and expenses among primary insurers," applied an equal shares approach in *Assurance Co. of Am. v. Ironshore Specialty Ins. Co.*, 2017 U.S. Dist. LEXIS 170453 (D. Nev. Oct. 12, 2017) (apportioning defense and indemnity equally among two insurers, one providing approximately 18 years of coverage and the other providing 9 years of coverage to common insureds). The court reasoned that the policies at issue and the absence of facts indicating when the construction work was performed and completed supported the application of the equal shares approach.

New Hampshire: The Supreme Court of New Hampshire adopted the pro rata, by limits and years approach in *EnergyNorth Natural Gas, Inc. v. Certain Underwriters at Lloyd's*, 934 A.2d 517 (N.H. 2007). In deciding whether to apply pro rata or "all sums" to the allocation question, the *EnergyNorth* court made the salient point that the problem presented by long-term damage cases presents an atypical question. The court explained "[t]he typical occurrence covered by a liability policy is something akin to a car accident. Losses of this nature are relatively easy to identify because damages are both immediate and finite." *Id.* at 521 (quoting *Pub. Serv. Co. v. Wallis & Cos.*, 986 P.2d 924, 935 (Colo. 1999)). By contrast, in long-term environmental pollution cases, "correlating degrees of damage to particular points along the loss timeline may be virtually impossible [,] [which] has led to substantial uncertainty as to how responsibility for such losses should be allocated where multiple insurers have issued successive policies to the insured over the period of time the damage was developing." *Id.* (quoting *Pub. Serv.*, 986 P.2d at 935). After considering the various methods of allocation, the *EnergyNorth* Court followed the New Jersey Supreme Court by adopting the pro rata, by limits and years method announced in *Owens-Illinois, Inc. v. United Ins. Co.*, 650 A.2d 974, 993–94 (N.J. 1994). Again, under this approach, loss is allocated among all triggered policies based on both the number of years a policy was on the risk as well as that policy's limits. *EnergyNorth*, 934 A.2d at 523. In support of its decision, the court explained that joint and several liability is inconsistent with the injury in fact trigger approach adopted in New Hampshire because it allows the policyholder to determine which policy will pay and therefore is triggered. *Id.* at 526 (citing *EnergyNorth Natural Gas, Inc. v. Certain Underwriters at Lloyd's*, 848 A.2d 715 (N.H. 2004)) (adopting the injury-in-fact trigger)). The court also criticized the joint-and-several approach, noting that it "rests on an assumption not in accordance with the development of the law: that at every point in the progression, the probable damages due to injury … from exposure to manifestation will be substantially the same," "creates a false equivalence between an insured who has purchased insurance coverage continuously for many years and an insured who has purchased only one year of insurance," it "does not solve the allocation problem; it merely postpones it." *Id.*

New Jersey: The New Jersey Supreme Court adopted the pro rata, by limits and years, method of allocation in the context of claims for bodily injury and property damage from exposure to asbestos. *Owens-Illinois, Inc. v. United Ins. Co.*, 650 A.2d 974 (N.J. 1994). In rejecting the "all sums" approach, the court concluded that "to convert the 'all sums' or 'ultimate net loss' language into the answer to apportionment when injury occurs over a period of years is like trying to place one's hat on a rack that was never designed to hold it. It does not work. The language was never intended to cover apportionment when continuous injury occurs over multiple years." *Id.* at 989. To spread the risk, the court followed *Armstrong World Industries, Inc. v. Aetna Casualty & Surety Co.*, 26 Cal. Rptr. 2d 35, 57 (Cal. Ct. App. 1993), and allocated damages on the basis of the extent of risk assumed, i.e., proration on the basis of policy limits, multiplied by years of coverage. *Id.* at 993; *see also Carter-Wallace, Inc. v. Admiral Ins. Co.*, 712 A.2d 1116 (N.J. 1998) (adopting a pro rata method of allocation, accounting for the time-on-the-risk and the degree of the risk assumed, in the context of claims for property damage caused by environmental contamination); *Potomac Ins. Co. of Ill. ex rel. OneBeacon Ins. Co. v. Pa Mfrs. Assoc. Ins. Co.*, 73 A.3d 465 (N.J. 2013) (reiterating *Owens-Illinois* and *Carter-Wallace* holdings in determining that non-settling insurer could seek contribution towards insured's defense from settling insurer); *The Travelers Indem. Co. v. Thomas & Betts Corp.*, 2017 U.S. Dist. LEXIS 117135, at *3 (D.N.J. July 26, 2017) ("The allocation for both defense and indemnity costs . . . are based on the degree of risk transferred as reflected by the purchase of insurance, regardless of the likelihood that the policy will answer a claim."); *Franklin Mut. Ins. Co. v. Metro. Prop. & Cas. Ins. Co.*, 968 A.2d 1191, 1192 (N.J. Super. Ct. App. Div. 2009) (holding that a separate *Owens-Illinois* allocation must be conducted for each policyholder in the context of continuous property damage involving multiple policyholders); *Quincy Mut. Fire Ins. v. Borough* *of Bellmawr*, 799 A.2d 499 (N.J. 2002) (holding that allocation must be reflected by actual days on the risk rather than rounding up by the year). New Jersey courts have found that the pro rata approach serves several public policy interests, including, "(1) maximizing resources to cope with environmental injury or damage; (2) giving the greatest incentive to insureds to acquire insurance; and (3) notions of simple justice." *Spaulding Composites Co. v. Aetna Cas. & Sur. Co.*, 819 A.2d 410, 417 (N.J. 2003) (holding that non cumulation clauses were unenforceable). *See also Cont'l Ins. Co. v. Honeywell Int'l, Inc.*, 234 N.J. 23, 62 (2018). The District Court for the District of New Jersey also held that when an insured purchased "increasing levels of excess and/or umbrella coverage," it was in essence transferring greater portions of its own risk to the insurers. *Thomas & Betts*, 2017 U.S. Dist. LEXIS 117135, at *10. As such, "to make an allocation in proportion to the degree of the risks transferred or retained during the years of exposure, the umbrella and excess per occurrence limits must be included in the allocation formula." *Id.* (internal citations omitted).

A New York trial court, applying New Jersey law, has held that damages must be allocated to all "triggered" policies during the applicable period, whether or not the proceeds from those policies can be collected (*i.e.*, the insurer is insolvent or the policies contain an applicable exclusion). *See Foster Wheeler L.L.C. v. Affiliated FM Ins. Co.*, 910 N.Y.S.2d 762 (N.Y. Sup. Ct. N.Y. Cty. 2010); *see also In re Liquidation of Integrity Ins. Co./Sepco Corp.*, 49 A.3d 428 (N.J. Super. Ct. App. Div. 2012) (holding that New Jersey's preference to apply pro-rata allocation *methodology in context of excess insurer in liquidation, rather than* all-sums allocation, would not have impeded administration of insurer's estate, and thus, favored application of pro rata allocation where excess insurer was domiciled in New Jersey).

The Appellate Division has held that in "environmental contamination cases, the initial discharge of contaminants is an occurrence that triggers coverage." *Mid-Monmouth Realty Assocs. v. Metallurgical Indus.*, 2017 N.J. Super. Unpub. LEXIS 993, at *32 (N.J. Super. Ct. App. Div. Apr. 21, 2017) (citing *Quincy*, 799 A.2d at 513-14). The court in *Mid-Monmouth* also held that "in the continuous trigger context, insurance policies covering the risk are triggered throughout the period of exposure, discovery, and remediation." *Id.* (citing *Owens-Illinois*, 650 A.2d at 984). *See also Cooper Indus., LLC v. Emplrs Ins. of Wausau*, 2017 N.J. Super. Unpub. LEXIS 3239, at *34-35 (N.J. Sup. Ct. Law Div. Oct. 16, 2017) (applying continuous trigger to environmental contamination case). The Appellate Division has also held that the "last pull of the trigger occurs with the initial manifestation of a toxic-tort personal injury." *Polarome Int'l, Inc. v. Greenwich Ins. Co.*, 404 N.J. Super. 241, 268 (N.J. App.

Div. 2008). *See also Air Master & Cooling, Inc. v. Selective Ins. Co. of Am.*, 452 N.J. Super. 35 (N.J. App. Div. 2017) (applying continuous trigger in construction defect context).

The New Jersey Supreme Court held that liability insurers covering a long-tail loss cannot seek contribution from the New Jersey Property-Liability Insurance Guaranty Association (a nonprofit, unincorporated association obligated to stand in the place of an insolvent insurer) for the *Carter-Wallace* shares of insolvent insurers unless the limits of all solvent insurers are exhausted. The court also rejected the argument that the insured would have to bear the burden of the insolvent insurer's *Carter-Wallace* allocation to the extent the Guaranty Association was not required to pay. *Farmers Mut. Fire Ins. Co. v. New Jersey Property-Liability Ins. Guar. Assoc.*, 74 A.3d 860 (N.J. 2013); *but see Ward Sand & Materials Co. v Transamerica Ins. Co.*, No. CAM-L-4130-09, 2013 N.J. Super. Unpub. LEXIS 3062 (Nov. 13, 2013), *aff'd*, 2016 N.J. Super. Unpub. LEXIS 59 (N.J. Super. Ct. App. Div. Jan. 12, 2016) (declining to follow *Farmers Mutual* because 2004 amendments to Guaranty Association statute, which made Guaranty Association payor of last resort, did not apply retroactively to insolvencies that occurred before 2004).

The New Jersey Supreme Court has also held that an insured must pay the full amount of its deductible for each triggered policy. *Benjamin Moore & Co. v. Aetna Cas. & Sur. Co.*, 843 A.2d 1094 (N.J. 2004). New Jersey's highest court has also endorsed the unavailability exception. *Champion Dyeing & Finishing Co. v. Centennial Ins. Co.*, 810 A.2d 68 (N.J. 2002).

New Mexico: No instructive authority.

New York: Historically, New York has been a pro rata jurisdiction. In *Consolidated Edison Co. of N.Y. v. Allstate Ins. Co.*, 774 N.E.2d 687 (N.Y. 2002), the New York high court made clear that certain occurrence-based CGL policies provide coverage only for bodily injury or property damage that occurs *"during the policy period."* Based on this fundamental principle, the court affirmed the trial court's decision to allocate damages "based on the amount of the time the policy was in effect in comparison to the over-all duration of the damage." *Id.* at 695. Many courts applying New York law followed *Consolidated Edison* and applied pro rata allocation broadly. *See, e.g., Roman Catholic Diocese of Brooklyn v. Nat'l Union Fire Ins. Co. of Pittsburgh, Pa.*, 991 N.E.2d 666, 676-77 (N.Y. 2013) (declining to allocate indemnity jointly-and-severally because extent of alleged sexual assault that occurred during particular policy period could not be determined); *Nat'l Union Fire Ins. Co. of Pittsburgh, PA v. Roman Catholic Diocese of Brooklyn*, 2017 N.Y. Misc. LEXIS 687 (Sup. Ct. N.Y. Cnty. Feb. 27,

2017) (same); *Crucible Materials Corp. v. Certain Underwriters at Lloyd's London & London Market Cos.*, 681 F. Supp. 2d 216, 226, 231–32 (N.D.N.Y. 2010) (discussing differences between pro rata under New York law and "all sums" allocation under Pennsylvania law, and holding that second-layer excess policy would not be reached based on pro rata by years allocation); *Air & Liquid Sys. Corp. v. Allianz Underwriters Ins. Co.*, No. 11–247, 2013 U.S. Dist. LEXIS 142359 (W.D. Pa. Sept. 27, 2013) (applying New York law to certain policies and rejecting policyholder's argument that policy language supported joint-and-several allocation).

In 2016, however, the New York Court of Appeals held that, in policies containing non-cumulation clauses, all sums is the appropriate allocation method. In *In the Matter of Viking Pump, Inc.*, 27 N.Y.3d 244 (2016), the court held: "We agree that it would be inconsistent with the language of the non-cumulation clauses to use pro rata allocation here. Such policy provisions plainly contemplate that multiple successive insurance policies can indemnify the insured for the same loss or occurrence by acknowledging that a covered loss or occurrence may 'also [be] covered in whole or in part under any other excess [p]olicy issued to the [insured] prior to the inception date' of the instant policy. *Id.* at 261. The court also noted that "[s]everal of the excess policies here also contain continuing coverage clauses within the non-cumulation and prior insurance provisions, reinforcing our conclusion that all sums—not pro rata—allocation was intended in such policies." *Id.* at 262. A few months later, the New York Appellate Division cited to both *Viking Pump* and *Consolidated Edison* in its allocation analysis, and applied pro rata allocation to policies that contained "during the policy period" language but did not contain a non-cumulation clause. *Keyspan Gas E. Corp. v. Munich Reins. Am., Inc.*, 143 A.D.3d 86, 95-96 (N.Y. Sup. Ct. App. Div. 2016).

More recently, in *Olin Corp. v. OneBeacon Am. Ins. Co.*, 864 F.3d 130 (2d Cir. 2017), the U.S. Court of Appeals for the Second Circuit addressed issues arising from underlying environmental property damage claims against an insured. The umbrella excess liability policies at issue contained a non-cumulation clause (which the court also referred to as a "prior insurance provision") and also had a "continuing coverage" provision. The Second Circuit held that, in accordance with *Viking Pump*, "all sums" allocation and vertical exhaustion applied to the policies in question. The court rejected the insurer's invitation to apply a "hybrid" approach in which: (1) pro-rata allocation and horizontal exhaustion would apply to the immediately underlying primary policies, which did not contain non-cumulation clauses; and (2) "all sums" allocation would apply to the policies that contained non-cumulation clauses. (Under the hybrid approach, the primary limits would not be exhausted).

Other courts applying New York law have since weighed in on the all-sums/ non-cumulation clause issue. In 2018, the New York Supreme Court, New York County, confirmed a referee's finding that "all sums" allocation was required under excess policies that contained a non-cumulation provision. *In re Liquidation of Midland Ins. Co.*, 2018 N.Y. Misc. LEXIS 4668 (N.Y. Sup. Ct. Aug. 18, 2018). The court rejected the contention that the policies' lack of "continuing coverage" clauses was sufficient to distinguish the policies from those at issue in *Viking Pump* (which did contain "continuing coverage" clauses). The *Midland* court found that the "continuing coverage" clause merely "reinforced" the Court of Appeal's all sums findings, and that the absence of such clauses was not sufficient to overrule the *Viking Pump* holding. The court also found that even though the policies at issue provided coverage on an "ultimate net loss" basis and not on an "all sums" basis (as in *Viking Pump*), the meaning of the terms was "essentially the same . . . because the insurer is obligated to indemnify the full extent of the policyholder's liability for claims covered under the policy." *Id.* at *20. The Appellate Division upheld this ruling. *See In re Liquidation of Midland Ins. Co.*, 98 N.Y.S.3d 195 (1st Dep't. 2019); *see also Carrier Corp. v. Allstate Ins. Co.*, 187 A.D.3d 1616, 1621 (4th Dep't. 2020) (upholding trial court decision finding that "[t]he non-cumulation and prior insurance provisions incorporated in the . . . excess policies" rendered all sums as the appropriate allocation method); *Mineweaser v. OneBeacon Ins. Co.*, 2018 U.S. Dist. LEXIS 91203, at *68-72 (W.D.N.Y. May 30, 2018) (all sums applies to excess policies with non-cumulation clauses, and thus, if the insured "exhausted the underling policy for any year in which plaintiff suffered an injury in fact, plaintiff [can] enforce the judgment against any excess policy that provided coverage excess to the underlying policy, up to the policy limit for that year, and then pursue successive layers of excess insurance for that year until the judgment is satisfied").

In *Danaher Corp. v. Travelers Indem. Co.*, 414 F. Supp. 3d 436 (S.D.N.Y. 2019), a federal district court found that pro rata allocation applies for policies with "occurs during the policy period" language, "at least where the policy does not contain a non-cumulation clause or other similar language evidencing the understanding that two or more insurance policies that do not overlap in time might indemnify the insured with respect to the same loss or occurrence." *Id.* at 451. However, there were also certain excess policies that contained non-cumulation clauses. The court held that all sums allocation "must be used to allocate costs . . . whenever an insurer's triggered policy contains a non-cumulation clause comparable to the clauses in" *Viking Pump*. *Id.* at 458. The court cited *Keyspan* for the proposition that because "the method of allocation is to be governed foremost by the particular language of the relevant insurance policy, a different conclusion is warranted with respect to [the] policies that do not contain non-cumulation clauses" than those that do. *Id.* at 459.

The Second Circuit previously held in *Olin Corp. v. American Home Assurance Co.*, 704 F.3d 89 (2d Cir. 2012), that an "all sums" method could be applied where the express policy language stated that the insurer would continue to protect the insured for injury or damage arising out of an "occurrence" during the policy period if injury or damage continued after the policy's termination. *Id.* at 101-02. In support of its decision, the Second Circuit also relied upon a clause treating all exposures to the same general conditions as a single occurrence. Proponents of pro rata allocation would argue that this rationale confuses the limitation on the number of limits with the insuring agreement, which expressly limits coverage only to injury or damage that occurs during the policy period. While the court in *Viking Pump* discusses *Olin*, the court ultimately rejected the argument that its holding supported a finding of pro rata allocation for policies that contain non-cumulation clauses. *Viking Pump*, 27 N.Y.3d at 263-64.

In 2018, the New York Court of Appeals expressly rejected the unavailability exception, holding that the policyholder, not the insurer, "bears the risk for those years during which . . . coverage was unavailable." *Keyspan Gas E. Corp. v. Munich Reins. Am., Inc.*, 31 N.Y.3d 51 (2018). The court cited *Viking Pump* in holding that because "the very essence of pro rata allocation is that the insurance policy language limits indemnification to losses and occurrences during the policy period, the unavailability rule cannot be reconciled with the pro rata approach." *Id.* at 63. *See also Olin Corp. v. Ins. Co. of N. Am.*, 218 F.Supp.3d 212, 218 (S.D.N.Y. 2016) ("New York permits allocation of costs relating to the duty to indemnify between the insurer and insured where the injuries occurred during covered and uncovered time periods.").

As for the Court of Appeal's holding on allocation of defense costs in *Continental Casualty Co. v. Rapid-American Corp.*, 609 N.E.2d 506 (N.Y. 1993), the court did not endorse "all sums"; it simply held that the trial court did not err in failing to allocate defense costs where the factual record did not permit. *See Olin Corp. v. Century Indem. Co.*, 522 F. App'x 78, 80 (2d Cir. 2013) (noting that allocation of defense costs "has not been definitively established under New York law," but finding it unnecessary to consider whether defense costs may be allocated to insured for periods of self insurance because evidence permitted no reasonable means of proration between covered and non-covered items); *Olin Corp v. Ins. Co. of N. Am.*, 218 F. Supp. 3d at 219 (where allocating defense costs is "guesswork," declining an insurer's "invitation to engage in such speculation"). Indeed, numerous courts have since held that allocation of defense costs is required under New York law. *See, e.g., Generali-U.S. Branch v. Caribe Realty Corp.*, No. 25499/91, 1994 N.Y. Misc. LEXIS 166 (N.Y. Sup. Ct. 1994); *NL Indus., Inc. v. Commercial Union Ins. Co.*, 926 F. Supp. 446, 463, *recons. granted in part*, 935 F. Supp. 513 (D.N.J. 1996); *SPX Corp. v. Liberty Mut. Ins. Co.*, 709 S.E.2d 441, 447 (N.C. Ct. App. 2011) (stating that *Rapid-Am.* "stands for the proposition that trial courts may either order that an individual insurer be required to pay 100% of any defense costs and later seek contribution from other applicable insurers, or order pro rata time-on-the-risk allocation of defense costs"); *Deutsche Bank Trust Co. Ams. v. Royal Surplus Lines Ins. Co.*, No. 06C-09-261 JAP, 2012 Del. Super. LEXIS 244 (Del. Super. Ct. July 12, 2012) (holding that defense costs were allocable among all triggered policies based on time-on-the-risk, but declining to allocate defense costs to insured because "once an insurer has a duty to defend one claim in a suit it must provide a defense to all claims to its insured") (citing *Rapid-Am.*, 609 N.E.2d at 514); *Travelers Indem. Co. v. Northrop Grumman Corp.*, No. 12 Civ. 3040, mem. at 7 (S.D.N.Y. Oct. 31, 2013) (applying pro rata allocation to defense costs because "it makes little sense to require a party to cover defense costs relating to coverage periods for which it cannot have any obligation"); *Greater N.Y. Mut. Ins. Co. v. Admiral Indem. Co.*, 2015 N.Y. Misc. LEXIS 519, at *20-21 (N.Y. Sup. Ct. Feb. 23, 2015) (when "other insurance" provisions in two policies are identical, both policies are considered primary insurers "and must contribute to the defense of [underlying claims] in 'equal shares'"). Confusion also lies whether New York law favors allocation of defense costs on an equal shares basis. *See, e.g., Cont'l Cas. Co. v. Employers Ins. Co. of Wausau*, 865 N.Y.S. 2d 855, 861 (N.Y. Sup. Ct. 2008); *New York Ins. Dep't v. Generali*, 844 N.Y.S.2d 13, 15 (N.Y. Sup. Ct. 2007); *Travelers Cas. & Sur. Co. v. Alfa Laval Inc.*, 954 N.Y.S.2d 23 (N.Y. Sup. Ct. 2012). But these are fact-specific decisions where the trial court did not afford an insurer that had shirked its obligation to defend the protection of pro rata allocation. *See id.* A Delaware trial court has held that, under New York law, defense costs should be allocated among all triggered policies on a pro rata basis according to time on the risk. *See Deutsche Bank Trust Co. Ams. v. Royal Surplus Lines Ins. Co.*, No. 06C-09-261, 2011 Del. Super. LEXIS 89 (Del. Super. Ct. Feb. 25, 2011) (involving claims of exposure to toxins by World Trade Center cleanup workers).

North Carolina: In *Radiator Specialty Co. v. Arrowood Indem. Co.*, 850 S.E.2d 624 (N.C. Ct. App. 2020) (unpublished), the appeals court stated: "The policies, by their language, are clear — any claims covered by a particular policy must be defended and indemnified by the insurer under that policy. By prorating plaintiff's costs and damages based upon 'time on the risk,' the trial court reallocated those damages, potentially imposing more costs on one party, and removing them from another, who might be differently obligated." The court concluded that any error was moot as the final allocation of damages corrected it. *Id.* at 14. The insured sought re-argument on the basis that the reallocation by the trial court was, in fact, a pro rata, time-on-the-risk allocation. Re-argument was denied. *See also Duke Energy Carolinas, LLC v. AG Ins. SA/NV*, No. 17-5594, 2020 NCBC LEXIS 70 (N.C. Super. Ct. June 5, 2020) (holding "all sums" allocation applied based on unique, non-standard language of policies containing a non-cumulation clause).

North Dakota: No instructive authority.

Ohio: Ohio courts presently take an "all sums" approach to allocation where the claim in question involves long-term and progressive injury or property damage and the exact timing of the relevant damage is not known or knowable. In *Goodyear Tire & Rubber Co. v. Aetna Casualty & Surety Co.*, 769 N.E.2d 835 (Ohio 2002), the Supreme Court of Ohio overturned the Ohio Court of Appeals' adoption of pro rata allocation. In adopting the "all sums" approach, the Ohio Supreme Court focused on the clause in the policies which required the insurers to "pay on behalf of the insured *all sums* which the insured shall become legally obligated to pay as damages." *Id.* at 840. Assuming that this term was clear and unambiguous, the *Goodyear* Court explained that "th[is] plain language of this provision is inclusive of all damages resulting from a qualifying occurrence. Therefore, we find that the 'all sums' allocation approach is the correct method." *Id.* at 841. Supporting this decision, the Ohio Supreme Court turned to *Keene Corp. v. Ins. Co. of N. Am.*, 667 F.2d 1034 (D.C. Cir. 1981), and agreed that "Goodyear [like the insureds in *Keene*] expected complete security from each policy that it purchased." *Goodyear*, 769 N.E.2d at 841. The "all sums" approach, according to the *Goodyear* Court, struck the correct balance between providing this expected security to the insured, while still allowing the insurers to seek contribution from one another. *Id.* The "all sums" approach was affirmed by the Supreme Court of Ohio in *Pennsylvania Gen. Ins. Co. v. Park-Ohio Indus., Inc.*, 930 N.E.2d 800 (Ohio 2010). An Ohio appellate court cited *Goodyear* in noting that simply because an insured "exhausted both primary policies before turning to umbrella/excess policies does not necessarily mean that [the insured] rejected an 'all sums' approach." *MW Custom Papers LLC v. Allstate Ins. Co.*, No. 25430, 2014 Ohio App. LEXIS 1022 (Ohio Ct. App. 2014). However, where the timing of damage is "known or knowable," the Supreme Court of Ohio has found that the "all sums" approach is not appropriate. *Lubrizol Advanced Materials, Inc. v. Nat'l Union Fire Ins. Co.*, 160 N.E.3d 701 (Ohio 2020). The *Lubrizol* case involved allegedly defective resin used to manufacture piping. The *Lubrizol* court found that it should be ascertainable how much resin was produced on a given date, when the resin was sold, when the piping was produced, when it was sold, and when it failed. *Id.* at 706. Because the court found that the timing of the damage was known or knowable, the insurer on the risk at the time that the damage occurred should be liable and an all sums approach should not be applied. The court sidestepped the question of whether policies that promise to pay "those sums" – as opposed to "all sums" - that the insured becomes legally obligated to pay creates a different coverage obligation.

The Sixth Circuit Court of Appeals affirmed a district court's decision holding that an insured's settlement with all of its primary insurers extinguished all claims against those insurers, including the contribution rights of the insured's excess insurers. *See GenCorp, Inc. v. AIU Ins. Co.*, 297 F. Supp. 2d 995, 999 (N.D. Ohio 2003), *aff'd per curium*, 138 F. App. 732 (6th Cir. 2005). The court also held, however, that the insured's settlements with its primary insurers constituted an election to allocate its damages horizontally among all primary policies. The insured therefore was bound by its allocation and foreclosed from proceeding against the excess insurers under a different methodology in which the entire loss would be allocated to a single policy year. *See id.* at 1007-08. Although the court claimed that it was not deciding whether Ohio law recognized "settlement credits," the practical effect of the ruling was to provide the excess insurers with a full credit for the primary limits. *See also Bondex Int'l, Inc. v. Hartford Acc. & Indem. Co.*, No. 1:03-CV-01322, 2007 U.S. Dist. LEXIS 7448 (N.D. Ohio Feb. 1, 2007) (holding that, although non-settling insurers could not seek contribution from settling insurer, the settlement "should reduce whatever award is made against [the non-settling insurers]"), *aff'd on other grounds*, 667 F.3d 669 (6th Cir. 2011); *OneBeacon Am. Ins. Co. v. Am. Motorists Ins. Co.*, 679 F.3d 456, 463 (6th Cir. 2012) (holding that "settlement can exhaust a settling insurer's policy, and that such exhaustion precludes a non-settling insurer from seeking equitable contribution from the settling insurers"); *IMG Worldwide, Inc. v. Westchester Fire Ins. Co.*, 2015 U.S. Dist. LEXIS 144868, at *8 (noting that "an excess carrier should be placed in the same position it would have been in absent any settlement between the insured and the primary carrier") (citing *OneBeacon*, 679 F.3d at 456; *Bondex*, 2007 U.S. Dist. LEXIS 7448).

Oklahoma: No instructive authority.

Oregon: The state legislature of Oregon has adopted "joint-and-several" allocation by statute with respect to environmental remediation claims. Or. Rev. Stat. § 465.480(3)(a) (2013) ("An insurer with a duty to pay defense or indemnity costs, or both, to an insured for an environmental claim under a general liability insurance policy that provides that the insurer has a duty to pay all sums arising out of a risk covered by the policy, must pay all defense or indemnity costs, or both, proximately arising out of the risk pursuant to the applicable terms of its policy, including its limit of liability, independent and unaffected by other insurance that may provide coverage for the same claim."). As amended, the statute permits an insurer that has paid all or part of an environmental claim to seek contribution from another insurer that: (1) "is liable or potentially liable to the insured"; and (2) "has not entered into a good-faith settlement agreement with the insured regarding the environmental claim." *Id.* § 465.480(4)(a). *See also Century Indem. Co. v. Marine Group, LLC*, Case No. 08-1375, 2016 U.S. Dist. LEXIS 60339 (D. Or. May 6, 2016) (concluding that Section 465.480 only provides allocation for "covered damages," not defense costs, and that the proper allocation method for defense costs related to environmental remediation claims under consecutive primary CGL insurers is pro rata by time on the risk); *Century Indem. Co. v. Marine Group, LLC*, 131 F. Supp.3d 1018 (D. Or. 2015) (concluding that the existence of a self-insured retention does not convert an insured to an insurer for purposes of allocation under Section 465.480); *Certain Underwriters at Lloyd's London v. Mass. Bonding & Ins. Co.*, 401 P.3d 1212 (Or. Ct. App. 2017) (addressing in detail, in the context of a contribution claim, when the 2013 amendments to the OECAA [Oregon Environmental Cleanup Assistance Act; ORS 465.475 to 465.484] are effective); *Evraz Inc., N.A. v. Cont'l Ins. Co.*, No. 08-00447, 2018 U.S. Dist. LEXIS 110108 (D. Or. Apr. 16, 2018) ("The language of Or. Rev. Stat. § 465.480(4) limits only contribution rights among insurers for environmental claims. . . . The statute has no effect on the relationship between the insured and its insurers. For example, it does not in any way restrict an insurer's right to seek an equitable offset based on amounts paid by another insurer.") (magistrate's findings and recommendations adopted at 2018 U.S. Dist. LEXIS 109152 (D. Or. June 29, 2018)); *Allianz Global Risks US Ins. Co. v. Ace Prop. & Cas. Ins. Co.*, (Or. 2021) ("The OECAA is thus consistent with our longstanding recognition of common-law inter-insurer contribution claims . . . as well as our decisions interpreting insurance policies as a matter of law according to their 'applicable terms.' The existence of side agreements, indemnification promises, or an insured's waiver of policy terms is simply irrelevant to the contribution rights set out in the OECAA.").

In *FountainCourt Homeowners' Ass'n v. FountainCourt Development., LLC*, the Supreme Court of Oregon declined to address the issue of allocation in an insurance coverage action for a construction defect and other progressive injury claims, concluding that the issue was preserved for review. 380 P.3d 916, 931 (2016). However, while declining to address the issue of allocation directly, the Oregon Supreme Court noted that the trial court had implicitly applied some variation of the "all sums" approach. *Id.* The Court also favorably cited to the Court of Appeal's decision in *Cascade Corp. v. American Home Assurance Co.*, 165 P.3d 1176 (Or. App. Ct. 2007), and noted that, while a pro rata approach is suitable in determining allocation among insurers in contribution actions, it does not always provide a basis for reducing the insurer's liability to its insured. *Id.*

Pennsylvania: The Supreme Court of Pennsylvania adopted the "all sums" method of allocation for purposes of claims involving asbestos bodily injuries. *J.H. France Refractories Co. v. Allstate Ins. Co.*, 626 A.2d 502 (Pa. 1993). The Pennsylvania Supreme Court held that each insurer on the risk was jointly-and-severally liable for defense and indemnity costs, and the insured could select the policy or policies under which it would be indemnified. *Id.* at 507–09. The court further held that, when a particular insurer's limits are exhausted, the insured may seek indemnification from any other insurer on the risk. *Id.* at 509; *see also Asten Johnson, Inc. v. Columbia Cas. Co.*, 562 F.3d 213, 226–27 (3d Cir. 2009) (citing *J.H. France* for the proposition that the joint-and-several approach to allocation applies in Pennsylvania); *Titeflex Corp. v. Nat'l Union Fire Ins. Co. of Pittsburgh, Pa.*, 88 A.3d 970, 980 (Pa. Super. Ct. 2014) (reiterating *J.H. France* holding that insured can recover full extent of its loss from any insurer or insurers on the risk); *Air & Liquid Sys. Corp. v. Allianz Underwriters Ins. Co.*, No. 11–247, 2013 U.S. Dist. LEXIS 142359 (W.D. Pa. Sept. 27, 2013) (same); *Gen. Refractories Co. v. First State Ins. Co.*, No. 04-3509, 2015 U.S. Dist. LEXIS 69727 (E.D. Pa. May 29, 2015) (finding that different sequence of insuring language in underlying policies did not create any special meaning and that the "all sums" approach in *J.H. France* and *Koppers* applied).

In *Pennsylvania National Mutual Casualty Insurance Co. v. St. John*, the Supreme Court of Pennsylvania held that the multiple trigger theory of liability adopted in *J.H. France* is an exception to the general rule under Pennsylvania law that the first manifestation rule governs trigger of coverage analysis for policies containing standard CGL language. 106 A.3d 1, 22 (Pa. 2014). The Pennsylvania high court declined to extend the multiple trigger theory of liability to all cases involving continuous and progressive bodily injury and property damage. *Id.* at 23. As a result of determining that the manifestation rule applied, the court held that only the insurance policy in effect when the property damage first manifested would cover the ensuing property damage. *Id.*

However, in *Pa. Mfrs. Ass'n Ins. Co. v. Johnson Matthey, Inc.*, 160 A.3d 285 (Pa. Commw. Ct. 2017), the Commonwealth Court of Pennsylvania held that the multiple trigger theory of liability adopted in *J.H. France* applies to environmental contamination cases involving undetected damage occurring over multiple policy periods. The court found that same policy reasons underlying the *J.H. France* case applied equally to pollution cases – namely that limiting coverage for environmental contamination claims to policies in effect at the time that contamination is first detected would present the same problematic scenario of permitting insurers to limit or terminate coverage, in anticipation of future claims that have not yet materialized but can be predicted with near certainty. *Id.* at 293.

The Third Circuit Court of Appeals held that, under Pennsylvania's "apportioned share set off rule," a non-settling insurer against which a judgment is entered is entitled to a set-off against that judgment to reflect the apportioned shares of settled insurers. *See Koppers Co., Inc. v. Aetna Cas. & Sur. Co.*, 98 F.3d 1440, 1454 (3d. Cir. 1996) (citing *Gould, Inc. v. Continental Cas. Co.*, 585 A.2d 16 (Pa. Super. Ct. 1991)).

Rhode Island: The issue of allocation does not present itself under Rhode Island law because the Supreme Court of Rhode Island has adopted a manifestation trigger of coverage. *CPC Int'l, Inc. v. Northbrook Excess & Surplus Ins. Co.*, 668 A.2d 647, 649 (R.I. 1995). Under a manifestation trigger, damages are allocated only to the year in which the property damage "(1) manifests itself, (2) is discovered or, (3) in the exercise of reasonable diligence is discoverable." *Textron, Inc. v. Aetna Cas. & Sur. Co.*, 754 A.2d 742, 746 (R.I. 2000). Because only one year is triggered under a manifestation trigger, only those policies in effect during the year of manifestation may be called upon to pay "all sums." *Emhart Indus., Inc. v. Century Indem. Co.*, 559 F.3d 57 (1st Cir. 2009). The duty to defend is the same yet different. Although the duty to defend exists only in the year of manifestation, all carriers on the risk have a duty to defend unless the year of manifestation can be readily ascertained by the complaint, or until the year of manifestation is established by the fact finder. *Id.*

Rhode Island federal courts have determined that equitable contribution for defense costs between insurers shall be allocated based on the insurers' time on the risk. *See Travelers Cas. & Sur. Co. v. Providence Wash. Ins. Co.*, C.A. No. 10-147 S, 2014 U.S. Dist. LEXIS 23536, at *2 (D.R.I. Feb. 25, 2014) (noting that insurer will contribute to past and future defense costs incurred by the insured based on the time on the risk calculation). In *Emhart Indus., Inc. v. Home Ins. Co.*, an insurance coverage dispute arising from the U.S. Environmental Protection Agency's efforts to remediate contamination from a Superfund Site, the district court found that an insurer owed a duty to defend the policyholder and owed the total costs, or "all sums," of the policyholder's defense of the underlying EPA action. 515 F. Supp. 2d 228, 250-57 (D.R.I. 2007) (The insurer did not owe indemnity costs as a jury found there was no coverage under its policies). On appeal, the U.S. Court of Appeals for the First Circuit rejected the insurer's argument that the district court should have adopted an allocation of the defense costs based on the insurer's "time-on-the-risk" and affirmed the district court's "all sums" approach. *Emhart, supra*, 559 F.3d at 70.

In a separate action, the same insurer sued a co-insurer for contribution towards the defense. *Century Indem. Co. v. Liberty Mut. Ins. Co.*, 815 F. Supp. 2d 508 (D.R.I. 2011). While no Rhode Island court has addressed allocation of defense costs in the context of a long-term progressive environmental injury, the district court noted that the Rhode Island Supreme Court has found it "proper to prorate defense costs between concurrent insurers, when…both insurers have wrongfully refused to defend an insured." *Id.* at 514 (citing *Peloso v. Imperatore*, 434 A.2d 274, 279 (R.I. 1981)). The district court determined that, if the Supreme Court found that defense costs should be prorated for concurrent insurers, then they should also be prorated for successive insurers. *Id.* at 520. Accordingly, the district court held that the defense costs should be allocated between the two insurers based on their time on the risk. *Id.* Notably, a non-settling insurer was left "holding the bag" in *INA v. Kaiser-Roth Corp.*, 770 A.2d 403 (R.I. 2001). In view of the insurer's failure to engage in good faith settlement discussions earlier, the court refused to permit First State to claim a setoff to reflect the sums that the insured had been obtained from other insurers.

South Carolina: The Supreme Court of South Carolina adopted the pro rata, time-on-the-risk approach to allocation in the context of indemnity for progressive damage cases. *Crossmann Cmtys. of N.C. v. Harleysville Mut. Ins. Co.*, 717 S.E.2d 589 (S.C. 2011). The Supreme Court further held that a policyholder must "bear a pro rata portion of the loss corresponding to any portion of the progressive damage period during which the policyholder was not insured or purchased insufficient insurance." *Id.* at 594. *See also Spartan Petroleum Co., Inc. v. Federated Mut. Ins. Co.* 162 F.3d 805 (4th Cir. 1998) (predicting that South Carolina high court would adopt pro rata, time-on-the-risk allocation and that policyholder would be responsible for "uninsured" periods.); *Builders Mut. Ins. Co. v. Wingard Props, Inc.*, No. 07-2179, 2010 U.S. Dist. LEXIS 104087 (D.S.C. Sept. 28, 2010) (holding, in context of progressive damage resulting from construction defect, that liability would be apportioned pro rata) (citing *Spartan Petroleum*, 162 F.2d 812). *But see Harleysville Grp. Ins. v. Heritage Cmtys., Inc.*, 420 S.C. 321, 803 S.E.2d 288 (2017) (concluding that underlying punitive damages were not subject to time-on-the-risk allocation, but refusing to create a "bright-line rule punitive damages may never be subject to allocation based on time on the risk"). Based on *Crossmann Communities*, the U.S. District Court for the District of Carolina held that, where damages are allocable pro rata, the policyholder is not entitled to prorate any deductibles, but must pay the full deductible for each policy triggered by the progressive damage. *Liberty Mut. Fire Ins. Co. v. J.T. Walker Indus., Inc.*, 817 F. Supp. 2d 784, 790 (D.S.C. 2011). The court reasoned that any progressive damage that takes place during the policy period is an "occurrence" that triggers the policy, and the policyholder is required to pay a full deductible for each "occurrence." *See id.* at 789. The court also declined to follow the Massachusetts Supreme Judicial Court's holding in *Boston Gas* that the policyholder was permitted to prorate deductibles because the continuous damage constituted a single "occurrence." The *J.T. Walker* court explained that viewing progressive damage as a series of "occurrences" was more consistent with the pro rata allocation method adopted in *Crossmann Communities*. *See id.* at 790. In *Builders Mut. Ins. Co. v. Island Pointe, LLC*, 847 S.E.2d 87 (S.C. 2020), the court addressed allocation, between covered and uncovered claims, and cited *Crossmann* for guidance: "[P]erfect precision in allocating damages is not always achievable. Where perfect precision is not achievable, a fair approximation must suffice." *Id.* at 96.

South Dakota: No instructive authority. *But see NorthWestern Corp. v. AEGIS*, No. 07-1174 (S.D. Cir. Ct. July 29, 2010), *reprinted in* 24–37 Mealey's Litig. Rep.: Insurance (Aug. 4, 2010) (applying the "all sums" method of allocation under Montana law).

Tennessee: In *Travelers Indem. Co. v. W.M. Barr & Co.*, 2011 U.S. Dist. LEXIS 159644 (W.D. Tenn. Oct. 31, 2011), a federal court denied an insurer's motion for summary judgment seeking to apply pro rata, time-on-the risk allocation. Instead, the court held: "So long as a lawsuit brought against Barr alleges benzene exposure during a period in which a Travelers policy was in force, Travelers must indemnify and defend such claims in their entirety, even if the injury at issue was in part suffered outside of the Travelers policy coverage period." *Id.* The court, however, noted that no Tennessee state court precedent existed.

Texas: In *Lennar Corp. v. Markel Am. Ins. Co.*, 413 S.W.3d 750, 759 (Tex. 2013), the Texas Supreme Court declined to apply pro rata allocation to the costs of remediating homes built with an exterior insulation and finish system. The court found that it was up to insurers who share responsibility for a loss to allocate it among themselves according to their subrogation rights. *Id.* at 759. Historically Texas's lower state courts have also applied a joint-and-several approach to allocation. *See Tex. Prop. & Cas. Ins. Guar. Ass'n v. Sw. Aggregates, Inc.*, 982 S.W.2d 600, 605 (Tex. App. Ct. 1998) (involving silicosis claims); *CNA Lloyds of Tex. v. St. Paul Ins. Co.*, 902 S.W.2d 657, 661 (Tex. App. 1995) (involving medical malpractice); *see also Great Am. Ins. Co. v. Hamel*, 444 S.W.3d 780 (Tex. App. Ct. 2014), *rev'd on other grounds*, 525 S.W.3d 655 (Tex. 2017) (noting that Texas law does not provide for "pro rata or any other form of allocation" between policies triggered by a single occurrence). Several Federal courts previously predicted that Texas would follow a pro rata approach. *See, e.g., Lafarge Corp. v. Hartford Cas. Ins. Co.*, 61 F.3d 389 (5th Cir. 1995) (applying pro rata, by time on the risk in environmental coverage action). However, these rulings predate *Lennar.*

Utah: The Supreme Court of Utah adopted the pro rata, by limits and years, method of allocation in the context of allocating defense costs for environmental property damage. *Sharon Steel Corp. v. Aetna Cas. & Sur. Co.*, 931 P.2d 127, 140 (Utah 1997). The court also held that the insured should be responsible for uninsured years. *Id.* at 141. Answering a certified question from the U.S. Court of Appeals for the Tenth Circuit (*see Ohio Cas. Ins. Co. v. Unigard Ins. Co.*, 564 F.3d 1192 (10th Cir. 2009)), the Utah Supreme Court reiterated its holding in *Sharon Steel* that costs should be apportioned using the pro rata, by limits and years, method. *Ohio Cas. Ins. Co. v. Unigard Ins. Co.*, 268 P.3d 180 (Utah 2012). Nevertheless, the Supreme Court declined to follow the portion of *Sharon Steel* that apportioned defense costs to the insured for periods when the insured was without coverage, reasoning that the specific policy language at issue in *Unigard* expressly gave each insurer control over its defense of the insured. *Id.* at 186. The *Unigard* court found it inequitable to apportion any defense costs to an insured that had no power either to select counsel or to settle suits. *Id.* As such, in accordance with *Sharon Steel* and consistent with the policy language specific to the case, the *Unigard* court modified the *Sharon Steel* formula in that defense costs were to be apportioned "between successive insurers according to their time on the risk and the amount of their policy limits. It then divides the portion of defense costs attributable to any periods during which the insured lacked coverage in the same proportions." *Id.* at 187. The Tenth Circuit subsequently reversed and remanded the case to the district court with directions to enter judgment consistent with the Supreme Court's answer. *Ohio Cas. Ins. Co. v. Unigard Ins. Co.*, 458 F. App. 702 (10th Cir. 2012). In *Chapman Constr., LC v. Cincinnati Ins. Co.*, No. 2:15-cv-172, 2015 U.S. Dist. LEXIS 180878 (D. Utah Sept. 22, 2015), a Utah federal court applied the pro rata, by time and limits, method of allocation to a construction defect claim. In *Md. Cas. Co. v. Mid-Continent Cas. Co.*, 725 F. App'x 699 (10th Cir. 2018), the appeals court concluded that, based on the rationale of *Sharon Steel* and *Unigard*, an insurer is not limited to a claim in equity against another insurer, but may also have recovery rights in contract) (construction defect claim).

Vermont: The Supreme Court of Vermont adopted the pro rata, time-on-the-risk method of allocation in the context of claims for environmental property damage. *Towns v. N. Sec. Ins. Co.*, 964 A.2d 1150 (Vt. 2008). In *Towns*, the court held that, where the insured sought coverage for continuous environmental damage, spanning successive policy periods, including one in which the insured "went bare," the insured's defense and indemnity expenses were allocable pro rata by time. *Id.* at 1167; *see also Bradford Oil Co., Inc. v. Stonington Ins. Co.*, 54 A.3d 983 (Vt. 2011) (allocating indemnity by time-on-the-risk). The Vermont Supreme Court also has applied a fact-based approach to allocation where the precise amount of property damage could accurately be determined in each year. *See Agency of Natural Res. v. Glens Falls Ins. Co.*, 736 A.2d 768 (Vt. 1999) (allocating damages based on volumes released in each year).

Virginia: In an environmental coverage dispute, a federal district court predicted that defense costs should be equitably allocated if damages can be readily apportioned among covered and uncovered years. *Morrow Corp. v. Harleysville Mut. Ins. Co.*, 101 F. Supp. 2d 422, 427, n.5 (E.D. Va. 2000) ("The sensible majority rule, which Virginia would likely adopt, is that when 'there is no reasonable means of prorating the costs of defense between the covered and the not-covered' periods, the insurer must bear the entire cost of the defense. *See Insurance Co. of North America v. Forty-Eight Insulations, Inc.*, 633 F.2d 1212, 1224 (6th Cir. 1980) (applying Michigan law). But, where defense costs can be readily apportioned, "the insured must pay its fair share for the defense of the non-covered risk," because the duty to defend arises solely under contract, and an insurer plainly has not contracted to pay defense costs for occurrences which took place outside the triggered policy periods. *Id.*").

Washington: The Supreme Court of Washington adopted the "all sums" method of allocation in an environmental property damage case. *Am. Nat'l Fire Ins. Co. v. B & L Trucking & Constr. Co.*, 951 P.2d 250 (Wash. 1998). The jury had found that the insured expected environmental property damage for more than five of the seven years in which property damage occurred. *Id.* at 259. Over a vigorous dissent, the insured was permitted to collect 100 percent of all damages by collapsing all property damage, expected or not, into any policy period of its choosing. *Id.* at 260; *see also Polygon N.W. Co. v. Am. Nat'l Fire Ins. Co.*, 189 P.3d 777, 789 (Wash. Ct. App. 2008) (citing *B&L Trucking* for the proposition that the "all sums" method of allocation applies in Washington); *Mutual of Enumclaw Ins. Co. v. OneBeacon Ins. Co.*, No. 64063-1-I, 2010 Wash. App. LEXIS 2341 (Wash. Ct. App. Oct. 11, 2010) (affirming "all sums" allocation in construction defect context); *Eagle Harbour Condo. Ass'n v. Allstate Ins. Co.*, No. C15-5312, 2017 U.S. Dist. LEXIS 54761 (W.D. Wash. Apr. 10, 2017) (applying "all sums" allocation to property damage claim); *Greenlake Condo. Ass'n v. Allstate Ins.Co.*, No. 14-1860, 2015 U.S. Dist. LEXIS 184729 (W.D. Wash. Dec. 23, 2015) (applying "all sums" allocation to property damage claim).

West Virginia: A West Virginia trial court adopted a modified version of "all sums" allocation with respect to an environmental property damage claim in *Wheeling Pittsburgh Corp. v. Am. Ins. Co.*, No. 93-C-340, 2003 W.V. Cir. LEXIS 3 (W. Va. Cir. Ct. Oct. 28, 2003). Significantly, although the court held that the policy language at issue did not limit coverage to property damage occurring during the policy period, the court found that equitable principles dictated that the policyholder be responsible for periods when it consciously decided to "go bare." "[T]he Court finds and concludes that, in seeking contribution, the Defendants' are not precluded from seeking to allocate liability to the Plaintiffs for those periods of time wherein the Plaintiffs either elected not to obtain insurance or chose to self insure." *Id.* at *53-54. In a dispute over coverage for asbestos-related bodily injury, a West Virginia federal trial court rejected a policyholder's invitation to apply a continuous trigger where the policies required the "last day of the last exposure" to occur during the policy period. *Homer Laughlin China Co. v. Cont' Cas. Co.*, No. 14-13, 2014 U.S. Dist. LEXIS 88632 (N.D. W. Va. June 27, 2014). The court reasoned that this language was materially distinguishable from the policy language at issue in *Keene. Id.*

Wisconsin: The Supreme Court of Wisconsin adopted the "all sums" method of allocation for purposes of claims involving bodily injury and property damage from asbestos exposure. *Plastics Eng'g Co. v. Liberty Mut. Ins. Co.*, 759 N.W.2d 613 (Wis. 2009). The court stressed that its decision was driven by the specific policy language at issue. *Plastics Eng'g*, 759 N.W.2d at 628. In particular, the majority rooted its decision on non-standard policy language that it found contemplated coverage "if an occurrence gives rise to Bodily Injury or Property Damage which occurs *partly before and partly within* the policy period." *Id.* at 618 (emphasis added). This language is in contrast to standard commercial general liability policies that expressly limit coverage to "bodily injury or property damage, which occurs during the policy period" or expressly define bodily injury and property damage as that which occurs *during the policy period. See also Westport Ins. Corp. v. Appleton Papers*, 787 N.W.2d 894 (Wis. Ct. App. 2010) (rejecting horizontal exhaustion); *Burgraff v. Menard, Inc.*, 875 N.W.2d 596 (Wis. 2016) (citing *Plastics Eng'g Co.*) (applying "all sums" allocation to auto accident claim based upon specific policy language at issue). A Wisconsin appellate court held that an insured has the right to select the manner and order in which policies within a triggered quota-share layer respond to a loss. *Cleaver Brooks, Inc. v. AIU Ins. Co.*, 839 N.W.2d 882, 889-92 (Wis. Ct. App. 2013); *see also Eaton Corp. v. Westport Ins. Co.*, 387 F. Supp. 3d 931 (E.D. Wis. 2019) (noting that both Wisconsin and Ohio have adopted all-sums allocation and rejecting insurers' argument that insured waived its right to use all-sums by entering into a settlement with other insurers in which it allocated losses for asbestos claims pro rata).

Wyoming: No instructive authority.

CHAPTER
19

Insurability of Punitive Damages

It is a question that is uttered by claims professionals and coverage counsel on a regular basis: Are punitive damages insurable in such and such state? In essence, what the questioner is often asking is whether the particular state's public policy permits a tortfeasor to insure against punitive damages that he or she may be legally obligated to pay. The answer provided is often one word: yes or no. While one of those two may be the right one generally, the issue is oftentimes much more complex than can be adequately answered with a single word. In fact, when all of the variations of the issue are considered, there may be as many as a dozen possible answers to the question.

The Supreme Court of Texas recognized the wide variation that exists over the insurability of punitive damages:

> The cases defy easy categorization, but it appears that: 19 states generally permit coverage of punitive damages; 8 states would permit coverage of punitive damages for grossly negligent conduct, but not for more serious conduct; 11 states would permit coverage of punitive damages for vicari-ously-assessed liability, but not directly-assessed liability; 7 states generally prohibit an insured from indemnifying himself against punitive damages; and the remainder have silent, unclear, or otherwise inapplicable law. States may fall into more than one category.

Fairfield Ins. Co. v. Stephens Martin Paving, L.P., 246 S.W.3d 653, 688 (Tex. 2008) (Hecht, J., concurring).[1]

---

1 The Texas Supreme Court categorized the states as follows: The nineteen states that generally **permit** coverage of punitive damages are Alabama, Alaska, Arizona, Delaware, Georgia, Hawaii, Idaho, Maryland, Mississippi, Montana, New Hampshire, New Mexico, North Carolina, South Carolina, Tennessee, Vermont, Washington, Wisconsin, and Wyoming. The eight states that would permit coverage of punitive damages for **grossly negligent** conduct, but not for more serious conduct are Arkansas, Iowa, Kentucky,

As the Texas high court demonstrated, the question of the insurability of punitive damages does not want for case law. The issue has been considered in every state, including, most of the time, by its highest court. Coverage for punitive damages has also been addressed in a few instances by state legislatures. The issue is a mature one and has well-defined battle lines. And as is often the case when an issue may turn on public policy considerations, judges are not shy about their feelings. Authors of opinions are frequently passionate in their views and dissenting opinions are not uncommon.

An award of punitive damages requires egregious conduct. *See State Farm Mut. Auto. Ins. Co. v. Campbell*, 538 U.S. 408, 419 (2003) ("[P]unitive damages should only be awarded if the defendant's culpability, after having paid compensatory damages, is so reprehensible as to warrant THE imposition of further sanctions to achieve punishment or deterrence."). Therefore, even before reaching the public policy considerations, it is not unreasonable to ask why coverage would exist in the first place, under the terms of an insurance policy, for conduct that was "so reprehensible." For example, coverage under a commercial general liability policy requires an "occurrence," defined as an accident. Surely any conduct that can support an award of punitive damages could not have been accidental. But consider that the issue also arises outside of "occurrence" based commercial general liability policies that provide coverage for "bodily injury" or "property damage." The availability of coverage for punitive damages arises in such contexts as the "personal injury" section of a commercial general liability (CGL) policy, which covers some intentional torts, as well as CGL policies that have nonstandard language, automobile policies, and professional liability policies. And sometimes this issue is simply not addressed at all.

In addition, while an award of punitive damages requires egregious conduct, there are many different levels of such conduct. This can have an important effect on the availability of insurance for both compensatory and punitive damages. For example, West Virginia's highest court held that where "the liability policy of an insurance

---

Louisiana, Nevada, Oregon, Virginia, and West Virginia. The eleven states that would permit coverage of punitive damages for **vicariously-assessed** liability, but not directly-assessed liability are California, Connecticut, Florida, Illinois, Indiana, Kansas, Kentucky, Minnesota, New Jersey, Oklahoma, and Pennsylvania. The seven states that generally **prohibit** an insured from indemnifying himself against punitive damages are Colorado, New York, North Dakota, Ohio, Rhode Island, South Dakota, and Utah. The states that have **silent, unclear, or otherwise inapplicable** law are Maine, Massachusetts, Michigan, Missouri, and Nebraska. *Stephens Martin Paving*, 246 S.W.3d at 688, nn.92–96. For further discussion, *see* the fifty-state survey of the insurability of punitive damages, *infra*.

company provides that it will pay on behalf of the insured all sums which the insured shall become legally obligated to pay as damages because of bodily injury and the policy only excludes damages caused intentionally by or at the direction of the insured, such policy will be deemed to cover punitive damages arising from bodily injury occasioned by gross, reckless or wanton negligence on the part of the insured." *Hensley v. Erie Ins. Co.*, 283 S.E.2d 227, 230 (W. Va. 1981). The court drew this distinction on the basis of its belief that gross, reckless, or wanton negligence does not carry the same degree of culpability as a purposeful or intentional tort, and, therefore, the right to insurance coverage should not be foreclosed. *Id.* at 233. In general, it is important to be mindful that the degree of culpability that gave rise to the award of punitive damages in the first place can have an impact on the insurance coverage issue.

The overarching public policy debate concerning insurance coverage for punitive damages is well illustrated by the competing arguments made in the two most frequently cited decisions on the issue— *Northwestern National Casualty Co. v. McNulty*, 307 F.2d 432 (5th Cir. 1962) (applying Florida law) and *Lazenby v. Universal Underwriters Insurance Co.*, 383 S.W.2d 1 (Tenn. 1964).

In *McNulty*, the Fifth Circuit Court of Appeals held that public policy precluded a tortfeasor from securing insurance coverage for punitive damages that were awarded against him for bodily injury that he caused while driving drunk. *McNulty*, 307 F.2d at 440. In the eyes of the *McNulty* court, to allow insurance for punitive damages would frustrate their purpose. *Id.* Since punitive damages are awarded for punishment and deterrence, it would serve no useful purpose if the party responsible for the wrong could shift the burden to its insurance company. *Id.* The court also described a global impact on the insurance market that it predicted would result if coverage for punitive damages were permitted:

> [Punitive] damages do not compensate the plaintiff for his injury, since compensatory damages already have made the plaintiff whole. And there is no point in punishing the insurance company; it has done no wrong. In actual fact, of course, and considering the extent to which the public is insured, the burden would ultimately come to rest not on the insurance companies but on the public, since the added liability to the insurance companies would be passed along to the premium payers. Society would then be punishing itself for the wrong committed by the insured.

Id.

The other side of the coin is *Lazenby*, where the Supreme Court of Tennessee was not convinced by the *McNulty* rationale for disallowing insurance coverage for punitive damages. *Lazenby*, 383 S.W.2d at 5. The Tennessee high court concluded that it was speculative that socially irresponsible drivers would be deterred from their wrongful conduct if coverage for punitive damages were not allowed. *Id.* "This State, in regard to the proper operation of motor vehicles, has a great many detailed criminal sanctions, which apparently have not deterred this slaughter on our highways and streets." *Id.*

The argument that there is a lack of any correlation between the insurability of punitive damages and irresponsible conduct was addressed with vigor by the Supreme Court of Wyoming in *Sinclair Oil Corp. v. Columbia Casualty Co.*, 682 P.2d 975 (Wyo. 1984). In holding that it was not against Wyoming public policy to insure against punitive damages, the court stated:

> We know of no studies, statistics or proofs which indicate that contracts of insurance to protect against liability for punitive damages have a tendency to make willful or wanton misconduct more probable, nor do we know of any substantial relationship between the insurance coverage and such misconduct. Neither is there any indication that to invalidate insurance contracts that protect against liability for punitive damages on grounds of public policy would have any tendency to deter willful and wanton misconduct.

Sinclair Oil, 682 P.2d at 981.

The competing rationales surrounding the insurability of punitive damages were also identified by the Supreme Court of Wisconsin in *Brown v. Maxey*, 369 N.W.2d 677 (Wis. 1985). On one hand, insurance for punitive damages would undermine their purpose and shift liability to the public in the form of higher insurance premiums. *Id.* at 687. On the other hand, the court observed that allowing insurance coverage for punitive damages is appropriate because public policy favors compelling an insurer to perform those obligations for which it contracted and received premium, the insurer could have excluded such coverage, there are alternative sanctions that can be imposed on an offender, and it is questionable whether punitive damages have a deterrent effect. *Id.*

While "public policy" is often the starting point, and most frequently debated aspect of the insurability of punitive damages, the analysis does not always end there. There are in fact many other facets and nuances surrounding the issue that must be considered.

Simply because coverage for punitive damages is not precluded by public policy does not per se create such coverage. The availability of coverage for punitive damages is still dependent upon the existence of policy language that includes it. Many courts resolve this issue by concluding that the policy language "all sums which the insured shall become legally obligated to pay as damages because of bodily injury" is broad enough to encompass punitive damages. *United Servs. Auto. Ass'n v. Webb*, 369 S.E.2d 196, 199 (Va. 1988). However, a specific exclusion for punitive damages has been given effect even if public policy does not prohibit such coverage. *See State Farm Mut. Auto. Ins. Co. v. Wilson*, 782 P.2d 727, 733–34 (Ariz. 1989). And the flip side—policy language that specifically covers punitive damages has been enforced, notwithstanding a general public policy prohibition against their insurability. *See Cont'l Cas. Co. v. Kinsey*, 499 N.W.2d 574, 580–81 (N.D. 1993). *But see Public Serv. Mut. Ins. Co. v. Goldfarb*, 425 N.E.2d 810, 814 (N.Y. 1981) (holding that coverage for punitive damages was impermissible even if an insurer agreed to provide such coverage and charged a premium for it).

It is also not uncommon for courts to preclude coverage for punitive damages on a public policy rationale, but make an exception for punitive damages that were awarded on the basis of vicarious liability. *Dayton Hudson Corp. v. Am. Mut. Liab. Ins. Co.*, 621 P.2d 1155, 1160 (Okla. 1980). ("In almost all jurisdictions which disallow insurance coverage for punitive damages, an exception is recognized for those torts in which liability is vicariously imposed on the employer for a wrong of his servant."). *See also Butterfield v. Giuntoli*, 670 A.2d 646, 655 (Pa. Super. Ct. 1995) ("[w]here corporate management commits an outrageous act, punishment is appropriate. Where the act is committed by … an agent, not pursuant to corporate policy or plan, the corporation, though vicariously liable for punitive damages, is entitled to insure against such damages") (alteration in original).

However, there are also situations where directly assessed punitive damages are uninsurable as a matter of law, vicariously assessed punitive damages are not, and a court nonetheless finds coverage for the directly assessed punitive damages. This can occur when the instructions given to the jury in the underlying action allowed for an award of punitive damages on the basis of both direct and vicarious liability— but the insurer did not request additional instructions or use special verdicts to have the jury's determination clarified. *E.g., U.S. Concrete Pipe Co. v. Bould*, 437 So. 2d 1061, 1065 (Fla. 1983).

The availability of insurance coverage for punitive damages also arises with frequency in the context of uninsured and underinsured motorist policies. It is not unusual for states to reach a different conclusion concerning coverage for punitive damages under such automobile policies than it does liability policies. The Supreme Court of Kentucky's decision in *Ky. Cent. Ins. Co. v. Schneider*, 15 S.W.3d 373 (Ky. 2000) provides a representative demonstration of how this issue is addressed nationally. A Kentucky statute provided "that every motor vehicle liability insurance policy shall provide coverage 'for the protection of persons insured thereunder who are legally entitled to recover damages from owners or operators of uninsured motor vehicles because of bodily injury, sickness or disease, including death.'" *Id.* at 374 (quoting KRS 304.20-020(1)).

The court held (and noted that its decision was consistent with the overwhelming majority of jurisdictions nationally) that *damages because of bodily injury* are regarded as compensatory damages, while punitive damages are not compensatory, but, rather, are damages awarded against a person to punish and to discourage him and others from similar conduct in the future. *Id.* at 374–75. The *Schneider* court also addressed a public policy component surrounding the issue: "In addition to the definitional distinction between compensatory and punitive damages ... most jurisdictions holding that punitive damages are not recoverable under the injured party's UM coverage also note that it would be antithetical to require the UM carrier to pay a penalty assessed against the wrongdoer, because the burden of payment would fall not upon the wrongdoer, or even the insurer of the wrongdoer, but upon the insurer of the innocent party." *Id.* at 375–76.

The following fifty-state survey of the insurability of punitive damages makes some references to the issue in the context of uninsured and underinsured motorist policies. However, as the focus of this book is liability insurance, this is not intended to be an exhaustive list.

50-State Survey: Insurability of Punitive Damages

Alabama: The Supreme Court of Alabama, without discussion of any public policy considerations, held that punitive damages were a "liability imposed by law," and, as such, within the coverage afforded by an automobile policy's insuring agreement, which provided: "To indemnify the assured ... against loss from the liability imposed by law upon the assured arising or resulting from claims upon the assured for damages by reason of the ownership, maintenance or use of any [automobile] ... if such claims are made on account of injury to persons." *Am. Fid. & Cas. Co. v. Werfel*, 164 So. 383, 383 (Ala. 1935); *see also Sua Ins. Co. v. Classic*

Home Builders, LLC, 751 F. Supp. 2d 1245, 1253 (S.D. Ala. 2010) (holding that punitive damages could not be considered when determining whether amount in controversy exceeded jurisdictional threshold because punitive damages could not be recovered) (policy at issue excluded punitive damages); *Admiral Ins. Co. v. Price-Williams*, 129 So. 3d 991 (Ala. 2013) (In holding that coverage was not owed for intentional conduct, because it was not "unexpected and accidental," court noted that its decision was in accord with the public policy in Alabama and elsewhere against indemnifying an insured for a loss resulting from his or her own intentional wrongdoing); *Wingard v. Lansforakringar AB*, No. 11-45, 2013 U.S. Dist. Lexis 141572 (M.D. Ala. Sept. 30, 2013) ("[T]here is a sufficient and substantial basis in Alabama law to conclude that Alabama's public policy that prohibits insurance companies from excluding coverage for punitive damages awards under the Alabama Wrongful Death Act is a substantial policy and a fundamental one."); *Graham v. FCA U.S. LLC* (*In Re Old Carco LLC*), No. 19-1901, 2020 U.S. App. LEXIS 16118 (2d Cir. May 20, 2020) (applying Alabama law and stating that the notion that Alabama law prohibits coverage for punitive damages "is not itself embodied in a statute" and is "not in a holding" from Alabama's highest court (*quoting Wingard v. Lansforakringar*)).

Alaska: The Supreme Court of Alaska acknowledged a general prohibition against coverage for punitive damages. *Providence Wash. Ins. Co. of Alaska v. City of Valdez*, 684 P.2d 861, 863 (Alaska 1984). However, the court also stated, assuming, without deciding, that public policy prohibited insurance coverage for punitive damages, such prohibition would not apply to vicarious liability or governmental entity defendants. *Id.* The court held that the relevant policy language provided coverage for punitive damages (a sum that the insured is legally obligated to pay as damages) and that punitive damages were not specifically excluded under the policy. *Id.*; *see also State Farm Mut. Auto. Ins. Co. v. Lawrence*, 26 P.3d 1074, 1079–80 (Alaska 2001) (concluding that a liability policy that does not specifically exclude punitive damages and provides that the insurer will "pay damages which an insured becomes legally liable to pay because of … bodily injury to others" affords coverage for punitive damages). The Supreme Court of Alaska held that punitive damages were insurable under an uninsured and underinsured motorist policy. *See Lawrence*, 26 P.3d at 180–81. Neither the policy language nor public policy precluded such result. *Id.*

Arizona: The Supreme Court of Arizona held that "any public policy considerations militating against an insurer providing coverage for punitive damages were outweighed by the public policy that an insurance company which admittedly took a premium for indemnifying against all liability for damages, should honor its obligation. … [T]herefore, … an express exclusion was required to eliminate coverage for punitive damages from general liability insurance because the insured was personally at risk if his liability insurance did not cover those damages. The essence of the transaction was the insured's purchase of indemnification against all damages for which he might be held liable." *State Farm Mut. Auto. Ins. Co. v. Wilson*, 782 P.2d 727, 733–34 (Ariz. 1989) (characterizing *Price v. Hartford Accident & Indem. Co.*, 502 P.2d 522 (Ariz. 1972)). But uninsured and underinsured insurers are not obligated to pay for punitive damages unless they specifically agreed to do so. *Wilson*, 782 P.2d at 736; *see also Irvin v. Lexington Ins. Co.*, No. 1 CA-CV 09-0270, 2010 Ariz. App. Unpub. LEXIS 53 (Ariz. App. Ct. Sept. 2, 2010) (examining various policy provisions and concluding that they were not sufficient to preclude coverage for punitive damages).

Arkansas: The Supreme Court of Arkansas held that punitive damages satisfied the policy's insuring agreement as they constituted a sum that the insured was legally obligated to pay as damages because of bodily injury. *S. Farm Bureau Cas. Ins. Co. v. Daniel*, 440 S.W.2d 582, 584 (Ark. 1969). The court also noted that it could not "find anything in the state's public policy that prevents an insurer from indemnifying its insured against punitive damages arising out of an accident, as distinguished from intentional torts." *Id.; see also Cal. Union Ins. Co. v. Ark. La. Gas Co.*, 572 S.W.2d 393, 394 (Ark. 1978) (reaffirming *Daniel*); *Med. Liab. Mut. Ins. Co. v. Alan Curtis Enters., Inc.*, No. 4:05-CV-01317 GTE, 2006 U.S. Dist. LEXIS 89180 (E.D. Ark. Dec. 8, 2006) (concluding that the phrase from *Daniel*—"as distinguished from intentional torts"—was *dicta*, and, therefore, leaving open the possibility that Arkansas public policy permits coverage for punitive damages for intentional torts); A.C.A. § 23-79-307(a)(8) ("Policies containing an exclusion for punitive damages must include a definition of punitive damages substantially similar to the following: 'Punitive damages' are damages that may be imposed to punish a wrongdoer and to deter others from similar conduct."). In *Cypress Ins. Co. v. Veal*, No. 19-00114, 2021 U.S. Dist. LEXIS 54037 (E.D. Ark. March 23, 2021), the court concluded that the punitive damages exclusion was enforceable as it defined "punitive damages" in a manner "substantially similar" to that provided in A.C.A. § 23-79-307(a)(8).

California: The Supreme Court of California held, based on a public policy rationale, that "an insured may not shift to its insurance company, and ultimately to the public, the payment of punitive damages awarded in the third party lawsuit against the insured as a result of the insured's intentional, morally blameworthy behavior against the third party." *PPG Inds., Inc. v. Transamerica Ins. Co.*, 975 P.2d 652, 658 (Cal. 1999); *see also* CAL. INS. CODE § 533 (Deering 2008) ("An insurer is not liable for a loss caused by the willful act of the insured; but he is not exonerated by the negligence of the insured, or of the insured's agents or others."). A California District Court stated that, in vicarious liability cases, where an employer is required to pay punitive damages as a result of the actions of one of his employees, courts have held that § 533 does not apply and the employer can be indemnified. *Certain Underwriters at Lloyd's of London v. Pac. Sw. Airlines*, 786 F. Supp. 867, 869 (C.D. Cal. 1996). No coverage existed for punitive damages under the state's uninsured motorist statute. *See Cal. State Auto. Ass'n Inter-Ins. Bureau v. Carter*, 164 Cal. App. 3d 257, 263 (Cal. Ct. App. 1985) (noting that while an insurance policy may provide broader coverage than that required under law, the policy at issue was virtually identical to the statute); *see also Riverport Ins. Co. v. Oakland Cmty. Hous., Inc.*, No. C 08-3883, 2009 U.S. Dist. LEXIS 60000 (N.D. Cal. July 13, 2009) (following *Transamerica* and holding that public policy prohibits insurer to provide coverage for punitive damages); *Howard v. Am. Nat. Fire Ins. Co.*, 187 Cal. App. 4th 498, 532–33 (Cal. Ct. App. 2010) (noting that insured may not place burden of paying punitive damages on insurer, but holding that court will not preclude coverage for settlement between insured and injured-plaintiff that may have included element for punitive damages without evidence of fraud or collusion, especially when settlement amount is not unreasonable); *Colorado Case Ins. Co. v. Candelaria Corp.*, No. EDCV 09-02123, 2010 U.S. Dist. LEXIS 31363 (C.D. Cal. Mar. 31, 2010) (determining that court apply California law because California's interest to exclude coverage for punitive damages would be impaired if court applied Arizona law, which allows punitive damages to be covered); *Paul Evert's RV Country, Inc. v. Universal Underwriters Ins. Co.*, 720 Fed. Appx. 412 (9th Cir. 2018) ("The California Supreme Court's decision in *PPG* controls. It bars Evert's RV from obtaining indemnification from its insurer for the underlying award of punitive damages assessed against Evert's RV's employees for their morally blameworthy behavior."); *Stem, Inc. v. Scottsdale Ins. Co.*, No. 20-02950, 2020 U.S. Dist. LEXIS 127486 (N.D. Cal. July 20, 2020) (finding that Scottsdale's policy "clearly excludes punitive damages" and citing *PPG* for the proposition that "[p]unitive damages are also not insurable under California law").

Colorado: The Supreme Court of Colorado held that both Colorado public policy and the insurance policy at issue prohibited an insurer from providing coverage for punitive damages. *Lira v. Shelter Ins. Co.*, 913 P.2d 514, 517 (Colo. 1996); *see also Universal Indem. Ins. Co. v. Tenery*, 39 P.2d 776, 779 (Colo. 1934) ("The injured will not be allowed to collect from a nonparticipating party [the tortfeasor's insurer], for a wrong against the public."); *Bohrer v. Church Mut. Ins. Co.*, 12 P.3d 854 (Colo. Ct. App. 2000) (holding that Colorado public policy also precluded coverage for post-judgment interest on punitive damages); *Ace Am. Ins. Co. v. Dish Network, LLC*, 173 F. Supp. 3d 1128 (D. Colo. 2016) (citing *Lira* and stating that "the tort of bad faith breach of an insurance contract does not encompass liability for punitive damages from the underlying lawsuit. The [*Lira*] court noted that the 'public policy of Colorado prohibits an insurance carrier from providing insurance coverage for punitive damages.'") (predicting that the Colorado Supreme Court would hold that an award of 500 dollars per violation under the TCPA "constitutes a penalty or an ilk of punitive damages which may not be covered by insurance under Colorado law."); *Nail v. Blue Donkey Transp., LLC*, No. 18-00159, 2018 U.S. Dist. LEXIS 171765 (E.D. Okla. Oct. 4, 2018) (applying Colorado law and citing to *Lira* to deny coverage for punitive damages).

Connecticut: The Supreme Court of Connecticut held that an award of statutory double damages for violating certain motor vehicle statutes was uninsurable. *Tedesco v. Md. Cas. Co.*, 18 A.2d 357, 359 (Conn. 1941). The court acknowledged a public policy rationale, but instead rested its decision on the construction of policy language that enabled it to avoid reaching a determination on such basis. *Id.* at 359. ("[T]he additional sum representing the doubling of the compensatory damages is, in its essence, a liability imposed, not for damages because of bodily injury, but as a reward for securing the punishment of one who has committed a wrong of a public nature."). In *Avis Rent A Car System v. Liberty Mutual Insurance Co.*, 526 A.2d 522 (Conn. 1987), the Supreme Court of Connecticut declined to follow *Tedesco* and held that, because Avis was only vicariously liable for statutory damages, and was not being punished for its own wrongdoing, coverage was available. *Id.* at 525–26. In *Bodner v. United States Automobile Ass'n*, 610 A.2d 1212 (Conn. 1992), the Supreme Court of Connecticut concluded that common law punitive damages were not insurable under an uninsured motorist policy. *Id.* at 1222; *see also Caufield v. Amica Mut. Ins. Co.*, 627 A.2d 466, 467–69 (Conn. App. Ct. 1993) (following *Bodner* and holding that double or treble statutory damages awarded for deliberately or with reckless disregard operating a motor vehicle in violation of certain statutes were not insurable under an uninsured motorist policy); *Anastasia v. General Cas. Co. of Wisconsin*, 59 A.3d 207 (Conn. 2013) (holding that insurer was entitled to reduction of its limits of liability for uninsured and underinsured motorist coverage by amount equal to sum of punitive damages paid to the insured); *Amica Mut. Ins. Co. v. Paradis*, No. HHDCV136041224S, 2014 Conn. Super. LEXIS 2640 (Conn. Super. Ct. Oct. 16, 2014) (referring to *Tedesco* and concluding that "the policy at issue expressly provides: 'We do not provide coverage for: fines, penalties, double or treble damages, punitive, exemplary or vindictive damages; or any other type of added conduct intended to punish or deter wrongful conduct rather than as compensation for actual damages.' This provision is consistent with the Supreme Court's holding that it is against public policy to insure against one's own liability for punitive damages."); *Nationwide Mut. Ins. Co. v. Pasiak*, 173 A.3d 888 (Conn. 2017) (distinguishing *Bodner* because it focused on policy considerations specific to uninsured motorist coverage and "*Bodner* did not involve, as does the present case, a policy expressly providing coverage for an intentional act, namely, false imprisonment.") ("[T]he plaintiffs do not contend that it would violate public policy to indemnify the defendant for compensatory damages awarded for the same intentional conduct. Common-law punitive damages under our law, which, unlike most jurisdictions, are limited to litigation costs, also help to make the injured plaintiff whole. . . . Accordingly, in the absence of a public policy reflected in our laws against providing such coverage, we conclude that, under the facts of the present case, the plaintiffs are bound to keep the bargain they struck, which includes coverage for common-law punitive damages for false imprisonment.").

Delaware: The Supreme Court of Delaware held that there was no evidence in the state of a public policy against insurance for punitive damages. *Whalen v. On-Deck, Inc.*, 514 A.2d 1072, 1074 (Del. 1986). "While the Superior Court and General Accident believe the purposes of punitive damages would be frustrated if such damages were insurable, we cannot infer from that concern a policy against such insurance. A wrongdoer who is insured against punitive damages may still be punished through higher insurance premiums or the loss of insurance altogether. More importantly, in light of the importance of the right of parties to contract as they wish, we will not partially void what might otherwise be a valid insurance contract as contrary to public policy in the absence of clear indicia that such a policy actually exists." *Id.* at 1074. The Supreme Court remanded the case to the trial court for a determination whether the policy language insured against punitive damages. *See also Brown v. United Water Delaware, Inc.*, No. 291, 2009, 2010 Del. Super. LEXIS 219 (Del. Super. Ct. May 20, 2010) (following *Whalen* and further declaring that "if there is no public policy against insuring for wanton conduct, there is no policy against a utility from limiting its liability for gross conduct") (noting that only Delaware state legislature may change *Whalen's* holding). The Supreme Court of Delaware held that both the policy language and public policy permitted coverage for punitive damages under an uninsured/underinsured motorist policy. *Jones v. State Farm Mut. Auto. Ins. Co.*, 610 A.2d 1352, 1353–54 (Del. 1992); *Stoms v. Federated Serv. Ins. Co.*, No. 14-01-163, 2014 Del. Super. LEXIS 602 (Del. Super. Ct. Nov. 20, 2014) (holding that "Delaware law provides that a plaintiff who would have been entitled to collect punitive damages from an uninsured motorist may collect the same damages from the insurance carrier. However, as the Court has found that Decedent is excluded from coverage by a valid and unambiguous Policy provision, the claim for punitive damages… is moot.") (*aff'd on other issues*, 125 A.3d 1102 (Del. 2015)).

District of Columbia: Although the District of Columbia has not formally decided whether punitive damages may be covered under an insurance policy, several courts have suggested that punitive damages awarded as a result of an intentional act would not be covered under an insurance policy. In *Salus Corp. v. Cont'l Cas. Co.*, 478 A.2d 1067 (D.C. Cir. 1984), the District of Columbia Court of Appeals overturned a trial court's decision that an insurer was not required to defend its insured in a punitive damages claim because the insured had "not yet been found to be guilty" of an intentional injury. *Id.* at 1070. "It may well be that once the 'ultimate liability' of Salus is determined, the contractual duty of the appellee-insurers to pay punitive damages would be negated by proof of Salus' intentional misconduct. However, that remains for future resolution." *Id.* at 1072; *see also Indep. Petrochemical Corp. v. Aetna Cas. and Sur. Co.*, 654 F. Supp. 1334, 1361 (D.D.C. 1986) ("When insured itself is not personally at fault but is only liable vicariously for another's wrongdoing, insurance for punitive damages is permitted. Public policy is not offended by covering any punitive damages imposed on plaintiffs since it appears that plaintiffs might be liable to the underlying claimants for the misfeasance of Bliss, not for any misconduct of their own.").

Florida: The Supreme Court of Florida held that the rationale for allowing punitive damages—punishment and deterrence—would be frustrated if such damages were covered by insurance. Thus, public policy precluded coverage for directly assessed punitive damages. *U.S. Concrete Pipe Co. v. Bould*, 437 So. 2d 1061, 1064 (Fla. 1983). However, the court also held that Florida public policy did not preclude coverage for punitive damages that were awarded when the insured is vicariously liable for another's wrong. *Id.* Nonetheless, coverage was permitted for directly assessed punitive damages because the instructions given to the jury in the underlying action allowed for an award of punitive damages on the basis of both direct and vicarious liability and the insurer did not request additional instructions or use special verdicts to have the jury's determination clarified. *Id.*; *see also First Specialty Ins. Co. v. Caliber One Indem. Co.*, 988 So. 2d 708, 713 (Fla. Dist. Ct. App. 2008) (no coverage for punitive damages under policy that defined "damages" as "compensatory amount" and that included an exclusion for "civil fines or penalties"); *Herendeen v. Mandelbaum*, 232 So. 3d 487 (Fla. Dist. Ct. App. 2017) ("Florida law does not allow indemnification against punitive damages.") (citing *Queen v. Clearwater Elec., Inc.*, 555 So. 2d 1262 (Fla. 2d DCA 1989) and *Concrete Pipe*); *Marino v. Greenberg*, No. 50-2016-CA-007297, 2018 Fla. Cir. LEXIS 4949 (Fla. Cir. Ct. Dec. 12, 2018) (reiterating *Concrete Pipe*); *Ranger Constr. Indus. v. Allied World Nat'l Assur. Co.*, No. 17-81226, 2019 U.S. Dist. LEXIS 220478 (S.D. Fla. Dec. 23, 2019) ("[W]hen the legislature enacted Florida Statute § 768.72 [changing the common law standard of culpability required to hold a defendant liable for punitive damages] it did not intend to change 50 years of Florida public policy regarding the uninsurability of punitive damages without making any indication that it was doing so.").

Georgia: The Supreme Court of Georgia held that the policy language at issue—all sums which the insured shall become legally obligated to pay as damages (1) *for* … mental anguish—included coverage for punitive damages. *Greenwood Cemetery, Inc. v. Travelers Indem. Co.*, 232 S.E.2d 910, 913 (Ga. 1977). The insurer argued that "for" meant "equivalent to" or "to the amount, value or extent of." *Id.* The insured argued that "for" meant "by reason of" or "because of or account of." *Id.* The Georgia high court concluded that the policy language was ambiguous and applied the interpretation that favored the insured. *Id.* The *Greenwood Cemetery* Court also rejected the insurer's argument that public policy precluded the insurability of punitive damages. *Id.* at 913–14; *see also Lunceford v. Peachtree Cas. Ins. Co.*, 495 S.E.2d 88, 89 (Ga. Ct. App. 1997) (concluding that because the phrase "because of bodily injury or property damage" was comparable to that which was construed in *Greenwood Cemetery*, the policy provided coverage for punitive damages). An insurer is relieved from its obligation to pay punitive damages if the policy explicitly excludes coverage for punitive damages. *Nationwide Mut. Fire Ins. Co. v. Kim*, 669 S.E.2d 517, 519–20 (Ga. Ct. App. 2008); *Alea London Ltd. v. Am. Home Services*, 638 F.3d 768, 779 (11th Cir. 2011) (applying Georgia law) (holding that policy exclusion for punitive damages did not apply to treble damages under the Telephone Consumer

Protection Act because "for the purposes of interpreting the coverage provided by an insurance contract governed by Georgia law, the TCPA's treble damages provision falls more on the compensatory than the punitive side") ("Alea could have drafted the Policy's punitive damages exclusion to expressly bar coverage for 'treble damages,' or all damages that were 'in any way non-compensatory,' or damages that were 'in part in the nature of punitive damages.' But it did not."); *Evanston Ins. Co. v. Mellors*, 141 F. Supp. 3d 1367 (S.D. Ga. 2015) (holding that the definition of damages: "the monetary portion of any judgment, award or settlement; provided, however, that Damages shall not include: (1) multiplied portions of damages in excess of actual damages, including trebling of damages; (2) taxes, criminal or civil fines, or penalties imposed by law; (3) sanctions; (4) matters which are uninsurable under the law pursuant to which this policy shall be construed; or (5) the return of or restitution of fees, profits or charges for services rendered" does not include damages that, "while punitive in nature, are not traditional 'punitive damages'"). In the uninsured motorist context, the Court of Appeals of Georgia held that "the legislative intention was to permit recovery of compensatory, and not punitive damages." *Bonamico v. Kisella*, 659 S.E.2d 666, 667 (Ga. Ct. App. 2008) (citation omitted); *Grange Prop. & Cas. Ins. Co. v. Smith*, No. 17-00199, 2019 U.S. Dist. LEXIS 143541 (N.D. Ga. Aug. 23, 2019) (addressing whether an insurer properly reserved its rights to preclude coverage for punitive damages).

Hawaii: "Coverage under any policy of insurance issued in this state shall not be construed to provide coverage for punitive or exemplary damages unless specifically included." Haw. Rev. Stat. § 431:10–240. *See Allstate Ins. Co. v. Takeda*, 243 F. Supp. 2d 1100, 1104 (D. Haw. 2003) (applying Haw. Rev. Stat. § 431:10–240 and concluding that, because the policy did not specifically include coverage for punitive damages, the insurer was not responsible for them); *State Farm Fire and Cas. Co. v. Wimberly*, 877 F. Supp. 2d 993 (D. Haw. 2012) (restated statute and *Takeda*); *United States Fire Ins. Co. v. Fea*, No. 16-00173, 2016 U.S. Dist. LEXIS 177554 (D. Haw. Dec. 1, 2016) (referring to *Takeda* and HAW. REV. STAT. § 431:10-240 and holding that "[u]nder Hawaii law, '[c]overage under any policy of insurance issued in [Hawaii] shall not be construed to provide coverage for punitive or exemplary damages unless specifically included.' The Policy does not specifically include coverage for punitive damages."); *State Farm Fire & Cas. Co. v. Shaun Ching*, No. 16-418, 2017 U.S. Dist. LEXIS 39503 (D. Haw. Feb. 24, 2017) (citing statute and holding that insurer was not responsible for punitive damages because its policy did not specifically include such coverage).

Idaho: The Supreme Court of Idaho held that punitive damages were covered under an automobile liability policy. *Abbie Uriguen Oldsmobile Buick, Inc. v. U.S. Fire Ins. Co.*, 511 P.2d 783, 789 (Idaho 1973). The court held that punitive damages were not specifically excluded by the terms of the policy. *Id.* The insurer promised "to pay on behalf of the insured *all* sums which the insured shall be legally obligated to pay as *damages* caused by the use of any automobile." *Id.* (emphasis added). On the subject of public policy, the *Uriguen Oldsmobile* Court concluded that it was not a prohibition against coverage for punitive damages. *Id.* The court adopted the oft-cited position of the Supreme Court of Tennessee in *Lazenby v. Universal Underwriters Insurance Co.*, 383 S.W.2d 1 (Tenn. 1964), which concluded that it is speculative that socially irresponsible drivers would be deterred from their wrongful conduct if coverage for punitive damages were not allowed. *Id.*

Illinois: The Appellate Court of Illinois adopted the rationale of *Northwestern National Casualty Co. v. McNulty*, 307 F.2d 432 (5th Cir. 1962), discussed in the introduction, and held that public policy prohibited insurance for liability for punitive damages that arose out of one's own misconduct. *Beaver v. Country Mut. Ins. Co.*, 420 N.E.2d 1058, 1060 (Ill. App. Ct. 1981). However, the *Beaver* Court did not disturb the rule set forth in *Scott v. Instant Parking, Inc.*, 245 N.E.2d 124 (Ill. App. 1969), that an employer may insure for punitive damages that are assessed on the basis of vicarious liability on account of the wrongful conduct of his employee. *Beaver*, 400 N.E.2d at 1061. *But see Nutmeg Ins. Co. v. E. Lake Mgmt. & Dev. Corp.*, No. 05 C 1328, 2006 U.S. Dist. LEXIS 85665 (N.D. Ill. Nov. 21, 2006), *aff'd on other grounds* 260 Fed. App'x 914 (7th Cir. 2008) (distinguishing *Beaver* and holding that a landlord's liability for two times damages for violating a municipal ordinance, concerning the handling of security deposits, were not uninsurable as a matter of public policy because such damages are recoverable whether a landlord's failure to comply with the ordinance was inadvertent or intentional); *W. World Ins. Co. v. Wendy Frieden & Frieden Prop. Mgmt., LLC*, No. 16-04038, 2018 U.S. Dist. LEXIS 230533 (C.D. Ill. Jul. 18, 2018) (reiterating *Beaver*'s distinction, between coverage for punitive damages against an individual versus an employer, and holding that no coverage owed) ("Here, the claims for punitive damages are based on Frieden's own willful and fraudulent conduct, not based on the bad acts of an employee."); *Ironshore Speciality Ins. Co. v. Akorn, Inc.*, No. 17-3541, 2021 U.S. Dist. LEXIS 109923 (N.D. Ill. June 11, 2021) ("line prohibiting the protection of insurance is drawn . . . not between negligent conduct and intentional conduct, but between negligent conduct and the kind of unintentional conduct for which punitive damages may be imposed") (discussing *Beaver* and rejecting various arguments to navigate around the prohibition on coverage for punitive damages under the facts at issue).

Indiana: An Indiana District Court held that "it would contravene public policy to allow [a] corporation to shift to an insurer the deterrent award imposed on account of the corporation's own wrongful acts; [but] it would not be inconsistent with public policy to allow the corporation to shift to an insurer the punitive damage award when that award is placed upon the corporation solely as a matter of vicarious liability." *Norfolk & W. Ry. Co. v. Hartford Accident & Indem. Co.*, 420 F. Supp. 92, 97 (N.D. Ind. 1976); *see also Executive Builders, Inc. v. Motorists Ins. Cos.*, No. IP00–0018-C-T/G, 2001 U.S. Dist. LEXIS 6775 (S.D. Ind. Mar. 30, 2001) (citing *Norfolk* in discussing public policy concerning the insurability of punitive damages). In *Commercial Union Insurance Co. v. Ramada Hotel Operating Co.*, 852 F.2d 298, 306 (7th Cir. 1988), the Seventh Circuit Court of Appeals, applying Indiana law, remanded the case to the District Court for the insurer to attempt to meet its burden that punitive damages were awarded based on the insured's direct liability and not vicarious; *Auto-Owners Ins. Co. v. Lake Erie Land Co.*, No. 212-184, 2014 U.S. Dist. LEXIS 62339 (N.D. Ind. May 6, 2014) (citing *Norfolk* and requiring parties to file supplemental briefs (1) "predicting how the Indiana Supreme Court would determine whether Indiana's public policy prohibits the insurability of an award of punitive damages assessed directly against a corporation on a theory of gross negligence and (2) the parties' position as to whether the question should be certified to the Indiana Supreme Court"). [Docket entries reflect that the case was dismissed before the court's ruling.]; *See also Westfield Ins. Co. v. Orthopedic & Sports Med. Ctr. of N. Ind., Inc.*, No. 14-1548, 2017 U.S. Dist. LEXIS 46119 (N.D. Ind. March 28, 2017) (referring to *Executive Builders* and noting that the parties were in agreement that the policies did not provide coverage for the punitive damages claims, in part because courts have held that such coverage is void as against public policy.).

Iowa: The Supreme Court of Iowa held that public policy did not preclude coverage for punitive damages. *Skyline Harvestore Sys., Inc. v. Centennial Ins. Co.*, 331 N.W.2d 106 (Iowa 1983). The court concluded that "[i]f the parties wish to contract for coverage of punitive damages, they may. If the insurance companies do not wish to provide such coverage, then they must exclude coverage of punitive damages specifically." *Id.* at 109. The court recognized that, by its decision, it was "elevat[ing] the public policy of freedom of contract for insurance coverage above the public policy purposes of punitive damages." *Id.*; *see also Grinnell Mut. Reinsurance Co. v.*

Jungling, 654 N.W. 2d 530, 540–41 (Iowa 2002) (following *Skyline Harvestore* and concluding that the public policy of freedom of contract for insurance coverage should prevail over the public policy reasons for barring coverage for the intentional act of fraud).

Kansas: The Supreme Court of Kansas held that punitive damages are uninsurable under Kansas law and public policy. *Koch v. Merchants Mut. Bonding Co.*, 507 P.2d 189, 195–96 (Kan. 1973). In 1984, the Kansas Legislature adopted KAN. STAT. ANN. § 40–2115, which states that it does not violate public policy to provide coverage for punitive damages that are assessed against an insured on the basis of vicarious liability, without the actual prior knowledge of such insured. However, in 1987, the Kansas Legislature adopted KAN. STAT. ANN. § 60–3701(d)(1), which states: "In no case shall exemplary or punitive damages be assessed pursuant to this section against: a principal or employer for the acts of an agent or employee unless the questioned conduct was authorized or ratified by a person expressly empowered to do so on behalf of the principal or employer." This is sometimes referred to as the "complicity rule." In *Hartford Accident and Indem. Co. v. Am. Red Ball Transit Co.*, 938 P.2d 1281 (Kan. 1997), the Supreme Court of Kansas held that section 40–2115 has no effect in cases where punitive damages are awarded on the basis of the complicity rule set in section 60–3701(d)(1). *Id.* at 1292; *see also Hackman v. Western Agr. Ins. Co.*, No. 103,967, 2011 Kan. App. Unpub. LEXIS 334 (Kan. Ct. App. May 6, 2011) ("Kansas public policy clearly prohibits an insurer from being liable to the insured for punitive damages.").

Kentucky: The Court of Appeals of Kentucky held that it was not against public policy to permit insurance for punitive damages that were imposed for a grossly negligent act of the insured rather than an intentional one. *Cont'l Ins. Cos. v. Hancock*, 507 S.W.2d 146, 151–52 (Ky. 1973). However, it was impossible to determine from the jury instructions what the basis was for authorizing compensatory and punitive damages. *Id.* Thus, the court "indulge[d] the presumption" that the punitive damages were awarded as a punishment for grossly negligent conduct and were therefore covered by the policy obligation to pay all sums which the insured shall be legally obligated to pay. *Id.* at 152. The court also held that punitive damages awarded on the basis of vicarious liability were insurable, whether the servant's act was intentional or grossly negligent. *Id.* at 151. The Supreme Court of Kentucky held that punitive damages were not insurable under an uninsured motorists policy that provided coverage for "damages … because of bodily injury." *Ky. Cent. Ins. Co. v. Schneider*, 15 S.W.3d 373, 374 (Ky. 2000). *See also West American Insurance Co. v.*

M&M Service Station Equipment Specialist, No. 16-00046, 2017 U.S. Dist. LEXIS 203773 (W.D. Ky. Dec. 12, 2017) ("The Policy's exclusion of coverage for punitive damages awards is unequivocal and unambiguous. Kentucky courts have held that such exclusions are enforceable.") (citing *Deerfield Ins. Co. v. Warren Cty. Fiscal Court*, 88 S.W.3d 867 (Ky. App. Ct. 2002)); *United Specialty Ins. Co. v. Cole's Place, Inc.*, No. 17-00326, 2018 U.S. Dist. LEXIS 67850 (W.D. Ky. Apr. 23, 2018), *aff'd on other grounds* 936 F.3d 386 (6th Cir. 2019) (discussing, but not needing to decide, whether, because the duty to defend is broader than the duty to indemnify, a policy's punitive damages exclusion did not apply to the duty to defend).

Louisiana: The Court of Appeal of Louisiana held that the language of two policies at issue—"(1) all sums the insured legally must pay as damages *because of* bodily injury or property damage ... [and] (2) indemnify the insured for ultimate net loss ... which the insured shall become legally obligated to pay as damages *because of* ... [p]ersonal injury"—included coverage for punitive damages. *Creech v. Aetna Cas. & Sur. Co.*, 516 So. 2d 1168, 1171 (La. Ct. App. 1987) (emphasis added). The *Creech* Court also held that Louisiana public policy did not preclude coverage for punitive damages, stating that "[p]ublic policy is better served by giving effect to the insurance contract rather than by creating an exclusion based on a judicial perception of public policy not expressed by the legislature." *Id.* at 1174. In the uninsured motorist context, LA. REV. STAT. § 22:1406(D)(1)(a)(i) allows an insurance policy to include an exclusion for punitive damages. *Pike v. Nat'l Union Fire Ins. Co.*, 796 So. 2d 696, 699–700 (La. Ct. App. 2001); *see also Indian Harbor Ins. Co. v. Bestcomp, Inc.*, No. 09-7327, 2010 U.S. Dist. LEXIS 139252 (E.D. La. Nov. 12, 2010) ("[T]he public policy excluding payment for punitive damages does not apply to costs and attorneys' fees incurred in the defense of a penal statute."); *Cazenave v. ANPAC La. Ins. Co.*, No. 16-1420, 2016 U.S. Dist. LEXIS 175728 (E.D. La. Dec. 20, 2016) (reiterating that "Louisiana law allows an insurer to exclude punitive damages from uninsured motorist coverage by the terms of the policy or contract."). An exclusion for punitive damages has been upheld in the context of a commercial automobile policy. *Dickerson v. Hapl*, No. 19-14763, 2020 U.S. Dist. LEXIS 203442 (E.D. La. Nov. 2, 2020) (granting partial summary judgment on the basis that a punitive damages exclusion applied to punitive damages sought as a result of a rear-end car accident) ("Louisiana courts have held punitive damage exclusions in insurance policies are enforceable when expressed in terms that are clear and unambiguous"); *Moreaux v. Clear Blue Ins. Co.*, No. 18-01255, 2021 U.S. Dist. LEXIS 29601 (W.D. La. Feb. 17, 2021) (non-UM case and citing *Pike* for the proposition that "Louisiana courts have routinely upheld punitive damages exclusions as valid and enforceable").

Maine: The Supreme Judicial Court of Maine held that insurers providing coverage under the provisions mandated by the uninsured motorist statute are not liable for punitive damages. *Braley v. Berkshire Mut. Ins. Co.*, 440 A.2d 359, 361–62 (Me. 1982). While the court did not address the issue in the liability insurance context, it did state that "[u]nder Maine law deterrence of the tortfeasor is 'the proper justification' for an award of punitive damages. Allowing punitive damages to be awarded against an insurance company can serve no deterrent function because the wrongdoer is not the person paying the damages. This has been recognized by many courts in the context of liability insurance." *Id.* at 362 (citations omitted) (quoting *Foss v. Me. Turnpike Auth.*, 309 A.2d 339, 345 (Me. 1973)). However, the *Braley* Court also noted that, in the liability context, the ability to raise the insured's premiums may achieve some small deterrent effect. *Id.* at 363.

Maryland: The Court of Appeals of Maryland held that it was not against public policy to permit coverage for punitive damages awarded for malicious prosecution. *First Nat'l Bank of Saint Mary's v. Fid. & Deposit Co.*, 389 A.2d 359, 362 (Md. 1978). Indeed, the court suggested that Maryland's public policy may be the exact opposite. *Id.* at 366. "[W]e strongly suspect that the common sense of the community as a whole would expect a judgment including exemplary damages to be satisfied through the insurance policies for which such small business people had paid. It would be outraged and have substantial difficulty in comprehending reasons for a holding to the contrary." *Id.*; *see also Bailer v. Erie Ins. Exch.*, 687 A.2d 1375, 1385 (Md. 1997) ("[W]e held [in *St. Mary's*] that it was not contrary to public policy to insure against liability for punitive damages awarded in a civil action for malicious prosecution, even though the punitive damages in legal theory are predicated upon malice."); *State Auto Prop. & Cas. Ins. Co. v. Moser*, No. 589-MDA-2017, 2018 Pa. Super. Unpub. LEXIS 1471 (Pa. Super. Ct. May 7, 2018) (applying Maryland law) ("[S]ince Maryland law holds that insurance coverage for punitive damages arising from both vicarious and direct liability does not offend public policy, Appellants were entitled to a declaration that coverage for punitive damages was available to them in this action.")

Massachusetts: The Supreme Judicial Court of Massachusetts held that punitive damages were not recoverable under an uninsured motorist policy. *Santos v. Lumbermens Mut. Cas. Co.*, 556 N.E.2d 983, 989 (Mass. 1990). "Requiring an insurance company to pay punitive damages to the insured would not serve to deter wrongdoing or punish the wrongdoer; rather it would result in payment of punitive damages by a party who was not a wrongdoer. In the underinsurance context, where the wrongdoer is not in a contractual relationship with the insurance company, there is not even the possible deterrent effect of higher premium rates." *Id.* at 990 (citations omitted). *See also Williamson-Green v. Interstate Fire & Cas. Co.*, No. 1684-03141-BLS2, 2017 Mass. Super. LEXIS 70 (Mass. Super. Ct. May 26, 2017) ("[T]he SJC [in *Santos*] carefully limited its holding to the underinsurance context, and stressed that it was not deciding 'whether a tortfeasor's insurer may be obliged to pay for punitive damages.' In any case, whether an insurance policy covers punitive damages does not control the scope of the insurer's liability for consequential damages if it mishandles settlement of a claim. If an insurance policy excludes coverage for punitive damages, that does not absolve an insurer from liability for all losses flowing from a breach of its duty to settle a claim, including for a foreseeable award of punitive damages against the insured.").

Michigan: A Michigan District Court held that coverage was available for punitive damages under a liability policy that provided coverage for damages because of bodily injury and that did not contain an explicit exclusion for punitive damages. *Meijer, Inc. v. Gen. Star Indem. Co.*, 826 F. Supp. 241, 246–47 (W.D. Mich. 1993), *aff'd* No. 94–1152, 61 F.3d 903 (Table) (6th Cir. 1995). The court concluded that "[t]o hold that punitive damages are not recoverable would create, in effect, an exclusion for which the parties did not negotiate and allow insurance companies to collect premiums for coverage of a risk that they voluntarily assumed and then escape their obligation to pay on a claim by a mere judicial declaration that the contract is void by reason of public policy." *Id.* at 247.

Minnesota: The Supreme Court of Minnesota held that "in most instances public policy should prohibit a person from insuring himself against misconduct of a character serious enough to warrant punitive damages." *Wojciak v. N. Package Corp.*, 310 N.W.2d 675, 680 (Minn. 1981). However, the *Wojciak* Court did not apply the rule because the punitive damages were awarded under a statute prohibiting retaliatory discharge of an employee that seeks workers' compensation benefits. *Id.* The court concluded that the punitive damages were awarded not only to punish employers and deter such conduct, but also to afford redress to employees who are victimized by retaliatory dismissal. *Id.* Punitive and exemplary damages awarded on the basis of vicarious liability are insurable. *See* Minn. Stat. § 60A.06, subd. 4. *But see Seren Innovations, Inc. v. Transcon. Ins. Co.*, No. A05–917, 2006 Minn. App. Unpub. LEXIS 535 (Minn. Ct. App. May 23, 2006) ("Absent policy language providing coverage for punitive damages, we will not create coverage where coverage does not exist, even if such coverage would fall within the vicarious-liability exception to the punitive-damages-coverage prohibition.").

Mississippi: The Supreme Court of Mississippi reaffirmed its holding in *Anthony v. Frith*, 394 So. 2d 867 (Miss. 1981) that an "insurance company's liability 'for all damages arising from bodily injury' includes punitive damages. However, the extent or limit of that liability for punitive damage is governed by the agreement of the parties as reflected by the actual language in the policy of insurance." *Old Security Cas. Ins. Co. v. Clemmer*, 455 So. 2d 781, 783 (Miss. 1984); *see also Shelter Mut. Ins. Co. v. Dale*, 914 So. 2d 698, 703 (Miss. 2005) (holding that Mississippi law did not prevent an insurer from excluding coverage for punitive damages by amendatory endorsement to its automobile liability policy); *State Farm Mut. Auto. Ins. Co. v. Daughdrill*, 474 So. 2d 1048, 1054 (Miss. 1985) (finding that Mississippi Uninsured Motorist Act did not require an uninsured motorist provision in an automobile policy to cover punitive damages that the insured is legally entitled to collect from the uninsured motorist); *Abel v. Allstate Prop. & Cas. Ins. Co.*, No. 14-00064, 2015 U.S. Dist. LEXIS 35852 (N.D. Miss. March 23, 2015) (citing *Daughdrill* and reiterating that "because the purpose of punitive damages is to punish a tortfeasor and deter others, '[s]uch an award against an insurance company does not deter or punish similar future conduct, and no punishment is imposed on the uninsured.'").

Missouri: The Supreme Court of Missouri has not addressed the availability of insurance coverage for punitive damages. Several Missouri appellate court decisions have addressed the issue and the results vary depending upon the policy language under consideration. *See DeShong v. Mid-States Adjustment, Inc.*, 876 S.W.2d 5 (Mo. Ct. App. 1994) (stating that punitive damages not covered under policy stating that the insurer will pay amounts the insured is "legally required to pay to compensate others for loss" because punitive damages are not compensatory in nature); *Heartland Stores, Inc. v. Royal Ins. Co.*, 815 S.W.2d 39, 40 (Mo. Ct. App. 1991) (finding that punitive damages were not covered under policy stating that the insurer will pay "all sums which the insured shall become legally obligated to pay as damages because of personal injury" because the policy was limited to compensation for personal injury and not sums awarded as punishment); *Schnuck Markets, Inc. v. Transamerica Ins. Co.*, 652 S.W.2d 206, 209 (Mo. Ct. App. 1983) ("Since punitive damages are never awarded merely because of a 'bodily injury' or 'personal injury' but only when the actor's conduct displays the requisite malice, we find they are not in the category of damages for 'bodily injury' or 'personal injury.'"); *Crull v. Gleb*, 382

S.W.2d 17, 22, 23 (Mo. Ct. App. 1964) (finding that policy language and public policy precluded coverage for punitive damages). *But see Colson v. Lloyd's of London*, 435 S.W.2d 42, 43, 46–47 (Mo. Ct. App. 1968) (finding that coverage for punitive damages permitted by the language of a False Arrest Insurance policy ("loss by reason of liability imposed by law upon the insured by reason of any false arrest") and public policy did not preclude coverage); *Argonaut Great Cent. Ins. Co. v. Valley Village, LLC*, No. 4-10CV2247, 2013 U.S. Dist. LEXIS 25016 (E.D. Mo. Feb. 25, 2013) (citing *Schnuck* and holding that a policy covering damages because of "bodily injury" or "personal injury" did not extend coverage for punitive damages).

Montana: "Insurance coverage does not extend to punitive or exemplary damages unless expressly included by the contract of insurance." MONT. CODE ANN. § 33–15–317. The statute followed the Supreme Court of Montana's decision in *First Bank Billings v. Transamerica Ins. Co.*, 679 P.2d 1217 (Mont. 1984), which held that insurance coverage of punitive damages is not contrary to public policy. The court concluded that "[i]insurance companies are more than capable of evaluating risks and deciding whether they will offer policies to indemnify all or some conduct determined by judges or juries to be malicious, fraudulent or oppressive." *Id.* at 1222. The court was also persuaded that it was necessary for punitive damages to be insurable given the lack of consistency surrounding their award. *Id.* Because judges and juries may award punitive damages for a broad range of conduct (willful, wanton, reckless, or unjustified) and different fact finders in similar fact situations may reach different conclusions concerning the availability of punitive damages, the court concluded that the argument for the denial of coverage was difficult to sustain. *Id. See also American Reliable Insurance Co. v. Lockard*, No. 17-04, 2018 U.S. Dist. LEXIS 399 (D. Mont. Jan. 2, 2018) (while policy's punitive damages exclusion and § 33–15–317 preclude indemnity for punitive damages, insurer still had a duty to defend a complaint where such duty was otherwise owed); *Homesite Ins. Co. v. Frost*, No. 20-0024, 2020 U.S. Dist. LEXIS 163535 (D. Mont. Sept. 8, 2020) (finding that punitive damages sought in a kidnapping case were uninsurable because the homeowner's policy issued to the kidnapper did not "expressly provide for coverage in the event of an award of punitive damages"; as a result the "claim in the Underlying Lawsuit does not fall within the scope of coverage").

Nebraska: Punitive damages are themselves not recoverable under Nebraska law. *See Abel v. Conover*, 104 N.W.2d 684, 688 (Neb. 1960) ("It has been a fundamental rule of law in this state that punitive, vindictive, or exemplary damages will not be allowed, and that the measure of recovery is all civil cases is compensation for the injury sustained. This rule is so well settled that we dispose of it merely by citation of cases so holding."); *Distinctive Printing & Packaging Co. v. Cox*, 443 N.W.2d 566, 574 (Neb. 1989) ("[P]unitive, vindictive, or exemplary damages contravene NEB. CONST. art. VII, § 5, and thus are not allowed in this jurisdiction.") *But see Cherry v. Burns*, 602 N.W.2d 477, 484 (Neb. 1999) (recognizing that punitive damages are recoverable in a civil rights action filed in Nebraska state court pursuant to 42 U.S.C. § 1983); *Factory Mut. Ins. Co. v. Nebraska Beef, Inc.*, No. 8:09CV159, 2010 U.S. Dist. LEXIS 9037 (D. Neb. Jan. 19, 2010) ("If the State of Nebraska wants to carve out an exception to allow private parties to pursue punitive damages on behalf of local school districts, it will have to explicitly say so. This court is not going to interpret the Nebraska Constitution, statutes, and caselaw to find this right of action, when there has been no clear directive on the part of the State of Nebraska to do so."); *Bamford, Inc. v. Regent Ins. Co.*, No. 13-200, 2014 U.S. Dist. LEXIS 190119 (D. Neb. June 12, 2014) (reiterating holding in *Distinctive Printing* that "Nebraska's Supreme Court has read the state Constitution to prohibit punitive damages."); *O'Brien v. Cessna Aircraft Co.*, 903 N.W.2d 432 (Neb. 2017) (reiterating that Nebraska law prohibits the award of "punitive, vindictive, or exemplary damages"); *Wolfbauer v. Ocwen Loan Servicing, LLC*, No. 18-13, 2018 U.S. Dist. LEXIS 59301 (D. Neb. Apr. 6, 2018) (same); *Trimble v. Helwig*, No. 19-5015, 2020 U.S. Dist. LEXIS 97170 (D. Neb. Jun. 2, 2020) (same).

Nevada: "An insurer may insure against legal liability for exemplary or punitive damages that do not arise from a wrongful act of the insured committed with the intent to cause injury to another." NEV. REV. STAT. ANN. § 681A.095. The Supreme Court of Nevada held that punitive damages are not recoverable under an uninsured motorist policy. *Siggelkow v. Phoenix Ins. Co.*, 846 P.2d 303, 305 (Nev. 1993). The court based its decision on an unwillingness to distort the purpose of punitive damages, as well as the policy language reasoning that "[u]nder no construction can the language 'for bodily injury' be read to include punitive damages. Punitive damages are not awarded for bodily injury." *Id.* (internal quotations omitted) (quoting *State Farm Mut. Ins. Co. v. Blevins*, 551 N.E.2d 955, 959 (Ohio 1990)). *See also United Specialty Ins. Co. v. Hachiman*, No. 16-02784, 2018 U.S. Dist. LEXIS 238031 (D. Nev. Feb. 15, 2018) (finding that a punitive damages exclusion stating "[t]his insurance does not apply to [p]unitive or exemplary damages" unambiguously applied with respect to the duty to indemnify claims for punitive damages; however, the language was ambiguous as it related to the insurer's duty to defend) (The court noted that "[i]f a claim otherwise falls within the Policy's scope of coverage, but punitive damages are sought as a remedy, it would not make sense for United to disclaim its duty to defend.").

New Hampshire: The Supreme Court of New Hampshire held that "public policy sanctions rather than opposes insuring for liability arising directly against the insured from intentional torts such as false arrest, slander or § 1983 actions." *Am. Home Assurance Co. v. Fish*, 451 A.2d 358, 360 (N.H. 1982). However, the specific policy at issue excluded "fines and penalties imposed by law" from the definition of "loss." *Id.* The *Fish* Court held that, because punitive damages are fines and penalties, no coverage was owed for such damages. *Id.*; *see also Weeks v. St. Paul Fire & Marine Ins. Co.*, 673 A.2d 772, 775 (N.H. 1996) ("Even assuming, without deciding, that the claims are penal, we have held an insurance company liable [in *Fish*] for exemplary or punitive damages where fines and penalties are not expressly excluded by the policy language."); *MacKinnon v. Hanover Ins. Co.*, 471 A.2d 1166, 1168–69 (N.H. 1984) (rejecting the insurer's argument that public policy precludes coverage for all consequences of intentional acts of harm).

New Jersey: The New Jersey Appellate Division noted that "New Jersey sides with those jurisdictions which proscribe coverage for punitive damage liability because such a result offends public policy and frustrates the purpose of punitive damage awards." *Johnson & Johnson v. Aetna Cas. & Sur. Co.*, 667 A.2d 1087, 1091 (N.J. Super. App. Div. 1995). The *Johnson & Johnson* Court also declined to decide whether an exception existed to allow coverage for punitive damages that are awarded on the basis of vicarious liability because there was no finding that the insureds were found to be vicariously liable. *Id. But see Chubb Custom Ins. Co. v. Prudential Ins. Co. of Am.*, 948 A.2d 1285, 1293 n.3 (N.J. 2008) (noting parenthetically that there has never been a declaration by itself or the legislature that punitive damages are uninsurable and observing that the legislature (N.J. STAT. § 17:30A-5) has at least implicitly recognized that it does not violate public policy to insure punitive damages); *Med-Plus, Inc. v. Am. Cas. Co. of Reading*, No. 16-2985, 2017 U.S. Dist. LEXIS 123553 (E.D.N.Y. Aug. 4, 2017) (citing *Johnson & Johnson*, *Fireman's Fund Ins. Co. v. Imbesi*, 826 A.2d 735 (N.J. Super. App. Div. 2003), foot note 3 in *Chubb v. Prudential*, noting that the New Jersey Supreme Court has not addressed the issue and concluding that "the best available authority suggests that, under . . . New Jersey law, punitive damages are not insurable as a matter of public policy").

New Mexico: The Supreme Court of New Mexico held that punitive damages are insurable so long as they are not excluded by the language of the policy. *Baker v. Armstrong*, 744 P.2d 170, 173–74 (N.M. 1987). "Citizens and their insurers should have the right to contract for insurance against the possibility of a judicial decision finding that a person's conduct rises above ordinary negligence and justifies punitive damages. If insurance companies market policies which consumers reasonably expect cover all damages, then the insurer should honor that contract. Contracts should be held invalid against public policy only if there is an evil tendency connected with the contract itself, and insurance coverage of punitive damages has not been related in any substantial way to the commission of wrongful acts." *Id.*; *see also Rummel v. St. Paul Surplus Lines Ins. Co.*, 945 P.2d 985, 989 (N.M. 1997) (discussing *Baker* and addressing whether excess follow form policies provide or exclude coverage for punitive damages); *Mid-Continent Cas. Co. v. I&W, Inc.*, No. 11-0329, 2015 U.S. Dist. LEXIS 178095 (D.N.M. Feb. 11, 2015) (citing *Baker* and *Rummel* and reiterating that public policy "requires coverage where the policy is broad enough to include coverage for punitive damages") ("specific or express language is not required in order to effectuate a punitive damage exclusion"); *Am. Auto. Ins. Co. v. First Mercury Ins. Co.*, No. 13-439, 2018 U.S. Dist. LEXIS 65980 (D.N.M. Apr. 19, 2018) (permitting insurer to seek indemnification from another insurer for punitive damages paid to settle claim against mutual insured).

New York: The highest court of New York held that punitive damages are uninsurable because, to allow coverage for them, would defeat their purpose. *Pub. Serv. Mut. Ins. Co. v. Goldfarb*, 425 N.E.2d 810, 814 (N.Y. 1981). Indeed, the New York Court of Appeals went so far as to say that coverage for punitive damages was impermissible even if an insurer agreed to provide such coverage and charged a premium for it. *Id.* However, the *Goldfarb* Court also stated that "if punitive damages are awarded on any ground other than intentional causation of *injury*—for example, gross negligence, recklessness or wantonness—indemnity for compensatory damages would be allowable even though indemnity for the punitive or exemplary component of the damage award would be barred as violative of public policy." *Id.* at 815. The policy articulated in *Goldfarb* applies equally to cases involving conduct that is less culpable than intentional, such as grossly negligent, wanton or so reckless as to amount to a conscious disregard of the rights of others. *Home Ins. Co. v. Am. Home Prods. Corp.*, 550 N.E.2d 930, 932–33 (N.Y. 1990). New York's highest court has also held that punitive damages awarded on the basis of vicarious corporate liability are not insurable. *Zurich Insurance Co. v. Shearson Lehman Hutton, Inc.*, 642 N.E.2d 1065, 1070 (N.Y. 1994); *see also McCabe v. St. Paul Fire and Marine Ins. Co.*, 914 N.Y.S.2d 814 (N.Y. App. Div. 2010) (following *Am. Home Prods.* by declaring that public policy precludes insurance companies from covering insured for punitive damages) (treating treble damages as uninsurable punitive damages); *CBS Corp. v. Eaton Corp.*, No. 07 Civ. 11344, 2010 U.S. Dist. LEXIS 32881 (S.D.N.Y. Mar. 30, 2010) (citing *Goldfarb* for proposition that insurer must defend insured when claim falls within policy coverage even though insured does not need to cover insured for punitive damages in the case); *Certain Underwriters at Lloyd's v. BDO Seidman LLP*, 957 N.Y.S.2d 263 (N.Y. Sup. Ct. 2012) (citing *Goldfarb*, *Zurich*, and *Am. Home Prods.* and holding that "New York public policy precludes insurance indemnification for punitive damages") (addressing whether an out-of-state punitive damages judgment was indemnifiable in New York); *J.P. Morgan Securities Inc. v. Vigilant Ins. Co.*, 992 N.E.2d 1076 (N.Y. 2013) (referencing *Zurich* in concluding that New York public policy overrides freedom to contract for punitive damages coverage, and citing *Goldfarb*, reaffirming that coverage depended on whether insured acted with intent to harm others.); *Tower Natl. Ins. Co. v. National Bus. Capital, Inc.*, No. 155786/2012, 2014 N.Y. Misc. LEXIS 3414 (N.Y. Sup. Ct. July 28, 2014) (holding that it was premature to determine whether the nature of any remedy imposed for a violation of the Telephone Consumer Protection Act was punitive or compensatory).

North Carolina: The Supreme Court of North Carolina held that it was not against the state's public policy to insure against punitive damages that are awarded for other than intentional conduct, such as for wanton or gross acts. *Mazza v. Med. Mut. Ins. Co. of N.C.*, 319 S.E.2d 217, 221–23 (N.C. 1984). The court emphasized that it was not deciding whether public policy prohibits insurance for intentional acts. *Id.* at 220. Turning to the policy language, the court rejected the insurer's argument that the term "damages" includes only those damages attributable to a particular injury, reasoning that "[t]he plain and ordinary meaning of the language used in the policy, particularly from the viewpoint of a layman, covers 'all damages' and contains no exclusion for punitive damages." *Id.* at 223. In *St. Paul Mercury Ins. Co. v. Duke University*, 849 F.2d 133 (4th Cir. 1988), the appeals court held that punitive damages, for intentional conduct, are insurable. "The *Mazza* court's reservation of the issue [concerning insurability of punitive damages for intentional conduct], however, is precisely that: a declaration of what the court was not deciding. To read a state court's refusal to decide an issue as a de facto decision of that issue would divest the state courts of their authority to determine state law." *Id.* at 136. *See also New S. Ins. Co. v. Kidd*, 443 S.E.2d 85, 88 (N.C. Ct. App. 1994) (examining North Carolina cases addressing coverage for punitive damages and noting that they all reached the same conclusion—the policy must explicitly state that it does not provide such coverage); *Universal Underwriters Ins. Co. v. Lallier*, 334 F. Supp. 3d

723 (E.D.N.C. 2018) (rejecting Universal's assertion that providing insurance coverage for a civil action, related to "heinous criminal acts," would be "tantamount to 'condoning insurance against the results' of Lallie's criminal acts" because "it is not against public policy to enforce an insurance policy that provides coverage for punitive damages arising from wanton or grossly negligent conduct").

North Dakota: The Supreme Court of North Dakota held that, in general, public policy precludes coverage for punitive damages. *Cont'l Cas. Co. v. Kinsey*, 499 N.W.2d 574, 580–81 (N.D. 1993). Specifically, N.D. CENT. CODE § 9–08–02 prohibits contracts that would exempt a person from being held responsible for the consequences of his wrongful intentional conduct and N.D. CENT. CODE § 26.1–32–04 precludes insurers from indemnifying insureds for losses caused by the insured's willful acts. *Id.* However, the specific insurance policy before the *Kinsey* Court expressly provided coverage for punitive damages. *Id.* at 577. Therefore, the court concluded that the insurer was obligated to pay for the punitive damages awarded. *Id.* at 581. But, in order to give effect to the legislature's objectives, the court held that the insurer was entitled to seek indemnity from its insured, who was prohibited by statute from being indemnified for injury caused by his own fraud or deceit. *Id.*; *See also Tibert v. Nodak Mut. Ins. Co.*, 816 N.W.2d 31 (N.D. 2012) (applying standard set in *Kinsey* and holding that insured could not receive indemnification for punitive damages it already paid to third party because, as in *Kinsey*, injured third party had been fully compensated, and wrongdoing insured had been held responsible).

Ohio: Punitive or exemplary damages against an insured are precluded under uninsured and underinsured motorist policies, as well as any other policy of casualty or liability insurance that is covered by sections 3937.01 to 3937.17 of Ohio's Revised Code. OHIO REV. CODE § 3937.182; *see also State Farm Mut. Ins. Co. v. Blevins*, 551 N.E.2d 955, 959 (Ohio 1990) (permitting coverage for punitive damages under an uninsured motorist policy if provided by the specific contractual language); *The Corinthian v. Hartford Fire Ins. Co.*, 758 N.E.2d 218, 221 (Ohio Ct. App. 2001) (addressing the history of section 3937.182 and holding that it does not preclude coverage for statutory punitive damages awarded without any finding of malice, intent, or ill will); *Neal-Pettit v. Lahman*, 928 N.E.2d 421 (Ohio 2010) (holding that attorney's fees awarded as a result of punitive damages were covered because (1) they could qualify as "damages which an insured person is legally obligated to pay" because of "bodily injury"; (2) they were not clearly and unambiguously within a policy exclusion for "punitive or exemplary damages, fines or penalties"; and (3) public policy did not serve as a prohibition); *Motorists Mut.*

Ins. Co. v. Dandy-Jim, Inc., 912 N.E.2d 659, 667 (Ohio Ct. App. 2009) (As a willful or knowing violation of the Telephone Consumer Protection Act is different from an intentionally malicious act that could give rise to punitive damages, the treble damages provision of the TCPA is not punitive in nature, and, therefore, public policy did not prohibit insurance coverage for treble damages under the TCPA); *Foster v. D.B.S. Collection Agency*, No. 01-CV-514, 2008 U.S. Dist. LEXIS 22264 (S.D. Ohio Mar. 20, 2008) (following *Corinthian*) ("[T]o the extent that Plaintiffs are awarded punitive damages pursuant to a statute without any finding of malice, ill will, or other similar culpability, Northland must indemnify Dickerson/D.B.S. against those damages. If punitive damages are awarded after a finding of malice, ill will, or other similar culpability, or are awarded other than pursuant to a statute, Ohio public policy forbids their indemnification."); *World Harvest Church v. Grange Mut. Cas. Co.*, No. 13AP-290, 2013 Ohio App. LEXIS 5994 (Ohio Ct. App. Dec. 24, 2013) (citing *Neal-Pettit* and holding that statute prohibited insurance coverage for punitive damages awarded under a commercial liability policy and public policy prohibited coverage for punitive damages based on insured's malicious conduct), *reversed* 68 N.E. 3d 738 (Ohio 2016) (addressing applicability of an abuse exclusion); *Stephens v. Grange Mut. Ins. Co.*, No. 2011-CA-102, 2012 Ohio App. LEXIS 4357 (Ohio Ct. App. Oct. 26, 2012) (holding that punitive damages were not insurable as a matter of public policy).

Oklahoma: The Supreme Court of Oklahoma adopted the rationale of *Nw. Nat'l Cas. Co. v. McNulty*, 307 F.2d 432 (5th Cir. 1962), discussed in the introduction, and held that public policy prohibited insurance for liability for punitive damages that arose out of one's own misconduct. *Dayton Hudson Corp. v. Am. Mut. Liab. Ins. Co.*, 621 P.2d 1155, 1160 (Okla. 1980). However, the *Dayton Hudson* Court held that the public policy prohibition against coverage for punitive damages did not apply to such damages that are assessed on the basis of vicarious liability. *Id.* In reaching its decision, the Supreme Court of Oklahoma made much of the fact that the employer itself may be guilty of reckless disregard in not discharging an unfit employee. *Id.* at 1161. If so, public policy would prohibit coverage for punitive damages assessed against the employer. *Id.*; *see also Magnus Foods, Inc. v. Cont'l Cas. Co.*, 36 F.3d 1491, 1499 (10th Cir. 1994) (applying Oklahoma law) (finding that the insurer bears the burden of requesting a special verdict or special interrogatories to determine if punitive damages were awarded based on direct or vicarious liability and if it is impossible to determine such basis, the punitive damages are presumed to be covered.); *Finley v. Atlas Computers, Inc.*, No. 10-CV-405, 2011 U.S. Dist. LEXIS 23285 (N.D. Okla.

Feb. 10, 2011) (citing *Magnum* for proposition that "public policy forbids insurance coverage for punitive damages, except when punitive damages liability arises solely under principles of vicarious liability"); *James River Ins. Co. v. Blue Ox Dance Hall, LLC*, No. 16-0151, 2017 U.S. Dist. LEXIS 84422 (N.D. Okla. May 31, 2017) ("As a matter of Oklahoma law, an insured may not ordinarily obtain coverage for punitive damages, because this would allow a culpable party to escape punishment for his wrongs and shift the burden to the premium payers of an insurance company."); *Am. Nat'l Prop. & Cas. Co v. Select Mgmt. Group., LLC*, No. 20-542, 2021 U.S. Dist. LEXIS 54515 (N.D. Okla. Mar. 23, 2021) (noting that, if an employer is held vicariously liable for the acts of its employee, a punitive damages award against the employer is insurable) ("In Oklahoma, insurers are generally not liable for punitive damages imposed against their insureds, the rationale being that allowing tortfeasors to shift the burden to an insurer would undermine the purpose of exemplary damages, which is to punish the wrongdoer and deter others from engaging in similar conduct. However, an exception exists where the insured has been held vicariously liable for the misconduct of its servant."). The Supreme Court of Oklahoma held that public policy precludes coverage for punitive damages under an uninsured motorist policy. *Aetna Cas. & Sur. Co. v. Craig*, 771 P.2d 212. 214–15 (Okla. 1989).

Oregon: The Supreme Court of Oregon held that it is not against public policy for an insurer to provide coverage for punitive damages. *Harrell v. Travelers Indem. Co.*, 567 P.2d 1013, 1021 (Or. 1977). Instead, the *Harrell* Court concluded that the insurability of punitive damages is based on a decision by the insurer whether it wishes to take on such risk, reasoning that "as long as insurance companies are willing, for a price, to contract for insurance to provide protection against liability for punitive damages to persons or corporations deemed by them to be 'good risks' for such coverage, and as long as liability for punitive damages continues to be extended to 'gross negligence,' 'recklessness,' and for other conduct, 'contrary to societal interests,' we are in agreement with those authorities which hold that insurance contracts providing protection against such liability should not be held by courts to be void as against public policy." *Id.* Thus, punitive damages were covered under an automobile liability policy that insured for "all sums which the insured shall become legally obligated to pay as damages because of … bodily injury." *Id.* at 1014.

Pennsylvania: The Pennsylvania Superior Court held that punitive damages are uninsurable as a matter of law. *Esmond v. Liscio*, 224 A.2d 793, 800 (Pa. Super. Ct. 1966). "To permit insurance against the sanction of punitive damages would be to permit such offenders to purchase a freedom of misconduct altogether inconsistent with the theory of civil punishment which such damages represent." *Id.* at 799. The Pennsylvania Superior Court has also held that public policy does not preclude the insurability of punitive damages that are awarded against an insured on the basis of vicarious liability. *Butterfield v. Giuntoli*, 670 A.2d 646, 655 (Pa. Super. Ct. 1995). However, in *Butterfield*, because the insurer did not seek special jury interrogatories or intervene in the underlying action, for purposes of securing a determination whether any punitive damages that may be awarded were on the basis of vicarious or direct liability, it could not sustain its burden to prove that the punitive damages that were awarded were excluded from coverage. *Id.; see also Whole Enchilada, Inc. v. Travelers Prop. Cas. Co. of Am.*, 581 F. Supp. 2d 677, 704–05 (W.D. Pa. 2008) (addressing non-insurability of punitive damages under Pennsylvania law) ("[T]he Court predicts that under Pennsylvania law, public policy does not permit [the insured] to shift its burden of paying for its willful non-compliance to [its insurer], in regard to either the statutory or punitive damages alleged by the Complaint."); *State Farm Fire & Cas. Co. v. Scalia*, No. 14-49, 2014 U.S. Dist. LEXIS 170015 (M.D. Pa. Dec. 9, 2014) ("State Farm is correct in its briefing that insurers do not have a duty to indemnify an insured with regard to an award of punitive damages. *See Aetna Cas. and Sur. Co. v. Roe*, 437 Pa. Super. 414, 650 A.2d 94, 100 (Pa. Super. 1994)."); *Dietz & Watson, Inc. v. Liberty Mut. Ins. Co.*, No. 14-4082, 2015 U.S. Dist. LEXIS 9815 (E.D. Pa. Jan. 28, 2015) ("Under Pennsylvania law, an insurer has no duty to indemnify its insured to the extent that any amounts paid by the insured are in satisfaction of claims for punitive damages. *Tig Ins. Co. v. Nobel Learning Communities, Inc.*, 2002 U.S. Dist. LEXIS 10870 (E.D. Pa. June 18, 2002)."); *Bensalem Racing Ass'n v. Ace Prop. & Cas. Ins. Co.*, No. 530 EDA 2017, 2017 Pa. Super. Unpub. LEXIS 4395 (Pa. Super. Ct. Oct. 31, 2017) (acknowledging Pennsylvania's rule that punitive damages, for direct liability, are not insurable but it is not against public policy to insure punitive damages awarded on the basis of vicarious liability).

Rhode Island: The Supreme Court of Rhode Island discussed the competing public policy arguments concerning the insurability of punitive damages. *Allen v. Simmons*, 533 A.2d 541, 543 (R.I. 1987). While the court concluded that punitive damages were uninsurable, it did not do so on the basis of a public policy rationale. *Id.* The *Allen* Court explained "[the insurer's] obligation in this dispute is set forth in simple and direct language that tells the insured and those claiming under the terms of the policy that the insurer will pay for the damages arising from bodily injuries or damages to one's property arising out of an automotive mishap. The damages for which [the insurer] is obligated to respond are set forth in the provisions to which we have just alluded. Punitive or exemplary damages are awarded, not to enrich or reward a plaintiff, but rather to serve as an object lesson both to the wrongdoer and to others who might be tempted to follow in his or her path." *Id.*; *But see Town of Cumberland v. R.I. Interlocal Risk Mgmt. Trust, Inc.*, 860 A.2d 1210, 1218–19 (R.I. 2004) (rejecting an interpretation of *Allen* that insurers cannot insure for actions that are contrary to public policy and held that Rhode Island public policy did not bar an insured from indemnification for intentional torts where the policy explicitly provided such coverage). However, on March 28, 2013, the Insurance Division of the Rhode Island Department of Business Regulation issued a Bulletin stating: "Punitive Damages are not insurable under Rhode Island law. The Department will, therefore, reject any form filing that includes insuring of punitive damages."

South Carolina: The Supreme Court of South Carolina held that punitive damages were covered under an automobile liability policy. *Carroway v. Johnson*, 139 S.E.2d 908, 910 (S.C. 1965). The court concluded that "[i]nsurers have the right to limit their liabilities and to impose whatever conditions they please on their obligations, provided they are not in contravention of some statutory inhibition or public policy." *Id.* The court did not address the public policy issue any further. However, it was presumably not a prohibition to coverage because the *Carroway* Court held that coverage was owed. *Id.* at 910. "The policy under consideration did not limit recovery to actual or compensatory damages. The language of the policy here is sufficiently broad enough to cover liability for punitive damages as such damages are included in the 'sums' which the insured is legally obligated to pay as damages because of bodily injury within the meaning of the policy." *Id.* In *S.C. State Budget & Control Board v. Prince*, 403 S.E.2d 643 (S.C. 1991), the Supreme Court of South Carolina relied upon *Carroway* and held that the policy language at issue encompassed punitive damages. *Prince*, 403 S.E.2d at 648. The court also rejected the insurer's public policy argument against providing coverage for intentional and malicious defamation reasoning that "[t]he [insurer] should not be permitted to deny coverage in the name of public policy when the language of its own policy specifically provides such coverage." *Id.*; *Harleysville Group Ins. v. Heritage Cmtys., Inc.*, 803 S.E.2d 288 (S.C. 2017) (citing *Carroway* and *Prince*) ("Because the policy does not unambiguously exclude punitive damages, we construe the policy language in favor of the insured to include punitive damages.") (insurer failed to meet its burden of showing the expected or intended policy exclusion operated to exclude coverage for punitive damages). *See also O'Neill v. Smith*, 695 S.E.2d 531, 534–36

(S.C. 2010) (holding that it did not violate public policy to allow plaintiff to seek recovery of punitive damages from its underinsured motorists insurer, after plaintiff entered into covenant shielding at-fault motorist's personal assets from liability).

South Dakota: The Supreme Court of South Dakota held that civil penalties awarded for an intentional violation of the Clean Water Act were punitive in nature and it would violate public policy to insure against them. *City of Fort Pierre v. United Fire & Cas. Co.*, 463 N.W. 2d 845, 848–49 (S.D. 1990); *see also St. Paul Fire & Marine Ins. Co. v. Engelmann*, 639 N.W.2d 192, 203 (S.D. 2002) (Dobberpuhl, J., concurring) (writing that a legislative expression of South Dakota's public policy that one may not insure against an intentional act is found at S.D. CODIFIED LAWS § 53–9-3, which provides that "[a]ll contracts which have for their object, directly or indirectly, to exempt anyone from responsibility for his own fraud or willful injury to the person or property of another or from violation of law whether willful or negligent, are against the policy of the law").

Tennessee: The Supreme Court of Tennessee held that the policy language at issue ("all sums which the insured shall become legally obligated to pay as damages because of bodily injury") included punitive damages, that it was speculative that socially irresponsible drivers would be deterred from their wrongful conduct if coverage for punitive damages were not allowed, and that coverage for punitive damages was not precluded on the basis of public policy. *Lazenby v. Universal Underwriters Ins. Co.*, 383 S.W.2d 1, 5 (Tenn. 1964). *See also Certain Underwriters at Lloyd's London v. Alkabsh*, No. 09-2711, 2011 U.S. Dist. LEXIS 26593 (W.D. Tenn. Mar. 15, 2011) (upholding a punitive damages exclusion as clear and unambiguous); *Unique Ins. Co. v. Perez*, No. 18-00040, 2019 U.S. Dist. LEXIS 110645 (M.D. Tenn. July 2, 2019) (upholding an exclusion for payment of "punitive damages arising from or resulting from actual or alleged malicious, intentional, fraudulent or reckless conduct"); *Shelter Mutual Ins. Co. v. Elliott*, No. 17-02859, 2018 U.S. Dist. LEXIS 222154 (W.D. Tenn. Dec. 6, 2018) (upholding a policy's exclusion for punitive damages). The Supreme Court of Tennessee held that punitive damages are precluded from the statutory requirement that all motor vehicle insurers provide uninsured motorist coverage. *Carr v. Ford*, 833 S.W.2d 68, 71 (Tenn. 1992). However, insurers are free to voluntarily offer uninsured motorist coverage for punitive damages.

Texas: The Supreme Court of Texas held that "the public policy of Texas does not prohibit insurance coverage of exemplary damages for gross negligence in the workers' compensation context." *Fairfield Ins. Co. v. Stephens Martin Paving, LP,*

246 S.W.3d 653, 670 (Tex. 2008). While the *Fairfield* Court's holding was limited to workers' compensation, the court also discussed the issue in other contexts. *Id.* at 668. For example, the court observed that Texas appellate courts have relied on public policy grounds to uniformly reject the insurability of exemplary damages under uninsured and underinsured motorists policies. *Id.* The *Fairfield* Court also stated that courts should consider valid arguments that businesses be permitted to insure against exemplary damages that are awarded on the basis of vicarious liability. *Id.* at 670. Looking outside the workers' compensation arena, the *Fairfield* Court left the door open to a public policy prohibition against the insurability of exemplary damages by noting that "extreme circumstances," involving extreme and avoidable conduct that causes injury, may justify such a conclusion. *Id.*; *see also Am. Int'l Specialty Lines Ins. Co. v. Res-Care, Inc.*, 529 F.3d 649, 663 (5th Cir. 2008) (applying Texas law) (citing *Fairfield* and holding that the circumstances before it (group-home neglect for mentally disabled individuals) demonstrated the kind of "avoidable conduct that causes injury" to justify a prohibition against coverage for punitive damages on public policy grounds); *Minter v. Great Am. Ins. Co. of N.Y.*, No. 09-10734, 2010 U.S. App. LEXIS 17985 (5th Cir. Aug. 27, 2010) (applying Texas law) (addressing *Fairfield*) (Texas public policy prohibited insurance coverage for an intoxicated insured, with two prior DWI convictions, who caused bodily injury); *Tesco Corp. v. Steadfast Ins. Co.*, No. 13-9, 2014 Tex. App. LEXIS 9682 (Tex. Ct. App. Aug. 28, 2014) ("[W]hen the insured is a corporation or business that must pay exemplary damages for the conduct of one or more of its employees and other employees and management are not involved in or aware of an employee's wrongful act, the purpose of exemplary damages may be achieved by permitting coverage so as not to penalize the many for the wrongful act of one. When a party seeks damages under these circumstances, courts should consider valid arguments that businesses be permitted to insure against them.") (quoting *Fairfield*); *Laine v. Farmers Ins. Exch.*, 325 S.W.3d 661, 666–67 (D. Tex. 2010) (addressing Texas law that has uniformly rejected, as against public policy, coverage for exemplary damages against a third-party tortfeasor under an insured's own uninsured or underinsured auto policy); *Farmers Tex. Cty. Mut. Ins. Co. v. Zuniga*, No. 04-16-00773, 2017 Tex. App. LEXIS 10725 (Tex. Ct. App. Nov. 15, 2017) ("Unlike other policies that contain a promise 'to pay all sums which the insured shall become legally obligated to pay as damages because of bodily injury,' the Farmers policy promises only to 'pay damages for bodily injury.' Based on the Policy's plain language, we hold that the Policy is not ambiguous and that it does not cover punitive damages.");

Frederking v. Cincinnati Ins. Co., No. 17-00651, 2020 U.S. Dist. LEXIS 88602 (W.D. Tex. May 20, 2020) (the application of *Fairfield* counseled against the insurability of punitive damages awarded against a drunk driver; citing several strong public policies of Texas: policies that require exemplary damages to serve the purposes of punishment and deterrence, and that exemplary damages must be borne by the wrongdoer; and policies that disfavor driving while intoxicated and that punish DWI offenders).

Utah: "No insurer may insure or attempt to insure against: (1) a wager or gaming risk; (2) loss of an election; (3) the penal consequences of a crime; or (4) punitive damages." UTAH CODE ANN. § 31A-20–101.

Vermont: The Supreme Court of Vermont held that the policy language "all sums as damages" means the whole amount due a plaintiff as damages, regardless of how characterized. *State v. Glens Falls Ins. Co.*, 404 A.2d 101, 105 (Vt. 1979). "The insurer drafts the contract and can easily include exclusions for punitive damages, or can bargain a higher premium. Where it does neither and uses the language involved here, coverage ought to be had." *Id.* The *Glens Falls* Court also rejected the insurer's argument that public policy precludes coverage for punitive damages. *Id.* Even with coverage for punitive damages, a deterrent effect still exists as such damages could exceed the insured's limit of liability and also subject the insured to an increase in premium. *Id.* Indeed, the *Glens Falls* Court concluded that VT. STAT. ANN. tit. 8, § 4203 [requiring that liability policies provide as follows: "The company shall pay and satisfy *any* judgment that may be recovered against the insured upon any claim covered by this policy to the extent and within the limits of liability assumed thereby. …" (emphasis added)] was a legislative declaration of a public policy favoring complete coverage. *Id.*

Virginia: "It is not against the public policy of the Commonwealth for any person to purchase insurance providing coverage for punitive damages arising out of the death or injury of any person as the result of negligence, including willful and wanton negligence, but excluding intentional acts. This section is declaratory of existing policy." VA. CODE ANN. § 38.2–227. The Supreme Court of Virginia held that punitive damages were covered under a policy that included an agreement to pay " 'all sums which the insured shall become legally obligated to pay as damages because of bodily injury … including death resulting therefrom.' The insurance company could have inserted the word 'compensatory' before the word 'damages,' or specifically excluded liability for punitive damages elsewhere in the policy, and resolved the ambiguity, but it did not." *United Sers. Auto. Ass'n v. Webb*, 369 S.E.2d 196, 199 (Va. 1988).

Washington: The Supreme Court of Washington held that it does not violate the state's public policy to provide coverage for punitive damages. *Fluke Corp. v. Hartford Accident & Indem. Company*, 34 P.3d 809, 812 (Wash. 2001). Turning to the policy language to determine if it provides coverage for punitive damages awarded for malicious prosecution, the *Fluke* Court observed that "[b]ecause the policy uses the general term 'damages,' makes no distinction between compensatory and punitive damages, and contains no exclusion for the payment of punitive damages, the insuring agreement appears to be a straightforward promise to indemnify Fluke for all damages, compensatory or punitive, that Fluke becomes legally bound to pay." *Id.* at 814.

West Virginia: The Supreme Court of Appeals of West Virginia held that where "the liability policy of an insurance company provides that it will pay on behalf of the insured all sums which the insured shall become legally obligated to pay as damages because of bodily injury and the policy only excludes damages caused intentionally by or at the direction of the insured, such policy will be deemed to cover punitive damages arising from bodily injury occasioned by gross, reckless or wanton negligence on the part of the insured." *Hensley v. Erie Ins. Co.*, 283 S.E.2d 227, 230 (W. Va. 1981). The *Hensley* Court also held that public policy did not preclude coverage for punitive damages arising from gross, reckless, or wanton negligence. *Id.* at 233. Only a purposeful or intention tort carries the degree of culpability that should foreclose the right to insurance coverage. *Id.* The *Hensley* Court acknowledged that an insurer can decline to insure against punitive damages by way of an express policy exclusion. *Id.; see also Camden-Clark Mem'l Hosp. Corp. v. St. Paul Fire and Marine Ins.*, 717 F. Supp. 2d 529, 538 (S.D.W.Va. 2010) (holding that, because jury verdict form did not distinguish whether punitive damages were awarded based on medical negligence or intentional conduct, insured had burden, under policy that did not contain a duty to defend, to establish that damages were for covered negligent conduct and it could not do so); *USF Ins. Co. v. Orion Dev. Ra XXX, LLC*, 756 F. Supp. 2d 749, 759 (N.D.W.Va. 2010) (declaring that insurer had no duty to provide coverage for punitive damages where specific punitive damages exclusion existed).

Wisconsin: The Supreme Court of Wisconsin held that the liability policy at issue provided coverage for punitive damages and that such coverage was not contrary to public policy. *Brown v. Maxey*, 369 N.W.2d 677, 688 (Wis. 1985). On the issue of policy language, the *Maxey* Court held that "[f]irst the punitive damage award in this case was a 'sum' that Maxey '[became] legally obligated to pay as damages.' The term 'damages' is sufficiently broad to cover liability for both compensatory and punitive damages. Punitive damages are not specifically excluded from the policy language. Second, it is clear that these punitive damages were awarded 'because of bodily injury.'" *Id.* at 686. Turning to the public policy question, the Wisconsin high court held that it was not a prohibition to coverage. *Id.* at 688. The court rejected the argument that allowing coverage for such awards will alleviate the deterrent effect of such awards. *Id.* Deterrence still exists because the insured's insurance premiums may rise, he may be unable to obtain insurance, the punitive damages may exceed the policy limits and his reputation in the community may be injured. *Id.*

Wyoming: The Supreme Court of Wyoming held that it is not against public policy "to insure against either liability for punitive damages imposed vicariously based on willful and wanton misconduct or personal liability for punitive damages imposed on the basis of willful and wanton misconduct." *Sinclair Oil Corp. v. Columbia Cas. Co.*, 682 P.2d 975, 981 (Wyo. 1984).

CHAPTER
20

First- and Third-Party Bad Faith Standards

Most insurance coverage issues involve just that—whether a particular claim is *covered* under the terms and conditions of a certain insurance policy. But sometimes there is an additional aspect to an otherwise "is it covered" scenario. In certain instances the insurance company's conduct in handling the insured's claim, or the process by which the insurer arrived at a determination that a claim is not covered, becomes the subject of a separate claim for damages. This additional aspect of the claims process is usually referred to under the general heading called "bad faith."

Bad faith—or breach of the duty of good faith, as it is also sometimes called—is one of, if not the most, complex aspects of insurance coverage. The question whether a particular claim is covered is usually a narrow one, largely tied to the application of certain facts to the language of the insurance policy and perhaps with resort to case law for guidance. In most cases there are only two possible answers to the question whether a claim is covered: yes or no. But bad faith is many times more faceted. Moreover, oftentimes one of the most important issues surrounding bad faith is determining the insurance company's mindset in handling the insured's claim or arriving at its coverage determination. The need for the insured to get inside the insurance company's head, so to speak, brings a significant subjective element into play. That subjective determinations are never ones to lend themselves to cut-and-dried answers, in any context, is an important source of the complexity of bad faith. *But see Georgetown Realty, Inc. v. Home Ins. Co.*, 831 P.2d 7, 13 (Or. 1992) (en banc) ("The insurer is negligent in failing to settle, where an opportunity to settle exists, if in choosing not to settle it would be taking an unreasonable risk—that is, a risk that would involve chances of unfavorable results out of reasonable proportion to the chances of favorable results. Stating the rule in terms of 'good faith' or 'bad faith' tends to inject an inappropriate subjective element—the insurer's state of mind—into the formula. The insurer's duty is best expressed by an objective test: Did the insurer exercise due care under the circumstances?") (quoting *Me. Bonding & Cas. Co. v. Centennial Ins. Co.*, 693 P.2d 1296, 1299 (Or. 1985) (en banc)).

Any discussion of bad faith must begin with an explanation of the two general types—first-party and third-party. In its most common form—and the subject of this chapter—third-party bad faith arises in the context of an insured being sued by a third-party and the insured's liability insurer takes over its defense. *Braesch v. Union Ins. Co.*, 464 N.W.2d 769, 773 (Neb. 1991). In this situation, "[a] conflict of interest is inherent in the insurer's control of settlement when … there is potential exposure in excess of the policy limits. A settlement demand within the policy limits highlights that conflict, inasmuch as it will be in the insured's interest for that demand to be met. Such a settlement is not necessarily in the insurer's best interest, however, for by going to trial the insurer might be able to avoid liability altogether, or obtain a judgment for an amount less than the demand." *Myers v. Ambassador Ins. Co., Inc.*, 508 A.2d 689 (Vt. 1986).

"It is this control of the litigation by the insurer coupled with differing levels of exposure to economic loss which gives rise to the 'fiduciary' nature of the insurer's duty." *Id.* If an insurance company fails to settle a claim, when there was an opportunity to do so within the policy limits, and such a settlement was reasonable, the insurer subjects the insured to the risk of a judgment in excess of the policy limits—for which the insured would be liable but the insurer would not. To put it another way, "[b]y taking such an unreasonable risk, the insurer would be gambling with the insured's money to the latter's prejudice." *Shuster v. S. Broward Hosp. Dist. Physicians' Prof. Liab. Ins. Trust*, 570 So. 2d 1362, 1367 (Fla. Ct. App. 1990), *aff'd*, 591 So. 2d 174 (Fla. 1992). "Although referred to as 'third-party bad faith,' the insurer's duty of good faith and fair dealing extends only to its insured, not the third party." *Nunn v. Mid-Century Ins. Co.*, 244 P.3d 116, 119 (Colo. 2010) (en banc).

The typical consequence for an insurer that, in bad faith, fails to settle a claim, when there was an opportunity to do so within policy limits, is liability for the full amount of the judgment—even the amount in excess of the policy limit. This is sometimes referred to as the "judgment rule," and the majority of states have adopted it. *See Econ. Fire & Cas. Co. v. Collins*, 643 N.E.2d 382, 385 (Ind. App. Ct. 1994) (rejecting the alternative "pre-payment rule"—which holds an insurer liable for a judgment in excess of policy limits only if part or all of the judgment has been paid by the insured—and instead adopting the "judgment rule" because it eliminates the insurer's ability to hide behind the financial status of its insured, and it recognizes that the entry of judgment itself against an insured constitutes actual damage—such as impairing the insured's credit and damaging the insured's reputation).

Another type of third-party bad faith—although not nearly as common as third-party bad faith in the "failure to settle within limits context" (and not the subject of this chapter)—involves a claim by an injured party brought directly against the tortfeasor's insurer. The most well-known source of third-party bad faith is the Supreme Court of California's adoption of it in *Royal Globe Insurance Co. v. Superior Court*, 592 P.2d 329 (Cal. 1979) (en banc). The court held that the Unfair Practices Act of the state's Insurance Code afforded a private party, *including a third-party claimant*, the right to sue an insurer for violation of the Act—addressing various unfair claims settlement practices. *Id.* The court further held that "it is inconceivable that the Legislature intended that such a litigant would be required to show that the insurer committed the acts prohibited by that provision 'with such frequency as to indicate a general business practice.'" *Id.*

However, just nine years later *Royal Globe* was overruled by *Moradi-Shalal v. Fireman's Fund Insurance Cos.*, 758 P.2d 58 (Cal. 1988) (en banc). The *Moradi-Shalal* Court concluded that "developments occurring subsequent to our *Royal Globe* decision convince us that it was incorrectly decided, and that it has generated and will continue to produce inequitable results, costly multiple litigation, and unnecessary confusion unless we overrule it." *Moradi-Shalal*, 758 P.2d at 63 (also noting that courts in eight states had expressly acknowledged, but declined to follow, *Royal Globe*; courts in nine states had implicitly rejected its holding; and only two states other than California recognized a statutory cause of action for private litigants—with the courts in those states rejecting *Royal Globe*'s conclusion that a single violation of their Unfair Practices Act is a sufficient basis for a suit for damages). While the *Moradi-Shalal* Court gave many reasons for its decision to overrule *Royal Globe*, a principal driver of its decision was a recognition of the adverse consequences that third-party bad faith would have on the general public vis-à-vis increased insurance premiums.

In contrast to coverage for insureds for injuries caused to third-parties, first-party bad faith involves claims by insureds for policy benefits for their *own* damages. *Universal Life Ins. Co. v. Giles*, 950 S.W.2d 48, 60 (Tex. 1997). While third-party bad faith dates back nearly a hundred years (*see Brassil v. Md. Cas. Co.*, 104 N.E. 622 (N.Y. 1914)), first-party bad faith is of more recent vintage—with many courts giving credit for its origin to the Supreme Court of California in *Gruenberg v. Aetna Insurance Co.*, 510 P.2d 1032 (Cal. 1973), where the court held:

> [I]n the case before us we consider the duty of an insurer to act in good faith and fairly in handling the claim of an insured, namely a duty not to withhold unreasonably payments due under a policy. ... That responsibility is not the

requirement mandated by the terms of the policy itself—to defend, settle, or pay. It is the obligation, deemed to be imposed by the law, under which the insurer must act fairly and in good faith in discharging its contractual responsibilities. Where in so doing, it fails to deal fairly and in good faith with its insured by refusing, without proper cause, to compensate its insured for a loss covered by the policy, such conduct may give rise to a cause of action in tort for breach of an implied covenant of good faith and fair dealing.

Gruenberg, 510 P.2d at 1037; *see also Nichols v. State Farm Mut. Auto. Ins. Co.*, 306 S.E.2d 616, 618 (S.C. 1983) ("The *Gruenberg* decision is premised on an implied covenant of good faith and fair dealing that neither party will do anything to impair the other's rights to receive benefits under the contract.").

Courts have used various rationales for adopting a cause of action in tort for first-party bad faith:

An insurance policy is not obtained for commercial advantage; it is obtained as protection against calamity. In securing the reasonable expectations of the insured under the insurance policy there is usually an unequal bargaining position between the insured and the insurance company. … Often the insured is in an especially vulnerable economic position when such a casualty loss occurs. The whole purpose of insurance is defeated if an insurance company can refuse or fail, without justification, to pay a valid claim. We have determined that it is reasonable to conclude that there is a legal duty implied in an insurance contract that the insurance company must act in good faith in dealing with its insured on a claim, and a violation of that duty of good faith is a tort.

State Farm Fire & Cas. Co. v. Nicholson, 777 P.2d 1152, 1155 (Alaska 1989) (quoting *Noble v. Nat'l Am. Life Ins. Co.*, 624 P.2d 866, 867–68 (Ariz. 1981) (en banc)); *see also Spencer v. Aetna Life & Cas. Ins. Co.*, 611 P.2d 149, 158 (Kan. 1980) (despite declining to adopt the bad faith tort, the court examined the rationales of many decisions that have and concluded that all of the arguments pertain to the unequal bargaining position between the insurer and insured and the public interest nature of the insurance industry); *Arnold v. Nat'l Cnty. Mut. Fire Ins. Co.*, 725 S.W.2d 165, 167 (Tex. 1987) (noting that, without a cause of action for first-party bad faith, insurers could arbitrarily deny coverage and delay payment of a claim with the penalty being limited to interest on the amount owed).

Some states have chosen to address bad faith by statute. *See Rose ex rel. Rose v. St. Paul Fire & Marine Ins. Co.*, 599 S.E.2d 673, 679 n.6 (W. Va. 2004) ("At least sixteen states, including West Virginia, also use statutes to impose various duties upon insurance companies to use 'good faith' toward a claimant throughout the settlement of a claim. These statutes—which, like West Virginia's, are usually patterned after the National Association of Insurance Commissioners' 'Model Unfair Trade Practices Act' or 'Model Unfair Claims Settlement Practices Act'— have been construed by courts to allow a claimant to bring an action against an insurance company for damages caused by a violation of the statute.")

While many do, not all states recognize a cause of action for first-party bad faith. Some states have declined to adopt such cause of action on the basis that adequate alternative remedies already exist to address insurer's improper behavior. *See Marquis v. Farm Family Mut. Ins. Co.*, 628 A.2d 644, 652 (Me. 1993) ("In view of the broad range of compensatory damages available in a contract action and in view of the statutorily provided remedies of interest on the judgment and attorney fees, we believe sufficient motivation presently exists to stifle an insurer's bad faith tendencies without the further imposition of the specter of punitive damages under an independent tort cause of action.") (quotations omitted). Other states have refused to recognize the tort on the basis that the relationship between the insurer and insured, in the first-party context, is not a fiduciary one. *See Best Place, Inc. v. Penn Am. Ins. Co.*, 920 P.2d 334, 343 (Haw. 1996) (adopting tort cause of action but citing decisions from several states that have refused to do so).

In general, the significance of a court's adoption of a cause of action for first-party bad faith is the opening of the door to an insured's recovery of damages in tort, rather than its recovery being limited to damages for breach of contract:

> [T]he requirement that contract damages be foreseeable at the time of contracting in some cases would bar recovery for damages proximately caused by the insurer's bad faith. The measurement of recoverable damages in tort is not limited to those foreseeable at the time of the tortious act; rather they include "[a] reasonable amount which will compensate plaintiff for *all* actual detriment proximately caused by the defendant's wrongful conduct."

White v. Unigard Mut. Ins. Co., 730 P.2d 1014, 1017–18 (Idaho 1986) (citations omitted and emphasis in original); *see also Tackett v. State Farm Fire & Cas. Ins. Co.*, 653 A.2d 254, 264 (Del. 1995) ("If the bad faith claim is viewed as an independent tort, the insured's recovery may include damages for emotional distress, as well as for economic loss. By contrast, if the bad faith claim is viewed as arising *ex contractu*, the damages generally are confined to the payment of money due, with interest for delay.").

Because first- and third-party bad faith address different risks for the insured, they are typically subject to different standards. In the third-party context, the insurer has the responsibility of defending the claim, usually has exclusive authority to accept or reject settlements and could subject the insured to liability in excess of the policy limits because of its refusal to settle within those limits. *Clearwater v. State Farm Mut. Auto. Ins. Co.*, 792 P.2d 719, 723 (Ariz. 1990) (en banc). In third-party situations, the insurance policy creates a fiduciary relationship—on account of the insured being wholly dependent upon the insurer to see that the insured's best interests are protected. *Beck v. Farmers Ins. Exch.*, 701 P.2d 795, 799 (Utah 1985).

This same risk, however, is generally seen as lacking in the context of first-party claims, where "[t]he insurer is not in a position to expose the insured to a judgment in excess of the policy limits through its unreasonable refusal to settle a case, nor is it in a position to otherwise injure the insured by virtue of its exclusive control over the defense of the case." *Lawton v. Great Sw. Fire Ins. Co.*, 392 A.2d 576, 581 (N.H. 1978).

On account of the potential harm to the insured being greater in the third-party context, the applicable standards for establishing first- and third-party bad faith often differ. *See Clearwater v. State Farm Mut. Auto. Ins. Co.*, 792 P.2d 719, 722 (Ariz. 1990) (en banc). And those differences can be substantial. For example, the Supreme Court of Colorado adopted a much higher standard for an insured to prove first-party versus third-party bad faith. *See Goodson v. Am. Standard Ins. Co. of Wis.*, 89 P.3d 409, 415 (Colo. 2004) (en banc) (first-party claimant must prove that the insurer either knowingly or recklessly disregarded the validity of the insured's claim; for third-party bad faith, the insured need only show that a reasonable insurer under the circumstances would have paid or otherwise settled the third-party claim, i.e., negligence standard).

Therefore, because of the different purposes between first-party and third-party bad faith, any comparison between the applicable standards for establishing each is apples to oranges. But even when only one type of bad faith is examined, i.e., the comparison is apples to apples, the standards also vary widely between states. For example, in the third-party bad faith context, compare *Asermely v. Allstate Ins. Co.*, 728 A.2d 461, 464 (R.I. 1999) (adopting a standard that resembles strict liability for an insurer that fails to settle within policy limits) with *Helmbolt v. LeMars Mut. Ins. Co., Inc.*, 404 N.W.2d 55, 57 (S.D. 1987) (recognizing that there are an array of factors—at least seven—to consider in determining whether an insurer's refusal to settle was bad faith).

The standard for third-party bad faith can also vary widely within the *same* state—a fact that did not go unnoticed by New York's highest court:

> [C]ourts have had some difficulty selecting a standard for actionable "bad faith" because of the need to balance the insured's rightful expectation of "good faith" against the insurer's equally legitimate contract expectations. Consequently, a divergence of authority has arisen concerning whether a bad-faith finding may be predicated on a showing of the insurer's recklessness or "gross disregard" for the insured's interests ... or whether a heightened showing of intentionally harmful, dishonest or disingenuous motive is required.

Pavia v. State Farm Mut. Auto. Ins. Co., 626 N.E.2d 24, 27 (N.Y. 1993) (citations omitted) (rejecting the insurer's proposed "sinister motive" standard and instead holding that "in order to establish a prima facie case of bad faith, the plaintiff must establish that the insurer's conduct constituted a 'gross disregard' of the insured's interests—that is, a deliberate or reckless failure to place on equal footing the interests of its insured with its own interests when considering a settlement offer").

Decisions addressing bad faith often contain neat and tidy rules describing the standard that an insured must satisfy to establish its insurer's bad faith in handling a claim. Such rules are usually expressed by a litany of adjectives describing various forms of inappropriate behavior by an insurer. These standards make for convenient sound bites. However, the question whether an insurer actually committed such conduct—given the highly factual nature of the inquiry—is oftentimes easier said than done. For this reason, knowing the bad faith standard is only the first step—an important, yet small one—in attempting to establish that an insurer committed bad faith in its handling of an insured's claim.

In addition to the core issues concerning bad faith, such as the extent to which the causes of action are recognized and the varying standards for establishing them, bad faith has also given rise to various collateral issues. For example, numerous courts have addressed whether bad faith sounds in tort or contract—as the first step to determining the appropriate statute of limitations for such action. *See Noland v.*

Va. Ins. Reciprocal, 686 S.E.2d 23, 34 n.30 (W. Va. 2009) (noting that a majority of the courts that have addressed the issue have held that a common law bad faith action sounds in tort) (holding that a common law bad faith action sounds in tort and a one-year statute of limitations applies); *see also Ash v. Continental Ins. Co.,* 932 A.2d 877, 885 (Pa. 2007) (holding that the duty of good faith is a statutorily-created tort and subject to a two-year statute of limitations) (rejecting the argument that an action for bad faith sounds in contract and is subject to a six-year statute of limitations).

Another collateral issue that arrives with regularity in the bad faith context is whether an excess insurer can maintain an action for bad faith against a primary insurer on account of the primary insurer's failure to settle a claim within its policy limits—resulting in a verdict that exceeds the primary policy's limits and reaches the excess policy. The majority of states allow an excess insurer to sue a primary insurer for bad faith refusal to settle within the primary policy limits. The rationale often adopted for permitting such cause of action is equitable subrogation. In other words, because the insured, if it did not have excess coverage, would have a cause of action against the primary insurer for bad faith refusal to settle, this right is transferred to the excess insurer. *See Fireman's Fund v. Ins. Co. v. Continental Ins. Co.,* 519 A.2d 202 (Md. 1987). *But see Fed. Ins. Co. v. Travelers Cas. & Sur. Co.,* 843 So. 2d 140, 143 (Ala. 2002) (holding that, in the absence of contrary contractual obligations, a primary insurer does not owe a duty of good faith to an excess insurer regarding settlement of a claim) (rejecting equitable subrogation as a basis for an excess insurer to maintain a bad faith action because the insured is not subject to a judgment that he would personally have to pay). *See also St. Paul Fire & Marine Ins. Co. v. Liberty Mut. Ins. Co.,* No. 13-00361 HG-BMK, 2014 U.S. Dist. LEXIS 47385 (D. Haw. Mar. 31, 2014) (certifying the following question to the Hawaii Supreme Court: May an excess liability insurer bring a cause of action, under the doctrine of equitable subrogation to the rights of the insured, against a primary liability insurer for failure to settle a claim against the mutual insured within the limits of the primary liability policy, when the primary insurer has paid its policy limit toward the settlement?).

Lastly, any discussion of bad faith is likely to turn to the potential damages recoverable. Like the standards to establish bad faith, the potentially recoverable damages are also subject to wide variation between states—with the question of the availability of punitive damages often coming into play. While this issue is beyond the scope of this chapter, the cases cited in the following fifty-state survey frequently address the nature of damages that can be awarded to an insured for its insurer's bad faith.

50-State Survey: First- and Third-Party Bad Faith Standards

Alabama: The Supreme Court of Alabama has recognized an intentional tort of bad faith in first-party insurance claims. *Chavers v. Nat'l Sec. Fire & Cas. Co.*, 405 So. 2d 1, 6 (Ala. 1981). Under Alabama law, there is only one tort of bad-faith, albeit two different options for proof thereof—"normal" (failure to pay) and "abnormal" (failure to investigate). *State Farm Fire & Cas. Co. v. Brechbill*, No. 1111117, 2013 Ala. LEXIS 126 (Ala. Sept. 27, 2013) (citing *Chavers*). "This tort has four elements plus a conditional fifth element as follows: (a) an insurance contract between the parties and a breach thereof by the defendant; (b) an intentional refusal to pay the insured's claim; (c) the absence of any reasonably legitimate or arguable reason for that refusal (the absence of a debatable reason); (d) the insurer's actual knowledge of the absence of any legitimate or arguable reason; (e) if the intentional failure to determine the existence of a lawful basis is relied upon, the plaintiff must prove the insurer's intentional failure to determine whether there is a legitimate or arguable reason to refuse to pay the claim." *Id.* (citing *Nat'l Sec. Fire & Cas. Co. v. Bowen*, 417 So. 2d 179, 183 (Ala. 1982)) ("Bad faith, then, is not simply bad judgment or negligence. It imports a dishonest purpose and means a breach of a known duty, i.e., good faith and fair dealing, through some motive of self-interest or ill will." (quoting *Gulf Atlantic Life Ins. Co. v. Barnes*, 405 So. 2d 916, 924 (Ala. 1981))); *see also Jones v. Alfa Mut. Ins. Co.*, 1 So. 3d 23, 32 (Ala. 2008) (addressing "normal" bad-faith-refusal-to-pay claim); *State Farm Fire & Cas. Co. v. Slade*, 747 So. 2d 293, 303–07 (Ala. 1999) (setting forth a lengthy discussion of the history of the state's bad faith law); *Butler v. Allstate Indem. Co., Inc.*, No. 09–838-WKW, 2011 U.S. Dist. LEXIS 45637 (M.D. Ala. Apr. 25, 2011) (discussing in detail whether the claim satisfied the elements for "normal" and "abnormal" bad faith); *Finger v. State Farm Fire & Cas. Ins. Co.*, No. 10–00192, 2011 U.S. Dist. LEXIS 72063 (S.D. Ala. July 5, 2011) (holding that insurer was entitled to affirmative defense of advice of counsel for a bad faith claim); *Walker v. Auto-Owners Ins. Co.*, No. 16-448, 2017 U.S. Dist. LEXIS 176703 (N.D. Ala. Oct. 25, 2017) ("Those arguable grounds for denying plaintiff's insurance claim preclude his cause of action for bad faith, even if Auto-Owners' decision to deny the claim was wrong, and even if plaintiff ultimately prevails on his other cause of action, for breach of the insurance contract. As the Alabama

Supreme Court has held, 'more than bad judgment or negligence is required in a bad-faith action.'") (quoting *Brechbill*); *Steele v. Liberty Ins. Corp.*, No. 18-01810, 2019 U.S. Dist. LEXIS 151204 (N.D. Ala. Sept. 5, 2019) (finding fifth element is satisfied based upon an insurer's "(1) intentional or reckless failure to investigate the claim, (2) intentional or reckless failure to properly subject the claim to a cognitive evaluation, (3) creation of its own debatable reason for denying the claim, or (4) reliance on an ambiguous portion of the policy as lawful basis to deny the plaintiff's claim") (noting that "[a]lthough not abundantly clear from the caselaw, this court understands the fifth element of an abnormal bad faith claim as replacing the fourth element of a normal bad faith claim, such that insurers cannot rely on their own willful ignorance to undermine the knowledge requirement").

"In the context of third-party insurance, [Alabama courts] have recognized liability of the insurer for bad-faith failure to settle and for bad-faith refusal to defend under circumstances where the obligation to afford a defense has been established." *Aetna Cas. & Sur. Co. v. Mitchell Bros., Inc.*, 814 So. 2d 191, 201 (Ala. 2001). For purposes of establishing third-party bad faith, Alabama permits recovery against an insurer in situations where such wrongful refusal was either negligent or intentional. *Chavers*, 405 So. 2d at 5. "In the third party context, therefore, counts based upon either negligence or bad faith are actionable. Furthermore, both counts may be joined in a single action with recovery proceeding from either. This is not to say, however, that a test for bad faith includes a negligence standard of conduct. In this jurisdiction negligence is not an element of bad faith." *Id.*; *see also Penn Nat'l Mut. Cas. Ins. Co. v. IPSCO Steel (Ala.), Inc.*, No. 07-0524-WS-M, 2008 U.S. Dist. LEXIS 4718 (S.D. Ala. Jan. 21, 2008) (addressing bad faith in the settlement context where insurer challenged coverage in a declaratory judgment action and insured settled the claim for less than policy limits); *Franklin v. Nat'l General Assurance Co.*, No. 13-103, 2015 U.S. Dist. LEXIS 7736 (M.D. Ala. Jan. 23, 2015) ("Alabama law does not incorporate the arguable-reason test as an element of a plaintiff's claim in a third-party bad-faith case. Rather, whether an insurance company acted in bad faith in the exercise of its settlement authority depends upon all the facts and circumstances. The facts and circumstances that are relevant to whether an insurer acted in bad faith in evaluating settlement of a third-party claim — culled from *Waters*, *Cosby*, and *Hollis* — include, but are not limited to, the following: (1) whether the insurer adequately investigated the facts of this case; (2) whether the insurer conducted a dishonest evaluation of the case; (3) how the insurer viewed its insured's liability; (4) whether the insurer considered the welfare of the insured; (5) whether there was an opportunity to settle the case within policy limits; (6) whether the insurer evaluated the anticipated range of a verdict, should it be adverse; (7) whether the insurer examined the financial risk to the insured in the event of an excess judgment in excess of the policy limits; (8) whether the insurer considered the strengths and weaknesses of all of the evidence from a liability and damages standpoint; (9) whether the insurer considered the history of the particular geographic area in cases of similar nature; and (10) whether the insurer considered the relative appearance, persuasiveness, and likely appeal of the claimant, the insured, and the witnesses at trial."); *Thomas v. Auto-Owners Ins. Co.*, 479 F. Supp. 3d 1218 (M.D. Ala. 2020) (rejecting insurer's argument that the "arguable reason" test applied and finding that the "totality of the circumstances" test laid out in *Franklin* is the appropriate test in a third-party bad faith failure-to-settle claim in Alabama) (noting that "[w]hether an insurer has a legitimate or arguable reason not to settle, such as the recommendations of defense counsel, is certainly one of the many facts and circumstances that can be considered").

Alaska: The Supreme Court of Alaska stated that "while the tort of bad faith in first-party insurance cases may or may not require conduct which is fraudulent or deceptive, it necessarily requires that the insurance company's refusal to honor a claim be made without a reasonable basis." *Hillman v. Nationwide Mut. Fire Ins. Co.*, 855 P.2d 1321, 1324 (Alaska 1993) (footnotes omitted) (joining Alaska precedent in declining to define the elements of first-party tortious bad faith); *accord Lockwood v. Gelco Gen. Ins. Co.*, 323 P.3d 691, 697 n.21 (Alaska 2014) ("Whether the insured must *also* show some sort of culpable mental state in addition to objective unreasonableness in a bad-faith insurance tort action is a matter left open by our case law.") (emphasis in original). "[W]here the insurer establishes that no reasonable jury could regard its conduct as unreasonable, the question of bad faith need not and should not be submitted to the jury." *Hillman*, 855 P.2d at 1325. *See also KICC-Alcan Gen. v. Crum & Forster Specialty Ins. Co.*, 242 F. Supp. 3d 869 (D. Alaska 2017) (noting that the Alaska Supreme Court has not defined the elements of a bad faith claim beyond the insured showing at least 'that the insurer's actions were objectively unreasonable under the circumstances (citing *Lockwood*) but noting that an Alaska District Cout has identified two elements: "(1) that the insurer 'lacked a reasonable basis for denying coverage' and (2) that the insurer 'had knowledge that no reasonable basis existed to deny the claim or acted in reckless disregard for the lack of a reasonable basis for denying the claim.'") (citing *United States v. CNA Fin. Corp.*, 168 F. Supp, 2d 1109, 1124 (D. Alaska 2001)); *Allen v. State Farm Mut. Auto Ins. Co.*, No. 15-0019,

2018 U.S. Dist. LEXIS 48993 (D. Alaska Mar. 26, 2018) (finding that violations of Alaska's Unfair Claim Settlement Practices Act, AS 21.36.125, does not require a finding of bad faith, but the conduct described in that statute could constitute evidence of bad faith).

In the third-party bad faith context, the Supreme Court of Alaska held that "[w]hen a plaintiff makes a policy limits demand, the covenant of good faith and fair dealing places a duty on an insurer to tender maximum policy limits to settle a plaintiff's demand when there is a substantial likelihood of an excess verdict against the insured." *Jackson v. Am. Equity Ins. Co.*, 90 P.3d 136, 142 (Alaska 2004); *see also Whitney v. State Farm Mut. Auto. Ins. Co.*, 258 P.3d 113 (Alaska 2011) (same); *Allstate Ins. Co. v. Herron*, 634 F.3d 1101 (9th Cir. 2011) (applying Alaska law) (addressing *Jackson* in the context of a time limit demand to settle); *Hinkle v. Crum & Forster Holding, Inc.*, 746 F. Supp. 2d 1047 (D. Alaska 2010) (finding that insurer was not liable for bad faith failure to settle because there was not a "substantial likelihood" of a judgment in excess of policy limits); *Allstate Ins. Co. v. Herron*, 634 F.3d 1101 (9th Cir. 2011) (applying Alaska law) ("[I]f Allstate breached its obligation to tender policy limits in response to Power's settlement offer, Herron would be entitled to coverage, even in excess of his policy, for his liability to Trailov and Kenick, regardless of any subsequent breach on his part."); *Attys. Liab. Prot. Soc'y, Inc. v. Ingaldson Fitzgerald, P.C.*, 838 F.3d 976 (9th Cir. 2016) ("We note that this is not a case where [the insurer] could have tendered a settlement to the policy limit, thereby avoiding an excess judgment against Ingaldson. At no time did the amount in controversy in the underlying dispute approach the policy's $2 million limit.").

Arizona: The Supreme Court of Arizona stated that "the insurer breaches the implied duty of good faith and fair dealing if it (1) acts unreasonably towards its insured, and (2) acts knowingly or with reckless disregard as to the reasonableness of its actions. We have stated that this standard permits an insurer to challenge a claim that is 'fairly debatable,'" but such belief is generally a fact question for the jury. *Clearwater v. State Farm Mut. Auto. Ins. Co.*, 792 P.2d 719, 723 (Ariz. 1990) (en banc); *accord Lennar Corp. v. Transamerica Ins. Co.*, 256 P.3d 635, 640–42 (Ariz. Ct. App. 2011) (determining "fairly debatable" based on such things as "judicial decisions interpreting the policy language and evidence of the understandings of these insurers and of the insurance industry in general concerning the meaning of the disputed policy language") (determining if insurer lacked an objectively reasonable basis for denying the claim and that the insurer knew or was conscious of the fact that it was acting unreasonably in denying the claim based on such things as "the insurers' subjective belief in the reasonableness of the coverage positions they took. Also relevant may be evidence of prior positions these insurers have taken in similar cases and these insurers' knowledge of judicial interpretations of the policy language in other cases and their knowledge of positions other insurers or industry groups have taken in other similar cases.") (addressing possible bad faith claim handling by insurer during the time of coverage litigation). "The appropriate inquiry is whether there is sufficient evidence from which reasonable jurors could conclude that in the investigation, evaluation, and processing of the claim, the insurer acted unreasonably and either knew or was conscious of the fact that its conduct was unreasonable." *Zilisch v. State Farm Mut. Auto. Ins. Co.*, 995 P.2d 276, 280 (Ariz. 2000) (en banc). "The insurer must intend the act or omission and must form that intent without reasonable or fairly debatable grounds." *Demetrullas v. Wal-Mart Stores Inc.*, 917 F. Supp. 2d 993, 1005 (D. Ariz. 2013) (quoting *Rawlings v. Apodaca*, 726 P.2d 565, 576 (Ariz. 1986) (en banc)); *City of Phoenix v. First State Ins. Co.*, No. 15-00511, 2016 U.S. Dist. LEXIS 119024 (D. Ariz. Sept. 2, 2016), *aff'd* 727 Fed. Appx. 296 (9th Cir. 2018) ("The good faith obligation applies to the processing of a claim as well as the ultimate coverage decision. An insurer may not delay an investigation, force an insured to jump through needless hoops, or lowball claims in the hopes that the insured will settle for less. Nor may an insurer deny a claim whose merits are not fairly subject to debate. Knowledge or reckless disregard of unreasonableness does not require intent to harm, but it requires something more than mistake or inadvertence. Insurance companies are far from perfect. Papers get lost, telephone messages misplaced and claims ignored because paperwork was misfiled or improperly processed. Such isolated mischances may result in a claim being unpaid or delayed. None of these mistakes will ordinarily constitute a breach of the implied covenant of good faith. An insurer must have a founded belief in its coverage position."); *Labertew v. Chartis Prop. Cas. Co.*, 363 F. Supp. 3d 1031 (D. Ariz. 2019) (rejecting argument that insurer acted in bad faith for failing to conduct an investigation when the complaint clearly did not fall within the policy's coverage); *Fid. Nat'l Title Ins. Co. v. Osborn III Partners LLC*, 483 P.3d 237 (Ariz. Ct. App. 2021) (finding that an insurer's position was fairly debatable where "its position was consistent with one branch of the conflicting federal authority").

In the third-party context, the Supreme Court of Arizona held that "th[e] duty of good faith requires an insurer to give equal consideration to the protection of the insured's as well as its own interests. If an insurance company fails to settle, and does so in bad faith, it is liable to the insured for the full amount of the judgment."

Hartford Accident & Indem. Co. v. Aetna Cas. & Sur. Co., 792 P.2d 749, 752 (Ariz. 1990) (en banc) (citation omitted); *see also Acosta v. Phoenix Indem. Ins. Co.*, 153 P.3d 401, 404 (Ariz. Ct. App. 2007) ("An insurer must weigh a number of factors, including the strength of the third party's claim and the financial risk to the insured in the event of a judgment in excess of the policy limits. In determining whether an insurer has given consideration to the interests of the insured, the test is whether a prudent insurer without policy limits would have accepted the settlement offer.") (citations and internal quotations omitted); *Essex Ins. Co. v. W.G.S., LLC*, No. CV 08-1402, 2010 U.S. Dist. LEXIS 18600 (D. Ariz. Mar. 2, 2010) ("In determining whether an insurer has breached its duty by failing to give equal consideration to an insured's interest in settling a third-party case, the Court considers the following factors, if applicable: (1) the strength of the injured claimant's case on the issues of liability and damages; (2) attempts by the insurer to induce the insured to contribute to a settlement; (3) failure of the insurer to properly investigate the circumstances so as to ascertain the evidence against the insured; (4) the insurer's rejection of advice of its own attorney or agent; (5) failure of the insurer to inform the insured of a compromise offer; (6) the amount of financial risk to which each party is exposed in the event of a refusal to settle; (7) the fault of the insured in inducing the insurer's rejection of the compromise offer by misleading it as to the facts; and (8) any other factors tending to establish or negate bad faith on the part of the insurer."); *Apollo Educ. Grp., Inc. v. Nat'l Union Fire Ins. Co.*, 480 P.3d 1225 (Ariz. 2021) (noting that Arizona courts have rejected the "fairly debatable" standard in determining whether an insurer has acted in bad faith in third-party cases, but has applied that standard in first-party cases) ("The heightened standard in third-party actions applies because of the different relationships and duties that exist between the parties. Where the insurer exclusively controls settlement, the insured bears a disproportionate share of the risk if the insurer fails to accept a reasonable settlement offer within policy limits . . . . Therefore, although the fairly debatable standard sufficiently protects both parties' interests where those circumstances are not present, it inadequately protects the insured's interests where the insurer has exclusive control, requiring the insurer to consider the insured's interests equally with its own interests.") (internal citations and quotations omitted).

Arkansas: The Supreme Court of Arkansas stated: "We have defined 'bad faith' as dishonest, malicious, or oppressive conduct carried out with a state of mind characterized by hatred, ill will, or a spirit of revenge. Mere negligence or bad judgment is insufficient so long as the insurer is acting in good faith. Moreover, the tort of bad faith does not arise from the mere denial of a claim; rather, there must be affirmative misconduct on the part of the insurer." *Switzer v. Shelter Mut. Ins. Co.*, 208 S.W.3d 792, 801 (Ark. 2005) (citations omitted); *see also Williams v. State Farm Mut. Auto. Ins. Co.*, No. 5:10CV00032 JLH, 2010 U.S. Dist. LEXIS 61613 (E.D. Ark. June 22, 2010) ("The standard for establishing a claim for bad faith is rigorous and difficult to satisfy.") (providing examples of cases where the Supreme Court of Arkansas has found bad faith); *Hortica-Florists' Mut. Ins. Co. v. Pittman Nursery Corp.*, 729 F.3d 846, 854 (8th Cir. 2013) (applying Arkansas law) ("As long as the insurer is acting in good faith, negligence or bad judgment alone are not enough to sustain a bad faith claim.") ("Because a legitimate controversy existed as to whether money was tangible property, and therefore the migrant workers suffered 'property damage' within the meaning of the CGL policy, Hortica's refusal to pay a claim under the CGL policy cannot constitute affirmative misconduct under Arkansas law. Nor was it negligent."); *Warren v. State Farm Fire & Cas. Co.*, No. 14-05112, 2014 U.S. Dist. LEXIS 115262 (W.D. Ark. Aug. 19, 2014) ("The facts as presently alleged by Plaintiff are conclusory in nature and do not otherwise rise to the level of what the Supreme Court of Arkansas considers 'characterized by hatred, ill will, or a spirit of revenge.' Examples of appropriately specific facts would include instances where an insurance agent lied by stating there was no insurance coverage; predicate facts demonstrating aggressive, abusive, and coercive conduct by a claims representative; and where a carrier intentionally altered insurance records to avoid a bad risk."); *Sims v. State Farm Mut. Auto. Ins. Co.*, 894 F.3d 941 (8th Cir. 2018) (an insurer's violation of its own claims manual was not sufficient to allege bad faith); *Flowers v. Am. Nat'l Prop. & Cas. Co.*, No. 19-00385, 2020 U.S. Dist. LEXIS 180095 (E.D. Ark. Sept. 30, 2020) (finding insured failed to adequately plead bad faith where complaint alleged that the insurer conducted an inadequate investigation, violated its own claims manual, engaged in the practice of lowballing during negotiations, and failed to communicate claims decisions).

In the third-party bad faith context, the Arkansas Court of Appeals stated that "an insurer is liable to its insured for a judgment in excess of the policy limits if the insurer's failure to settle the claim was due to fraud, bad faith, or negligence." *Kirkwood v. State Farm Mut. Auto. Ins. Co.*, No. CA 95-359, 1996 Ark. App. LEXIS 360 (Ark. Ct. App. May 29, 1996) (interpreting *Members Mut. Ins. Co. v. Blissett*, 492 S.W.2d 429 (Ark. 1973) and *Tri-State Ins. Co. v. Busby*, 473 S.W.2d 893 (Ark. 1971)). *See also Williams v. State Volunteer Mut. Ins. Co.*, No. 11-04007, 2011 U.S. Dist. LEXIS 111462 (W.D. Ark. Sept. 28, 2011) ("Williams' argument that the large amount of the ultimate judgment against Dr. Soeller is evidence that State Volunteer acted negligently is untenable. If the Court were to allow the case to advance based on such purported evidence, insurance companies would be exposed to claims in any case in which the jury returned a verdict in excess of policy limits, regardless of any consideration of the reasonableness of their decision not to settle. Williams may argue that, in hindsight, State Volunteer exercised poor judgment in declining to settle the claim. Bad judgment, however, cannot be equated with negligence.").

California: The Supreme Court of California stated that a cause of action exists in tort for breach of an implied covenant of good faith and fair dealing where an insurer "fails to deal fairly and in good faith with its insured by refusing, without proper cause, to compensate its insured for a loss covered by the policy." *Gruenberg v. Aetna Ins. Co.*, 510 P.2d 1032, 1037 (Cal. 1973) (en banc); *see also Major v. W. Home Ins. Co.*, 87 Cal. Rptr. 3d 556, 568 (Cal. Ct. App. 2009) ("In first party cases, the implied covenant of good faith and fair dealing obligates the insurer to make a thorough investigation of the insured's claim for benefits, and not to unreasonably delay or withhold payment of benefits. If the insurer 'without proper cause' (i.e., unreasonably) refuses to timely pay what is due under the contract, its conduct is actionable as a tort.") (citing *Gruenberg*, 510 P.2d at 1037); *Richards v. Sequoia Ins. Co.*, 124 Cal. Rptr. 3d 637, 642 (Cal. Ct. App. 2011) (addressing damages recoverable for bad faith); *Maslo v. Ameriprise Auto & Home Ins.*, 173 Cal. Rptr. 3d 854, 859 (Cal. Ct. App. 2014) ("To fulfill its obligation, an insurer must give at least as much consideration to the interests of the insured as it gives to its own interests.") ("[W]hile an insurance company has no obligation under the implied covenant of good faith and fair dealing to pay every claim its insured makes, the insurer cannot deny the claim without fully investigating the grounds for its denial. By the same token, denial of a claim on a basis unfounded in the facts known to the insurer, or contradicted by those facts, may be deemed unreasonable. A trier of fact may find that an insurer acted unreasonably if the insurer ignores evidence available to it which supports the claim. The insurer may not just focus on those facts which justify denial of the claim. An insurer's good or bad faith must be evaluated in light of the totality of the circumstances surrounding its actions.") (citations and internal quotations omitted).

In 2016, the California Court of Appeal set forth the following recitation of the state's bad faith law: "To establish bad faith, the Paslays must demonstrate misconduct by State Farm more egregious than an incorrect denial of policy benefits. The law implies in every contract, including insurance policies, a covenant of good faith and fair dealing. The obligation imposed on the insurer under the covenant is not the requirement mandated by the terms of the policy itself … . It is the obligation … under which the insurer must act fairly and in good faith in discharging its contractual responsibilities. In the context of a bad faith claim, an insurer's denial of or delay in paying benefits gives rise to tort damages only if the insured shows the denial or delay was unreasonable. Under this standard, an insurer denying or delaying the payment of policy benefits due to the existence of a genuine dispute with its insured as to the existence of coverage liability or the amount of the insureds coverage claim is not liable in bad faith, even though it might be liable for breach of contract. That is because when there is a genuine issue as to the insurer's liability under the policy for the claim asserted by the insured, there can be no bad faith liability imposed on the insurer for advancing its side of that dispute. An insurer may thus obtain summary adjudication of a bad faith cause of action by establishing that its denial of coverage, even if ultimately erroneous and a breach of contract, was due to a genuine dispute with its insured. The genuine dispute doctrine does not relieve an insurer of its obligation to thoroughly and fairly investigate, process and evaluate the insured's claim. A genuine dispute exists only where the insurer's position is maintained in good faith and on reasonable grounds. Those grounds include reasonable reliance on experts hired to estimate repair benefits owed under the policy. The reasonableness of the insurer's decision is assessed by reference to an objective standard. The application of the genuine dispute doctrine becomes a question of law where the evidence is undisputed and only one reasonable inference can be drawn from the evidence." *Paslay v. State Farm General Ins. Co.*, 248 Cal. App. 4th 639, 652-53 (2016) (citations and internal quotes omitted). *See also Pulte Home Corp. v. Am. Safety Indem. Co.*, 14 Cal. App. 5th 1086 (2017) (finding bad faith where insurer made an unreasonable reading of its policy language and "inexplicably disregarded case law known to it"); *Karawit v. Geico Gen. Ins. Co.*, No. 642233, 2018 Cal. Super. LEXIS 13380 (Cal. Super. Ct. Aug. 10, 2018) ("An insurer's reliance on the advice of counsel is evidence the insurer had proper cause to deny an insured's claim, and did not act unreasonably. The defense of reliance on the advice of counsel is established where the insurer proves it acted in good faith reliance on the advice of counsel, that it made a full disclosure of all relevant facts to counsel and, that counsel acted on the basis of facts counsel determined by counsel's own investigation on behalf of the insurer.").

For purposes of third-party bad faith, the Supreme Court of California held that "the insurer must settle within policy limits when there is substantial likelihood of recovery in excess of those limits. … An insurer that breaches its implied duty of good faith and fair dealing by unreasonably refusing to accept a settlement offer within policy limits may be held liable for the full amount of the judgment against the insured in excess of its policy limits." *Kransco v. Am. Empire Surplus Lines Ins. Co.*, 2 P.3d 1, 9 (Cal. 2000); *see also Sasaguchi v. Commerce W. Ins. Co.*, No. B209546, 2009 Cal. App. Unpub. LEXIS 4182 (Cal. Ct. App. May 28, 2009) (rejecting the argument that an underlying excess judgment is not a prerequisite to an insured's cause of action against its insurer for breach of the duty to settle) ("An insurer's refusal to settle within policy limits while the underlying action is pending presents only the possibility that a judgment might be rendered in excess of policy limits. An excess judgment in the underlying action against the insured is necessary to establish the damages for which the insurer may be liable in a subsequent bad faith action.") (citations and internal quotations omitted); *DeWitt v. Monterey Ins. Co.*, 138 Cal. Rptr. 3d 705 (Cal. Ct. App. 2012) (discussing in depth California's case law regarding insurer's failure to accept a reasonable settlement offer); *Reid v. Mercury Ins. Co.*, 162 Cal. Rptr. 3d 894, 904 (Cal. Ct. App. 2013) (finding insurer cannot be liable for failure to settle where there was no settlement offer from the motorist); *Madrigal v. Allstate Indem. Co.*, No. 14-4242, 2015 U.S. Dist. LEXIS 187462 (C.D. Cal. Dec. 7, 2015) ("To prevail on a claim for breach of the implied covenant of good faith and fair dealing, an insured must show: that the claimant brought a claim against the insured that was covered by the insurer's insurance policy; (2) that the insurer failed to accept a reasonable settlement demand for an amount within policy limits; (3) the insurer's failure to accept the settlement demand was unreasonable, which means without proper cause; and (4) a monetary judgment was entered against the insured for a sum greater than the policy limits. Factors that a jury may consider in determining whether the offer to settle was reasonable include whether: (1) [the offer's] terms are clear enough to have created an enforceable contract resolving all claims had it been accepted by the insurer, (2) all of the third party claimants have joined in the demand, (3) it provides for a complete release of all insureds, and (4) the time provided for acceptance did not deprive the insurer of an adequate opportunity to investigate and evaluate its insured's exposure.") (*aff'd*, 2017 U.S. App. LEXIS 10643 (9th Cir. June 15, 2017); *McDaniel v. Gov't Emples. Ins. Co.*, 681 Fed. Appx. 614 (9th Cir. 2017) (noting that "an insurer's negligence is insufficient to constitute an 'unreasonable refusal' to accept a settlement offer" and that constructive or implied knowledge also cannot supply the "requisite degree of culpability to establish bad faith"); *Trees, LLC v. Liberty Mut. Fire Ins. Co.*, No. 17-04774, 2018 U.S. Dist. LEXIS

233753 (N.D. Cal. July 25, 2018) (It's true that many bad faith cases contemplate the fact pattern of an insurance company settling claims against one insured and leaving the other insured entirely without coverage. But it does not follow that an insurance company can automatically insulate itself from a bad faith claim simply by leaving some coverage to the non-settling insured where the insurer's actions harm the interests that insured contracted to protect.") (internal citations omitted). *See also Barickman v. Mercury Casualty Co.*, 2 Cal. App. 5th 508 (2016), *Graciano v. Mercury General Corp.*, 231 Cal. App. 4th 414 (2014) and *Pinto v. Farmers Ins. Exchange*, 61 Cal. App. 5th 676 (Cal. Ct. App. 2021) addressing bad faith failure to settle in detail.

Colorado: The Supreme Court of Colorado stated that "[i]n addition to proving that the insurer acted unreasonably under the circumstances, a first-party claimant must prove that the insurer either knowingly or recklessly disregarded the validity of the insured's claim. This standard of care reflects a reasonable balance between the right of an insurance carrier to reject a non-compensable claim submitted by its insured and the obligation of such carrier to investigate and ultimately approve a valid claim." *Goodson v. Am. Standard Ins. Co. of Wis.*, 89 P.3d 409, 415 (Colo. 2004) (en banc) (citation and internal quotation omitted). "[A]n insurer may challenge claims which are fairly debatable and will be found to have acted in bad faith only if it has intentionally denied (or failed to process or pay) a claim without a reasonable basis." *Fincher ex rel. Fincher v. Prudential Prop. & Cas. Ins. Co.*, Nos. 08-1109, 08-1159, 2010 U.S. App. LEXIS 8134 (10th Cir. Apr. 20, 2010) (applying Colorado law); *see also Sanderson v. Am. Family Mut. Ins. Co.*, 251 P.3d 1213, 1218 (Colo. Ct. App. 2010) ("[F]air debatability is not a threshold inquiry that is outcome determinative as a matter of law, nor is it both the beginning and the end of the analysis in a bad faith case."). In 2008, the General Assembly enacted COLO. REV. STAT. § 10-3-1115 (improper denial of claims) and -1116 (unreasonable delay or denial of benefits). *See Kisselman v. Am. Family Mut. Ins. Co.*, 292 P.3d 964 (Colo. Ct. App. 2011) (discussing and distinguishing § 10-3-1115 and § 10-3-1116 from common law bad faith claims and holding that statutes created new private cause of action, imposed new standard of liability on insurers, and applied prospectively); *Vaccaro v. Am. Family Ins. Grp.*, 275 P.3d 760, 759 (Colo. Ct. App. 2012) (same); *State Farm Mut. Auto. Ins. Co. v. Fisher*, 419 P.3d 985 (Colo. Ct. App. May 7, 2015) (rejecting insurer's argument that, under section 10-3-1115, an insurer's decision to delay or deny payment of a 'fairly debatable' UIM claim cannot be unreasonable as a matter of law) ("[U]nlike a common law insurance bad faith claim, in which the insured has to prove both that the insurer acted unreasonably under the circumstances and that the insurer knowingly or recklessly disregarded the validity of the insured's claim, the only element at issue in a statutory claim [under section 10-3-1115] is whether an insurer denied benefits without a reasonable basis. Whether a claim is 'fairly debatable' . . . goes as much to the knowledge or recklessness prong of common law bad faith as it does to unreasonable conduct. . . . So even if a plaintiff's claim for UIM benefits were 'fairly debatable' in the common law context, that would not alone establish that the defendant's actions . . . were reasonable as a matter of law.") (*aff'd on other grounds* 418 P.3d 501 (Colo. 2018)); *Thompson v. State Farm Mut. Auto Ins. Co.*, 457 F. Supp. 3d 998 (D. Colo. 2020) (discussing methods for determining insurance industry standards for purposes of statutory bad faith claims, including the use of Colorado's Unfair Competition - Deceptive Trade Practices Act and expert testimony) (noting that fair debatability "weighs against a finding that the insurer acted unreasonably" but is not outcome determinative, particularly where multiple courts have found that an issue of material fact exists); *Peerless Indem. Ins. Co. v. Colclasure*, No. 16-424, 2017 U.S. Dist. LEXIS 22193 (D. Colo. Feb. 16, 2017) ("[T]he majority of decisions in this district have concluded that the plain language of § 10-3-1115 does not preclude commercial general liability insureds from bringing a statutory bad faith claim.").

Section 10-3-1116 provides: "(1) A first-party claimant as defined in section 10-3-1115 whose claim for payment of benefits has been unreasonably delayed or denied may bring an action in a district court to recover reasonable attorney fees and court costs and two times the covered benefit. . . . (4) The action authorized in this section is in addition to, and does not limit or affect, other actions available by statute or common law, now or in the future. Damages awarded pursuant to this section shall not be recoverable in any other action or claim." Section 10-3-1115 provides: "(1) (a) A person engaged in the business of insurance shall not unreasonably delay or deny payment of a claim for benefits owed to or on behalf of any first-party claimant. . . . (2) Notwithstanding section 10-3-1113 (3), for the purposes of an action brought pursuant to this section and section 10-3-1116, an insurer›s delay or denial was unreasonable if the insurer delayed or denied authorizing payment of a covered benefit without a reasonable basis for that action."

Turning to the third-party context, the *Goodson* Court stated that "[b]ecause of the quasi-fiduciary nature of the insurance relationship in a third-party context, the standard of conduct required of the insurer is characterized by general principles of negligence. To establish that the insurer breached its duties of good faith and fair dealing, the insured must show that a reasonable insurer under the circumstances would have paid or otherwise settled the third-party claim." 89 P.3d at 415 (citations omitted); *see also Nunn v. Mid-Century Ins. Co.*, 244 P.3d 116, 123 (Colo. 2010) (en banc) ("[A]lthough entry of a stipulated judgment in excess of policy limits is sufficient to establish actual damages for a bad faith failure to settle claim, the actual amount of damages for which an insurer will be liable will depend on whether the stipulated judgment is reasonable."), *as modified on denial of reh'g* (Jan. 10, 2011); *State Farm Mut. Auto Ins. Co. v. Goddard*, 484 P.3d 765 (Colo. Ct. App. 2021) (citing *Goodson* and *Nunn*) ("Although a finding that the insurer appeared to act unreasonably — thereby allowing an insured to enter into a *Nunn* agreement — and a finding that the insurer actually acted unreasonably — resulting in a finding of bad faith on the part of the insurer — are likely to go hand in hand, it is conceivable that an insurer may appear to have acted unreasonably in rejecting a policy-limits offer, but not actually acted unreasonably in settling the claim. Under that scenario, the insured would not have breached the insurance contract and the insurer would not have acted in bad faith.").

Connecticut: A Connecticut trial court expressly adopted the Supreme Court of California's rule in *Gruenberg v. Aetna Insurance Co.*, 510 P.2d 1032 (Cal. 1973) that allows for recovery of consequential damages where there has been a showing of bad faith by the insurer. *Grand Sheet Metal Prods. Co. v. Prot. Mut. Ins. Co.*, 375 A.2d 428, 430 (Conn. Super. Ct. 1977). "Where an insurer fails to deal fairly and in good faith with its insured by refusing without proper cause to compensate its insured for a loss covered by the policy such conduct may give rise to a cause of action in tort for breach of an implied covenant of good faith and fair dealing." *Id.; see also Nationwide Mut. Ins. Co. v. Mortensen*, No. 3:00-cv-1180 (CFD), 2009 U.S. Dist. LEXIS 74870 (D. Conn. Aug. 24, 2009) (continuing to rely on *Grand Sheet* as authority for a tort action for breach of the duty of good faith and fair dealing). The Supreme Court of Connecticut held that "bad faith is not actionable apart from a wrongful denial of benefit under the policy." *Capstone Bldg. Corp. v. Am. Motorists Ins. Co.*, 67 A.3d 961, 988 (Conn. 2013) (refusing to "extend bad faith actions to allegations based solely on a failure to investigate where the investigation is not mandated under the policy"); *see also De La Concha of Hartford, Inc. v. Aetna Life Ins. Co.*, 849 A.2d 382, 388 (Conn. 2004) ("Bad faith in general implies both actual or constructive fraud, or a design to mislead or deceive another, or a neglect or refusal to fulfill some duty or some contractual obligation, not prompted by an honest mistake as to one's rights or duties, but by some interested or sinister motive. ... Bad faith means more than mere negligence; it involves a dishonest purpose."); *Mead v. Burns*, 509 A.2d 11, 18 (Conn. 1986) (holding that it is possible to state a cause of action under the Connecticut Unfair Trade Practices Act, Conn. Gen. Stat. § 42-110a *et seq.*, for a violation of the Connecticut Unfair Insurance Practices Act, Conn. Gen. Stat. § 38a-816 *et seq.*); *PHL Variable Ins. Co. v. Charter Oak Trust*, No. HHDCV1060126218, 2013 Conn. Super. LEXIS 721 (Conn. Super. Ct. Mar. 27, 2013) (noting the various ways Connecticut jurisprudence defines "bad faith"); *Carney v. Allstate Ins. Co.*, No. 16-00592, 2017 U.S. Dist. LEXIS 119435 (D. Conn. Feb. 14, 2017) ("A mere dispute over the discretionary application or interpretation of a contract term is insufficient to warrant a finding of bad faith"); *Rood v. Covenant Ins. Co.*, No. 156059856, 2018 Conn. Super. LEXIS 3375 (Conn. Super. Ct. Oct. 15, 2018) (finding that "a person due money can sue an insurance company for at least the financial consequences of an insurer's alleged deliberate torment and delay in paying what it actually owed") (distinguishing *Captstone* on the basis that "the Supreme Court neither considered the facts here nor embraced them in its holding" and "the idea that there is no circumstance in which an insurer can be responsible for bad faith misconduct on a claim it paid is too much to swallow"); *Heroux v. State Farm Fire & Cas. Co.*, No. 206127358, 2021 Conn. Super. LEXIS 680 (Conn. Super. Ct. May 4, 2021) ("Intentionally forcing policy holders to litigate for sums due under a contract of insurance, and the use of their superior economic strength to frustrate and leverage an inadequate settlement from policy holders as a business practice is, in the court's view, the essence of bad faith.").

In the context of third-party bad faith, a Connecticut trial court noted the lack of Connecticut appellate authority concerning the type of conduct which would constitute bad faith for failure to settle a claim within the policy limits, following a demand for settlement. *Hernandez v. Allstate Ins. Co.*, No. CV040413243S, 2006 Conn. Super. LEXIS 2403 (Conn. Super. Ct. Aug. 9, 2006). The *Hernandez* Court concluded that "'[b]ad [f]aith' entails more than mere negligence, carelessness, or inadvertence. It implies a design to mislead or to deceive another, or a neglect or refusal to fulfill some duty or contractual obligation, not promoted by an honest mistake. Bad faith involves a dishonest purpose." *Id.* (citations omitted). *See also Carford v. Empire Fire & Marine Ins. Co.*, No. CV065001946, 2012 Conn. Super. LEXIS 2147 (Conn. Super. Ct. Aug. 21, 2012) ("Connecticut has long recognized a cause of action for negligent failure to settle a claim. In situations analogous to that presented by this case courts have applied varying standards by which to determine whether or not an insurer is liable to an insured for failing to settle a claim. These may be generally summarized as a requirement of good faith and honest judgment on the part of the insurer or one that the insurer should use that care and diligence which a person of ordinary prudence would exercise in the management of his own business.").

Delaware: The Supreme Court of Delaware stated that "[i]f a claim arises concerning a breach of the terms of th[e] [insurance] agreement, whether it be a dispute over coverage, or an exclusion or delay in payment of a claim, the remedy should be for breach of contract." *Tackett v. State Farm Fire & Cas. Ins. Co.*, 653 A.2d 254, 264 (Del. 1995). "A lack of good faith, or the presence of bad faith, is actionable where the insured can show that the insurer's denial of benefits was clearly without any reasonable justification." *Id.* (citation and internal quotation omitted); *see also Arrowood Indem. Co. v. Hartford Fire Ins. Co.*, 774 F. Supp. 2d 636 (D. Del. 2011) ("Where an insurer fails to investigate or process a claim or delays payment in bad faith, it is in breach of the implied obligations of good faith and fair dealing underlying all contractual obligations. Stating a claim for breach of the duty of good faith and fair dealing under Delaware law requires that the plaintiff allege a specific implied contractual obligation, a breach of that obligation by the defendant, and resulting damages to the plaintiff.") (citations and internal quotations omitted); *Enrique v. State Farm Mut. Auto. Ins. Co.*, 142 A.3d 506 (Del. 2016) ("We have recognized that an insured has a cause of action for breach of the implied covenant of good faith when the insurer refuses to honor its obligations under the policy and clearly lacks reasonable justification for doing so. A mere delay in paying benefits is insufficient to constitute bad faith, but delays attributed to a 'get tough' policy, *i.e.*, a general business practice of claims denial without a reasonable basis, may subject the insurer to a bad faith claim."); *RSUI Indem. Co. v. Murdock*, 248 A.3d 887 (Del. 2021) (finding that the proper inquiry for determining whether an insurer acted in good faith is "whether the insurer [was] aware of facts and circumstances, at the time of denial, that support a bona fide dispute as to whether the loss is covered"); *Henlopen Hotel v. United Nat'l Ins. Co.*, No. 18-09-212, 2020 Del. Super. LEXIS 1524 (Del. Super. Ct. 2020) (concluding that "[w]here an insurer's denial of coverage is premised on a theory sufficiently well-supported as to resist summary judgment, they are entitled to contest coverage and cannot be subject to an 'extra-contractual' claim for bad faith").

In the third-party context, "liability of an insurance carrier to its policyholder in excess of policy limits is based on the tortious conduct of the insurance carrier, which under the policy has sole control of the defense." *Stilwell v. Parsons*, 145 A.2d 397, 402 (Del. 1958); *see also McNally v. Nationwide Ins. Co.*, 815 F.2d 254, 259 (3d

Cir. 1987) (applying Delaware law) (discussing *Stilwell* and finding that "[w]hen a judgment in excess of the policy limits might be obtained by the claimant, the good faith standard is satisfied only if the insurer acts in the same way as would a reasonable and prudent man with the obligation to pay all of the recoverable damages") (citation and internal quotation omitted); *Gruwell v. Allstate Ins. Co.*, 988 A.2d 945, 949 (Del. Super. Ct. 2009) ("[N]o case has been brought to the Court's attention which undermines the legal principle for which [*Stilwell*] was cited by the Third Circuit [in *McNally*].")*; Christiana Care Health Servs. v. PMSLIC Ins. Co.*, No. 14-1420, 2015 U.S. Dist. LEXIS 148048 (D. Del. Nov. 2, 2015) (Although it cites the laws of other jurisdictions for support, PMSLIC acknowledges that there is no statement of Delaware law to the effect that an insurer's duty to settle is not triggered unless there is a within-limits settlement demand. In Delaware, whether an insurer acted in bad faith is a fact-specific question of the reasonableness of its actions. In light of PMSLIC's inability to demonstrate that the bright line rule it advances is the law of Delaware, I conclude that Counts II-III of the Complaint state a claim even though Christiana Care does not allege that the Houghtons made a within-limits settlement demand.").

District of Columbia: A District of Columbia District Court concluded that a tort for bad faith breach of contract is not recognized under District of Columbia law. *Fireman's Fund Ins. Co. v. CTIA*, 480 F. Supp. 2d 7 (D.D.C. 2007). The *CTIA* Court chose to follow *Washington v. Government Employees Insurance Co.*, 769 F. Supp. 383 (D.D.C. 1991) and was also persuaded by the fact that courts in Maryland have not recognized a bad faith claim against an insurer in a first-party context. *CTIA*, 480 F. Supp. 2d at 11. "[A] tort must exist in its own right independent of the contract, and any duty upon which the tort is based must flow from considerations other than the contractual relationship." *Choharis v. State Farm Fire & Cas. Co.*, 961 A.2d 1080, 1089 (D.C. Cir. 2008) (following *CTIA* and Maryland's view to conclude that a tort for bad faith breach of contract is not recognized under District of Columbia law); *Tolson v. Hartford Fin. Servs. Grp.*, No. 16-440, 2017 U.S. Dist. LEXIS 160732 (D.D.C. Sept. 29, 2017) ("In the District of Columbia, an insured may sue an insurer in tort where the injury to the insured is an independent injury over and above the mere disappointment of the insured's hope to receive his contracted-for benefit. Put another way, the tort must exist in its own right independent of the contract, and any duty upon which the tort is based must flow from considerations other than the contractual relationship. The D.C. Court of Appeals has specifically declined to recognize a tort for bad faith by insurance companies in the handling of policy claims, including failure to conduct good faith investigation of insured's claims.") (citing *Choharis*); *Gebretsadike v. Travelers Home & Marine Ins. Co.*, 694 Fed. Appx. 2 (D.C. Cir. 2017) ("[T]he district court correctly concluded that District of Columbia law does not recognize a tort claim for bad faith in the context of a contractual relationship. . . . To the extent that claim could also have been construed as a contract law claim for breach of the implied covenant of good faith and fair dealing, there is nothing in the record to indicate that appellee acted in 'bad faith' or engaged in 'conduct that is arbitrary and capricious' in its dealings with appellant."); *Burks Cos. v. Howard Univ.*, No. 16-2312, 2018 U.S. Dist. LEXIS 225203 (D.D.C. May 9, 2018) (citing *Gebratsadike*) (holding that insured failed to state a claim for breach of the implied covenant of good faith and fair dealing because it did not allege that the insurer violated "community standards of decency, fairness or reasonableness" or that the insurer's conduct was arbitrary and capricious).

Third-party bad faith—No instructive authority. *See* Maryland. "When District of Columbia law is silent, it has been the practice of the federal courts in this Circuit to turn to the law of Maryland for historical and geographical reasons." *Gray v. Am. Express Co.*, 743 F.2d 10, 17 (D.C. Cir. 1984).

Florida: FLA. STAT. ANN. § 624.155 created a statutory cause of action for first-party bad faith and also codified prior Supreme Court of Florida decisions authorizing a third party to bring a bad faith action under common law. *See Macola v. Gov't Emps. Ins. Co.*, 953 So. 2d 451, 456 (Fla. 2006). First-party claims for breach of the covenant of good faith and fair dealing based on the insurer's failure to investigate and assess the insured's claim within a reasonable time period "are actually statutory bad-faith claims that must be brought under section 624.155 of the Florida Statutes." *Chalfonte Condo. Apartment Ass'n, Inc. v. QBE Ins. Corp.*, 695 F.3d 1215, 1227 (11th Cir. 2012) (applying Florida law) ("Since the statute's enactment, both federal and Florida courts have found that section 624.155 extends bad-faith actions to the first-party context.") (discussing the history of Florida law on bad-faith claims before and after § 624.155). This statute authorizes a cause of action against an insurer for, among other things, "[n]ot attempting in good faith to settle claims when, under all the circumstances, it could and should have done so, had it acted fairly and honestly toward its insured and with due regard for her or his interests." FLA. STAT. ANN. § 624.155(1)(b)(1). Florida applies a totality of the circumstances approach to bad faith determinations. *State Farm Mut. Auto. Ins. Co. v. Laforet*, 658 So. 2d 55, 62–63 (Fla. 1995). "[A]t least five factors should be taken into account: (1) whether the insurer was able to obtain a reservation of the right to deny coverage if a defense were provided; (2) efforts or measures taken by the insurer to resolve the coverage dispute promptly or in such a way as to limit any potential prejudice to the insureds; (3) the substance of the coverage dispute or the weight of legal authority on the coverage issue; (4) the insurer's diligence and thoroughness in investigating the facts specifically pertinent to coverage; and (5) efforts made by the insurer to settle the liability claim in the face of the coverage dispute." *Id.* The second, third, and fourth factors should be considered in a first-party cause of action. *Id.* at 63. "There must be a causal connection between the damages claimed and the insurer's bad faith." *Perera v. U.S. Fid. & Guar. Co.*, 35 So. 3d. 893, 903–04 (Fla. 2010) (holding that assignee of insured could not recover an excess verdict against a primary insurer where the insured had adequate excess limits, an excess insurer was willing to settle without any contribution from the primary insurer, insured did not face exposure in excess of the limits of the combined policies, and the excess insurer did not bring a bad faith claim against the primary insurer or assign its claim to the underlying plaintiff); *Wiggins v. Allstate Prop. & Cas. Ins. Co.*, 94 F. Supp. 3d 1276 (S.D. Fla. 2015) ("To demonstrate good faith, an insurer must investigate the facts, give fair consideration to a settlement offer that is not unreasonable under the facts, and settle, if possible, where a reasonably prudent person, faced with the prospect of paying the total recovery, would do so. Because the duty of good faith involves diligence and care in the investigation and evaluation of the claim against the insured, negligence is relevant to the question of good faith.") (also setting out the five-part totality of the circumstances factors for bad faith) ("In examining a bad faith claim, the factfinder must examine the insurer's 'entire conduct in the handling of the claim, including the acts or omissions of the insurer in failing to ensure payment of the policy limits within the time demands.'"); *Cousin v. GEICO Gen. Ins. Co.*, 719 Fed. Appx. 954 (11th Cir. 2018) (concluding that, while Florida bad faith law focuses on the conduct of the insurer, "the insured's—or, as here, the insured's lawyer's—actions are part of the 'totality of the circumstances,' especially to the extent that they impede the insurer's good faith duty to investigate facts and give fair consideration to settlement").

Moreover, this statute "authorizes a third party to file a bad-faith claim directly against the liability insurer without an assignment by the insured upon obtaining judgment in excess of the policy limits." *State Farm Fire & Cas. Co. v. Zebrowski*, 706 So. 2d 275, 277 (Fla. 1997); *see also Macola*, 953 So. 2d at 456 (explaining that the statute codified the court's prior decisions authorizing a third party to bring a bad-faith action under common law). "While evidence of carelessness may be relevant to proving bad faith, Florida has expressly stated that the standard for determining liability in an excess judgment case is bad faith rather than negligence." *Novoa v. GEICO Indem. Co.*, No. 13-10704, 2013 U.S. App. LEXIS 20779 (11th Cir. Oct. 15, 2013) (internal quotations omitted) ("To fulfill the duty of good faith, an insurer does not have to act perfectly, prudently, or even reasonably. Rather, insurers must 'refrain from acting solely on the basis of their own interests in settlement.'" (quoting *Laforet*)) *(but see Harvey,* addressed blow); *Goheagan v. Am. Vehicle Ins. Co.*, 107 So. 3d 433, 438 (Fla. Dist. Ct. App. 2012) ("Bad faith may be inferred from a delay in settlement negotiations which is willful and without reasonable cause. ... Where liability is clear, and injuries so serious that a judgment in excess of policy limits is likely, an insurer has an affirmative duty to initiate settlement negotiations."); *Welford v. Liberty Mut. Ins. Co.*, No. 16-14054, 2017 U.S. App. LEXIS 24081 (11th Cir. Nov. 29, 2017) ("While Liberty did not make a pre-suit settlement offer, there was no affirmative duty under applicable Florida law to do so, and even if there was, such a duty would have been inapplicable because Middleton was not clearly liable for the accident.").

The Florida Supreme Court has noted that both Florida and federal courts at times miss the mark regarding the application of Florida's bad faith precedent. *Harvey v. GEICO Gen. Ins. Co.*, 259 So. 3d 1 (Fla. 2018). The *Harvey* court rejected the Eleventh Circuit's statement in *Novoa v. GEICO Indem. Co.* that "an insurer need not act prudently or even reasonably" on the basis that it misconstrued Florida's well-established bad faith precedent. *Id.* at 8. The *Harvey* court also concluded that the Fourth District Court of Appeals misstated Florida's bad faith law "when it stated that an insurer cannot be liable for bad faith 'where the insured's own actions or inactions result, at least in part, in an excess judgment.'" *Id.* The court noted that "[n]othing in our precedent can be read to suggest that an insurer cannot be found liable for bad faith merely because the insured could have attempted on his own to avoid the excess judgment. In fact, our precedent states just the opposite." *Id.* Further, the Fourth District's statement was "fundamentally inconsistent with this Court's precedent, which could not be clearer in stating that 'the focus in a bad faith case is not on the actions of the claimant but rather on those of the insurer in fulfilling its obligations to the insured.'" *Id.* at 11. "[T]his Court has never held or even suggested that an insured's actions can let the insurer off the hook when the evidence clearly establishes that the insurer acted in bad faith in handling the insured's claim." *Id.* See *Ilias v. USAA General Indemnity Company*, No. 20-834, 2021 U.S. Dist. LEXIS 117879 (M.D. Fla. June 24, 2021) ("While *Harvey* does instruct that negligence is relevant to determining bad faith and perhaps 'muddie[d] the waters between negligence and bad faith,' *Harvey* plainly states that 'negligence is not the standard' for liability in a bad-faith action. *Harvey* thus reaffirmed longstanding Florida precedent that requires a plaintiff in a bad-faith action to prove that an insurer's actions surpassed mere negligence. So USAA's actions, though potentially negligent to some degree, did not rise to the level of bad faith.") (internal citations omitted).

Georgia: A Georgia statute provides that "[i]n the event of a loss which is covered by a policy of insurance and the refusal of the insurer to pay the same within 60 days after a demand has been made by the holder of the policy and a finding has been made that such refusal was in bad faith, the insurer shall be liable to pay such holder, in addition to the loss, not more than 50 percent of the liability of the insurer for the loss or $5,000.00, whichever is greater, and all reasonable attorney's fees for the prosecution of the action against the insurer." GA. CODE ANN. § 33-4-6. "Bad faith for purposes of ... § 33-4-6 is any frivolous and unfounded refusal in law or in fact to pay according to the terms of the policy." *King v. Atl. Cas. Ins. Co.*, 631 S.E.2d 786, 788 (Ga. Ct. App. 2006); *see also Tiller v. State Farm Mut. Auto. Ins. Co.*, No. 13-10988, 2013 U.S. App. LEXIS 22396 (11th Cir. Nov. 4, 2013) (applying Georgia law) (holding that to state a claim for breach of the implied duty of good faith and fair dealing, insured must allege a breach of the first-party insurance contract); *American Safety Indemnity Co. v. Sto Corp.*, 802 S.E.2d 448 (Ga. Ct. App. 2017) ("[B]ad faith is shown by evidence that under *the terms of the policy* upon which the demand is made and under the facts surrounding the response to that demand, the insurer had no good cause for resisting and delaying payment.") (emphasis in original); *Majesko v. Nationwide Mut. Ins. Co.*, No. 16-222, 2017 U.S. Dist. LEXIS 193831 (N.D. Ga. Jan. 24, 2017) ("Bad faith penalties, however, are not authorized where the insurance company has *any reasonable ground to contest the claim* and where there is a disputed question of fact.") (emphasis in original); *Lee v. Mercury Ins. Co.*, 808 S.E.2d 116 (Ga. Ct. App. 2017) (The rule that "[p]enalties for bad faith are not authorized where the insurance company has any reasonable ground to contest the claim and where there is a disputed question of fact" applies even if genuine issues of fact exist with regard to whether the insurer's conduct in denying the claim, in part, may have been based upon bad faith"); *Montgomery v. Travelers Home & Marine Ins. Co.*, No. 01042021, 2021 Ga. App. LEXIS 268 (Ga. Ct. App. June 9, 2021) ("The advice of an independent consultant may provide an insurer with a reasonable ground to contest an insured's claim under the policy, entitling the insurer to summary judgment on a claim for bad faith penalties. As a matter of law, it is reasonable for an insurer to deny a claim based on such advice unless the advice is patently wrong and the error was timely brought to the insurer's attention, or unless the advice is in the nature of mere pretext for an insurer's unwarranted prior decision to deny the claim.") (internal citations and quotations omitted).

Addressing third-party bad faith, the Supreme Court of Georgia stated that "the insurer had a duty to its insured to respond to the plaintiff's deadline to settle the personal injury claim within policy limits when the insurer had knowledge of clear liability and special damages exceeding the policy limits. Our holding in *Southern General Insurance Co. v. Holt* [416 S.E.2d 274 (Ga. 1992)] was consistent with the general rule that the issue of an insurer's bad faith depends on whether the insurance company acted reasonably in responding to a settlement offer." *Cotton States Mut. Ins. Co. v. Brightman*, 580 S.E.2d 519, 521 (Ga. 2003); *see also Butler v. First Acceptance Ins. Co., Inc.*, 652 F. Supp. 2d 1264 (N.D. Ga. 2009) (addressing *Brightman* and failure to settle in detail and holding that both insured and insurer put forward evidence which could persuade a reasonable jury as to their respective positions whether, under the totality of the circumstances, the insurer did not act as an ordinarily prudent insurer or put its own interests above those of its insured); *Equipco Intern., LLC v. Certain Underwriters at Lloyd's, London*, 739 S.E.2d 797, 799 (Ga. Ct. App. 2013) (noting that bad faith claims under Georgia's insurance code are generally between insured and insurers, but § 33-4-7 "allows third parties to bring bad faith claims directly against insurers in certain limited circumstances"); *First Acceptance Ins. Co. of Ga. v. Hughes*, 826 S.E.2d 71 (Ga. 2019) ("An insurance company's 'bad faith in refusing to settle depends on whether the insurance company acted reasonably in responding to a settlement offer, bearing in mind that, in deciding whether to settle, the insurer must give the insured's interests the same consideration that it gives its own. . . To the extent that this Court's decisions have been deemed to be unclear, "we take this opportunity to clarify that an insurer's duty to settle arises when the injured party presents a valid offer to settle within the insured's policy limits.") (clarifying that "*Miller* [*v. Ga. Interlocal Risk Mgmt. Agency*, 501 S.E.2d 589 (Ga. Ct. App. 2019)] does not require that an insurer settle part of multiple claims" and that, in this instance, settlement of multiple claims, including the most serious claim was in the insured's best interest); *GEICO Indem. Co. v. Whiteside*, 857 S.E.2d 654 (Ga. 2021) ("Regardless of the type of coverage at issue, the unreasonableness of the insurer's conduct is at the heart of a negligent or bad faith failure-to-settle claim, and the reasonableness of the insurer's actions or decisions must be judged at the time they were taken or made.") (finding that an insurer who had no notice of a lawsuit against its insured was not categorically relieved of liability from a bad faith failure to settle suit).

Hawaii: The Supreme Court of Hawaii stated that "[t]he breach of the express covenant to pay claims … is not the *sine qua non* for an action for breach of the implied covenant of good faith and fair dealing. The implied covenant is breached, whether the carrier pays the claim or not, when its conduct damages the very protection or security which the insured sought to gain by buying insurance." *Guajardo v. AIG Hawai'i Ins. Co., Inc.*, 187 P.3d 580, 587 (Haw. 2008) (citation and internal quotation omitted). "[A]n action for the tort of 'bad faith' will lie when an insurance company unreasonably handles or denies payment of a claim. … [C]onduct based on an interpretation of the insurance contract that is reasonable does not constitute bad faith." *Id.* (citation and internal quotation omitted). "In general, whether an insurer has acted in bad faith is a question of fact." *Willis v. Swain*, 304 P.3d 619, 637 (Haw. 2013) (citing *Guajardo*) ("The special relationship between the insurer and the insured and the conduct of the insurer toward the insured is what gives rise to the tort of bad faith, not solely the existence of a contract."). *See also Port Lynch, Inc. v. Samsung Fire & Marine Ins. Co.*, No. 11–000398, 2013 U.S. Dist. LEXIS 152678 (D. Hawaii Oct. 24, 2013) ("[T]he insured need not show a conscious awareness of wrongdoing or unjustifiable conduct, nor an evil motive or intent to harm the insured. An unreasonable delay in payment of benefits will warrant recovery for compensatory damages.... However, conduct based on an interpretation of the insurance contract that is reasonable does not constitute bad faith. In addition, an erroneous decision not to pay a claim for benefits due under a policy does not by itself justify an award of compensatory damages. Rather, the decision not to pay a claim must be in 'bad faith.'") (quoting *Best Place, infra*.); *Aloha Petroleum, Ltd. v. National Union Fire Ins. Co. of Pittsburgh, PA*, No. 13–0296, 2014 U.S. Dist. LEXIS 92660 (D. Hawaii July 8, 2014) (providing detailed discussion of Hawaii bad faith law); *State Farm Fire & Cas. Co. v. GP West, Inc.*, 190 F. Supp. 3d 1003 (D. Hawaii 2016) ("Construing Hawaii law, this district has previously stated that an insurer that relies on governing law in denying a claim cannot be said to have acted in bad faith. Additionally, in determining whether an insurer acted in bad faith by denying coverage to an insured under a policy, conduct based on an interpretation of the insurance contract that is reasonable does not constitute bad faith."); *Arc in Haw. v. Db Ins. Co.*, No. 20-00123, 2021 U.S. Dist. LEXIS 113918 (D. Hawaii June 17, 2021) (insurer who "denied coverage based on an ambiguous policy provision and an unsettled question of law" did not act in bad faith) (noting that the insurer "reasonably interpreted the Policies in considering the subject issues with an absence of Hawaii appellate law on point").

In the context of third-party bad faith, a Hawaii District Court, following the analysis of the Supreme Court of Hawaii's seminal decision on bad faith in *Best Place, Inc. v. Penn America Insurance Co.*, 920 P.2d 334 (Haw. 1996) and the California Supreme Court's decision in *Gruenberg, supra*, stated that—for purposes of determining whether an insurer, who does not accept a reasonable settlement offer within policy limits is liable for violation of its duty to act in good faith regarding the interests of the insured—the focus is on the reasonableness of the insurer's actions. *Tran v. State Farm Mut. Auto. Ins. Co.*, 999 F. Supp. 1369, 1372 (D. Haw. 1998); *see also Enoka v. AIG Haw. Ins. Co., Inc.*, 128 P.3d 850, 865 (Haw. 2006) (discussing the difference between first-party bad faith and third-party bad faith); *St. Paul Fire & Marine Ins. Co. v. Liberty Mut. Ins. Co.*, 353 P.3d 991 (Haw. 2015) ("[W]e hold that an excess liability insurer can bring a cause of action, under the doctrine of equitable subrogation, against a primary liability insurer who in bad faith fails to settle a claim within the limits of the primary liability policy, when the primary insurer has paid its policy limit toward settlement.") (not addressing the standard for establishing bad faith).

Idaho: The Supreme Court of Idaho stated that "the mere failure to immediately settle what later proves to be a valid claim does not of itself establish 'bad faith.' … [T]he insured must show the insurer 'intentionally and unreasonably denies or delays payment.' An insurer does not act in bad faith when it challenges the validity of a 'fairly debatable' claim, or when its delay results from honest mistakes." *White v. Unigard Mut. Ins. Co.*, 730 P.2d 1014, 1020 (Idaho 1986) (citations and internal quotations omitted). "A claim for bad faith exists where (1) the insurer intentionally and unreasonably denied or withheld payment, (2) the claim was not fairly debatable, (3) the denial or failure to pay was not the result of a good faith mistake, and (4) the resulting harm is not fully compensable by contract damages." *Lakeland True Value Hardware, LLC v. Hartford Fire Ins. Co.*, 291 P.3d 399, 404–05 (Idaho 2012) (citations and internal quotations omitted); *see also Nord Excavating Inc. v. Northland Ins. Co.*, No. CV08-450, 2010 U.S. Dist. LEXIS 37039 (D. Idaho Apr. 14, 2010) (same); *Weinstein v. Prudential Prop. & Cas. Ins. Co.*, 233 P.3d 1221 (Idaho 2010) ("The tort of bad faith breach of insurance contract … is founded upon the unique relationship of the insurer and the insured, the adhesionary nature of the insurance contract including the potential for overreaching on the part of the insurer, and the unique, 'non-commercial' aspect of the insurance contract." (quoting *White* at 1020)). "In order to prove his bad faith claim, [the insured] must establish that [he] was entitled to recover under the [Policy]." *Rizzo v. State Farm Ins. Co.*, 305 P.3d 519, 528 (Idaho 2013) (internal quotations omitted); *see also Dave's Inc. v. Linford*, 291 P.3d 427, 436 (Idaho 2012) ("Although the tort of bad faith is not a breach of contract claim, to find that the insurer committed bad faith there must also have been a duty under the contract that was breached."); *Naccarato v. Liberty Northwest Ins. Corp.*, No. 13-00390, 2015 U.S. Dist. LEXIS 7459 (D. Idaho Jan. 21, 2015) ("Although there appear to be disputed material facts sufficient to establish one or more of the elements of a bad faith claim, such as whether the delay was due to a good faith mistake, Mr. Naccarato has not carried his burden with respect to the fourth element. As discussed, Mr. Naccarato has not established that he was either entitled to or that he can provide any evidence of extra-contractual damages."); *Botai v. Safeco Ins. Co.*, No. 14-00445, 2017 U.S. Dist. LEXIS 57127 (D. Idaho Mar. 22, 2017) ("Idaho recognizes a tort action, distinct from an action on the contract, for an insurer's bad faith in settling the first party claims of its insured. Insurers have a common law duty to their insureds to settle first party claims in good faith. A breach of that duty will give rise to an action in tort."); *Cedillo v. Farmers Ins. Co.*, 408 P.3d 886 (Idaho 2017) (noting that "[p]oor claims management standing alone is not enough to make out a bad faith claim" and that whether a claim is fairly debatable includes a dispute about the amount of claimed damages).

In the third-party bad faith context, the Supreme Court of Idaho adopted the "equality of consideration" test to determine whether the insurer breached its duty of good faith in rejecting a settlement offer made by a third party. *Truck Ins. Exch. v. Bishara*, 916 P.2d 1275, 1280 (Idaho 1996). The insurer must give "equal consideration" to the interests of its insured in deciding whether to accept an offer of settlement. *Id.* The court adopted several factors for determining whether an insurer acted in bad faith for failing to settle a claim, including, among others, whether the insurer failed to communicate with the insured concerning compromise offers and the amount of financial risk to each of the parties. *Id.* at 1279–80. "The other five factors to be considered are: the strength of the injured claimant's case on the issues of liability and damages; whether the insurer has thoroughly investigated the claim; the failure of the insurer to follow the legal advice of its own attorney; any misrepresentations by the insured which have misled the insurer in its settlement negotiations; and any other factors which may weigh toward establishing or negating the bad faith of the insurer." *McKinley v. Guar. Nat'l Ins. Co.*, 159 P.3d 884, 888 (Idaho 2007) (citing *Bishara*).

Illinois: The Supreme Court of Illinois stated that "[m]ere allegations of bad faith or unreasonable and vexatious conduct, without more, … do not constitute [a bad faith tort action]." *Cramer v. Ins. Exch. Agency*, 675 N.E.2d 897, 904 (Ill. 1996) (noting that the implied duty of good faith and fair dealing "is not generally recognized as an independent source of duties giving rise to a cause of action in tort"). In such case of insurer misconduct, an insured's remedy is limited to a breach of contract action with a right to recover extra-contractual damages set out in 215 ILL. COMP. STAT. ANN. § 5/155. *Id.* "Courts therefore should look beyond the legal theory asserted to the conduct forming the basis for the claim. In cases where a plaintiff actually alleges and proves the elements of a separate tort, a plaintiff may bring an independent tort action, such as common law fraud, for insurer misconduct." *Id.* (citations omitted); *see also W. Howard Corp. v. Indian Harbor Ins. Co.*, No. 1:10–CV–7857, 2011 U.S. Dist. LEXIS 70069 (N.D. Ill. June 29, 2011) (discussing *Cramer*) ("Where an insurer has engaged in 'unreasonable or vexatious conduct,' § 155 of the Illinois Insurance Code allows an insured to recover attorney's fees and extracontractual damages. … The Supreme Court of Illinois has explained that this statute, while not the exclusive remedy for tortious conduct by an insurer, essentially substitutes for a separate tort of 'bad faith.'"). *But see Hess v. Travelers Cas. & Sur. Co. of Am.*, No. 11 C 1310, 2011 U.S. Dist. LEXIS 134509 (N.D. Ill. Nov. 22, 2011) (noting that a claim for punitive damages for a "bad faith" refusal to pay on the policy is not a claim permitted under Illinois law); *Soto v. Country Mut. Ins. Co.*, No. 2-16-0720, 2017 Ill. App. Unpub. LEXIS 943 (Ill. Ct. App. May 11, 2017) ("The purpose of section 155 is to provide a remedy to insureds who encounter unnecessary difficulties resulting from an insurance company's vexatious and unreasonable refusal to honor its contract with the insured. Section 155 was intended to make lawsuits by policyholders economically feasible and to punish insurers. Further, by holding insurance companies responsible for the expense resulting from an insured's efforts to prosecute claims, section 155 discourages insurance companies from exploiting their superior financial position and vexatiously failing to perform legitimate contractual obligations."); *Charter Props. v. Rockford Mut. Ins. Co.*, 119 N.E.3d 15 (Ill. Ct. App. 2018) (finding evidence of improper claims practices, such as a failure to provide a written explanation for a denial or to complete the investigation and determine liability in the prescribed time period is "relevant and tends to support a section 155 claim") ("Plaintiff's expert's opinion comports with common sense that an insurer owes a duty of good faith and fair dealing to provide an estimate so the insured can proceed knowing the scope of coverage."). 215 ILCS 5/155 provides as follows: "In any action by or against a company wherein there is in issue the liability of a company on a policy or policies of insurance or the amount of the loss payable thereunder, or for an unreasonable delay in settling a claim, and it appears to the court that such action or delay is vexatious and unreasonable, the court may allow as part of the taxable costs in the action reasonable attorney fees, other costs, plus an amount not to exceed any one of the following amounts: (a) 60% of the amount which the court or jury finds such party is entitled to recover against the company, exclusive of all costs; (b) $60,000; (c) the excess of the amount which the court or jury finds such party is entitled to recover, exclusive of costs, over the amount, if any, which the company offered to pay in settlement of the claim prior to the action."

Addressing third-party bad faith, the Supreme Court of Illinois stated that "[t]he duty of an insurance provider to settle arises when a claim has been made against the insured and there is a reasonable probability of recovery in excess of policy limits and a reasonable probability of a finding of liability against the insured." *Haddick ex rel. Griffith v. Valor Ins.*, 763 N.E.2d 299, 304 (Ill. 2001); *see also R.C. Wegman Constr. Co. v. Admiral Ins. Co.*, 629 F.3d 724 (7th Cir. 2011) (applying Illinois law) (finding that insured stated claim that its insurer breached implied duty of good faith when insurer did not notify insured that a judgment in excess of limits was a nontrivial probability in time for insured to have placed excess insurer on notice); *Founders Ins. Co. v. Shaikh*, 937 N.E.2d 1186, 1192 (Ill. Ct. App. 2010) ("A cause of action against an insurer arises if the insurer's refusal to settle a claim within the policy limits amounts to negligence or bad faith."); *McCabe v. Daimier AG*, 948 F. Supp. 2d 1347, 1364 (N.D. Ga. 2013) (applying Illinois law) ("[B]reach of the covenant of good faith and fair dealing is not an independent cause of action under Illinois law except in the narrow context of cases involving an insurer's obligation to settle with a third party who has sued the policy holder.") (citation and internal quotations omitted); *Powell v. Am. Serv. Ins. Co.*, 7 N.E.3d 11 (Ill. Ct. App. 2014) (addressing "what constitutes a sufficient pleading of 'a reasonable probability' as it relates to recovery in excess of the policy limits or a finding of liability against the insured in a third-party action."); *Rogers Cartage Co. v. Travelers Indem. Co.*, 103 N.E. 3d 504 (Ill. Ct. App. 2018) ("Courts consider a number of factors to decide whether an insurer's actions constitute bad faith [failure to settle], including (1) potential for an adverse verdict, (2) potential for damages in excess of policy limits, (3) refusal to negotiate, (4) communication with the insured, (5) adequate investigation and defense, and (6) advice of the insurance company's own adjusters and defense counsel") ("[W]e agree with plaintiffs that an insurer may not overcome section 155 damages by cloaking its bad faith under the guise of a bona fide dispute. The trial court correctly reasoned, 'No Illinois case supports the contention that raising a bona fide dispute over coverage entitles an insurance company to mislead and threaten its insured in an attempt to sabotage settlement negotiations.' Even though Travelers defended Rogers under reservation of rights for a lengthy period of time, Travelers' mishandling and mismanagement of settlement negotiations was so egregious that an award under section 155 is warranted."); *Hobbs v. USAA Gen. Indem Co.*, No. 20-262, 2021 U.S. Dist. LEXIS 44686 (S.D. Ill. Mar. 10, 2021) ("Whether an insurer's failure to respond or delayed response constitutes negligence or bad faith depends on the circumstances of the case. The appropriate time for response should take into account such factors as the complexity of the case, the complexity of the offer, and the state of the negotiations (i.e., has the settlement offer come close on the heels of the initial claim, or has the insurer already had significant amounts of investigation time).") (internal citations and quotations omitted).

Indiana: The Supreme Court of Indiana noted that Indiana has long recognized a cause of action in tort for a breach of an insurer's duty to deal in good faith with its insured. *Freidline v. Shelby Ins. Co.*, 774 N.E.2d 37, 40 (Ind. 2002). "[A] good faith dispute about whether the insured has a valid claim will not supply the grounds for recovery in tort for the breach of the obligation to exercise good faith. On the other hand, an insurer that denies liability knowing there is no rational, principled basis for doing so has breached its duty. To prove bad faith, the plaintiff must establish, with clear and convincing evidence, that the insurer had knowledge that there was no legitimate basis for denying liability." *Id.* (citations omitted); *see also Kartman v. State Farm Mut. Auto. Ins. Co.*, 634 F.3d 883, 890 (7th Cir. 2011) (applying Indiana law) ("Under Indiana law, an insurer's obligation of good faith and fair dealing with respect to the discharge of its contractual obligation arises in tort and includes the "obligation to refrain from (1) making an unfounded refusal to pay policy proceeds; (2) causing an unfounded delay in making payment; (3) deceiving the insured; and (4) exercising any unfair advantage to pressure an insured into a settlement of his claim.") (citation and internal quotations omitted); *Ind. Ins. Co. v. Kopetsky*, 11 N.E.3d 508 (Ind. Ct. App. 2014) ("Poor judgment and negligence do not amount to bad faith; the additional element of conscious wrongdoing must also be present. Further, a finding of bad faith requires evidence of a state of mind reflecting dishonest purpose, moral obliquity, furtive design, or ill will."); *Villasat Winding Ridge v. State*

Farm Fire & Cas. Co., 942 F.3d 824 (7th Cir. 2019) ("The mere fact that State Farm's initial estimate was less than the award does not suggest culpability. At best, it may suggest that State Farm's first inspection was inadequate. But this alone does not constitute bad faith."); *Travelers Indem. Co. v. Johnson*, 440 F. Supp. 3d 980 (N.D. Ind. 2020) (discussion of the history of Indiana's bad faith law). The Indiana Court of Appeal has clarified that an insurer owes a duty of good faith and fair dealing to an insured who is not the policyholder on a contract of insurance. *Schmit v. Allstate Prop. & Cas. Ins. Co.*, 141 N.E.3d 1251 (Ind. Ct. App. 2020) ("[W]e observe that no published Indiana Supreme Court or Court of Appeals case has squarely held that an insurer does not owe a duty of good faith and fair dealing to an insured, named or unnamed, who is not the policyholder. To the extent that the cases mentioned in the trial court's order may suggest that no such duty exists, we believe that such a proposition is untenable and unjust.").

Turning to third-party bad faith, in *Catt v. Affirmative Insurance Co.*, No. 08-243, 2009 U.S. Dist. LEXIS 37443 (N.D. Ind. Apr. 30, 2009), the Northern District of Indiana noted a split in Indiana law over the appropriate standard for third-party bad faith. Without taking a position, the court cited support for a standard that the insured must prove that the insurer acted with a "dishonest purpose, moral obliquity, furtive design, or ill will." (citation omitted). The *Catt* Court also cited support for the "fiduciary duty standard" or "negligence and/or bad faith" standard. *See also Robertson v. Med. Assurance Co., Inc.*, No. 2:13-CV-107-JD, 2014 U.S. Dist. LEXIS 46010 (N.D. Ind. Apr. 3, 2014) (noting that Indiana law is unsettled as to whether common law permits a third party to assert an insured's bad faith claim against its insurer through the doctrine of equitable subrogation), *certified question accepted by* 11 N.E.3d 913 (Ind. Jun. 30, 2014) (*rendered moot*, 2015 Ind. LEXIS 434 (Ind. May 19, 2015)); *Woodruff v. Am. Family Mut. Ins. Co.*, No. 12-00859, 2014 U.S. Dist. LEXIS 62038 (S.D. Ind. May 5, 2014) ("There is a dispute of fact regarding the inferences that could be drawn from these facts, and a reasonable factfinder could infer that American Family's refusal to settle for the policy limits, or to offer even its reserve during mediation, was unreasonable and a breach of their duty to deal with Mr. Key in good faith by not giving adequate consideration to his potential financial exposure at trial, and whether American Family placed its interests over that of its insured. . . . It has long been recognized in Indiana that insurance companies have the right to assert a good faith defense to liability, and even the right to fail in that defense. However, the Court agrees that insurers should not have an unfettered right to 'gamble' with insureds' money, and it is for the trier of fact to determine whether, under the circumstances, American Family's gamble was unreasonable.") ("[T]o recover actual damages in an excess judgment case, regardless of whether American Family attempts to distinguish a 'bad faith' claim from 'breach of duty to deal in good faith,' the insured (or in this case, the Trustee) does not need to meet the same standard of proof as is required for punitive damages [clear and convincing evidence]."); *Cincinnati Ins. Co. v. Selective Ins. Co. of Am.*, No. 18-00956, 2021 U.S. Dist. LEXIS 36360 (S.D. Ind. Feb. 25, 2021) ("[T]he Indiana Supreme Court has not held that there is no cause of action for negligent failure to settle a claim, nor has it expressly disavowed *Certain Underwriters [of Lloyd's & Companies v. Gen. Acc. Ins. Co. of Am.*, 909 F.2d 228 (7th Cir. 1990)]'s view that Indiana does recognize this cause of action.").

Iowa: The Supreme Court of Iowa held that "to establish a claim for first-party bad faith, the insured must prove two facts: (1) that the insurer had no reasonable basis for denying benefits under the policy and, (2) the insurer knew, or had reason to know, that its denial was without basis. The first element is objective, the second subjective. If a claim is fairly debatable, the insurer is entitled to debate it, whether the debate concerns a matter of fact or law. Whether a claim is fairly debatable is appropriately decided by the court as a matter of law." *United Fire & Cas. Co. v. Shelly Funeral Home, Inc.*, 642 N.W.2d 648, 657 (Iowa 2002) (citations and internal quotation omitted); *see also Weitz Co., LLC v. Lloyd's of London*, 574 F.3d 885, 892 (8th Cir. 2009) (applying Iowa law) ("However, [b]ad faith may be inferred from a flawed or inadequate investigation by the insurer. As such, [i]t is appropriate, in applying the test, to determine whether a claim was properly investigated and whether the results of the investigation were subjected to a reasonable evaluation and review.") (citations and internal quotations omitted) (alteration in original); *Villarreal v. United Fire & Cas. Co.*, 873 N.W.2d 714 (Iowa 2016) (discussing several differences between a breach of contract and bad-faith claim -- calling it a "different animal" – which involves the knowing failure to exercise an honest and informed judgment); *Van Der Weide v. Cincinnati Ins. Co.*, No. 14-4100, 2017 U.S. Dist. LEXIS 101735 (N.D. Iowa June 30, 2017) (failure to investigate can lead to an inference of bad faith); *Luigi's Inc. v. United Fire & Cas. Co.*, 959 N.W.2d 401 (Iowa 2021) ("[T]o establish bad faith [the insured] must do more than show the investigation wasn't as 'thorough or all-encompassing' as [the insured] would have liked.") (The insurer "had no obligation to disregard the opinion of its own expert in favor of the insured's expert's opinion"); *Thornton v. Am. Interstate Ins. Co.*, 940 N.W.2d 1 (Iowa 2020) (addressing bad faith in the worker's compensation context and discussing Iowa bad faith law in general).

In the third-party bad faith context, the Supreme Court of Iowa stated: "If the insurer has exercised good faith in its dealings with the insured and if the settlement proposal has been fully and fairly considered and decided against, based upon an honest belief that the action could be defeated or the judgment held within the policy limits, and in which respect ... counsel have honestly expressed their conclusion, the insurer cannot be held liable [for an excess verdict] even though there is a mistake of judgment in arriving at its conclusion." *Johnson v. Am. Family Mut. Ins. Co.*, 674 N.W.2d 88, 90 (Iowa 2004) (quoting *Henke v. Iowa Home Mut. Cas. Co.*, 97 N.W.2d 168, 173 (Iowa 1959)); *Walter v. Grinnell Mut. Reinsurance Co.*, 734 N.W.2d 486 (Iowa Ct. App. 2007) ("[T]he reasonableness of an insurer's rejection of a settlement offer within policy limits must be judged from the point of view of one who is exposed to the entire risk. That standard differs from the first-party bad-faith test whether a claim is fairly debatable.").

Kansas: The Supreme Court of Kansas held that the tort of bad faith is not recognized in Kansas. *Spencer v. Aetna Life & Cas. Ins. Co.*, 611 P.2d 149, 158 (Kan. 1980). The *Spencer* Court reached this decision on the basis that "[t]he legislature has provided several remedies for an aggrieved insured and has dealt with the question of good faith first party claims. Statutory law does not indicate the legislature intended damages for emotional suffering to be recoverable by an aggrieved insured through a tort of bad faith. Where the legislature has provided such detailed and effective remedies, we find it undesirable for us to expand those remedies by judicial decree." *Id.; see also Payless Shoesource, Inc. v. Travelers Cos., Inc.*, 569 F. Supp. 2d 1189, 1200 (D. Kan. 2008) ("[A] party may still assert other types of tort actions against his or her insurer, such as fraud or misrepresentation."), *aff'd*, 585 F.3d 1366 (10th Cir. 2009); *Classico, LLC v. United Fire & Cas. Co.*, 386 P.3d 529 (Kan. Ct. App. 2016) ("In its amended petition and in the pretrial order, Classico acknowledged that the tort of bad faith was not recognized in Kansas but asserted that it was challenging the holding in *Spencer* because Kansas did not have sufficient statutory remedies to protect the insured. Our Supreme Court has given no indication that it is abandoning the position taken in *Spencer*.").

In the third-party bad faith context, the Supreme Court of Kansas rejected the decisions of other courts that have held that an insurer is liable for an excess verdict only if it fails to exercise good faith in considering settlement offers within the policy limits. *Bollinger v. Nuss*, 449 P.2d 502, 508 (Kan. 1969). Instead the court adopted a more stringent standard, holding that "[p]ublic policy dictates that the insured's interests be adequately [protected], and we believe this may be best accomplished by holding that both due care and good faith are required of the insurer in reaching the decision not to settle." *Id.* "Something more than mere error of judgment is necessary to constitute bad faith. The company cannot be required to predict with exactitude the results of a trial; nor does the company act in bad faith where it honestly believes, and has cause to believe, that any probable liability will be less than policy limits." *Id.* at 514; *see also Associated Wholesale Grocers, Inc. v. Americold Corp.*, 934 P.2d 65, 90 (Kan. 1997) ("[A]n insurance company should not be required to settle a claim when there is a good faith question as to whether there is coverage under its insurance policy."); *Brockmann v. Bd. of Cnty. Comm'rs of Shawnee*, Nos. 09-3042, 09-3051, 2010 U.S. App. LEXIS 25073 (10th Cir. Dec. 8, 2010) (applying Kansas law) ("[E]ven if General Casualty had acted in bad faith, the refusal to defend was not a factor in the excess judgment, and an insurer is not liable for an excess judgment without a showing that the excess judgment is traceable to an insurer's bad faith refusal to defend."); *Kannaday v. Ball*, 631 Fed. Appx. 635 (10th Cir. 2015) (listing the following factors in determining whether insurer's failure to settle was in bad faith: "(1) the strength of the injured claimant's case on the issues of liability and damages; (2) attempts by the insurer to induce the insured to contribute to a settlement; (3) failure of the insurer to properly investigate the circumstances so as to ascertain the evidence against the insured; (4) the insurer's rejection of advice of its own attorney or agent; (5) failure of the insurer to inform the insured of a compromise offer; (6) the amount of financial risk to which each party is exposed in the event of a refusal to settle; (7) the fault of the insured in inducing the insurer's rejection of the compromise offer by misleading it as to the facts; and (8) any other factors tending to establish or negate bad faith on the part of the insurer.") (quoting *Bollinger*); *Blann v. Rogers*, 22 F. Supp. 3d 1169 (D. Kan. 2014) (setting forth a detailed discussion of the *Bollinger* factors in finding that insurer's failure to settle was in bad faith); *Progressive Northwestern Ins. Co. v. Gant*, 957 F.3d 1144 (10th Cir. 2020) (predicting that the Kansas Supreme Court would not find an insurer in breach of the duty of good faith for failing to "investigate and disclose information about their insurance coverage with other companies"); *Gruber v. Estate of Marshall*, 482 P.3d 612 (Kan. Ct. App. Jan. 22, 2021) (finding insurer "acted negligently and in bad faith because it failed to offer the voluntary settlement as required by its policy, not because of a general duty to settle").

Kentucky: Under Kentucky law, "[b]ad faith claims generally fall into two categories: (1) first-party bad faith, where the insured sues the insurer for failing to use good faith to resolve the insured's claim, and (2) third-party bad faith, where the victim of the insured's tortious behavior sues the insurer for failure to reach a settlement with the victim in good faith." *Shaheen v. Progressive Cas. Ins. Co.*, No. 5:08-CV-00034-R, 2012 U.S. Dist. LEXIS 120475 (W.D. Ky. Aug. 24, 2012) (discussing various discovery standards dependent on which category the claim falls under). The Supreme Court of Kentucky held that "an insured must prove three elements in order to prevail against an insurance company for alleged refusal in bad faith to pay the insured's claim: (1) the insurer must be obligated to pay the claim under the terms of the policy; (2) the insurer must lack a reasonable basis in law or fact for denying the claim; and (3) it must be shown that the insurer either knew there was no reasonable basis for denying the claim or acted with reckless disregard for whether such a basis existed. ... [A]n insurer is ... entitled to challenge a claim and litigate it if the claim is debatable on the law or the facts." *Wittmer v. Jones*, 864 S.W.2d 885, 890 (Ky. 1993) (citation omitted) (addressing requirements for insured to recover for an insurer's alleged bad-faith refusal to pay a claim under the Kentucky Unfair Claims Settlement Practices Act); *see also Crutchfield ex rel. Crutchfield v. Transamerica Occidental Life Ins. Co.*, 894 F. Supp. 2d 971 (W.D. Ky. 2012) ("A single test under Kentucky law exists for the merits of bad-faith claims, whether brought by a first- or third-party claimant or brought under common law or statute.") (citation and internal quotations omitted); *Scott v. Deerbrook Ins. Co.*, 714 F. Supp. 2d 670, 676 (E.D. Ky. 2010) ("[B]efore a cause of action for violation of the UCSPA exists, there must be evidence sufficient to warrant punitive damages. Punitive damages are warranted where there is proof of bad faith sufficient for the jury to conclude that there was conduct that was outrageous, because of the defendant's evil motive, or his reckless indifference to the rights of others.") (citations and internal quotes omitted); *Exel, Inc. v. Liberty Mut. Fire Ins. Co.*, No. 2010–CA–001148-MR, 2011 Ky. App. Unpub. LEXIS 382 (Ky. Ct. App. May 6, 2011) ("To establish a private cause of action for a claim of bad faith under the UCSPA, one cannot rely merely upon a 'technical violation' of the UCSPA. ... Indeed, a condition precedent to bringing a statutory bad faith action is that the claimant was damaged by reason of the violation of the statute. Absent actual damage, there can be no cause of action premised upon an allegation of bad faith under the UCSPA.") (citations and internal quotes omitted); *Hollaway v. Direct Gen. Ins. Co. of Miss.*, 497 S.W.3d 733 (Ky. 2016) ("Despite the relatively straightforward directives in the KUCSPA regarding insurers' behavior in the course of investigating and settling claims, Kentucky law still imposes a tall burden of proof on plaintiffs seeking to recover on a theory of bad faith.") (explaining that the third element of *Wittmer* requires "evidence that the insurer's conduct was outrageous, or because of his reckless indifference to the rights of others"); *Caudill v. N.H. Ins. Co.*, No. 2014-CA-000921, 2016 Ky. App. Unpub. LEXIS 393 (Ky. Ct. App. July 10, 2016) ("The evidentiary threshold is high indeed. Evidence must demonstrate that an insurer has engaged in outrageous conduct toward its insured. Furthermore, the conduct must be driven by evil motives or by an indifference to its insureds' rights. Absent such evidence of egregious behavior, the tort claim predicated on bad faith may not proceed to a jury. Evidence of mere negligence or failure to pay a claim in timely fashion will not suffice to support a claim for bad faith. Inadvertence, sloppiness, or tardiness will not suffice; instead, the element of malice or flagrant malfeasance must be shown."); *Ind. Ins. Co. v. Demetre*, 527 S.W.3d 12 (Ky. 2017) (finding that an insured under a liability policy is entitled to bring a bad faith action) ("The essence of liability insurance is that the insured is indemnified in the event of a third-party claim and, if necessary, has counsel to represent his or her interest in litigation. A liability insured who seeks these benefits owed under a policy of insurance is most assuredly making his or her own claim."); *Messer v. Universal Underwriters Ins. Co.*, 598 S.W.3d 578 (Ky. Ct. App. 2019) (holding that "reserves do not evidence an admission of coverage, fault, or liability by the insurer").

As to third-party bad faith for failure to settle, the Supreme Court of Kentucky held that "the 'various factors' to be considered in determining the existence of bad faith are (1) whether the plaintiff offered to settle for the policy limits or less, (2) whether the insured made a demand for settlement on the insurer, and (3) the probability of recovery and of a jury verdict which would exceed the policy limits." *Motorists Mut. Ins. Co. v. Glass*, 996 S.W.2d 437, 451 (Ky. 1997) (citation and internal quotation omitted); *Caudill, supra* (reciting elements from *Glass* and noting that "[i]t is not bad faith to refuse a demand to settle for a sum in excess of the policy limits"); *Watson v. United States Liab. Ins. Co.*, No. 2018-000475, 2019 Ky. App. LEXIS 94 (Ky. Ct. App. May 24, 2019) ("[T]hird-party claims against insurers generally cannot be maintained, and thus cannot accrue, until after: (1) a judgment fixing liability against the insured has been entered; or (2) the insured becomes legally obligated to pay pursuant to terms of the insurance contract."); *Mosley v. Arch Spec. Ins. Co.*, No. 2018-0586, 2021 Ky. LEXIS 148 (Ky. June 17, 2021) (rejecting application of "fairly debatable standard in third-party bad faith actions) (noting a "paucity of guidance in [Kentucky's] third-party-bad-faith precedent").

Louisiana: A Louisiana statute provides: "An insurer, including but not limited to a foreign line and surplus line insurer, owes to his insured a duty of good faith and fair dealing. The insurer has an affirmative duty to adjust claims fairly and promptly and to make a reasonable effort to settle claims with the insured or the claimant, or both. Any insurer who breaches these duties shall be liable for any damages sustained as a result of the breach." LA. REV. STAT. ANN. § 22:1973A. Section 22:1973B sets forth a list of acts which, if knowingly committed or performed by an insurer, constitute a breach of the insurer's duties imposed in Subsection A. *See also Reed v. State Farm Mut. Auto. Ins. Co.*, 857 So. 2d 1012, 1021 (La. 2003) (addressing an "arbitrary, capricious, or without probable cause" standard to prove a statutory violation) ("arbitrary" is defined as an act "based on random choice or personal whim, rather than reason or system"; "capricious" means "given to sudden and unaccountable changes in behavior"); *Buffman Inc. v. Lafayette Co.*, 36 So. 3d 1004, 1024 (La. Ct. App. 2010) ("Further, the phrase 'arbitrary, capricious, or without probable cause' is synonymous with 'vexatious,' and a 'vexatious failure to pay' is one that is 'unjustified, without reasonable or probable cause or excuse.' These phrases describe an insurer whose willful refusal to pay is not accompanied by a good-faith defense.") (citations omitted), *abrogated in part by Durio v. Horace Mann Ins. Co.*, 74 So. 3d 1159 (La. 2011) (addressing calculation of penalties for violation of duty of good faith and fair dealing); *Wood v. Allstate Indem. Co.*, 15-2327, 2017 U.S. Dist. LEXIS 6999 (W.D. La. Jan. 18, 2017) ("Louisiana law provides a penalty for an insurer's failure to pay a claim within thirty days after it has received satisfactory proof of loss if the failure is arbitrary, capricious, or without probable cause. LA. R.S. § 22:1892(B)(1). It also provides that an insurer owes a duty of good faith and fair dealing to an insured and provides a penalty for the insurer's failure to pay a claim within sixty days after receiving satisfactory proof of loss if the failure was arbitrary, capricious, or without probable cause. §§ 22:1973(A), (B)(6), (C). These two statutes prohibit 'virtually identical' conduct, the primary difference being the time periods allowed for payment."); *Cooper v. Farmers Ins. Exch.*, 210 So. 3d 829 (La. Ct. App. 2016) ("[P]enalties and attorney's fees are inappropriate when the insurer has a reasonable basis to defend the claim and was acting in good faith reliance on that defense. This is especially true when there is a reasonable and legitimate question as to the extent and causation of a claim; bad faith should not be inferred from an insurer's failure to pay within the statutory time limits when such reasonable doubt exists."); *Jones v. Gov't Emples. Ins. Co.*, 220 So. 3d 915 (La. Ct. App. 2017) ("We cannot say that the delay in making tender while GEICO litigated the application of Georgia law as a coverage defense rises to the level of arbitrary and capricious conduct so as to warrant the imposition of penalties and attorney fees…[T]he fact that the appeal of the choice of law issue resulted in a 2-1 split decision, with one judge dissenting, demonstrates the potential merit and reasonableness of GEICO's position. The fact that a majority disagreed with GEICO on the choice of law issue is not evidence that GEICO's position was baseless or made in bad faith."); *Lamar Adver. Co. v. Zurich Am. Ins. Co.*, No. 18-1060, 2021 U.S. Dist. LEXIS 69754 (M.D. La. Apr. 12, 2021) (finding that an insured has a cause of action for its insurer's post-litigation conduct) (noting there "is disagreement on the issue").

In the context of third-party bad faith, the Supreme Court of Louisiana held that "when an insurer has made a thorough investigation and the evidence developed in the investigation is such that reasonable minds could differ over the liability of the insured, the insurer has the right to choose to litigate the claim, unless other factors, such as a vast difference between the policy limits and the insured's total exposure, dictate a decision to settle the claim." *Smith v. Audubon Ins. Co.*, 679 So. 2d 372, 377 (La. 1996). "The determination of good or bad faith in an insurer's deciding to proceed to trial involves the weighing of such factors, among others, as the probability of the insured's liability, the extent of the damages incurred by the claimant, the amount of the policy limits, the adequacy of the insurer's investigation, and the openness of communications between the insurer and the insured." *Id.* In *Kelly v. State Farm Fire & Cas. Co.*, 169 So. 3d 328 (La. 2015) the Supreme Court of Louisiana held that "an insurer can be found liable for a bad-faith failure-to-settle claim under La. R.S. 22:1973(A), notwithstanding that the insurer never received a firm settlement offer." *Id.* at 341. "[W]e see no practical reason why the insurer's obligation to act in good faith should be made subject to the tenuous possibility that an insurer will receive a firm settlement offer. Instead, the insurer's obligation to act in good faith is triggered by knowledge of the particular situation, which knowledge the insurer has an affirmative duty to gather during the claims process." *Id. See Richard v. USAA Cas. Ins. Co.*, No. 17-00175, 2019 U.S. Dist. LEXIS 3703 (M.D. La. Jan. 8, 2019) ("Conducting a 'thorough investigation' [as discussed in *Audubon*] is only the first step that an insurance company must take in order to discharge its duties to its insured when making the determination to litigate. Should there be other mitigating factors, such as those delineated in *Kelly*, a court may conclude that even if a thorough investigation was completed, or even in light of the results of such investigation, the insurance company still should not have proceeded to litigation.").

Maine: The Supreme Judicial Court of Maine refused to adopt an independent tort action for bad faith. *Marquis v. Farm Family Mut. Ins. Co.*, 628 A.2d 644, 652

(Me. 1993). The court reasoned that "[i]n view of the broad range of compensatory damages available in a contract action and in view of the statutorily provided remedies of interest on the judgment and attorney fees, we believe sufficient motivation presently exists to stifle an insurer's bad faith tendencies without the further imposition of the specter of punitive damages under an independent tort cause of action." *Id.* (citation and internal quotation omitted); *see also* Me. Rev. Stat. tit. 24, § 2436-A (listing conduct by an insurer that gives rise to an action by an insured for damages, costs and disbursements, reasonable attorney's fees, and interest on damages at the rate of 1½ percent per month); *Perry v. Hanover Ins. Grp., Inc.*, No. 20-301, 2021 U.S. Dist. LEXIS 22877 (D. Me. Feb. 8, 2021) (finding that, "under Maine law, a violation of the obligation of good faith and fair dealing cannot sustain an independent cause of action").

Turning to third-party bad faith, "[t]he existence of a cause of action in Maine for damages for an insurer's bad faith failure to settle within policy limits is unsettled." *State Fire & Cas. Co. v. Haley*, 916 A.2d 952, 956 (Me. 2007) (Dana, J., dissenting) (discussing cases from 1899 and 1950 and concluding that any conflict should be resolved "by expressly declaring that Maine law imposes upon insurers a good faith duty to settle within the limits of a policy when faced with the possibility of a substantial excess judgment against the insured").

Maryland: Historically, Maryland did not recognize a tort action against an insurer for bad faith failure to pay a first-party insurance claim. *Johnson v. Fed. Kemper Ins. Co.*, 536 A.2d 1211, 1213 (Md. Ct. Spec. App. 1988). "Because [a first-party claim] … involves a claim by the insured against the insurer, rather than a claim by a third party against both the insurer and insured, there is no conflict of interest situation requiring the law to impose any fiduciary duties on the insurer. Instead, the situation is a traditional dispute between the parties to a contract." *Id.* at 1213; *see also Harris v. Keystone Ins. Co.*, No. CCB-13-2839, 2013 U.S. Dist. LEXIS 167942 (D. Md. Nov. 26, 2013) (indicating that Maryland does not recognize a tort claim based on insurer's bad faith investigation of a first-party claim). However, in 2007, Maryland enacted a statute that "provides that a plaintiff can recover expenses and litigation costs, including reasonable attorneys' fees, as well as interest on those costs, in an action seeking 'to determine coverage that exists under [an] insurance policy,' if the plaintiff can show that 'the insurer failed to act in good faith' with respect to the insurance claim." Md. Code Ann., Ins. § 27-1001(e)(2)(ii); Md. Code Ann., Cts. & Jud. Proc. § 3-1701(d)(1)–(2). The statute defines "good faith" as making "an informed judgment based on honesty and diligence supported by evidence the insurer knew or should have known at the time the insurer made a decision on a claim." *Schwaber Trust Two v. Hartford Accident & Indem. Co.*, 636 F. Supp. 2d 481, 484–85 (D. Md. 2009); MD. CODE ANN., CTS. & JUD. PROC. § 3-1701(a)(4). However, no such action may be brought in court unless certain administrative requirements, as set out in MD. CODE ANN., INS. § 27-1001, are first satisfied. The administrative process can itself result in an award of damages. *See also Thompson v. State Farm Mut. Auto. Ins. Co.*, 9 A.3d 112 (Md. Ct. Spec. App. 2010) (addressing generally procedural issues under the relatively new statute); *Charter Oak Fire Co. v. Am. Capital Ltd.*, No. 09-0100, 2017 U.S. Dist. LEXIS 122156 (D. Md. Aug. 3, 2017), *aff'd* 760 Fed. Appx. 224 (4th Cir. 2019) ("Assessing whether an insurer acted in good faith requires an evaluation of the insurer's efforts to obtain information related to the loss, accurately and honestly assess this information, and support its conclusion regarding coverage with evidence obtained or reasonably available. This 'totality of the circumstances' standard has been summarized as requiring an insurer to meet standards of reasonable investigation, honest assessment, and reasonable explanation. The following factors are considered when determining if an insurer meets the aforementioned standards: [(1)] efforts or measures taken by the insurer to resolve the coverage dispute promptly or in such a way as to limit any potential prejudice to the insureds; [(2)] the substance of the coverage dispute or the weight of legal authority on the coverage issue; [and] [(3)] the insurer's diligence and thoroughness in investigating the facts specifically pertinent to coverage."); *Bierman Family Farm, LLC v. United Farm Family Ins. Co.*, 265 F. Supp. 3d 633 (D. Md. 2017) (complaint failed to allege a plausible claim for bad faith because it lacked "any facts indicative of Defendant's bad faith beyond the initial breach of the insurance policy contract") ("It is well-settled under Maryland law that an insured claiming that an insurer has failed to pay policy benefits may only pursue contract remedies."); *Schwartz v. Travelers Prop. Cas. Ins. Co.*, No. 20-1919, 2021 U.S. Dist. LEXIS 52260 (D. Md. Mar. 19, 2021) (noting that, in assessing the totality of the circumstances factors, courts consider "the insurer's efforts to obtain information related to the loss, accurately and honestly assess this information, and support its conclusion regarding coverage with evidence obtained or reasonably available").

Maryland recognizes a bad faith cause of action for an insurer's failure to settle a claim within policy limits. *Mesmer v. Md. Auto. Ins. Fund*, 725 A.2d 1053, 1062 (Md. 1999) ("[F]or an insurer to measure up to the good faith test, its action in refusing to settle must consist of an informed judgment based on honesty and diligence. Furthermore, the insurer's negligence, if any there be, is relevant in determining whether or not it acted in good faith.") (quoting *State Farm Mut. Auto. Ins. v. White*, 236 A.2d 269, 273 (Md. 1967)); *Cook v. Nationwide Ins. Co.*, No. 13-882, 2013 U.S. Dist. LEXIS 143237 (D. Md. Oct. 3, 2013) ("[T]he presence of one or more of the following acts or circumstances may affect the 'good faith' posture of the insurer: the severity of the plaintiff's injuries giving rise to the likelihood of a verdict greatly in excess of the policy limits; lack of proper and adequate investigation of the circumstances surrounding the accident; lack of skillful evaluation of plaintiff's disability; failure of the insurer to inform the insured of a compromise offer within or near the policy limits; pressure by the insurer on the insured to make a contribution towards a compromise settlement within the policy limits, as an inducement to settlement by the insurer; and actions which demonstrate a greater concern for the insurer's monetary interests than the financial risk attendant to the insured's predicament.") (quoting *White*).

Massachusetts: A Massachusetts statute lists several prohibited unfair claim settlement practices, including refusing to pay claims without conducting a reasonable investigation based upon all available information and failing to effectuate prompt, fair, and equitable settlements of claims in which liability has become reasonably clear. MASS. ANN. GEN. LAWS ch. 176D, § 3(9)(d), (f); *see also Hopkins v. Liberty Mut. Ins. Co.*, 750 N.E.2d 943, 947–48 (Mass. 2001) (addressing MASS. ANN. GEN. LAWS ch. 176D, § 3(9)); *Gore v. Arbella Mut. Ins. Co.*, 932 N.E.2d 837, 845 (Mass. Ct. App. 2010) ("The statute protects the interests of both claimants and insureds against unfair insurance claim settlement practices. With respect to claimants, it was enacted to encourage the settlement of insurance claims ... and discourage insurers from forcing claimants into unnecessary litigation to obtain relief.") (citation and internal quotes omitted); *Chery v. Metro. Prop. & Cas. Ins. Co.*, 948 N.E.2d 1278, 1280–81 (Mass. Ct. App. 2011) ("[T]here is support in the summary judgment record for Chery's claim that Metropolitan's conduct caused her emotional distress, not only as a result of having to commence litigation but also out of concern for the negative effect her unpaid medical bills might have on her creditworthiness. Metropolitan's efforts to discount these allegations as insufficient to establish quantifiable damages for intentional infliction of emotional distress are unavailing. A plaintiff seeking redress under c. 93A is not required to show a quantifiable amount of actual damages as an element of her claim. Rather, a plaintiff is required to show only that she suffered some loss caused by the defendant's allegedly unlawful conduct."); *Silva v. Steadfast Insurance Company*, 35 N.E.3d 401 (Mass. Ct. App. 2015) ("General Laws c. 93A, the Massachusetts Consumer Protection Act, protects consumers and businesses alike from unfair business practices that are 'immoral, unethical, oppressive, or unscrupulous; or within the bounds of some statutory, common-law or other established concept of unfairness.' Similarly, [G. L.] c. 176D, § 3, prohibits 'unfair or deceptive acts or practices in the business of insurance,' and § 3(9) enumerates acts and omissions that constitute unfair claim settlement practices." However, c. 176D, § 3, does not itself provide a private right of action. To proceed against an insurer who has violated G. L. c. 176D, § 3(9), a plaintiff must bring a claim under G. L. c. 93A, § 9 or § 11."); *Graf v. Hospitality Mut. Ins. Co.*, No. HDCV2010-00429, 2015 Mass. Super. LEXIS 80 (Mass. Super. Ct. June 29, 2015) ("The law in regard to an insurer's obligation to settle liability claims is well established in Massachusetts. G.L.c. 93A, § 2(a) states that 'unfair or deceptive acts or practices in the conduct of any trade or commerce are hereby declared unlawful.' G.L.c. 176D, § 3, in turn, prohibits 'unfair or deceptive acts or practices in the business of insurance, including, in subsection 9(f), the failure 'to effect prompt, fair and equitable settlements of claims in which liability has become reasonably clear.' The Supreme Judicial Court has declared that the former statute incorporates the latter and, therefore, an insurer that fails to effectuate a prompt, fair and equitable settlement of claims in which liability has become reasonably clear, by definition, has violated the prohibitions in [c. 93A] against the commission of unfair or deceptive acts or practices. Taken together, c. 93A and c. 176D require an insurer . . . promptly to put a fair and reasonable offer on the table when liability and damages become clear, either within the thirty-day period set forth in G.L.c. 93A, § 9(3), or as soon thereafter as liability and damages make themselves apparent."); *Silva v. Norfolk & Dedham Mut. Fire Ins. Co.*, 75 N.E.3d 1132 (Mass. Ct. App. 2017) (reciting rule that "[t]o determine when an insured's liability became 'reasonably clear' an objective test is used. The fact finder determines 'whether a reasonable person, with knowledge of the relevant facts and law, would probably have concluded, for good reason, that the insure[d] was liable to the plaintiff'") (concluding that the insurer did not act in bad faith because "[a]lthough fault for the accident may have been clear, the 'damages attributable to [McQuinn] … [were] still the subject of good faith disagreement'"); *River Farm Realty Trust v. Farm Family Cas. Ins. Co.*, 943 F.3d 27 (1st Cir. 2019) ("Disparity in amounts offered and amount awarded may, of course, be relevant, but cannot be subject to per se rules, and depends on the totality of the facts.") (noting that the "mere fact that the initial opening estimate, likely made before all the damage manifested itself, was less than what [the insurer] later offered does not mean that it was outside the scope of reasonableness…The passage of time between initial estimate and final award and the nature of the damage are also relevant."). Mass. Ann. Gen. Laws ch. 93A is complex and has been the subject of numerous judicial decisions. Resort to the statute and case law is recommended.

In the third-party bad faith context, the Supreme Judicial Court of Massachusetts adopted the following test to determine if an insurer is liable for bad faith for failure to settle a claim within policy limits: "The test is not whether a reasonable insurer might have settled the case within the policy limits, but rather whether no reasonable insurer would have failed to settle the case within the policy limits." *Hartford Cas. Ins. Co. v. N.H. Ins. Co.*, 628 N.E.2d 14, 18 (Mass. 1994). *See also Anderson v. Am. Int'l Group, Inc.*, No. MICV2003-01212-B, 2014 Mass. Super. LEXIS 48 (Mass. Super. Ct. April 8, 2014) ("This test requires the insured (or its excess insurer) to prove that the plaintiff in the underlying action would have settled the claim within the policy limits and that, assuming the insurer's unlimited exposure (that is, viewing the question from the point of view of the insured), no reasonable insurer would have refused the settlement offer or would have refused to respond to the offer."); *Boyle v. Zurich American Insurance Company*, 36 N.E.3d 1229 (Mass. 2015) ("The judge found, in essence, that although Zurich blundered badly in its reading of the legal landscape, its unsuccessful efforts to settle the Boyles' claims as C&N's assignees represented a negligent miscalculation, rather than 'conduct involving dishonesty, fraud, deceit or misrepresentation.' Similarly, the judge's finding that Zurich's settlement efforts, while misguided, were made in good faith, entails the conclusion that Zurich's conduct was not 'willful or knowing' in the sense necessary to warrant an award of multiple damages."); *Williamson-Green v. Interstate Fire & Cas. Co.*, No. 1684 CV 03141, 2017 Mass. Super. LEXIS 70 (Mass. Super. Ct. May 26, 2017) ("If an insurer breaches its duty to settle a claim, the insured party may recover from the insurer for 'all losses' that were 'foreseeable consequences' of the failure to settle, even if those losses exceed what is covered by the insurance policy...The losses recoverable by the insured include all consequential damages caused by the insurer's breach of its duty to settle; the insured's recovery is not limited to compensatory damages awarded against it in the underlying tort action."); *Rawan v. Continental Cas. Co.*, 483 Mass. 654 (Mass. 2019) ("[T]he statute [G. L. c. 176D, § 3 (9) (f)] has not been interpreted to require the effectuation of settlements as opposed to good faith efforts to effectuate settlement.").

Michigan: Michigan does not recognize an independent tort claim for bad-faith breach of an insurance contract. *Casey v. Auto Owners Ins. Co.*, 729 N.W.2d 277, 286 (Mich. Ct. App. 2006); *see also No Limit Clothing, Inc. v. Allstate Ins. Co.*,

No. 09-13574, 2011 U.S. Dist. LEXIS 2875 (E.D. Mich. Jan. 12, 2011) ("Michigan courts—and federal courts applying Michigan law—have long held that breach of an insurance contract, even if done in bad faith, does not give rise to a separate and independent tort claim. ... Rather, there must exist some tortious conduct wholly independent of the contractual breach.") (citations omitted); *Hall v. State Farm Fire & Cas. Co.*, No. 13-14575, 2014 U.S. Dist. LEXIS 190915 (E.D. Mich. Feb. 10, 2014) ("In this case, the substance of the cause of action for bad-faith handling of an insurance claim is legally indistinguishable from the accompanying cause of action for breach of contract. Therefore, a separate tort action cannot be maintained for the failure to pay under an insurance contract - even if the non-payment is done in bad-faith."); *Andreson v. Progressive Mich. Ins. Co.*, No. 345864, 2019 Mich. App. LEXIS 8152 (Mich. Ct. App. Dec. 19, 2019) ("[O]ur Courts' recognition of a claim for bad faith refusal to settle appears to apply only in situations where the claimant's insurer is defending an action and refuses/neglects to settle *on behalf of* the claimant. Despite being a doubtful position, for purposes of this appeal only we will assume there exists the potential that an action could lie for bad faith in failing or refusing to settle a claim brought against the insurer by its insured.") (ultimately concluding insured failed to present evidence of bad faith) (emphasis in the original).

However, Michigan does recognize a bad faith cause of action for an insurer's failure to settle a claim within policy limits. In *Commercial Union Ins. Co. v. Liberty Mutual Insurance Co.*, 393 N.W.2d 161, 164 (Mich. 1986), the Supreme Court of Michigan described the standard for liability as follows: "Good-faith denials, offers of compromise, or other honest errors of judgment are not sufficient to establish bad faith. Further, claims of bad faith cannot be based upon negligence or bad judgment, so long as the actions were made honestly and without concealment. However, because bad faith is a state of mind, there can be bad faith without actual dishonesty or fraud. If the insurer is motivated by selfish purpose or by a desire to protect its own interests at the expense of its insured's interest, bad faith exists, even though the insurer's actions were not actually dishonest or fraudulent." (citations omitted). The court then set forth twelve factors for the fact finder to consider in deciding whether or not the insurer's failure to settle was in bad faith. *Id.* at 165–66 ("[A] claim of bad faith cannot be based upon negligence or bad judgment if the actions were made honestly and without concealment."). *See also Tibble v. Am. Physicians Capital*, No. 306964, 2014 Mich. App. LEXIS 2088 (Mich. Ct. App. Oct. 28, 2014) ("[A]lthough the trial court erred when it failed to include the words 'arbitrary' and 'intentional' in the instructional definition of bad faith, the error does not require reversal. On balance, the applicable law regarding bad faith was adequately and fairly presented to the jury. AP Capital was not prevented from arguing that its failure to settle did not constitute bad faith, and no expert witness unambiguously testified that bad faith equaled negligence.") (listing the twelve supplemental factors that a fact-finder may consider in determining whether bad faith existed, such as failure to solicit a settlement offer or initiate settlement negotiations when warranted under the circumstances and failure to accept a reasonable compromise offer of settlement when the facts of the case or claim indicate obvious liability and serious injury); *Stryker Corp. v. XL Ins. Am., Inc.*, No. 17-66, 2018 U.S. Dist. LEXIS 140216 (W.D. Mich. Aug. 17, 2018) ("[W]here the insurer exercises control over the settlement of a claim on behalf of the insured, the insurer has a duty to act in such a way that advances the interests of the insured. If an insurer unreasonably or arbitrarily refuses to settle a claim within the policy limits because it is motivated by its own interests rather than the interests of the insured, then the insurer may have acted in bad faith, and may be liable for an amount greater than its policy limit.") (noting "there is no Michigan case law expressly holding that an insurer has a duty to act in good faith when deciding which claim to pay first" but recognizing "such a duty is consistent with longstanding Michigan precedent that a duty of good faith is implied in most contracts") (concluding "there is nothing unusual about extending the duty of good faith to this case, where an insurance contract implicitly gives the insurer discretion to choose the order in which to pay the claims against its insured"); *Trident Fasteners v. Selective Ins. Co.*, No. 19-983, 2021 U.S. Dist. LEXIS 68266 (W.D. Mich. Apr. 8, 2021) (finding that the insured could not argue bad faith because the insured was never sued and "the duties of good faith at issue only come into play after a lawsuit is filed against the insured") ("Selective was therefore acting within its rights when it refused to consent to Tenneco's settlement offer and instead promised to defend Trident.").

Minnesota: Historically, Minnesota did not recognize a cause of action for bad-faith breach of an insurance contract absent an independent tort. *Sather v. State Farm Fire & Cas. Ins. Co.*, No. C3-01-1268, 2002 Minn. App. LEXIS 277 (Minn. Ct. App. Mar. 12, 2002) (citing *Haagenson v. Nat'l Farmers Union Prop. & Cas. Co.*, 277 N.W.2d 648, 652 (Minn. 1979)). "A malicious or bad-faith motive in breaching a contract does not convert a contract action into a tort action." *Haagenson*, 277 N.W.2d at 652. However, in 2008, Minnesota adopted MINN. STAT. § 604.18, which provides, in general, that an insured may be awarded one-half of the amount of its claim recovery that is in excess of the amount offered by the insurer at least ten days prior to trial (up to $250,000), if the insured can show the absence of a reasonable basis for denying the benefits of the insurance policy and that the insurer knew of a lack of a reasonable basis or acted in reckless disregard of the lack of a reasonable basis. Further, the insured may also be awarded its reasonable attorney's fees, not to exceed $100,000, to prove such violation. *See also Friedberg v. Chubb & Son, Inc.*, 800 F. Supp. 2d 1020 (D. Minn. 2011) (addressing § 604.18 in some detail) ("The first prong is an objective standard that asks whether a reasonable insurer would have denied or delayed payment of the claim under the facts and circumstances. Under this prong, courts consider whether the claim was properly investigated and whether the results of the investigation were subjected to reasonable evaluation and review. Whether an insurer has acted reasonably in good or bad faith is measured against what another reasonable insurer would have done in a similar situation. The second prong is subjective and turns on what the insurer knew and when. Knowledge of the lack of a reasonable basis may be inferred and imputed to an insurer where there is reckless indifference to facts or proofs submitted by the insured. But when a claim is fairly debatable, the insurer is entitled to debate it, whether debate concerns a matter of fact or law. Whether a claim is fairly debatable implicates the question whether the facts necessary to evaluate the claim are properly investigated and developed or recklessly ignored and disregarded.") (citations omitted); *Wilbur v. State Farm Mut. Auto. Ins. Co.*, 892 N.W.2d 521 (Minn. 2017) (holding that, under the plain language of Minn. Stat. § 604.18, subd. 3, "proceeds awarded" to an insured are capped by the insurance policy's limit); *Selective Ins. Co. v. Sela*, 413 F. Supp. 3d 861 (D. Minn. 2019) ("For a number of reasons, the Court does not believe that the Minnesota Supreme Court would hold that every contract of insurance contains an implied covenant that imposes a broad duty on insurers to act 'reasonably' or 'properly' in handling claims. Policyholders have been making claims—and insurers have been denying claims—since Minnesota became a state in 1858. The Minnesota Supreme Court and the Minnesota Court of Appeals have issued hundreds of decisions in denial-of-benefits cases. And yet, with one arguable exception [*Western National Mutual Insurance Company v. Prospect Foundry*, No. A17-0992, 2018 Minn. App. Unpub. LEXIS 287 (Minn. Ct. App. Apr. 16, 2018)], neither the Minnesota Supreme Court nor the Minnesota Court of Appeals has ever suggested that the implied covenant of good faith and fair dealing imposes on insurers a broad obligation to act 'reasonably' in handling claims. Indeed, the very reason why the Minnesota Legislature enacted Minn. Stat. § 604.18 in 2008 was because the common law did not provide a cause of action against insurers who acted unreasonably in handling claims.") (rejecting

Prospect Foundry on the basis that "the key language quoted above appears in a three-sentence footnote in an unpublished decision, and the language is dicta"); *Shaw Farm Bureau Prop. & Cas. Ins. Co.*, No. 20-534, 2020 U.S. Dist. LEXIS 112383 (D. Minn. June 26, 2020) ("The Court cannot conclude that Defendant acted in bad faith when there is no controlling legal authority in the relevant jurisdiction interpreting the valued policy statute or similar insurance policy in the manner proposed by Plaintiffs. This is particularly true because courts that have considered the issue in other states have reached contradictory conclusions").

Minnesota recognizes a bad faith cause of action for an insurer's failure to settle a claim within policy limits. *Short v. Dairyland Ins. Co.*, 334 N.W.2d 384, 388 (Minn. 1983) ("The insurer's duty of good faith is breached in situations in which the insured is clearly liable and the insurer refuses to settle within the policy limits and the decision not to settle within the policy limits is not made in good faith and is not based upon reasonable grounds to believe that the amount demanded is excessive."); *see also Am. Family Mut. Ins. Co. v. Donaldson*, No. 12-2855 (PAM/FLN), 2013 U.S. Dist. LEXIS 88942 (D. Minn. June 25, 2013) ("This duty to exercise good faith includes an obligation to view the situation as if there were no policy limits applicable to the claim, and to give equal consideration to the financial exposure of the insured. The duty of good faith is breached when (1) the insured is clearly liable, (2) the insurer refuses to settle within the policy limits, and (3) the insured is personally exposed to a judgment in excess of the policy limits.") (citing *Short*); *Hawkins, Inc. v. Am. Int'l Specialty Lines Ins. Co.*, No. A07–1529, 2008 Minn. App. Unpub. LEXIS 1218 (Minn. Ct. App. Oct. 14, 2008) ("The fiduciary duty that the insurer owes to the insured is measured by the standard of 'good faith,' meaning that the insurer must view the situation as if there were no policy limits applicable to the claim, and … give equal consideration to the financial exposure of the insured.") (citation and internal quotations omitted). When coverage is debatable, the insurer has a right to dispute coverage. *See Trueblood v. MMIC Ins.*, No. 20-6378, 2021 Minn. Dist. LEXIS 73 (Minn. Dist. Ct. Feb. 11, 2021) ("If the insurer in bad faith fails to settle the liability action against its insured within the policy's limits, it is liable for contractual damages measured by the amount of the insured's liability above the policy limits.") (finding no bad faith where "Plaintiff had no liability in excess of the policy limits and did not personally have to pay any money toward the underlying settlement").

Mississippi: The Supreme Court of Mississippi held that punitive damages may not be imposed in "cases in which a carrier is determined to have merely reached an incorrect decision in denying a given claim. The issue of punitive damages should not be submitted to the jury unless the trial court determines that there are jury issues with regard to whether: 1) The insurer lacked an arguable or legitimate basis for denying the claim, *and* 2) The insurer committed a willful or malicious wrong, or acted with gross and reckless disregard for the insured's rights." *Am. Income Life Ins. Co. v. Hollins*, 830 So. 2d 1230, 1239–40 (Miss. 2002) (quoting *State Farm Mut. Auto. Ins. Co. v. Grimes*, 722 So. 2d 637, 641 (Miss. 1998)), *overruled by Mladineo v. Schmidt*, 52 So. 3d 1154, 1166 (Miss. 2010) (overruling *Hollins* to the extent that it contradicts well-settled precedent regarding an insured's duty to read his or her policy); *see also G & B Invs., Inc. v. Henderson In re Evans*, 460 B.R. 848, 901 (Bankr. S.D. Miss. 2011) ("To prevail on its claim for bad faith [delaying full payment], [insured] must establish three elements by clear and convincing evidence. First, [insured] must demonstrate that the claim or obligation was in fact owed. Second, the insured must demonstrate that the insurer has no arguable reason to refuse to pay the claim or to perform its contractual obligation. Third, the insured must demonstrate that the insurer's breach of the insurance contract results from an intentional wrong, insult, or abuse as well as from such gross negligence as constitutes an intentional tort.") (citations and internal quotations omitted); *Chapman v. Coca-Cola Bottling Co.*, 180 So. 3d 676 (Miss. Ct. App. 2015) ("[T]he fact that an insurer's decision to deny benefits may ultimately turn out to be incorrect does not in and of itself warrant an award of punitive damages if the decision was reached in good faith. Where an insurance carrier denies or delays payment of a valid claim, punitive damages will not lie if the carrier has a reasonable cause for such denial or delay."); *GuideOne Elite Ins. Co. v. Mount Carmel Ministries*, 676 Fed. Appx. 269 (5th Cir. 2017) (finding that an insurer did not act in bad faith when it "relied on the majority rule in interpreting both Mississippi law and the policy" in the absence of any authority from the Mississippi Supreme Court); *Knight v. Allstate Prop. & Cas. Ins. Co.*, No. 18-115, 2019 U.S. Dist. LEXIS 143435 (N.D. Miss. Aug. 23, 2019) ("Plaintiffs' position is essentially that Allstate should be required to tender the amount of its last offer [] made during negotiations to settle this matter prior to the lawsuit being filed — an offer which Plaintiffs refused to accept as full settlement of the claim. Plaintiffs, however, have cited no Mississippi case supporting the position that an insurer is required to tender payment unconditionally for an offer that was unaccepted by its insured as a full resolution of the case. According to Plaintiffs' argument, Allstate must make this payment — an amount which Plaintiffs assert represents the 'undisputed' portion of the claim — despite Plaintiffs' refusal to accept the amount as full resolution of the case and release Allstate from further responsibility — and then continue to negotiate the remaining amount of the claim, or allow the fact finder to determine the value of the claim at trial. Further, Plaintiffs assert that Allstate's failure to tender this payment unconditionally amounts to bad faith. The court finds this position to be unsupported by Mississippi law.").

In the context of third-party bad faith, the Supreme Court of Mississippi adopted the following standard: "[W]hen suit covered by a liability insurance policy is for a sum in excess of the policy limits, and an offer of settlement is made within the policy limits, the insurer has a fiduciary duty to look after the insured's interest at least to the same extent as its own, and also to make a knowledgeable, honest and intelligent evaluation of the claim commensurate with its ability to do so. If the carrier fails to do this, then it is liable to the insured for all damages occasioned thereby." *Hartford Accident & Indem. Co. v. Foster*, 528 So. 2d 255, 265 (Miss. 1988); *see also Lexington Ins. Co. v. Hattiesburg Med. Park Mgmt. Corp.*, No.07CV26, 2007 U.S. Dist. LEXIS 49598 (S.D. Miss. July 6, 2007) (addressing *Foster's* "failure to settle" cause of action in the context of an insurer's alleged duty to make a sufficient settlement offer without a demand   from the claimant); *Hemphill v. State Farm Mut. Auto. Ins. Co.*, 805 F.3d 535 (5th Cir. 2015) ([("[O]ver the thirty-three years since *Hartford*, no case from either the Mississippi Supreme Court or a Mississippi intermediate appellate court has suggested or even hinted that the Mississippi Supreme Court would hold that an insurer has a duty to make a settlement offer absent a settlement offer by the claimant. Therefore, this Court makes an *Erie* guess that the Mississippi Supreme Court would not impose such a duty under the circumstances presented herein."); *Heritage Props., Inc. v. Ironshore Specialty Ins. Co.*, No. 17-637, 2018 U.S. Dist. LEXIS 9598 (S.D. Miss. Jan. 22, 2018) ("[I]n the context of a third-party insurance claim—like the one here—there is no duty to investigate beyond the allegations of the underlying complaint 'unless some facts are presented that would make an investigation reasonable and necessary.'").

Missouri: A Missouri statute provides that "if the insurer has failed or refused for a period of thirty days after due demand therefor prior to the institution of the action, suit or proceeding, to make payment under and in accordance with the terms and provisions of the contract of insurance, and it shall appear from the evidence that the refusal was vexatious and without reasonable cause, the court or jury may, in addition to the amount due under the provisions of the contract of insurance and interest thereon, allow the plaintiff damages for vexatious refusal to pay and attorney's fees as provided in section 375.420." Mo. Rev. Stat. § 375.296;

see also Hensley v. Shelter Mut. Ins. Co., 210 S.W.3d 455, 465–66 (Mo. Ct. App. 2007) (addressing in detail the proof required to recover under § 375.420) ("Several factual scenarios have been recognized as indicative of a vexatious and recalcitrant attitude. They include: (1) the insurer's delay or refusal to pay the mortgagee; (2) the insurer's denial of liability without stating any ground for denial; (3) the inadequacy of the insurer's investigation of the claim (4) the explanation given by the insurer for denying the claim; and (5) the insurer's disparate treatment of coinsureds.") (citations omitted); *Midwest Special Surgery, P.C. v. Anthem Ins. Cos.*, No. 09646, 2010 U.S. Dist. LEXIS 16403 (E.D. Mo. Feb. 24, 2010) ("A vexatious refusal to pay claim requires a plaintiff to show: (1) an insurance policy; (2) the insurer's refusal to pay; and (3) refusal without reasonable cause or excuse.") (citing *Hensley*). However, "Missouri has not yet recognized a cause of action for bad faith, sometimes referred to as a breach of the covenant of good faith and fair dealing, arising out of a first-party insurance contract. The Supreme Court of Missouri has had the opportunity to adopt such a common law cause of action, but declined to do so." *Millman v. Provident Life & Accident Ins. Co.*, No. 14-05073, 2014 U.S. Dist. LEXIS 101626 (W.D. Mo. July 25, 2014); *Allstate Indem. Co. v. Dixon*, No. 14-03489, 2016 U.S. Dist. LEXIS 109790 (W.D. Mo. Aug. 18, 2016) ("[T]he continued open question of whether Allstate has an arson defense to the Dixons' insurance claim necessarily precludes a finding by the Court, at the summary judgment stage, that Allstate acted without reasonable cause or excuse when it refused to pay the Dixons' claim. Such a question of reasonableness belongs in the hands of the fact-finder once it has determined whether the Dixons are entitled to recover under the insurance policy."); *Easter v. Farmers Ins. Co.*, No. 13-3412, 2014 U.S. Dist. LEXIS 39950 (W.D. Mo. Mar. 26, 2014) ("[B]ecause this suit is by the insured against the insurance company, plaintiff's remedy is limited to that provided by the law of contract plus a claim for vexatious refusal to pay. Missouri law prohibits a claim by an insured against an insurance company for breach of good faith and fair dealing."); *Markley v. Allied Prop. & Cas. Ins. Co.*, No. 16-03315, 2017 U.S. Dist. LEXIS 220083 (W.D. Mo. Sept. 18, 2017) (noting ["[c]ourts have uniformly applied *Overcast* [*v. Billings Mut. Ins. Co.*], 11 S.W.3d 62 (Mo. 2001) (en banc)] to prohibit first-party claims for breach of good faith and fair dealing").

Missouri recognizes a bad faith cause of action for an insurer's failure to settle a claim within policy limits. *Ganaway v. Shelter Mut. Ins. Co.*, 795 S.W.2d 554, 556 (Mo. Ct. App. 1990) (citing *Zumwalt v. Utils. Ins. Co.*, 228 S.W.2d 750 (Mo. 1950)) (explaining that a bad faith action for refusal to settle sounds in tort, not in contract, and requires a showing that the insurer acted in bad faith, rather than negligently); *see also Shobe v. Kelly*, 279 S.W.3d 203, 210 (Mo. Ct. App. 2009) (discussing factors considered in a bad faith determination); *Johnson v. Allstate Ins. Co.*, 262 S.W.3d 655, 662 (Mo. Ct. App. 2008) ("An insurer's bad faith in refusing to settle is a state of mind, which is indicated by the insurer's acts and circumstances and can be proven by circumstantial and direct evidence. Circumstances that indicate an insurer's bad faith in refusing to settle include the insurer's not fully investigating and evaluating a third-party claimant's injuries, not recognizing the severity of a third-party claimant's injuries and the probability that a verdict would exceed policy limits, and refusing to consider a settlement offer.") (citation omitted); *Emp'rs Mut. Cas. Co. v. Luke Draily Constr. Co.*, No. 10-00361, 2010 U.S. Dist. LEXIS 124114 (W.D. Mo. Nov. 23, 2010) ("While the policy behind BFFS [bad faith failure to settle] is generally to protect insured parties facing judgments that should have been settled, the case law contradicts [the insurer's] argument that a judgment is an essential element. [The insured] will have to show damages of some sort, but [the insurer] has failed to show that the lack of a judgment against [the insured] in excess of the policy limit is fatal to its BFFS counterclaim."). "To succeed on [a] bad faith failure to settle claim, Plaintiff must prove the following elements: (1) liability insurer has assumed control over negotiation, settlement, and legal proceedings brought against the insured; (2) the insured has demanded that the insurer settle the claim brought against the insured; (3) the insurer refuses to settle the claim within the liability limits of the policy; and (4) in so refusing, the insurer acts in bad faith, rather than negligently." *Purscell v. TICO Ins. Co.*, 959 F. Supp. 2d 1195, 1200 (W.D. Mo. 2013) (internal quotations omitted), *aff'd* 790 F.3d 842 (8th Cir. 2015) ("We also disagree with the premise that an insurer's attempt to reach a global settlement of competing claims, without ever denying the responsibility to pay the full policy limits, can serve as evidence that the insurer is placing its own interests over that of its insured. It was in Purscell's interest to have all three claims against him settled within the policy limits. When a global settlement could not be reached, Infinity appropriately filed an interpleader action. . . . In addition, the record does not show Infinity ever had a reasonable opportunity to settle Tim Carr's individual claim within the policy limits in any event."); *Scottsdale Ins. Co. v. Addison Ins. Co.*, 448 S.W.3d 818 (Mo. 2014) ("[A]n insurer's obligation to act in good faith when settling a third-party claim is part of what the insured pays for with its premiums. When the insurer refuses to settle, the insured loses the benefit of an important obligation owed by the insurer. This loss is suffered regardless of whether there is an excess judgment or settlement. Therefore, an excess judgment is not required to maintain an action against an insurer for bad faith refusal to settle."); *Zurich Am. Ins. Co. v. Fluor Corp.*, No. 16-00429, 2019 U.S. Dist. LEXIS 168333 (E.D. Mo. Sept. 30, 2019) (concluding that an insurer's disclaimer of coverage, made after the insurer engaged in bad faith conduct, is irrelevant to and cannot defeat a claim for bad faith failure to settle) ("From a common-sense standpoint, Zurich's proposal would allow insurers to undertake the defense of a claim, bar the insured from voluntarily making payment on the claim, fail to act in good faith with regard to settlement opportunities, and later evade [bad faith failure to settle] liability for this conduct by procuring a determination at trial or otherwise that coverage was non-existent—a fact that was not established at the time of the alleged bad-faith conduct."); *Sprint Lumber, Inc. v. Union Ins. Co.*, No. 82930 and 82939, 2021 Mo. App. LEXIS 431 (Mo. Ct. App. Apr. 6, 2021) ("[I]f an insurer wrongly denies coverage, denies even a defense under a reservation of rights, and then completely refuses to engage in settlement negotiations, it cannot avoid liability for bad faith failure to settle by its wrongful refusal to assume control of the proceedings.") (finding Section 375.296 inapplicable to third-party loss) (noting that the insured conflated "the indemnity insurer's obligation to pay covered losses (under its policy of indemnity) with its obligation to provide a defense (and the resulting damages it may be obligated to pay its insured because it violated its duty to provide a defense)").

Montana: A Montana statute provides that "(1) An insured or a third-party claimant has an independent cause of action against an insurer for actual damages caused by the insurer's violation of subsection (1), (4), (5), (6), (9), or (13) of 33-18-201 [Unfair claim settlement practices]. (2) In an action under this section, a plaintiff is not required to prove that the violations were of such frequency as to indicate a general business practice. (3) An insured who has suffered damages as a result of the handling of an insurance claim may bring an action against the insurer for breach of the insurance contract, for fraud, or pursuant to this section, but not under any other theory or cause of action. An insured may not bring an action for bad faith in connection with the handling of an insurance claim. (4) In an action under this section, the court or jury may award such damages as were proximately caused by the violation of subsection (1), (4), (5), (6), (9), or (13) of 33-18-201. Exemplary damages may also be assessed in accordance with 27-1-221." Mont. Code Ann. § 33-18-242. Some of the prohibited conduct under § 33-18-201 includes "(1) misrepresent pertinent facts or insurance policy provisions relating to coverages at issue; ... (4) refuse to pay claims without conducting a reasonable investigation based upon all available information; (5) fail to affirm or deny coverage of claims within a reasonable time after proof of loss statements have been completed." *See also Northland Cas. Co. v. Mulroy*, No. 13-232, 2016 U.S. Dist. LEXIS 104982 (D. Mont. Aug. 9, 2016), *rev'd in part, remanded in part on other grounds* 713 Fed. Appx. 713 (9th Cir. 2018) ("Because the Court has ruled that there was no coverage for Mulroy's injuries under the CGL policy, and that Northland breached neither its duty to defend nor its duty to indemnify, Mulroy's UTPA claim fails as a matter of Montana law.") (noting that, *under* Mont. Code Ann. § 33-18-242(5), "[a]n insurer may not be held liable under this section if the insurer had a reasonable basis in law or in fact for contesting the claim or the amount of the claim, whichever is in issue"); *Estate of Gleason v. Cent. United Life Ins. Co.*, 350 P.3d 349 (Mont. 2015) (undertaking discussion of several issues under § 33-18-242); *Butler v. Unified Life Ins. Co.*, No.17-50, 2017 U.S. Dist. LEXIS 214161 (D. Mont. Dec. 15, 2017) ("[T]he UTPA only bars common law claims against insurers that originate from the actual handling of an insurance claim. When an insured's claim is based on conduct that occurred before the claims handling process, the claim is not barred by the UTPA.") (internal citations omitted).

Montana recognizes a bad faith cause of action for an insurer's failure to settle a claim within policy limits, which leads to an excess judgment. *Fowler v. State Farm Mut. Auto. Ins. Co.*, 454 P.2d 76, 78–79 (Mont. 1969) ("It has been held that a policy of this type places a fiduciary duty on the insurance company to look after the interests of the insured as well as its own, thus requiring it to consider fairly the insured's liability for the excess when evaluating an offer of settlement within the policy limits. Failure to do so is bad faith and renders the company liable for its breach of fiduciary duty in the amount of any judgment over the policy limits.") (citation and internal quotation omitted). "[A]n insurer does not act in bad faith in rejecting a settlement if it had a reasonable basis in law or fact to contest the claim or the amount of the claim." *State Farm Mut. Auto. Ins. Co. v. Freyer*, 312 P.3d 403, 418 (Mont. 2013) ("To determine whether an insurer had a reasonable basis in law … for contesting the claim or amount of the claim, it is necessary first to survey the legal landscape as it existed during the relevant time period.") (citation and internal quotations omitted); *see also Gibson v. W. Fire Ins. Co.*, 682 P.2d 725, 731 (Mont. 1984) ("Malice on the part of the insurer is not a necessary component to impose liability upon an insurer for bad faith refusal to settle. This is so because the failure to settle may have been the result of either bad faith or negligence, and there is no clear distinction in Montana between the two terms in such cases.") (addressing whether insurer's failure to settle was in bad faith by reviewing six factors from *Jessen v. O'Daniel*, 210 F. Supp. 317 (D.Mont.1962), *aff'd sub nom. Nat'l Farmers Union Prop. & Cas. Co. v. O'Daniel*, 329 F.2d 60 (9th Cir. 1964)) (no one *Jessen* factor is decisive, and all of the circumstances must be considered as to whether the insurer acted in good faith) ("The jury found by special verdict that Western was guilty of bad faith in the handling of the claim, and we hold that the evidence fully supports the jury verdict. The failure of Western through its agents to follow established standards of investigation, evaluation, negotiation, and communication with its insured are the deciding factors upon which we base this conclusion."); *Northland Cas. Co. v. Mulroy*, No. 13-232, 2015 U.S. Dist. LEXIS 94631 (D. Mont. July 21, 2015), *rev'd in part and vacated in part on other grounds*, 713 Fed. Appx. 713 (9th Cir. 2018) ("[T]he Montana Supreme Court has never held an insurer liable in bad faith for failing to settle within policy limits when it had a reasonable basis in law or fact for contesting coverage."); *Draggin' Y Cattle Co. v. Junkermier, Clark, Campanella, Stevens, P.C.*, 439 P.3d 935 (Mont. 2018) ("In addition to allowing private rights of action for violations of certain duties expressed in the UTPA, § 33-18-242(3), MCA, preserves an insured's common-law right to bring a breach of contract claim. Every insurance contract includes a covenant of good faith and fair dealing, which we have long recognized gives rise to a duty to accept a reasonable offer within policy coverage limits.") (declining to impose, as a matter of law, "a new obligation on a defending insurer…to file a declaratory judgment action before the resolution of the liability case, when the Legislature has provided an express cause of action and remedies for violations of duties expressed in the UTPA" but noting that the failure to file a declaratory judgment action is not abandonment of an insured, but "could be part of an alleged violation of § 33-18-201(5), MCA").

Nebraska: The Supreme Court of Nebraska adopted the following test for bad faith in the context of first-party claims: "To show a claim for bad faith, a plaintiff must show the absence of a reasonable basis for denying benefits of the [insurance] policy and the defendant's knowledge or reckless disregard of the lack of a reasonable basis for denying the claim. It is apparent, then, that the tort of bad faith is an intentional one. 'Bad faith' by definition cannot be unintentional." *Braesch v. Union Ins. Co.*, 464 N.W.2d 769, 777 (Neb. 1991) (adopting the standard in *Anderson v. Cont'l Ins. Co.*, 271 N.W.2d 368, 376 (Wis. 1978)); *Locke v. Std. Ins. Co.*, No. 14-2, 2014 U.S. Dist. LEXIS 128006 (D. Neb. Sept. 12, 2014) ("[A]n insurance company has a right to debate a claim that is 'fairly debatable,' or subject to a reasonable dispute, without being subject to a bad faith claim. Whether a claim is fairly debatable is appropriately decided by the court as a matter of law, and such determination is based on the information available to the insurance company at the time the demand is presented."); *LeRette v. Am. Med. Sec., Inc.*, 705 N.W.2d 41 (Neb. 2005) ("The LeRettes' evidence did not indicate that United Wisconsin's experts' opinions were unsound or false or that there was an absence of a reasonable basis to deny benefits."); *Hayes v. Metro Prop. & Cas. Ins. Co.*, 908 F.3d 370 (8th Cir. 2018) ("While Met is correct that there must have been a contract at some point in time in order for there to be a bad faith claim, Met cannot insulate itself from a bad faith claim by creating the fiction that a contract never existed by voiding or rescinding it 'ab initio.' The cases Met cites do not stand for the proposition that an insurer can do what it did here—discover there is liability after eighteen months of 'investigating' and rescind based upon misrepresentation evidence that was within its knowledge five days after the fire…Alleging that Hayes was never a 'policyholder' because Met rescinded the contract eighteen months after the fire occurred is more than a bit of a stretch.").

Nebraska recognizes a bad faith cause of action for an insurer's failure to settle a claim within policy limits. *Olson v. Union Fire Ins. Co.*, 118 N.W. 2d 318, 323 (Neb. 1962) ("If the insurer has exercised good faith in all of its dealings under its policy, if the settlement which it has rejected has been fully and fairly considered and has been based on an honest belief that the insurer could defeat the action or keep the judgment within the limits of the policy, and if its determination is based on a fair review of the evidence after reasonable diligence in ascertaining the facts, accompanied by competent legal advice, a court will not subject the insurer to liability in excess of policy limits if it ultimately turns out that its determination is a mistaken one."). *See also Bamford, Inc. v. Regent Ins. Co.*, 822 F.3d 403 (8th Cir. 2016) ("Here, the jury could have concluded that Regent—by relying on valuations received from mediators, counsel, and internal adjusters—reasonably embraced a low value for the Davises' claims early in the case, but ultimately acted in bad faith in failing to reassess the value of the claims in light of case developments and advice from its own players that the low value was inaccurate.").

Nevada: "The Supreme Court of Nevada adopted the cause of action called 'bad faith' in *United States Fidelity & Guaranty Co. v. Peterson*, 540 P.2d 1070 (Nev. 1975). The duty to deal fairly and in good faith then is implied by common law. Breach of the covenant of good faith and fair dealing is a tort. An insurer breaches the duty of good faith when it refuses without proper cause to compensate its insured for a loss covered by the policy. An insurer is without proper cause to deny a claim when it has an actual or implied awareness that no reasonable basis exist to deny the claim. Thus, the insurer is not liable for bad faith for being incorrect about policy coverage as long as the insurer had a reasonable basis to take the position that it did." *Pioneer Chlor Alkali Co., Inc. v. Nat'l Union Fire Ins. Co.*, 863 F. Supp. 1237, 1242 (D. Nev. 1994) (citations and internal quotation omitted); *see also Allstate Ins. Co. v. Miller*, 212 P.3d 318, 324 (Nev. 2009) ("This court has defined bad faith as an actual or implied awareness of the absence of a reasonable basis for denying benefits of the [insurance] policy.") (citation and internal quotes omitted) (alteration in original); *Nelson v. Safeco Ins. Co. of Ill.*, No. 10- 241, 2011 U.S. Dist. LEXIS 23820 (D. Nev. Mar. 8, 2011) ("Under Nevada law, 'bad faith' exists where insurer denies claim without any reasonable basis and with knowledge that no reasonable basis exists to deny claim.") (citation and internal quotations omitted); *USF Ins. Co. v. Smith's Food & Drug Ctr., Inc.*, 921 F. Supp. 2d 1082, 1093 (D. Nev. 2013) ("Poor judgment or negligence on the part of an insurer does not amount to bad faith. …[D]uty of good faith arises by law irrespective of the insurance contract's terms, and flows from Nevada law's recognition of an implied covenant of good faith and fair dealing in every contract."); *Am. Access Cas Co. v. Cruz*, No. 16-0173, 2018 Nev. Dist. LEXIS 362 (Nev. Dist. Ct. Feb. 14, 2018) ("The Nevada Supreme Court has repeatedly held that a bad-faith action applies to more than just an insurer's denial or delay in paying a claim. An insurer's failure to adequately inform an insured of a settlement offer may also constitute grounds for a bad-faith claim. Failure to adequately inform an insured is a factor to consider in a bad faith claim. A primary liability insurer's duty to its insured continues from the filing of the claim until the duty to defend has been discharged.") (internal citations and quotations omitted); *Goodrich v. Garrison Prop. & Cas Ins. Co.*, No. 18-00562, 2021 U.S. Dist. LEXIS 49083 (D. Nev. Mar. 16, 2021) ("An insurer's failure to properly investigate an insured's claim can support a claim for bad faith under Nevada Law. However, evidence that an insurer failed to properly investigate is only probative insofar as it supports the ultimate conclusion that an insurer denied a claim without a reasonable basis to do so."). Nevada law also permits a cause of action under NEV. REV. STAT. § 686A.310, which addresses the manner in which an insurer handles an insured's claim whether or not the claim is denied. *Pioneer Chlor*, 863 F. Supp. at 1243; *see also Turk v. TIG Ins. Co.*, 616 F. Supp. 2d 1044, 1052–53 (D. Nev. 2009) (addressing the elements of § 686A.310); *Bucca v. Allstate Indem. Ins.*, No. 14-01903, 2016 U.S. Dist. LEXIS 119163 (D. Nev. Sept. 1, 2016) ("It is not necessary for Allstate to show that it conducted a perfect investigation, arrived at the right conclusion, or to show that actual fraud occurred.

At this stage, Allstate is required to show only that it had a 'reasonable basis for disputing coverage.' Allstate discovered several indications of fraud, and thus did not act in bad faith in denying the claim.").

In the context of third-party bad faith, "the litmus test is whether the insurer, in determining whether to settle a claim, [gave] as much consideration to the welfare of its insured as it [gave] to its own interests." *Landow v. Med. Ins. Exch. of Cal.*, 892 F. Supp. 239, 240–41 (D. Nev. 1995) (citation and internal quotation omitted) (alteration in original) (court's analysis of the standard is minimal but it makes clear that California law provides guidance); *see also Miller*, 212 P.3d at 322 ("Because a primary insurer's exercise of its right and duty to defend includes settlement duties and an insurer must give equal consideration to the insured's interest, we hold that the covenant of good faith and fair dealing includes a duty to adequately inform the insured of settlement offers. This includes reasonable offers in excess of the policy limits. Failure to adequately inform an insured is a factor to consider in a bad-faith claim and, if established, can be a proximate cause of any resulting damages."); *Hicks v. Dairyland Ins. Co.*, No. 10–15650, 2011 U.S. App. LEXIS 13419 (9th Cir. June 30, 2011) (applying Nevada law) (holding that the demand at issue was not a "reasonable settlement offer" within the meaning of *Miller* because it established an unreasonable time limit and did not afford insurer sufficient information with which to evaluate the claim); *Sharp Plumbing, Inc. v. National Fire & Marine Ins. Co.*, No. 09–00783, 2013 U.S. Dist. LEXIS 181074 (D. Nev. Dec. 27, 2013) ("[A]n insurer can be liable for bad faith failure to settle even where a demand exceeds policy limits if the insured is willing and able to pay the amount of the proposed settlement that exceeds policy coverage.") (quoting *Miller*); *Kelly v. CSE Safeguard Ins., Co.*, No. 08–0088, 2011 U.S. Dist. LEXIS 111136 (D. Nev. Sept. 27, 2011) ("The implied covenant requires the insurer to settle the case within policy limits when there is a substantial likelihood of recovery in excess of those limits. See *Murphy v. Allstate Ins. Co.*, 17 Cal.3d 937, 941 (Cal.1976). The duty to settle is 'implied in law to protect the insured from exposure to liability in excess of coverage as a result of the insurer's gamble—on which only the insured might lose.' *Id.* When the insurer breaches its duty to settle, the insured has been allowed to recover excess award over policy limits and other damages. *Id.*"); *Kalberer v. Am. Family Mut. Ins. Co.*, 692 Fed. Appx. 488 (9th Cir. 2017) ("There is no evidence in the record suggesting that American Family had knowledge that there was 'no reasonable basis' for its decision to proceed to trial. The 'worst-case scenario' estimates of potential liability found in the record are not evidence that American Family knew or should have known that trial would produce an unfavorable outcome; rather, they demonstrate that American Family was proactive in its cost-benefit analyses of the expected values of trial or settlement. And of course, the benefit of hindsight— i.e. the knowledge gained post facto that the jury verdict was not favorable—cannot serve as an evidentiary basis to show American Family acted unreasonably *prior* to trial. The evidence shows that American Family both reasonably and subjectively believed that proceeding to trial was a rational course.") (emphasis in original); *Colony Ins. Co. v. Colo. Cas. Ins. Co.*, No. 12-01727, 2018 U.S. Dist. LEXIS 111818 (D. Nev. July 3, 2018) ("The Court finds that Colorado was acting in bad faith when it failed to reasonably settle Bustillos' personal injury claim within its policy limit when it was clear that All Temp was liable and when the claim would have settled within the policy limit. At a time when liability was clear, Colorado unreasonably failed to settle the claim. It was also clear that at that time, failure to settle the claim would increase the future settlement amount for Bustillos' claim. Colorado had no reasonable basis for contesting liability or delaying settlement at the time when the claim could have been settled within Colorado's policy limit.").

New Hampshire: New Hampshire does not recognize a tort action for first-party bad faith. *See Bennett v. ITT Hartford Grp., Inc.*, 846 A.2d 560, 564 (N.H. 2004) ("A breach of contract standing alone does not give rise to a tort action; however, if the facts constituting the breach of the contract also constitute a breach of duty owed by the defendant to the plaintiff independent of the contract, a separate tort claim will lie."). "In a given case the [insurer] may in fact have reason to know that its failure or delay in payment will cause the insured severe financial injuries. Whether the defendant had knowledge of the facts and reason to foresee the injury will normally be a question of fact for the jury." *Lawton v. Great Sw. Fire Ins. Co.*, 392 A.2d 576, 579–80 (N.H. 1978); *Lessard v. Vt. Mut. Ins. Co.*, No. 12-236, 2013 U.S. Dist. LEXIS 26904 (D.N.H. Feb. 27, 2013) ("[T]he New Hampshire Supreme Court has made clear that [n]ot every delay or refusal to settle or pay a claim under the policy will constitute a breach of the contract. Moreover, allegations of an insurer's wrongful refusal or delay to settle a first-party claim do not state a cause of action in tort. But, [w]here the [insurer's] failure to make prompt payment under the policy is to *coerce the insured* into accepting less than full performance of the insurer's contractual obligations, . . . there is a breach of this covenant [of good faith and fair dealing].") (emphasis in original); *Elizabeth Skrekas & a v. State Farm Fire and Cas. Co.*, No. 2015-0368, 2017 N.H. LEXIS 108 (N.H. May 12, 2017) (distinguishing *Bennett* on the basis that insurer who undertook investigation to determine "whether its insurance contract with the plaintiffs required it to pay for the loss" did not owe a duty to the insureds independent of the insurance contract).

In the third-party bad faith context, "an insurer owes a duty to its insured to exercise due care in defending and settling claims against the insured, and that a breach of that duty will give rise to a cause of action by the insured." *Allstate Ins. Co. v. Reserve Ins. Co.*, 373 A.2d 339, 340 (N.H. 1976); *see also Gelinas v. Metropolitan Property & Liab. Ins. Co.*, 551 A.2d 962 (N.H. 1988) ("Various standards, such as bad faith and negligence, have been used to determine the liability of an insurer in failing to settle a third-party claim within policy limits. New Hampshire, however, has specifically adopted a negligence standard. The negligence standard is defined as how a reasonable man might act under the same circumstances.").

New Jersey: The Supreme Court of New Jersey adopted the "fairly debatable" standard to establish first party bad faith. *Pickett v. Lloyd's*, 621 A.2d 445, 453 (N.J. 1993). "To show a claim for bad faith, a plaintiff must show the absence of a reasonable basis for denying benefits of the policy and the defendant's knowledge or reckless disregard of the lack of a reasonable basis for denying the claim." *Id.* (citation and internal quotes omitted). "Under the 'fairly debatable' standard, a claimant who could not have established as a matter of law a right to summary judgment on the substantive claim would not be entitled to assert a claim for an insurer's bad-faith refusal to pay the claim." *Id.* at 454; *see also Markel Int'l Ins. Co., Ltd. v. Centex Homes, LLC*, No. 05-3540 (GEB), 2006 U.S. Dist. LEXIS 4780 (D.N.J. Feb. 1, 2006) ("To establish a bad faith claim in the insurance context under New Jersey law, a plaintiff must show two elements: (1) the insurer lacked a 'fairly debatable' reason for its failure to pay a claim, and (2) the insurer knew or recklessly disregarded the lack of a reasonable basis for denying the claim. To establish a bad faith claim, the entity seeking coverage must be able to establish, as a matter of law, a right to summary judgment on the substantive claim. If the entity cannot establish a right to summary judgment, the bad faith claim fails.") (citing *Pickett*); *Badiali v. New Jersey Mfrs. Ins. Group*, 107 A.3d 1281 (N.J. 2015) ("A finding of bad faith against an insurer in denying an insurance claim cannot be established through simple negligence. Moreover, mere failure to settle a debatable claim does not constitute bad faith. Rather, to establish a first-party bad faith claim for denial of benefits in New Jersey, a plaintiff must show that no debatable reasons existed for denial of the benefits.") (citing *Pickett*); *Johnson v. Encompass Ins. Co.*, No. 17-3527, 2018 U.S. Dist. LEXIS 94775 (D.N.J. June 6, 2018) ("Mere negligent inattention to a claim is not sufficient [to prove bad faith], for example, when a claim is lost in a computer processing system") (citing *Pickett*); *Parko Props. v. Mercer Ins. Co.*, No. 4137-17, 2020 N.J. Super. Unpub. LEXIS 2268 (N.J. Super. App. Div. Nov. 19, 2020) (finding the insurer's decision to deny coverage was fairly debatable because there was "no binding New Jersey precedent" interpreting the insurer's policy form).

In the third-party bad faith context, "an insurer, having contractually restricted the independent negotiating power of its insured, has a positive fiduciary duty to take the initiative and attempt to negotiate a settlement within the policy coverage." *Rova Farms Resort, Inc. v. Investors Ins. Co. of Am.*, 323 A.2d 495, 507 (N.J. 1974). The only exception being if the insurer, "by some affirmative evidence, demonstrates there was not only no realistic possibility of settlement within policy limits, but also that the insured would not have contributed to whatever settlement figure above that sum might have been available." *Id.* "The proposed rule is a simple one to apply and avoids the burdens of a determination whether a settlement offer within the policy limits was reasonable." *Id.* at 510; *see also Am. Hardware Mut. Ins. Co. v. Harley Davidson of Trenton, Inc.*, Nos. 03-4170, 03-4348, 04-1398, 2005 U.S. App. LEXIS 3166 (3d Cir. Feb. 22, 2005) (applying New Jersey law) (noting the distinction between *Pickett* and *Rova Farms*) ("*Rova Farms*, not *Pickett*, protects insureds who are relegated to the sidelines in third-party litigation from the danger that insurers will not internalize the full expected value of a claim due to a policy cap."); *N.J. Mfrs. Ins. Co. v. Nat'l Cas. Co.*, 992 A.2d 837, 841 (N.J. Super. Ct. App. Div. 2010) ("[U]nder *Rova Farms*, an insurer that fails to negotiate in good faith with a party who asserts a claim against its insured is not automatically liable for any judgment in excess of the policy limit. Instead, the insurer may avoid such liability if it can show that there was no realistic possibility of a settlement within the policy limits and that its insured—or in this case the excess carrier—would not have contributed whatever amount above the policy limit would have been required to settle the case."); *Wood v. N.J. Mfrs. Ins. Co.*, 21 A.3d 1131, 1132 (N.J. 2011) ("We conclude that a *Rova Farms* claim that an insurer in bad faith failed to settle a claim within the policy limits, thereby in fact exposing its insured to liability for any excess, represents a traditional contract claim that the insurer breached the implied covenant of good faith and fair dealing and to which the right to trial by jury attaches."); *State Nat'l Ins. Co. v. Cnty. of Camden*, No. 08-5128, 2014 U.S. Dist. LEXIS 43229 (D.N.J. Mar. 31, 2014) (addressing whether the "fairly debatable" standard in *Pickett* applies in the context of a third-party bad faith claim) ("Even though no bright-line rule has been established in the case law as to whether the "fairly debatable" standard only applies to first-party claims, and there is no specific case that precludes the application of that standard here [in the third-party context], the Court finds that the rationale of *Rova Farms* is more applicable to this action than the rationale of *Pickett*."); *Ellington v. Cure Auto Ins.*, No. A-2470-16T4, 2017 N.J. Super. Unpub. LEXIS 1831 (N.J. Super. App. Div. July 20, 2017) ("Considering the allegations of the complaint and the fiduciary duties of CURE under the principles governing our narrow scope of review, we can readily glean from the complaint a bad faith cause of action. Construing the complaint with liberality, it clearly alleges facts and circumstances demonstrating CURE did not take the initiative and attempt to negotiate a settlement within its policy coverage. To the contrary, the complaint alleges CURE disregarded an opportunity to explore settlement within its policy limits and then waited nearly eleven months — long after it knew the personal injury plaintiffs would no longer accept the policy limits to settle — before following up with them or tendering the policy limits."); *Penn Nat'l Ins. Co. v. Group C Communs., Inc.* Nos. 0754-15 & 0808-15, 2018 N.J. Super. Unpub. LEXIS 1833 (N.J. Super. App. Div. July 30, 2018) (noting that "[n]o reported New Jersey decision has addressed whether *Pickett's* 'reasonably debatable' standard applies to an insured's bad faith refusal to settle claim") ("Without deciding the issue, we acknowledge the appeal of the Third Circuit's rationale [that *Pickett's* 'reasonably debatable standard' does not apply to an insurer's bad faith refusal to settle"]. An insurer who, while exclusively controlling the litigation, acts in bad faith and refuses to settle a third-party claim within its insured's policy limits exposes the insured to personal liability. The situation therefore presents different concerns from those posed by a suit where the insurer acts in bad faith and wrongfully denies contractual benefits to the insured under its policy of insurance."); *Brightview Enter. Solutions, LLC v. Farm Family Cas. Ins. Co.*, No. 20-7915, 2020 U.S. Dist. LEXIS 191474 (D.N.J. Oct. 15, 2020) (holding that a jury verdict in excess of policy limits is not necessary; rather, "a plaintiff need only allege that it was exposed to liability exceeding its policy limits").

New Mexico: The Supreme Court of New Mexico adopted the following standard for recovering damages in tort for first-party bad faith: "[T]here must be evidence of bad faith or a fraudulent scheme. We further announced that 'bad faith' means any frivolous or unfounded refusal to pay. We have defined 'frivolous or unfounded' as meaning an arbitrary or baseless refusal to pay, lacking any support in the wording of the insurance policy or the circumstances surrounding the claim[.]" *Sloan v. State Farm Mut. Auto. Ins. Co.*, 85 P.3d 230, 236–37 (N.M. 2004) (citing *State Farm Gen. Ins. Co. v. Clifton*, 527 P.2d 798, 800 (N.M. 1974)). "[A]n insurer acts in bad faith when it denies a first party claim for reasons that are frivolous or unfounded." *Am. Nat'l Prop. & Cas. Co. v. Cleveland*, 293 P.3d 954, 958 (N.M. Ct. App. 2012) ("To be liable for bad faith, the insurer must lack a founded belief, and the founded belief is absent when the insurer fails to undertake an investigation adequate to determine whether its position is tenable."). *See also* N.M. Stat. Ann. § 59A-16-30 (authorizing private right of action against insurer for violation of New Mexico's Trade Practices and Frauds Article of the Insurance Code); *Dydek v. Dydek*, 288 P.3d 872 (N.M. Ct. App. 2012) (interpreting § 59A-16-30 in determining the proper measure of damages); N.M. Stat. Ann. § 13-1702 (governing bad faith failure to pay a first party claim); *Ortiz v. Safeco Ins. Co. of Am.*, 207 F. Supp. 3d 1216 (D.N.M. 2016) ("An insurer can act in bad faith in its handling of a claim for reasons other than its refusal to pay a claim in full. An insurer can act in bad faith by: misrepresenting pertinent facts concerning coverage under the policy; failing to timely and fairly investigate an insured's claim; failing to timely evaluate an insured's claim; exploiting an insured's vulnerable position; and unreasonable delay in notifying the insured about the status of the claim."); *Progressive Cas. Ins. Co. v. Vigil*, 413 P.3d 850 (N.M. 2018) (restating *Sloan*); *Nilson v. Peerless Indem. Ins. Co.*, 484 F. Supp. 3d 1050 (D.N.M. 2020) (predicting that the Supreme Court of New Mexico would not recognize a cause of action for a breach of fiduciary duty in the insurance context).

In the third-party bad faith context, New Mexico recognizes a common-law cause of action for bad-faith failure to settle within policy limits, but not for negligent failure to settle. An insured must show that the insurer's refusal to settle was based on a dishonest judgment, meaning that the insurer has failed to honestly and fairly balance its own interests and the interests of the insured. *Sloan*, 85 P.3d at 237. "In caring for the insured's interests, the insurer should place itself in the shoes of the insured and conduct itself as though it alone were liable for the entire amount of the judgment." *Id.* (quoting *Dairyland Ins. Co. v. Herman*, 954 P.2d 56, 61 (N.M. 1997)). *See also Dairyland Ins. Co. v. Herman*, 134 F.3d 382 (10th Cir. 1998) (applying New Mexico law) ("The implied covenant of good faith and fair dealing imposes a duty on an insurer to settle a claim against its insured within policy limits whenever there is a substantial likelihood of recovery in excess of policy limits."); *Am. Guar. & Liab. Ins. Co. v. Liberty Mut. Fire Ins. Co.*, No. 13-277, 2015 U.S. Dist. LEXIS 180111 (D.N.M. Feb. 17, 2015) ("It is that precise issue—whether New Mexico would recognize a bad faith failure to settle claim in the absence of a firm settlement offer—that was addressed by the Tenth Circuit in *Hobbs* [*City of Hobbs v. Hartford Fire Ins. Co.*, 162 F.3d 576 (10th Cir. 1998)] and that must be addressed by the Court in this case. Because no intervening decision of the New Mexico Supreme Court has resolved the issue, this Court is bound to follow the Tenth Circuit's prediction in *Hobbs* that New Mexico would allow a bad faith failure to settle claim in the absence of a firm settlement offer.").

New York: The Court of Appeals of New York held that an insurer that breaches its contract is liable for those risks foreseen or which should have been foreseen at the time the contract was made. *Bi-Economy Mkt., Inc. v. Harleysville Ins. Co.*, 886 N.E.2d 127, 130 (N.Y. 2008). "To determine whether consequential damages were reasonably contemplated by the parties, courts must look to the nature, purpose and particular circumstances of the contract known by the parties ... as well as what liability the defendant fairly may be supposed to have assumed consciously, or to have warranted the plaintiff reasonably to suppose that it assumed, when the contract was made." *Id.* (citations and internal quotes omitted) (alteration in original). The dissent discusses issues related to the insurer's standard of conduct. *Id.* at 133–35 (Smith, J., dissenting); *see also Panasia Estates, Inc. v. Hudson Ins. Co.*, 886 N.E.2d 135 (N.Y. 2008) (companion case to *Bi-Economy* and decided the same day); *Goldmark, Inc. v. Catlin Syndicate Ltd.*, No. 09-CV-3876, 2011 U.S. Dist. LEXIS 18197 (E.D.N.Y. Feb. 24, 2011) ("This Circuit has consistently held that *Bi-Economy* stands for the proposition that consequential damages are permitted when they derive from an insurer's bad faith refusal to pay an insured's claim and such damages were reasonably contemplated by both parties at the time of the contract's execution. ... Plaintiff's argument, therefore, that its only obligation in seeking consequential damages is to prove that such damages were reasonably contemplated at the time of execution is erroneous. Cases have virtually uniformly held that, after *Panasia Estates* and *Bi-Economy*, a plaintiff simply cannot sustain a claim for consequential damages without showing that defendants lacked good faith in processing [plaintiff's] claim.") (citations and internal quotes omitted); *Orman v. GEICO Gen. Ins. Co.*, 964 N.Y.S.2d 61 (N.Y. Sup. Ct. 2012) (holding that plaintiffs' claim for breach of contract was duplicative of their claim for breach of the covenant of good faith and fair dealing as they did not allege any consequential damages resulting from insurer's refusal to pay benefits). "New York law does recognize a cause of action for an insurer's extra-contractual bad faith upon well-pleaded allegations that: (1) the insurer denied coverage as a result of 'gross negligence'; and (2) the insurer lacked even an 'arguable' basis for denying coverage under the standards of a reasonable insurer." *Bartlett v. Nationwide Mut. Fire Ins. Co.*, No. 12-CV-435-A, 2013 U.S. Dist. LEXIS 22320 (W.D.N.Y. Feb. 19,

2013); *see also Kurzdorfer v. GEICO Gen. Ins. Co.*, No. 12-CV-781-A, 2013 U.S. Dist. LEXIS 14858 (W.D.N.Y. Feb. 4, 2013) (holding that a plaintiff need not necessarily allege an independent tort against an insurer to state a cause of action for extra-contractual bad faith); *Brown v Government Employees Ins. Co.*, No. 524696, 2017 N.Y. App. Div. LEXIS 8821 (N.Y. App. Div. Dec. 14, 2017) ("Although the Court of Appeals did not specifically consider the issue of whether damages were available for emotional distress when it decided *Bi-Economy* and *Panasia*, we conclude that it did not implicitly abandon the long-standing rule that damages for emotional distress for breach of contract are available only in certain limited circumstances, such as a willful breach accompanied by egregious and abusive behavior."); *Orient Overseas Assoc. v XL Ins. Am., Inc.*, 18 N.Y.S.3d 381 (N.Y. App. Div. 2015) ("In *Bi-Economy*, while the Court mentioned that the plaintiff asserted a claim for 'bad faith claims handling,' it did not discuss that claim at all and, instead, focused its discussion on plaintiff's breach of contract claim seeking consequential damages. Thus, there is no compelling authority indicating that a separate, non-contractual claim exists for 'bad faith claims handling.'"); *D.K. Prop., Inc. v. National Union Fire Ins. Co. of Pittsburgh, Pa.*, 168 A.D.3d 505 (N.Y. App. Div. 2019) (noting there is "no heightened pleading standard requiring plaintiff to explain or describe how and why the 'specific' categories of consequential damages alleged were reasonable and for[e]seeable at the time of contract") (finding that whether consequential damages, such as "engineering costs, painting, repairs, monitoring equipment, and moisture abatement to address water intrusion, loss of rents, and other expenses attributable to mitigating further damage to the property" were "for[e]seeable should not be decided on a motion to dismiss and must await a fully developed record"); *R&R Third Props., LLC v. Federal Ins. Co.*, 191 A.D.3d 444 (N.Y. App. Div. 2021) (finding that consequential damages are permitted even if an insurer did not act in bad faith) ("[E]ven if Federal did not act in bad faith, it would not be entitled to summary dismissal of the claim for consequential damages, because it failed to establish that such damages were not 'within the contemplation of the parties as the probable result of a breach at the time of or prior to contracting.'").

On the subject of third-party bad faith, the Court of Appeals of New York rejected the insurer's proposed "sinister motive" standard and instead held that "in order to establish a prima facie case of bad faith, the plaintiff must establish that the insurer's conduct constituted a 'gross disregard' of the insured's interests—that is, a deliberate or reckless failure to place on equal footing the interests of its insured with its own interests when considering a settlement offer. In other words, a bad-faith plaintiff must establish that the defendant insurer engaged in a pattern of behavior evincing a conscious or knowing indifference to the probability that an insured would be held personally accountable for a large judgment if a settlement offer within the policy limits were not accepted." *Pavia v. State Farm Mut. Auto. Ins. Co.*, 626 N.E.2d 24, 27–28 (N.Y. 1993); *see also In re AXIS Reinsurance Co. REFCO Related Ins. Litig.*, No. 07-CV-07924-JSR, 2010 U.S. Dist. LEXIS 33377 (S.D.N.Y. Mar. 7, 2010) ("There is no formula to determine whether an insurer acted in good faith. Among the factors this Court must consider are "plaintiffs' likelihood of success on the issue of liability, the potential damages award, the financial burden on each party if the insurer refuses to settle, whether the claim was properly investigated, the information available to the insurer when the demand for settlement was made, and, finally, any other relevant proof tending to establish or negate the insurer's good faith in refusing to settle.") (quoting *Pinto v. Allstate Ins. Co.*, 221 F.3d 394, 400 (2d Cir. 2000)); *Doherty v. Merch. Mut. Ins. Co.*, 903 N.Y.S.2d 836 (N.Y. App. Div. 2010) (competing majority and dissenting opinions, examining many factors in the claim, on whether the insurer's failure to settle was bad faith under the *Pavia* standard); *Phelps v. GEICO Indem. Co.*, No. 12-1585, 2015 U.S. Dist. LEXIS 39830 (N.D.N.Y. Mar. 30, 2015) ("New York Courts consider several factors to determine whether a defendant insurer acted with gross disregard in electing not to settle a claim. Generally, these factors include the following: (1) whether the insurer in good faith considered the insured's interests as well as its own when making decisions as to settlement; (2) whether the insured lost an actual opportunity to settle the claim at a time when all serious doubts about the insured's liability were removed; (3) whether the insurer's investigatory efforts prevented it from making an informed evaluation of the risks of refusing settlement; (4) what, if any, attempts were made by the insurer to settle plaintiff's claim and at what point during the underlying action those attempts were made; (5) whether the insurer informed the insured of settlement negotiations; (6) the potential magnitude of damages and the financial burden to each party may be exposed to as a result of a refusal to settle; and (7) whether any other evidence . . . tends to establish or negate the insurer's bad faith in refusing to settle."); *Sea Tow Servs. Int'l v. St. Paul Fire & Marine Ins. Co.*, 699 Fed. Appx. 70 (2d Cir. 2017) ("STSI may take issue with St. Paul's pre-settlement strategy, but a 'difference of opinion between carrier and insured' does not by itself constitute bad faith. At most, STSI proffered evidence that St. Paul's strategy inadequately factored in a hypothetical scenario under which STSI might have been liable to Triplecheck, its franchisee, for contractual indemnification—a hypothetical scenario, it should be emphasized, that never came to pass. Such counterfactual thought experiments do not establish bad faith."); *Gov't Emples. Ins. Co. v. Diane Sanco*, No. 12-5633, 2018 U.S. Dist. LEXIS 209652 (E.D.N.Y. Dec. 10, 2018) ("[W]hile *Bi-Economy* involved a bad-faith claim against a first-party insurer, rather than a liability insurer, no court has yet held that *Bi-Economy's* expansion of consequential damages does not apply to third-party claims; indeed, at least one court has applied *Bi-Economy* to permit consequential damages in a third-party case. Other courts have assumed that *Bi-Economy* applies to third-party bad-faith claims, while still precluding consequential damages based on the language of the insurance contracts at issue.") (internal citations omitted).

North Carolina: North Carolina recognizes a private right of action in general for unfair methods of competition in or affecting commerce. *See* N.C. GEN. STAT. § 75-1.1(a). While there is no private right of action against an insurer that engages in unfair methods of competition and unfair and deceptive acts or practices in the business of insurance, in violation of N.C. GEN. STAT. § 58-63-15 (Unfair Claim Settlement Practices), a court may look to N.C. GEN. STAT. § 58-63-15(11) for examples of conduct to support a finding of liability under the broader standards of N.C. GEN. STAT. § 75-1.1. *See Gray v. N.C. Ins. Underwriting Ass'n*, 529 S.E.2d 676, 683 (N.C. 2000) (holding that an "insurance company that engages in the practice of '[n]ot attempting in good faith to effectuate prompt, fair and equitable settlements of claims in which liability has become reasonably clear,' N.C.G.S. § 58-63-15(11)(f), also engages in conduct that embodies the broader standards of N.C.G.S. § 75-1.1 because such conduct is inherently unfair, unscrupulous, immoral, and injurious to consumers") ("[S]uch conduct that violates subsection (f) of N.C.G.S. § 58-63-15(11) constitutes a violation of N.C.G.S. § 75-1.1, as a matter of law, without the necessity of an additional showing of frequency indicating a 'general business practice,' N.C.G.S. § 58-63-15(11)."); *see also Defeat The Beat, Inc. v. Underwriters At Lloyd's London*, 669 S.E.2d 48, 53–54 (N.C. Ct. App. 2008) ("In order to establish a violation of N.C. Gen. Stat. § 75-1.1, a plaintiff must show: (1) an unfair or deceptive act or practice, (2) in or affecting commerce, and (3) which proximately caused injury to plaintiffs; a court may look to the types of conduct prohibited by N.C. Gen. Stat. § 58-63-15(11) for examples of conduct which would constitute an unfair and deceptive act or practice."). "To state a claim of an insurer's bad faith refusal to pay a claim, at a minimum, [the insured] must plausibly allege an insurer's refusal to pay a valid claim and bad faith." *Martinez v. Nat'l Union Fire Ins. Co.*, 911 F. Supp. 2d 331, 337 (E.D.N.C. 2012); *Biltmore Ave. Condo. Ass'n v. Hanover Am. Ins.*

Co., No. 15-00043, 2017 U.S. Dist. LEXIS 33147 (W.D.N.C. Mar. 8, 2017), *aff'd* 706 Fed. Appx. 144 (4th Cir. 2017) ("The fact that Hanover's interpretation may be legally incorrect does not establish bad faith. Advocating a position that is ultimately determined to be incorrect does not necessarily demonstrate a lack of good faith in attempting to settle a claim. Further, the fact that both parties present reasonable yet conflicting interpretations of the Policy language suggests that the existence of coverage was anything but 'reasonably clear.'") (addressing § 58-63-15(11)(f), which prohibits an insurer from "not attempting in good faith to effectuate prompt, fair and equitable settlements of claims in which liability has become reasonably clear"); *New Hickory Pizza, Inc. v. TIG Ins. Co.*, No. 16-00164, 2017 U.S. Dist. LEXIS 142091 (W.D.N.C. Aug. 31, 2017) ("Plaintiff has failed to allege sufficient facts to make plausible that Defendant ever recognized the claim at issue here as valid. The denial letters unambiguously made clear that Defendant did not recognize the claim and provided reasons based on language in the Policy.") (finding that "allegations of a failure to reasonably investigate are not in themselves sufficient with respect to the first element of a bad faith settlement claim"); *Browder v. State Farm Fire & Cas. Co.*, No. 20-00026, 2020 U.S. Dist. LEXIS 243021 (W.D.N.C. Dec. 28, 2020) (rejecting insurer's argument that bad faith does not exist because the insurer "never accepted Plaintiffs' claim as valid") ("If a claim for bad faith could be avoided simply by never stating that an insurance claim is valid, then no insurance company that refused to pay a claim, regardless of the merits or circumstances of that decision, could ever be guilty of bad faith. This seems unreasonable, and the Court is unpersuaded that such a bright-line rule should apply to the insurance context.").

On the subject of third-party bad faith, a North Carolina District Court held that "the duty of the insurer in the exercise of its contract right to settle a pending liability claim or suit, is "to act diligently and in good faith in effecting settlements within policy limits and, if necessary to accomplish that purpose, to pay the full amount of the policy." *Coca-Cola Bottling Co. of Asheville, N.C. v. Md. Cas. Co.*, 325 F. Supp. 204, 206 (W.D.N.C. 1971) (citation and internal quotation omitted). "Although the insurer may be unreasonable as seen in retrospect, it is liable for recovery beyond its policy limits only if it acts with wrongful or fraudulent purpose or with lack of good faith; an honest mistake of judgment is not actionable." *Id.* "In order to recover punitive damages for the tort of an insurance company's bad faith refusal to settle, a plaintiff must prove: (1) a refusal to pay after recognition of a valid claim; (2) bad faith; and (3) aggravating or outrageous conduct. In this context, bad faith means not based on honest disagreement or innocent mistake. The third element ... may be shown by fraud, malice, gross negligence, insult, rudeness, oppression, or wanton and reckless disregard of plaintiff's rights. North Carolina courts have recognized that a low settlement offer in violation of N.C. GENERAL STATUTE § 58-63-15(11) (h) is also a factor contributing to aggravated conduct." *Guessford v. Penn. Nat'l Mut. Cas. Ins. Co.*, 983 F. Supp. 2d 652, 671–72 (M.D.N.C. 2013) (citations and internal quotations omitted). *See also Lovell v. Nationwide Mut. Ins. Co.*, 424 S.E.2d 181 (N.C. Ct. App. 1993), *aff'd* 334 N.C. 682 (N.C. 1993) (discussed in *Guessford* and addressing bad faith failure to settle, but not in a typical excess verdict situation); *DENC, LLC v. Phila. Indem. Ins. Co.*, 454 F. Supp. 3d 552 (M.D.N.C. 2020) ("While the Court agrees that DENC was just as guilty of posturing during the settlement process as Philadelphia was, Philadelphia, not DENC, is the wrongdoer here: Philadelphia sent conflicting coverage letters and wrote a deceptive denial letter. Its failure to make a reasonable settlement offer that gave any weight at all to Philadelphia's deceptive conduct in sending the denial letter means that for nearly two years, Philadelphia engaged in an unwarranted refusal to settle. While the Court will take DENC's settlement conduct into account…Philadelphia does not get off the hook for all of the attorneys' fees incurred by DENC…merely because DENC might have done a better job negotiating or because Philadelphia made a last-minute offer that was finally reasonable.") (addressing bad faith failure to settle, outside of the typical excess verdict situation).

North Dakota: North Dakota recognizes a cause of action for bad faith if an insurer acts unreasonably in handling an insured's claim by failing to compensate the insured, without proper cause, for a loss covered by the policy. *Hanson v. Cincinnati Life Ins. Co.*, 571 N.W.2d 363, 369–70 (N.D. 1997); *see also Seifert v. Farmers Union Mut. Ins. Co.*, 497 N.W.2d 694, 698 (N.D. 1993) ("[T]he fact most significant to the question of bad faith was the refusal of the insurer to pay its insured's claim, despite the insurer's knowledge that the insured had incurred a payable loss.") (citing *Corwin Chrysler-Plymouth, Inc. v. Westchester Fire Ins. Co.*, 279 N.W.2d 638, 644 (N.D. 1979)); *Fetch v. Quam*, 623 N.W.2d 357, 361 (N.D. 2001) ("This duty of good faith imposed on an insurer, which has its genesis in the contractual relationship between the insurer and its policyholders, is implied by law to include a duty of fair dealing in paying claims, providing defense to claims, negotiating settlements, and fulfilling all other contractual obligations. … The gravamen of the test for bad faith is whether the insurer acts unreasonably in handling an insured's claim. … Whether an insurer has acted in bad faith is ordinarily a factual question to be determined by the trier of fact.") (citations omitted). "An insurer has a duty to act fairly and in good faith in

482 General Liability Insurance Coverage

dealing with its insured, including a duty of fair dealing in paying claims, providing defenses to claims, negotiating settlements, and fulfilling all other contractual obligations." *Johnson v. Auto-Owners Ins. Co.*, No. 3:07-87, 2009 U.S. Dist. LEXIS 22278 (D.N.D. Mar. 19, 2009) (citing *Hartman v. Miller*, 656 N.W.2d 676, 680 (N.D. 2003)); *Star Ins. Co. v. Cont'l Res., Inc.*, No. 12-121, 2013 U.S. Dist. LEXIS 191767 (D.N.D. Feb. 20, 2013) ("The failure to provide a defense to an insured who is covered by a policy as alleged by P&W is, as a matter of law, an unreasonable act unless there was proper cause for refusing to defend. However, the mere fact that an insurer's position as to coverage is determined to be erroneous does not automatically equate with bad faith."); *Mau v. Twin City Fire Ins. Co.*, No. 16-325, 2017 U.S. Dist. LEXIS 174582 (D.N.D. Oct. 3, 2017) ("The gravamen of the test for bad faith is whether the insurer acts unreasonably in handling an insured's claim. An insurer acts unreasonably by failing to compensate an insured for a loss covered by a policy, unless the insurer has a proper cause for refusing payment. It is axiomatic there is no breach of the duty of good faith and fair dealing when there is no potential for coverage."); *Selective Way Ins. Co. v. CSC Gen. Contrs., Inc.*, 994 F.3d 952 (8th Cir. 2021) (noting that "[t]he mere fact that an insurer's position is held invalid by the courts does not necessarily mean it acted in bad faith"; rather, the insurer must act "unreasonably in handling an insured's claim by failing to compensate the insured, without proper cause, for a loss covered by the policy").

North Dakota does not appear to have conclusively formulated a bad faith standard for establishing an insurer's liability for an excess verdict following its failure to settle a suit within policy limits. For some guidance, *see Fetch v. Quam*, 623 N.W.2d 357 (N.D. 2001) and cases discussed therein.

Ohio: Ohio recognizes a cause of action in tort for bad faith if "an insurer fails to exercise good faith in the processing of a claim of its insured where its refusal to pay the claim is not predicated upon circumstances that furnish reasonable justification therefor. Intent is not and has never been an element of the reasonable justification standard." *Zoppo v. Homestead Ins. Co.*, 644 N.E.2d 397, 400 (Ohio 1994) (citation and internal quotation omitted); *see also McCurdy v. Hanover Fire & Cas. Ins. Co.*, 964 F. Supp. 2d 863, 874 (N.D. Ohio 2013) ("The burden is on the plaintiff to establish bad faith, it is not a defendant's burden to establish it acted in good faith."); *Palmer v. Grange Mut. Cas. Co.*, No. 2008-T-0124, 2009 Ohio App. LEXIS 3389 (Ohio Ct. App. Aug. 7, 2009) ("To withstand a motion for summary judgment in a bad faith claim, an insured must oppose such a motion with evidence which tends to show that the insurer had no reasonable justification for refusing the claim, and the insurer either had actual knowledge of that fact or intentionally failed to determine whether there was any reasonable justification for refusing the claim.") (quoting *Tokles & Sons, Inc. v. Midwestern Indemn. Co.*, 605 N.E.2d 936 (Ohio 1992)); *Belsito v. Allstate Prop. & Cas. Ins. Co.*, No. 10–988, 2011 U.S. Dist. LEXIS 72758 (N.D. Ohio July 7, 2011) ("An insurer fails to exercise good faith in processing an insurance claim when its refusal to pay the claim is not predicated upon circumstances that furnish reasonable justification therefor. Denial of a claim is not reasonably justified when it is done arbitrarily and capriciously. However, denial of a claim may be reasonably justified when the claim was fairly debatable and the refusal was premised on either the status of the law at the time of the denial or the facts that gave rise to the claim. The test, therefore, is not whether the defendant's conclusion to deny benefits was correct, but whether the decision to deny benefits was arbitrary or capricious, and there existed a reasonable justification for the denial.") (citations and internal quotes omitted); *Harris v. Transamerica Advisors Life Ins. Co.*, 77 N.E.3d 577 (Ohio Ct. App. 2017) ("Even where a claim is ultimately paid, the insurer's 'foot-dragging' in handling and evaluating the claim may support a bad-faith cause of action."); *Ballard v. Nationwide Ins. Co.*, 46 N.E.3d 170 (Ohio Ct. App. 2015) ("There are two types of bad faith claims: (1) when an insurer breaches its duty of good faith by intentionally refusing to pay an insured's claim where there is no lawful basis for the refusal coupled with actual knowledge of that fact; and (2) when an insurer breaches its duty of good faith by intentionally refusing to pay an insured's claim where the insurer intentionally failed to determine whether there was any lawful basis for such refusal."); *Brumitt v. Seeholzer*, No. 16-020, 2019 Ohio App. LEXIS 1664 (Ohio Ct. App. Apr. 26, 2019) (finding "that evidence of alleged violations of the [Unfair Claims Settlement Practices Act] does not constitute evidence of bad faith" because "the Ohio Administrative Code does not create a private cause of action for violation of its rules"); *Harsh v. Geico Gen. Ins. Co.*, No. 17-00814, 2019 U.S. Dist. LEXIS 74464 (S.D. Ohio May 2, 2019) (finding that an insurer can act in bad faith by withholding a policy limits payment until after a declaratory judgment coverage action was completed).

In the third-party bad faith context, an "insurer cannot be held liable in tort for mere negligence on its part in failing or refusing to settle or compromise a claim brought against the insured for an amount within the policy limit, but that to be held liable in tort for its failure or refusal in this respect so as to entitle the insured to recover for the excess of the judgment over the policy limit it must have been guilty of fraud or bad faith." *Hart v. Republic Mut. Ins. Co.*, 87 N.E.2d 347, 349 (Ohio

1949) (citations and internal quotation omitted). *See also Siemientkowski v. State Farm Ins. Co.*, No. 85323, 2005 Ohio App. LEXIS 3908 (Ohio Ct. App. Aug 18, 2005) (addressing *Hart* and third-party bad faith); *Calich v. Allstate Ins. Co.*, No. 21500, 2004 Ohio App. LEXIS 1439 (Ohio Ct. App. Mar. 31, 2004) (addressing *Hart* and third-party bad faith); *NL Corp., Inc. v. Seneca Specialty Ins. Co.*, No. 28927, 2021 Ohio App. LEXIS 1558 (Ohio Ct. App. May 7, 2021) ("NL argues that, even if an insurer does not have a duty to defend, it can still be held liable for bad faith. The Ohio Supreme Court has held that '[a]n insurer fails to exercise good faith in the processing of a claim of its insured where its refusal to pay the claim is not predicated upon circumstances that furnish reasonable justification therefor.' We have said that 'refusal to pay' encompasses more than the outright denial of a claim…But those cases dealt with an insured's claim against its own insurer, not the insurer's treatment of a third-party claim. The Fourth District, citing several Ohio courts that have applied *Zoppo's* reasonable-justification standard to 'duty to defend' cases, has concluded that the standard applies to any bad-faith claim. We question whether the handling of a third-party claim that is settled within policy limits should be viewed in the same light as a direct claim of the insured against its own insurance company.") (internal citations omitted).

Oklahoma: Under Oklahoma law, "[t]he elements of a bad faith claim against an insurer for delay in payment of first-party coverage are: (1) claimant was entitled to coverage under the insurance policy at issue; (2) the insurer had no reasonable basis for delaying payment; (3) the insurer did not deal fairly and in good faith with the claimant; and (4) the insurer's violation of its duty of good faith and fair dealing was the direct cause of the claimant's injury. The absence of any one of these elements defeats a bad faith claim." *Ball v. Wilshire Ins. Co.*, 221 P.3d 717, 724 (Okla. 2009). "If there is a legitimate dispute concerning coverage or no conclusive precedential legal authority requiring coverage, withholding or delaying payment is not unreasonable or in bad faith." *Id.* at 725; *see also Platner v. State Farm Mut. Auto. Ins. Co.*, No. 09-CV-0353, 2010 U.S. Dist. LEXIS 48840 (N.D. Okla. May 18, 2010) ("The critical question in a bad faith claim is whether the insurer had a good faith belief, at the time its performance was requested, that it had a justifiable reason for withholding [or delaying] payment under the policy.") (quoting *Ball*, 221 P.3d at 725); *Bannister v. State Farm Mut. Auto. Ins. Co.*, 692 F.3d 1117, 1128 n.11 (10th Cir. 2012) (applying Oklahoma law) ("[A]n insurer's violation of the [Oklahoma Unfair Claims Settlement Practices Act] does not give rise to an inference of bad faith in the context of [a] tort action."); *Phelps v. State Farm Mut. Auto. Ins. Co.*,

No. 2014-208, 2015 U.S. Dist. LEXIS 101651 (W.D. Ok. Aug. 4, 2015) ("Under Oklahoma law, when an insurer denies a claim based on the existence of a legitimate dispute, there can be no inference of bad faith. However, a legitimate dispute as to coverage will not act as an impenetrable shield against a valid claim of bad faith. In other words, even where there is a legitimate business dispute, a jury may decide the issue of bad faith if there is evidence that the insurer did not actually rely on that legitimate basis to deny coverage or that the insurer acted improperly in other ways.") (citations and internal quotes omitted); *Smith v. Am. Nat'l Prop. & Cas. Co.*, No. 20-00115, 2020 U.S. Dist. LEXIS 240642 (N.D. Okla. Dec. 22, 2020) ("Oklahoma law does not require the insurer's position in a dispute to be correct to avoid liability. Even if the jury finds for the plaintiff on the dispute and renders a verdict for breach of an insurance contract, this does not mean the insurer acted in bad faith."); *United States Liab. Ins. Co. v. Paul*, No. 19-677, 2020 U.S. Dist. LEXIS 243199 (N.D. Okla. Dec. 11, 2020) ("[T]he court concludes that Paul has not submitted evidence from which a reasonable juror could conclude that USLIC's handling of Paul's insurance claim was tortious. While the court infers that USLIC did not look beyond the pleadings to analyze whether coverage was possible, when a bad faith claim is premised on inadequate investigation, the insured must make a showing that material facts were overlooked or that a more thorough investigation would have produced relevant information. . . . Paul's marital status was not material or relevant to that determination. Accordingly, USLIC's failure to interview Paul and, as a result, failure to learn that Paul was never married to Destiny Spillers, is not evidence that USLIC overlooked material facts or failed to garner relevant information.").

In the third-party bad faith context, the Supreme Court of Oklahoma held that "the minimum level of culpability necessary for liability against an insurer to attach is more than simple negligence, but less than the reckless conduct necessary to sanction a punitive damage award against said insurer." *Badillo v. Mid Century Ins. Co.*, 121 P.3d 1080, 1094 (Okla. 2005). "[T]he insured's interests must be given faithful consideration and the insurer must treat a claim being made by a third party against its insured's liability policy as if the insurer alone were liable for the entire amount of the claim." *Id.* at 1093 (citation and internal quotes omitted); *Watson v. Farmers Ins. Co., Inc.*, No. 12-CV-391-JD-PJC, 2014 U.S. Dist. LEXIS 73155 (N.D. Okla. May 29, 2014) ("It is true that, under Oklahoma law, an insurer has no duty to deal fairly and in good faith with a third party. However, an insurance company does owe duties to its insured when dealing with a third party's claim against its insured.") (citations omitted); *Dabbs v. Shelter Mut. Ins. Co.*, No. 15-00148, 2019 U.S. Dist. LEXIS 166716 (W.D. Okla. Sept. 27, 2019) ("[T]here is simply no evidence on the record creating a dispute of fact that Defendant acted with bad faith. For example, there is no evidence that Defendant ignored undisputed facts supporting a claim. . . . Here, there is no indication of excess delays on Defendant's part. To the contrary, Defendant, according to the record, engaged the process from the outset and acted swiftly in attempting to resolve possible competing claims on a limited policy. Defendant retained counsel for Plaintiff and remained actively involved in ongoing litigation. There is no evidence that retained counsel was incompetent or conflicted. Plaintiff points out that Defendant failed to investigate retained counsel's qualifications, experience, or reputation. But Plaintiff points to no authority obligating Defendant to do so, and the Court cannot locate any. Even drawing all reasonable inferences in Plaintiff's favor, these facts do not allege more than mere negligence, and to sustain a bad faith claim, mere negligence is not enough.").

Oregon: Oregon does not recognize a tort action for first-party bad faith. *See Emp'rs' Fire Ins. Co. v. Love It Ice Cream Co.*, 670 P.2d 160, 165 (Or. Ct. App. 1983) ("[A]n insurer's bad faith refusal to pay policy benefits to its insured sounds in contract and is not an actionable tort in Oregon."); *see also Great Am. Ins. Co. v. Or. Landmark*, No. 10–3147-TC, 2011 U.S. Dist. LEXIS 64103 (D. Or. Apr. 6, 2011) ("It is well settled in Oregon law that an injured contracting party may sue for negligence only if the other party is subject to a standard of care independent of the terms of the contract. An insurer's bad faith refusal to pay policy benefits to its insured sounds in contract and is not an actionable tort in Oregon. Here, it is clear Great American did not owe any special duty to defendants, and any duty owed defendants was set forth in the policy contract.") (citing *Love It* and *Georgetown Realty, infra.*); *Russell v. Liberty Mut. Ins. Co.*, No. 13-00163, 2013 U.S. Dist. LEXIS 108534 (D. Or. Aug. 2, 2013) ("Oregon law does not allow first-party bad faith claims. That is, an insurer's bad faith refusal to pay policy benefits to its insured sounds in contract and is not an actionable tort in Oregon.") (internal quotations omitted); *Foraker v. USAA Cas. Ins. Co.*, No. 14-87, 2017 U.S. Dist. LEXIS 116895 (D. Or. July 26, 2017) (rejecting argument that a negligence *per se* claim may be brought when an insurer violates ORS § 746.230 (the Unfair Settlement Claims Practices Act)) (explaining that, under *Georgetown Realty*, "an insurer may be liable to its insured in tort when the insurer is subject to a standard of care that exists independent of the contract and without reference to the specific terms of the contract, such as when the insurer undertakes the duty to defend, thereby creating a special relationship with concomitant duties"); *Bates v. Bankers Life & Cas. Co.*, 408 P.3d 1081 (Or. 2018) (rejecting argument that an elder financial abuse action is appropriate "whenever an insurance company incorrectly denies an insurance claim" involving an elderly person) ("Allegations that an insurance company, in bad faith, delayed the processing of claims and refused to pay benefits owed to vulnerable persons under an insurance contract do not state a claim under ORS 124.110(1)(b) for wrongful withholding of 'money or property.'"); *Veloz v. Foremost Ins. Co. Grand Rapids*, 306 F. Supp. 3d 1271 (D. Or. 2018) ("Oregon courts have not provided much clarity in describing which actions constitute a breach of the duty of good faith. While it is clear that not every breach of the duty of good faith claim requires a breach of contract, it is not clear whether every breach of contract is necessarily also a breach of the duty of good faith. It does not appear that this question has been confronted by the Oregon appellate courts, this Court, or the Ninth Circuit...") ("It does not appear that Oregon law requires bad faith. Nonetheless, even in the absence of a bad faith requirement, it seems unlikely that every breach of contract claim is a per se breach of the duty of good faith...There likely are cases where an insurer's interpretation of policy language is so patently unreasonable that denial alone could support a breach of good faith claim, but that is because an insurer's adoption of a truly beyond-the-pale interpretation of contractual language is evidence that the insurer was willing to disregard the objectively reasonable contractual expectations of the insured. Here, however, defendant adopted a plausible yet ultimately incorrect reading of the contract language. Under such circumstances, a breach of the duty of good faith claim requires evidence of something beyond the mere breach of contract to proceed."); *Foraker v. USAA Cas. Ins. Co.*, 345 F. Supp. 3d 1308 (D. Or. 2018) ("The Court is unable to find supporting precedent that—even if USAA acted reasonably and in good faith—it breached its obligation of good faith and fair dealing merely by offering substantially less in settlement negotiations than the amount Foraker ultimately recovered at trial.") (holding that, "[s]imply violating O.R.S. § 746.230(1) (g), without more" does not "automatically mean an insurer has breached the covenant of good faith and fair dealing").

In the context of third-party bad faith, the Supreme Court of Oregon adopted a negligence standard. *Georgetown Realty, Inc. v. Home Ins. Co.*, 831 P.2d 7, 14 (Or. 1992) (en banc). "The insurer is negligent in failing to settle, where an opportunity to settle exists, if in choosing not to settle it would be taking an unreasonable risk—that is, a risk that would involve chances of unfavorable results out of reasonable proportion to the chances of favorable results. Stating the rule in terms of 'good faith' or 'bad faith' tends to inject an inappropriate subjective element—the insurer's state of mind—into the formula. The insurer's duty is best expressed by an objective test: Did the insurer exercise due care under the circumstances?" *Id.* at 13 (quoting *Me. Bonding & Cas. Co. v. Centennial Ins. Co.*, 693 P.2d 1296, 1299 (Or. 1985) (en banc)); *see also Alexander Mfg., Inc. v. Ill. Union Ins. Co.*, 666 F. Supp. 2d 1185, 1207 (D. Or. 2009) ("The insurer must approach an opportunity to settle by considering the interests of the insured equally with its own. An insurer that, through bad faith or negligence, breaches its duty to the insured, may be liable to the insured for the amount of any excess verdict.") (citations omitted); *Goddard v. Farmers Ins. Co.*, 179 P.3d 645 (Or. 2008) (en banc) (discussing *Georgetown Realty* and *Farris v. U.S. Fid. & Guar. Co.*, 587 P.2d 1015 (Or. 1978) in relation to bad faith failure to defend and bad faith failure to settle); *Forge Underwriting v. Greenspan*, No. 19-810, 2019 U.S. Dist. LEXIS 225679 (D. Or. Dec. 3, 2019) (finding no bad faith because "even if the acts of Forge and Starr amounted to a refusal to settle within policy limits, such a claim sounds in contract only").

Pennsylvania: A Pennsylvania statute provides that, "In an action arising under an insurance policy, if the court finds that the insurer has acted in bad faith toward the insured, the court may take all of the following actions: (1) [award interest (as specified in the statute)]. (2) Award punitive damages against the insurer. (3) Award court costs and attorney fees against the insurer." 42 PA. CONS. STAT. § 8371. In *Rancosky v. Wash. Nat'l Ins. Co.*, 170 A.3d 364 (Pa. 2017), the Pennsylvania Supreme Court held that "to prevail in a bad faith insurance claim pursuant to Section 8371, a plaintiff must demonstrate, by clear and convincing evidence, (1) that the insurer did not have a reasonable basis for denying benefits under the policy and (2) that the insurer knew or recklessly disregarded its lack of a reasonable basis in denying the claim. We further hold that proof of the insurer's subjective motive of self-interest or ill-will, while perhaps probative of the second prong of the above test, is not a necessary prerequisite to succeeding in a bad faith claim. Rather, proof of the insurer's knowledge or reckless disregard for its lack of reasonable basis in denying the claim is sufficient for demonstrating bad faith under the second prong." *Id.* at 377. The decision sets forth the history of bad faith law nationally, as well as Pennsylvania's § 8371, adopted in 1990. The court noted that it "has not had occasion to consider the precise contours of bad faith claims arising under Section 8371 since its enactment." *Id.* at 373. The court explained that the Superior Court's "longstanding two-pronged test, first articulated in *Terletsky [v. Prudential Property & Cas. Ins. Co.*, 649 A.2d 680 (Pa. Super. Ct. 1994)]*, presents an appropriate framework for analyzing bad faith claims under Section 8371" and the "*Terletsky*" test, and its imposition of a recklessness standard for liability under the second prong, comports with the historical development of bad faith in Pennsylvania and effectuates the intent of the General Assembly in enacting Section 8371." *Id.* at 376. Thus, decisions addressing *Terletsky* would seemingly remain relevant. *Berg v. Nat'l Mut. Ins. Co.*, 189 A.3d 1030 (Pa. Super. Ct. 2018) ("Our law imposes a duty of good faith and fair dealing on insurance companies, and § 8371 provides for punitive damages in the event of insurer bad faith. Thus, the law provides insureds with a means of addressing any misconduct by their insurers. The relative power and wealth of the insurer as compared to the insured is not relevant to whether bad faith occurred in a particular case, unless some factual basis can be shown that the insurer used its wealth to engage in bad faith."); *Ironshore Specialty Ins. Co. v. Conemaugh Health Sys.*, 423 F. Supp. 139 (W.D. Pa. 2019) ("[A]ctions constituting bad faith are not limited solely to a denial of coverage—bad faith may also include a lack of investigation, unnecessary or unfounded investigation, failure to communicate with the insured, or failure to promptly acknowledge or act on claims. Bad faith can also include poor claims-handling, the insurer's failure to act with diligence or respond to the insured, scattershot investigation, and similar conduct. Failure to properly defend litigation against an insured may also give rise to bad faith liability. Payment of the claim does not grant immunity from liability for bad faith. Bad faith claims may arise from conduct before, during, or after litigation. Further, the use of litigation in bad faith to evade a duty that a policy requires can give rise to a claim under § 8371.") (internal citations omitted).

The standard in Pennsylvania for third-party bad faith is as follows: "[W]hen there is little possibility of a verdict or settlement within the limits of the policy, the decision to expose the insured to personal pecuniary loss must be based on a bona fide belief by the insurer, predicated upon all of the circumstances of the case, that it has a good possibility of winning the suit. While it is the insurer's right under the policy to make the decision as to whether a claim against the insured should be litigated or settled, it is not a right of the insurer to hazard the insured's financial well-being. Good faith requires that the chance of a finding of nonliability be real and substantial and that the decision to litigate be made honestly." *Cowden v. Aetna Cas. & Sur. Co.*, 134 A.2d 223, 228 (Pa. 1957); *see also Birth Ctr. v. St. Paul Cos., Inc.*, 787 A.2d 376, 385 (Pa. 2001) (addressing damages recoverable for bad faith failure to settle) ("Where, as here, the insured can prove that it sustained damages in excess of the verdict, the insurer's payment of the excess has little to do with the insured's damages. Accordingly, the insurer's payment of the excess should not free it from other known or foreseeable damages it has caused its insured to incur."); *McMahon v. Med. Protective Co.*, 92 F. Supp. 3d 367 (W.D. Pa. 2015) (discussing *Cowden* and predicting, following a review of Pennsylvania case law on the issue, that entry of an excess verdict is not a prerequisite for a third-party bad faith claim under Pennsylvania common law); *Angeli v. Liberty Mut. Ins. Co.*, No. 18-703, 2020 U.S. Dist. LEXIS (M.D. Pa. 2020) (citing *Cowden* and *Birth Control* standards for bad faith refusal to settle).

Rhode Island: A Rhode Island statute permits an action against an insurer that "wrongfully and in bad faith refused to pay or settle a claim made pursuant to the provisions of the policy, or otherwise wrongfully and in bad faith refused to timely perform its obligations under the contract of insurance." R.I. GEN. LAWS § 9-1-33. "Bad faith is established when the proof demonstrates that the insurer denied coverage or refused payment without a reasonable basis in fact or law for the denial. The standard that this Court employs in making that determination is the 'fairly debatable' standard. According to that standard, an insurer is entitled to debate a claim that is fairly debatable. That inquiry turns on whether there is sufficient evidence from which reasonable minds could conclude that in the investigation, evaluation, and processing of the claim, the insurer acted unreasonably and either knew or was conscious of the fact that its conduct was unreasonable." *Imperial Cas. & Indem. Co. v. Bellini*, 947 A.2d 886, 893 (R.I. 2008) (citations and internal quotes omitted); *New York Life Ins. Co. v. Ortiz*, No. 14-74, 2015 U.S. Dist. LEXIS 134097 (D.R.I. Sept. 30, 2015) ("[B]ecause New York Life seeks to deposit the policy proceeds into the registry of this Court, there has been no 'refus[al] to pay or settle [Ortiz's] claim.' Moreover, before a bad-faith claim can even be considered, a plaintiff must prove that the insurer breached its obligation under the insurance contract.") (addressing § 9-1-33); *Summit Ins. Co. v. Stricklett*, No. 2012-5368, 2017 R.I. Super. LEXIS 26 (R.I. Super. Ct. Jan. 19, 2017) ("Although an insurer is obligated to consider reasonable settlement offers, they are not obligated to search out and encourage adversaries when they rationally conclude that their insured was not at fault.") ("The Alves suggest that a reasonable insurer would have employed an expert in accident reconstruction before denying the claim. However, Summit easily determined the sequence of events, the lack of contradictory evidence, and multiple witness statements corroborating the events. An insurance company need not always retain an expert to resolve a claim where there is minimal (if any) evidence in support of it."); *Geovera Specialty Ins. Co. v. Poulton*, No. 16-432, 2017 U.S. Dist. LEXIS

165539 (D.R.I. Sept. 26, 2017) ("While the slight delay in initially responding to [an insured's] request for a defense in the state court action may provide relevant evidence to resolve a claim for bad faith, it does not, on its own, provide a basis for maintaining a claim for bad faith") (fining that an insurer did not act in bad faith by offering to defend the insured under a general reservation of rights and thereafter filing a declaratory judgment action to determine its obligations under the policy).

Rhode Island sets a low threshold for insureds to establish third-party bad faith: "If the insurer declines to settle the case within the policy limits, it does so at its peril in the event that a trial results in a judgment that exceeds the policy limits, including interest. If such a judgment is sustained on appeal or is unappealed, the insurer is liable for the amount that exceeds the policy limits, unless it can show that the insured was unwilling to accept the offer of settlement. The insurer's duty is a fiduciary obligation to act in the best interests of the insured. Even if the insurer believes in good faith that it has a legitimate defense against the third party, it must assume the risk of miscalculation if the ultimate judgment should exceed the policy limits." *Asermely v. Allstate Ins. Co.*, 728 A.2d 461, 464 (R.I. 1999); *see also DeMarco v. Travelers Ins. Co.*, 26 A.3d 585 (R.I. 2011) ("[W]hen an insurer is faced with multiple claimants with claims that in the aggregate exceed the policy limits, the insurer has a fiduciary duty to engage in timely and meaningful settlement negotiations in a purposeful attempt to bring about settlement of as many claims as is possible, such that the insurer will thereby relieve its insured of as much of the insured's potential liability as is reasonably possible given the policy limits and the surrounding circumstances. … In meeting this duty, the insurer must negotiate as if there were no policy limits applicable to the claims and as if the insurer alone would be liable for the entire amount of any excess judgment. … The insurer must exercise its best professional judgment throughout this process, always keeping in mind the best interests of its insured and the necessity of minimizing its insured's possible eventual direct liability. As with the *Asermely* rule when it is applied in the single claimant situation, in order to show that an insurer has violated its fiduciary duty in a multiple claimant case, the insured (or a party to whom the rights of the insured have been assigned) need not demonstrate that the insurer acted in bad faith but only that the insurer did not act reasonably and in its insured's best interests in light of the surrounding circumstances.").

South Carolina: The Supreme Court of South Carolina stated that "if an insured can demonstrate bad faith or unreasonable action by the insurer in processing a claim under their mutually binding insurance contract, he can recover consequential damages in a tort action. Actual damages are not limited by the contract. Further, if he can demonstrate the insurer's actions were willful or in reckless disregard of the insured's rights, he can recover punitive damages." *Nichols v. State Farm Mut. Auto. Ins. Co.*, 306 S.E.2d 616, 619 (S.C. 1983), *superseded by statute as stated in Duncan v. Provident Mut. Life Ins. Co. of Phila.*, 427 S.E.2d 657 (S.C. 1993). "An insured may recover damages for a bad faith denial of coverage if he or she proves there was no reasonable basis to support the insurer's decision to deny benefits under a mutually binding insurance contract." *Cock-N-Bull Steak House, Inc. v. Generali Ins. Co.*, 466 S.E.2d 727, 730 (S.C. 1996) (quoting *Dowling v. Home Buyers Warranty Corp., II*, 400 S.E.2d 143, 144 (S.C. 1991)); *see also Liberty Mut. Fire Ins. Co. v. J.T. Walker Indus., Inc.*, No. 08-2043, 2010 U.S. Dist. LEXIS 30690 (D.S.C. Mar. 30, 2010) ("South Carolina has recognized the rule that [b]ad faith is a knowing failure on the part of the insurer to exercise an honest and informed judgment in processing a claim. ... [A]n insurer acts in bad faith where there is no reasonable basis to support the insurer's decision.") (citation and internal quotes omitted) (alteration in original); *BMW of N. Am., LLC v. Complete Auto Recon Servs., Inc.*, 731 S.E.2d 902, 907 (S.C. Ct. App. 2012) ("The elements of a cause of action for bad faith refusal to pay first party benefits under a contract of insurance are: (1) the existence of a mutually binding contract of insurance between the plaintiff and the defendant; (2) refusal by the insurer to pay benefits due under the contract; (3) resulting from the insurer's bad faith or unreasonable action in breach of an implied covenant of good faith and fair dealing arising on the contract; (4) causing damage to the insured."); *Ball v. USAA Life Ins. Co.*, No. 16-00041, 2017 U.S. Dist. LEXIS 150648 (D.S.C. Sept. 18, 2017) ("DiLisio found USAA's materiality conclusion to be reasonable because USAA's underwriter found the misrepresentation to be material using the company's guidelines and the Swiss Re Underwriting Manual (the 'Swiss Manual'). As an initial matter, it is clear that DiLisio did not conduct his own evaluation. Thus, he does not appear to know whether the underwriter correctly applied the company guidelines or the Swiss Manual. Instead, he assumes the guidelines were applied correctly and relies on the fact that the Swiss Manual is 'commonly used' to find that the decision was reasonable. Of course, the Swiss Manual was only one of the tools used in the evaluation. DiLisio does not appear to be familiar with USAA's company guidelines. Ultimately, DiLisio's answer reveals that he did not actually evaluate whether USAA's conclusion was a reasonable one. At best, he evaluated whether the process used to reach that conclusion was a reasonable one. The distinction is significant, as the law allows an insured to recover bad faith damages where there is no 'reasonable basis' for denying coverage. An insurer is not excused simply because it used 'reasonable processes,' if it nevertheless reached an unreasonable conclusion."); *Agape Senior Primary Care, Inc. v. Evanston Ins. Co.*, 304 F. Supp. 3d 492 (D.S.C. 2018) ("There must be some cases where the coverage issue is so close that a bad faith cause of action does not arise as a matter of law. Surely the law cannot provide that every time a carrier improperly denies coverage, it is guilty of acting in bad faith. Some cases present such a close call that a bad faith claim fails as a matter of law. This is such a case.").

In the third-party bad faith context, "a liability insurer owes its insured a duty to settle a personal injury claim covered by the policy, if settlement is the reasonable thing to do. An insurer who unreasonably refuses or fails to settle a covered claim within the policy limits is liable to the insured for the entire amount of the judgment obtained against the insured regardless of the limits contained in the policy." *Doe v. S.C. Med. Malpractice Liab. Joint Underwriting Ass'n*, 557 S.E.2d 670, 674 (S.C. 2001) (citations and internal quotes omitted); *Vanderhall v. State Farm Mut. Auto. Ins. Co.*, No. 14-518, 2015 U.S. Dist. LEXIS 39965 (D.S.C. Mar. 30, 2015), *aff'd* 632 Fed. Appx. 103 (4th Cir. 2015) ("Thus, the critical question raised by a motion for summary judgment in a bad faith refusal to settle case is whether, taking the evidence in a light most favorable to the nonmoving party, there sufficient evidence upon which a reasonable jury could find that the carrier acted without any reasonable basis? In other words, assuming that a valid offer of settlement had been made by Plaintiff to State Farm, was there any reasonable basis for State Farm to propose the insertion of the additional language that the settlement was 'inclusive of all economic damages, known and unknown, and any liens, assignments or statutory rights of recovery?'") (holding that "[s]ince there was clearly a potential benefit to the insured, there was a reasonable basis for the Defendant to have proposed the additional language and such action cannot, as a matter of law, constitute the basis of a claim of bad faith"); *Reeves v. S.C. Mun. Ins. & Risk Fund*, No. 28034, 2021 S.C. LEXIS 71 (S.C. June 19, 2021) (finding no bad faith where the insurer satisfied a judgment in excess of its policy limits after trial without exposing the insured to excess liability) ("While it is conceivable an insurer may subject itself to liability for consequential damages for bad faith conduct in some other respect, we do not condone the idea an insurer may incur bad faith liability for simply taking a case to the jury, when the insurer satisfied the judgment after trial without exposing the insured to excess liability."); *Columbia Ins. Co. v. Waymer*, No. 20-1266, 2021 U.S. App. LEXIS 18568 (4th Cir. June 22, 2021) (noting that "South Carolina courts have not weighed in on whether a lack of time to investigate constitutes an objectively reasonable basis for refusing to accede immediately to a short-fuse demand to pay the policy limits" but predicting that an insurer is permitted reasonable time to investigate a claim and that no obligation exists to accept a settlement offer without time to conduct an investigation).

South Dakota: South Dakota recognizes that an insurer's violation of its duty of good faith and fair dealing constitutes a tort, even though it is also a breach of contract. *Stene v. State Farm Mut. Auto. Ins. Co.*, 583 N.W.2d 399, 403 (S.D. 1998). "[F]or proof of bad faith, there must be an absence of a reasonable basis for denial of policy benefits [or failure to comply with a duty under the insurance contract] and the knowledge or reckless disregard [of the lack] of a reasonable basis for denial, implicit in that test is our conclusion that the knowledge of the lack of a reasonable basis may be inferred and imputed to an insurance company where there is a reckless disregard of a lack of a reasonable basis for denial or a reckless indifference to facts or to proofs submitted by the insured." *Id.* (citation and internal quotation omitted) (alteration in original); *see also Fed. Beef Processors, Inc. v. Royal Indem. Co.*, No. CIV. 04-5005, 2008 U.S. Dist. LEXIS 80658 (D.S.D. Oct. 9, 2008) ("Integral to the inquiry of whether there was (1) an absence of a reasonable basis for denial and (2) knowledge or a reckless disregard of the lack of a basis for denial, is whether a claim was properly investigated and whether the results of the investigation were subjected to a reasonable evaluation and review.") (citation and internal quotation omitted). "However, an insurance company … may challenge claims which are fairly debatable and will be found liable only where it has intentionally denied (or failed to process or pay) a claim without a reasonable basis. When evaluating whether an insurer has engaged in bad faith, we must look to the facts and law available to [the] [i]nsurer at the time it made the decision to deny coverage." *Bertelsen v. Allstate Ins. Co.*, 833 N.W.2d 545, 554 (S.D. 2013) (alterations in original) (citations and internal quotation marks omitted). *See also Lewison v. Western Nat'l Mut. Ins. Co.*, No. 13-4031, 2014 U.S. Dist. LEXIS 98399 (D.S.D. July 21, 2014) ("[W]hile a reasonable investigation into an insured's claim is required, plaintiffs' arguments imply that Western National was required to perform a perfect investigation. Such is not the law in South Dakota."); *Hill v. Auto Owners Ins. Co.*, No. 14-5037, 2015 U.S. Dist. LEXIS 59877 (D.S.D. May 5, 2015) ("Genuine questions of material fact as to plaintiffs' claim that Auto Owners acted in bad faith when it denied their claim for hail damage remain, such as whether there actually was hail damage, how obvious that hail damage should have been, and whether Auto Owners knew or should have known that the investigation into the damage was unreasonable.

Questions of fact also remain on whether Auto Owners acted in bad faith when it allegedly designed its claims handling process to allow its adjusters to build a case for denying valid claims. Ultimately, these questions are for a jury to determine."); *Harvieux v. Progressive N. Ins. Co.*, 915 N.W.2d 697 (S.D. 2018) (rejecting insured's claims of "companywide bad faith by Progressive through its employee-bonus plan and other internal claims policies" because although the insured "presented evidence from unrelated cases suggesting the internal policies of Progressive were contrary to the terms of Progressive's insurance contracts with its insureds and that such internal policies were unreasonable," the insured failed to present any evidence that her claims were not fairly debatable or that Progressive's internal policies caused Progressive to unreasonably investigate or evaluate her claim); *Sapienza v. Liberty Mut. Fire Ins. Co.*, 389 F. Supp. 3d 648 (D.S.D. 2019) ("According to the Supreme Court of South Dakota, requiring equal consideration in the first-party context-- where the insurer does not act like a fiduciary as it does when considering whether to settle a claim by a third party against its insured--could fundamentally alter the rights and obligations of insureds and insurers contained in the express contractual provisions of the policy.") (noting that "the Supreme Court of South Dakota has always focused on an insurer's unreasonable refusal to settle a claim against its insured when discussing third-party bad faith") (internal quotations omitted).

For purposes of third-party bad faith, in the context of an insurer's failure to settle, the Supreme Court of South Dakota has recognized that there are an array of factors to consider in determining whether an insurer's refusal to settle is equivalent to a breach of its good faith duty: "(1) the strength of the injured claimant's case on the issues of liability and damages; (2) attempts by the insurer to induce the insured to contribute to a settlement; (3) failure of the insurer to properly investigate the circumstances so as to ascertain the evidence against the insured; (4) the insurer's rejection of advice of its own attorney or agent; (5) failure of the insurer to inform the insured of a compromise offer; (6) the amount of financial risk to which each party is exposed in the event of a refusal to settle; (7) the fault of the insured in inducing the insurer's rejection of the compromise offer by misleading it as to the facts; and (8) any other factors tending to establish or negate bad faith on the part of the insurer." *Helmbolt v. LeMars Mut. Ins. Co., Inc.*, 404 N.W.2d 55, 57 (S.D. 1987) (quoting *Kunkel v. United Sec. Ins. Co. of N.J.*, 168 N.W.2d 723, 727 (S.D. 1969)).

Tennessee: A Tennessee statute provides that, if an insurer refuses "to pay a loss within sixty (60) days after a demand has been made by the policyholder, the insurer shall be liable to pay the policyholder, in addition to the loss, a sum not exceeding

25% on the liability for the loss; provided, that it is made to appear to the court or jury trying the case that the refusal to pay the loss was not in good faith, and that the failure to pay inflicted additional expense, loss, or injury including attorney fees upon the holder of the policy or fidelity bond; and provided, further, that the additional liability, within the limit prescribed, shall, in the discretion of the court or jury trying the case, be measured by the additional expense, loss, and injury including attorney fees thus entailed." TENN. CODE ANN. § 56-7-105; *see also Wilson v. State Farm Fire & Cas. Co.*, 799 F. Supp. 2d 829 (E.D. Tenn. 2011) ("This statute is penal in nature and must be strictly construed. The plaintiff has the burden of proving bad faith on the part of the insurer. ... The bad faith penalty is not recoverable in every refusal of an insurance company to pay a loss. An insurance company is entitled to rely upon available defenses and refuse payment if there is substantial legal grounds that the policy does not afford coverage for the alleged loss.") (citations omitted); *Burge v. Farmers Mut. of Tenn.*, No. M2016-01604, 2017 Tenn. App. LEXIS 235 (Tenn. Ct. App. Apr. 13, 2017) ("In the case before us, Insurer argues that it had 'substantial legal grounds' for failing to pay Plaintiffs' claim and therefore the statutory bad faith penalty was inappropriate. We disagree. A simple inquiry would have disclosed that only one mortgage encumbered the insured property, i.e., the mobile home. Insurer did not have substantial legal grounds supporting its position that Plaintiffs materially misrepresented the number of mortgages on the insured mobile home. To make matters worse, the record indicates that the Insurer compounded the problem by failing to process Plaintiffs' claim in a diligent manner. If Insurer had explained its position to Plaintiffs during the months after the fire, they could have provided any additional documents that Insurer needed in order to clarify any confusion about the mortgage. Instead, the proof presented at trial indicated that the Insurer failed to respond to Plaintiffs' calls, failed to formally deny the claim, and failed to provide an explanation for its refusal to pay until its written discovery responses after the litigation was filed and nearly two years after the fire occurred. We must therefore agree with the trial court's conclusion that Insurer's refusal to pay the loss was not in good faith."); *Cox Paradise, LLC v. Erie Ins. Exch.*, No. 20-01068, 2020 U.S. Dist. LEXIS 218611 (W.D. Tenn. Nov. 23, 2020) ("To succeed in a § 56-7-105 action, a plaintiff must establish the following: (1) 'the policy of insurance must, by its terms, have become due and payable,' (2) 'a formal demand for payment must have been made,' (3) 'the insured must have waited 60 days after making [its] demand before filing suit (unless there was a refusal to pay prior to the expiration of the 60 days),' and (4) 'the refusal to pay must not have been in good faith.'"); *Johnson v. Arch*

Specialty Ins. Co., No. 19-22172020, U.S. Dist. LEXIS 64010 (W.D. Tenn. Apr. 13, 2020) ("Plaintiffs plead that Arch refused their insurance claim in bad faith. They allege, inter alia, that the losses to the Properties are clearly compensable under the Policy, that '[t]here is no reasonable coverage dispute or other justifiable reason for [Arch's] refusal,' that Arch 'refus[ed] to pay Plaintiffs' claim without conducting a reasonable investigation based on all available information,' and that Arch failed to 'promptly provide Plaintiffs with a reasonable and accurate explanation for its refusal to pay their claim in full.'") (insurer argued that it relied on an engineering report that losses to the properties resulted from deteriorated roofing and not from a winter storm).

For purposes of third-party bad faith, the Supreme Court of Tennessee stated that "[m]ere negligence is not sufficient to impose liability for failure to settle. Moreover, an insurer's mistaken judgment is not bad faith if it was made honestly and followed an investigation performed with ordinary care and diligence. However, negligence may be considered along with other circumstantial evidence to suggest an indifference toward an insured's interest. The question of an insurance company's bad faith is for the jury if from all of the evidence it appears that there is a reasonable basis for disagreement among reasonable minds as to the bad faith of the insurance company in the handling of the claim." *Johnson v. Tenn. Farmers Mut. Ins. Co.*, 205 S.W.3d 365, 371 (Tenn. 2006). *See also For Senior Help v. Westchester Fire Ins. Co.*, No. 19-001262021, U.S. Dist. LEXIS 13256 (M.D. Tenn. Jan. 25, 2021) ("[Insurer] is not entitled to summary judgment on the bad faith failure to settle claim as a matter of law, purely on the basis that it provided a defense subject to a reservation of rights. By providing a defense, it incurred a duty to negotiate settlement in good faith as an integral part of that defense, and it may be held liable if it failed to do so.") ("Moreover, the ROR letters Westchester sent to Medex made it clear that Medex was required to obtain its 'prior consent before offering or agreeing to pay an amount which is in excess of the per Claim Retention in order to settle any Claim.' In other words, irrespective of Westchester's reservation of rights, it appears to have had exclusive control over the investigation and settlement of FSH's claim against Medex.").

Texas: The Supreme Court of Texas held that a "bad faith claimant … [must] prove that a carrier failed to attempt to effectuate a settlement after its liability has become reasonably clear." *Universe Life Ins. Co. v. Giles*, 950 S.W.2d 48, 55 (Tex. 1997) (clarifying the "no reasonable basis for denial of a claim" standard originally adopted in *Arnold v. Nat'l Cnty. Mut. Fire Ins. Co.*, 725 S.W.2d 165 (Tex. 1987)); *see* *also State Farm Fire & Cas. Co. v. Simmons*, 963 S.W.2d 42 (Tex. 1998) (discussing the evidence that supported a jury's finding that an insurer breached its duty of good faith and fair dealing); *Columbia Lloyds Ins. Co. v. Mao*, No. 02–10–00063-CV, 2011 Tex. App. LEXIS 2180 (Tex. Ct. App. Mar. 24, 2011) ("An insurer breaches its duty of good faith and fair dealing by denying or delaying a claim when the insurer's liability has become reasonably clear. The focus is not on whether an insured's claim was valid, but on the reasonableness of the insurer's conduct in rejecting the claim. Evidence of coverage, standing alone, will not constitute evidence of bad faith denial. Evidence showing only a bona fide coverage dispute does not rise to the level of bad faith. Nor is bad faith established when a trier of fact, using hindsight, decides the insurer was simply wrong about the proper construction of the terms of the policy. As long as an insurer has a reasonable basis to deny payment of a claim, even if that basis is eventually determined to be erroneous, the insurer is not liable for the tort of bad faith. But insurers do have a duty to conduct a reasonable investigation of a claim and cannot insulate themselves from bad faith liability by investigating a claim in a manner calculated to construct a pretextual basis for denial. To withstand a no-evidence motion for summary judgment, a plaintiff in a bad faith case must present evidence that the insurer failed to attempt a prompt, fair settlement when the insurer's liability has become reasonably clear.") (citations omitted); *Anderson v. Am. Risk Ins. Co.*, No. 01-15-00257, 2016 Tex. App. LEXIS 6538 (Tex. Ct. App. June 21, 2016) ("[A]bsent a breach of contract, the insured cannot maintain a common law bad faith claim in Texas unless the insurer commit[s] some act, so extreme, that would cause injury independent of the policy claim or fails to timely investigate the insureds claim."); *State Farm Lloyds v. Webb*, No. 09-15-00408, 2017 Tex. App. LEXIS 4025 (Tex. Ct. App. May 4, 2017) ("The experts in this case disagreed on whether the plumbing leak caused Webb's foundation damages, and State Farm's adjusters believed it was reasonable to rely on its expert's report. We conclude that when State Farm denied Webb's claim, liability was not reasonably clear, and based on the findings of its expert, State Farm had a reasonable basis to deny the claim. Webb offered no evidence showing that State Farm failed to conduct a reasonable investigation, that English's report was not objectively prepared, or that State Farm's reliance on English's report was unreasonable."); *Tex. Windstorm Ins. Ass'n v. James*, No. 13-17-00401, 2020 Tex. App. LEXIS 6719 (Tex. Ct. App. Aug. 20, 2020) ("While evidence that shows an insurer was incorrect about the factual basis for its denial of the claim is not evidence of bad faith, the complete disregard of a reliable estimate may be.").

In addition, a Texas statute provides that "[a] person who sustains actual damages may bring an action against another person for those damages caused by the other person engaging in an act or practice: (1) defined by Subchapter B to be an unfair method of competition or an unfair or deceptive act or practice in the business of insurance." TEX INS. CODE § 541.151. Subchapter B includes § 541.060 (Unfair Settlement Practices), which provides, among other things, that it is an unfair method of competition or an unfair or deceptive act or practice in the business of insurance to engage in the following unfair settlement practices with respect to a claim by an insured or beneficiary: failing to attempt in good faith to effectuate a prompt, fair, and equitable settlement of a claim with respect to which the insurer's liability has become reasonably clear. TEX INS. CODE § 541.060(a)(2)(A). In *USAA Tex. Lloyds Co. v. Menchaca*, 545 S.W.3d 479 (Tex. 2018), the Texas Supreme Court re-affirmed the five rules set out in *USAA Tex. Lloyds Co. v. Menchaca*, No. 14-0721, 2017 Tex. LEXIS 361 (Tex. Apr. 7, 2017), which sought to address the relationship between contract claims based upon an insurance policy and tort claims based upon the Insurance Code. *Id.* at 484. In issuing its decision, the court sated that "[b]ecause an insurer's statutory violation permits an insured to receive only those 'actual damages' that are 'caused by' the violation, we clarify and affirm the general rule that an insured cannot recover policy benefits as actual damages for an insurer's statutory violation if the insured has no right to those benefits under the policy." *Id.* at 495. *See also Tex. Friends Chabad-Lubavitch, Inc. v. Nova Cas. Co.*, No., 2021 U.S. Dist. LEXIS 90964 (S.D. Tex. May 12, 2021) ("No reasonable juror could find that Defendant failed to provide a reasonable explanation for denying coverage. Arguably Defendant did not provide this explanation 'promptly,' as § 541.060(a) (3) requires, but Plaintiff does not assert lack of promptness as a ground for its § 541.060(a)(3) claim. Defendant was not required to respond to arguments that Plaintiff has not made").

For purposes of third-party bad faith, the Supreme Court of Texas held that "there must be coverage for the third-party's claim, a settlement demand within policy limits, and reasonable terms such that an ordinarily prudent insurer would accept it, considering the likelihood and degree of the insured's potential exposure to an excess judgment. When these conditions coincide and the insurer's negligent failure to settle results in an excess judgment against the insured, the insurer is liable under the Stowers Doctrine for the entire amount of the judgment, including that part exceeding the insured's policy limits." *Phillips v. Bramlett*, 288 S.W.3d 876, 879 (Tex. 2009) (internal quotation omitted) (citing *G.A. Stowers Furniture Co. v. Am.*

Indem. Co., 15 S.W.2d 544 (Tex. Comm'n App. 1929)); *see also Tex. Farmers Ins. Co. v. Soriano*, 881 S.W.2d 312, 314–15 (Tex. 1994) ("To impose a *Stowers* duty on an insurer when there is a single claim, a settlement demand must propose to release the insured fully in exchange for a stated sum of money. ... A demand above policy limits, no matter how reasonable, does not trigger the *Stowers* duty to settle.") (citations omitted); *McDonald v. Home State Cnty. Mut. Ins. Co.*, No. 01-09-00838-CV, 2011 Tex. App. LEXIS 2149 (Tex. Ct. App. Mar. 24, 2011) ("In the context of a *Stowers* lawsuit, evidence concerning claims investigation, trial defense, and conduct during settlement negotiations is necessarily subsidiary to the ultimate issue of whether the claimant's demand was reasonable under the circumstances, such that an ordinarily prudent insurer would accept it. Given the tactical considerations inherent in settlement negotiations, an insurer should not be held liable for failing to accept an offer when the offer's terms and scope are unclear or are the subject of dispute.") (citations and internal quotations omitted); *Seger v. Yorkshire Ins. Co.*, 503 S.W.3d 388 (Tex. 2016) ("To recover under a *Stowers* cause of action, the Segers must prove that their claim meets all of the *Stowers* elements, beginning with coverage. *Stowers* Insurers are not obligated to defend against or offer to settle a claim that is not within the scope of coverage.") (addressing whether a policy was unenforceable for statutory reasons, thereby precluding insurers from pleading or proving that policy exclusions precluded coverage); *Mumford v. State Farm Mut. Auto. Ins. Co.*, No. 14-282, 2015 U.S. Dist. LEXIS 179749 (E.D. Tex. Apr. 29, 2015) ("State Farm does not direct the court to any case in which a court has held that an insurer acted reasonably as a matter of law in rejecting an injured's *Stowers* demand."); *In re Farmers Tex. Cty Mut. Ins. Co.*, 621 S.W.3d 261 (Tex. 2021) (concluding that the insured did not have a viable claim for negligent failure to settle, where "insurer chose to settle claims against its insured within policy limits but obtained a release that was contingent on the insured paying $100,000 of the $350,000 settlement") ("[W]e see no reason to extend *Stowers* to impose potential extra-contractual damages on an insurer in cases where an insured has no liability in excess of policy limits. In such cases, the contract between the insured and insurer sets out the carrier's obligations and protects the insured."); *Ryan v. New York Marine & Gen. Ins. Co.*, No. 19-629, 2020 U.S. Dist. LEXIS 180380 (W.D. Tex. Sept. 30, 2020) (holding that the *Stowers* standard applies to both statutory and common-law third party claims) (noting that, although "Texas law does not support a common law cause of action for breach of the duty of good faith and fair dealing with respect to a third-party claimant, it does not preclude an insured from pursuing a statutory claim under Chapter 541, as NYM implies").

Utah: The Supreme Court of Utah held that a violation of the good faith duty to bargain or settle under an insurance contract gives rise to a claim for breach of contract and not a tort action. *Beck v. Farmers Ins. Exch.*, 701 P.2d 795, 798 (Utah 1985). "[T]he implied obligation of good faith performance contemplates, at the very least, that the insurer will diligently investigate the facts to enable it to determine whether a claim is valid, will fairly evaluate the claim, and will thereafter act promptly and reasonably in rejecting or settling the claim. The duty of good faith also requires the insurer to deal with laymen as laymen and not as experts in the subtleties of law and underwriting and to refrain from actions that will injure the insured's ability to obtain the benefits of the contract." *Christiansen v. Farmers Ins. Exch.*, 116 P.3d 259, 262 (Utah 2005) (quoting *Beck*, 701 P.2d at 801) (alteration in original); *see also U.S. Fid. v. U.S. Sports Specialty*, 270 P.3d 464, 470–71 (Utah 2012) ("Bad faith is merely the inverse of the implied covenant of good faith and fair dealing that inheres in all insurance contracts.") ("If an insurer acts reasonably in its evaluation of a claim, it cannot be liable for violating the covenant, even if the insurer initially denies a claim that is later determined to be covered by the policy."); *Borandi v. USAA Cas. Ins. Co.*, 13-141, 2014 U.S. Dist. LEXIS 178527 (D. Utah Dec. 29, 2014) ("Under Utah law, whether there has been a breach of good faith and fair dealing is a factual issue, generally inappropriate for decision as a matter of law. However, whether an insured's claim is fairly debatable under a given set of facts is . . . a question of law."); *Matthews v. Pa. Life Ins. Co.*, No. 12-896, 2014 U.S. Dist. LEXIS 104965 (D. Utah July 29, 2014) ("The denial of a claim is reasonable if the insured's claim is 'fairly debatable.' If an insurer denies an insured's claim that is fairly debatable, then the insurer is entitled to debate it and cannot be held to have breached the implied covenant if it chooses to do so.") (*aff'd* 606 Fed. Appx. 460 (10th Cir. 2015)); *Fire Ins. Exch. v. Oltmanns*, No. 20160304, 2017 Utah LEXIS 182 (Utah Nov. 21, 2017), *aff'd* 416 P.3d 1148 (Utah 2018) ("It was more than fair for Fire Insurance to argue that its policy's 'jet ski' exclusion applied to bodily injuries resulting from the use of an Aquatrax. In litigating whether the 'jet ski' exclusion encompassed Aquatrax accidents, Fire Insurance put forward substantial usage evidence suggesting that the term 'jet ski' is, in Fire Insurance's words, a 'genericized term for any type of personal watercraft.' Fire Insurance's argument is bolstered by the fact that 'jet ski' is frequently treated as a generic term in cases, ordinances, and dictionaries. The cited dictionaries, ordinances, and cases show that the public uses the trademarked term 'jet ski' generically, at least on occasion. That suggests that the scope of the term may be fairly debatable."); *Owners Ins. Co. v. Dockstader*, No. 18-173, 2019 U.S.

Dist. LEXIS 42623 (D. Utah Mar. 14, 2019) (finding that where an insurance carrier seeks a declaratory judgment as to coverage under an insurance policy, "there is no basis for a bad faith claim for refusal to settle a claim"), *aff'd* 2021 U.S. App. LEXIS 19369 (10th Cir. June 29, 2021) (addressing insurer's handling of a settlement in the face of a coverage defense); *Christensen v. Mid-Century Ins. Co.*, No. 19-00164, 2020 U.S. Dist. LEXIS 23511 (D. Utah Feb. 10, 2020) (noting that neither punitive nor exemplary damages may be recovered in a bad faith action, as bad faith claims sound in contract).

In the third-party bad faith context, the Supreme Court of Utah held that "the best view is that [the insurer] must act in good faith and be as zealous in protecting the interests of its insured as it would in looking after its own. Whether it discharges that duty may depend upon various considerations including the certainty or uncertainty as to the issues of liability, injuries, and damages." *Ammerman v. Farmers Ins. Exch.*, 430 P.2d 576, 579 (Utah 1967). "It is therefore essential that the provisions of the contract be given effect and that the company have a reasonable latitude of discretion to decide whether it will accept a proposed settlement. Otherwise the policy limit would mean nothing and it would be all but impossible to determine the correct amount of premiums to be charged and the reserves necessary to cover potential losses." *Id.; see also Rupp v. Transcontinental Ins. Co.*, 627 F. Supp. 2d 1304, 1319, 1324 (D. Utah 2008) (discussing *Ammerman* and settlement in excess of limits) (predicting that the Utah Supreme Court would hold that claims are not barred as a matter of law by the voluntary payment and "legal action limitation" conditions, nor that an insured facing the significant likelihood of an excess judgment is required to take the case to trial before a cause of action for bad faith accrues); *State Farm Fire & Cas. Co. v. Inevat, LLC*, No. 17-00901, 2018 U.S. Dist. LEXIS 97075 (D. Utah. June 8, 2018) (noting that a bad faith failure to reasonably engage in settlement discussions could likely exist prior to final disposition of the underlying third-party claim) ("[T]he wisdom of a rule that only envisions the formation of bad faith after final disposition of the underlying third party claim is debatable. It seems likely that a factual scenario could exist under which final judgment would not be the only acceptable form of evidence. At present, however, this case does not present that scenario. Indeed, without something more concrete---a final disposition, the rejection of offers where the insured is 'facing the significant likelihood of an excess judgment,' or an 'unreasonable' decision to proceed to trial---the court is presented with a theoretical conflict as to what may or might happen that, at this juncture, proves too nebulous to support the claim.").

Vermont: The Supreme Court of Vermont held that the state "recognizes a claim for tortious bad faith brought by an insured against its own insurer when an insurer not only errs in denying coverage, but does so unreasonably. To establish a claim for bad faith, a plaintiff must show that (1) the insurer had no reasonable basis to deny the insured the benefits of the policy, and (2) the company knew or recklessly disregarded the fact that it had no reasonable basis for denying the insured's claim." *Peerless Ins. Co. v. Frederick*, 869 A.2d 112, 116 (Vt. 2004); *see also Fine Paints of Eur., Inc. v. Acadia Ins. Co.*, No. 2:08-CV-81, 2009 U.S. Dist. LEXIS 24188 (D. Vt. Mar. 24, 2009) ("If the claim is 'fairly debatable,' then the insurer will not be found liable."); *Town of Ira v. Vt. League of Cities & Towns*, 109 A.3d 893 (Vt. 2014) ("We agree with the trial court that insurer's position was fairly debatable as a matter of law. As the trial court found, we have not yet decided this question. Although we have found that the decisions from other jurisdictions in favor of the Town's position are persuasive, this does not mean that all precedents support the Town. Although we reject its reasoning, we do not find . . . the chief case relied upon by insurer, as off-point as the Town argues."); *Murphy v. Patriot Ins. Co.*, 106 A.3d 911 (Vt. 2014) ("Sloppy or negligent claims handling does not rise to the level of bad faith. In a first-party bad faith claim, an imperfect investigation, standing alone, is not sufficient cause for recovery if the insurer in fact has an objectively reasonable basis for denying the claim.") (citations and internal quotes omitted); *Garcia v. Farm Family Ins. Co.*, No. 465-5-15, 2019 Vt. Super. LEXIS 107 (Vt. Super. Ct. Aug. 28, 2019) (noting "an insurer cannot delegate its duty to act in good faith and avoid liability by saying 'they did it, not us'").

For purposes of third-party bad faith, the Supreme Court of Vermont stated that "[t]he insurer's fiduciary duty to act in good faith when handling a claim against the insured obligates it to take the insured's interests into account. The company must diligently investigate the facts and the risks involved in the claim, and should rely only upon persons reasonably qualified to make such an assessment. If demand for settlement is made, the insurer must honestly assess its validity based on a determination of the risks involved." *Myers v. Ambassador Ins. Co. Inc.*, 508 A.2d 689, 691 (Vt. 1986); *see also Vt. Ins. Mgmt., Inc. v. Lumbermens' Mut. Cas. Co*, 764 A.2d 1213 (Vt. 2000) ("Third-party bad faith claims arise because of the control an insurer has over the defense of underlying liability claims and the conflict of interest that may develop between insured and insurer over settlement.").

Virginia: Virginia treats first-party bad faith as a matter of contract and not tort law. *A&E Supply Co., Inc. v. Nationwide Mut. Fire Ins. Co.*, 798 F.2d 669, 676 (4th

Cir. 1986) (applying Virginia law) (allowing recovery of foreseeable consequential damages). A Virginia statute allows an insured to recover costs and reasonable attorneys' fees in a declaratory judgment action brought by the insured against the insurer, if the trial court determines that the insurer was not acting in good faith when it denied coverage or refused payment under the policy. VA. CODE ANN. § 38.2-209; *Kenney v. Indep. Order of Foresters*, 744 F.3d 901, 910 (4th Cir. 2014) (applying Virginia law) ("[C]ourts that have interpreted … [§ 38.2-209] have declined to recognize a separate cause of action in tort for bad-faith dealing over an insurance contract."). Adopting a reasonableness standard, the Supreme Court of Virginia held that "[a] bad-faith analysis generally would require consideration of such questions as whether reasonable minds could differ in the interpretation of policy provisions defining coverage and exclusions; whether the insurer had made a reasonable investigation of the facts and circumstances underlying the insured's claim; whether the evidence discovered reasonably supports a denial of liability; whether it appears that the insurer's refusal to pay was used merely as a tool in settlement negotiations; and whether the defense the insurer asserts at trial raises an issue of first impression or a reasonably debatable question of law or fact." *Cuna Mut. Ins. Soc'y v. Norman*, 375 S.E.2d 724, 727 (Va. 1989); *see also Nationwide Mut. Ins. Co. v. St. John*, 524 S.E.2d 649, 651 (Va. 2000) (adopting the same standard as *Norman* for purposes of VA. CODE ANN. § 8.01-66.1, which addresses bad faith damages in the context of motor vehicle claims); *Yorktowne Shopping Ctr., LLC v. Nat'l Sur. Corp.*, No. 10-1333, 2011 U.S. Dist. LEXIS 63880 (E.D. Va. June 15, 2011) (restating the standard from *Norman*); *Great Am. Ins. Co. v. GRM Mgmt., LLC*, No. 14-295, 2014 U.S. Dist. LEXIS 164147 (E.D. Va. Nov. 24, 2014) ("[O]ur district has identified that the Fourth Circuit held that, in a first-party Virginia insurance relationship, liability for bad faith conduct is a matter of contract, with the contract itself and general contract law governing the measure of recovery. Although Virginia law on the implied duty of good faith and fair dealing is not exceptionally clear, the Fourth Circuit and this district court clearly recognize such a duty. This Court cannot find a Virginia case repudiating such a duty[.]") (citations and internal quotes omitted); *Jeb Stuart Auction Servs., LLC v. West Am. Ins. Co.*, No. 14-00047, 2016 U.S. Dist. LEXIS 78243 (W.D. Va. June 16, 2016) (undertaking review of each *Norman* factor and concluding that insurer's position was undertaken in good faith, therefore insured not entitled to recover its attorneys' fees under § 38.2-209); *Allied Prop. & Cas. Ins. Co. v. Zenith Aviation, Inc.*, No. 18-264, 2019 U.S. Dist. LEXIS 234302 (E.D. Va. July 2, 2019) (finding that an insurer did not act in bad faith because it had asserted an objectively reasonable, honestly held coverage position); *S. Boston Energy LLC v. Hartford Steam Boiler Specialty Ins. Co.*, No. 18-596, 2019 U.S. Dist. LEXIS 138847 (E.D. Va. Aug. 15, 2019) ("The law does not require an insurer's investigation to be perfect, and certainly downward adjustments are necessary in many insurance claims. However, this investigation-- where the insurer adjusted the claim downward by over half the claimed amount, where this adjustment was based on mere estimates by engineers who had never viewed the turbine in person, where the insured's invoices were found to be 'largely reasonable' and no evidence of quote comparisons has been presented, and where the final adjusted claim amount skirts just below the deductible reeks of bad faith. The investigation was not reasonable and the denial of coverage was not supported by the evidence.").

For purposes of third-party bad faith, the Supreme Court of Virginia held that "[a] decision not to settle must be an honest one. It must result from a weighing of probabilities in a fair manner. To be a good faith decision, it must be an honest and intelligent one in the light of the company's expertise in the field. Where reasonable and probable cause appears for rejecting a settlement offer and for defendant [*sic*] the damage action, the good faith of the insurer will be vindicated." *Aetna Cas. & Sur. Co. v. Price*, 146 S.E.2d 220, 228 (Va. 1966) (citation omitted).

Washington: Under Washington law, an action for first-party bad faith sounds in tort and in order to establish bad faith, an insured is required to show the breach of duty was unreasonable, frivolous or unfounded. *St. Paul Fire & Marine Ins. Co. v. Onvia, Inc.*, 196 P.3d 664, 668 (Wash. 2008) (en banc) (citations and internal quotes omitted); *see also Smith v. Safeco Ins. Co.*, 78 P.3d 1274, 1277–78 (Wash. 2003) (en banc) (addressing reasonableness of the insurer's conduct). In addition, in 2007, Washington enacted the Insurance Fair Conduct Act, which authorizes a cause of action by a first party claimant who is unreasonably denied a claim for coverage. WASH. ADMIN. CODE § 48.30.015. The aggrieved party shall be entitled to recover the actual damages sustained, the costs of the action, including reasonable attorneys' fees and litigation costs. § 48.30.015(1). The court may also award treble damages. § 48.30.015(2). Further, such damages are available if the insurer violates WASH. ADMIN. CODE §§ 284-30-330, 284-30-350, 284-30-360, 284-30-370, and 284-30-380. WASH. ADMIN. CODE § 48.30.015(5). In general, these provisions set forth, in detail, a litany of claims handling practices, such as prompt acknowledgment of communications, prompt investigation of claims, prompt settlements, and misrepresentation of policy provisions. As a result, there is a low threshold for the possible imposition of treble damages. *See also Coventry Assocs. v. Am. States Ins. Co.*, 961 P.2d 933, 937 (Wash. 1998) (en banc) (holding that an insured may maintain an action against its insurer for bad faith investigation of its claim and violation of the Consumer Protection Act (WASH. REV. CODE ANN. § 19.86.010) regardless of whether the insurer was ultimately correct in determining coverage did not exist); *Perez-Crisantos v. State Farm Fire & Cas. Co.*, 389 P.3d 476 (Wash. 2017) ("In 2007, the legislature passed, and the voters of this state ratified, the Insurance Fair Conduct Act (IFCA), RCW 48.30.015. IFCA gives insureds a new cause of action against insurers who unreasonably deny coverage or benefits. RCW 48.30.015(1). IFCA also directs courts to grant attorney fees and authorizes courts to award triple damages if the insurer either acts unreasonably or violates certain insurance regulations. RCW 48.30.015(2)-(3), (5). These regulations broadly address unfair practices in insurance, not just unreasonable denials of coverage or benefits. RCW 48.30.015(5). We are asked to decide whether IFCA also created a new and independent private cause of action for violation of these regulations in the absence of any unreasonable denial of coverage or benefits. We conclude it did not[.]"); *State Farm Fire & Cas. Co. v. Justus*, 398 P.3d 1258 (Wash. Ct. App. 2017) ("We note that recently *Perez-Crisantos* held that the IFCA does not create an independent cause of action for regulatory violations. . . . We note, however, that *Perez-Crisantos* continues to recognize that insurers may be sued under insurance regulations through a CPA or bad faith action."); *Perez-Cristanos v. State Farm Fire & Cas. Co.*, 389 P.3d 476 (Wash. 2017) ("We respectfully disagree…that legislative intent supports creating an implicit IFCA cause of action. IFCA explicitly creates a cause of action for first party insureds who were 'unreasonably denied a claim for coverage or payment of benefits.' IFCA does not state it creates a cause of action for first party insureds who were unreasonably denied a claim for coverage or payment of benefits or 'whose claims were processed in violation of the insurance regulations listed in (5),' which strongly suggests that IFCA was not meant to create a cause of action for regulatory violations."); *Am. Best Food, Inc. v. ALEA London, Inc.*, 229 P.3d 693, 700 (Wash. 2010) (en banc) (holding that the insurer's failure to defend, based upon a questionable interpretation of law, was unreasonable and, therefore, the insurer acted in bad faith as a matter of law) ("An insurer acts in bad faith if its breach of the duty to defend was unreasonable, frivolous, or unfounded. We specifically disapprove of language to the contrary.") (citations omitted); *Onvia, Inc.*, 196 P.3d at 669 ("[T]hird-party insured has a cause of action for bad faith claims handing that is not dependent on the duty to indemnify, settle, or defend."); *Zhaoyun Xia v. ProBuilders Specialty Ins.*

Co., 400 P.3d 1234 (Wash. 2017) ("An insurer acts in bad faith if the refusal to defend was unreasonable, frivolous, or unfounded.") (holding that insurer's breach of the duty to defend was in bad faith, despite that the court adopted a never before applied test for purposes of interpreting the pollution exclusion); *Enters. LLC v. Houston Specialty Ins. Co.*, No. 17-676, 2018 U.S. Dist. LEXIS 18605 (W.D. Wash. Feb. 5, 2018) (finding that application of the wrong duty to defend standard constituted bad faith) ("Evidence of bad faith abounds here. There are a number of instances throughout the chronology of this event where Defendant acted in contravention of Washington law. The first and most egregious is its use of extrinsic evidence (e.g., the determination, based on the King County Assessor's website, that Williams Court was a condominium building) to deny a defense to its insured... Additionally, HSIC claimed in its declination letter that Plaintiff began and concluded its work outside of the coverage periods, and that Plaintiff's subcontractors did not maintain CGL insurance, information which is found nowhere in the complaint."); *Travelers Prop. Cas. Co. v. N. Am. Terrazzo Inc.*, No. 19-1175, 2020 U.S. Dist. LEXIS 212797 (W.D. Wash. Nov. 13, 2020) (finding that an insurer acted in bad faith by conducting an inadequate investigation and then filing a declaratory judgment action "when it knew or should have known that it could not prove an essential element of its claims due to the inadequate investigation"). Washington's bad faith laws are complex and have been the subject of numerous judicial decisions. Resort to the statutes and case law is recommended.

For purposes of third-party bad faith, "[a]n insurer breaches its affirmative duty to make a good faith effort to settle by negligently or in bad faith failing to settle a claim against the insured within its policy limits." *Smith v. Safeco Ins. Co.*, 50 P.3d 277, 281 (Wash. Ct. App. 2002) *rev'd on other grounds by* 78 P.3d 1274 (Wash. 2003); *Cox v. Cont'l Cas. Co.*, No. C13-2288, 2014 U.S. Dist. LEXIS 68081 (W.D. Wash. May 16, 2014) ("Continental's contention that it was precluded from attempting to settle within limits because Washington law prohibits any consideration of the policy limits can be dismissed out of hand. Clearly, in order to limit the insured's personal exposure, the insurance company must take into consideration the point at which a settlement or judgment would cease to affect only the funds available under the policy and begin to encroach on the insured's personal assets. Washington law is clear on that point."); *2FL Singh v. Zurich Am. Ins. Co.*, 428 P.3d 1237 (Wash Ct. App. 2018) ("We conclude there is no bright-line rule absolutely excusing an insurer from its duty to defend once coverage is exhausted in an excess exposure case involving multiple claimants. The existence of bad faith 'requires us to set aside traditional rules regarding harm and contract damages because insurance contracts are different.' If the insurer acted in bad faith when negotiating a settlement that exhausted the policy limits, the insurer cannot then use the exhaustion of policy limits as the basis for denying defense coverage. Even when the contractual language is unambiguous, there may still be a valid concern that the insurer has attempted to circumvent its duty to defend by making an early escape from the litigation.").

West Virginia: A West Virginia statute sets forth various unfair methods of competition and unfair or deceptive acts or practices in the business of insurance. W. VA. CODE ANN. § 33-11-4; *see also Taylor v. Nationwide Mut. Ins. Co.*, 589 S.E.2d 55, 59–60 (W. Va. 2003) ("[A]n implied private cause of action may exist for a violation by an insurance company of the unfair settlement practice provisions of [W. VA. CODE ANN. § 33-11-4(9)] …. [P]ast acceptance of an implied cause of action for a statutory violation is deeply ingrained.") (citations and internal quotation omitted); *United Bankshares, Inc. v. St. Paul Mercury Ins. Co.*, No. 6:10-cv-00188, 2010 U.S. Dist. LEXIS 117922 (S.D. W. Va. Nov. 4, 2010) ("[W]e hold that to maintain a private action based upon alleged violations of W. Va. Code § 33-11-4(9) *in the settlement of a single insurance claim*, the evidence should establish that the conduct in question constitutes more than a single violation of W. Va. Code § 33-11-4(9), that the violations arise from *separate, discrete acts or omissions in the claim settlement*, and that they arise from a habit, custom, usage, or business policy of the insurer, so that, viewing the conduct as a whole, the finder of fact is able to conclude that the practice or practices are sufficiently pervasive or sufficiently sanctioned by the insurance company that the conduct can be considered a 'general business practice' and can be distinguished by fair minds from an isolated event.") (emphasis in original) (quoting *Dodrill v. Nationwide Mut. Ins. Co.*, 491 S.E.2d 1, 13 (W. Va. 1996)) (holding that the plaintiffs' allegations, that the defendants wrongfully denied the plaintiffs' claims, failed to issue a timely coverage decision, and refused to settle the plaintiffs' claims brought under three separate insuring clauses, were sufficient to state claims for violations of multiple sections of the UTPA based on repeated acts by the defendants over nearly one year) ("[T]he plaintiffs have alleged 'separate, discrete acts or omissions, each of which constitute violations of different sub-paragraphs of W. Va. Code § 33-11-4(9).'") (quoting *Dodrill*, 491 S.E.2d at 12–13); *Skiles v. Mercado*, No. 15-3865, 2016 U.S. Dist. LEXIS 4580 (S.D. W.Va. Jan. 4, 2016) ("Presumably the denial of coverage letters were two violations, and a reasonable fact finder could conclude that leaving Plaintiff to defend the suits against him constituted further UTPA violations based on the refusal to indemnify, and a reasonable fact finder could further conclude that those later UTPA violations are necessary to establish the sort of general business practice the UTPA requires for liability based on handling a single claim."); *Moses Enters., LLC v. Lexington Ins. Co.*, No. 19-0477, 2021 U.S. Dist. LEXIS 76798 (S.D. W.Va. Apr. 21, 2021) ("[T]he Court finds a lack of support for Plaintiff's assertion that simply mishandling an insurance claim is a violation of the Act. While each violation of the Act may amount to mishandling a claim, the Court is not inclined to hold that the inverse in necessarily true. Surely an insurer does not violate the law each time it mishandles a claim.").

For purposes of third-party bad faith, the Supreme Court of Appeals of West Virginia held that "wherever there is a failure on the part of an insurer to settle within policy limits where there exists the opportunity to so settle and where such settlement within policy limits would release the insured from any and all personal liability, that the insurer has prima facie failed to act in its insured's best interest and that such failure to so settle prima facie constitutes bad faith towards its insured." *Shamblin v. Nationwide Mut. Ins. Co.*, 396 S.E.2d 766, 776 (W. Va. 1990). The *Shamblin* Court went on to describe the "insurer's burden to prove by clear and convincing evidence that it attempted in good faith to negotiate a settlement, that any failure to enter into a settlement where the opportunity to do so existed was based on reasonable and substantial grounds, and that it accorded the interests and rights of the insured at least as great a respect as its own." *Id.*; *see also Strahin v. Sullivan*, 647 S.E.2d 765, 770–71 (W. Va. 2007) ("In assessing whether an insurer is liable to its insured for personal liability in excess of policy limits, the proper test to be applied is whether the reasonably prudent insurer would have refused to settle within policy limits under the facts and circumstances, bearing in mind always its duty of good faith and fair dealing with the insured. Further, in determining whether the efforts of the insurer to reach settlement and to secure a release for its insured as to personal liability are reasonable, the trial court should consider whether there was appropriate investigation and evaluation of the claim based upon objective and cogent evidence; whether the insurer had a reasonable basis to conclude that there was a genuine and substantial issue as to liability of its insured; and whether there was potential for substantial recovery of an excess verdict against its insured. Not one of these factors may be considered to the exclusion of the others.") (noting that, in *Shamblin*, the court declined to adopt a strict liability standard whereby an insurer would have been liable any time it refused to settle within policy limits, but, rather, chose to add a negligence component creating a hybrid "negligence-strict liability" standard) ("[T]o recover under *Shamblin*, there must not only be a negligent refusal to accept a settlement offer by the insurer, but also subsequent harm to the insured. In other words, the insured's personal assets must be at risk."); *Stidd v. Erie Ins. Prop. & Cas. Co.*, No. 2018 U.S. Dist. LEXIS 243630 (N.D. W.Va. Apr. 25, 2018) (citing *Shamblin*) (finding question of bad faith failure to settle where the adjuster made "a settlement offer at the lowest end of the authorized range, considering the proof of damages and the claims presented").

Wisconsin: The Supreme Court of Wisconsin recognized a bad faith claim sounding in tort, although arising out of a contractual relationship. *Jones v. Secura Ins. Co.*, 638 N.W.2d 575, 579 (Wis. 2002) (citing *Anderson v. Cont'l Ins. Co.*, 271 N.W.2d 368 (Wis. 1978)). "To show a claim for bad faith, a plaintiff must show the absence of a reasonable basis for denying benefits of the policy and the defendant's knowledge or reckless disregard of the lack of a reasonable basis for denying the claim." *Id.* at 579–80 (quoting *Anderson*, 271 N.W.2d at 376); *Eagle Fuel Cells-ETC Inc. v. Acuity*, 838 N.W.2d 866 (Wis. Ct. App. 2013) ("[T]o prevail on a bad faith claim, an insured must establish three elements: (1) that the policy's terms obligated the insurer to pay the claim; (2) that the insurer lacked a reasonable basis in law or fact to deny the claim; and (3) that the insurer either knew there was no reasonable basis to deny the claim or acted with reckless disregard for whether such a basis existed."); *see also Brethorst v. Allstate Prop. & Cas. Ins. Co.*, 798 N.W.2d 467, 483 (Wis. 2011) ("Given our analysis of the requirements for a first-party bad faith claim, we conclude that the insured may not proceed with discovery on a first-party bad faith claim until it has pleaded a breach of contract by the insurer *as part of a separate bad faith claim* and satisfied the court that the insured has established such a breach or will be able to prove such a breach in the future. Stated differently, an insured must plead, in part, that she was entitled to payment under the insurance contract and allege facts to show that her claim under the contract was not fairly debatable. To go forward in discovery, these allegations must withstand the insurer's rebuttal.") (emphasis in original) (addressing in detail the history of Wisconsin's bad faith law and standard civil jury instructions for first-party bad faith); *Advance Cable Co., LLC v. Cincinnati Ins. Co., LLC*, 788 F.3d 743 (7th Cir. 2015) ("The courts of Wisconsin permit insured parties to bring bad faith claims against their insurance providers. A plaintiff bringing such a claim must show two things: the absence of a reasonable basis for denying benefits of the policy and the defendant's knowledge or reckless disregard of the lack of a reasonable basis for denying the claim. The Supreme Court of Wisconsin has characterized the first of these elements as objective, and the second as subjective. The objective element tests whether the insurer properly investigated the claim and whether the results of the investigation were subject to a reasonable evaluation and review. The subjective element asks whether the insurer was aware that there was no reasonable basis for denial, or that it displayed reckless disregard of a lack of a reasonable basis for denial or a reckless indifference to facts or to proofs submitted by the insured.") (citations and internal quotes omitted); *Williams v. Travelers Home & Marine Ins. Co.*, 402 F. Supp. 3d 499 (E.D. Wis. 2019) (declining to recognize bad-faith claims against agents, independent adjusters, and other entities that are not in privity with the insured) ("An insurance agent owes a duty to the insurer who employs him. A new duty to the insured would conflict with that duty and interfere with its faithful performance. This would be poor policy. Further, in most cases a duty between agents and insureds would be redundant, because the insurer also would be liable for unreasonable investigation or claims handling.").

For purposes of third-party bad faith, the Supreme Court of Wisconsin held that "[t]he insurer has the right to exercise its own judgment in determining whether a claim should be settled or contested. But exercise of this right should be accompanied by considerations of good faith. In order to be made in good faith, a decision not to settle a claim must be based on a thorough evaluation of the underlying circumstances of the claim and on informed interaction with the insured." *Mowry v. Badger State Mut. Cas. Co.*, 385 N.W.2d 171, 178 (Wis. 1986) (citation and internal quotation omitted); *see also Roehl Transp., Inc. v. Liberty Mut. Ins. Co.*, 784 N.W.2d 542, 555 (Wis. 2010) ("For the very reasons our cases have concluded that an insurance company becomes liable for the tort of bad faith when it fails to act in good faith and exposes its insured to liability over policy limits, we likewise conclude that an insurance company may be liable for the tort of bad faith when the insurance company fails to act in good faith and exposes the insured to liability for sums within the deductible amount.") (containing a lengthy explanation and history of third-party bad faith in Wisconsin); *Brethorst*, 798 N.W.2d. at 476 ("Significantly, a bad faith claim arises from the contractual relationship between the parties, but is not a contract action. The purpose behind providing a bad faith cause of action to an insured is to 'protect against the risk that an insurance company may place its own interests above those of the insured and that the recovery available to the insured for breach of contract would not fully compensate the insured for the resulting harms.'") (discussing third-party bad faith and quoting *Roehl*).

Wyoming: The Supreme Court of Wyoming held that an insurer's breach of the duty of good faith gives rise to an independent tort action. *McCullough v. Golden Rule*

Ins. Co., 789 P.2d 855, 858 (Wyo. 1990). "[T]he appropriate test to determine bad faith is the objective standard whether the validity of the denied claim was not fairly debatable." *Id.* at 860. "The tort of bad faith can be alleged only if the facts pleaded would, on the basis of an objective standard, show the absence of a reasonable basis for denying the claim, i.e., would a reasonable insurer under the circumstances have denied or delayed payment of the claim under the facts and circumstances." *Id.* at 860 (citation omitted); *see also Cathcart v. State Farm Mut. Auto. Ins. Co.*, 123 P.3d 579, 591 (Wyo. 2005) ("Whether a claim is 'fairly debatable' necessarily implicates the question whether the facts necessary to evaluate the claim are properly investigated and developed or recklessly ignored and disregarded. ... Moreover, [t]he logical premise of the debatable ... standard is that if a realistic question of liability does exist, the insurance carrier is entitled to reasonably pursue that debate without exposure to a claim of violation of its duty of good faith and fair dealing.") (citations and internal quotations omitted). "Nonetheless, 'even if a claim for benefits is fairly debatable, the insurer may breach the duty of good faith and fair dealing by the manner in which it investigates, handles or denies a claim.'" *Sonnett v. First Am. Title Ins. Co.*, 309 P.3d 799, 807 (Wyo. 2013) (quoting *Matlack v. Mountian W. Farm Bureau Mut. Ins. Co.*, 44 P.3d 73, 81 (Wyo. 2002)); *Hasbrouck v. Starr Indem. & Liab. Co.*, No. 13-174, 2014 U.S. Dist. LEXIS 148489 (D. Wyo. Oct. 17, 2014) (discussing distinction between bad faith denial of payment and bad faith delay of payment); *Cornhusker Cas. Co. v. Skaj*, 786 F.3d 842 (10th Cir. 2015) ("Vincent's substantive bad-faith claim founders on the first prong of Wyoming's test: the absence of *any* reasonable basis for denying his claim. To satisfy this component of the standard, a litigant must show that a reasonable insurer under the circumstances would not have acted as it did by denying . . . the claim. Wyoming caselaw makes clear that an insurer enjoys a wide berth in this regard—*viz.*, if a realistic question of liability does exist, the insurance carrier is entitled to reasonably pursue that debate without exposure to a bad-faith claim. Moreover, the Wyoming Supreme Court has clarified that the realistic-question aspect of the 'fairly debatable' standard is not the same as asking whether there actually was coverage under the policy. This means that, under Wyoming law, it is not necessarily an act of bad faith for an insurer to deny . . . payment of benefits where the underlying incident objectively may be seen as being covered by a policy exclusion, particularly where there is no controlling authority within the jurisdiction.") (emphasis in original); *Interstate Fire & Cas. Co. v. Apt. Mgmt. Consultants LLC*, 328 F. Supp. 3d 1241 (D. Wyo. 2018) ("Interstate, through the adjuster, its own representatives, and counsel, did investigate the claim and evaluated it as one with little risk of a punitive damages award…Interstate [and the insureds] were never in the dark. The fact that Interstate rejected [an insured's] demands to settle the case within the policy limits and [failure to] consider the case as one where there was significant exposure to punitive damages is not the type of claim handling that is beyond the pale. No threats were made; no unreasonable reports or statements were required by the insurer…The Court does recognize that the handling of the claim was far from perfect and flawed; however, a bad faith claim does not provide relief to [the insureds] in these circumstances."); *Lexington Ins. Co. v. Precision Drilling Co., L.P.*, 951 F.3d 1185 (10th Cir. 2020) (finding that "two different interpretations of statutory language, with one ultimately being unsuccessful, does not create an unreasonable withholding of payment").

For purposes of third-party bad faith, the Supreme Court of Wyoming held that good faith means "a bona fide belief by the insurer that it had a good possibility of winning the lawsuit or that the claimant's recovery in the lawsuit would not exceed the limits of the insurance policy." *Gainsco Ins. Co. v. Amoco Prod. Co.*, 53 P.3d 1051, 1058 (Wyo. 2002) (citation and internal quotation omitted). "The governing standard is whether a prudent insurer would have accepted the settlement offer if it alone were to be liable for the entire judgment. This is an objective, rather than a subjective, standard." *Id.* (citation and internal quotation omitted).

CHAPTER

21

The ALI Restatement of the Law of Liability Insurance[1]

[A] Introduction: The Restatement and Attendant Controversy

As of May 2018 (the date of final approval; publication in 2019), insurance is the subject of a Restatement, specifically the *Restatement of the Law, Liability Insurance* (hereinafter "RLLI"), prepared by the American Law Institute ("ALI"). There was considerable insurer opposition to what began as a "Principles" project[2] and was converted to a Restatement, both to portions of the document and even to the entire project. Policyholder counsel have also objected to significant portions of the RLLI. For a discussion of the debate over and politics of the RLLI, *see* Jeffrey W. Stempel & Erik S. Knutsen, Stempel and Knutsen on Insurance Coverage § 14.15 (4th ed. 2016 & Supp. 2021); Jeffrey W. Stempel, *Hard Battles Over Soft Law*, 69 Cleve. St. L. Rev. 605 (2021).

Restatements, of course, are well known to law students and lawyers. A Restatement is designed to collect and synthesize the law of a given area. In addition to those concerning Torts and Contracts, the ALI has published Restatements regarding Judgments, Conflict of Laws, Foreign Relations, and other areas of law. The Restatement format has "black letter" sections setting forth a Rule, followed by Comments and Illustrations concerning the Rule, followed by a Reporter's Note, which is something of a mini-treatise, collecting caselaw regarding the black letter and commentary such as treatises and law review articles. Restatements were among the first projects undertaken by the ALI, which was formed in 1923 by prominent lawyers, judges, and academics seeking improvement of American law.

---

1 This chapter represents the work of solely author Stempel.

2 A Principles project is distinguished from a Restatement in that the former is less tethered to existing law and has greater freedom to adopt an approach regarded as superior even if it lacks support in existing law or has even been rejected by courts. However, a Restatement need not adopt as a rule only positions embraced by the majority of courts. *See* ALI Revised Style Manual (Jan. 2015).

Summarizing, the ALI notes that "Restatements are primarily addressed to courts. They aim at clear formulations of common law and its statutory elements or variations and reflect the law as it presently stands or might appropriately be stated by a court." A Restatement rule should have at least some support in caselaw but need not be the majority rule. Rather, in examining the legal landscape, the ALI may embrace the judicial approach viewed as superior if it is the minority rule, even a distinct minority.

That position has met with some criticism by those who assert that "restating" the law should permit little or no deviance from the majority rule. In response to insurer criticisms of the RLLI, the ALI deferred final consideration until the May 2018 Annual Meeting (Rather than the 2017 Meeting at which it was slated for final approval). But the RLLI, despite being recommitted for review, was not changed dramatically before it was approved at the ALI's 2018 Annual Meeting and formally published in 2019.

Among those opposed to the RLLI – or are least some portions of it – were the National Association of Mutual Insurance Companies, the National Conference of Insurance Legislators, and the Defense Research Institute ("DRI"), which announced shortly before the May 2017 ALI Meeting that it was officially "opposed to the adopting of the Proposed Final Draft" of the RLLI because it had "grave concerns over several portions of this body of work," contending that "[m]any provisions are at odds with the common law of insurance, and their adoption will impeded the ability of our members to represent policyholders and insurers."[3] The DRI also argued that "the proposed draft may engender more insurance coverage controversies and litigation.

Subsection [B] of this Chapter examines some of the initial judicial decisions to cite to the RLLI. Subsection [C] compares and contrasts applicable provisions of the RLLI with this book's findings regarding state law, referred to as "*Key Issues*." Subsection [D] reviews the overall structure and content of the RLLI.

[B]   Judicial Citations to the RLLI

The RLLI was first cited while it was still a *Principles* project for the rather uncontroversial proposition that where a complaint alleges facts that would, if true, give rise to potentially covered liability, an insurer with a duty to defend must defend.

---

3 *See* Letter of May 16, 2017 to "Fellow DRI Members" from John E. Cuttino, DRI President.

See Hanover Am. Ins. Co. v. Balfour, 594 Fed. Appx. 526, 543 (10th Cir. Jan. 16, 2015) (applying Oklahoma law) (citing § 15 of *Principles of the Law, Liability Insurance,* Tentative Draft No. 2 (revised) (July 23, 2014). Its first citing as a Restatement was equally undramatic. *See Wisconsin Pharmacal Co., LLC v. Nebraska Cultures of Calif., Inc.*, 876 N.W.2d 72, 95. n.21 (Wis. 2016) (noting that RLLI did not address economic loss doctrine issue before the court).

In the ensuring five years, the RLLI has been cited in roughly 50 cases, with some cases producing multiple opinions. A pattern of sorts has emerged. Most cases citing the RLLI do so in conjunction with making an uncontroversial pronouncement of basic insurance law or practice. *See, e.g., Inn One Home v. Colony Specialty Ins. Co.*, 2021 U.S. Dist. LEXIS 33451, at *20 (D. Vt. Feb. 23, 2021) (citing RLLI § 35(2) and noting distinction between prevailing notice-prejudice rule for occurrence policies and general rule that claims-made insurer need not prove prejudice from late notice to avoid coverage).

A significant number cite the RLLI as consistent with applicable, controlling state law precedent. *See, e.g., Evanston Ins. Co. v. Desert Life Mgmt*, 434 F. Supp. 3d 1051 (D.N.M. 2020) (noting RLLI treatment of insuring agreements, exclusions, and exceptions to exclusions that is consistent with existing state law).

Some cases note that the RLLI differs from the state law that in any event trumps the RLLI, which is only "soft" law suggesting an approach and need not be followed by courts that are unpersuaded. *See, e.g., Westminster Am. Ins. Co. v. Spruce 1530, LLC*, 2021 U.S. App. LEXIS 7932 (3d Cir. Mar. 18, 2021) (noting that long-standing state precedent permits insurer to cease defense at trial level when potentially covered claims eliminated and that this takes precedence over RLLI § 18 provision stating that duty to defend continues until absence of potentially covered claim affirmed on appeal).

Sometimes, the division of opinion on an issue noted in commentary about the RLLI prompts a court to certify a question to a state's high court for guidance. *See, e.g., Cincinnati Ins. Co. v. Selective Ins. Co.*, 2021 U.S. Dist. LEXIS 36360 at *4, n. 2 (S.D. Ind. Feb. 25, 2021) (noting different state approaches to insurer settlement obligations and certifying question of whether Indiana recognizes a cause of action for negligent failure to settle) (quoting Leo P. Martinez, *Restatement of the Law of Liability Insurance and the Duty to Settle*, 68 RUTGERS U.L. REV. 155, 159 (2015)). *But see Tapestry on Central Condo. Ass'n v. Liberty Ins. Underwriters Inc.*, 2021 U.S. Dist. LEXIS 59924 at *45-*46 (D. Ariz. Mar. 29, 2021) (declining to certify to Arizona

Supreme Court question of applicability of RLLI § 15 because situation not ripe for such review in light of fact disputes to be determined).

In only a comparatively small subset of cases citing the RLLI is the court making a merits-based assessment of the RLLI provision at issue. *See, e.g., Burka v. Garrison Prop. & Cas. Co.*, 2021 U.S. Dist. LEXIS 32447 at *18-*19 (D. Me. Feb. 22, 2021) (agreeing with RLLI § 18 that insurer may not terminate defense upon adjudication eliminating a covered cause of action until appeal rights are exhausted) (*reconsideration denied*, 2021 U.S. Dist. LEXIS 80475 (D. Me. April 27, 2021)). As noted below, a significant amount of judicial attention to the RLLI has involved insurer efforts to seek recoupment of funds spent defending claims lacking a potential for coverage. *See, e.g., Nautilus Ins. Co. v. Access Medical, LLC*, 482 P.3d 683 (Nev. 2021); *Catlin Specialty Ins. Co. v. CBL & Assocs. Props.*, 2018 Del. Super. LEXIS 342 (Del. Super. Ct. Aug. 9, 2018).

As one commentator and insurer counsel summarized:

In many cases, the court's use of the RLLI has been benign, simply citing it for a general principles of coverage law and it played no part in the decision. Insurers have also prevailed in cases where the RLLI was included in the discussion. There have been a few cases that an insurer lost and the RLLI was included in the court's analysis. But, in some of those cases, it is clear that the court would have found against the insurer anyway – for other reasons. Importantly for insurers, courts have not undone any pro-insurer precedent in favor of adopting a different rule pronounced in the RLLI. In general, of the thousands of coverage decisions handed down [since ALI adoption of the final version of the RLLI in 2018], there are few where insurers can pin a loss on the RLLI. The reality of the RLLI for insurers – so far at least – has not equated with the dire predictions [of some insurers and counsel during the drafting process of the RLLI]. None of this is to say that insurers are out of the woods on the RLLI. For sure, there are some places in the RLLI that offer courts an opportunity to adopt a novel approach on an issue that could be very detrimental to insurers.[4]

---

4 Randy Maniloff, *Coverage Opinions*, Vol. 10, Iss. 2 (March 8, 2021)

[C]   The RLLI and *Key Issues* Chapters: Comparing the ALI Rules and State Rules

Chapter 3: Late Notice Defense Under "Occurrence" Policies: Is Prejudice to the Insurer Required?

Regarding occurrence policies, RLLI § 35 reflects the "notice-prejudice" rule found in nearly all states. If a policyholder's notice to the insurer is late, this generally will only bar coverage if the insurer can demonstrate prejudice to the insurer due to the late notice, although a few states place the burden of proof on the policyholder to prove lack of prejudice. RLLI § 35 also addresses claims-made policies and, like the majority of state law, gives much stricter application to the notice provisions of a claims-made policy than to an occurrence policy. However, RLLI § 35(2)(a)-(c) provides some exceptions to this (discussed in Section [D] below) that have attracted some insurer criticism.[5]

Chapter 5: Duty to Defend Standard: "Four Corners" or Extrinsic Evidence?

There is some division among the states on what information can be considered by an insurer to determine if it is obligated to defend its insured. All states start with the four corners/eight corners approach of looking at the face of the complaint and the face of the insurance policy. If the facts as alleged in the complaint create a potential for coverage the insurer has a duty to defend. Then most states also provide that even if the face of the complaint fails to allege facts implicating coverage, an insurer aware of additional facts creating a potential for coverage must defend. And most of those states permit the insured to provide such facts to the insurer. Some states permit consideration of extrinsic evidence not only to bring a matter within potential coverage but also to preclude a potential for coverage. But this generally takes place only in narrow circumstances such as those recognized in the RLLI.

RLLI § 13 adopts what might be called the "4-corners plus" approach of looking at the face of the complaint but being willing to consider additional information creating the required potential for coverage. It generally rejects the use of extrinsic evidence to eliminate a duty to defend created by allegations of the complaint.

---

5 RLLI § 35 is discussed in *Alps Prop. & Cas. Ins. Co. v. Unsworth Laplante, Pllc*, 2021 U.S. Dist. LEXIS 101035 (D. Vt. Jan. 25, 2021) (enforcing notice provisions of claims-made policy and finding no prejudice required for insurer's application of provision to defeat coverage); *Darwin Nat'l Assur. Co. v. Ky. State Univ.*, 2021 Ky. App. LEXIS 31 (Ky. Ct. App. Mar. 19, 2021) (same). *See also Nadkos, Inc. v. Preferred Contractors Ins. Co. Risk Retention Group LLC*, 34 N.Y. 1 (2019) (distinguishing between late notice, disclosure of coverage, and disclosure of grounds for reserving rights or denying coverage).

Exceptions to this limitation are "facts as to which there is no genuine dispute" that "establish as a matter of law" one of the following: (a) the defendant is not an insured under the policy through which defense is sought; (b) the vehicle involved in a case is not a covered vehicle under the policy in question (and the defendant has no other basis for asserting coverage); (c) the claim was inexcusably reported late under a claims-made policy; (d) the action is subject to a prior claim or related claim exclusion in a claims-made policy; or (e) the insurance policy has been "properly cancelled."

Chapter 6: Insured's Right to Independent Counsel

RLLI §§ 16 and 17 address whether an insured is entitled to be defended with counsel of its choice, *i.e.*, independent counsel as opposed to "panel counsel" selected by the insurer. Section 16 provides that when an insurer with a duty to defend "provides the insured notice of a ground for contesting coverage under § 15 (the RLLI section regarding reservation of rights), and "there are facts at issue that are common to the legal action" and to the coverage dispute that could be affected by the conduct of the defense to the insured's detriment, the insurer must then "provide an independent defense of the action."

The RLLI black letter does not deal directly with other types of conflicts of interest such as whether an insurer appointed attorney has sufficient incentive to defend vigorously if the claim is viewed as one likely to fall outside coverage once facts are adjudicated. Comment b. to RLLI § 16 acknowledges the issue and takes the position that insurers and panel counsel have adequate incentive to defend because of potential liability for failure to provide an adequate defense, including bad faith liability, as well as liability for any failure to make reasonable settlement decisions that results from an inadequate defense.

The black letter of RLLI § 16 does not directly bar insurer-appointed defense counsel from sharing potentially coverage-defeating information with the insurer. But RLLI § 11 takes a forcefully pro-policyholder view in that regard, stating that "[a]n insurer does not have the right to receive any information of the insured that is protected by attorney-client privilege, work-product immunity, or a defense lawyers' duty of confidentiality under rules of professional conduct, if that information could be used to benefit the insurer at the expense of the insured."

RLLI § 17 also states that in situations in which independent counsel (an "independent defense" in the language of the RLLI) is required: (1) the insurer then loses the right to conduct the defense; (2) the insured may select defense counsel and "related service providers;" (3) the insurer must pay the reasonable defense costs "on an ongoing basis in a timely manner;" (4) the insurer may not associate in the defense of the action; and (5) the insured's provision of information to the insurer is subject to RLLI § 11.

Chapter 7: Insurer's Right to Reimbursement of Defense Costs

Pursuant to the RLLI § 21, an insurer with a duty to defend may not be reimbursed for defense costs related to claims not potentially covered unless the policy has express language to that effect or there is an express agreement in that regard. This is the RLLI's attempt to deal with what is frequently referred to as the "*Buss*" issue, so named after a famous California Supreme Court case. *See Buss v. Superior Court*, 939 P.2d 766 (Cal. 1997). Since that decision, several significant courts (most prominently Pennsylvania and Illinois: *see General Agents Insurance Co. of America v. Midwest Sporting Goods Co.*, 828 N.E.2d 1092, 1102-03 (Ill 2005); *American & Foreign Ins. Co. v. Jerry's Sport Center, Inc.*, 2 A.3d 526, 546 (Pa. 2010)) have rejected *Buss* and denied recoupment, at least for standard language CGL policies. Chapter 7 of *Key Issues* provides a discussion of the history and development of the issue as well as a state-by-state scorecard. Insurers have opposed RLLI § 21 and argued in favor of the *Buss* approach.

Two days after the May 2017 ALI Annual Meeting, a federal district court in Indiana (which lacked authoritative state precedent) cited § 21 in rejecting a recoupment claim. *See Selective Ins. Co of Am. v. Smiley Body Shop, Inc.*, 260 F. Supp. 3d 1023 (S.D. Ind. 2017). One must be careful not to overstate the importance of § 21 in the court's analysis. The court was also well aware of the precedential landscape generally and cited cases rejecting recoupment that it found more persuasive than cases approving recoupment.

Although the black letter of § 21 leaves some room for argument, a full review of the Comments and Reporters' Note to the Section strongly suggests that an insurer cannot create a right of recoupment that is not in the policy simply by agreeing to defend pursuant to a reservation of rights that includes a purported right to seek recoupment. *See* Reporters Note a ("The default rule is no recoupment of defense costs") (italics in original). *See, e.g., Texas Ass'n of Counties County Gov't Risk Mgmt. Pool v. Matagorda Country*, 52 S.W.3d 128, 131 (Tex. 2000) ("a unilateral reservation-of-rights letter cannot create rights not contained in the insurance policy") (citing *Shoshone First Bank v. Pac. Employers Ins. Co.*, 2 P.3d 510, 515-16 (Wyo. 2000) (both cases cited in Reporter's Note a to RLLI § 21).

Since *Smiley Body Shop, supra*, courts have diverged on the issue. Some have cited the RLLI § 21 favorably in denying recoupment. *See, e.g., Continental Cas. Co. v. Winder Labs.*, 2021 U.S. Dist. LEXIS 103013 at *11-*12 (N.D. Ga. April 20, 2021) (but noting it is minority approach); *Hayes v. Wis. & S. R.R., LLC*, 2021 U.S. Dist. LEXIS 10175 (E.D. Wis. Jan. 20, 2021); *Twin City Fire Ins. Co. v. Hartman*, 2017 U.S. Dist. LEXIS 227524 (N.D. Ga. Feb. 28, 2017). Others have rejected § 21, at least in part. *See, e.g., Marcus v. Allied World Ins. Co.*, 384 F. Supp. 3d 115 (D. Me. 2019); *Catlin Specialty Ins. Co. v. CBL & Assocs. Props.*, 2018 Del. Super. LEXIS 342 (Del. Super. Ct. Aug. 9, 2018); *CGA, Inc. v. Kiewit Infrastructure West Co.*, 2020 U.S. Dist. LEXIS 10151 (D. Haw. Jan 22, 2020) (differentiating case from typical insurance duty to defend because defense was pursuant to indemnity clause but permitting recoupment of fee expenditures).

The most extensive judicial discussion of the provision is found in *Nautilus Ins. Co. v. Access Medical, LLC*, 482 P.3d 683 (Nev. 2021). The origin of the decision began with a business dispute that prompted a claim of mismanagement and an allegation that one of the insureds had misappropriated funds, improperly interfered with business relationships, and was not authorized to distribute particular medical products. The insurer contended these allegations did not constitute defamation claims sufficient to trigger personal injury coverage pursuant to the applicable liability policy, but agreed to defend pending the outcome of its declaratory judgment action, upon which it prevailed in federal trial court. *See Nautilus Ins. Co. v. Access Med., LLC*, 2016 U.S. Dist. LEXIS 132300 (D. Nev. Sept. 27, 2016) (cross-claim does not sufficiently allege publication of false statements by the policyholder and thus does not amount to defamation claim triggering potential for personal injury coverage pursuant to general liability policy). The Ninth Circuit affirmed the finding of no duty to defend and certified to the Nevada Supreme Court the following question:

> Is an insurer entitled to reimbursement of costs already expended in defense of its insureds where a determination has been made that the insurer owed no duty to defend and the insurer expressly reserved its right to seek reimbursement in writing after defense has been tendered but where the insurance policy contains no reservation of rights?

482 P.2d at 685-686.

In a 4-3 decision, the Court answered the question "yes." The majority concluded that if the matter lacked any potentially covered claims, and there was no duty to defend, the insurer had conferred a benefit to the policyholder to which it was not entitled and that had been accepted by the policyholder, thus using a restitution analysis for supporting the insurer's claims. *See* 482 P.2d at 688-690, citing American Law Institute, Restatement (Third) of Restitution and Unjust Enrichment § 35 (2011) ("RRUE"). *See also* 482 P.3d at 690:

> when a court holds that there was never a duty to defend, it is holding that the claims were never even potentially covered by the policy. Therefore, when the insurer reserved its right to seek reimbursement, it was not extracting an amendment to a contract that would otherwise govern its defense. No contract governed its defense. In these circumstances, the is no reason it cannot reserve a right it has, not pursuant to the contract, but pursuant to the law of restitution.

The majority also applied a public policy analysis reasoning that a contrary rule would put insurers in an untenable position in that they face significant pressure to defend under doubtful circumstances in order to avoid excess liability of the policyholder and allegations of bad faith and unfair claims handling. *See* 482 P.2d at 690-691. The majority further found that taking this approach did not improperly undermine or deviate from the terms of the insurance policy contract, which was subject to overarching principles of contract law.

The Nautilus majority self-consciously noted its agreement with California, in particular *Scottsdale Ins. Co. v. MV Transportation Co.*, 115 P.3d 460 (Cal. 2005), noting the RLLI but only for its acknowledgment that § 21 represented a minority view in caselaw. *See* 482 P.3d at 689. By contrast, the RRUE was favorably cited a half-dozen times in the majority opinion.

The dissenters, however, embraced RLLI § 21 and its rationale while viewing RRUE § 35 as inapplicable because of the existence of an "express, written contract" – the insurance policy, which made no provision for recoupment. They argued that under Nevada law, the restitution theory of the majority was therefore foreclosed. *See* 482 P.3d at 692 (citing cases). The dissent also faulted the insurer for failing to timely pursue a declaratory judgment, waiting more than nine months after the duty to defend dispute surfaced before commencing the action. *Id.* at 692, n. 1 (citing RRUE § 35 cmt. a (restitution apt only where it is impossible to obtain a legal determination prior to date claimed performance due)).

The dissent took particular issue with the majority's willingness to permit the insurer to attempt to condition defense on agreement to a recoupment action, taking the view that a unilateral reservation of rights cannot create contract rights for the insurer. 482 P.3d at 694-95 (quoting *Am. & Foreign Ins. Co. v. Jerry's Sport Ctr., Inc.*, 2 A.3d 526, 539 (Pa. 2010) and citing other cases rejecting recoupment). Regarding RLLI § 21, the dissent noted, as had the § 21 Comments and Reporters' Note, that although a majority of decisions permitted recoupment, the modern trend has been to the contrary.

Without doubt, *Nautilus* was a significant if narrow (4-3) victory for insurers, with *Coverage Opinions* describing it as the "Biggest ALI Restatement Case to Date" and the "first decision to use the RLLI in the process of making new law" in the jurisdiction at issue. But, as also noted by *Coverage Opinions*, the *Nautilus* Court was not using the RLLI to alter existing law but rather to provide supplementary guidance. The RRUE arguably played a larger role in the decision than did the RLLI.

Consequently, some restraint in celebration is required of insurers viewing the decision. *Nautilus*, unlike *Buss v. Superior Court*, involved a situation where a court ruled that the claims the insurer defended **all** had **no** potential for coverage. *Accord, Catlin Specialty Ins. Co. v. CBL & Assocs. Props.*, 2018 Del. Super. LEXIS 342 (Del. Super. Ct. Aug. 9, 2018) (insurer defended matter in which no claims qualified for duty to defend and then sought recoupment). Thus far, it appears there is not a judicial decision rejecting § 21 that has involved a mixture of potentially covered and uncovered claims as in *Buss*.[6] For both insurers and policyholder, the majority and dissenting opinions in *Nautilus* provide helpful analysis that can be deployed in arguing the issue.

Chapter 8: Prevailing Insured's Right to Recover Attorney's Fees in Coverage Litigation
As discussed in Chapter 8 of *Key Issues*, the "vast majority of states provide a mechanism of some sort for a prevailing insured in a coverage action to recover its attorney's fees" but there is wide variance as to the conditions required for such

---

6 The situation in *Buss v. Superior Court*, 939 P.2d 766 (Cal. 1997) was extreme in that only one of 27 counts of a complaint involved a potentially covered claim, which undoubtedly influenced the court in finding recoupment apt. But there was that one potentially covered claim and, as opponents of *Buss* and recoupment have noted, the standard general liability policy states that the insurer will defend "suits" involving potentially covered claims, an argument that has proven persuasive to courts rejecting recoupment in such situations, as detailed in Ch. 7.

an exception to the 'American Rule' that each side bears its own legal costs. Courts normally have broad discretion in this area and most use it cautiously. A "few states maintain strict adherence to the American Rule and do not allow" any fee shifting in favor of policyholders who prevail in coverage litigation.

RLLI §§ 47-50 touch on recovery of counsel fees. Section 47 governing "Remedies Potentially Available" in liability insurance litigation notes that counsel fees may be awarded to a prevailing party "when provided by state law or the policy").

RLLI § 47 notes that if a policyholder spends its own funds on defense because of an insurer's breach of the duty to defend, the policyholder may recover those costs as a remedy in litigation. Where an insurer has been found to have acted in bad faith (defined in RLLI § 49), one of the remedies may be an award of "reasonable attorneys' fees and other costs incurred by the insured in the legal action establishing the insurer's breach." *See* RLLI § 50(1).

Chapter 9: Number of Occurrences

The RLLI provides some guidance in this area in that it endorses the prevailing "cause" test for counting occurrences, which is the clear majority rule, rather than an "effects" test. *See* RLLI § 38 ("all bodily injury, property damage, or other harm caused by the same act or event constitutes a single accident or occurrence"). The RLLI Comments and Reporters' Note also provide a discussion of variants of the cause test and three illustrations that can provide useful guidance, all of which is consistent with Chapter 9 of *Key Issues*, which notes the degree of malleability of the concept and often seeming inconsistencies between many of the cases in this regard.

Chapter 16: Trigger-of-Coverage for Latent Injury and Damage Claims

As discussed in *Key Issues*, Chapter 16, latent injury situations present "vexing claims" such as those "caused by exposure to hazardous substances" where "injuries often evolve slowly." Asbestos and hazardous waste claims form the bulk of such coverage litigation to date and have produced a rich but varied body of precedent catalogued in Chapter 16. RLLI § 33 addresses trigger and essentially takes the approach of applying an actual injury or injury-in-fact trigger for occurrence policies. For claims-made policies, the claim (and usually required timely reporting) is the trigger. But § 33(1) is perhaps frustratingly vague, at least in its black letter, in failing to endorse a particular metric for determining trigger. Instead, it states that "[w]hen a liability insurance policy provides coverage based on the timing of a harm, event, wrong, loss, activity, occurrence, claim, or other happening, the determination of when that harm, event, wrong, loss, activity, occurrence, claim, or other happening took place is a question of fact."

RLLI § 33(2) provides that a policy may define trigger to take place at a more specific time "even if it would be determined for other purposes to have taken place at a different time." Decoded, this means that an insurance policy may "batch" related claims as taking place at the time of first onset or deem all claims of a certain type to related back to a certain date, or use other such provisions in the policy.

Chapter 18: Allocation of Latent Injury and Damage Claims

Regarding allocation, RLLI § 41 adopts the view that the coverage responsibility for consecutively triggered liability insurers should be allocated by time on the risk, the position advanced by most insurers facing long-tail claims. In contrast, policyholders almost always prefer the "all sums" approach in which each triggered insurer is responsible for responding fully (to the extent of policy limits) in connection with such claims.

Some controversy exists regarding the degree to which "pro-ration" rather than the "all-sums" approach favored by policyholders is the majority rule or even whether it is the majority rule in light of recent trends and the number of large jurisdictions (e.g., California, Ohio) that have adopted the all-sums approach. As noted in Chapter 18, the issue can be more nuanced than just picking one approach or another. But on balance, it appears pro-ration has more judicial support. Consequently, RLLI § 41 may be particularly influential and accordingly has been criticized by policyholders. *But see Nooter Corp. v. Allianz Ins. Co.*, 536 S.W.3d 251 (Mo. Ct. App. 2017) (rejecting pro-ration by time on risk and adopting all-sums approach despite RLLI endorsement of proration).

Chapter 19: Insurability of Punitive Damages

As detailed in Chapter 19, there is considerable variation among the states regarding the insurability of punitive damages. In addition, as discussed in the Chapter, answering the question as to insurability is "oftentimes much more complex than can be answered with a single word." Further, "when all of the variations of the issue are considered, there may be as many as a dozen possible answers to the question." RLLI § 45, which takes the view that the insurability of punitive damages is a policy choice to be made by individual states, will not end this division. However, unless state law makes punitive damages uninsurable as a matter of public policy, the RLLI view is that such damages are presumptively insurable unless otherwise stated in the policy.

In addition, if an insurer's failure to defend or make reasonable settlement decisions results in a verdict in excess of policy limits that includes punitive damages (that could have been avoided had the insurer settled and avoided a trial), the policyholder is entitled to recovery of such amounts from the insurer even if punitive damages are generally not insurable in the jurisdiction. *See* RLLI § 27, Comment e ("the amount of [a] punitive-damages award is included in the consequential damages owed for breach of the insurer's duty"). This is a direct disapproval of the state supreme court decisions in *PPG Industries, Inc. v. Transamerica Ins. Co.*, 975 P.2d 652 (Cal. 1999) and *Lira v. Shelter Ins.* Co., 913 P.2d 514 (Colo. 1996), both of which were 4-3 decisions. The RLLI expressly adopts the approach of the dissenters in those cases. *See* Comment e & Reporters' Note e.

Chapter 20: First- and Third-Party Bad Faith Standards
The RLLI is concerned only with third-party bad faith. In § 49, the RLLI defines bad faith as an insurer's failure "to perform under a liability insurance policy: (a) [w]ithout a reasonable basis for its conduct; and (b) [w]ith knowledge of its obligation to perform or in reckless disregard of whether it had an obligation to perform." As detailed in Chapter 20, states differ in that some regard unreasonable conduct alone as bad faith while at the other extreme some decisions appear almost to require specific intent to injury the policyholder. The RLLI combination of unreasonable assessment of a claim for coverage and knowledge or reckless disregard about the unreasonableness accords with the approach of a plurality of jurisdictions and perhaps a majority. But as noted in Chapter 20, "[t]he standard for third-party bad faith can also vary widely" not only between states but "within the *same* state" (italics in original).

Former Chapter 22 (3d ed.; eliminated in 4ᵗʰ ed. and 5ᵗʰ ed.): The Reasonable Expectations Approach to Insurance Policy Interpretation
The RLLI (in §§ 3 and 4) endorses consideration of policyholder reasonable expectations for resolving unclear language but does not support a strong view of the concept that overrides clear policy language. Rather, policyholder expectations must be at least consistent with a reading of the policy language that would square with those expectations. The majority of courts will consider reasonable expectations where policy language is unclear but ordinarily will not resort to expectations as an interpretative tool unless the policy text is ambiguous.

***Key Issues* Chapter Topics Not Expressly Addressed by the RLLI**

Perhaps because it is a document aimed at liability insurance as a genre rather than at specific provisions of a general liability policy, the RLLI does not address in any significant way: Choice of Law (Chapter 2 of this volume); Coverage for Innocent Co-Insureds (Chapter 10); Whether Emotional Injury Is Bodily Injury (Chapter 11); whether Faulty Workmanship is an "Occurrence" (Chapter 12); the Permissible Scope of Indemnification in Construction Contracts (Chapter 13); the Qualified Pollution Exclusion (Chapter 14); or the "Absolute" Pollution Exclusion (Chapter 15). Despite the number of sections of the RLLI devoted to the duty to defend and related issues, the RLLI also does not specifically address Coverage for Pre-Tender Defense Costs (Chapter 4).

[D]   An Overview of the Structure and Content of the RLLI

Definitions and Interpretation

After addressing some general concepts, the RLLI covers liability insurance topics in roughly the order they arise in litigation. Section 1 provides some fourteen (14) definitions. RLLI § 2 addresses "insurance-policy interpretation," noting that unless otherwise provided in the RLLI or by other law, "the ordinary rules of contract interpretation apply to the interpretation of liability insurance policies."

RLLI § 3 provides that terms are to be interpreted according to their "plain meaning," which is "the single meaning to which the language of the term is reasonably susceptible when applied to facts of the claim at issue in the context of the entire insurance policy." Prior drafts of § 3 expressed a more intent or purpose-based focus and were controversial, engendering particular opposition from insurers and business that viewed the prior versions as insufficiently deferential to policy text. The section was revised in response

Comments to § 3 identify "[g]enerally accepted sources of plain meaning" and the role of custom, practice, and usage in construing text. Notably, Comment b states that "dictionaries, court decisions, statutes and regulations, and secondary authority such as treatises and law-review articles" should not ordinarily be deemed extrinsic evidence but instead are "legal authorities that courts consult when determining the lain meaning of an insurance policy term" which, like contract construction generally, is a question of law for the court rather than a question of fact for the jury.

Comment c also expresses a receptive attitude toward custom, practice and usage. Consequently, although the black letter of § 3 focuses on policy text, commentary supports a broader, more eclectic approach to determining policy meaning. It remains to be seen which figurative fork in the § 3 road will be followed by courts. To date, § 3 appears not to have been expressly cited by any court.

RLLI § 4(1) states the traditional view that a term "is ambiguous if there is more than one meaning to which the language of the term is reasonably susceptible when applied to the facts of the claim at issue in the context of the entire insurance policy." Where the court finds a term to be ambiguous, § 4(2) follows the prevailing approach that interprets the ambiguous language "against the party that supplied the term, unless that party persuades the court that a reasonably person in the policyholder's position would not give the term that interpretation."

Waiver and Estoppel

RLLI §§ 5 & 6 address waiver and estoppel, respectively, restating traditional doctrine. They have been essentially uncontroversial.

Misrepresentation

Regarding misrepresentation, RLLI § 7(1) makes any statement of fact in an application for insurance a representation rather than a warranty or covenant. RLLI § 7(2) permits the insurer to deny a claim or rescind the entire policy on the basis of an "incorrect" representation if the representation is "material" and was "reasonably relied" upon by the insurer in issuing or renewing the policy. A material representation is one that would have prompted a "reasonable insurer" to "not have issued the policy" or to "have issued the policy only under substantially different terms."

The RLLI adoption of an objective approach to determining materiality may place some pressure on jurisdictions using the subjective standard (most prominently California) to reconsider their approach – although where a state has a long-established subjective approach, RLLI-spurred change is unlikely but may take place in states with unclear or inconsistent precedent on the point.

The Duty to Defend and Related Issues

Sections 10 through 23 of the RLLI address the duty to defend. RLLI § 10 provides that "unless otherwise stated in the policy or limited by applicable law," the insurer issuing a policy with a duty to defend has control over the defense and settlement of the action, "including the selection and oversight of defense counsel" as well as the "right to receive from defense counsel all information relevant to the defense or settlement of the action" unless the information is confidential as provided in RLLI § 11. RLLI § 11(2) provides that "an insurer does not have the right to receive any information of the insured that is protected by attorney-client privilege, work-product immunity, or a defense lawyer's duty of confidentiality under the rules of professional conduct if that information could be used to benefit the insurer at the expense of the insured." While issues of client identity and disclosure of information can create difficulties for defense counsel, it is an accepted occupational hazard and has not made §§ 10 and 11 controversial.

Potential Insurer Liability for Defense Counsel Conduct

Section 12, which continues to attract some controversy, presumptively adopts the prevailing view that an insurer is not liable for the negligence of insurer-selected counsel providing a defense to the policyholder/defendant. The insurer is not vicariously liable for counsel's errors (§ 12 cmt. e). *But see Arch Ins. Co. v. Kubicki Draper, LLP*, 2021 Fla. LEXIS 898 (Fla. June 3, 2021), decided not long before the publication of this edition. The Florida high court held that, while the insurer was not in privity with the defense counsel (the insured was, as the client), the insurer could pursue a claim against the lawyer on a subrogation basis.

However, § 12(1) provides that if the insurer "fails to take reasonable care" in selecting defense counsel, "the insurer is subject to liability for the harm caused by any subsequent negligent act or omission of the selected counsel that is within the scope of the risk that made the selection of counsel unreasonable."

Section 12(2) further provides for liability of the insurer "when the insurer directs the conduct of the counsel with respect to the negligent act or omission in a manner that overrides the duty to counsel to exercise independent professional judgment."

Although not expressly stated in the black letter or commentary, it is quite clear that the mere existence of insurer litigation guidelines required of counsel will not alone constitute such liability-creating direction of counsel and that potential liability will be a fact-specific inquiry that will most likely require rather obviously unreasonable insurer conduct to create liability.

For example, Illustration No. 4 to § 12 involves an insurer, that contrary to the recommendation of counsel, directs counsel not to incur the costs of an independent medical examination and a damages expert to refute plaintiff's calculation of damages in a case with sufficiently serious injuries that plaintiff obtains a judgment in excess of policy limits against the policyholder. Under this scenario, the insurer is deemed factually and legally responsible for the entire judgment. However, per Illustration No. 5, the insurer is not subject to liability if "defense counsel independently chose not to conduct an independent medical examination" or to retain damages experts in the matter.

Regarding selection of counsel, § 12 cmt. c "takes no position" on the issue of whether retention of counsel without liability insurance constitutes lack of reasonable care in selecting counsel but can be read in conjunction with Comment e as suggesting that this is the case. Both comments justify insulating insurers from liability for defense counsel negligence where counsel has malpractice insurance on the ground that counsel is then in a position to access and spread risk that is as good as that of the insurer.

RLLI § 12 was discussed at some length in *Progressive Northwestern Ins. Co. v. Gant*, 957 F.3d 1144 (10th Cir. 2020) (trial court opinion at 2018 U.S. Dist. LEXIS 163624 (D. Kan. Sept. 25, 2018)), which rejected a claim of insurer liability due to alleged negligence in selecting defense counsel, with a purported reputation for aggressive tactics and resistance to settlement, that was an alleged cause of a judgment in excess of policy limits.

Allegations of insurer liability were also rejected in *Sapienza v. Liberty Mut. Fire Ins. Co.*, 389 F. Supp. 3d 648 (D.S.D. 2019) and 2019 U.S. Dist. LEXIS 179017 (D.S.D. Oct. 16, 2019), a case perhaps better know for the state supreme court decision holding that the cost of rectifying building encroachment constitutes covered general liability damages rather than uncovered injunctive relief. *See Sapienza v. Liberty Mut. Fire. Ins. Co.*, 2021 S.D. LEXIS 64 (S.D. June 2, 2021).

Determining Whether a Defense is Owed

RLLI § 13(1) sets forth the prevailing rule on when the duty to defend is triggered and states that the duty is triggered if the allegations of the claim, "if proved, would be covered by the policy, without regard for the merits of those allegations." More controversial is § 13(2)(b) that provides that the insurer must also defend when it is aware of "[a]ny additional allegation known to the insurer, not contained in the complaint, or comparable document stating the legal action, that a reasonable insurer would regard as an actual or potential basis for all or part of an action." *See also W. Hills Dev. Co. v. Chartis Claims, Inc.*, 385 P.3d 1053, 1055 (Or. 2016) (noting RLLI adoption of four corners/eight-corners approach generally). The RLLI does not adopt the more pronounced pro-policyholder position of requiring a liability insurer to investigate and seek facts that create a potential for coverage.

Terminating the Duty to Defend

RLLI § 13(3) states that once the duty to defend is triggered, it remains in effect unless the insurer prevails in a declaratory judgment terminating the duty or the case is resolved or "unless facts as to which there is no genuine dispute establish as a matter of law" that one of the following situations exists: the defendant is "not an insured" under the applicable policy (§ 13(3)(a)); the "vehicle involved in the accident is not a covered vehicle" under the applicable policy (§ 13(3)(b)); the claim "was reported late under a claims-made-and-reported policy" and the late notice is not excused (§ 13(3)(c)); the action is subject to a prior litigation or related claim exclusion in a claims-made policy (§ 13(3)(d)); the policy has been "properly cancelled" (§ 13(3)(e)); or "[t]here is no duty to defend under a similar, narrowly defined exception to the complaint-allegation rule recognized by the courts in the applicable jurisdiction." (§ 13(3)(f)).

Defense Requirements

When the duty to defend is operative, RLLI § 14(1) sets forth the "basic obligations" of the duty while § 15 addresses reservation of rights. The defending insurer must make "reasonable efforts to defend the insured from all of the causes of action and remedies sought in the action, including those not even potentially covered by the liability insurance policy." RLLI § 14(3) also sets forth the common understanding that "[u]nless otherwise stated in the policy" defense costs are "in addition to policy limits" and are borne by the insurer rather than merely reimbursed after payment by the policyholder.

Reservations of Rights

Regarding reservation of rights, RLLI § 15 largely codifies existing precedent and practice by providing counsel an extensive template or even what one might call a roadmap for properly defending (which is based on the potential for coverage standard) pursuant to a reservation of the insurer's right to contest ultimate coverage of the claim (which is based on an actual facts standard). Section 15 provides that an insurer defending a legal action "may reserve the right to contest coverage for an action *before* undertaking the defense of the action if it gives *timely* notice to the insured of *any* ground for contesting coverage of which it knows or should know." (RLLI § 15(1) (emphasis added)). Once defense of an action has begun, the insurer that has been defending without reservation may later reserve rights if the insurer "learns of information that provides a ground for contesting coverage" so long as it gives notice to the policyholder within a reasonable time.

RLLI § 15(3) provides that to be effective, notice of a reservation of rights "must include a written explanation of the ground, including the specific insurance-policy terms and facts upon which the potential ground for contesting coverage is based, in language that is understandable by a reasonable person in the position of the insured."[7] Where the insurer lacks sufficient information to make a decision, it may initially reserve rights but must then conduct a reasonably diligent investigation of the matter and provide a "final answer" (to borrow a game-show phrase) as to its position within a reasonable time. *See generally Tapestry on Central Condo. Ass'n v. Liberty Ins. Underwriters Inc.*, 2021 U.S. Dist. LEXIS 59924 (D. Ariz. Mar. 29, 2021) at *45-*46 (declining to certify to Arizona Supreme Court question of applicability of § 15 and whether policyholder need show prejudice use insurer's failure to reserve rights as bar to insurer coverage defense).

When Independent Counsel Is Required

RLLI § 16 addresses the issue of when an insurer must provide "independent" (meaning not insurer-selected) defense counsel to the policyholder. That duty is triggered when "there are facts at issue that are common to the legal action for which the defense is due and to the coverage dispute, such that the action could be defended in a manner that would benefit the insurer at the expense of the insured." When a conflict requiring independent counsel arises under § 16, RLLI § 17 provides that the insurer "does not have the right to defend the legal action," and the policyholder "may select defense counsel and related service providers" although the insurer "has the right to associate in the defense of the legal action."

In funding independent counsel, the insurer "is obligated to pay the reasonable fees of the defense counsel and related service providers on an ongoing basis in a timely manner." Provision of information regarding the defense to the insurer by the policyholder is governed by RLLI § 11(1) which provides that the insured "does not waive rights of confidentiality with respect to third parties by providing . . . information protected by attorney-client privilege, work-product

---

7   *See* Randy Maniloff, *When a Reservation of Rights Letter is Not Effective*, Law360 (Jan. 25, 2017). *See, e.g., Hoover v. Maxum Indem. Co.*, 730 S.E.2d 413, 417 (Ga. 2012) (unclear ROR letter construed against insurer; letter "not valid if it does not fairly inform the insured of the insurer's position."); *Advantage Buildings & Exteriors, Inc. v. Mid-Continent Casualty Co.* 449 S.W.3d 16, 22-24 (Mo. Ct. App. 2014) (failure to clearly explain basis for reservation of rights makes ROR letter ineffective and insurer is estopped to deny coverage).

immunity, or other confidentiality protections." Section 11(2) states that the insurer does not have the right to such information "if that information could be used to benefit the insurer at the expense of the insured."

Although the current "reasonable fees" language of § 16(3) does not expressly set the fees of independent counsel at panel counsel rates, as do some courts and California by legislation (Calif. Civ. Code § 2860), this is the presumptively logical starting place for determining reasonable rates.

Terminating the Duty to Defend

Termination of the duty to defend is governed by RLLI § 18, which states that the duty "terminates only upon the occurrence of one or more of the following events" and then lists these events, including: explicit waiver by the insured of its right to a defense of the action; final adjudication of the action; final adjudication or dismissal of part of the action that eliminates any basis for coverage of any remaining components of the action; settlement of the action that fully and finally resolves the entire action; partial settlement of the action (consented to by the insured) that eliminates any basis for coverage of remaining components of the action; exhaustion of the applicable policy limit; a correct insurer determination that there is no duty to defend; or final adjudication that there is no duty to defend.

When Multiple Insurers Have Defense Obligations

RLLI § 20 sets forth a regime for governing situations in which "multiple" insurers have a duty to defend. In essence, § 20 adopts a modified version of the "targeted tender" approach of several jurisdictions, perhaps most notably Illinois, which allows the policyholder to designate the insurer it wishes to respond and then off-loads to multiple-triggered insurers the task of working out their respective responsibilities so that the policyholder is not harmed by multiple insurers each waiting for another to make the first move.

Coverage of Defense Costs Without a Duty to Defend

RLLI § 22 discusses liability policies that do not provide for an ongoing duty to defend but instead reimburse the policyholder for defense costs incurred in connection with a potentially covered claim. *See Morden v. XL Specialty Ins.*, 177 F. Supp. 3d 1320, 1340-41 (D. Utah 2016) (noting RLLI distinction between duty to defend and duty to pay policies). For such policies, the "scope of the insurer's defense-cost obligation is determined using the rules governing the duty to defend stated" in RLLI §§ 13, 18-20 and 23. The insurer is subject to the reservation of rights protocols set forth in § 15. Regarding the time period for reimbursing the policyholder's defense expenditures, RLLI § 22(3) punts a bit by saying that in the absence of a specific policy provision, "the insurer's obligation to pay defense costs is determined based on all the facts and circumstances, unless otherwise provided in the policy."

Consequences of Breach of the Duty to Defend

Particularly controversial was an earlier draft of RLLI § 19 that provided that an insurer in breach of the duty to defend lost the right to contest coverage, even if the breach was not in bad faith. Final RLLI § 19 simply states that "[a]n insurer that breaches the duty to defend a legal action forfeits the right to assert any control over the defense or settlement of the action." *See Nationwide Mut. Fire Ins. Co. v. D.R. Horton, Inc.*, 2016 U.S. Dist. LEXIS 160148 at *20, n. 6 (S.D. Ala. Nov. 18, 2016) (citing earlier draft of RLLI on this point). The more controversial former § 19(2) provided that "[a]n insurer that breaches the duty to defend without a reasonable basis for its conduct must provide coverage for the legal action for which the defense was sought, notwithstanding any ground for contesting coverage that the insurer could have preserved by providing a proper defense under a reservation of rights. . . ."

Insurers prefer a rule that limits the penalty for a non-bad faith breach of the duty to defend to the simple remedy of reimbursing defense costs incurred by the policyholder that should have been defended by the insurer. A majority of states have adopted this approach. With the removal of former § 19(2), insurers gained some ground regarding the final version of the RLLI as compared to earlier drafts. However, § 50(2) and commentary notes that forfeiture of coverage defenses may be an apt remedy where an insurer's breach of the duty to defend was in bad faith.

An earlier RLLI draft embraced the minority rule of automatic loss of coverage defenses for breach of the duty to defend. A substantial minority of states uses this approach that strips the breaching insurer of coverage defenses. The more recent former § 19(2) used what many deemed a hybrid standard of "bad faith lite" as the prerequisite to losing coverage defenses. By contrast, the RLLI now appears to have acceded to the majority rule that a mere breach of the duty to defend, unless particularly unreasonable or unusually blameworthy, will not strip the insurer of coverage defenses.

Insurer Recoupment of Defense Expenditures

RLLI § 21 deals with the issue of recoupment of defense costs expended by the insurer in connection with uncovered claims. It provides that "[u]nless otherwise stated in the insurance policy or otherwise agreed to by the insured, an insurer may not seek recoupment of defense costs from the insured, even when it is subsequently determined that the insurer did not have a duty to defend or pay defenses costs." As noted above in discussion of the RLLI relationship to *Key Issues* Ch. 7, § 21 has to date been one of the more litigated provisions of the Restatement.

The "Duty to Settle"

RLLI §§ 24-28 deal with settlement and what has traditionally been termed an insurer's "duty" to settle. Helpfully, the RLLI does not use this potentially misleading term and instead speaks of an insurer's "Duty to Make Reasonable Settlement Decisions," which is discussed in detail in RLLI § 24(1), which provides that an insurer controlling defense of a case "has a duty to the insured to make reasonable settlement decisions." RLLI § 24(2) defines a reasonable settlement as "one that would be made by a reasonable insurer who bears the sole financial responsibility for the full amount of the potential judgment." Further, per § 24(3), the "insurer's duty to make reasonable settlement decisions includes the duty to make its policy limits available to the insured for the settlement of a covered legal action that exceeds those policy limits if a reasonable insurer would do so in the circumstances." This provision has attracted some criticism from insurers. RLLI § 25, cmt. a notes that a "reservation of the rights does not eliminate the duty to make reasonable settlement decisions, but there is no such duty for noncovered actions" (italics removed).

Policyholder Settlement Options

Where the insurer is defending, but is unwilling to settle or has failed to settle, the policyholder is permitted to take affirmative action, without violating the standard policy language giving insurers control of case resolution and requiring cooperation of the policyholder, provided that several requirements are satisfied, including that: the insurer is given the opportunity to participate in the settlement process; the insurer declines to withdraw its reservation of rights after receiving prior notice of the proposed settlement; it would be reasonable for a person who bears the sole financial responsibility for the full amount of the potential covered judgment to accept the settlement; and a settlement of covered and uncovered claims is allocated reasonably.

Where there are multiple actions against the policyholder, the insurer's duty to settle of course remains but becomes more complicated in situations where it appears the cumulative value of the claims will exceed policy limits. In such cases, RLLI § 26(1) states that "the insurer has a duty to the insured to make a good-faith effort to settle the actions in a manner that minimizes the insured's overall exposure." Section 26(2) provides that the insurer may satisfy this duty by interpleading the policy limits to the court, naming all known claimant and continuing to pay defense costs until settlement, final adjudication of the matter, or a declaration that the "insurer does not have a duty to defend or to pay the defense costs."

Remedies When Insurers Unreasonably Fail to Settle

RLLI § 27 adopts the widely used "excess judgment" measure of damages for breach of the duty to make reasonable settlements. RLLI § 28 provides that where an underlying insurer has breached the duty to make reasonable settlement decisions, "an excess insurer has an equitable right of subrogation for loss incurred as a result."

The Duty to Cooperate

RLLI § 29 and § 30 address the duty to cooperate and adopt the prevailing view that the policyholder must cooperate with the insurer in defending a suit, providing specifics, but also stating that the breach of the cooperation duty will not bar coverage unless "the insurer demonstrates that the failure caused or will cause prejudice to the insurer" (§ 30(1)).

Insuring Agreements and Exclusions

After addressing the duties of defense and cooperation, the RLLI provides an explanation of concepts and terms. For example, RLLI § 31(1) notes that an "insuring clause" is "a term in a liability insurance policy that grants insurance coverage" while § 31(3) adopts the universal judicial position that such clauses are to be "interpreted broadly." The RLLI also notes that a provision of a policy may be a coverage-granting insuring clause even when it is not so denominated in the policy. RLLI § 32(2) states that "[w]hether a term in an insurance policy is an exclusion does not depend on where the term is in the policy or the label associated with the term in the policy." Exclusions are to be "interpreted narrowly" while "[a]n exception to an exclusion narrows the application of the exclusion" and "does not grant coverage beyond that provided in the insuring clauses in the insurance policy" (§ 32(5)). RLLI § 32(4) provides that "[u]nless otherwise stated in the insurance policy, words in an exclusion regarding the expectation or intent of the insured refer to the subjective state of mind of the insured."

Trigger

RLLI § 33 deals with trigger of coverage and, although not using that language, reflects prevailing law regarding trigger. For example, if an occurrence policy is triggered by injury to the claimant, the time of initial injury constitutes trigger. But an insurer can specify that all potentially covered injury is deemed to have arisen at a particular time. In effect, claims-made policies do this by making the claim against the policyholder the trigger of coverage rather than focusing on the date of injury to the claimant as do occurrence policies.

Conditions

RLLI §§ 34 deals with conditions in the insurance policy, defining a condition as "an event under the control of an insured, policyholder, or insurer that, unless excused, must occur, or must not occur, before performance under the policy becomes due under the policy" (§ 34(1)). As with insuring clauses and exclusions, RLLI § 34(2) provides that "[w]hether a term in a liability insurance policy is a condition does not depend on where the term is located in the policy or the label associated with the term in the policy." Consistent with the view that failure to adhere to certain policy provisions should not result in disproportionate forfeiture, RLLI § 34(3) provides that "failure of an insured to satisfy cooperation conditions . . . does not relieve the insurer of its obligations under the policy unless the failure caused prejudice to the insurer."

Notice

RLLI § 35 provides that for occurrence basis policies, late or defective notice by a policyholder "excuses an insurer from performance of its obligations . . . only if the insurer demonstrates that it was prejudiced as a result." However, for claims-made policies, a stricter view applies and the insurer can avoid coverage when notice is late without regard to prejudice unless, per § 35(2): the policy does not contain an extended reporting period; the claim at issue is made too close to the end of the policy period to allow the insured a reasonable time to satisfy the condition; and the insured reports the claim to the insurer within a reasonable time.

Assignment

RLLI § 36 deals with assignment of rights under a policy and adopts standard contract law, which generally supports liberal assignment as a means of maximizing the utility of property and contract rights. It further provides in § 36(2) that "[r]ights of an insured under an insurance policy relating to a specific claim that has been made against the insured may be assigned without regard to an anti-assignment condition or other term in the policy restricting such assignments."

This portion of the RLLI adopts the long-standing view that after a claim has been made, assignment of the policy does not increase the insurer's risk because when the events giving rise to the claim took place, the insured on the risk was the original insured. *See Ocean Accident & Guaranty Corp. v. Southwestern Bell Telephone Co.*, 100 F. 2d 441 (8th Cir. 1932).

Somewhat less clear in case law is a situation that takes place when the original policyholder's conduct has given rise to a number of claims that may be the first wave of claims yet to come (perhaps even the metaphorical tip of the iceberg) as is the case involving product liability or other mass torts or mini-mass torts. RLLI § 37(3)(a)-(c) addresses such situations.

Policy Limits and Number of Occurrences

RLLI § 37 addresses policy limits, defining the term, including the distinction between per-occurrence limits and aggregate limits, while § 38 takes a brief, generalist stab at the vexing issue of determining the number of occurrences that does little more than state the prevailing common law rule of "cause" analysis (rather than "effects" analysis) in broad terms.

Attachment of Excess Insurance Policies

Regarding attachment, RLLI § 39 takes as a presumptive rule the approach of *Zeig v. Massachusetts Bonding Co.*, 23 F.2d 665 (2d Cir. 1928) (applying New York law) and provides that an excess insurer must attach when the underlying limits are satisfied by payment from any source -- RLLI § 39 then backs away from the *Zeig* approach if it is "otherwise stated in the excess insurance policy." For example, if the excess policy has language stating that the underlying limit can be satisfied only by payment by the underlying insurer(s) (and nobody else), this language presumptively controls. Policyholder counsel oppose this provision while insurer counsel support it.

Allocation of Insurer Responsibility and Contribution

RLLI § 41(1) states unless altered by a term in the policy, "when indivisible harm occurs over multiple policy periods, the amount of any judgment entered in or settlement of any liability action arising out of that harm is subject to pro rata allocation under occurrence-based liability policies" and in § 41(1)(a) endorses pro-ration by time on the risk.

RLLI takes the view that when multiple insurers are consecutively triggered by claims of injury taking place in a number of policy periods over several years (or, in the case of asbestos or pollution claims, potentially several decades), each insurer's coverage responsibility can be pro-rated by time on the risk and policy limits rather than requiring each triggered insurer to be responsible for "all sums" (or "those sums" in more recent policy language) covered up to the policy limits. Case law in the area has been split. *See Key Issues*, Ch. 18. *See also Nooter Corp. v. Allianz Underwriters Ins. Co.*, 2017 Mo. App. LEXIS 977, at *33 (Mo. Ct. App. Oct. 17, 2017) (citing RLLI in the course of defining terms and surveying jurisdictional split on the allocation issue).

Regarding contribution, RLLI § 42(1) states that "[a]n insurer that indemnifies an insured for a legal action has a right of contribution against any other insurer with an indemnification obligation to that insured for that action" if certain conditions are met. Where multiple insurers are involved, with some settling coverage matters with the policyholder, RLLI § 43 provides that "[i]n determining the declarations of rights and amount of any judgment to be entered against a liability insurer with respect to the insurer's obligation to provide coverage for a legal action brought against an insured, the amount of the insured's losses that are subject to the declaration or judgment are reduced by the amount paid for those losses by any insurers that settled with and were released by the insured with respect to that legal action."

Public Policy and Punitive Damages

RLLI § 44 deals with terms that are imposed by operation of law, stating that a "term that is required by law to be included in a liability insurance policy is so included by operation of law notwithstanding its absence in the written policy" (§ 44(1)). A liability insurance policy term is unenforceable on public-policy grounds if legislation provides that it is unenforceable or the interests in its enforcement is clearly outweighed in the circumstances by a public policy against the enforcement of such term (§ 44(2)).

Regarding claims against the policyholder that may allege more than mere negligence (e.g., recklessness, willful, wanton conduct), RLLI § 45(1) provides that unless "barred by legislation or judicially declared public policy," insurance policies provide at least potential coverage for such claims – the types of claims that may create punitive damages liability – and that allegations of bad conduct do not relieve an insurer of the duty to defend unless otherwise provided in the policy or a clear legislative or judicial ruling that such claims are not insurable under the applicable law.

Regarding payment of settlements or judgments, RLLI § 45(2) provides that "[e]xcept as barred by legislation or judicially declared public policy, a term in a liability insurance policy providing coverage for civil liability arising out of aggravated fault is enforceable," including civil liability for: criminal acts, expected or intentionally caused harm, fraud, or other conduct involving aggravated fault." RLLI § 45(3) states that issues of coverage in such situations are "a question of interpretation governed by the ordinary rules of insurance-policy interpretation."

Known Liabilities

RLLI § 46 addresses a "known liability" (and contrasts it with a known risk), providing that "[u]nless otherwise stated in the policy, a liability insurance policy provides coverage for a known liability only if that liability is disclosed to the insurer during the application or renewal process for the policy" (§ 46(1)). A "liability is known only when, prior to the inception of the policy period, the policyholder knows that, absent a settlement, an adverse judgment establishing the liability in an amount that would reach the level of coverage provided under the policy is substantially certain" (§ 46(2)).

Remedies

RLLI §§ 47 and 48 address the remedies that may be available to insurers and policyholders in disputes over the policy. Such damages include an award of compensatory damages, a declaration of rights, court costs and counsel fees for the prevailing party, and "[i]f so provided in the liability insurance policy or otherwise agreed to by the parties," recoupment of defense costs (§ 47(4)). This last provision takes the sting out of RLLI § 21 that generally bars recoupment because liability insurers usually promise in the policy to defend "suits" rather than only "covered claims." An insurer that wants to establish a right to recoupment can do this through the policy – and need not have such a right judicially created.

RLLI § 48 sets forth an extensive list of damages that "an insured may recover for breach of a liability policy," including all reasonable costs of the defense of a potentially covered legal action that have not already been paid by the insurer, all amounts required to indemnify the insured for a covered legal action that have not already been paid by the insurer, reasonable attorneys' fees and other costs incurred in the legal action establishing the insurer's breach of the duty to defend, other foreseeable losses caused by breach of the policy, and, in the case of a breach of the duty to make reasonable settlement decisions, the damages stated in RLLI § 27, which are largely the amount of the judgment in excess of the policy limits. This is an extensive array of damages. But in order to recover even a single item of these damages, a policyholder will need to prevail in its action against the insurer, at least in part.

Bad Faith

The RLLI § 49 test for holding an insurer in bad faith requires that the insurer fail "to perform under a liability insurance policy" and that this be "[w]ithout a reasonable basis for [the insurer's] conduct" and "[w]ith knowledge of its obligation to perform or in reckless disregard of whether it had an obligation to perform." RLLI § 50 provides as damages for bad faith breach: reasonable attorneys' fees and other costs incurred by the insured; "[a]ny other loss to the insured proximately caused by the insurer's bad-faith conduct;" and, if available pursuant to applicable state law, punitive damages.

Made in United States
Troutdale, OR
12/09/2023

15583275R00306